2_

9

AT THIS THEATRE

AT THIS THEATRE

110 Years of Broadway Shows, Stories, and Stars

ROBERT VIAGAS AND LOUIS BOTTO

APPLAUSE
THEATRE & CINEMA BOOKS

AN IMPRINT OF
HAL•LEONARD®

An Imprint of Hal Leonard Corporation
New York

Published in 2010 by Applause Theatre & Cinema Books
An Imprint of Hal Leonard Corporation
7777 West Bluemound Road
Milwaukee, WI 53213

Trade Book Division Editorial Offices
19 West 21st Street, New York, NY 10010

Except where otherwise noted, all photographs in this book are from the archives of the Theatre
Collection at the Museum of the City of New York. These include the following photographs by
Martha Swope: p. 245: *Your Arms Too Short to Box with God* and *Morning's at Seven*; p. 51: *Ain't
Misbehavin'*; p. 238: *Peter Pan* and *Private Lives*; p. 407: *Cats*; p. 309: *Applause*; p. 230: *Ain't
Misbehavin'* and *Children of a Lesser God*; p. 329: *A Chorus Line*; p. 78: *Butterflies Are Free*; p. 77:
For Colored Girls Who Have Considered Suicide/When the Rainbow is Enuf; p. 92: *Dancin'*; p. 184:
Plaza Suite; p. 185: *Piaf*; p. 20: *A View from the Bridge*; p. 145: *Lena Horne: The Lady and Her
Music*; p. 277: *Side by Side by Sondheim*; p. 211: *Pippin*; p. 213: *Dreamgirls*; p. 7: *The Little Foxes*;
p. 317: *1776*; p. 102: *Candide*; p. 103: *Evita*; p. 113: *Same Time, Next Year* and *The Dresser*; p. 64:
Joseph and the Amazing Technicolor Dreamcoat; p. 255: *The Wiz* and *The Act*; p. 290: *Annie*; p.
124: *The Man Who Came to Dinner* and *The Caine Mutiny Court-Martial*; p. 174: *The Pirates of
Penzance*.

Editor's note: All PLAYBILL covers in this book are from the magazine's archives or the private
collections of the authors. Unfortunately, the people at PLAYBILL had no idea that someday these
covers would be used in a book and have stamped some of them with dates and other marks. We
show the covers exactly as they appear in the archives.

Printed in China through Colorcraft Ltd., Hong Kong

Book design by Damien Castaneda

The Library of Congress Control number for the 2004 edition: 2002105517

ISBN 978-1-55783-764-6

www.applausepub.com

CONTENTS

FOREWORD

I WAS AROUND SEVEN OR EIGHT THE first time I heard the word Broadway. Not being from New York, I thought Broadway was literally one big theatre.

The only person I knew who had been to the "Broadway Theatre" was my mom's friend Bobby. She was visiting one afternoon and described a show she had just seen in New York. The plot sounded utterly preposterous to me, but positively delicious.

Grown people dressed up as cats? Licking themselves, stretching and preening, and, what's more, singing and dancing? It was too much. My mind reeled. She described the old, fat, wise cats, the young, mischievous cats, and the elaborate makeup that brought them to life. She described the giant cat tire, and the huge boxes they leapt around on, the mysterious fog that overtook the stage, and the magic that hung in the air.

Then she told us about her favorite moment in the show. When the beautiful old lady cat sang a song about grief and longing. And as her pain grew, the music grew with aching and yearning until it crested with the final moment of anguish. "My heart jumped up into my throat," Bobby said emphatically. "It was beautiful."

Her words hung in the air, her descriptions so vivid in my mind. My eyes were wide, the hairs on the back of my neck were standing up, I felt like I might burst.

And that's when I knew. I wanted to be someone like that old lady cat making people's hearts jump up into their throats at the Broadway Theatre in *Cats*.

Her description of what took place that night stayed with me for days. I spent that summer going to garage sales looking for Broadway cast albums. I got swept away to the world of *South Pacific*, I pretended I was the eighth Von Trapp child in *The Sound of Music*, and I was a redheaded orphan with a hard-knock life in *Annie*. And I believed that all of this magic was created on a single stage.

Now, twenty-five years later, every day when I walk by the Winter Garden Theatre, I think about my mom's friend describing *Cats*. It makes me smile that I thought all this joy came from one little building.

I've had the good fortune to work in some of the most legendary theatres in the world, each with its own secrets and stories to tell. Many of those secrets and stories I found in an earlier edition of the very book you're holding now, *At This Theatre*.

I learned about the Marquis, where Annie got her gun and I made my Broadway debut.

I learned about the Palace Theatre, where every night I rode up to my dressing room in Lauren Bacall's elevator, or sometimes crept up the secret Judy Garland staircase just to spy on the house.

And I learned about the St. James Theatre, where the waiters of the Harmonia Gardens sang "Hello, Dolly!" to Carol Channing and where Yul Brynner ruled his kingdom.

The day I learned that Broadway was actually a whole neighborhood of theatres was a bit like learning that Santa didn't exist. But now . . . it doesn't diminish the enchantment that I first felt when listening to Bobby's story. In fact, it makes it all the sweeter, because as we all know, magic isn't made in one theatre, it's made in every theatre. It's made "at this theatre."

—CHEYENNE JACKSON

PREFACE TO THE 2010 EDITION

THE FIRST EDITION OF *AT THIS THEATRE* was published in 1984 to mark the one hundredth anniversary of PLAYBILL's founding. It was written in just a few months in an almost supernatural burst of creativity by Louis Botto, a lifelong lover of theatre and PLAYBILL's senior editor.

The second edition was published in 2001, covering the years 1900 to 2000. I was honored to serve as editor of that edition, working closely with Mr. Botto as he chronicled the developments of the late twentieth century and added chapters on the New Amsterdam Theatre and other playhouses renovated and relit during the Forty-second Street theatrical renaissance.

The continued popularity of that edition, along with the renewed energy of Broadway over the past decade (plus the 125th anniversary of PLAYBILL in 2009), prompted a further update, covering the busy years of the early twenty-first century, when records were being broken up and down the Great White Way for attendance, long runs, and box office income. What you hold in your hands is not just an update, but a comprehensive and beautiful redesign courtesy of Damien Castaneda of PLAYBILL's partner, Applause Books.

A deep bow to my colleague Mr. Botto for having the faith to allow me to pen this update on his masterpiece. I've tried to preserve something of his authoritative tone, his eye for detail, his taste for pungent backstage anecdotes, his occasional dry commentary, and his never-ending quest to discover synonyms for the word *performances*.

The book's focus remains on the traffic on the boards—the plays themselves. However, important incidents in the lives of these theatres sometimes occurred offstage, as well, and I have included them.

Two theatres have been removed from this edition of *At This Theatre*: the Mark Hellinger and the City Center. And two have been added: Studio 54 and the Stephen Sondheim Theatre/Henry Miller's Theatre. Even in 2000, it had been more than a decade since a Broadway show was presented at either of the deleted theatres. The Hellinger was leased to the Times Square Church in 1989 and subsequently sold to them. The last legitimate show there was *Legs Diamond* in 1988. It's not a Broadway theatre anymore. As for the City Center, it remains home to the "Encores!" series of American musicals in concert and to certain productions by Manhattan Theatre Club. But these attractions are contractually Off-Broadway. The last Broadway production there was a revival of *The Music Man* in 1980. The City Center of the twenty-first century is primarily the home of ballet and classical music, all of which have taken it outside the realm of this book.

On the other hand, we're delighted to add two theatres long presumed "lost": former disco Studio 54 (originally a Broadway theatre—opened in 1927 as the Gallo Opera House) and the 1918-vintage Henry Miller's Theatre, recently rechristened the Stephen Sondheim Theatre. Both have been renovated and restored to legitimacy, and both have embarked on ambitious schedules of Broadway productions under the auspices of Roundabout Theatre Company. This edition of *At This Theatre* welcomes them back into the Broadway fold with all-new full chapters that chart their history back to the laying of the first brick.

Since the 2001 edition, several of the Broadway theatres have celebrated their centenaries and many more are nearing that milestone, meaning that most theatregoers have spent their entire lives passing through their lobbies, sitting in their seats, gazing up at their chandeliers and murals, and waiting for their curtains to rise. These theatres are like old friends. For some of us, they are virtual members of the family. To visit them means not only seeing a new show, but taking a moment to wonder, "What else did I see here?" "What famous stars stood on that stage?" "What great shows first saw the spotlight here?" *At This Theatre* was created to answer those questions. The third edition was created to answer those questions for a whole new generation of theatregoers.

—ROBERT VIAGAS
MAY 2010

PREFACE TO THE 2002 EDITION

AT THIS THEATRE IS AN EXPANDED version of the popular feature of the same name that has appeared since the 1930s in PLAYBILL magazine, which serves as the program of the professional legitimate theatre in the United States. While attending a Broadway show, theatregoers are fond of reading this page to discover the names of other productions and stars they have seen in the past at this same theatre. The feature offers instant nostalgia, and that is the primary purpose of this book.

It was the idea of Joan Alleman, former editor-in-chief of PLAYBILL, to expand "At This Theatre" to book form as one of the observances of the magazine's centennial in 1984. PLAYBILL, which was founded by Frank Vance Strauss, an Ohio advertising man, has brought a century of playgoing pleasure to theatregoers by combining magazine features with a theatre program, offering a rich memento of the show they have seen.

This expanded *At This Theatre* contains the informal history of forty theatres that were built as either legitimate houses or movie palaces and that are currently operating as legitimate theatres. The only exception is the Mark Hellinger, a theatre with a rich history, currently leased as a church. Theatres that were formerly nightclubs are not included, nor are theatres that have been demolished or that have reverted to showing films or other uses, such as the Eltinge on Forty-second Street.

Even in this expanded form, *At This Theatre* is not a complete history of all shows that these forty theatres have ever housed. Hundreds of short-lived productions are omitted. Some shows have moved from theatre to theatre; these productions are listed at the theatre where they first played and also in other theatres if they had extended runs after they moved.

A number of legitimate theatres have had name changes in their long years of operation. The names that appear in the chapter headings are the current names of these theatres, but all significant name changes are included in each history.

It has not been possible to chronicle ownership changes of every house. The original builders and owners are noted, as well as the current owners, but many who came in between are not mentioned.

The entire cast of a show is not listed, unless the production had a very small cast. Other credits—-author, director, producer, set designer, composer, lyricist, librettist, costume and lighting designers, choreographers, et al.—are listed when the contribution was notable.

Unfortunately, due to a fire, PLAYBILL magazine's "theatre-by-theatre" listing of productions that have played in each house goes back only as far as 1924. To determine shows that played in theatres before that year, it has been necessary to refer to the following sources: *Notable Names in the Theatre*; *The New York Times Theatre Reviews*; *A Pictorial History of the American Theatre*, by Daniel Blum; *Twentieth Century Theatre*, by Glenn Loney; *The Encyclopedia of the Musical Theatre*, by Stanley Green; *Broadway*, by Brooks Atkinson; *The City and the Theatre*, by Mary C. Henderson; *Documents of American Theater History*, by William C. Young; and *Our Theatres To-day and Yesterday*, by Ruth Crosby Dimmick.

Other sources include the Theatre World annuals, edited successively by Daniel Blum and John Willis; the Best Plays annuals, edited successively by Burns Mantle, John Chapman, John Kronenberger, Henry Hewes, Otis L. Guernsey Jr., and Jeffrey Sweet; *The World of Musical Comedy* and *Ring Bells! Sing Songs!*, both by Stanley Green; *The Tony Award*, by Isabelle Stevenson, and the www.tonyawards.com website; *The Magic Curtain*, by Lawrence Langner; *Vintage Years of the Theatre Guild*, 1928—1939, by Roy S. Waldau; *A Pictorial History of the Theatre Guild*, by Norman Nadel; *Revue*, by Robert Baral; *Complete Book of the American Musical Theater*, by David Ewen; *Matinee Tomorrow*, by Ward Morehouse; *Stage and Theatre Arts* magazines; *The Rodgers and Hammerstein Fact Book*, edited by Stanley Green; and *The Passionate Playgoer*, by George Oppenheimer.

All PLAYBILL magazines are from the files of PLAYBILL or from my own collection, or the collection of my editor, Robert Viagas. Souvenir programs, sheet music, and "heralds" (inserts placed in theatre programs to advertise a show playing in another theatre) are from my own collection.

All photographs [in the 1984 edition] are from the collection of the Museum of the City of New York. Unfortunately, not all actors are credited on some photographs, and in some cases it has proven impossible to verify their names. Some actors changed the spelling of

their names or changed their names entirely. These changes have been noted.

I am grateful to Arthur, Philip, and Joan Birsh for the completion and publication of this book. I appreciate the hard work of graphic artists Julie Meridy and Michelle Thompson in bringing its look up-to-date. Pat Cusanelli and Gary Pearce deserve thanks for their work in saving and processing the artwork and treating the delicate original pieces from my collection with such care. I thank the team at Applause Theatre and Cinema Books for being so supportive in returning this volume to print. Most of all I wish to thank Philip Birsh, president and publisher of PLAYBILL, for securing the services of Robert Viagas as editor of this book. He has been a diligent aide and helpful deadline taskmaster and has also provided a sorely needed index.

—LOUIS BOTTO
SENIOR EDITOR, PLAYBILL

PREFACE TO THE 1984 EDITION

PLAYBILL MAGAZINE IS COMMEMORATING its centennial in 1984. as part of such celebrations it is considered traditional to put out "the book." Being a quite traditional company and a bit of an institution in our own right, we have published *At This Theatre*. There is no shortage of books about the theatre. However, our volume is special in several ways.

First and foremost, we are privileged to have Louis Botto, senior editor on our staff, bring his astonishing knowledge to this project. In addition, many of the most interesting illustrations are reproductions of items in his fabulous personal collection of theatre memorabilia.

The organization of this volume is unique. Our popular "At This Theatre" feature reflects the organization of day-to-day life at PLAYBILL Magazine, where, in reality, we do not serve shows, we serve theatres. Our thinking, printing, deliveries, and files are all organized by theatre. Organizing by theatre in these pages results in an unusual and interesting slant on theatre history.

We have chosen to illuminate the history of only those theatres now served by PLAYBILL Magazine, for any other choice would result in an encyclopedic project. Even so, it was possible to include only a fraction of the interesting and amusing material available.

We are grateful to be part of the tradition and to be able to look through this volume and be able to say, without exception, "PLAYBILL was there!"

—ARTHUR T. BIRSH
PUBLISHER, PLAYBILL

MAIN LEVEL FOYER

THEATRE FLOOR PLAN

ACKNOWLEDGEMENTS

Primary thanks go to PLAYBILL chairman Arthur Birsh, former editor Joan Alleman and original author Louis Botto, who first conceived of capturing the history of the Broadway theatres, in the pages of PLAYBILL, and then between the covers of a book.

Thanks for the third edition go especially to PLAYBILL publisher Philip Birsh, and Applause publisher John Cerullo, who decided it was time for an update.

Among those who helped with research on the updated and new chapters: Tiffany Nixon at Roundabout Theatre Company, Marty Jacobs at the Museum of the City of New York, and the Mandelbaum brothers at PhotoFest.

We salute the photographers, especially Joan Marcus, Carol Rosegg, Paul Kolnik, and their colleagues, whose images grace these pages.

A special hats-off to Stanley Stark, the artist whose theatre sketches grace the first pages of nearly all the chapters. And thanks to PLAYBILL staffers who took the new photos of the theatre exteriors: David Gewirtzman, Matt Blank, and Krissie Fullerton.

The handsome design of the new edition was the work of Damien Castaneda, and copy editor Angela Buckley bravely waded through eleven decades of names.

A personal thank-you to Catherine Ryan, who did a first edit on the chapters; Jil Simon, who coordinated the project at PLAYBILL; and Marybeth Keating, who coordinated the project at Applause Books.

And a belated thank-you to PLAYBILL's Oldyna Dynowska, who worked closely with original author Louis Botto to transfer his typewritten manuscript into computerized form for the 2001 edition of this book and was not thanked properly therein. Oldyna, we're finally square.

STAGE

INTRODUCTION

FOR WHAT MAY BE LONGER THAN living memory, one of the most popular editorial features in PLAYBILL has been a column titled "At This Theatre," a short history of the most famous plays and musicals of the past that were performed in the theatre the audience is currently attending. PLAYBILL has served some of our theatres for over one hundred years. Appearing whenever space permits, this well-read feature gives theatregoers a chance to learn of performances they have only heard about and to reminisce about those they came to see.

When he joined PLAYBILL thirty-two years ago, Louis Botto, an avid theatre buff and respected theatre historian, was given the chore of maintaining these columns in the nearly forty theatres we were serving. As part of the PLAYBILL centennial in 1984, it seemed fitting that these mini histories be combined into an illustrated book. The first edition, long out of print, was followed by a second edition in 2001, which updated and expanded the historical array, adding a welcome index. Robert Viagas, PLAYBILL's founding online editor, armed with his encyclopedic knowledge of theatre, edited the second and is coauthor of this third edition, which adds the highlights of each theatre from yet another decade.

My own history with PLAYBILL goes back for more than fifty years. I can remember when we set all special copy for each theatre (including "Cast in Order of Appearance," "Who's Who," "Scenes," and the "At This Theatre" column), on then antiquated linotype machines, casting hot lead slugs and locking them in gigantic frames. We had special trolleys to bring these half-ton chases to our lumbering letterpresses. To dry the ink, the paper had to pass over open gas flames. A sheet-feeding error could and did start significant blazes. We printed day and night to supply Broadway. The "At This Theatre" column had no pictures. Pictures were rare in PLAYBILL and very hard to print on our aged machines. Color was unthinkable, appearing only on preprinted interleaves purchased from offset printers.

Happily, today our theatre editions are filled with illustrations, of course, in full color. The digital age has also made our *At This Theatre* books more attractive, colorful, and informative. I love books, feeling the weight, letting the pages slip in a stream under my thumb. *At This Theatre* is my idea of how to look back at the rich history of PLAYBILL on Broadway.

—ARTHUR BIRSH
PUBLISHER OF PLAYBILL
FROM 1964 TO 1994

THEATRE CHRONOLOGY

NEW AMSTERDAM—October 26, 1903

LYCEUM—November 2, 1903

BELASCO—October 16, 1907 (as the Stuyvesant)

LUNT-FONTANNE—January 10, 1910 (as the Globe)

WINTER GARDEN—March 10, 1911

HELEN HAYES—March 12, 1912 (as the Little)

CORT—December 20, 1912

PALACE—March 24, 1913

LONGACRE—May 1, 1913

SAM S. SHUBERT—September 29, 1913

BOOTH—October 16, 1913

BROADHURST—September 27, 1917

AMERICAN AIRLINES—October 2, 1918 (as the Selwyn)

GERALD SCHOENFELD—October 10, 1917 (as the Plymouth)

AMBASSADOR—February 11, 1921

MUSIC BOX—February 21, 1921

WALTER KERR—March 21, 1921 (as the Ritz)

DAVID T. NEDERLANDER—September 1, 1921 (as the National)

IMPERIAL—December 25, 1923

AL HIRSCHFELD—November 11, 1924 (as the Martin Beck)

RICHARD RODGERS—December 24, 1924 (as the 46th Street)

BROADWAY—December 25, 1924 (as the B.S. Moss)

AUGUST WILSON—April 13, 1925 (as the Guild)

EUGENE O'NEILL—November 25, 1925 (as the Forrest)

SAMUEL J. FRIEDMAN—December 7, 1925 (as the Biltmore)

BROOKS ATKINSON—February 15, 1926 (as the Mansfield)

BERNARD B. JACOBS—January 11, 1927 (as the Royale)

JOHN GOLDEN—February 24, 1927

MAJESTIC—March 28, 1927

ST. JAMES—September 26, 1927

STEPHEN SONDHEIM—April 1, 1918 (as Henry Miller's)

STUDIO 54—November 7, 1927 (as the Gallo Opera House)

NEIL SIMON—November 22, 1927 (as the Alvin)

ETHEL BARRYMORE—December 20, 1928

VIVIAN BEAUMONT—October 21, 1965

CIRCLE IN THE SQUARE—November 15, 1972

GEORGE GERSHWIN—November 28, 1972

MINSKOFF—March 13, 1973

MARQUIS—August 10, 1986

HILTON—January 18, 1998 (as the Ford Center for the Performing Arts)

AT THIS THEATRE

AL HIRSCHFELD
THEATRE

THE AL HIRSCHFELD THEATRE SERVES
as the western outpost of the Times Square theatre district, being located just west of Eighth
Avenue at 302 West Forty-fifth Street.

This distinctive-looking playhouse opened
in 1924 as the Martin Beck Theatre and was
described by the *New York Times* as the only
theatre in America designed in the Byzantine
style. Beck, the vaudeville mogul who built the
house, conceived the building's style and
entrusted its design and execution to San
Francisco architect G. Albert Lansburgh. The
theatre is distinguished by its unusually large
foyer and promenade, and its details of
wrought iron and stained glass. With a seating
capacity of 1,200 (today 1,437) and dressing
rooms for 200 actors, the house was ideal for

A Great Big New Musical Comedy

THE AL HIRSCHFELD THEATRE

PRIVATE EYES

Top left: Standard program cover for the Martin Beck Theatre in the 1920s.

Center: PLAYBILL for *The Sound of Music* (1998).

Left: PLAYBILL for *Guys and Dolls* (1992).

Bottom lower left: Eva Clark, Wilda Bennett, and Leeta Corder in *Madame Pompadour*, the Martin Beck's first show (1924).

Bottom right: Glenn Anders and Claudette Colbert in Eugene O'Neill's *Dynamo* (1930).

musicals and spectacular productions. Curiously, it has in its more than eighty years of operation housed many distinguished dramatic plays, some of which were definitely not spectacular.

The Martin Beck opened on November 11, 1924, with a Viennese operetta, *Mme. Pompadour*, adapted by playwright Clare Kummer, but the public was wearying of schmaltzy operettas at this time and the show ran for a moderate eighty performances.

The theatre had better luck in 1925 when *Captain Jinks* arrived. This was a musical version of Clyde Fitch's play *Captain Jinks of the Horse Marines*, which had made a star of Ethel Barrymore. In this version the marine captain (J. Harold Murray) is in love with a world-famous dancer, Trentoni (Louise Brown). Also in the cast was comedian Joe E. Brown as a hack driver. Five collaborators worked on the musical, and it ran for 167 performances.

One of the most sensational plays ever produced on Broadway, John Colton's *The Shanghai Gesture*, made waves on February 1, 1926. It starred Florence Reed as Mother Goddam, the owner of a notorious Shanghai whorehouse. It was her most famous role.

Seeking revenge on a Britisher who once dumped her to marry an Englishwoman, she lures him to her brothel and sells his own daughter off as a prostitute. Then, discovering that the daughter she had by the Britisher has turned into a dope fiend, she strangles her to death. The critics scoffed at this purple melodrama, but audiences loved it and kept the Martin Beck full for 210 performances.

Next, the Martin Beck booked a comedy that turned out to be its biggest hit to that time: *The Shannons of Broadway*, written by actor James Gleason, who also starred in it. Playing a vaudevillian, he and his wife (Lucile Webster) have comic adventures when they buy and operate a hotel in New England. The popular comedy ran for 288 performances.

Beginning in December 1928, the prestigious Theatre Guild began producing a number of fascinating plays at the Martin Beck, featuring the famed Theatre Guild Acting Company. Their first production, an antiwar play called *Wings Over Europe*, was chosen by Burns Mantle as one of the year's ten best. Next, in February 1929, they presented Eugene O'Neill's unusual play *Dynamo*, which pitted religion against science and starred Claudette

Colbert, Dudley Digges, Glenn Anders, and Helen Westley. Despite its offbeat attraction, the play lasted only sixty-six performances.

More successful was *The Camel Through the Needle's Eye* (1929), a play about an illegitimate girl (Miriam Hopkins) who meets a man (Claude Rains) and makes a success out of him by going into the dairy business with him. The excellent cast also included Henry Travers, Helen Westley, and Morris Carnovsky. The play ran for 195 performances.

Theatre Guild productions included a Russian play, *Red Rust* (1929), with Lee Strasberg, Luther Adler, and Franchot Tone, who would soon be prominent in the Group Theatre; Philip Barry's metaphysical play *Hotel Universe* (1930), in which guests at a French villa recall incidents from their youth that had a profound influence on their lives, brilliantly acted by Franchot Tone, Ruth Gordon, Glenn Anders, Katherine Alexander, Morris Carnovsky, and others; and *Roar China!* (1930), a play about a Chinese rebellion in which an enormous British warship occupied the vast reaches of the Martin Beck stage.

In 1931 the Theatre Guild moved its successful production of Maxwell Anderson's *Elizabeth the Queen*, starring Lunt and Fontanne, from the Guild Theatre to the Martin Beck. The Lunts next appeared at this theatre in one of their acting triumphs, Robert E. Sherwood's romantic comedy *Reunion in Vienna* (1931).

Between those two shows the Martin Beck housed the first production of the Group Theatre, made up of younger members of the Theatre Guild who had been responsible for the presentation of *Roar China!* Their inaugural presentation was Paul Green's *The House of Connelly*, and it was produced under the auspices of the Theatre Guild. Chosen as one of the year's ten best, it was staged by Lee Strasberg and Cheryl Crawford and dealt with the clash of generations in an aristocratic southern family. The critics were very receptive to the production.

In 1932 the Abbey Irish Theatre Players

Top left: Katharine Hepburn flops in *The Lake* (1933).

Top center: Maurice Evans and Katharine Cornell in *Saint Joan* (1936).

Top right: Katharine Cornell and Basil Rathbone in *Romeo and Juliet* (1934).

Bottom left: Alfred Lunt, Lynn Fontanne, and Henry Travers in *Reunion in Vienna* (1931).

Bottom right: Burgess Meredith and Peggy Ashcroft in *High Tor* (1936).

(including Barry Fitzgerald) presented a season of repertory, including such Irish classics as *The Far-off Hills, Juno and the Paycock, Playboy of the Western World,* and *The Shadow of a Gunman.*

In December 1933, Broadway waited with great anticipation for the return of Katharine Hepburn to the stage. Her chosen vehicle was a British play, *The Lake,* directed by Jed Harris. Hepburn had gone to Hollywood and become a superstar in a very short time, and so eminent was she that Harris forbade the rest of the cast (including many distinguished actors) to speak to her offstage. The play opened, and Hepburn's nervous performance inspired the famed Dorothy Parker crack "She ran the gamut of emotions—from A to B." The general opinion was that Miss Hepburn flopped in *The Lake.*

Sidney Howard's documentary play *Yellow Jack* (1934), written with Paul de Kruif and adapted from de Kruif's book *The Microbe Hunters,* opened next. It was based on the true record of Walter Reed and the researchers who discovered that the killer yellow fever was propagated by mosquitoes. The large cast included James Stewart, Edward Acuff, Myron McCormick, and Sam Levene as Marine privates who volunteered to be bitten by the deadly insects. The play ran only seventy-nine per-

formances but was admired by the critics.

The D'Oyly Carte Opera Company played a four-month season at the Martin Beck in 1934, followed by Katharine Cornell as a radiant Juliet in *Romeo and Juliet,* with Basil Rathbone as Romeo, Brian Aherne as Mercutio, Orson Welles as Tybalt, and Edith Evans as the Nurse. Cornell was hailed for her luminous performance, and the sumptuous production, with magical sets by Jo Mielziner and dances by Martha Graham, ran for seventy-eight performances. Cornell followed her Juliet with two other productions at the Martin Beck: a revival of her beloved gem *The Barretts of Wimpole Street* (1935), with Brian Aherne, Burgess Meredith, and Brenda Forbes; and John Van Druten's antiwar play *Flowers of the Forest* (1935), with Cornell, Meredith, and Margalo Gillmore.

A major dramatic event occurred at the Martin Beck on September 25, 1935. Maxwell Anderson's *Winterset* opened and proved to be a fascinating and controversial blank-verse drama. Starring Burgess Meredith, Margo, Richard Bennett, and Eduardo Ciannelli, the tragedy dealt with a son's quest for his father's murderer. The action took place beneath the Brooklyn Bridge, and Jo Mielziner's majestic set was one of his greatest designs. The play won the first award as Best Play of the season conferred by the newly formed New York

Drama Critics Circle. It ran for 195 performances.

On March 9, 1936, Katharine Cornell returned in glory to this theatre in her acclaimed revival of Shaw's *Saint Joan*. Brilliantly directed by her husband, Guthrie McClintic, who piloted all her plays, the production was hailed as a work of art. Maurice Evans was the Dauphin, and the large cast also included Brian Aherne, Arthur Byron, Eduardo Ciannelli, Kent Smith, George Coulouris, and the future film idol Tyrone Power Jr.

The D'Oyly Carte Opera Company paid a return visit with their repertory in 1936, followed by another Maxwell Anderson play, a fantasy called *High Tor*, which won the second Best Play award conferred by the New York Drama Critics Circle. The fanciful play starred Burgess Meredith and British actress Peggy Ashcroft, and featured young Hume Cronyn. It was set on top of an actual mountain on the Hudson called High Tor and involved the young man who owned it and who refused to sell it. Ghosts of ancient Dutch sailors waiting for the return of Henry Hudson's boat added comic relief, and the refreshing play ran for 171 performances.

The remainder of the 1930s found the Martin Beck occupied by Ina Claire in an unsuccessful adaptation of Trollope's *Barchester Towers* (1937); a revival of *Victoria Regina*, with Helen Hayes repeating her celebrated role (1938); another engagement of the D'Oyly Carte Opera Company (1939); and Helen Hayes again, this time in a modern murder-trial play, *Ladies and Gentlemen* (1939), adapted by her husband, Charles MacArthur, and Ben Hecht from a Hungarian play. It was a moderate success, running for 105 performances.

In 1940 *Lady in Waiting*, a dramatization of Margery Sharp's popular novel *The Nutmeg Tree*, boasted a sterling comic performance by Gladys George but ran for only 87 performances. On April 1, 1941, Lillian Hellman's prophetic play *Watch on the Rhine*, starring Paul Lukas, Lucile Watson, Mady Christians, and George Coulouris, stunned audiences with its antifascist theme. Directed by Herman Shumlin and brilliantly acted, the play won the Best American Play award conferred by the New York Drama Critics Circle and ran for 378 performances. John Steinbeck's adaptation of his novel *The Moon Is Down* (1942) was next, but did not achieve great success. The popular comedy hit *My Sister Eileen* moved here from the Biltmore Theatre and stayed for four months. The Lunts arrived in November 1942 with *The Pirate*, S. N. Behrman's colorful adaptation of an idea in a play by Ludwig Fulda. It gave Lunt an opportunity to walk a tightrope and pretend he was a notorious pirate whom Fontanne idolizes. This bizarre burlesque ran for 176 performances.

One of the Martin Beck's biggest hits was Behrman's adaptation of Franz Werfel's play *Jacobowsky and the Colonel* (1944), starring Louis Calhern, Oscar Karlweis, Annabella, J. Edward Bromberg, and E. G. Marshall. The adventurous story involved a comical and enterprising refugee named Jacobowsky (Karlweis), an aristocratic Polish colonel (Calhern), and a beautiful blonde (Annabella) fleeing together in a car from Nazi-occupied France. The comedy ran for 417 performances.

In March 1945 Tallulah Bankhead and Donald Cook opened in *Foolish Notion*, Philip Barry's most foolish play. This misguided venture was followed by the rollicking Bernstein/Comden/Green musical *On the Town*, which moved in from the 44th Street Theatre for a stay of five months. Next came the melodious Harold Arlen/Johnny Mercer musical *St. Louis Woman* (1946), with Pearl Bailey, Rex Ingram, Juanita Hall, and the Nicholas Brothers, directed by Rouben Mamoulian; Eugene O'Neill's *The Iceman Cometh* (1946), with James Barton, Dudley Digges, E. G. Marshall, Nicholas Joy, Tom Pedi, and Jeanne Cagney; Nancy Walker in a musical, *Barefoot Boy with Cheek* (1947), adapted by Max

Shulman from his humorous book of the same name; Katharine Cornell, Godfrey Tearle, Kent Smith, Eli Wallach, Maureen Stapleton, Charlton Heston, Lenore Ulric, and Douglass Watson in a revival of Shakespeare's *Antony and Cleopatra* (1949); unsuccessful revivals of Shaw's *You Never Can Tell* and Jerome Kern's *Sally* (1948); and Katharine Cornell in one of her poorest productions, *That Lady* (1949), in which she performed with a black patch over her eye.

During the 1950s at the Martin Beck, Helen Hayes appeared in *The Wisteria Trees* (1950), Joshua Logan's adaptation of *The Cherry Orchard* set in America's Deep South. Gilbert Miller unveiled his sumptuous production of *Ring Round the Moon* (1950), Christopher Fry's translation of Jean Anouilh's charade with music. Maureen Stapleton, Eli Wallach, Don Murray, and Phyllis Love gleamed in Tennessee Williams's *The Rose Tattoo* (1951), with Stapleton and Wallach winning Tony Awards for their performances and

Top left: Frank Langella as the Count in *Dracula* (1977).

Top right: Geraldine Page and Paul Newman in *Sweet Bird of Youth* (1959).

Bottom: Philip Bosco and Carol Burnett ham it up in *Moon Over Buffalo* (1995).

Ernie Sabella and Mary Elizabeth Mastrantonio in the 2002 revival of *Man of La Mancha*. (Photo by Joan Marcus)

the play winning a Tony as the best drama of the season.

Maxwell Anderson's *Barefoot in Athens* was a failure in 1951, and Truman Capote's *The Grass Harp* flopped in 1952. Arthur Miller's *The Crucible* (1953), with Arthur Kennedy, Beatrice Straight, E. G. Marshall, Walter Hampden, and Madeleine Sherwood, focused on the Salem witch hunts as a metaphor for anticommunist hysteria in then-contemporary America but was more successful when it was later revived Off-Broadway.

On October 15, 1953, one of the Martin Beck's most memorable productions opened: John Patrick's enchanting comedy *The Teahouse of the August Moon*. The production won five Tony Awards, including Best Actor (David Wayne) and Best Play, and stayed at the Martin Beck for 1,027 performances. Also starring John Forsythe and Paul Ford, *Teahouse* delighted with its comical depiction of the American occupation of Okinawa island.

On October 30, 1956, Shaw's *Major Barbara* was successfully revived. The production,

directed by Charles Laughton, also starred Laughton and Cornelia Otis Skinner, plus Burgess Meredith, Glynis Johns, and Eli Wallach. It moved to the Morosco to make way for the Beck's next tenant, *Candide*, a musical version of the Voltaire classic with music by Leonard Bernstein, book by Lillian Hellman, and lyrics by Richard Wilbur, John Latouche, Leonard Bernstein, and Dorothy Parker. With these geniuses at the helm, the production (directed by Tyrone Guthrie) should have been a triumph, but it was not. However, the cast album captured the brilliance of the score, and the show has had two (drastically revised) revivals on Broadway.

A minor Tennessee Williams play, *Orpheus Descending*, with Maureen Stapleton, Cliff Robertson, and Lois Smith, lasted only 68 performances in 1957; but a flimsy comedy, *Who Was That Lady I Saw You With?*, with Mary Healy, Peter Lind Hayes, and Ray Walston, managed to last 208 times. The final show of the 1950s at the Beck was a Tennessee Williams winner, *Sweet Bird of Youth*, with Geraldine

Jennifer Westfeldt and Donna Murphy as the Sherwood sisters sing "Ohio" in the 2003 revival of *Wonderful Town*. (Photo by Paul Kolnik)

Page giving an unforgettable performance as a fading movie star who is living with a young hustler (Paul Newman). It ran for 375 performances.

On April 14, 1960, a jubilant hit came to the Martin Beck. *Bye Bye Birdie*, an exuberant musical parody of early rock and roll and the gyrating Elvis Presley, was an instant hit and won the following Tony Awards: Best Musical, Best Book (Michael Stewart), Best Score (Charles Strouse and Lee Adams), Best Direction and Best Choreography (Gower Champion), and Best Supporting Actor (Dick Van Dyke). The gifted cast also included Chita Rivera, Paul Lynde, Dick Gautier (as a Presley clone), Kay Medford, and Michael J. Pollard. It ran for 607 performances.

During the 1960s the Martin Beck hosted a number of shows that moved there from other houses. Some highlights that originated at the Beck during this decade included Jerry Herman's *Milk and Honey* (1961), about the new Israel; Anne Bancroft, Barbara Harris, Gene Wilder, and Zohra Lampert in a revival of Brecht's *Mother Courage and Her Children* (1963), staged by Jerome Robbins; Colleen Dewhurst and Michael Dunn in Edward Albee's adaptation of Carson McCullers's *The Ballad of the Sad Café* (1963); Jessica Tandy, Hume Cronyn, and Robert Shaw in Friedrich Durrenmatt's *The Physicists* (1964), directed by Peter Brook; and Buddy Hackett and Richard Kiley in the rowdy musical *I Had a Ball* (1964).

The Royal Shakespeare Company's mesmerizing production of *The Persecution and Assassination of Jean-Paul Marat as Performed by the Inmates of the Asylum of Charenton under the Direction of the Marquis de Sade* brought nudity—and a startling sense of the stage's possibilities—to Broadway in 1965.

Highlights of the late 1960s included Jessica Tandy, Hume Cronyn, Rosemary Murphy, and Marian Seldes in Edward Albee's *A Delicate Balance* (1966); Leslie Uggams, Robert Hooks, Lillian Hayman, and Allen Case in the Tony Award—winning musical *Hallelujah, Baby!* (1967), by Betty Comden, Adolph Green, and Jule Styne; and the long-running musical *Man of La Mancha*, which moved here from the downtown ANTA Theatre (1968).

The Martin Beck Theatre remained in the

Beck family until 1966. The theatre is currently owned and operated by Jujamcyn Theaters, which has kept the house in the finest condition.

During the early 1970s, the Martin Beck had a run of plays and musicals that did not last very long. The most notable were Edward Albee's *All Over* (1971), with Jessica Tandy, Colleen Dewhurst, Betty Field, and George Voskovec; a musical version of *The Grass Harp* (1971), starring Barbara Cook; and a British import, *Habeas Corpus* (1975), with June Havoc, Rachel Roberts, Richard Gere, Celeste Holm, Jean Marsh, and Paxton Whitehead.

The streak of flops ended on October 20, 1977, when Frank Langella opened in the title role of *Dracula*, and the Martin Beck became a happy haven for thrill seekers for 925 performances. Langella was succeeded by Raul Julia and David Dukes. The much-publicized Broadway debut of Elizabeth Taylor in *The Little Foxes* had a sellout run in 1981.

The Martin Beck's 1980s tenants included a baseball musical, *The First* (1981); Robert Altman's *Come Back to the Five and Dime Jimmy Dean, Jimmy Dean* (1981), with Cher making her Broadway debut; Angela Lansbury in *A Little Family Business* (1982); and the Royal Shakespeare Company's splendid revival of Shakespeare's *All's Well That Ends Well* (1983).

In 1984 Liza Minnelli and Chita Rivera opened here in *The Rink*, a musical by Terrence McNally, John Kander, and Fred Ebb. Rivera won a Tony Award for her performance. The following year, John Lithgow starred in a stage adaptation of Rod Serling's successful TV and movie story *Requiem for a Heavyweight*, but it was short-lived (three performances). Also doomed was a revival of the musical *Take Me Along* (based on Eugene O'Neill's nostalgic comedy *Ah, Wilderness!*), which closed on its opening night in 1985.

The Stephen Sondheim/James Lapine musical *Into the Woods* fared much better in 1987 and ran for 765 performances. The interweaving of classic fairy tales (e.g., "Cinderella," "Rapunzel," "Little Red Riding Hood," and "Jack and the Beanstalk") won Tony Awards for Best Book of a Musical (Lapine), Best Original Score (Sondheim), and Leading Actress in a Musical (Joanna Gleason). The producers advertised the production by attaching a huge inflatable leg and spiked

Left to right: Peter Kapetan,Eric Lajuan Summers, Stephen Lynch, Matthew Saldivar, andKevin Cahoon sing about the joys of bachelorhood in "Single" in the 2006 musical *The Wedding Singer.* (Photo by Joan Marcus)

boots to the front of the theatre, to make it appear that the Giant of the beanstalk was sitting atop the Martin Beck!

On November 12, 1989, the musical *Grand Hotel* opened, based on the popular Vicki Baum novel, with a book by Luther Davis; songs by Robert Wright, George Forrest, and Maury Yeston; and direction and choreography by Tommy Tune. Performed without intermission, the musical detailed the lives and intrigues of guests at the Grand Hotel in Berlin in 1928. This atmospheric musical was nominated for eleven Tony Awards and won the following: Best Featured Actor in a Musical (Michael Jeter), Best Costume Design (Santo Loquasto), Best Musical Director (Tommy Tune), Best Choreography (Tune), and Best Lighting Design (Jules Fisher). During rehearsals, Yeston (*Nine, Titanic*) was brought in to supply additional music and lyrics to a project Wright and Forrest had been developing for more than two decades. The musical ran for 1,077 performances and ended its long run in 1992 at the Gershwin Theatre.

Another huge hit played at this theatre when the classic 1950 musical *Guys and Dolls*, by Frank Loesser, Jo Swerling, and Abe Burrows, was revived in 1992. The stars this time included Nathan Lane, Faith Prince, Peter Gallagher, Josie de Guzman, Scott Wise, and Walter Bobbie, and the revival received a rapturous reception. It ran for 1,143 performances—nearly as long as the original—and won the following Tony Awards: Best Musical Revival, Best Actress in a Musical (Prince), Best Musical Director (Jerry Zaks), and Best Scenic Design (Tony Walton).

My Thing of Love, a play about a broken marriage, opened on May 3, 1995, starring Laurie Metcalf, but lasted for only thirteen performances.

On October 1, 1995, Carol Burnett and Philip Bosco brought convulsive slapstick to the Martin Beck in Ken Ludwig's farce *Moon Over Buffalo*. Not all critics were amused. Some found that the comedy about a hammy theatrical troupe appearing at a Buffalo theatre strained too hard to be funny. Nevertheless, both Burnett (in her first Broadway appearance since 1964) and Bosco received Tony Award nominations for their performances. They were ably supported by Jane Connell, Randy Graff, and others, and ran for 308 performances. Later in the run the two

Edward Hibbert (center) battles for control of his briefcase with most of the cast of the backstage murder mystery musical, *Curtains* (2007). (Photo by Joan Marcus)

leads were succeeded by Lynn Redgrave and Robert Goulet. An unusual aspect of the production was that a fascinating documentary called *Moon Over Broadway* was filmed by D. A. Pennebaker backstage during the creation and rehearsals of this comedy, which vividly detailed the bickering and problems that ensue when "the show must go on." The show is also remembered for its poster, which consisted of a rebus: a crescent moon hanging over the figure of a bison.

The famed magician David Copperfield brightened the 1996 holiday season at this theatre with his lavish magic show *Dreams & Nightmares*. Described as "an intimate evening of grand illusion," the spectacle was created and performed by Copperfield with startling special effects. Francis Ford Coppola served as the creative advisor. The sold-out extravaganza completed a limited run of fifty-four performances.

A new production of the 1977 musical *Annie* received a very mixed reception in March 1997. Nell Carter played Miss Hannigan and Brittny Kissinger was Annie, but they did not enjoy the success of Dorothy Loudon or Andrea McArdle of the original production.

The show received a Tony Award nomination for Best Revival but didn't win. It ran for 238 performances.

Rebecca Luker starred as Maria in a beautifully mounted 1998 revival of *The Sound of Music* directed by Susan H. Schulman. During the 533-performance run, TV star Richard Chamberlain stepped into the role of Captain von Trapp, with eighteen-year-old Laura Benanti at his side to sing "Do Re Mi" as Maria in her Broadway debut.

A nostalgic event occurred at this theatre on November 18, 1999. A new production of Cole Porter's classic 1948 *Kiss Me, Kate* (which had been the first musical to win a Tony Award) opened to vociferous cheers. The splendid book by Sam and Bella Spewack deftly combined Shakespeare's *The Taming of the Shrew* with the backstage antics of a theatrical troupe performing a musical version of the comedy in Baltimore. Porter's score is considered to be his best. In the new production the leads were played by Brian Stokes Mitchell, Marin Mazzie, Amy Spanger, and Michael Berresse. A nostalgic note: the original leads in 1948 were Alfred Drake, Patricia Morison, Lisa Kirk, and Harold Lang. Morison, the only surviving member of this quartet, attended the 1999 opening night and looked radiant.

Kiss Me, Kate received twelve Tony Award nominations and won the following: Best Musical Revival; Best Orchestrations (Don Sebesky); Best Costumes (Martin Pakledinaz); Best Musical Direction (Michael Blakemore), and Best Leading Actor in a Musical (Mitchell).

In response to the box office plunge that followed the September 11, 2001, terrorist attack on the World Trade Center, the cast of *Kiss Me, Kate* made a memorable eleventh-

hour effort to save the show. In a dramatic curtain speech at what was to have been the final performance on September 23, it was announced that in addition to taking a 25 percent pay cut, the company volunteered to allocate an additional quarter of their salaries to buy tickets to the show and donate them to the rescue workers who had a hand in the recovery effort. The gesture helped keep *Kate* running through December 2001, when it closed after 881 performances.

John Lithgow took the role of corrupt newspaper columnist J. J. Hunsecker, and Brian d'Arcy James played the increasingly desperate press agent Sidney, in *Sweet Smell of Success*, a dark musical adaptation of the classic film of the same name. The powerhouse collaborative team of Marvin Hamlisch (music), John Guare (book), Craig Carnelia (lyrics), and Nicholas Hytner (direction) was unable to deliver a hit. The show opened on March 14, 2002, and closed after 109 performances.

In December 2002 Brian Stokes Mitchell brought his lush baritone to the role of knight-errant Don Quixote in a revival of *Man of La Mancha* opposite Mary Elizabeth Mastrantonio as Aldonza and Ernie Sabella as Sancho. Paul Brown's set featured a huge semicircular staircase that embraced the playing space and rose into the heavens. Mitchell sang "The Impossible Dream (The Quest)" 304 times.

On June 21, 2003, the Martin Beck Theatre

was renamed the Al Hirschfeld Theatre in honor of the caricaturist who had spent eight decades capturing the spirit of evanescent theatre performances with his distinctive looping sketches. The theatre's new marquee was topped with a self-portrait of Hirschfeld outlined in neon. When first installed, the figure in the drawing seemed to be using its own head as an inkwell, with a well of bright red "ink" that gave the portrait a macabre aspect. Blue neon was soon substituted.

Actors in the next few shows reported backstage mischief from an allegedly supernatural source—reputedly Beck's ghost, who apparently was unhappy with the name change. The problem seemed to abate after a plaque acknowledging Beck was installed in a prominent place in the inner lobby.

The first show in the rechristened playhouse was a revival of the musical *Wonderful Town*, starring Donna Murphy and Jennifer Westfeldt as two Ohio sisters adapting to life in Greenwich Village. Murphy earned raves for a performance that had her climbing the set for "Conga!" but her frequent absences due to illness became tabloid fodder and cut into the box office. Actress Brooke Shields followed her into the role of Ruth, but Kathleen Marshall's lauded revival (which originated at the City Center Encores! series) closed after 497 performances.

The Hirschfeld got its third big musical revival in a row beginning May 4, 2005, with *Sweet Charity*, starring Christina Applegate as the hapless taxi dancer Charity Hope Valentine. The show nearly closed out of town when Applegate broke her foot in an onstage misstep. But, in grand Broadway tradition, she insisted that the show go on. She went into intensive physical therapy while understudy Charlotte d'Amboise played the rest of the tryout. With help from choreographer Wayne Cilento, Applegate returned to the stage for the Broadway opening and performed a showstopping version of the Cy Coleman/Dorothy Fields song "Bravest Individual" with costar Denis O'Hare. The show ran 279 performances.

The songwriting team of Matthew Sklar and Chad Beguelin made its Broadway debut April 27, 2006, with *The Wedding Singer*, a musical adaptation of the popular Adam Sandler film comedy about a musician who plays at wedding after wedding while his own love life is a mess. Directed by John Rando, the 285-performance show was an homage to 1980s pop culture, complete with a giant version of the pioneering video game Pong projected on the curtain during the intermission. Stephen Lynch played the title role, with Laura Benanti and Felicia Finley as his love interests. Rita Gardner, the original Luisa in *The Fantasticks* forty-six years earlier, had a notable role as his rapping grandmother.

Broadway veterans Kander and Ebb delved into a backstage murder mystery in Curtains, a traditional tuner that opened March 22, 2007, and won a Tony Award for leading man David Hyde Pierce as a police detective who dreams of starring in a musical. The score contained the limelight anthem "Show People." Rupert Holmes stepped in after the death of lyricist Fred Ebb during the show's long gestation, and composer Kander supplied his own words for the heartfelt song "I Miss the Music," about a songwriter who has lost his partner. The show stayed for 511 performances.

Composer/lyricist/librettist Jill Santoriello worked a reported eighteen years on her labor of love, a musical adaptation of Charles Dickens's *A Tale of Two Cities*, which finally got its Broadway debut here September 18, 2008. Despite a powerhouse performance by James Barbour as reformed alcoholic Sidney Carton, who gives his life for the girl he loves, the pop opera was judged to be too similar to *Les Misérables* and managed only sixty performances.

The Hirschfeld got its first true blockbuster in years with the March 31, 2009, revival of *Hair*, which arrived after a hot-ticket engagement at the Delacorte Theatre in Central Park the previous summer. Director Diane Paulus tapped into the original spirit of the 1960s antiwar musical and had leads Gavin Creel and Will Swenson invite the audience onto the stage each night for a joyous singing of "Let the Sun Shine In." Though the producers initially had trouble raising money in the worst days of the winter 2009 recession, Hair quickly recouped and settled in for a long run at the Hirschfeld.

AMBASSADOR
THEATRE

THE AMBASSADOR WAS THE FIRST OF six new theatres that the Shuberts built on West Forty-eighth and West Forty-ninth streets in the early 1920s. The plot at 215 West Forty-ninth Street presented a challenge to veteran theatre architect Herbert J. Krapp, being too narrow for a conventional theatre layout. The resourceful Krapp responded with an unorthodox configuration, placing the auditorium diagonally on the site. Its auditorium is wide rather than deep, offering an excellent view of the stage from all seats.

There have been some erroneous reports that this theatre opened with the Shuberts' famous operetta *Blossom Time*. Not so. The Ambassador welcomed a musical called *The Rose Girl* as its inaugural production on

scapino!

February 11, 1921, starring Marjorie Gateson. It was a success.

In May of 1921, a soldier revue called *Biff! Bing! Bang!* amused theatregoers. Later that year *Blossom Time* did open at the Ambassador, and it was this theatre's first smash hit. A musical biography of composer Franz Schubert, it featured melodies adapted by fellow composer Sigmund Romberg from Schubert's themes. The showstopper was "Serenade." The operetta, which ran for 576 performances, became a perennial Shubert revival.

Operettas were the rage in the 1920s, and the Ambassador had its share of them. After *Blossom Time* came *The Lady in Ermine* (1922), a European import with added numbers by Al Goodman, who conducted pit orchestras for many Broadway shows, and by Romberg, whose "When Hearts Are Young" was the hit of the show. This success was followed by *Caroline* (1923), an American adaptation of a German operetta by Edward Kunneke, starring Tessa Kosta. Next came Victor Herbert's last show, *The Dream Girl* (1924), a fantasy that involved Fay Bainter and Walter Woolf in one of those "dream" plots, which takes them back to the fifteenth century. There were some Sigmund Romberg interpolations in this operetta, too, which was produced after Herbert's death.

A change of fare came to the Ambassador in 1925 when a highly successful revival of Shaw's *Candida*, starring Katharine Cornell, who became famed for her interpretation of the leading role, moved from the Eltinge Theatre to this house. More drama arrived when William A. Brady brought in his production of F. Scott Fitzgerald's *The Great Gatsby* (1926), adapted by Owen Davis and starring James Rennie as Gatsby, Florence Eldridge as Daisy, and Elliott Cabot as Tom Buchanan. Directed by George Cukor, the future great film director, the play ran for 113 performances.

The Ambassador returned to musicals with a solid hit, *Queen High*, which ran for almost four hundred performances in 1926—27. It starred Charles Ruggles. From September 1927 until December 1929, the Ambassador had a string of quick flops. The few exceptions were an exciting police drama, *The Racket*

(1927), starring Edward G. Robinson, Norman Foster, and John Cromwell, which ran for 120 performances and was named one of the year's ten best plays; and *Little Accident*, a play by Floyd Dell and Thomas Mitchell, with Mitchell starring as a man about to marry one woman when he discovers he is the father of another woman's child. This hit comedy moved from the Morosco Theatre and played for six months at the Ambassador.

In December 1929 *Street Scene*, Elmer Rice's Pulitzer Prize—winning play that took place in front of a Manhattan tenement house, moved from the Playhouse and completed its run of 601 performances at the Ambassador. *The Last Mile*, a prison drama by John Wexley, starring Spencer Tracy, Joseph Spurin-Calleia, and Henry O'Neill, moved from the Sam H. Harris Theatre to the Ambassador in October 1930. This lauded drama, one of the year's ten best, served as the springboard for Spencer Tracy's career in Hollywood.

Highlights of the 1930s at this theatre included *Are You Decent?* (1934), a comedy by Crane Wilbur in which Claudia Morgan announced to two suitors that she wished to have a baby without bothering with matrimony; *Kill That Story* (1934), a George Abbott/Philip Dunning production about a newspaperman whose wife unjustly divorces him because she believes he's having an affair with a stenographer at the newspaper; and Lucile Watson and Percy Kilbride in *Post Road* (1935), a comedy about kidnapping that moved here from the Masque Theatre.

Ayn Rand's fascinating courtroom drama *The Night of January 16* (1935), starring Doris Nolan and Walter Pidgeon, featured a jury selected from the audience at each performance to decide if Nolan was guilty of murder.

Other 1930s highlights: the Abbey Theatre Players from Dublin in a season of repertory, including *Katie Roche*, *The Plough and the Stars*, *The Playboy of the Western World*, and *Juno and the Paycock* (1937); and Danny Kaye making his Broadway debut in *The Straw Hat Revue* (1939), with Imogene Coca, Alfred Drake, and Jerome Robbins in the cast, spoofing Broadway shows and current trends.

In 1935 the Shuberts sold their interest in this theatre; they did not buy it back until 1956. During those two decades, the Ambassador did not always function as a legitimate theatre. It was, on different occasions, leased as a movie theatre and as a studio for radio and TV.

The Ambassador returned to legitimacy on November 16, 1941, with *Cuckoos on the*

Hearth, an insane comedy that moved here from the Mansfield Theatre, with Percy Kilbride, Janet Fox, and Howard St. John. Then two years elapsed before the theatre again housed a play. The Messrs. Shubert brought in a revival of *Blossom Time* in 1943, but it lasted for only forty-seven performances. Edward Chodorov's successful drama *Decision* moved here from the Belasco in 1944; the critically disdained but popular comedy *School for Brides*, starring Roscoe Karns, moved here from the Royale in 1944.

For the next twelve years, the Ambassador was leased to radio and television networks. In 1956 the Shuberts once again became the owners and reopened the refurbished house with a comedy, *The Loud Red Patrick*, starring David Wayne and Arthur Kennedy. It was not suc-

cessful, and neither was the next tenant, Tallulah Bankhead in *Eugenia*, adapted from Henry James's *The Europeans*.

In 1957 Meyer Levin's adaptation of his book *Compulsion*, about the famous Leopold/Loeb murder trial in Chicago, played for 140 performances with Dean Stockwell and Roddy McDowall as the murderers and Ina Balin as one of their college classmates. In March 1958 Tyrone Power and Faye Emerson played Adam and Eve in George Bernard Shaw's *Back to Methuselah* for twenty-nine performances. George C. Scott made his Broadway debut at the Ambassador with Judith Anderson in the 1958 drama *Comes a Day* and caused an immediate sensation by strangling a bird onstage (a prop, we hope). In 1959 Melvyn Douglas, E. G. Marshall, and Jean Dixon appeared in *The Gang's All Here*, a play about the scandalous Harding administration in Washington, D.C.

The 1960s at the Ambassador brought Paddy Chayefsky's *The Tenth Man* (1961) from the Booth Theatre; Gladys Cooper in an interesting adaptation of E. M. Forster's *A Passage to India* (1962); Joseph Cotten, Patricia Medina (his wife), Russell Collins, and John Beal in Joseph Hayes's drama about corruption in big business, *Calculated Risk* (1962); *Stop the World—I Want to Get Off* (1963), the celebrated Anthony Newley/Leslie Bricusse musical, transferred from the Shubert Theatre; Ira Wallach's *Absence of a Cello* (1964), with Fred Clark giving a comic performance; and appearances by the Paul Taylor Dance Company and Charles Aznavour (1965).

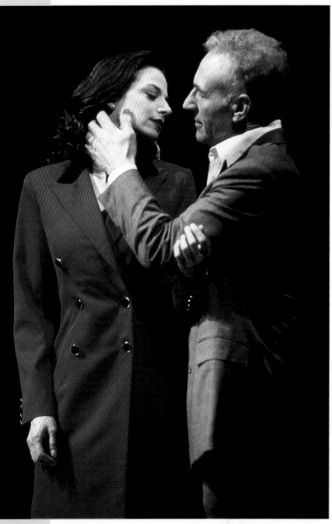

Right: Frances Conroy and Patrick Stewart in Arthur Miller's *The Ride Down Mt. Morgan* (2000).

The second half of the decade brought Robert Preston and Rosemary Harris in James Goldman's witty play *The Lion in Winter* (1966), about Henry II and Eleanor of Aquitaine; Robert Anderson's captivating playlets under the collective title *You Know I Can't Hear You When the Water's Running* (1967), starring Martin Balsam, Eileen Heckart, and George Grizzard; and *We Bombed in New Haven* (1968), the unsuccessful Joseph Heller play about men at war, starring Jason Robards Jr.

On January 22, 1969, the Ambassador hosted an experimental musical, *Celebration*, from the writers of *The Fantasticks*, Tom Jones and Harvey Schmidt. Called by Jones a "ritual experience. With laughs. And a few naked girls," *Celebration* enacted a battle between winter and summer in the persons of an old rich man and an orphan lad who vie for the love of a young woman named Angel. Starring Keith Charles, Susan Watson, and Ted Thurston, it stayed for 109 performances.

The 1970s brought unusual and varied fare to this theatre. A revival of Sandy Wilson's spoof of 1920s musicals, *The Boy Friend* (1970), starring Sandy Duncan and Judy Carne, did not fare as well as the original. Paul Sills's *Story Theatre* (1970) turned out to be a delightful entertainment that presented children's classic stories with dance, song, narration, and pantomime. Melvin Van Peebles's *Ain't Supposed to Die a Natural Death* (1971) offered an original look at the black experience. Subsequent productions included Jim Dale in a lively revival of *Scapino* (1974) that featured the startling stunt of Dale dashing out into the audience balancing on the backs of seats; Estelle Parsons in a one-woman tour de force, *Miss Margarida's Way* (1977), which treated the audience as a classroom of misbehaving children; a marvelous revue of Eubie Blake songs called *Eubie!* (1978); a revival of the gospel musical *Your Arms Too Short to Box with God* (1980); *Dancin'* (1980), the Bob Fosse dance triumph that moved here from the Broadhurst; and a 1983 revival of Arthur Miller's revised

version of *A View from the Bridge*, with potent performances by Tony Lo Bianco, Rose Gregorio, James Hayden, Alan Feinstein, and Robert Prosky.

In 1985 this theatre housed *Leader of the Pack*, a revue of bouncy, early 1960s pop songs by Ellie Greenwich. In 1987 *Barbara Cook: A Concert for the Theatre* opened here, followed by a revival of the musical *Dreamgirls*. A revival of *Ain't Misbehavin'* in 1988 (with a reunion of the 1978 musical's original cast) proved popular, staying for nearly six months, though the Brazilian revue *Oba Oba '90* managed only forty-five performances.

In 1989 Rex Harrison, Glynis Johns, and Stewart Granger starred in a revival of W. Somerset Maugham's witty comedy *The Circle*. Granger made his Broadway debut in this play. Unfortunately, it was his only appearance on Broadway, as well as Harrison's last. Both were deceased a short time afterward. The play ran for 208 performances.

Red Buttons on Broadway, a solo show featuring the comedian, played a short engagement at the Ambassador, then was followed by a big hit: the Off-Broadway musical *Bring in 'da Noise, Bring in 'da Funk*, which transferred from the Public Theatre to Broadway on April 25, 1996. Described as a "performance piece," the unique entertainment was based on an idea by Savion Glover (who choreographed and starred in it) and George C. Wolfe. Produced by the New York Shakespeare Festival, it thrilled critics and audiences with its vivid sketches of African-American history as expressed through dynamic dancing and singing. The musical earned nine Tony Award nominations and won the following: Best Direction of a Musical (Wolfe), Best Choreography (Glover), Best Featured Actress in a Musical (Ann Duquesnay), and Best Lighting (Jules Fisher). The hit ran for 1,130 performances.

In February 1999 a new production of Clark Gesner's 1967 Off-Broadway musical *You're a Good Man, Charlie Brown* opened and won Tony Awards for its two featured performers, Kristin Chenoweth and Roger Bart. Chenoweth's performance of the interpolated song "My New Philosophy" by Andrew Lippa made her a star. The production was also nominated for Best Musical Revival and Best Direction of a Musical (Michael Mayer).

Arthur Miller's drama *The Ride Down Mt. Morgan* opened here on April 9, 2000, to mixed reviews. Critics felt that it was an unfinished work. The play, about a charismatic bigamist whose two families meet after he's injured in a car accident, starred Patrick Stewart and Frances Conroy. Stewart caused controversy after one performance by making a curtain speech and accusing the play's producers of not properly publicizing the production. He was censured by Actors' Equity and ordered to apologize. The drama earned a Best Play Tony nomination and a Best Featured Actress nomination for Conroy and played for 120 performances. It was the final Broadway opening of a new play for playwriting titan Arthur Miller, who died in 2005.

On March 11, 2001, the Ambassador hosted a transfer of Lonny Price and Linda Kline's Off-Broadway hit *A Class Act*, a musical biography of idiosyncratic *A Chorus Line* lyricist Ed Kleban (1939—1987) using his many fine, but largely unpublished, songs to tell the story of his life, which had been cut short by cancer. The show finally gave the songs the Broadway airing Kleban had craved.

Kate Burton earned a Tony nomination for her performance of the title role in the October 4, 2001, revival of Henrik Ibsen's *Hedda Gabler*. The Ambassador housed the 2002 Pulitzer Prize—winning drama *Topdog/Underdog*, making its author, Suzan-Lori Parks, the first African-American woman to be accorded that honor. Jeffrey Wright and rapper Mos Def starred in the drama about two brothers, named Booth and Lincoln, who wind up reenacting the assassination of the president. It stayed at the Ambassador for 144 performances.

For the rest of the decade, the Ambassador Theatre was the laboratory for a highly successful experiment in serial stunt casting. The theatre was booked throughout that period with the Tony-winning 1996 revival of *Chicago*, which had opened at the Richard Rodgers Theatre and spent a period at the Shubert before settling in for the long haul at the Ambassador starting January 29, 2003.

Producers Fran and Barry Weissler had kept their 1994 revival of *Grease!* running long past its natural expiration date by bringing in celebrities from other media for short engagements, usually in supporting roles. When *Chicago*'s box office moxie began to flag, they tried the same policy (though applying now to leading roles) with tremendous success, bringing in the likes of Marilu Henner, Melanie Griffith, and Ashlee Simpson as Roxie, and Usher, George Hamilton, Alan Thicke, and Tom Wopat as Billy Flynn. The leads may have changed, but many in the supporting ensemble stayed with the show year after year and became adept at handling the "put-ins" of these celebrities.

Also contributing to the revival's longevity was the 2002 film version of *Chicago*, which won the Oscar for Best Picture. Far from harming the prospects of the Broadway version, the movie made the property a known quantity throughout the world, and tourists visiting New York were sold for many years on the opportunity to see what was billed as the *real Chicago* "live on Broadway."

Chicago celebrated its tenth anniversary in 2006 with a reunion of the many performers who had played the roles, with special guest Chita Rivera from the original 1975 production on hand to sing and dance in the opening number, and the others alternating in the various songs and scenes.

Tom Wopat (center) stars as Billy Flynn in *Chicago* the musical. (Photo by Paul Kolnik)

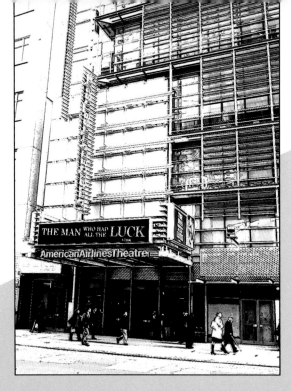

AMERICAN AIRLINES

THEATRE

THE AMERICAN AIRLINES THEATRE was originally the Selwyn Theatre, built by brothers Arch and Edgar Selwyn, celebrated producers of the 1910s. George Keister was the architect, and the intimate theatre (1,051 seats) with one balcony was designed in the Italian Renaissance style.

The October 3, 1918, opening-night program boasted of the Selwyn as the most modern theatre in New York. This was the height of World War I, and the program also had this startling message on the back cover: "BUY LIBERTY BONDS. Every German or Austrian in the United States, unless known by years of association to be absolutely loyal, should be treated as a potential spy. Keep your eyes and ears open. Whenever any suspicious act or dis-

The ensemble cast of the courtroom drama *Twelve Angry Men* (2004). (Photo by Joan Marcus)

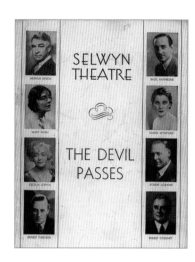

Left to right: Cover and billboard page from the program distributed on the opening night of the Selwyn Theatre in 1918. The play was *Information, Please.*

Libby Holman sings "Something To Remember You By" to MacMurray in *Three's a Crowd.*

Program for *Tickle Me* (1926), the hit musical by Otto Harbach, Oscar Hammerstein II, and Frank Mandel.

Program from *The Devil Passes* (1932).

loyal word comes to your notice, communicate at once with the Bureau of Investigation of the Department of Justice, 15 Park Row, New York. We are at war with the most merciless and inhumane nation in the world."

Unfortunately, the opening production at the Selwyn was not memorable. The acclaimed actress and playwright Jane Cowl starred in *Information Please*, written by her and Jane Murfin. It was a flop. However, Cowl (famed for her portrayal of Juliet in Shakespeare's tragedy) redeemed herself in the next play, *The Crowded Hour.*

In 1919, two popular actors, Holbrook Blinn and Alan Dinehart, starred in a socialist drama called *The Challenge* by Eugene Walter. It ran for seventy-two performances.

The Selwyn's first hit was a World War I musical, *Buddies*, by George V. Hobart, music and lyrics by B. C. Hilliam. According to Gerald Bordman in his excellent volume *American Musical Theatre*, one song was partially written by Cole Porter. The musical took place in Normandy shortly after the Armistice. A shy Yank (Roland Young) is in love with a French girl named Julie (Peggy Wood) but is too bashful to woo her. She's in love with him, but to arouse his interest, she flirts with his best buddy, Sonny (Donald Brian). It works. Critics raved about the three leads, and the musical ran for 259 performances, although the score was considered mediocre.

On August 17, 1920, a musical called *Tickle Me* opened at this theatre. It had book and lyrics by Otto Harbach, Oscar Hammerstein II, and Frank Mandel, and music by Herbert Stothart. The popular comic Frank Tinney starred in it and employed his usual bit about talking to the audience during the show. The plot revolved around a company of actors who

travel to Tibet to shoot a film. The show ran for six months, which in those days was considered substantial.

The Circle, W. Somerset Maugham's brilliant high comedy, proved popular at the Selwyn in 1921. Its distinguished cast included Leslie Carter, in her comeback; John Drew, who had also been away from the stage for several years; Estelle Winwood; and John Halliday. The plot involves a titled Englishwoman who had abandoned her husband and daughter and eloped with her lover. When the two elopers return to her estate years later, they discover that their son's wife is about to abandon him and run off with her lover. The circle is completed when the young elopers borrow the old elopers' car to take them to London. This high-society fluff ran for 175 performances.

In 1921 a tragic incident occurred involving this theatre. At the time, several of the theatres on Forty-second Street supplemented their income by showing silent movies. In May 1921 the theatre was screening the silent film of *A Connecticut Yankee in King Arthur's Court.* Katharine Hepburn was visiting her aunt in New York with her young brother Tom and took him to see the film. In the movie there was a scene in which a man devised a way to hang himself without dying. The next morning, when Hepburn went to wake her brother, she found him hanging dead in his upstairs bedroom. Hepburn's father told the press that his son was merely trying to emulate the false hanging, but to this day there is a belief that he committed suicide, as he had a history of depression.

A modest musical hit called *The Blue Kitten*, by Otto Harbach and William Clay Duncan, opened on January 13, 1922. It starred two old-timers—Joseph Cawthorn and Lillian Lorraine—and told of a headwaiter who tries to conceal his station in life so his daughter can marry a socialite. Although the score was pronounced inferior, the musical ran for 140 performances.

The famous actress Alla Nazimova appeared here in 1923 in a turgid drama called *Dagmar*, by Louis Anspacher, adapted from a French play. The sexually promiscuous heroine (Nazimova) promises her latest lover that he can kill her if she is ever unfaithful to him. Sure enough, she winds up with her throat slit. This turkey played fifty-six times.

An improbable drama called *The Guilty One* opened on March 20, 1923. Written by Michael Morton and Peter Traill, it told of a married woman who gets involved in the murder of her lover. It lasted only thirty-one performances.

A short-lived drama (fifteen performances) opened at the Selwyn on April 17, 1923. Called *Within Four Walls*, by Glen Macdonough, it depicted a man who returns to

Greenwich Village the day before his family home is to be demolished, which leads to a lot of nostalgic flashback scenes.

A whimsical musical titled *Helen of Troy, New York* arrived here on June 19, 1923. Written by two of the century's greatest wits, George S. Kaufman and Marc Connelly, with a score by Bert Kalmar and Harry Ruby, *Helen* told of a woman (Helen Ford) who works in a collar factory in Troy, New York, but loses her job because she falls in love with the boss's son. She later invents the semisoft style of collar, which becomes highly commercial and wins back her lover. Paul Frawley and Queenie Smith also glowed in this frolic. It ran for 191 performances. As a promotional stunt, the producers sent out cardboard shirt collars with the name of the show and theatre on them.

A musical comedy called *Battling Butler*, starring the popular actor Charles Ruggles, arrived on October 8, 1923. Written by Ballard MacDonald, adapted from a British musical, *Battling Butler* had music by Walter L. Rosemont. The plot told of Alfred Butler, who so strongly resembles a boxer called Battling Butler that he's able to pass himself off as the pugilist. The real Battling Butler then urges him to take his place in the ring. The *New York Times* proclaimed that "musical comedies are getting better," and the show prospered for 288 performances.

Three plays of short duration next appeared. *Puppets*, a melodrama by Frances Lightner, had two actors in it who would

Top: Jennifer Cody, Kelly O'Hara, Peter Benson and Joyce Chittick lead union members singing "7 1/2 Cents" in the 2006 revival of *The Pajama Game*. (Photo by Joan Marcus)

Bottom: Carla Gugino and Peter Krause in Arthur Miller's *After the Fall* (2004). (Photo by Joan Marcus)

become popular movie stars: Fredric March and Miriam Hopkins. Their play about a puppeteer lasted only fifty-four performances, in 1925. *The Sapphire Ring*, by Laszlo Lakatos, starred Helen Gahagan and Frank Conroy. This play about fidelity in marriage disappeared after thirteen performances. A comedy thriller called *The Gorilla*, by Ralph Spence, featured two comic detectives and a gorilla in a spooky house. This one departed after fifteen performances, although it was made into several films.

On November 10, 1925, *Charlot's Revue*, the second edition of the famed British revue, returned with three of its original stars: Beatrice Lillie, Gertrude Lawrence, and Jack Buchanan. Lillie repeated her hilarious routine called "March with Me," which had fractured Broadway in 1924, and a new song, "A Cup of Coffee, a Sandwich and You," proved a hit. Although not as sensational as the 1924 edition, the 1926 *Charlot's* still managed to amuse audiences for 138 performances.

On May 25, 1926, something different opened at this theatre. Fakir Rahman Bey, in his first visit to the United States, demonstrated practices of Fakirism, including body rigidity, thought reading, hypnotism, burial alive, and talismans. He cavorted for three weeks.

A minor comedy called *The Man from Toronto*, by Douglas Murray, opened late in the season and tarried for only twenty-eight performances. It concerned a woman who is forced by a will to marry a man she's never met, so she pretends to be the maid of the house to see if she likes him. She does.

A fun musical, *Castles in the Air*, came to the Selwyn via Chicago in September 1926. Starring Vivienne Segal, J. Harold Murray, Bernard Granville, and Gregory Ratoff, it concerned two college cutups who mistakenly enter an exclusive club, thinking it's a hotel. In order to stay, one of them pretends to be a Latvian prince, and Segal is smitten. Her wealthy uncle sees through the ruse and, to cure his niece, rents a Latvian castle, where he intends to expose the fake prince. As usual in 1920s musicals, the prince turns out to be real, and he and the niece live happily ever after. The book and lyrics were by Raymond W. Peck and the music by Percy Wenrich. It played for 160 performances.

In 1927—28, the Broadway season that witnessed the production of a record 270 shows, the Selwyn had its ups and downs. *The Mating Season*, a farce by William A. Grew, started things badly. It expired after twenty-four showings. A revue called *The Manhatters* fared a bit better, running for sixty-eight performances. Three future movie stars—Alison Skipworth, Miriam Hopkins, and Douglas Montgomery—couldn't save Avery Hopwood's *The Garden of Eden*, which was cast out after twenty-three performances.

Nightstick, a melodrama by John Wray, the Nugents, and Elaine Stern Carrington, ran for fifty-two performances, then returned for thirty-two more. In the cast were Thomas Mitchell, Lee Patrick, and playwright Wray. Patrick played a woman who has two love interests: a prisoner (Wray) and a detective (Mitchell). Of course, the detective wins out.

The Selwyn's biggest hit arrived on

Left to right: Swoosie Kurtz, Lily Rabe, and Byron Jennings in the 2006 revival of Shaw's *Heartbreak House*. (Photo by Joan Marcus)

December 28, 1927. *The Royal Family*, by George S. Kaufman and Edna Ferber, was a thinly disguised farce about two royal families of the theatre, the Barrymores and the Drews, although the authors denied this. Suffice to say that Ethel Barrymore took great umbrage at the play and stopped speaking to Kaufman. The family in the play was called Cavendish and, certainly, the madcap Anthony Cavendish, actor, philanderer, alcoholic, and outrageous charlatan, could be no one but John Barrymore. The role was played to the hilt by Otto Kruger. The erratic Jed Harris produced this huge success, which filled the Selwyn for 345 performances. The comedy was revived as recently as 2009, and composer William Finn spent years working on a musical version—in an age when Drew and Barrymore descendant Drew Barrymore is continuing her family's tradition of acting (and cutting up).

Producer Arch Selwyn was instrumental in bringing some of Britain's greatest revues to Broadway. In November 1928 he imported Noël Coward's triumphant *This Year of Grace*, the first revue in which Coward supplied all the music, lyrics, and sketches. He and Beatrice Lillie headed the show, and it was pronounced the acme of wit and melody. Three Coward classics were sung: "A Room with a View," "Dance, Little Lady," and "World Weary," which Lillie sang sitting on a stool while biting an apple. Under the personal direction of C. B. Cochran, the stylish revue had dances by Tilly Losch and Max Rivers, and sets and costumes by Oliver Messel, G. E. Calthrop, Norman Hartness, and Doris Zinkeisen. Beatrice Lillie's sketches—at a bus stop and on the Lido—were hilarious. The sophisticated romp ran for 158 performances.

This gem was followed by a dreadful revue called *Keep It Clean*, in 1929. The tasteless material included a risqué song about the marriage of Charles Lindbergh to Anne Morrow, and a hapless imitation of the great Beatrice Lillie. After sixteen performances, this mess expired.

The Selwyn was graced with another stylish London revue, *Wake Up and Dream*, in 1929. The show starred Jack Buchanan, Jessie Matthews, and the ethereal dancer Tilly Losch, who beautifully interpreted Cole Porter's song "What Is This Thing Called Love?" This was another C. B. Cochran revue, and it was applauded for 138 performances.

By now, the Selwyn had become a prime house to showcase splendid revues. The next offering, *Three's a Crowd*, starring the great trio of Clifton Webb, Fred Allen, and Libby Holman (who had glittered in *The Little Show* on Broadway), proved that. The skilled cast also included Tamara Geva, Portland Hoffa (Mrs. Fred Allen), and Fred MacMurray. Howard Dietz and Arthur Schwartz wrote most of the music, but a squad of composers and lyricists contributed such gems as "Body and Soul" (danced by Webb and Geva in a strikingly lighted set by Hassard Short) and "Something to Remember You By." The sketches were mostly by Dietz. Allen was riotous in a scene ribbing Admiral Byrd at the North Pole. Albertina Rasch staged the memorable dances, and Hassard Short received an award from General Electric for his dazzling lighting. The revue ran for 272 performances.

The Selwyn had serious troubles in the Depression years. It housed eleven consecutive flops and, under new ownership, started showing films in 1934. In the 1950s it tried an experiment, attempting to combine films with live drama, but audiences weren't interested.

The Selwyn continued showing films into the 1990s. But late in that decade, as part of the

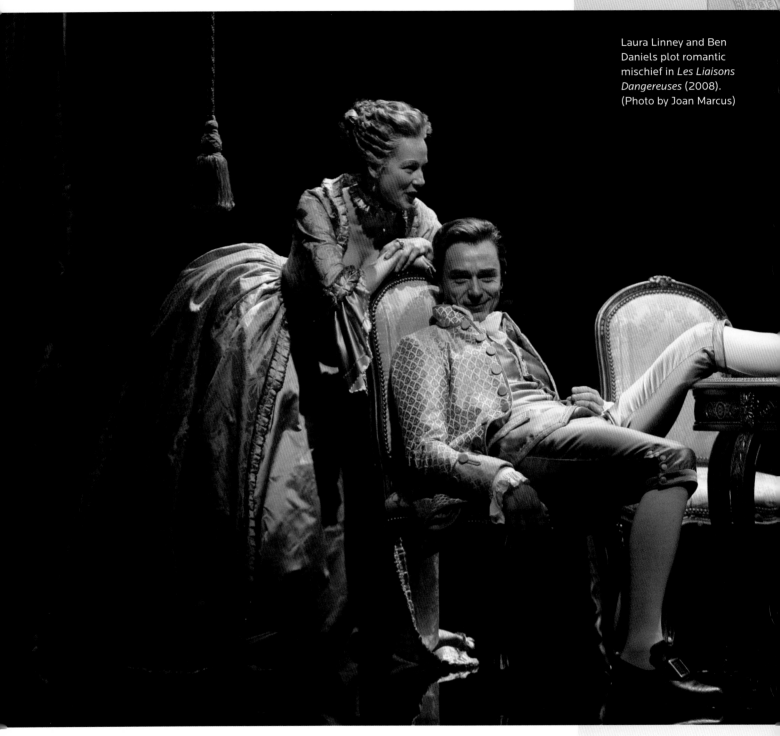

Laura Linney and Ben Daniels plot romantic mischief in *Les Liaisons Dangereuses* (2008). (Photo by Joan Marcus)

Forty-second Street renaissance, the Roundabout Theatre Company, the not-for-profit troupe that had been operating out of temporary quarters at the Criterion Center in Times Square, announced that it would take control of the Selwyn from the New 42nd Street redevelopment organization, restore the theatre, and make it the company's permanent home.

The theatre straddles the block between Forty-second and Forty-third streets. The main auditorium is on the Forty-third Street side, but the main entrance is on the more heavily traveled Forty-second Street side, formerly connected by a promenade auditorium that ran through a small office building. The renovation project proceeded despite the untimely collapse of that building on December 30, 1997. A new office tower, complete with a prime rehearsal space called the New 42nd Street Studios, was built in its place.

Also at this time, Roundabout announced that it would rechristen the Selwyn the American Airlines Theatre, as part of a deal for the patron company to donate $8.5 million

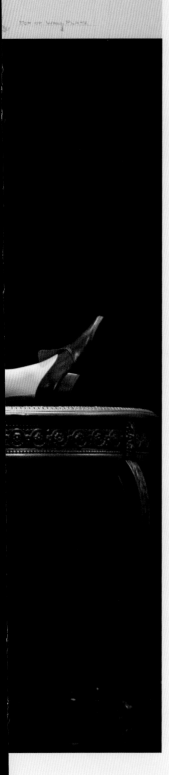

over ten years toward the project's expected $21 million cost.

The former Selwyn was magnificently restored and reduced to a more intimate capacity of 750 seats. A reception area for the exclusive use of subscribers offered a view of the offices of the *New York Times*, at least until that newspaper decamped to its new headquarters on Eighth Avenue in 2007. The *Daily News* reported that the restoration wound up costing $25 million but extolled the theatre's wider seats and expanded leg room, the restored Renaissance-style murals, and the reddish-brown interior with a huge domed ceiling in blue, and little blue domes at the back. Most important, critic Howard Kissel of the *News* praised the theatre's acoustics.

The American Airlines Theatre opened on July 27, 2000, with a revival of Kaufman and Hart's 1939 comedy *The Man Who Came to Dinner*, starring Nathan Lane as Sheridan Whiteside, a thinly disguised, acerbic portrait of critic Alexander Woollcott. Both the comedy and the new theatre on Forty-second Street were warmly welcomed back.

The old Selwyn Theatre, which had turned its back on the legitimate theatre for so many decades, now seemed eager to make up for lost time. As a subscription house, the American Airlines presented two to five shows a year during its first decade in operation, logging the most new productions of any Broadway theatre during that period. Because all of them were scheduled as limited runs, they tended to run the same length of time whether they were successful or not, though two of them (*Twelve Angry Men* and *The Pajama Game*) stayed at the American Airlines Theatre for more than one hundred performances, and one (*The 39 Steps*) transferred to a long commercial run at other theatres.

On November 24, 2000, David Leveaux directed a revival of Harold Pinter's 1978 drama *Betrayal*, showing the effects of infidelity on a marriage, with the scenes presented in reverse chronological order. Juliette Binoche, Liev Schreiber, and John Slattery played the love triangle. A variation on that scenario came next, with Jennifer Ehle, Dominic West, and Alan Cumming playing a soigné ménage à trois in a tepidly received March 2001 revival of Noël Coward's *Design for Living*, directed by Joe Mantello.

Another revival of a British play arrived in July 2001 when Cherry Jones and David Warner starred as daughter and father in a well-received production of George Bernard Shaw's critique of capitalism, *Major Barbara*. Dana Ivey added to her repertoire of acerbic mothers as Lady Britomart, and rising actor Denis O'Hare drew attention as Adolphus.

Scott Elliott assembled a starry all-female cast for his November 8, 2001, revival of *The Women*, Clare Boothe Luce's portrait of her gender at its worst and best. The production featured two titillating moments. One was a full-frontal nude scene by the always daring Jennifer Tilly, upon emerging from a bath. The other was the curtain call, in which all the women, including other featured performers Kristen Johnston, Cynthia Nixon, Rue McClanahan, Amy Ryan, and Mary Louise Wilson, took their bows clad in 1930s underwear.

Roundabout presented its first original play at the American Airlines Theatre on February 7, 2002: Heather McDonald's drama about religion and perseverance, *An Almost Holy Picture*. Kevin Bacon gave a distinguished performance in this solo play about a former minister who in Act I goes on a spiritual journey across America, and then endures Job-like trials with his new family in Act II. John Dosset played the role on Wednesday and Sunday matinees.

Roundabout reached deeply into the playbox and pulled out a bit of history, Arthur Miller's very first (but rarely revived) Broadway play, *The Man Who Had All the Luck*, subtitled "a fable," about a young man who believes his success is due to good fortune of a supernatural nature. The May 1, 2002, production starred Chris O'Donnell, who at the time was known for playing comic-book sidekick Robin in the film *Batman and Robin*.

High-strung comedian Mario Cantone performed his standup show *An Evening with Mario Cantone* for four performances on "dark" nights when Roundabout was out of *Luck*.

A revival of Rodgers and Hart's uproarious musical *The Boys from Syracuse*—the first on Broadway since the 1938 original—followed on August 18, 2002, but critics turned thumbs-down on Scott Ellis's production. The retelling of Shakespeare's *Comedy of Errors* with songs like "This Can't Be Love" and "Sing for Your Supper" was judged a disappointment, despite game performances by Tom Hewitt, Chip Zien, Lee Wilkoff, Jonathan Dokuchitz, and Erin Dilly.

Joe Dowling, who held artistic directorship of the Abbey Theatre in Dublin and the Guthrie Theatre in Minneapolis, staged a January 2003 production of Molière's *Tartuffe* with Henry Goodman as the great religious hypocrite, Brian Bedford as Orgon, and J. Smith-Cameron as the mischievous maid Dorine.

The Roundabout went from classic comedy to black comedy with its next play, an April 2003 revival of Peter Nichols's *A Day in the Death of Joe Egg*. Eddie Izzard and Victoria Hamilton made their Broadway debuts as the desperate parents of a severely disabled child, the title character, played by nine-year-old Madeleine Martin in the first of several disturbing child roles she would play in coming years in *The Pillowman* and *August: Osage County*. Izzard, Hamilton, and the production itself were all nominated for Tony Awards.

The Soviet-born comedian Yakov Smirnoff attempted to modulate his Cold War—era shtick in a solo show, *As Long as We Both Shall Laugh*, which played on *Joe Egg*'s "dark" nights. It attracted capitalists for fifteen performances.

The Tony-winning musical *Big River* got an unorthodox but applauded revival in July 2003, courtesy of the North Hollywood—based Deaf West Theatre Company. The cast combined deaf, hearing-impaired, and hearing actors working together to tell the classic American story of Huckleberry Finn and his journey down the Mississippi. Some of the Roger Miller score was sung outright by the characters; some was performed using the graceful beauty of American Sign Language, with others singing the words. Huck was played by a deaf actor, Tyrone Giordano. Jim was played by hearing actor Michael McElroy (Tony nomination). The original 1985 Huck, Daniel Jenkins, returned in the role of Mark Twain, who served as narrator of this production. The show was nominated as Best Revival of a Musical at the 2004 Tony Awards.

Patrick Stewart played a homeless man who tries to work his way into dominance over two men who give him a job and a place to stay in the November 9, 2003, revival of Harold Pinter's *The Caretaker*. Directed by David Jones, the three strove for a more humorous version of Pinter's "comedy of menace."

Ben Hecht and Charles MacArthur's classic American farce *Twentieth Century* got a classy revival March 25, 2004, starring Alec Baldwin as the down-but-not-out Broadway producer Oscar Jaffe, and Anne Heche as the movie star he must woo and sign for his last-chance Broadway comeback. Walter Bobbie directed the frantic action aboard the coaches of the Twentieth Century Limited, a luxury express train from Chicago to New York, with sets designed by John Lee Beatty and elegant period costumes by William Ivey Long.

Arthur Miller's 1964 drama *After the Fall* got its first Broadway revival here on July 29, 2004, with Peter Krause as Quentin and Carla Gugino as Maggie in a thinly disguised dramatization of the playwright's real-life failed marriage to movie icon Marilyn Monroe. Set in a limbo that reminded some critics of an airport waiting area (designed by Richard Hoover), Michael Mayer's production was judged a disappointment. Ben Brantley of the *New York Times* wrote, "Peter Krause certainly appears to be feeling no pain. Or joy. Or any of the stronger emotions, pleasant or unpleasant, that crop up in between."

The longest run of any Roundabout show at the American Airlines so far was logged by its October 28, 2004, revival of Reginald Rose's tense courtroom drama *Twelve Angry Men*. Boyd Gaines, Philip Bosco, and James Rebhorn led a fine-tuned ensemble of jurors whose deliberations cause them gradually to shift from eleven-to-one in favor of conviction of an alleged murderer, to twelve-to-zero in favor of acquittal. Originally scheduled for a run of a few weeks, the production (directed by Scott Ellis) proved so popular that it was extended multiple times and amassed a total of 228 performances. It was nominated for a Tony Award as Best Revival of a Play and won the Drama Desk Award in that same category.

Kate Burton and Lynn Redgrave played daughter and mother in an austere June 2005 revival of W. Somerset Maugham's *The Constant Wife*, with Michael Cumpsty as Burton's husband. Both actresses earned Tony nominations, as did the production.

Richard Greenberg, who had enjoyed Tony-winning success with *Take Me Out*, followed it with a less enthusiastically received comedy, *A Naked Girl on the Appian Way*, on October 6, 2005. Directed by Doug Hughes, it was the story of a cookbook author (Jill Clayburgh, returning after a long absence from Broadway) and her husband (Richard Thomas), who try to cope with (among other

Michael Cerveris as Tesman and Mary-Louise Parker as the title character in Ibsen's *Hedda Gabler* (2009). (Photo by Joan Marcus)

things) their adopted children wanting to marry. The production also marked Matthew Morrison's first Broadway assignment after *The Light in the Piazza*. Critics said the play lacked focus, and the story's connection with the eye-catching title proved tenuous.

One of the greatest successes of the Roundabout's tenure at the American Airlines Theatre arrived February 23, 2006. Kelli O'Hara and crooner Harry Connick Jr. proved to have sparkling chemistry in the leading roles of *The Pajama Game*, the 1954 Adler and Ross musical about a strike at a Midwest pajama factory. The revival played an extended run of 129 performances and might have continued longer if the stars hadn't made other commitments. (It won the 2007 Tony Award as Best Revival of a Musical and Best Choreography (Kathleen Marshall).

Swoosie Kurtz donned a wig of red curls and Philip Bosco donned a gray cloud of whiskers to play the roles of Hesione Hushabye and Captain Shotover in what the *New York Times* called a "rippingly good" revival of Shaw's *Heartbreak House* in fall 2006.

Things got mysterious the following March when Annie Parisse and Alan Tudyk starred in Daniel Sullivan's revival of Craig Lucas's *Prelude to a Kiss*, a *Twilight Zone*—like story of an old man (John Mahoney) who magically switches bodies with a woman in the bloom of youth (Parisse), leaving her husband (Tudyk) to figure out what happened and how to undo the switch.

John Van Druten's rarely seen 1940 play *Old Acquaintance* got a polished revival in June of 2007, starring Harriet Harris and Margaret Colin as women whose friendship is tested when one of them goes through a divorce. The lush townhouse sets were by Alexander Dodge. Diane Davis earned favorable notice as the daughter of one of the women, who starts to come between them.

In October 2007 Broadway got to see a rare production of George Bernard Shaw's *Pygmalion*, a 1913 play that has become overshadowed by its successful 1956 musical adaptation, *My Fair Lady*. David Grindley directed a cast that toplined Jefferson Mays as Henry Higgins, Boyd Gaines as Colonel Pickering, and film actress Claire Danes making her Broadway debut as the cockney flower girl, Eliza Doolittle.

One of the longest-running nonmusical plays of the 2000s opened at the American Airlines Theatre on January 15, 2008. It was a transfer of the London hit *The 39 Steps*, based on the Alfred Hitchcock film of the same title but telling the story with four actors playing dozens of characters through the use of quick-change and a treasure chest of other classic theatrical tricks and techniques. The virtuoso ensemble of Charles Edwards, Jennifer Ferrin, Arnie Burton, and Cliff Saunders played the thriller for pure, high-energy comedy. The show proved so successful that, at the conclusion of its limited run, it transferred to a commercial production at the Cort Theatre, and subsequently at the Helen Hayes, where it ran through January 2010, and enjoyed a simultaneous national tour.

Laura Linney, Ben Daniels, and Mamie Gummer were featured in the May 1, 2008, revival of Christopher Hampton's *Les Liaisons Dangereuses*, a drama about sexual games that turn into cruelty in 1780s France. Some critics said the actors lacked the high style for the parts, but the production proved popular with subscribers.

Frank Langella unfurled a majestic Sir Thomas More in an October 7, 2008, revival of

A Man for All Seasons, Robert Bolt's drama about a man who must choose between his duty to his king and his duty to God. You can tell that story just isn't going to end well, but Langella earned a Tony nomination for bringing weary grandeur to his inevitable fall.

Critics and audiences were less reverent about the January 2009 revival of Ibsen's *Hedda Gabler*, starring Mary-Louise Parker as an almost sadistic Hedda and Michael Cerveris as a clueless Tesman. Ben Brantley of the *New York Times* wrote that Parker "traded in her usual air of easy, quirky spontaneity for the robotic petulance of an I-hate-everybody adolescent in a yearlong sulk."

Matthew Broderick followed in a tepidly received April 26, 2009, revival of Christopher Hampton's *The Philanthropist*.

British author Patrick Marber rewrote August Strindberg's *Miss Julie* in his October 2009 play *After Miss Julie*, taking the story of a doomed romance between a male servant and the daughter of his aristocrat boss and moving it to England in the days after World War II when the Labour Party took control of Parliament. Sienna Miller and Johnny Lee Miller (no relation) played the lovers, whose sexual passion is constantly at war with their class-conscious upbringing. Marin Ireland provided a dose of common sense as the man's heartbroken wife.

A revival of Noël Coward's *Present Laughter* greeted 2010 with Victor Garber in the role of the comically put-upon playwright, Harriet Harris as his tart-tongued secretary, and Brooks Ashmanskas leaping across the stage as mad young playwright Roland Maul.

When leading lady Megan Mullally abruptly withdrew from a planned April 2010 Roundabout revival of Terrence McNally's *Lips Together, Teeth Apart*, the production was canceled. In its place, subscribers got to see Sherie Rene Scott in *Everyday Rapture*, an expanded version of her club show, which told how the star of *Dirty Rotten Scoundrels* and *The Last Five Years* adapted to life in the big city after growing up in a Kansas Mennonite community.

The naming contract for the American Airlines Theatre was scheduled to expire in 2010, but as of this volume's deadline time there was no word on whether the old Selwyn Theatre would continue as the American Airlines, or adopt the moniker of a new sponsor.

Johnny Lee Miller is teased by Sienna Miller in Patrick Marber *After Miss Julie* (2009). (Photo by Joan Marcus)

AUGUST WILSON
THEATRE

THE AUGUST WILSON THEATRE AT 245
West Fifty-second Street originated as the Guild
Theatre, built by the Theatre Guild to be used as
a home base for its own repertory company. The
Guild, which began presenting plays on
Broadway in 1919, had been using the Garrick
Theatre for many of its shows. But after its
fourth season its directors decided to build a
theatre of their own so that the Guild's fifteen
thousand subscribers and its acting company
and school could prosper in comfort and luxury.

In his book *The Magic Curtain*, Lawrence
Langner, the founder of the Guild, wrote that the
theatre was built in the then popular "pseudo-
Italian style." It was designed by C. Howard
Crane, Kenneth Franzheim, and Charles Bettis,
in consultation with set designers Norman Bel

Top left: Helen Hayes as the Egyptian queen in the Guild's opening production of Shaw's *Caesar and Cleopatra* (1925).

Top center and right: Alfred Lunt and Lynn Fontanne in *The Second Man* (1927) and *Elizabeth the Queen* (1930).

Bottom left: Earle Larimore and Alice Brady in Eugene O'Neill's masterly *Mourning Becomes Electra* (1931).

Bottom center: Gene Lockhart and George M. Cohan in Eugene O'Neill's *Ah, Wilderness!* (1933).

Bottom right: Ina Claire and Van Heflin in S.N. Behrman's captivating comedy, *End of Summer* (1936).

Geddes and the Guild's Lee Simonson. According to Langner, the Guild Theatre was one of the company's greatest failures. The stage was made so large that there was little room left for dressing rooms or even audience space. "We made the ghastly mistake," he wrote, "of providing a theatre with all the stage space necessary for a repertory of plays without enough seating capacity to provide the income necessary to support the repertory." The theatre had 914 seats (later increased). Nevertheless, the Guild Theatre building was one of the most impressive legitimate houses in Manhattan, and a novel aspect of it was that the auditorium was not on street level but on the second story of the edifice.

The Guild Theatre debuted with great fanfare on the evening of April 13, 1925. President Calvin Coolidge officially opened the theatre by pushing an electric button in Washington, D.C., throwing the lights on a lush production of Shaw's *Caesar and Cleopatra*, starring Helen Hayes as the Egyptian queen and Lionel Atwill as Caesar. The critics were kind, and the revival managed to run for 128 performances.

The Guild Theatre's next production was also a Shaw revival—*Arms and the Man*—and this offering proved even more successful. It

starred the Guild's foremost acting couple, Alfred Lunt and Lynn Fontanne, and it prospered for 181 performances.

Ferenc Molnar, one of the Guild's favorite playwrights, provided the theatre's next show, a romantic play called *The Glass Slipper*, starring June Walker, Lee Baker, and Helen Westley, but audiences attended it for only sixty-five performances. Since the Guild had fifteen thousand subscribers, each play it produced ran a few weeks for the subscribers. If the reviews were good and the show was a hit, it could be moved to a larger theatre, while the Guild continued with its repertory at its own house.

From the mid-1920s on, the Guild presented its company in a great variety of plays, many of them by foreign authors. Stars such as Lunt and Fontanne, Edward G. Robinson, Dudley Digges, Helen Westley, Philip Loeb, Armina Marshall (Mrs. Lawrence Langner), Henry Travers, Clare Eames, and many artists who would later establish the Group Theatre appeared at the Guild Theatre in plays that usually ran for fifty or more performances. The Lunts appeared together at the Guild Theatre in Franz Werfel's bizarre play *Goat Song* (1926), C. K. Munro's *At Mrs. Beam's* (1926), Werfel's *Juarez and*

THE DARK IS LIGHT ENOUGH

Left to right: Katharine Cornell and Tyrone Power as they appeared on the PLAYBILL cover for Christopher Fry's *The Dark Is Light Enough* (1955).

Helen Hayes as a wealthy-aristocrat-turned-scrubwoman in Mary Chase's comic fairy tale, *Mrs. McThing* (1952).

Mona Freeman (in touring cast) and Edward G. Robinson in *Middle of the Night* (1956).

Raymond Massey and Christopher Plummer in the Pulitzer Prize-wining drama, *J.B.* (1958).

Maximilian (1926), a dramatization of Dostoyevsky's *The Brothers Karamazov* (1927), S. N. Behrman's witty comedy *The Second Man* (1927), Shaw's *The Doctor's Dilemma* (1927), Sil-Vara's *Caprice* (1928), and another Behrman comedy, *Meteor* (1929).

The Lunts did not always appear as a team, however. At the Guild Theatre, Lunt appeared without Fontanne as Marco Polo in Eugene O'Neill's *Marco Millions* (1928); and Lynn appeared without Alfred in a revival of Shaw's *Pygmalion* (1926).

Other interesting productions presented at the Guild during the 1920s that did not star the Lunts were Edward G. Robinson in Pirandello's *Right You Are if You Think You Are* (1927); a straight version of *Faust* (1928), with Dudley Digges as Mephistopheles, Helen Chandler as Margaret, and George Gaul as Faust; Alice Brady, Otto Kruger, Frank Conroy, Gale Sondergaard, and Claude Rains in *Karl and Anna* (1929); and the same stars (except Sondergaard) in Romain Rolland's *The Game of Love and Death* (also 1929). During these years, the Theatre Guild practiced "alternating repertory," which meant that its actors would perform in one play for a week (perhaps at the John Golden or Martin Beck theatres), then report to the Guild Theatre the following week and appear in a different production. Lawrence Langner wrote in "The Magic Curtain" that this plan was highly successful and that the 1920s constituted the Guild's golden era.

The 1930s changed the Theatre Guild's operating system. The "alternating repertory" became too difficult to manage, and the Depression did not help the Guild's economic

situation. Although it continued to present fine actors in excellent plays, many flops drained the company's resources.

In 1930 the Guild Theatre housed a revival of Turgenev's *A Month in the Country*, with Nazimova, Dudley Digges, and Henry Travers. It was successful, and during the run Katharine Hepburn joined the cast. It was her first job with the Guild, and she was to play an important role in its survival in years to come.

Some highlights of the 1930s at this theatre included the third edition of the popular revue *The Garrick Gaieties* (1930), with Imogene Coca, Cynthia Rodgers, Edith Meiser, and many others, who were joined during the run by the young Rosalind Russell, making her Broadway debut; the Lunts in Maxwell Anderson's verse play *Elizabeth the Queen* (1930), which moved from the Guild to the larger Martin Beck Theatre; and Lynn Riggs's lovely *Green Grow the Lilacs* (1931), which would save the Guild in 1943 when it was adapted as the landmark musical *Oklahoma!*

On October 26, 1931, the Guild Theatre hosted one of its greatest triumphs: Eugene O'Neill's five-hour trilogy (with a dinner intermission) *Mourning Becomes Electra*. O'Neill based his three plays on Aeschylus's *Oresteia* but changed the locale to New England during the Civil War. The tragedy, which starred Nazimova, Alice Brady, Earle Larimore, and Lee Barker, was hailed by critics as a masterpiece. The eminent critic Joseph Wood Krutch wrote: "It may turn out to be the only permanent contribution yet made by the 20th century to dramatic literature." The play posed a fashion problem to first-nighters. The performance started at 5:00 p.m..

Should they wear evening clothes or afternoon wear? Critic George Jean Nathan wore afternoon clothes, but when he saw financier Otto Kahn arrive in evening clothes, Nathan ran home at intermission to change. Kahn also ran home and changed to afternoon wear.

Other 1930s highlights included Beatrice Lillie and Hope Williams in a revival of Shaw's *Too True to Be Good* (1932); Nazimova, Henry Travers, Claude Rains, Sydney Greenstreet, and Jessie Ralph in an adaptation of Pearl Buck's novel *The Good Earth* (1932); Ina Claire in one of her greatest high-comedy performances in S. N. Behrman's *Biography* (1932); Judith Anderson, Humphrey Bogart, Shirley Booth, and Leo G. Carroll in *The Mask and the Face* (1933), translated by Somerset Maugham from an Italian play; George M. Cohan and Gene Lockhart in Eugene O'Neill's only comedy, *Ah, Wilderness!* (1933); Maxwell Anderson's *Valley Forge* (1934), with Philip Merivale as General George Washington; Jimmy Savo, Eve Arden, Charles Walters, and Ezra Stone in a colorful revue, *Parade* (1935); the Lunts, Richard Whorf, and Sydney Greenstreet in an inspired revival of *The Taming of the Shrew* (1935); Ina Claire, Osgood Perkins, Van Heflin, Mildred Natwick, and Shepperd Strudwick in another Behrman gem, *End of Summer* (1936); and Sylvia Sidney, Leslie Banks, and Evelyn Varden in Ben Hecht's *To Quito and Back* (1937).

Despite brilliant acting, some of these plays ran barely longer than fifty performanc-

es, and there were many in between that ran fewer. By the end of 1938 the Guild found itself in such financial straits that it began renting the Guild Theatre to other producers. In October 1938 Gilbert Miller presented J. B. Priestley's *I Have Been Here Before*, but it failed; and in December, Herman Shumlin presented Max Reinhardt's production of Thornton Wilder's *The Merchant of Yonkers*, starring Jane Cowl and featuring Percy Waram, June Walker, and Nydia Westman. This farce was a curious flop. Wilder later rewrote it as *The Matchmaker*, which was a hit; then it was turned into *Hello, Dolly!*

William Saroyan's first Broadway play, with a Group Theatre cast—*My Heart's in the Highlands*—played a brief but acclaimed run in 1939, followed in February 1940 by Saroyan's *The Time of Your Life*, which won both the Pulitzer Prize and the New York Drama Critics Circle Award and moved to the Guild Theatre from the Booth. In the early 1940s the Guild had a series of short-lived plays at their theatre—a revival of *Ah, Wilderness!*, with Harry Carey; Frederic March, and Florence Eldridge in *Hope for a Harvest*; Celeste Holm and Jessie Royce Landis in *Papa Is All*; Paul Muni, Jessica Tandy, and Alfred Drake in *Yesterday's Magic*; Stuart Erwin and Lillian Gish in *Mr. Sycamore*; and finally, a Russian drama called *The Russian People*.

With all these disasters, the Theatre Guild decided to lease its theatre as a radio playhouse in 1943, and it remained so until 1950.

At this time, the federally chartered American National Theatre and Academy bought the theatre and renamed it the ANTA Playhouse. Lawrence Langner observed: "ANTA has now taken it over, and are operating it on a tax-free basis with subsidies and concessions from all the unions, which will make their burden far less than ours; and I wish them better luck with the building than we had." In 1944 the Theatre Guild moved out of the Guild Theatre to an imposing town house on West Fifty-third Street.

The beautifully renovated ANTA Playhouse opened auspiciously on November 26, 1950, with Judith Anderson, Marian Seldes, and Alfred Ryder in *The Tower Beyond Tragedy*, by Robinson Jeffers. The critics hailed Anderson's acting, but the verse tragedy based on the Electra theme played for only thirty-two performances. On Christmas Eve 1950, Santa brought a gilt-edged gift to this beleaguered theatre: Gloria Swanson

Left: **Diana Sands and Alan Alda in the 1964 comedy *The Owl and the Pussycat*.**

Above: PLAYBILLs for *Carrie* (1987), *City of Angels* (1989), and *Smokey Joe's Cafe* (1995).

and José Ferrer in a revival of Hecht and MacArthur's comedy *Twentieth Century*. It was so successful that it was moved to the Fulton Theatre. The ANTA Play Series continued with revivals of *Mary Rose* (1951); Molière's *L'École des Femmes*, performed in French by Louis Jouvet and company; *Desire under the Elms* (1952), with Karl Malden, Douglas Watson, and Carol Stone, directed by Harold Clurman; and *Golden Boy* (1952), with John Garfield, Lee J. Cobb, and Jack Klugman. During this time, a genuine hit moved to the ANTA—Mary Chase's delightful fantasy *Mrs. McThing* (1952), starring Helen Hayes, Ernest Borgnine, Jules Munshin, and Brandon de Wilde—but it tarried briefly before moving to the Morosco. In 1955 Katharine Cornell, Tyrone Power, and Christopher Plummer appeared in Christopher Fry's "winter comedy" *The Dark Is Light Enough*. The light burned out after sixty-nine performances. A musical version of *Seventh Heaven*, with Chita Rivera, Beatrice Arthur, Gloria DeHaven, Ricardo Montalban, and Kurt Kasznar, had just forty-four showings. ANTA's star-studded revival of *The Skin of Our Teeth* (1955) had Helen Hayes, Mary Martin, George Abbott, Florence Reed, and Don Murray in the cast. It played successful engagements in Paris, Washington, D.C., and Chicago before coming to the ANTA.

In 1956 the Lunts returned to the theatre where they had performed so often for the Guild. Their vehicle, *The Great Sebastians*, was one of their poorest. A melodramatic comedy by Howard Lindsay and Russel Crouse in which they played a mind-reading act, the play managed to last 174 performances.

On February 8, 1956, the ANTA Theatre finally housed a play that enjoyed a relatively long run (477 performances). Edward G. Robinson returned to this theatre, where he had acted for the Guild many times, and garnered superlatives for his performance in Paddy Chayefsky's *Middle of the Night*, about a fifty-three-year-old man who falls in love with a twenty-four-year-old woman, played by Gena Rowlands. June Walker, Anne Jackson, and Martin Balsam were also in the cast. Joshua Logan produced and directed.

The success of the Chayefsky play at the ANTA turned the tide for this house. After engagement by the *Dancers of Bali* and *Dancers of India*, it booked several hits that enjoyed substantial runs. *Say, Darling* (1958), a comedy about the troubles encountered when producing a Broadway musical, was satiric fact rather than fiction. It was plainly about the backstage shenanigans in getting *The Pajama Game* produced on Broadway. David Wayne, Vivian Blaine, Johnny Desmond, and Constance Ford were in the cast, but Robert Morse stole the show doing an outrageous impersonation of a flamboyant producer/director said to be inspired by Hal Prince. The comedy ran for 332 performances.

The ANTA's next tenant won the Pulitzer Prize. It was *J. B.* (1958), a verse drama by Archibald MacLeish, with Pat Hingle as J. B. (Job), Raymond Massey as Mr. Zuss (God), and Christopher Plummer as Nickles (Satan). Elia Kazan directed the biblical drama, which ran for 364 performances.

Critics praised Rex Harrison's acting in Anouilh's comedy *The Fighting Cock* (1959), but audiences supported it for only eighty-seven performances. Next came a healthy hit, *A Thurber Carnival* (1960), described as "a new entertainment patterned after the revue form," by James Thurber, with music by Don Elliott. The show was a series of humorous sketches based on the *New Yorker* magazine wit's writings and performed with charm by Tom Ewell, Peggy Cass, Paul Ford, John McGiver, Alice Ghostley, and others.

Highlights of the 1960s included Hugh Wheeler's *Big Fish, Little Fish* (1961), with Jason Robards Jr., Hume Cronyn, Martin Gabel, Elizabeth Wilson, and George Grizzard, directed by Sir John Gielgud; Robert Bolt's distinguished historical play *A Man for All Seasons* (1961), which won six Tony Awards, including Best Play, Best Actor (Paul Scofield), and Best Director (Noel Willman), later brought Faye Dunaway into the cast and ran for 640 performances; and James Baldwin's *Blues for Mister Charlie* (1964), with Diana Sands, Al Freeman Jr., John McCurry, Rosetta Le Noire, Pat Hingle, and Rip Torn, directed by Burgess Meredith.

Sands returned to the ANTA with Alan Alda in the two-character comedy *The Owl and the Pussycat* (1964), which ran for 421 performances. Peter Shaffer's *The Royal Hunt of the Sun* (1965) starred Christopher Plummer as Spanish conqueror Pizarro and George Rose as Ruiz, with David Carradine as the leader of the Incas. Next came engagements by the National Repertory Theatre (1967) and the American Conservatory Theatre (1969); Len Cariou in the American Shakespeare Festival's production of *Henry V* (1969); and a revival of *Our Town* (1969) with Henry Fonda, Ed Begley, Elizabeth Hartman, Harvey Evans, Mildred Natwick, John Beal, and Margaret Hamilton.

The 1970s brought Helen Hayes, James Stewart, and Jesse White in a revival of *Harvey* (1970), jointly produced by ANTA and the Phoenix Theatre; engagements of the dance companies of Alvin Ailey, Louis Falco, Pearl Lang, Paul Taylor, Nikolais, and the Dance Theatre of Harlem (all in 1971); the musical *Purlie* from the Broadway Theatre, which played for seven months in 1971; Julie Harris in a Tony Award—winning performance in *The Last of Mrs. Lincoln* (1972); Elizabeth Ashley, Keir Dullea, Fred Gwynne, and Kate Reid in a revival of *Cat on a Hot Tin Roof* (1974); the exuberant black musical *Bubbling Brown Sugar* (1976), which ran for 766 performances; Charles Repole in a revival of Eddie Cantor's 1920s hit *Whoopee* (1979), from the Goodspeed Opera House; and Maggie Smith in Tom Stoppard's *Night and Day* (1979).

Derek Jacobi starred in a Russian drama, *The Suicide*, in 1980, for sixty performances. A musical version of Dickens's *David Copperfield*, its title shortened to *Copperfield*, had a brief run of thirteen performances in 1981. *Annie* moved in from the Alvin across the street for one month, followed by the campy musical *Oh, Brother!*, based on Shakespeare's *The Comedy of Errors*, with the action transferred to the contemporary Middle East. It had the misfortune to open while the memory of American hostages in Iranian captivity was still fresh in people's memories, and it lasted just three performances. It was followed by the Pilobolus Dance Theatre (1981).

In August 1981 the ANTA theatre was acquired by Jujamcyn Theatres and subsequently renamed the Virginia Theatre, in honor of Mrs. Virginia M. Binger, owner of Jujamcyn along with her husband, James Binger. Richard G. Wolff, then president of Jujamcyn Theatres, supervised the renovation of the theatre and announced the firm's intention of booking both legitimate attractions and dance companies at the Virginia.

In June 1982 a musical called *Play Me a Country Song* had a very brief run here; and in December of that year, Eva LeGallienne revived her adaptation of *Alice in Wonderland* (coauthored with Florida Friebus) for a brief run. This was followed by a superlative new production of the 1936 Rodgers and Hart musical *On Your Toes*, which won a Tony Award for Best Revival of the season and another Tony for its brilliant ballet star, Natalia Makarova. It played 505 performances.

Emily Mann's *Execution of Justice*, a docudrama of the trial of Dan White, who murdered George Moscone, mayor of San Francisco, and City Supervisor Harvey Milk, had a short run in 1986 and was succeeded later that year by Ian McKellen in *Wild Honey*. The following year brought a Canadian production of *The Mikado* and a musical version of the macabre Stephen King novel *Carrie*, which eked out five performances but inspired a small, devoted cult. The show, which starred Betty Buckley and Linzi Hateley, became the gold standard for Broadway musical cataclysms when author Ken Mandelbaum titled a book on the subject *Not Since Carrie*.

Ray Cooney's British smash *Run for Your Wife* did not repeat its success in New York. A new production of the hit musical *Shenandoah* failed to run as long as the original, but it was followed by the successful musical *City of Angels*, which won six Tony Awards: Best Musical, Best Score (Cy Coleman, David Zippel), Best Book (Larry Gelbart), Best Actor in a Musical (James Naughton), Best Featured Actress in a Musical (Randy Graff), and Best Scenic Designer (Robin Wagner). A film noir mystery-within-a-musical about a troubled

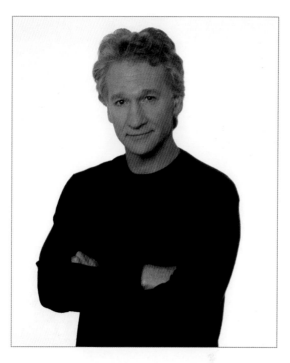

Comedian Bill Maher in his 2003 political show *Bill Maher: Victory Begins at Home.*

writer and the cool detective character he creates in his novels (the latter sections performed with black-and-white costumes and sets), *City of Angels* ran 878 performances here from 1989 to 1992, setting a new house record.

In the spring of 1992, another hit musical arrived—*Jelly's Last Jam*, an impressionistic biography of jazz pioneer Jelly Roll Morton, which won a Tony Award for its star, Gregory Hines, and one for featured actress Tonya Pinkins. A new production of the Lerner and Loewe classic *My Fair Lady* opened in 1993 and starred Richard Chamberlain as Henry Higgins, Melissa Errico as Eliza Doolittle, and Julian Holloway as Alfred P. Doolittle (the role his father Stanley Holloway had created in the original 1956 production). The *New York Times* stated that it was a touring show and looked it. It ran for only 165 performances and received no Tony nominations.

On March 2, 1995, a megahit musical arrived at the Virginia. *Smokey Joe's Café*, a revue featuring the hit 1950s—1960s songs of Jerry Leiber and Mike Stoller ("Stand by Me," "On Broadway," "Hound Dog," "Spanish Harlem," and many others) was praised for its brilliant performers and dancing. It dazzled for 2,036 performances, making it the longest-running musical revue in Broadway history. It received seven Tony Award nominations, and its cast album won a Grammy Award.

The Virginia Theatre's next tenant was a theatrical oddity called *The Wild Party*, based on a 1928 poem by Joseph Moncure March, with music and lyrics by Michael John LaChiusa and a book by LaChiusa and George C. Wolfe (who also directed). It was produced in April 2000 by the New York Shakespeare Festival/Joseph Papp Public Theater and starred Mandy Patinkin, Toni Collette, and Eartha Kitt. The production will forever carry an asterisk next to its title, owing to the fact that another musical with the same name, based on the same poem, but with book, music, and lyrics by Andrew Lippa, was produced Off-Broadway by the Manhattan Theatre Club at almost the same time, from February 24 to April 9, 2000. The Manhattan Theatre Club's production received better reviews, but the Broadway version had some wild admirers and received seven Tony Award nominations. It ran for just sixty-eight performances, a costly flop for the Public Theatre.

For the next two years the Virginia was booked with a series of dramas and dramatic musicals that tackled tough questions of politics, race, religion, and history. In fall 2000 the Virginia hosted a revival of *Gore Vidal's "The Best Man,"* with the author's name added to the original title to avoid confusion with a concurrent film of the same name. Examining the morality of a fictional 1950s presidential race, it opened in the midst of the 2000 presidential campaign, which saw George W. Bush battle Vice President Al Gore for the White House. Viewers found many parallels between life and art. The producers set up a voting booth in the lobby so ticket holders could cast nonbinding votes on the outcome of the 2000 contest. Voters at the Virginia overwhelmingly went for Gore, but the general election had a surprise in store.

Musical leading man Brian Stokes Mitchell lent his baritone to a nonmusical project, *King Hedley II*, an installment of August Wilson's ten-play cycle about the saga of American blacks in the twentieth century, known variously as the "Pittsburgh Cycle" or the "Century Cycle." Each play stood for a decade, and *King Hedley II* represented the 1980s, telling the story of an ex-convict trying to scrape together the money to open a video store and rebuild his life. Viola Davis and Leslie Uggams costarred in the production, which stayed at the Virginia for seventy-two performances in late spring 2001.

Laura Linney and Liam Neeson did battle with the forces of ignorance in a lauded revival of Arthur Miller's witch-hunt drama *The Crucible* for 101 performances, starting March 7, 2002.

The Rodgers and Hammerstein Organization

Maureen McGovern as Marmee and Sutton Foster as Jo in the 2005 musical adaptation of *Little Women*. (Photo by Paul Kolnik)

granted Tony-winning playwright David Henry Hwang (*M. Butterfly*) permission to rewrite Oscar Hammerstein II's libretto to the team's 1958 musical *Flower Drum Song*, in part to make it more intrinsically Asian-American, while keeping the original score intact. The result, which starred Lea Salonga and Randall Duk Kim, delved deeper into the story of a girl who comes from communist China to San Franciso's Chinatown in the 1950s to fulfill a prearranged marriage contract. One of the more spectacular additions was an opening scene enacting the girl's harrowing escape from Maoist China, set to the show's song "A Hundred Million Miracles." Opening October

Robert Spencer, John Lloyd Young, Daniel Reichard, and Christian Hoff as the Four Seasons in the biographical 2005 musical, *Jersey Boys*. (Photo by Joan Marcus)

17, 2002, the revision ran 169 performances.

Standup comedian Bill Maher jabbed hard at the American political follies in his solo comedy show *Bill Maher: Victory Begins at Home*, which opened March 5, 2003, in the final days before the United States launched its invasion of Iraq. The show earned a Tony nomination as Best Theatrical Event despite a limited run of just sixteen performances.

Just in time for the Halloween season in 2003, a long-running Off-Broadway musical comedy, *Little Shop of Horrors*, got a revival that was also its Broadway debut. Starring Hunter Foster as the mousy florist's clerk and Kerry Butler as his long-stemmed rose Audrey, the Alan Menken/Howard Ashman musical benefited from a Broadway budget in building its main special effect, an ever-growing man-eating plant that can also sing R & B. Directed by Jerry Zaks and costarring Douglas Sills as a sadistic dentist, the production was up in the chair at the Virginia for 372 performances.

Louisa May Alcott's novel *Little Women* would seem to have been a natural for musical adaptation, with its story of Jo, a plucky young woman who prevails over personal tragedy and learns to stand on her own two feet in Civil War America. But Broadway's first musicalization did not arrive until January 23, 2005, with the opening of *Little Women*, starring the picture-perfect Sutton Foster in the exhausting main role, and singer Maureen McGovern as her beloved Marmee. The show had music by Jason Howland, book by Allan Knee, and lyrics by Mindi Dickstein. Foster's showstopper was to have been "Astonishing," but audiences did not respond with the expected ardor, and the show lasted only 137 performances.

In summer 2005 Jujamcyn announced that the Virginia Theatre would be renamed the August Wilson Theatre in honor of the author of onetime tenant *King Hedley II*. Wilson didn't live to see the rechristening ceremony. He died of liver cancer on October 2, 2005. His widow, Constanza Romero, and his second daughter, Azula Carmen Wilson, attended the October 16, 2005, ceremony.

The new moniker proved lucky for this theatre. November 6 saw the opening of a resounding hit, *Jersey Boys*. At the time, Broadway seemed flooded with shows derided by critics as "jukebox musicals," which that tried to hammer a rock band's songbook into something that resembled a Broadway musical score. But with *Jersey Boys*, librettists Marshall Brickman and Rick Elice figured out ways to use the Bob Gaudio—Bob Crewe songs of the pop singing group The Four Seasons in a variety of witty ways to tell about, illustrate, comment upon or just reenact key moments from the band members' rise from blue-collar hoodlums to international stars. Directed by Des McAnuff, the show was nominated for eight Tony Awards and won four, including Best Musical and Best Actor in a Musical (John Lloyd Young as lead singer Frankie Valli).

Jersey Boys continued to fill the August Wilson Theatre with music and nostalgia for the rest of the decade and beyond.

BELASCO
THEATRE

THE HISTORY OF THE BELASCO
Theatre on Forty-fourth Street, between Broadway and Avenue of the Americas, can be very confusing. David Belasco, the flamboyant playwright/actor/producer/director and set designer, who was called "the bishop of Broadway" because he always dressed in priestly garments, had two Belasco Theatres at different times. The first, located on Forty-second Street, was Oscar Hammerstein's Republic Theatre until Belasco leased it and named it for himself. (It still stands today as an Off-Broadway playhouse under the name "New Victory Theatre.") On October 16, 1907, the impresario opened his own theatre on Forty-fourth Street, but he called it the Stuyvesant. In 1910, when the Forty-second Street theatre

Left: Program Cover for the Belasco's first musical success, Vincent Youmans' buoyant *Hit the Deck* (1927).

Right: David Belasco always wore priestly garb but was not known to practice celibacy.

Below: Tad Mosel's play caught on after it won a Pulitzer Prize. PLAYBILL covers from the original Broadway production of *The Rocky Horror Show* (1975), and Janet McTeer's revival of *A Doll's House* (1997).

reclaimed its Republic name, Belasco renamed his Forty-fourth Street theatre the Belasco, and that name has remained ever since.

Because Belasco was more interested in spectacular, realistic stage sets than in great plays, he made certain that his theatre, designed by architect George Keister, was a marvel of technical wizardry. It cost $750,000 and had a permanent dimmer board with sixty-five dimmers, an elevator stage that could be lowered for set changes, space for set and lighting studios, and a private backstage elevator that ascended to his sumptuous apartments for himself and his leading ladies. Belasco may have worn clerical garments, but there is no evidence that he practiced celibacy.

Our Theatres Today and Yesterday, published by Ruth Crosby Dimmick in 1913, had this description of the Belasco Theatre: "This was the first theatre to be built in an enclosed rectangular court. It is broad and shallow, seats about 1,100 persons and allows each a clear view of the stage at such close range that opera glasses are superfluous. The decorations are artistic to the Belasco degree. No chandeliers or brackets are visible, the lights being enclosed between the roof and almost flat ground glass globes. A feature of the house is the absence of an orchestra and the unique manner in which the rising of the curtain is

announced by the sounding of a muffled gong."

The Stuyvesant Theatre's opening bill was a new play by Belasco and two collaborators, Pauline Phelps and Marion Short, titled *A Grand Army Man* (1907). The interesting cast included David Warfield, Jane Cowl, and Antoinette Perry (the actress for whom the Tony Awards are named).

In September 1908 Belasco had a big hit in *The Fighting Hope*, starring Blanche Bates, but in 1909 he topped this with a shocker called *The Easiest Way*, by Eugene Walter. As critic Brooks Atkinson said years later, "*The Easiest Way* was a scandal, a sensation and a success—the three bright 'S's' of show business." Frances Starr played a mediocre actress of loose morals who tries to reform but finds virtue dull and vice exciting. Her famous curtain line to her maid, "Dress up my body and paint my face. I'm going back to Rector's to make a hit and to hell with the rest," caused women in the audience to faint and priests to denounce the play from their pulpits.

On September 17, 1910, Belasco rechristened the Stuyvesant Theatre in his own name. A hit soon followed: On October 4 he had another success with a German play, *The Concert*. Leo Ditrichstein, who translated the play, also starred as a violinist whose wife cures him of his amorous adventures. The play ran for 264 performances.

Top left: Melvyn Douglas and Helen Gahagan married after appearing in Belasco's last production, *Tonight or Never* (1930).

Top center: Luther Adler, Elia Kazan, Roman Bohnen, and Francis Farmer in the Group Theatre's *Golden Boy* (1931).

Top right: The cast of *Ain't Misbehavin'*, which moved from another theatre to the Belasco in 1981.

Bottom left: Jules (John) Garfield and Morris Carnovsky in Odets's *Awake and Sing* (1935).

Bottom right: Baby Face Martin is gunned down on Norman Bel Geddes's massive waterfront set for Sidney Kingsley's *Dead End* (1935).

Belasco wrote his own next hit, *The Return of Peter Grimm*, starring David Warfield as a man who returns from the dead. The fantasy ran for 231 performances, but Warfield almost drove the cast insane with his onstage practical jokes. One night he secreted Limburger cheese in a bowl of tulips, and when actress Janet Dunbar buried her face in the flowers during the play's climax, she almost passed out.

During these early years of the Belasco Theatre, its owner was celebrated for his development of such stars as Blanche Bates, Frances Starr, Lenore Ulric, Ina Claire, Katharine Cornell, and Jeanne Eagles. He was also famed for his insistence that if a play called for a scene in a laundry, the set designer had better provide a real laundry where people could actually take clothes to be washed and ironed. For one play he duplicated a Child's Restaurant.

In 1917 Ina Claire scored a tremendous success in a Cinderella play, *Polly with a Past*, that ran for 315 performances. Jeanne Eagles, who would later achieve immortality as Sadie Thompson in *Rain*, proved an instant hit in *Daddies* (1918) with George Abbott, and it played for 340 performances. The sexy Lenore Ulric was good for 223 performances in *The Son-Daughter* (1919), a play about China by Belasco and George Scarborough.

Ulric became a big Belasco star in the 1920s, featured in such seamy dramas as *Kiki* (1921), *The Harem* (1924), *Lulu Belle* (1926), and *Mima* (1928). Other celebrated stars who played the Belasco at this time were Lionel Barrymore in *Laugh, Clown, Laugh!* (1923) and Katharine Cornell in *Tiger Cats* (1924).

Surprisingly, the Belasco Theatre booked a musical in 1927 and it was one of the theatrical highlights of the 1920s. *Hit the Deck* had a captivating score by Vincent Youmans, and the production brightened the Belasco for 352 performances. Louise Groody, Charles King, and Brian Donlevy were in the cast.

Two more hits played the house before the end of the decade: *The Bachelor Father*, with C. Aubrey Smith and June Walker, and *It's a Wise Child*, starring Humphrey Bogart. The latter was a snappy comedy that amused for 378 performances.

David Belasco's last production at his theatre was a success. In November 1930 he presented Melvyn Douglas and Helen Gahagan in a continental romance called *Tonight or Never*. The stars fell in love not only onstage, but offstage. They married and remained husband and wife for the rest of their lives. Mrs. Douglas later tried to trade the stage for a career in politics but found herself up against rising star Richard

Christopher Walken in
James Joyce's musical
The Dead (2000).

Top: Margaret Colin and Thomas Derrah satirize the Kennedys in *Jackie* (1997).

Bottom: The company recaptures the past in the "Loveland" number from *Follies* (2001). (Photo by Joan Marcus)

Nixon, who tried to paint her as a communist.

David Belasco died in New York on May 14, 1931, at age seventy-one. His theatre was then leased to Katharine Cornell Productions, Inc. and Cornell's husband, Guthrie McClintic, produced and directed the first play under the new management. It was S. N. Behrman's witty comedy *Brief Moment*, but it must have caused the ghost of David Belasco (often seen in the theatre) unrest, because it numbered among its cast the vitriolic critic Alexander Woollcott, who had panned many of Belasco's plays. Woollcott played himself in *Brief Moment*—a fat, lazy, snippy dilettante—and one of the biggest laughs in the show occurred when an actress had this line to say to him: "If you were a woman what a bitch you would have made."

Cornell appeared in two plays under her own management at this theatre: *Lucrece*, translated from the French by Thornton Wilder (1932), and Sidney Howard's *Alien Corn* (1933). The Belasco was next leased to Hazel L. Rice, wife of playwright Elmer Rice, who provided the theatre with two plays, *Judgment Day* (1934) and *Between Two Worlds* (1934), neither of which succeeded.

The famous Group Theatre's association with the Belasco began in December 1934, when it moved its production of *Gold Eagle Guy* there from the Morosco. Some of the Group's illustrious members who appeared in this play included Clifford Odets, Morris Carnovsky, Luther and Stella Adler, Sanford Meisner, and J.

Edward Bromberg. On February 19, 1935, the Group Theatre made theatrical history with its production of Odets's *Awake and Sing*, featuring its acting company (including Jules Garfield, who later changed his name to John Garfield). The Odets sting was at its sharpest in this chronicle of the volcanic life of a Jewish family living in the Bronx.

On the evening of October 28, 1935, a play opened at the Belasco that would have delighted David Belasco. It was Sidney Kingsley's *Dead End*, and it ran for 684 performances, the longest-running play in the Belasco's history to this day. Produced and designed by the famed Norman Bel Geddes, it featured a realistic set of a dead-end street on Manhattan's East River that Belasco himself would have cheered. The Dead End Kids, unknown young actors who became famous overnight and later made endless films in Hollywood, actually dove into the orchestra pit, where the East River supposedly flowed. The play, which was a social tract on how dead-end boys grow up to be gangsters, featured a short, haunting performance by Marjorie Main as a notorious gangster's mother. She repeated her role in the superb movie version of the play.

Another memorable play came to this theatre in 1937 when the Group Theatre presented Odets's *Golden Boy*, starring Luther Adler as the boxer/violinist and Frances Farmer as his unlucky girlfriend. Expertly directed by Harold Clurman, the play ran for 248 perform-

ances. Two more Group Theatre productions followed: Odets's *Rocket to the Moon* (1938) and Irwin Shaw's *The Gentle People*, starring Sylvia Sidney, Franchot Tone, Lee J. Cobb, Sam Jaffe, Karl Malden, and Elia Kazan.

A sorry spectacle in 1940 was a comedy called *My Dear Children*, starring a weary and shamelessly ad-libbing John Barrymore in his last Broadway appearance. A more rewarding play was *Johnny Belinda* (1940), with Helen Craig giving a moving performance as a deaf-mute. Amusement was provided by *Mr. and Mrs. North* (1941), about a husband/wife detective team, and by *Dark Eyes* (1943), a comedy about Russian expatriates by Eugenie Leontovich and Elena Miramova, who also starred in the hit play.

A cause célèbre occurred at the Belasco in 1944. A play called *Trio*, with Richard Widmark, Lois Wheeler, and Lydia St. Clair, dealt with lesbianism. For some bizarre reason, no theatre wanted this drama, although it was written with taste. It finally opened at the Belasco on December 29, 1944, but its troubles were not over. The critics did not think it was a very good play, but they agreed that it was not lurid in its approach and that it deserved to have a hearing. Unfortunately, public officials disagreed, and *Trio* was forced to close after two months when the owners of the Belasco refused to renew the producer's lease.

Kiss Them for Me in 1945 was notable as the first play in which the great talents of Judy

Left: Stanley Tucci and Edie Falco as two misfits seeking love in *Frankie and Johnny in the Clair de Lune* (2003). (Photo by Joan Marcus)

Right: Molly Ringwald and Jayne Atkinson in *Enchanted April* (2003). (Photo by Carol Rosegg)

Denzel Washington as Marcus Brutus in the 2005 modern-dress production of Shakespeare's *Julius Caesar*. (Photo by Joan Marcus)

Holliday were noticed. Her performance as a tramp with an honest approach to her profession helped to land her the lead in *Born Yesterday* (1946) that would make her a star. Other 1940s highlights included Arthur Laurents's *Home of the Brave* (1945); a rollicking revival of *Burlesque* (1946), starring Bert Lahr and Jean Parker; Gertrude Berg in *Me and Molly* (1948); and Alfred de Liagre Jr.'s mesmerizing production of *The Madwoman of Chaillot* (1948), with gloriously loony performances by Martita Hunt and Estelle Winwood.

From mid-1949 until November 1953, the Belasco Theatre was leased to NBC as a radio playhouse. On November 5, 1953, it returned to the legitimate fold with a glittering hit, George S. Kaufman and Howard Teichmann's comedy *The Solid Gold Cadillac*, starring the incomparable Josephine Hull as a small stockholder who causes a big ruckus at a shareholders meeting. The satire ran for 526 performances.

Shows worthy of mention in the 1950s include Odets's *The Flowering Peach* (1954), with Menasha Skulnik as Noah; *Will Success Spoil Rock Hunter?* (1955), starring Jayne Mansfield, Orson Bean, Martin Gabel, and Walter Matthau; and Noël Coward's return to Broadway in a thin play of his own, *Nude with Violin*, alternating (1957—58) with some performances of *Present Laughter* to relieve the tedium.

In November 1960 a beautiful play came to the Belasco. Tad Mosel's *All the Way Home*,

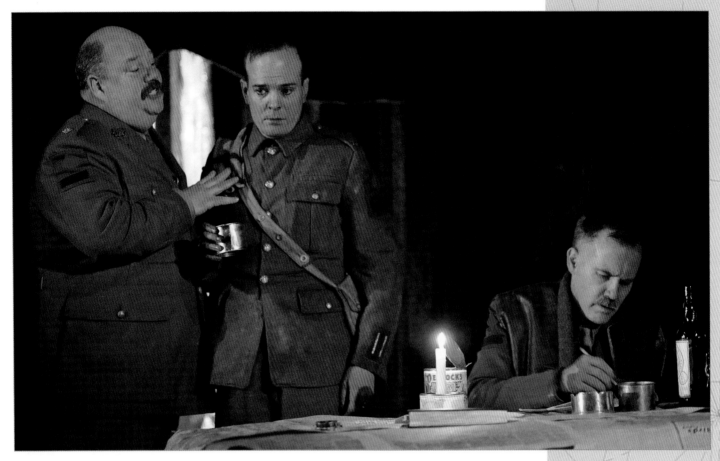

adapted from James Agee's novel *A Death in the Family*, starred Arthur Hill, Lillian Gish, Colleen Dewhurst, and Aline MacMahon. It etched with feeling the impact of a young father's death on his family. It was awarded the Pulitzer Prize and the New York Drama Critics Circle Award as the best play of the season.

Write Me a Murder (1961), by Frederick Knott, was an offbeat thriller with Denholm Elliott, Ethel Griffies, and Kim Hunter; Sam Levene was his Seventh Avenue best in a popular comedy, *Seidman and Son* (1962); Nicol Williamson gave a lacerating performance in John Osborne's *Inadmissable Evidence* (1965).

The Killing of Sister George (1966)—which was much more explicit about lesbians than the exiled *Trio*—ran for 205 performances unmolested. *Does a Tiger Wear a Necktie?* (1969) offered the Broadway debut of Al Pacino as a drug addict, and his electrifying performance won him a Tony Award.

Oh! Calcutta!, which moved to the Belasco in 1971 from the downtown Eden Theatre, had the entire cast in the nude and also featured some of the most explicitly sexual revue sketches and dances ever performed in the legitimate theatre.

For the next two decades, the Belasco's most successful tenants were long-run musicals that moved there from other theatres. In 1980 *Your Arms Too Short to Box with God* moved in from the Ambassador; and in 1981 *Ain't Misbehavin'* transferred from the Plymouth to run for an additional year at the Belasco.

For years, actors who appeared at this theatre and backstage personnel claimed that they saw the ghost of David Belasco in his priestly garb, usually sitting in an unoccupied box on opening nights. A caretaker at the theatre also told newspapers that he sometimes heard the creaky elevator chains rattling backstage, although Belasco's private elevator hasn't worked for years. According to an article that appeared in the *New York Times*, the Belasco ghost had never been seen in the theatre since *Oh! Calcutta!* played there. The theory was that the nude show may have been too much realism, even for Belasco. However, the ghost seems to have recovered and has been spotted numerous times throughout the 2000s.

The Belasco housed the original 1975 production of British import *The Rocky Horror Show* (later made into a cult film with much of the Broadway cast); Colleen Dewhurst in *An Almost Perfect Person*; Uta Hagen and Charles Nelson Reilly in *Charlotte*; Elizabeth Ashley in

Left to right: John Ahlin, Jefferson Mays, and Boyd Gaines prepare for battle in the 2007 revival of *Journey's End*. (Photo by Paul Kolnik)

Hide and Seek; Jonathan Pryce in Dario Fo's *Accidental Death of an Anarchist*; the New York Shakespeare Festival repertory of *Macbeth/As You Like It/Romeo and Juliet*; the musical *The Prince of Central Park*; and Len Cariou starring as a troubled Vietnam veteran in Steven Tesich's *The Speed of Darkness*.

During the 1991—92 season, Tony Randall's National Actors Theatre inaugurated its first season here with three revivals: Arthur Miller's *The Crucible*, Feydeau's *The Little Hotel on the Side*, and Ibsen's *The Master Builder*. The puppet show *A Little More Magic*, produced by the Famous People Players of Canada, played a limited engagement there in 1994.

The following year, British actor Ralph Fiennes played *Hamlet* and won a Tony Award for his performance. Later in 1995 Alexander H. Cohen and Max Cooper presented Ellen Burstyn in a religious drama called *Sacrilege*. Nicol Williamson starred in *Jack*, a one-man show about John Barrymore, in 1996. In 1997 Margaret Colin played Jacqueline Kennedy in a cartoon-like satire on the Kennedy family, called *Jackie*. That same year, a stunning production of *A Doll's House* won a Best Actress Tony Award for British actress Janet McTeer as Nora and a Best Supporting Actor Tony for Owen Teale. In 1998 Jane Alexander returned to the stage in the play *Honour*. In 1999 Lincoln Center Theater presented a new production of Anouilh's *Ring Round the Moon* with Toby Stevens, Marian Seldes, Fritz Weaver, Simon Jones, and Joyce Van Patten.

A famous James Joyce short story served as the basis for an unusual musical that transferred from Off-Broadway's Playwrights Horizons to the Belasco on January 11, 2000. *James Joyce's The Dead* painted a portrait of a group of Dubliners who gather on a snowy Christmas Eve to sing together. Like the story, the musical revealed the powerful emotions moving just below the surface of the merry proceedings. Among the stellar cast were Blair Brown, Christopher Walken, Sally Ann Howes, Daisy Eagan, Alice Ripley, Emily Skinner, Stephen Spinella, and Marni Nixon. The musical received five Tony Award nominations.

The Belasco greeted the new century in April 2001 with a revival of Stephen Sondheim's and James Goldman's memory musical *Follies*, starring Blythe Danner, Treat Williams, Judith Ivey, and Gregory Harrison. Though paying tribute to David Belasco's con-

temporary Florenz Ziegfeld, that musical brought the playhouse full circle: Ziegfeld's *Follies* was inaugurated the same year that the Belasco opened its doors, 1907.

British actor Simon Callow imported his hit London solo show *The Mystery of Charles Dickens* to the Belasco in April 2002 but quickly found that most Americans lacked the detailed familiarity with Dickens's characters (other than those in *A Christmas Carol*) required to enjoy Peter Ackroyd's play. It was off to the hulks after twenty recitations.

Better luck was had on August 8, 2002 with the Broadway debut of Terrence McNally's Off-Broadway hit *Frankie and Johnny in the Clair de Lune*, about two also-rans who come in first with each other one late night. Edie Falco played the waitress and Stanley Tucci played the cook in the widely praised production, which was nominated for a Tony Award as Best Revival of a Play. Tucci, who was nominated for a Tony as Best Actor for the performance, also earned headlines for going out of character on more than one occasion to tongue-lash audience members who allowed their cell phones to ring. From this and numerous other complaints that accrued, New York City voted in February 2003 to ban cell phone use at plays, movies, and concerts (though enforcement would prove spotty to nonexistent).

The Belasco hosted two short runs in 2003. First up was Matthew Barber's romantic comedy *Enchanted April*, based on a novel about a group of middle-aged women whose vitality and vigor are reborn when they stay at a beachside house in Italy. The play provided a tour de force for Jayne Atkinson, who was nominated for a Tony Award.

In fall of that year, Mark Hamill of *Star Wars* fame played a gay dance teacher who develops a warm relationship with one of his students, an older woman, in *Six Dance Lessons in Six Weeks*. There had been intense competition among older actresses to play the student role, but in the end it went to Polly Bergen, who had appeared here in the 2000 revival of *Follies*, as Carlotta. But the production got indifferent reviews and waltzed through only twenty-eight performances.

Frank Wildhorn, composer of *Jekyll & Hyde*, *The Scarlet Pimpernel*, and *The Civil War*, brought his next show to Broadway on August 19, 2004. It was *Dracula: The Musical*, the second of three big-budget vampire musi-

Rocker Stew stars in his semi-autobiographical musical *Passing Strange* (2008). (Photo by Michael Daniel)

cals to come and go quickly in the 2000s. Tom Hewitt starred as the iron-poor Transylvanian count. Melissa Errico costarred as Mina, the woman he hopes to lure into the world of the undead. Christopher Hampton and Don Black shared credit for the book and lyrics, which hewed a little closer than usual to the original Bram Stoker novel. But despite some dandy special effects, audiences just didn't turn out to see vampires sing. It lasted 157 performanc-es, the longest run of the three bloodsucking musicals.

Fans of Denzel Washington lined up along Forty-fourth Street in April 2005 to see their favorite movie star play Brutus in William Shakespeare's political-assassination drama *Julius Caesar* (the play's twentieth document-ed Broadway production). Director Daniel Sullivan populated the stage with Jessica Hecht as Portia, Tamara Tunie as Calpurnia,

Patrick Page as Decius Brutus, and William Sadler as Caesar. Reviews were mixed, but after it played out its scheduled run of eighty-one performances, producers were able to bank a $1 million profit. Problems with the lights during the run were variously ascribed to ghosts and to the grand old theatre starting to feel its age—the Belasco celebrated its centenary in 2007.

Meanwhile, Lincoln Center Theater leased the Belasco for an April 17, 2006, revival of Clifford Odets's groundbreaking drama *Awake and Sing!*, starring Zoë Wanamaker, Mark Ruffalo, Ben Gazzara, Jonathan Hadary, and Pablo Schreiber. Bartlett Sher's meticulous production won the 2006 Tony Award as Best Revival of a Play.

With the United States still in the teeth of twin wars in Iraq and Afghanistan, the English ushered over their hit revival of R. C. Sherriff's 1927 drama *Journey's End* on February 22, 2007. Staged with its heart in its throat by director David Grindley, *Journey's End* shows the last days of an English regiment on the front lines of World War I, as they all gradually realize they are about to be sacrificed in a frontal attack against the Germans. Audiences may have found the subject to be too painful while American soldiers were still engaged in battle. Despite reverent reviews and a Tony Award as Best Revival of a Play, audiences could no longer be coaxed to come after 125 performances. The production so impressed the few people who actually got to see it that it became, for a time, a cause célèbre for theatre lovers. The comparatively short run helped illustrate the erosion of traditional critics' power in the Internet age.

A unique theatrical creation opened at the Belasco on February 28, 2008. *Passing Strange*, which transferred here from the Public Theater, was the brainchild of a musician who went by the single name "Stew" (born Mark Stewart), who developed the show as a sort of rock cantata with co-composer Heidi Rodewald. Stew's book and lyrics told the semi-autobiographical story of a black California teenager who decides to tear free of his middle-class upbringing and embrace bohemian Europe on a quest to find his true self. The show was performed by Stew's onstage band with actors moving in and out of various characters. Daniel Breaker played Stew's younger alter ego, Youth, while Stew himself served as narrator of the story and lead singer. The show won a Tony Award for Best Book and played 165 performances. The final two performances were filmed by director Spike Lee and later released as a film.

A revival of David Mamet's *American Buffalo* flashed through the Belasco in eight performances during November 2008, with critics unwilling to give a nickel for the production that starred John Leguizamo, Cedric the Entertainer, and Haley Joel Osment.

Lincoln Center Theater again leased the Belasco in April 2009 and again engaged Bartlett Sher, this time to direct a revival of August Wilson's drama *Joe Turner's Come and Gone* with Ernie Hudson, Aunjanue Ellis, and Chad L. Lewis. Roger Robinson won a Tony Award as Best Featured Actor in a Play for his performance as Bynum Walker, the mystical "rootworker" in this drama about a stranger who arrives at a Pittsburgh boardinghouse on a singular quest.

Newly elected President Barack Obama took some political heat in spring 2009 for snatching time off from dealing with a deep recession to see *Joe Turner*. But the president said the trip fulfilled a promise to his wife, First Lady Michelle Obama. It was observed at the time that the Belasco was one of the few remaining theatres with a separate entrance for the balcony—originally designed in part to create a segregated audience. The first black president of the United States entered through the front door. After *Joe Turner* wrapped up its limited run in early summer 2009, the Belasco was closed by the Shubert Organization for an extensive 102nd-anniversary renovation. Aside from amenities like new seats and enlarged restrooms, the Shuberts had the building's extensive interior stained glass cleaned and restored, and elegant light fixtures dating to the Tiffany era were taken from storage in the Shubert Archive and returned to service. Restorers also meticulously removed gray paint that had been daubed over original mezzanine murals by Everett Shinn. According to Shubert archivist Regan Fletcher, the freshly revealed murals show allegorical human fixtures that embody the various emotions Belasco hoped to evoke in his eponymous playhouse.

The Belasco was scheduled to reopen in fall 2010 with Lincoln Center Theater's musical *Women on the Verge of a Nervous Breakdown*, by David Yazbek and Jeffrey Lane, inspired by the 1988 Pedro Almodóvar film.

BERNARD B. JACOBS

THEATRE

THE JACOBS THEATRE AT 242 WEST
Forty-fifth Street was one of six legitimate theatres built by the Chanin Brothers in the 1920s.
Over the years it bore the names John Golden
Theatre and Royale Theatre (twice) but was
rechristened after the longtime president of
the Schubert Organization in 2005.

In describing the new house, the *New York
Times* reported that it was "comfortable, with
plenty of leg room around the seats." The theatre was done in modern Spanish style and had
two murals, collectively titled *Lovers of Spain*,
by Willy Pogany; the general color scheme was
cardinal red, orange, and gold. Not surprisingly, once again the architect was the busy
Herbert J. Krapp.

With a seating capacity of a little over one

thousand, the theatre opened on January 11, 1927, as the Royale. The inaugural offering was a musical comedy called *Piggy*. The popular comic Sam Bernard played a monocled Englishman whose son (Paul Frawley) falls in love with an American girl. Brooks Atkinson in the *Times* called it an "average musical comedy" and highly praised the dancing of Goodee Montgomery, whom he identified as the daughter of the late and still lamented Dave Montgomery of the famed Montgomery and Stone team. The following day, the *Times* carried a correction. Miss Goodee was Montgomery's niece. Shortly after this show opened, the producer changed its title (a very rare practice in the theatre) to *I Told You So*, and it ran for seventy-nine performances.

The Royale's next musical, *Judy*, starred the bubbly Queenie Smith and the romantic Charles Purcell. One of the songs was titled "When Gentlemen Grew Whiskers and Ladies Grew Old." *Judy* pleased the nostalgia crowd for 104 performances.

A musical version of Oscar Wilde's *The Importance of Being Earnest*, retitled *Oh, Earnest!*, did not last long, but a black revue called *Rang Tang* fared better in 1927, running for 119 performances. The dancing in this show was highly praised by the critics. The *Times* referred to the revue as "a blackamoor folderol."

Winthrop Ames's Gilbert and Sullivan Opera Company moved into the Royale in September 1927 and performed *The Mikado*, *Iolanthe*, and *The Pirates of Penzance* for a very successful three months. A popular (but aging) entertainer named Mitzi next appeared in *The Madcap*, a very silly musical about an older woman (Mitzi) who pretends to be much younger in order to win rich Lord Clarence

Top left to right: Standard program cover for *Royale* in the 1920s and early 1930. Back cover of souvenir program for *New Faces of 1952*. Herald for Ina Claire in George Kelly's romantic comedy *The Fatal Weakness* (1946).

Bottom left: John Halliday and Jane Cowl in S.N. Behrman's thoughtful comedy, *Rain from Heaven* (1935).

Bottom center: Freida Inescort and Selena Royle in Rachel Crother's comedy *When Ladies Meet* (1932).

Bottom right: Sir Laurence Olivier in John Osborne's *The Entertainer* (1958).

Top left to right:
PLAYBILL covers for
Yasmin Reza's *Art* and
Andrew Lloyd Webber's
Song & Dance.

Audrey Christie and Sam
Levene in Moss Hart's
theatre comedy *Light Up
The Sky* (1948).

Julie Andrews (center) and
flappers in Sandy Wilson's
spoof of the 1920s musi-
cals, *The Boy Friend* (1954).

Bottom left: Bette Davis
in Tennessee Williams's
The Night of the Iguana
(1961).

Bottom center: Lauren
Bacall in the long-run-
ning comedy *Cactus
Flower* (1965).

Bottom right: Martin
Sheen (seated), Irene
Dailey and Jack
Albertson in *The Subject
Was Roses* (1964).

Steeple (Sydney Greenstreet). Arthur Treacher was also in this nonsense, which ran for 103 performances.

After its yearlong musicals-only diet, the Royale played its first straight show in 1928. It was *Sh! The Octopus*, described by an overzealous press agent as a "sneaky, snaky, slimy mystery." The murderous doings took place in a lighthouse, and since there is little prospect that this show will be revived (though it was filmed), it can be revealed that the plot turned out to be nothing but a dream.

The Royale had its first bona fide hit on April 9, 1928, when Mae West starred in her own play, *Diamond Lil*, a melodrama set in the 1890s Bowery. This devil's brew bubbled for 323 performances. The year 1929 ended at the Royale with an item called *Woof Woof*, a musical that featured not one, but two live whippet races onstage. They ran only 46 times.

The Second Little Show, a successor to the highly successful revue *The Little Show*, opened at the Royale on September 2, 1930, but did not measure up to the first edition. Although the score was by the illustrious Howard Dietz and Arthur Schwartz, it was a song by Herman Hupfeld that swept the nation—"Sing Something Simple." The show managed only sixty-three performances. A popular farce called *Stepping Sisters* played two engagements at this theatre in 1930—31. Mae West returned to the Royale in 1931 with her latest play, *The Constant Sinner*, but it wasn't sinful enough and ran for only sixty-four performances. West announced that she might do some matinees of *Macbeth* and play Lady Macbeth herself, but the project, unfortunately, never got off the ground. Instead, Fritz Leiber and his Chicago Civic Shakespeare Society arrived in *The Merchant of Venice*

(1931). His company included Helen Menken, Tyrone Power (Sr.), William Faversham, Pedro De Cordoba, Viola Roache, and Whitford Kane.

Rachel Crothers had a hit play, *When Ladies Meet*, which opened at the Royale on October 6, 1932, starring Frieda Inescort, Walter Abel, Spring Byington, and Selena Royle.

The Theatre Guild production of Maxwell Anderson's exposé of corruption in the nation's capital, *Both Your Houses*, was brilliantly acted by Shepperd Strudwick, Morris Carnovsky, Walter C. Kelly, Mary Philips, J. Edward Bromberg, and others, but it managed to play for only seventy-two performances. A comedy called *Every Thursday*, starring Queenie Smith, opened in May of 1934, and it was the last play at the Royale before the theatre changed its name for the first time.

John Golden, the famous theatrical producer, owned the John Golden Theatre on West Fifty-eighth Street between Broadway and Seventh Avenue, but he lost it in 1933. In 1934 he leased the Royale and renamed it the Golden Theatre. The first production under the new management was Norman Krasna's comedy *Small Miracle*, which opened on September 26, 1934. Directed by George Abbott, this unusual play took place in a theatre lobby and chronicled the lives of the theatre's patrons who congregated there. The large cast included Ilka Chase, Joseph Spurin-Calleia, Myron McCormick, and Elspeth Eric. It prospered for 118 performances.

In November 1934, the Abbey Theatre Players from Dublin opened at the Golden in a repertory of plays that changed weekly. Headed by Barry Fitzgerald, the company presented such Irish classics as *The Plough and the Stars*, *The Far-off Hills*, *The Shadow of the Glen*, *The Playboy of the Western World*, and *Drama at Inish*. On Christmas Eve the Theatre Guild presented one of S. N. Behrman's most thoughtful drawing-room comedies, *Rain from Heaven*, with Jane Cowl, John Halliday, Lily Cahill, Ben Smith, and Thurston Hall. Contemporary issues—fascism, Nazism, communism, Lindbergh hero worship—were brilliantly discussed by intellectuals of opposing viewpoints during a country weekend in England.

The remainder of 1935 was devoted to a comedy, *The Bishop Misbehaves*, starring Walter Connolly, which moved here from the Cort Theatre, and an acerbic play, *A Touch of Brimstone*, with Roland Young as a very nasty theatrical producer who took perverse delight in mistreating people. (Shades of Jed Harris?)

During 1936 the Golden Theatre had a series of short-run shows. Some of the more interesting ones were the return of eighty-year-old actor William Gillette, after four years of retirement, in a revival of *Three Wise Fools*, with Charles Coburn; Nazimova in *Ghosts*, which returned after a tour and played for a month at a $1.65 top (reasonable even for that time); and *Double Dummy*, a "farce-satire" about contract bridge, with Martha Sleeper, Dudley Clements, and John McGovern.

Above: Blair Brown, Michael Cumpsty, and Philip Bosco in the Tony-winning play, *Copenhagen* (2000). (Photo by Joan Marcus)

Audra McDonald and rapper Sean Combs (a.k.a. P. Diddy) in *A Raisin in the Sun* (2004). (Photo by Joan Marcus)

From 1937 until 1940 the Golden ceased functioning as a legitimate playhouse. It became the CBS Radio Theatre. Undaunted, producer John Golden leased the Masque Theatre next door and rechristened it the John Golden Theatre. It has remained so ever since.

In October 1940 the former Golden Theatre was taken over by the Magoro Operating Corporation, which restored this theatre's original name: the Royale. To review: first, this theatre was the Royale, then it became the Golden, then the CBS Radio Theatre, then the Royale again, and, years later, the Jacobs.

The hit Cole Porter musical *DuBarry Was a Lady* moved from the 46th Street Theatre to the Royale on October 21, 1940, minus one of its stars—Ethel Merman—who was succeeded by Gypsy Rose Lee. Bert Lahr was still the star of the show. It stayed for two months. This was followed by Elmer Rice's *Flight to the West* (1940), from the Guild Theatre, and Ethel Barrymore in her hit *The Corn Is Green* (1940), which transferred from the National Theatre. Paul Muni returned in a revival of Elmer Rice's *Counsellor-at-Law* (1942), one of his earlier hits. It ran for 258 performances. The daffy ZaSu Pitts arrived in a melodramatic farce, *Ramshackle Inn* (1944), and her Hollywood fans supported this ramshackle play for 216 performances.

The critics scorned *School for Brides*, a Chicago hit that came east with Roscoe Karns and a bevy of beauties in the summer of 1944,

but the public bought it for 375 performances. Michael Todd's spectacular production of *Catherine Was Great*, with the mistress of triple entendre, Mae West, moved here from the Shubert and pulverized the local yokels for three more months. Another sex comedy that was a smash in Chicago—*Good Night, Ladies* (1945)—came east and was assassinated by the New York drama critics. The public listened to the scribes this time and the farce left after 78 performances. A stage adaptation of Lillian Smith's best-seller *Strange Fruit* expired after 60 performances in 1945.

The distinguished veteran producer Arthur Hopkins presented Louis Calhern as Justice Oliver Wendell Holmes and Dorothy Gish as his loving wife in Emmet Lavery's *The Magnificent Yankee* in January 1946, and it ran a respectable 160 performances. Tennessee Williams's first Broadway play, *The Glass Menagerie*, with triumphant performances by the great Laurette Taylor, Eddie Dowling, Julie Haydon, and Anthony Ross, moved here from the Playhouse in 1946. This was followed by a moderately successful revival of *The Front Page*, with Lew Parker and Arnold Moss. The radiant Ina Claire returned to the stage in George Kelly's amusing comedy *The Fatal Weakness*, about a romantic woman (Claire) who loves to attend weddings, even if the groom happens to be a former husband of hers.

A stylish revival of Wilde's *The Importance of Being Earnest* starred John Gielgud (who also staged it), Margaret Rutherford, and Robert Flemyng in 1947 and achieved a run of eighty-one performances. Gielgud and Flemyng returned to the Royale in May in a revival of William Congreve's artificial bore *Love for Love*, which left town after forty-eight showings.

In December 1947 Judith Anderson returned from a triumphant tour in *Medea* and continued to kill her helpless babes for five more months. Moss Hart's acidulous comedy about theatre folks trying out a show in Boston, *Light Up the Sky*, arrived in November 1948 and provoked hilarity for 214 performances. Sam Levene played a vulgar producer, Audrey Christie acted his loudmouth wife, and Broadway insisted that the characters were modeled after Billy Rose and his then wife, Olympic swimmer Eleanor Holm.

Alfred de Liagre's memorable production of *The Madwoman of Chaillot* moved here from

Bradley Cooper and Julia Roberts in Richard Greenberg's drama *Three Days of Rain* (2006). (Photo by Joan Marcus)

the Belasco in 1949 and stayed for four months. *Dance Me a Song*, an intimate revue, was not a hit, but it served to introduce the delightful comic Wally Cox, who wrote his own very funny monologues. This was followed by a revival of Shaw's *The Devil's Disciple*, with Maurice Evans, Dennis King, Victor Jory, and Marsha Hunt, staged by Margaret Webster for 111 performances. Next came a London hit, Christopher Fry's verse play *The Lady's Not for Burning*, starring John Gielgud (who also directed), Richard Burton, and Pamela Brown, which made pleasant rhymes for 151 performances. Sidney Kingsley's powerful dramatization of Arthur Koestler's novel *Darkness at Noon* moved here from the Alvin and played for three more months in 1951.

Borscht Capades, described as an "English Yiddish revue," pleased the critics and ran for 90 performances. Another revue—Leonard Sillman's *New Faces of 1952*, which opened here on May 16, 1952—turned out to be the best show of this series and one of the finest revues

in Broadway history. Staged by the great revue director John Murray Anderson, the cast included such bright talents as Paul Lynde, Ronny Graham, June Carroll, Eartha Kitt, Robert Clary, Alice Ghostley, Carol Lawrence, and many others. The smash ran for 365 performances and was one of the few Broadway revues that was filmed by Hollywood.

Billy Rose presented a stage adaptation of André Gide's novel *The Immoralist*, with Geraldine Page as a woman who has married a homosexual, played by Louis Jordan. In the cast was the young James Dean as a North African homosexual who attempts to lure the husband to the local date grove. The daring play ran for 104 performances in 1954.

A British musical, *The Boy Friend*, by Sandy Wilson, opened at the Royale on September 30, 1954, and captivated Manhattan. This diverting parody of 1920s musicals introduced Julie Andrews to Broadway, and she was a delight. The spoof ran for 485 performances. This theatre had another smash hit in Thornton

Martin Short wears a fat suit as Jimminy Glick with Capathia Jenkins in his pseudo-autobiographical musical *Martin Short: Fame Becomes Me* (2006). (Photo by Paul Kolnik)

Wilder's *The Matchmaker*, which opened on December 5, 1955. The play had a very curious history. Wilder first wrote it as *The Merchant of Yonkers*, but it flopped on Broadway in 1938, despite direction by the famed Max Reinhardt and Jane Cowl and Percy Waram in the leading roles. But this raucous version—staged by Tyrone Guthrie and vividly performed by Ruth Gordon, Loring Smith, Robert Morse, Eileen Herlie, and Arthur Hill—rang the cash register for 486 performances. Guthrie won a Tony Award for his galvanic staging of this comedy, which was later adapted as the celebrated musical *Hello, Dolly!*

The Tunnel of Love, a minor comedy by Joseph Fields and Peter DeVries, managed to run for 417 performances in 1957, probably because of the popularity of its leading man, Tom Ewell. Nancy Olson, Darren McGavin, and Elizabeth Wilson were also in this comedy about a childless suburban couple who wish to adopt a baby.

Laurence Olivier gave a memorable performance as a seedy vaudeville actor in John Osborne's rather boring play *The Entertainer* (1958), an allegory of modern England. The cast included Olivier's wife, Joan Plowright; Brenda de Banzie; Peter Donat; and Jeri Archer, who played Britannia as a topless statue who did not move. David Merrick, the pro-

ducer of this British play, did not allow Archer to take a curtain call, stating that she would be too distracting to the audience.

The 1950s came to a dazzling close at this theatre with the lunatic French revue *La Plume de Ma Tante*, which opened on November 11, 1958, and stayed for 835 performances. Robert Dhery conceived, wrote, and starred in this uproarious vaudeville explosion, and the entire cast won a Special Tony Award for "contribution to the theatre."

Highlights of the 1960s at this theatre included Laurence Olivier and Anthony Quinn in Jean Anouilh's *Becket* (1960), which moved here from the St. James; *From the Second City* (1961), a hit Chicago revue with Alan Arkin, Barbara Harris, Paul Sand, and others; Tennessee Williams's *The Night of the Iguana* (1961), starring Bette Davis, Patrick O'Neal, Alan Webb, and Margaret Leighton, who won a Tony Award for her luminous performance; and Charles Boyer in S. N. Behrman's high comedy about an art dealer, *Lord Pengo* (1962), with Agnes Moorehead, Brian Bedford, and Henry Daniell.

Coral Browne and Keith Michell followed in Anouilh's *The Rehearsal* (1963); Margaret Leighton, John Williams, Alan Webb, Peter Donat, and Douglas Watson in Enid Bagnold's *The Chinese Prime Minister* (1964); Frank D. Gilroy's *The Subject Was Roses* (1964), the Pulitzer Prize—winning play with Jack Albertson (who won a Tony Award for his performance), Irene Dailey, and Martin Sheen; Jason Robards in Eugene O'Neill's *Hughie* (1964); and Lauren Bacall, Barry Nelson, Robert Moore, and Brenda Vaccaro in *Cactus Flower* (1965), adapted by Abe Burrows from a French comedy. It ran for 1,234 performances.

The last hit of the 1960s at the Royale featured Donald Pleasence starring in Robert Shaw's play *The Man in the Glass Booth* (1968), directed by Harold Pinter.

The 1970s brought Robert Marasco's chilling *Child's Play* (1970), with Ken Howard, Pat Hingle, Fritz Weaver, and David Rounds; Michael Weller's fascinating portrait of the 1960s generation, *Moonchildren* (1972); and the record-breaking musical *Grease*, which moved to the Royale from the Broadhurst in 1972 and stayed until April 13, 1980. It became the longest-running musical in Broadway history, with 3,388 performances. (In September 1983 it was surpassed by *A Chorus Line*, and subse-

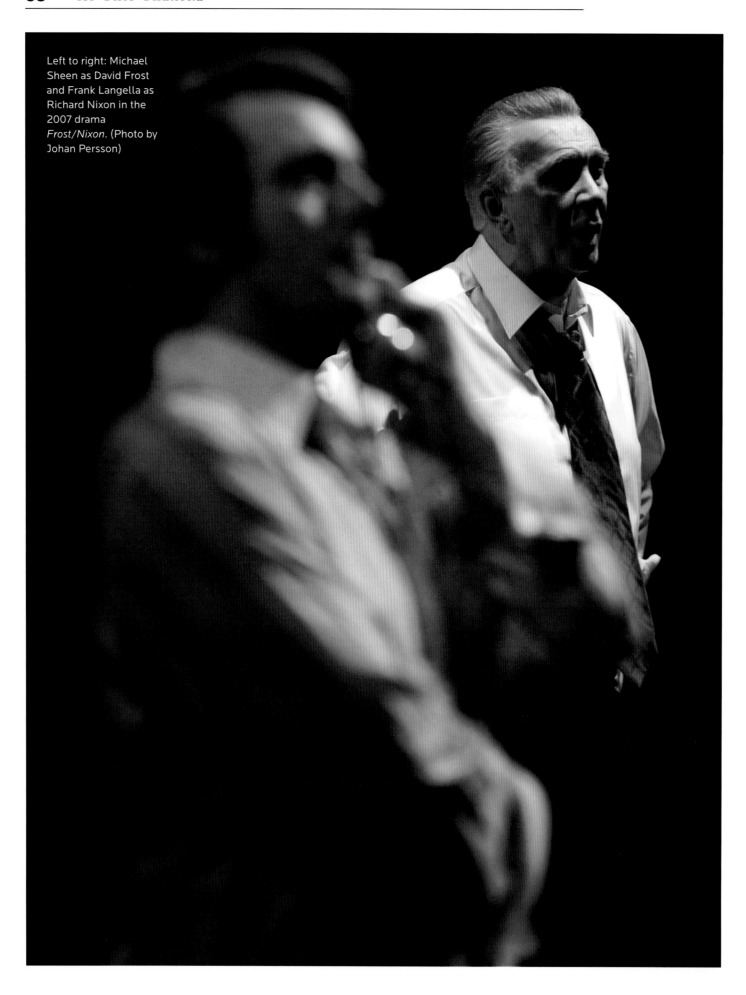

Left to right: Michael Sheen as David Frost and Frank Langella as Richard Nixon in the 2007 drama *Frost/Nixon*. (Photo by Johan Persson)

quently by others.)

An unusual event occurred at this theatre in February 1980. The British play *Whose Life Is It Anyway?*, in which Tom Conti had won a Tony Award for his performance as a man paralyzed from the neck down, was revised to make the hero a heroine. Mary Tyler Moore played the part in the revised version, which ran at the Royale for ninety-six performances. The experiment was considered a success.

Next came a screwball musical, *A Day in Hollywood/A Night in the Ukraine*, which moved here from the John Golden Theatre and won a Tony Award for Priscilla Lopez as Best Featured Actress in a Musical and another for co-choreographers Tommy Tune and Lopez's fellow *A Chorus Line* alumnus Thommie Walsh. Actually a double bill, the show consisted of a first-act tribute to movie musicals and a second-act adaptation of a short Chekhov play as a vehicle for the Marx Brothers. The curious amalgam lasted 588 performances.

In December 1981 *Duet for One*, by Tom Kempinski, starred Anne Bancroft and Max von Sydow, and was directed by William Friedkin. The following month, *Joseph and the Amazing Technicolor Dreamcoat*, Andrew Lloyd Webber and Tim Rice's first musical (though not their first on Broadway), moved here from the Entermedia Theatre and ran until September 1983. The following April *The Human Comedy*, a musical version of Saroyan's novel of the same name (with music by *Hair*'s Galt MacDermot), had a brief run here. That fall Alec McCowen played a limited engagement in his one-man show *Kipling*. In 1985 Carroll O'Connor and Frances Sternhagen starred in *Home Front* for a brief run, followed by Rosemary Harris, Dana Ivey, George N. Martin, and Patrick McGoohan in the absorbing British play *Pack of Lies*, by Hugh Whitemore. Harris received a Drama Desk Award for her performance.

September 1985 brought Bernadette Peters in a Tony Award—winning performance in *Song & Dance* by Andrew Lloyd Webber, Don Black, and Richard Maltby Jr. Among the excellent dancers in this British import were Charlotte and Christopher d'Amboise, Scott Wise, Victor Barbee, and Cynthia Onrubia. The offbeat musical, another double bill at the Royale, ran for 474 performances. Next came a revival of the famed 1926 play *Broadway*, by George Abbott and Philip Dunning. It coincided with Mr. Abbott's one hundredth birthday,

and he directed the production. Unfortunately, the critics found the play to be dated and it ran for only four performances.

It was succeeded at the Royale by *Roza*, a musical directed by Harold Prince and starring Georgia Brown, but this, too, had a short run: twelve performances. The story of a woman who cares for the unwanted children of Paris prostitutes was based on *La Vie Devant Soi*, by French author Romain Gary.

Serious Money, by Caryl Churchill, a devastating satire on the British stock market in the Thatcher era, moved here from the New York Shakespeare Festival in February 1988 but did not repeat its London success, lasting only fifteen performances. May 3, 1988, brought the Broadway debut of rock star Madonna in David Mamet's *Speed-the-Plow*, also starring Ron Silver (who won a Tony Award for his dynamic performance) and Joe Mantegna. Most critics were not impressed with Madonna's thespian abilities. Nevertheless, the drama about a pair of would-be Hollywood film producers ran for 278 performances.

In March 1989 Ken Ludwig's hilarious farce *Lend Me a Tenor* opened and played here for more than a year. The superlative cast included Philip Bosco (Tony Award), Victor Garber, Ron Holgate, Tovah Feldshuh, and Jane Connell, and the director was Jerry Zaks (Tony Award). Next Herb Gardner's *Conversations with My Father* opened and won a Tony Award for Judd Hirsch. Also starring Tony Shalhoub and David Margulies, it ran here for a year.

The 1994 attraction was the acclaimed Royal National Theatre production of J. B. Priestley's thriller *An Inspector Calls*, with dazzling direction by Stephen Daldry. It starred Rosemary Harris, Philip Bosco, and Kenneth Cranham and featured Jane Adams and Marcus D'Amico. Adams won a Tony Award as Best Featured Actress in a Play. Stunning stage effects included a pounding rainstorm onstage in Act I and an Act II climax in which the house set turned inside-out, disgorging its contents. The show closed in 1995 after 454 performances.

In 1996 Tony Randall's National Actors Theatre presented a well-received revival of the 1955 play *Inherit the Wind*, by Jerome Lawrence and Robert E. Lee. This absorbing drama about the famed 1925 Scopes "Monkey Trial" in Tennessee, charging an educator with teaching evolution, was hailed for the savage performance of George C. Scott as Henry Drummond. Unfortunately, Scott became seriously ill during the short run and had to be replaced by Randall. The production closed after only forty-five performances.

On September 19, 1996, *Skylight*, a London hit, opened here with the stars of the British production, Michael Gambon and Lia Williams. The domestic drama by David Hare took place in a depressing flat in London and involved former lovers who attempt to rekindle their love. The production received four Tony Award nominations and ran for 116 performances.

Stars of the present and future were packed into the tiny seven-member cast of the November 1997 musical *Triumph of Love*, adapted by James Magruder, Jeffrey Stock, and Susan Birkenhead from the Marivaux play. Betty Buckley, F. Murray Abraham, Susan Egan, Kevin Chamberlin, Nancy Opel, Christopher Sieber, and Roger Bart were featured in the chamber musical, which managed

a run of only eighty-three performances.

On March 1, 1998, *Art*, an international hit by Yasmina Reza, translated by Christopher Hampton, opened to rave reviews. It starred Alan Alda, Victor Garber, and Alfred Molina as long-standing buddies whose friendship is shattered over an expensive white-on-white painting that Garber's character has bought. Performed without intermission, the comedy gave Molina a show-stopping monologue about his battles with his mother-in-law over his impending wedding. During the play's long run Alda was succeeded by Brian Cox, Judd Hirsch, and Buck Henry; Garber by Henry Goodman, Joe Morton, and George Segal; and Molina by David Haig, George Wendt, and Wayne Knight. *Art* won a Best Play Tony Award and received two other Tony nominations.

A new production of Arthur Miller's 1968 play *The Price* opened here on November 15, 1999, starring Jeffrey DeMunn, Bob Dishy, Lisbeth Mackay, and Harris Yulin. It was well received. The drama involves two brothers who have been estranged for sixteen years.

Left: Left to right: Nicole Ansari and Brian Cox in Tom Stoppard's *Rock 'n' Roll* (2007). (Photo by Johan Persson)

Right: The teen-aged ensemble of the 2008 Jason Robert Brown musical, *13*. (Photo by Joan Marcus)

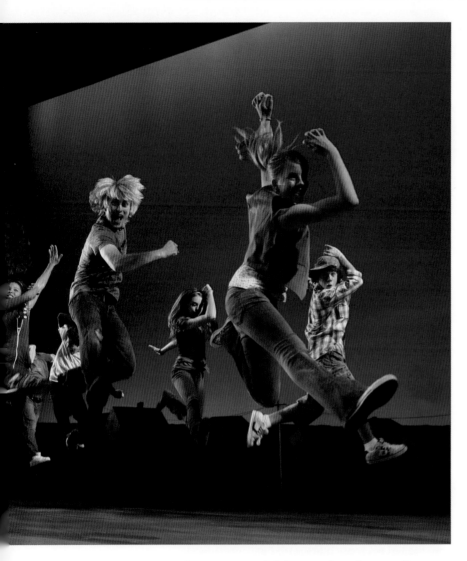

production of this intellectual drama was hailed for its thoughtful content and ran for 326 performances. The play was recorded with its original cast by Fynsworth Alley.

Gary Sinise earned glowing reviews as the rebellious Randle McMurphy in a revival of Dale Wasserman's mental hospital drama *One Flew Over the Cuckoo's Nest*, which opened April 8, 2001, and stayed on Broadway through July. Amy Morton played the tyrannical Nurse Ratched.

Monologuist John Leguizamo took audiences on a tour through his fractured love life and his decision start a family in the solo drama *Sexaholix . . . A Love Story*, for three months starting December 2, 2001.

Billy Crudup visited for two months in April 2002 with a revival of *The Elephant Man*, also starring Kate Burton. Both actors earned Tony Award nominations. Comedian Jackie Mason brought his sixth solo comedy show, *Prune Danish*, to the Royale on October 22, 2002, but it had one of his shortest runs, five weeks.

Film stars brought two short-lived revivals of 1980s classics to the Jacobs in 2003. Whoopi Goldberg played the demanding jazz singer Ma Rainey (opposite Charles S. Dutton) in a revival of August Wilson's *Ma Rainey's Black Bottom* in February. Danny Glover recreated his original 1982 Broadway performance as Willie, one of two black servants who watch their white childhood friend transform into a racist teenager, in a June revival of Athol Fugard's South African drama *"MASTER HAROLD" . . . and the boys*. The production was directed by Lonny Price, who had originated the role of Master Harold in that earlier production.

Nilo Cruz's drama *Anna in the Tropics* came to Broadway in November 16, 2003, having already won the Pulitzer Prize after its regional debut. Jimmy Smits, Priscilla Lopez, and Daphne Rubin-Vegas were featured in this drama about passions that erupt when a new *Lector*—one who reads to the workers—is hired at a family-run cigar-making business in South Florida. The production stayed at the Jacobs for 113 performances.

Rapper Sean "P. Diddy" Combs went legit April 26, 2004, in a revival of Lorraine Hansberry's classic *A Raisin in the Sun*, about a black family in conflict over how to spend an inheritance. He wisely surrounded himself with top acting talent, notably Phylicia Rashad and Audra McDonald as his mother and wife, respectively. Both women won Tony Awards

One a successful doctor, the other a policeman, they meet again in an attic to dispose of their late father's belongings and to battle over the past that the furniture represents. The drama was directed by actor James Naughton and ran for 128 performances.

A lauded British play, *Copenhagen*, opened at the Royale Theatre on April 11, 2000. Starring Philip Bosco, Blair Brown, and Michael Cumpsty, it told the complex tale, based on actual people and events, of a 1941 meeting between two brilliant physicists—German Werner Heisenberg and Danish Niels Bohr—plus the latter's wife, Margrethe Bohr. The two men had collaborated on work that led to unlocking the power of the atom but were now on opposing sides in World War II. The meeting ended in personal disaster—but may have prevented Hitler from developing nuclear weapons. Written by Michael Frayn and directed by Michael Blakemore, the drama won the following Tony Awards: Best Play, Best Direction, and Best Featured Actress (Blair Brown). The American for their performances. Critics saluted Combs for giving a much more complex and creditable performance than they had expected in his Broadway debut. The production was filmed for cable TV broadcast in 2008. It was nominated for three Emmy Awards, including Outstanding Made-for-Television Movie, and it won the Humanitas Prize when it was shown at the Sundance Film Festival.

Actress Edie Falco, then at the height of her fame from playing Carmella on TV's *The Sopranos*, returned to Broadway November 14, 2004, in a revival of Marsha Norman's Pulitzer-winning suicide drama *'night, Mother*. But critics felt it lacked the spark of the original, and it survived for only two months.

Another 1980s drama got a better-received revival in May 2005 when Liev Schreiber, Alan Alda, Tom Wopat, and Jeffrey Tambor led the ensemble in director Joe Mantello's production of David Mamet's Pulitzer-winning *Glengarry Glen Ross*, about a group of real-estate salesmen pushed to the edge when an aggressive new manager is brought on board. It won the Tony Award as Best Revival of a Play and ran for 137 performances.

On May 9, 2005, shortly after the opening of *Glengarry*, the theatre was renamed in honor of Bernard B. Jacobs (1916—1996), who had been president of the Shubert Organization for more than two decades.

Oscar nominee Julia Roberts drew crowds to the Jacobs Theatre in April 2006 when she made her Broadway debut in *Three Days of Rain*, Richard Greenberg's mystery drama that uses the same three actors to play members of a younger generation in Act I, and then their own parents in Act II. Despite a publicity blitz, neither Roberts nor the show impressed critics, and the production did not extend its seventy-performance limited run.

Comedian Martin Short, a Tony winner for *Little Me*, parodied show-business autobiographies with the musical revue *Martin Short: Fame Becomes Me*, which boasted a score by the *Hairspray* team of Marc Shaiman and Scott Wittman. Though the show followed the general outline of Short's career, Short, Wittman, Shaiman, and Daniel Goldfarb had fun making up vast swaths of it, including a time when Short supposedly costarred as a fence in a movie that looked a lot like *The Wizard of Oz*, and when he played Jesus's stepbrother in a sequel to *Godspell*. Short wasn't afraid to share

the spotlight with an A-team supporting cast he dubbed "Comedy All Stars": Capathia Jenkins, Brooks Ashmanskas (Tony nomination), Mary Birdsong, Nicole Parker, and composer Shaiman himself on the piano. This entertaining nonsense opened August 17, 2006, and stayed for 165 performances.

Frost/Nixon transferred here from London's Donmar Warehouse Theatre on April 22, 2007. Peter Morgan's hit UK drama purported to show what happened behind the scenes in 1977 when English talk-show host David Frost conducted a series of interviews with former President Richard M. Nixon, in which Nixon is shown to have admitted authorizing the Watergate break-ins that eventually brought down his presidency. *Frost/Nixon* presented one marvelous performance, by Michael Sheen as Frost, and one titanic performance, by Frank Langella as Nixon. Langella showed Nixon as foxy, often paranoid, and sometimes alcoholic. But he also made a good case for Nixon's side of the story. The performance won him the 2007 Tony Award as Best Actor in a Play. And when Langella and Sheen recreated their roles in the 2008 movie version, Langella was nominated for the Oscar as Best Actor in a Leading Role.

British playwright Tom Stoppard was born and spent his early days in the Eastern European country of Czechoslovakia. He returned to his roots there with his November 4, 2007, drama *Rock "n' Roll*, about the 1968 "Prague Spring," when the communist government of that country briefly relaxed control before the Soviet army was called in. The play opened in the shadow of Stoppard's epic *The Coast of Utopia*, which had won the Tony for Best Play just a few months earlier. Trevor Nunn directed a cast led by Rufus Sewell and Sinéad Cusack. It stayed until early March 2008.

Film star Morgan Freeman starred in Clifford Odets's *The Country Girl* as an alcoholic has-been leading man trying to make a comeback. Despite a glowing performance by Frances McDormand as his long-suffering wife, the production lasted less than three months after its April 27, 2008, opening.

Composer Jason Robert Brown had won the Tony Award for Best Score for his debut Broadway effort, *Parade*, in 1998. Since then he had attracted a devout following of fans who loved his passionate and resolutely original songs for Off-Broadway shows like *The Last Five Years*. None of his projects enjoyed pro-

PLAYBILL®
JOHN GOLDEN THEATRE

The original Broadway cast of Yasmina Reza's 2009 drama *God of Carnage* (left to right): Marcia Gay Harden, Hope Davis, Jeff Daniels, and James Gandolfini. (Photo by Joan Marcus)

longed runs, and when it was announced in 2008 that Brown would be returning to Broadway with a musical called *13*, which had a completely original score with an original book by Robert Horn and Dan Elish, Brown's fans were in ecstasy. The show dealt with a Jewish boy whose mother moves him to an unwelcoming new town just as he is about to celebrate his Bar Mitzvah, given at age thirteen. All the characters in the show were similarly supposed to be thirteen or thereabouts, and to keep things even realer, not only was the entire cast populated by teen actors like Allie Trimm and Graham Phillips, but the musicians in the orchestra were also teens The show opened October 5, 2008, but the bad luck of the title must have been working overtime, because *13* got slammed into the lockers by the critics and, to Brown fans' chagrin, class was dismissed after just 105 performances.

One of the biggest hits of the 2008—9 season was Yasmina Reza's comedy *God of Carnage*, a portrait of two middle-class couples whose veneer of civilization quickly wears away when their two sons get involved in a schoolyard fight. The spare one-act play was performed by a stellar four-person ensemble consisting of TV and film stars James Gandolfini, Marcia Gay Harden, Jeff Daniels, and Hope Davis. The production opened March 22, 2009, and immediately zoomed to sellout status. All four actors were nominated for Tony Awards; Harden won Best Actress in a Play. Director Matthew Warchus was named Best Director of a Play, and the script took the Tony as Best Play of 2009.

The production took the unusual step of going on hiatus for several months in summer 2009 but was immediately restored to SRO status when the original cast came back in the fall. Since then, the production attracted star replacements from the worlds of stage, film, and television, including Lucy Liu, Jimmy Smits, Annie Potts, Christine Lahti, and Janet McTeer.

BOOTH
THEATRE

THIS WARM, INTIMATE THEATRE WAS
a joint venture of the aristocratic producer
Winthrop Ames, owner of the even smaller
Little Theatre, and impresario Lee Shubert.
Their aim was to offer theatregoers a cozy
house for the viewing of dramas and comedies.
It was named the Booth in remembrance of
another Booth Theatre in Manhattan (named
for actor Edwin Booth), in which Ames's father
had held financial interest.

The 668-seat (later augmented to 785)
Booth Theatre on West Forty-fifth Street was
built back-to-back with the Shubert Theatre
and shared Shubert Alley with it. According to
newspapers at the time of the Booth's opening,
the theatre was designed by architect Henry B.
Herts in early Italian Renaissance style, with

Graphic PLAYBILL covers for four Booth Theatre hits.

designs in sgrafitto in brown and ivory, colors which harmonize with the exterior of the theatre, which is yellow brick and ivory terra cotta." An unusual feature of the Booth was a wall that partitioned the entrance from the auditorium, preventing street and lobby noises and drafts from coming to the interior of the house. Woodwork and walls were in neutral tints of driftwood gray; draperies, upholstery, carpeting, and the house curtain were in various shades of mulberry. Chandeliers and appliqués along the wall gave the impression of candlelight. The theatre contained numerous Booth souvenirs, including the actor's favorite armchair, a statue of him, and many handbills and posters of Booth's appearances.

The Booth opened with fanfare on October 16, 1913, with the first American production of Arnold Bennett's play *The Great Adventure*, dramatized by him from his novel *Buried Alive*. The stars were Janet Beecher and Lyn Harding, and the fascinating plot dealt with a famous artist who is pronounced dead and who decides to go along with the erroneous obituary. Unfortunately, the play lasted only fifty-two performances.

The Booth's first hit was *Experience*, an allegorical play with music, in which William Elliott played a character who symbolized Youth. It ran for 255 performances in 1914—15. This was followed by another success, *The Bubble*, starring Louis Mann, which had a run of 176 showings.

On February 5, 1917, the distinguished producer/director Arthur Hopkins piloted a hit called *A Successful Calamity*, by Clare Kummer, starring William Gillette, Estelle Winwood, Roland Young, and William Devereaux. Later that year, *DeLuxe Annie*, with Jane Grey and Vincent Serrano, proved to be another good show.

The year 1918 started out with a huge hit for the Booth. Ruth Gordon, Gregory Kelly, Paul Kelly, and Neil Martin appeared in a delightful adaptation of Booth Tarkington's *Seventeen*. There were two hits the following year: Janet Beecher and Lowell Sherman in a mystery called *The Woman in Room 13* and a comedy called *Too Many Husbands*.

The Roaring Twenties at the Booth began rousingly with a lively melodrama, *The Purple Mask*, with Leo Ditrichstein, Brandon Tynan, and Lily Cahill in a cloak-and-dagger masquerade set in Napoleon's time. Alexander Woollcott loved it and wrote in the *New York Times* that Tom Sawyer and Penrod would have, too. This swashbuckler was followed by a charming play, *Not So Long Ago*, a nostalgic Cinderella tale set in early New York, with Eva Le Gallienne giving an enchanting performance as a poor girl who marries a rich boy. She was supported by Sidney Blackmer and Thomas Mitchell. The Booth went back to melodrama in November 1920 with a rousing adaptation of Mark Twain's *The Prince and the Pauper*, with actress Ruth Findlay playing the dual roles of the title and with William Faversham and Clare Eames in other choice parts.

Highlights of the 1920s at the Booth included George Arliss as the Raja of Ruka in a lush adventure play, *The Green Goddess* (1921), set in the Himalayas, which ran for 440 performances. A. A. Milne's engrossing play *The Truth About Blayds* (1922), starred O. P. Heggie as Blayds, a famed poet who reveals that someone else wrote all his poems, with Leslie Howard, Frieda Inescort, and Ferdinand Gottschalk helping to keep his secret. Austin Strong's unforgettable *Seventh Heaven* (1922) featured Helen Menken and George Gaul as the poor

Alfred Lunt and Lynn Fontanne in their joyous hit *The Guardsman* (1924).

Leslie Howard in John Galsworthy's engrossing drama *Escape* (1927).

Clockwise from top left:
Program-cover motif
for a 1921 Booth
Theatre production.

Kaufman and Hart's
1936 Pulitzer Prize
comedy, *You Can't Take
It with You*.

Souvenir program for
Noël Coward's enchant-
ing comedy, *Blithe
Spirit* (1942).

Shirley Booth and
Sidney Blackmer in
William Inge's poignant
play, *Come Back, Little
Sheba* (1950).

Risë Collins and
Trazana Beverley in *For
Colored Girls Who Have
Considered
Suicide/When the
Rainbow Is Enuf* (1976).

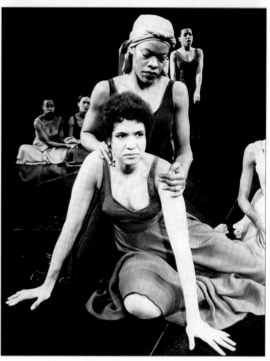

lovers in a Parisian garret. They moved in for 683 performances.

Next came *Dancing Mothers* (1924), a daring play in which a mother (played by Mary Young) rebels against her flapper daughter (Helen Hayes) and philandering husband (Henry Stephenson) by going wild herself and walking out on them. Edna Ferber and George S. Kaufman's *Minick* (1924) provided a gentle portrait of an old man going to live with his son and daughter-in-law.

Alfred Lunt and Lynn Fontanne appeared at the Booth in their fourth play together, Molnar's *The Guardsman* (1924), a Theatre Guild production so successful that it moved to the Booth from the Garrick Theatre. The 1920s continued with publisher Horace Liveright's startling modern-dress production of *Hamlet* (1925), which depicted Basil Sydney as the melancholy Dane in a dinner suit, King Claudius (Charles Waldron) in flannels, and Ophelia (Helen Chandler) in flapper frocks; *The Patsy* (1925), a winning comedy starring Claiborne Foster; Winthrop Ames's 1926 production of a fanciful Philip Barry comedy, *White Wings* (a fancy term for street cleaners),

which should have lasted longer than twenty-seven performances; Ruth Gordon, Roger Pryor, and Beulah Bondi in Maxwell Anderson's timely comedy about youth, *Saturday's Children* (1927); and Leslie Howard and Frieda Inescort in John Galsworthy's excellent drama *Escape* (1927), brilliantly produced and staged by Winthrop Ames.

The Grand Street Follies of 1928, an annual topical revue that spoofed current plays and players, featured James Cagney tapping and Dorothy Sands stopping the show with her impression of Mae West playing Shakespeare; Cagney, Sands, and others returned to do parodies for *The Grand Street Follies of 1929*. The last show of the 1920s at the Booth was a contemporary comedy of ill manners called *Jenny* (1929), starring Jane Cowl as an actress who

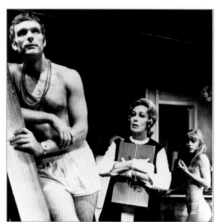

tries to straighten out a wayward family but ends up running off with the father of the house, capitally played by Guy Standing.

During the 1930s some fifty shows played the Booth, many of them quick failures and a number of them transferred from other theatres. Among the most noteworthy tenants were Margaret Sullavan in her Broadway debut, in a shabby play called *A Modern Virgin* (1931); Rose Franken's drama about family tyranny, *Another Language* (1932), splendidly acted by Margaret Wycherly, Margaret Hamilton, Glenn Anders, Dorothy Stickney, and John Beal; *No More Ladies* (1934), an intelligent comedy about infidelity, by A. E. Thomas, starring Lucile Watson and Melvyn Douglas; and Gladys Cooper making her Broadway debut with Raymond Massey and Adrianne Allen in Keith Winter's *The Shining Hour* (1934), another play about infidelity.

Also seen were John Van Druten's "comedy of women," called *The Distaff Side* (1934), superbly acted by Sybil Thorndike, Mildred Natwick, Estelle Winwood, and Viola Roache; J. B. Priestley's *Laburnum Grove* (1935), in which Edmund Gwenn pretended to be a counterfeiter in order to get rid of sponging relatives who

wished to borrow money from him; and Melvyn Douglas, Cora Witherspoon, Claudia Morgan, Violet Heming, Elsa Maxwell, Blanche Ring, and Tom Ewell—a million-dollar cast—all wasted in a maudlin play called *De Luxe* (1935), by novelist Louis Bromfield and John Gearon.

The radiant Grace George starred in a chilling drama, *Kind Lady* (1935), about a rich old lady held captive in her own home by a gang of clever thieves headed by Henry Daniell. The 1930s continued with *Blind Alley* (1935), another thriller, with Roy Hargrave as a gangster who is destroyed when a psychologist (George Coulouris) he is holding captive delves into his mind; a classical Chinese drama, *Lady Precious Stream* (1936), starring Helen Chandler, Bramwell Fletcher, and Clarence Derwent; *Sweet Aloes* (1936), a British play by Joyce Carey, with Miss Carey, Evelyn Laye, and Rex Harrison making his Broadway debut; and a rowdy farce about

Top: Playbills for *Having Our Say* (1995), Edward Albee's *Seascape* (2005), and *Dame Edna: The Royal Tour* (1999).

Center left: Alan Arkin, Anne Jackson, and Eli Wallach in *Luv* (1964).

Center right: Keir Dullea, Eileen Heckart, and Blythe Danner in the long-running *Butterflies Are Free* (1969).

Bottom: Patti LuPone and Peter Riegert reminisce in Mamet's *The Old Neighborhood* (1997).

Barry Humphries in one of his flamboyant creations for *Dame Edna: The Royal Tour* (1999).

Left to right: Michael Stuhlbarg and Billy Crudup in Martin McDonagh's *The Pillowman* (2005). (Photo by Joan Marcus)

wrestling, *Swing Your Lady* (1936).

Henry Travers and Josephine Hull headed an insane family of lovable eccentrics in Kaufman and Hart's Pulitzer Prize comedy *You Can't Take It with You* (1936), which ran almost two years at the Booth. There followed Montgomery Clift, Jessie Royce Landis, Morgan James, and Onslow Stevens in *Dame Nature* (1938), a sexual drama adapted from the French by actress Patricia Collinge; Philip Barry's arresting drama *Here Come the Clowns* (1938), with Eddie Dowling, Madge Evans, Doris Dudley, and Russell Collins; and a bright, richly designed revue, *One for the Money* (1939), by Nancy Hamilton and Morgan Lewis, with future stars Alfred Drake and Gene Kelly, along with Keenan Wynn, Grace McDonald, and Brenda Forbes.

Another Pulitzer Prize play brought the 1930s to a close at the Booth: William Saroyan's daffy comedy *The Time of Your Life*, with Eddie Dowling, Julie Haydon, Gene Kelly, William Bendix, Edward Andrews, and Celeste Holm.

In the 1940s the Booth had fewer productions than in the preceding decade, but more long-running hits. The decade started out with a sequel to the revue *One for the Money* called, aptly, *Two for the Show*, by the same authors. This edition boasted a memorable song, "How High the Moon," and comic and tuneful per-

formances by *One for the Money* veterans Drake and Wynn, along with Betty Hutton, Eve Arden, Richard Haydn, Brenda Forbes, Tommy Wonder, Eunice Healey, and Nadine Gae. On February 12, 1941, a genuine hit called *Claudia* came to the Booth and stayed for a little over a year. Written by Rose Franken, the touching play about a childlike wife made a star out of Dorothy McGuire and brought back to the stage the famed Belasco actress Frances Starr to play Claudia's mother, with Donald Cook as her husband.

Noël Coward's blissful comedy *Blithe Spirit* moved from the Morosco to the Booth in 1942, with Clifton Webb, Peggy Wood, Leonora Corbett, and Mildred Natwick, and the merry spooks stayed for a year. Another huge hit, *The Two Mrs. Carrolls* (1943), starring Elisabeth Bergner, Victor Jory, Vera Allen, and Irene Worth, thrilled Booth audiences with its homicidal plot and stayed for 585 performances.

A war drama, *The Wind Is Ninety*, had a remarkable cast (Kirk Douglas, Wendell Corey, Joyce Van Patten and her brother "Dickie," Blanche Yurka, and Bert Lytell) and played for more than a hundred performances in 1945. *You Touched Me!* (1945), by Tennessee Williams and Donald Windham, had fine performances by Montgomery Clift and Edmund Gwenn but was a lesser Williams work. Bobby

Top left: left to right: Frances Sternhagen and George Grizzard on the beach in Edward Albee's *Seascape* (2005). (Photo by Joan Marcus)

Top right: Nathan Lane as a teacher losing his battle with demons in a 2006 revival of *Butley*. (Photo by T. Charles Erickson)

Clark added burlesque touches to Molière's *The Would-Be Gentleman*, with June Knight and Gene Barry; Ben Hecht and Charles MacArthur's psychological murder mystery *Swan Song* played for 158 performances; and a revival of Synge's *The Playboy of the Western World* (1946) had Burgess Meredith, Mildred Natwick, J. C. Nugent, Julie Harris, and, making her Broadway debut, Maureen Stapleton.

Additional 1940s hits included Norman Krasna's farce-comedy *John Loves Mary* (1947), with Nina Foch, Tom Ewell, and William Prince; Gilbert Miller's revival of Molnar's bubbly comedy *The Play's the Thing* (1948), with Louis Calhern, Ernest Cossart, Arthur Margetson, and Faye Emerson making her Broadway debut; James B. Allardice's comedy *At War*

with the Army (1949), staged by Ezra Stone, with Gary Merrill giving an excellent performance; and Grace George, Walter Hampden, Jean Dixon, and John Williams in a pleasant religious drama, *The Velvet Glove* (1949).

The 1950s began auspiciously with William Inge's first Broadway play, *Come Back, Little Sheba*, with Shirley Booth and Sidney Blackmer winning Tony Awards for their powerful performances. Beatrice Lillie was the toast of the town in the hilarious revue *An Evening with Beatrice Lillie* (1952), in which she sang some of her most celebrated songs and acted in some of her most outlandish sketches with Reginald Gardiner for 278 performances. A popular comedy called *Anniversary Waltz* (1954), directed by Moss Hart and starring his wife, Kitty Carlisle, and Macdonald Carey, moved from the Broadhurst to the Booth and stayed for ten months; *Time Limit* (1956), a taut drama about the Korean War by Henry Denker and Ralph Berkey, starred Richard Kiley, Arthur Kennedy, Allyn McLerie, and Thomas Carlin and played for 127 performances.

Gore Vidal's science fiction delight, *Visit to a Small Planet* (1957), starring Cyril Ritchard as a comic extraterrestrial and Eddie Mayehoff as an imbecilic general, ran for nearly a year. William Gibson's *Two for the Seesaw* (1958), an enchanting two-character love story starring Henry Fonda and Anne Bancroft, ran for almost two years; and Paddy Chayefsky's *The Tenth Man*, about the exorcism of a dybbuk in suburban Mineola, with Gene Saks as a rabbi and Jack Gilford, George Voskovec, Jacob Ben-Ami, and Lou Jacobi giving sublime performances, played 623 times.

Highlights of the 1960s included Julie Harris, Walter Matthau, William Shatner, Gene Saks, and Diana van der Vlis in the continental comedy *A Shot in the Dark* (1961); Murray Schisgal's outré comedy *Luv* (1964), directed by Mike Nichols, with Eli Wallach, Anne Jackson, and Alan Arkin as three miserable creatures who cavort on a bridge, which lasted for 901 performances; Flanders and Swann, the British comedy team, in *At the Drop of Another Hat* (1966), a follow-up to their popular two-man revue *At the Drop of a Hat*; and Harold Pinter's sinister play *The Birthday Party* (1967), his first full-length work on Broadway.

Next came one of the Booth's most popular tenants, Leonard Gershe's *Butterflies Are Free*, the story of a blind man, his kooky neighbor, and his overprotective mother, which stayed for 1,128 performances. The cast featured Keir Dullea, Blythe Danner (who made her

Broadway debut and won a Tony Award for her luminous acting), and Eileen Heckart (later replaced by Gloria Swanson).

In 1972 the Booth housed another Pulitzer Prize play, Joseph Papp's production of *That Championship Season* (1972), by actor Jason Miller, which moved from the downtown New York Shakespeare Festival and played for almost two years at the Booth. Other attractions of the decade included Terrence McNally's zany *Bad Habits* (1974), two playlets about therapy, which moved uptown from the Astor Place Theatre; Cleavon Little in Murray Schisgal's *All Over Town* (1974), directed by Dustin Hoffman; a revival of Jerome Kern's 1915 musical *Very Good*

Eddie (1975), from the Goodspeed Opera House in Connecticut; and Ntozake Shange's *For Colored Girls Who Have Considered Suicide/When the Rainbow Is Enuf* (1976), an exalted program of poetry acted by an extraordinary cast of black artists for 742 performances.

The Elephant Man (1979), Bernard Pomerance's enthralling study of a disfigured man who strives to keep his humanity though he is displayed in a carnival freak show, was enhanced by memorable performances from Philip Anglim, Kevin Conway, and Carole Shelley. The drama moved from Off-Broadway's Theatre at Saint Peter's Church to the Booth and won the New York Drama Critics Circle Award for Best Play and three Tony Awards.

In 1975 the Booth was home to a unique, though failed, experiment on the part of the New York Shakespeare Festival's Joseph Papp, who was then flush from the phenomenal success of *A Chorus Line* at the neighboring Shubert Theatre. Advertising "Broadway for bupkes" (Yiddish for "very little money"), he booked the Booth for what was to have been a subscription series of Broadway dramas at a cost of just $10. The series did not survive the failure of its first offering, Dennis J. Reardon's *The Leaf People*, which closed after eight performances.

In 1979 the famed interior designer Melanie Kahane, who had redone four other Shubert Organization theatres, was hired to restore the Booth to its original elegance and grandeur. "What I've tried to do with these old houses is get back to the beginning and then modernize them in some way," she told PLAY-BILL at the time. "The Booth was a sad old sack. All in brown. I kept the brown below—to anchor—then put light beige on top. The light color brings your eye up, so you notice the detail." Kahane characterized the Booth as "very Jacobean." She got rid of the delicate French chandeliers, which she felt didn't belong in that house, and restored the elegant old theatre in the short space of three weeks.

Most of the thousands of theatre fans who visit the One Shubert Alley memorabilia store don't realize it is actually one of the Booth's converted former dressing rooms.

In November 1981 *Mass Appeal*, by Bill C. Davis, directed by Geraldine Fitzgerald, was another successful transfer from Off-Broadway to the Booth. This religious drama, first presented at the Circle Repertory Theatre and the Manhattan Theatre Club, featured

Left: Vanessa Redgrave as author Joan Didion in her autobiographical play, *The Year of Magical Thinking* (2007). (Photo by Brigitte Lacombe)

Ciarán Hinds (far right) played the devil come to earth on Christmas Eve in *The Seafarer*, with (left to right) Jim Norton, Sean Mahon, Conleth Hill, and David Morse. (Photo by Joan Marcus)

excellent performances by Milo O'Shea as a luxury-loving priest and Michael O'Keefe as his rebellious protégé.

The Booth's 1980s tenants included the Royal Shakespeare Company's production of *Good*, by the British playwright C. P. Taylor, starring Alan Howard as an intellectual German in Frankfurt in 1933 who turns into a rabid Nazi; *Total Abandon*, a short-lived play by Larry Atlas, starring Richard Dreyfuss as a parent who is guilty of child abuse and murder; and *Sunday in the Park With George*, a unique musical by Stephen Sondheim and James Lapine, in which an Impressionist painting comes to life. Mandy Patinkin and Bernadette Peters starred.

It won the Pulitzer Prize for Drama.

Herb Gardner's *I'm Not Rappaport* (1985) brought the Best Play Tony Award to the Booth, with its story of a feisty old codger who tries to hold on to life and dignity in his relationships with his friend, his daughter, and a young woman he meets in Central Park. It played for 890 performances. Judd Hirsch won the Tony as Best Actor in a Play.

The London hit *Shirley Valentine* (1989) struck a chord with its story of a working-class woman who grows tired of being taken for granted by her family and makes the bold step of abandoning them to pursue her dream of going to Greece. Pauline Collins won a Tony

Award for her performance in Willy Russell's solo play, which occupied the Booth for 324 performances.

The year 1990 brought *Once on This Island*, the Broadway debut of the songwriting team Lynn Ahrens and Stephen Flaherty, later to create *My Favorite Year*, *Ragtime*, and *Seussical*. Their first Broadway production retold a Caribbean tale about a peasant girl whose romance with a handsome aristocrat is aided by spirits of the land, air, and water. The bittersweet fairy-tale musical lasted 469 performances and earned the team a Tony nomination for Best Score.

In 1992 a British play, *Someone Who'll Watch Over Me* by Frank McGuinness, was splendidly acted by Stephen Rea, Alec McCowen, and James McDaniel and ran for 216 performances. It was nominated for two Tony Awards: Best Play and Best Actor in a Play (Rea). The following year, *The Twilight of the Golds* by Jonathan Tolins had an interesting premise—a pregnant woman learns, via genetic testing, that her future son will be gay—but the critics dismissed the theme as shallow. It closed after twenty-nine performances. On April 24, 1994, Arthur Miller's *Broken Glass*, starring Amy Irving, Ron Rifkin, and David Dukes, explored the theme of American Jews during the Holocaust. But the play drew mixed reviews, with several critics finding the work "unfinished." It closed after seventy-three performances.

In December of that year, *A Tuna Christmas* arrived for a limited engagement. A sequel to the 1982 hit *Greater Tuna*, the show was once again performed by two actors— Jaston Williams and Joe Sears (who cowrote it with Ed Howard). They portrayed a variety of characters in the small town of Tuna, Texas. Sears was nominated for a Best Actor Tony for his versatile performance.

Having Our Say arrived at the Booth on April 6, 1995. Mary Alice and Gloria Foster starred as the Delany sisters, the daughters of a former slave, whose lives encompassed a century of African-American history. Both of the play's real-life subjects were more than one hundred years old when the play opened and attended one of the performances. The play was adapted by Emily Mann from the sisters' autobiography. The play achieved 308 performances and received the following Tony Award nominations: Best Play (Mann), Best Director of a Play (Mann), and Best Actress (Alice).

Left to right: Aaron Tveit, Alice Ripley, and J. Robert Spencer in the Pulitzer Prize-winning musical *Next to Normal* (2009). (Photo by Joan Marcus)

The Booth was filled with laughter when Jackie Mason brought his one-man comedy show *Love Thy Neighbor* there in 1996. With his hilarious barbs at contemporary society, the comic kept audiences happy for 236 performances. Another one-man comedy show moved to the Booth from the Helen Hayes Theatre on January 29, 1997. It was the popular hit *Defending the Caveman*, written and performed by Rob Becker. During the run at the Booth Becker was succeeded by Michael Chiklis. The comedy closed June 21, 1997, after 645 performances (at the Hayes and the Booth combined). It was the last long run at the Booth for more than a decade.

David Mamet's *The Old Neighborhood* opened on November 19, 1997, offering a collection of three memory plays about the Chicago neighborhood where the author grew up. Performed without intermission, the plays starred Peter Riegert, Patti LuPone, Vincent Guastaferro, and Rebecca Pidgeon (Mrs. Mamet). The production received mixed reviews and ran for 197 performances.

An Evening with Jerry Herman, a revue of Herman's songs, opened on July 28, 1998, with the composer/lyricist at the piano, assisted by actor Lee Roy Reams, singer Florence Lacey, and Jared Egan on bass. The entertainment had a lukewarm reception and departed after twenty-eight performances.

Caustic comic Sandra Bernhardt insulted showbiz celebrities in her one-woman show *I'm Still Here . . . Dammit!*, to the delight of some theatregoers and the chagrin of others. Her profane barbs ceased after fifty-one airings.

David Hare's provocative one-man show *Via Dolorosa* showcased his vivid recollections of Jews and Arabs he met on a visit to the West Bank. Opening on March 18, 1999, as a production of the Lincoln Center Theater, it enthralled audiences for eighty-five performances.

On October 17, 1999, the Booth enjoyed a riotous explosion with the opening of *Dame Edna: The Royal Tour*. Australian actor Barry Humphries, who for years had delighted audiences with his impersonation of a flamboyant, eccentric "housewife superstar" called Dame Edna, captivated critics and audiences with this entertainment that involved much audience participation. Humphries won a special Tony Award for his brilliant impersonation and flung gladiolas at audiences until July 2, 2000.

In November 2000 Lily Tomlin brought her celebrated 1985 one-woman show *The Search for Signs of Intelligent Life in the Universe* back to Broadway for a limited engagement. Written and directed by Jane Wagner, the tour de force had earned Tomlin the 1986 Tony Award for Best Leading Actress in a Play.

It was followed on February 17, 2002, by another successful monodrama, *Bea Arthur on Broadway*, featuring the reminiscences of the costar of the original *Mame, The Threepenny Opera*, and TV's *Maude*. Judd Hirsch and Ben Vereen starred in a short-lived revival of Herb Gardner's *I'm Not Rappaport* in summer 2002.

Film star Paul Newman made his first appearance on Broadway in nearly forty years, playing the Stage Manager in a November 2002 revival of Thornton Wilder's classic *Our Town* (fifty-nine performances, limited run). The production was presented in part as a fund-raiser by Westport Country Playhouse in Westport, Connecticut, for which Newman's wife, actress Joanne Woodward, served as artistic director. Newman earned a Tony nomination as Best Actor in a Play for what also turned out to be his final Broadway performance. The production also featured Jayne Atkinson as Mrs. Gibbs, Frank Converse as Dr. Gibbs, Jane Curtin as Mrs. Webb, and Stephen Spinella as Simon Stimson.

The Retreat from Moscow (October 23, 2003) was not a military play; rather, it was a portrait of a dysfunctional family, led by John Lithgow and Eileen Atkins as the parents whose marriage is stalled and likely terminal. The title comes from the name of a painting that occupied the attention of the leading man. William Nicholson's play ran 148 performances.

Eve Ensler, who had achieved an international hit with her Off-Broadway collection *The Vagina Monologues*, about women's thoughts on their private parts, returned with *The Good Body*, a solo show about how women relate to the rest of their bodies, especially their weight. The November 15, 2004, production did not achieve the earlier show's cult-hit status and closed after forty performances.

Broadway got a touch of horror with Martin McDonagh's acclaimed drama *The Pillowman*, about a writer named Katurian (Billy Crudup), who is questioned and tortured by police (Jeff Goldblum and Îeljko Ivanek). The constables have noticed that a series of gruesome local child murders closely resemble those in some of Katurian's stories. It turns out that the stories were inspired by events in the writer's own childhood, and soon his brother (Michael Stuhlbarg) adds to the plot's many twists and turns. Winner of the 2004 Olivier Award in its Royal National Theatre premiere in London, *The Pillowman* opened on Broadway April 10, 2005, and ran 185 performances, winning Tony Awards for its sets and costumes, and the 2005 New York Drama Critics' Circle Award for Best Foreign Play.

George Grizzard and Frances Sternhagen starred as the human couple in a November 2005 revival of the Pulitzer-winning drama *Seascape*, formally titled *Edward Albee's Seascape* for this production. Elizabeth Marvel and Frederick Weller played the human-sized reptiles who rise from the sea and overcome mutual suspicion to find a common—*humanity* is certainly not the right word, but understanding.

Ralph Fiennes and Cherry Jones starred in a May 2006 revival of Brian Friel's *Faith Healer*, about a traveling layer-on-of-hands who believes he may actually have performed a bona fide miracle. However, the Tony Award for Best Featured Actor in a Play went to Ian McDiarmid, who played the healer's devoted longtime manager.

In an October 2006 revival of Simon Gray's *Butley*, Nathan Lane presented a portrait of a teacher whose anger and cynicism have poisoned all the personal and professional relationships in his life.

Manhattan's intelligentsia were thrilled when novelist Joan Didion announced in the pages of the *New York Times* that she was working on her first full-length play for Broadway, an adaptation of her 2005 novel *The Year of Magical Thinking*, which would offer an autobiographical account of the stages she went through in accepting the illness and eventual death of both her husband, novelist John Gregory Dunne, and her daughter, Quintana Roo Dunne Michael. The result opened March 29, 2007, with Vanessa Redgrave playing Didion on a nearly bare set. Some critics found it more gentle and contemplative than they had expected. It ran 144 performances.

The devil came down to Dublin for an extraordinarily high-stakes card game on Christmas Eve in Conor McPherson's drama *The Seafarer*, directed by the author. Jim Norton won a Tony Award for his performance in an ensemble that included Conleth Hill and Ciarán Hinds. The production opened December 6, 2007, and ran 133 performances.

Laurence Fishburne presented an inspiring portrait of Supreme Court Justice Thurgood Marshall in George Stevens Jr.'s. solo drama *Thurgood* for a limited engagement of 126 performances starting April 30, 2008.

Nineteen years after its regional debut, and a year after a hit Off-Broadway revival, Horton Foote's *Dividing the Estate* finally was mounted on Broadway with a sterling cast that featured Elizabeth Ashley, Penny Fuller, Gerald McRaney, and the playwright's daughter, Hallie Foote. But it had the misfortune of opening November 20, 2008, just a few months after another acclaimed dysfunctional family drama, the Pulitzer-winner *August: Osage County*, which was still playing across the street at the Music Box. Some critics (and audiences) found them to be too similar in tone. *Dividing the Estate* lasted only through January 4, 2009.

The Booth was occupied very briefly—for five performances—in February 2009 by a chamber musical called *The Story of My Life*, which transferred here after acclaimed engagements at the Canadian Stage Company and Goodspeed Musicals. New York critics were not similarly impressed, saying the story of a famous writer (Will Chase) and the devoted friend he neglects (Malcolm Gets) insufficiently plumbed the characters. The show had music and lyrics by Neil Bartram and a book by Brian Hill.

Alice Ripley gave one of the great musical theatre performances of her generation in *Next to Normal*, the story of a woman whose mental illness worsens despite all therapy, which tears her family apart. She feels trapped in her marriage but is actually trapped by the memories of her beloved son, who died while still a child. The unorthodox show, with music by Tom Kitt and book and lyrics by Brian Yorkey, offered no happy ending but did offer several rewarding roles played by Ripley (Tony Award as Best Actress in a Musical), J. Robert Spencer (Tony nomination), Jennifer Damiano (Tony nomination), and Aaron Tveit. The production opened at the Booth on April 15, 2009, after a decade-long development process and engagements at Second Stage Theatre Off-Broadway at Arena Stage in Washington, D.C. The show was nominated for a total of eleven 2009 Tony Awards. Yorkey and Kitt won the Tony for Best Score.

The Booth has always been an ideal house for dramas, comedies, and intimate musical shows.

BROADHURST
THEATRE

GEORGE H. BROADHURST, THE ANGLO-
American dramatist (1866—1952), came to
America in 1886. In addition to writing popular
plays, he managed theatres in Milwaukee,
Baltimore, and San Francisco before he opened
his own self-named New York theatre in association with the Shubert brothers.

Located at 235 West Forty-fourth Street,
right next door to the Shubert Theatre, the
Broadhurst was designed by architect Herbert
J. Krapp, one of the major theatre designers of
that era. With a seating capacity of 1,155 (later
augmented to 1,186) and a wide auditorium that
offered unobstructed views of the stage, the
theatre was constructed to house both musicals
and straight fare, which it has done successfully for more than ninety years.

The Broadhurst's opening show was George Bernard Shaw's *Misalliance* on September 27, 1917, starring Maclyn Arbuckle. This was the first New York production of Shaw's philosophical 1910 comedy, and it ran for only fifty-two performances. It was not performed again on Broadway until a City Center revival in 1953.

In 1918 the Broadhurst had a hit musical in *Ladies First*, starring Nora Bayes and comic William Kent. This suffragette show (the Nineteenth Amendment wouldn't recognize women's right to vote until 1920) centered on a woman (Bayes) who dares to run for mayor against her boyfriend. She loses the election but wins the boy. The show had a score by A. Baldwin Sloane. During the run at the Broadhurst, one George Gershwin song, "Some Wonderful Sort of Someone," was interpolated.

The Broadhurst had two hits in 1919. Rachel Crothers's *39 East* was a comedy of manners that starred Alison Skipworth, Henry Hull, and Constance Binney. Later in the run Hull was replaced by Sidney Blackmer and Binney by a striking young actress named Tallulah Bankhead. On December 30 Jane Cowl scored one of her early successes in a romantic drama called *Smilin' Through*, which she coauthored with Allan Langdon Martin. Cowl played a ghost in some scenes and the ghost's niece in others, serving to confuse critic Alexander Woollcott, who complained that these quick-change tricks belonged more to vaudeville than to the legitimate theatre. But audiences loved *Smilin' Through* for 175 performances.

In September 1921 George Broadhurst brought his American version of the British play *Tarzan of the Apes* to his theatre. The *New York Times*'s critic labeled the show "rather astonishing." A British actor, Ronald Adair, played Tarzan, and there were real lions and monkeys onstage, but the Ape Man managed to swing from tree to tree for only thirteen performances.

In November 1921 Lionel Barrymore won plaudits for his acting in a French play called *The Claw*, in which he played a politician who is ruined by a conniving woman. Critic Alexander Woollcott reported in the *New York Times* that the play was attended by "the most bronchial audience of the season that coughed competitively through each scene and applauded with vehemence at its conclusion."

One of the most popular themes of this era—that of two generations of lovers from the same family—cropped up again in the musical *Marjolaine*, starring Peggy Wood. It ran for 136 performances in 1922. In 1923 *The Dancers*, the London play by Sir Gerald Du Maurier in which Tallulah Bankhead had made her dazzling British debut, came to the Broadhurst with Richard Bennett and Florence Eldridge. It was a hit. Later in the year a revue called

Clockwise from top left: Program covers for the Broadhurst, 1926.

Katharine Cornell as Iris March in the sensational Michael Arlen play, *The Green Hat* (1925).

PLAYBILL cover for *Amadeus*, Peter Shaffer's prize-winning play (1980).

Illustration of Sarah Jessica Parker cavorting as Princess Winnifred in the musical *Once Upon A Mattress* (1996).

PLAYBILL cover for *Fosse* (1999).

Top left: Lee Tracy and Sylvia Field in the classic Jed Harris production of *Broadway* (1926).

Top right: The tense operating scene in Sidney Kingsley's Pulitzer Prize-winning play, *Men in White* (1933).

Above: PLAYBILL covers for *Private Lives* (1992), *Long Day's Journey Into Night* (1996), and *Proposals* (1997).

Topics of 1923, with Alice Delysia, frolicked for 143 performances.

On February 12, 1924 (the same day that George Gershwin's famous *Rhapsody in Blue* had its Manhattan premiere), the Broadhurst celebrated Lincoln's birthday with a distinguished hit, *Beggar on Horseback*, by George S. Kaufman and Marc Connelly. This expressionistic play focused on a composer (Roland Young) who almost marries into a stuffy rich family but is saved from this fate by an extended surrealistic dream about how life would be with them. It caused a sensation, ran for 224 performances, and is still regarded as a classic of its genre.

Another sensation was caused by Katharine Cornell in *The Green Hat* (1925), by Michael Arlen. Based on Arlen's shocking novel of the same name, the play was considered extremely daring. It dealt with a bride

(Cornell) whose husband commits suicide on their honeymoon. The audience learns later that the husband threw himself out of a hotel window because he had a venereal disease. The excellent cast included Leslie Howard, Margalo Gillmore, Eugene Powers, and Paul Guilfoyle. The play was staged by Cornell's husband, Guthrie McClintic.

One of the Broadhurst's greatest entertainments opened on September 16, 1926. Jed Harris, the boy wonder, brought his production of *Broadway* to the Broadhurst, and it hit Times Square like a thunderbolt. Written by Philip Dunning and George Abbott, it mesmerized first-nighters and subsequent audiences with its kaleidoscopic view of life in a New York nightspot called the Paradise Club. A jazz band, dancing girls, a fast-talking hoofer perfectly played by Lee Tracy, gangsters, bootleggers, murderers, and nightclub habitués thronged the Broadhurst stage and electrified theatregoers for 603 performances. Winston Churchill once declared that this was his favorite show of all time.

Winthrop Ames brought his production of *The Merchant of Venice* to the theatre in 1928. With George Arliss as Shylock and Peggy Wood as Portia, it managed to run for a respectable seventy-two performances.

On October 10, 1928, Bert Lahr achieved immortality in a raucous musical, *Hold Everything*, by DeSylva, Brown, and Henderson. Lahr played a punch-drunk boxer named Gink Schiner who was given to making strange sounds like "gnong, gnong, gnong"; these utterances later became his trademark. The cast also included the beloved Victor Moore, Jack Whiting, Ona Munson, and Betty Compton, but it was Lahr who got the raves and who kept the musical running for 413 performances. The hit song was "You're the Cream in My Coffee."

The Broadhurst had another winner in 1929, *June Moon*. A satire on Tin Pan Alley's songwriters, the play was written by George S. Kaufman and Ring Lardner, and it kept the Broadhurst shaking with laughter for 272 performances. Norman Foster played a lyricist who writes an imbecilic hit tune, "June Moon." The tart Jean Dixon, Philip Loeb, and Linda Watkins gave comic support to this tuneful cartoon.

Rodgers and Hart came back from Hollywood in 1931 with a new musical, *America's Sweetheart*, that naturally spoofed the movie capital. The two young hopefuls who go to Hollywood were played by beautiful Harriette Lake (who subsequently went to Hollywood for real and became Ann Sothern) and Jack Whiting. There was one hit song, the infectious Depression lament "I've Got Five Dollars," and acerbic performances by Jeanne Aubert and Inez Courtney, but the book by Herbert Fields was proclaimed dull and dirty, and the show ran for only 135 performances.

Norman Bel Geddes, set designer extraordinaire, tackled Shakespeare's *Hamlet* at the Broadhurst in 1931. He adapted the play; designed its sets, costumes, and lighting; and directed it. Raymond Massey was the Melancholy Dane, Mary Servoss was Gertrude, Celia Johnson was Ophelia, and Colin Keith-Johnston was Laertes. Wrote Brooks Atkinson in the *New York Times*, "Mr. Bel Geddes has hacked and transposed until no idle philosophy is left to trip up his scenery. What he has left is, to this department, an incoherent, flat and unprofitable narrative." The production expired after twenty-eight performances.

Philip Barry restored art to the Broadhurst with his finely written high comedy *The Animal Kingdom* in 1932. Leslie Howard gave one of his most ingratiating performances as a man who marries the wrong woman. The blue-chip cast included Frances Fuller, Ilka Chase, and William Gargan. It was Barry at his best.

Claude Rains and the fetching Jean Arthur could not save a drama called *The Man Who Reclaimed His Head* in 1932. Also in the cast, as a maid, was Lucille Lortel, who later became a patroness of the Off-Broadway movement and renamed the Theatre de Lys in Greenwich Village after herself.

The Broadway team of George Abbott and Philip Dunning produced another hit in 1932,

One of the dazzling numbers from Bob Fosse's *Dancin'* (1978).

Left: Helen Hayes in her triumphant *Victoria Regina* (1935).

but not of their authorship. They presented Hecht and MacArthur's rambunctious farce *Twentieth Century*, which took place onboard the Twentieth-Century Limited luxury train en route from Chicago to New York. Moffat Johnston played an egomaniacal Broadway producer (said to be inspired by Jed Harris) trying to get a famous actress (Eugenie Leontovich) to sign a contract with him. Directed with express-train speed by Abbott, the comedy delighted for 154 performances and later became the basis for the musical *On the Twentieth Century*.

Another highlight of the 1930s included the Group Theatre's realistic production of Sidney Kingsley's hospital drama *Men in White*, which won the Pulitzer Prize for the 1933—34 season. Starring Alexander Kirkland, Luther Adler, J. Edward Bromberg, Morris Carnovsky, and Russell Collins, it also featured such Group luminaries as Clifford Odets and Elia Kazan.

Upper left: Dan Stone as Jesus in *Godspell*, the long-running musical that moved from Off-Broadway to the Broadhurst (1976).

Top center: Harold Lang and Vivienne Segal in the superlative 1952 revival of *Pal Joey*, which ran longer than the original production.

Top right: Colleen Dewhurst, Arthur Hill, and Ingrid Bergman in O'Neill's *More Stately Mansions* (1967).

Bottom left: Humphrey Bogart achieves fame as the killer in *The Petrified Forest* (1935).

Bottom right: Ellen March and cast members of the record-breaking musical *Grease* (1972).

Staged by Lee Strasberg, the play contained an operation scene that held audiences spellbound with its chilling realism.

Eva Le Gallienne brought her Civic Repertory Company to the Broadhurst in 1934 and performed with Ethel Barrymore (and Barrymore's children, Ethel and Samuel Colt) in Rostand's costume play *L'Aiglon*. Without Ethel, Le Gallienne also presented and acted in *Hedda Gabler* and *The Cradle Song*.

On January 7, 1935, Leslie Howard returned to the Broadhurst in Robert E. Sherwood's *The Petrified Forest*. He enthralled audiences with his portrayal of an intellectual wanderer who allows a gangster to kill him so that he may leave his insurance money to a lovely young woman who wishes to study art in Paris. The gangster was played so vividly by Humphrey Bogart that Leslie Howard brought him to Hollywood to repeat his performance in the film version, which made him a star.

Helen Hayes scored perhaps her greatest triumph in *Victoria Regina* in 1935, playing the queen from a young girl to an aged monarch with remarkable physical changes. Gilbert Miller's lavish production and staging, and the

enormous cast, including Vincent Price as Prince Albert, made this one of the Broadhurst's most memorable events.

The remainder of the 1930s included Ruth Gordon's brilliant Nora in *A Doll's House*, which moved from the Morosco in 1938; Dodie Smith's charming family-reunion play *Dear Octopus* (1939); the great Bill Robinson in Mike Todd's splashy production of *The Hot Mikado* (1939); and Carmen Miranda's cyclonic Broadway debut in *The Streets of Paris* (1939), a lusty revue also starring Bobby Clark, Abbott and Costello, Luella Gear, Gower (Champion) and Jeanne, and Jean Sablon.

During the 1940s, musicals, revues, and comedies brightened the Broadhurst. Ed Wynn convulsed his fans in *Boys and Girls Together* (1940), with Jane Pickens and the dancing DeMarcos. George Jessel, Bert Kalmar, and Harry Ruby created a lively musical about a burlesque troupe, *High Kickers* (1941). Jessel, Sophie Tucker, Betty Bruce, and a cast of burlesque comics turned it into a hit. Eva Le Gallienne and Joseph Schildkraut sent shivers down the spine in the mystery melodrama *Uncle Harry* (1942). Dorothy Kilgallen's hus-

Billy Crystal in a re-creation of his boyhood home for the autobiographical play, *700 Sundays* (2004).

band, Richard Kollmar, produced and starred in *Early to Bed* (1943), a Fats Waller musical about a track team that mistakes a bordello for a hotel. It ran for 380 performances despite bad reviews.

Agatha Christie's *Ten Little Indians*, with practically the entire cast ending as stiffs, enjoyed success in 1944. *Follow the Girls* (1945), a noisy musical with Jackie Gleason and Gertrude Niesen, moved from the New Century to the Broadhurst and stayed for almost a year. *Three to Make Ready* (1946), the third and last of the revue series by Nancy Hamilton and Morgan Lewis, starred Ray Bolger, Gordon MacRae, Brenda Forbes, Arthur Godfrey, Harold Lang, and Carleton Carpenter and ran five months after it moved to the Broadhurst from the Adelphi. Helen Hayes returned in *Happy Birthday* (1946), a comedy by Anita Loos about a shy Newark, New Jersey, librarian, and the sentimental play ran for 564 performances.

From 1948 to 1950, four revues played the Broadhurst. They were *Make Mine Manhattan*, with Sid Caesar, David Burns, Sheila Bond, Joshua Shelley, and Kyle MacDonnell; Nancy Walker, Jackie Gleason, Hank Ladd, and Carol Bruce in *Along Fifth Avenue*; Charles Gaynor's delirious *Lend an Ear* (which moved from the National Theatre), with Carol Channing, Yvonne Adair, William Eythe, Gene Nelson, and Jenny Lou Law; and Jean and Walter Kerr's *Touch and Go*, with Nancy Andrews, Peggy Cass, Dick Sykes, Kyle MacDonnell, Helen Gallagher, and Jonathan Lucas.

The 1950s brought some long-running hits to the Broadhurst, but *Romeo and Juliet*, with Olivia de Havilland and Douglas Watson, was not one of them. It achieved only 49 performances in 1951. An interesting musical, *Flahooley*, with Barbara Cook, Ernest Truex, Jerome Courtland, Irwin Corey, Yma Sumac, and the Bil Baird Marionettes, managed only 40 performances in 1951 but later attracted a small cult following. A musical version of *Seventeen* (1951) fared much better, playing for 180 performances. A revival of the 1940 Rodgers and Hart musical *Pal Joey* (1952), with Vivienne Segal repeating her role as the lusty Vera, who keeps the young Joey (Harold Lang) in a luxurious love nest, was even more successful than the original production, running for 540 performances.

Katharine Cornell starred in a fair melo-

drama, *The Prescott Proposals* (1953), by Howard Lindsay and Russel Crouse. Kitty Carlisle and Macdonald Carey had a comparatively long run in a vapid comedy, *Anniversary Waltz* (1954). Sidney Kingsley turned comic with a madcap play, *Lunatics and Lovers* (1954), starring Buddy Hackett, Dennis King, Sheila Bond, and Vicki Cummings, which had a healthy run.

Also in the 1950s, Shirley Booth found a suitable vehicle in William Marchant's *The Desk Set* (1955); Rosalind Russell made *Auntie Mame* immortal (1956); and *The World of Suzie Wong* (1958), a bit of pseudo-Oriental romantic claptrap starring William Shatner and France Nuyen, managed to last for 508 performances.

The last show of the 1950s—the musical *Fiorello!* by Jerome Weidman, George Abbott, Sheldon Harnick, and Jerry Bock—brought another Pulitzer Prize to this theatre. Tom Bosley played the beloved Mayor Fiorello H. La Guardia and won a Tony for his performance. The show also won Tony Awards for Best Musical, Best Direction (Abbott), Best Book (Weidman and Abbott), Best Music (Bock), Best Lyrics (Harnick), and Best Producers of a Musical (Robert Griffith and Harold Prince).

In 1962 Noël Coward's musical *Sail Away* sailed into the Broadhurst, with Elaine Stritch as a hostess on a luxury liner, but it was all too dated and chichi for 1960s audiences and it departed for London after 167 performances. Richard Rodgers fared better with *No Strings*, the first musical for which he wrote both music and lyrics, with a book by Samuel Taylor. The show moved here from the Fifty-fourth Street Theatre and starred Richard Kiley and Diahann Carroll. They made beautiful music together for 580 performances.

Other interesting Broadhurst bookings in the 1960s included the Tom Jones and Harvey Schmidt musical *110 in the Shade* (1963); the British import *Oh What a Lovely War* (1964); and another British musical, *Half a Sixpence* (1965), starring Tommy Steele.

On November 20, 1966, a cherished musical came to this theatre: *Cabaret*, a musical version of John Van Druten's play *I Am a Camera*, which in turn was adapted from Christopher Isherwood's stories about his youthful days in Berlin, dazzled audiences with its innovative direction by Harold Prince and Joel Grey's mesmerizing performance as the leering nightclub Emcee. The brilliant show

The cast of the John Lennon musical *Lennon* (2005). (Photo by Joan Marcus)

won the following Tony Awards: Best Musical, Best Musical Director (Prince), Best Music and Lyrics (Fred Ebb and John Kander), Best Supporting Actor (Grey), Best Supporting Actress (Peg Murray), Best Set Designer (Boris Aronson), and Best Costumes (Patricia Zipprodt). It ran for 1,166 performances, but not all at the Broadhurst.

Next at this theatre was Eugene O'Neill's *More Stately Mansions*, starring Ingrid Bergman, Colleen Dewhurst, and Arthur Hill, directed by José Quintero; and Woody Allen's *Play It Again, Sam*, starring Allen, Tony Roberts, and Diane Keaton.

By the 1970s the revue genre was dead and the Broadhurst fare veered from dramas and comedies to musicals. Highlights included Sada Thompson's brilliant portrayal of three sisters and their mother in *Twigs* (1971), by George Furth; *Grease*, a rock musical about the aftereffects of "summer love" on high school students in the 1950s, which moved from the downtown Eden Theatre to the Broadhurst and became (briefly) the longest-running musical in Broadway history (after a move to the Royale); Neil Simon's uproarious comedy about two veteran comics, *The Sunshine Boys* (1972); John Wood in a marvelous revival of William

Gillette's *Sherlock Holmes* (1974); Katharine Hepburn and Christopher Reeve in Enid Bagnold's curious comedy *A Matter of Gravity* (1976); and the wonderful musical *Godspell* (1976), based on the Gospel According to St. Matthew, which moved from its long Off-Broadway run to the Broadhurst, where it added another 527 performances.

Preston Jones's ambitious work *A Texas Trilogy* (1976) was not as successful in New York as it had been in Washington, D.C. Larry Gelbart's *Sly Fox* (1976), a wild adaptation of Ben Johnson's *Volpone*, featured George C. Scott and Bob Dishy giving bravura performances. Bob Fosse's dance explosion, *Dancin'* (1978), a revue spotlighting Fosse's flashy choreography and Broadway's best dancers, ran at the Broadhurst for almost three years (becoming the theatre's longest-running show) before moving to the Ambassador Theatre.

Dancin' was followed by another triumph. On December 17, 1980, Peter Shaffer's acclaimed London play *Amadeus* opened at the theatre, with Ian McKellen as Salieri, Tim Curry as a comic Mozart, and Jane Seymour as the composer's wife. The season's most distinguished offering, it won the Tony Award for Best Play and McKellen won as Best Actor. This drama was followed by the musical *The Tap Dance Kid*, about a talented youngster who is driven by the need to dance.

In 1984 Dustin Hoffman starred in a new production of Arthur Miller's *Death of a Salesman*; this was followed by a gender-switched revised version of Neil Simon's *The Odd Couple* starring Sally Struthers and Rita Moreno as the mismatched roommates; a new production of O'Neill's *Long Day's Journey into Night* starring Jack Lemmon and Bethel Leslie; a return engagement of *The Life and Adventures of Nicholas Nickleby*; Neil Simon's popular *Broadway Bound*, which won a Tony Award for Linda Lavin; Andrew Lloyd Webber's musical *Aspects of Love*; Joan Collins in a revival of Noël Coward's *Private Lives*; the short-lived *Shimada*; and Andre Heller's strange vaudeville evening, *Wonderhouse*.

The Broadhurst next served as home for Harold Prince's multi—Tony Award—winning musical *Kiss of the Spider Woman*, with a score by Kander and Ebb and a book by Terrence McNally, starring Chita Rivera, Brent Carver, and Anthony Crivello, all of whom won Tony Awards for their performances. The musical,

about prisoners in a Brazilian jail who escape into fantasies culled from movie musicals, had a long run of 906 performances.

The New York Shakespeare Festival brought George C. Wolfe's production of *The Tempest* to the Broadhurst on November 1, 1995. Patrick Stewart was praised for his performance as Prospero. The revival thrived for seventy-one performances. The next tenant at this theatre, in March 1996, was an unsuccessful comedy thriller called *Getting Away with Murder* by Stephen Sondheim and George Furth. In the cast were John Rubinstein, Christine Ebersole, Terrence Mann, and others, but the critics found the play neither thrilling nor funny. It expired after seventeen performances.

Just in time for Christmas 1996, a new production of the musical *Once upon a Mattress* arrived, but it did not enjoy the success of the 1959 production, which had brought stardom to Carol Burnett. Sarah Jessica Parker, Jane Krakowski, Lewis Cleale, and David Aaron Baker headed the cast of the new version, and the show, despite mostly negative reviews, managed to run for 187 performances.

On April 29, 1998, David Hare's *The Judas Kiss* opened for a limited engagement. It starred Liam Neeson as Oscar Wilde and Tom Hollander as his lover, Lord Alfred Douglas. The play received mixed reviews, with some critics feeling that Neeson was miscast as the voluptuary poet. It ran for thirty-eight performances.

A blockbuster came to the Broadhurst on January 14, 1999: *Fosse*, an exuberant dance revue spotlighting the choreography of Bob Fosse from his Broadway and Hollywood musicals. The razzle-dazzle spectacle found immediate favor with audiences and went on to win the 1999 Tony Award as Best Musical. Some of the numbers were repeats from the earlier Fosse revue—*Dancin'*—but were brilliantly recreated by Ann Reinking, Chet Walker, and Gwen Verdon and explosively performed by thirty-two dancers. It ran more than 1,100 performances.

Two of our greatest modern actors, Ian McKellen and Helen Mirren, were locked in marital battle in a revival of August Strindberg's *Dance of Death* from October 2001 to January 2002.

Modern special effects and a new song were added to the Stephen Sondheim/James Lapine musical *Into the Woods* for an April 2002 revival that featured Vanessa Williams as the Witch and John McMartin as the Narrator.

It won the Tony Award as Best Revival of a Musical and ran 279 performances.

It was followed March 27, 2003. by another tuner, *Urban Cowboy*, based on a popular 1980 film. But the urban cowboy fad was long over by the time the musical came along, and director Lonny Price ultimately drew on thirty songwriters to stitch together the score, which was heard only sixty times. Most of the best original songs were supplied by Jason Robert Brown, who also served as the show's music director and started off Act II at the piano, leading the orchestra in playing one of his pieces, "That's How Texas Was Born." For many in the audience, it was the high point of the show.

The creators of the musical *Never Gonna Dance* sought to recapture the swirling magic of the Fred Astaire and Ginger Rogers films. Libretttist Jeffrey Hatcher threaded a treasure chest full of Jerome Kern song gems into a made-up story. Director Michael Greif worked with choreographer Jerry Mitchell to present limber leads Noah Racey and Nancy Lemenager in a series of showcase dances, including a memorable one set on a series of upright girders meant to be the top of an under-construction skyscraper. Critics judged that these efforts fell short, however, and the production, which opened on December 4, 2003, closed on February 15, 2004, after forty-four previews and eighty-four regular performances.

Comedian Billy Crystal managed to be both funny and moving in his solo show *700 Sundays*, a memoir of his childhood on Long Island, and especially of his father, a jazz aficionado who ran a record store in Manhattan. The production won the Tony Award as Best Theatrical Event and ran 163 performance starting December 5, 2004. It also set a new record for a single week's box-office take for a nonmusical production on Broadway: $1,061,688 for the week ending May 22, 2005. It held the record for more than four years.

The idea of having multiple actors play rock superstar John Lennon in the biographical jukebox musical *Lennon* might have looked good on paper, which may be why his widow, Yoko Ono, approved director/librettist Don Scardino's brainchild. Will Chase, Chuck Cooper, Terrence Mann, Chad Kimball, and others each got their crack at a different facet of the great Beatle, but audiences were confused. Moreover, the sketchily biographical show put much greater emphasis on Lennon's later years with Ono, giv-

ing short shrift to his years with the Beatles. The production opened August 14, 2005, and said "good night" forty-nine performances later.

Opening April 23, 2006, Alan Bennett's London hit *The History Boys* took up the issue of sexual impropriety by a beloved teacher directed at students at an English boys' academy. Richard Griffiths won the Tony Award for his performance as the motorcycle-riding pedagogue, and the play was named the best of 2006 by the Tony voters. It ran 185 performances and was made into a film with key members of the original cast.

Barely three and a half years after completing its original Broadway run, Boublil and Schönberg's *Les Misérables* got a November 9, 2006, revival widely criticized as premature. Nevertheless, with Alexander Gemignani as the steadfast Jean Valjean, Norm Lewis as the implacable Javert, Gary Beach as the slimy Thénardier, and Celia Keenan-Bolger as the tragic Eponine, the production was welcomed back by audiences for a further 463 performances.

There was talk around Broadway for several years about a revival of *Cat on a Hot Tin Roof* that would feature an all African-American cast. Onetime actress and dancer Debbie Allen waited until she had assembled a stellar cast, and the production opened March 6, 2008, with James Earl Jones as Big Daddy, Phylicia Rashad as Big Mama, Anika Noni Rose as a juicy Maggie, and, making his Broadway debut, Terrence Howard as a deeply brooding Brick. This powerful, sexy production gave 125 performances.

Paparazzi and fans mobbed the Broadhurst stage door each night for a glimpse of the star of the September 2008 revival of *Equus*. Daniel Radcliffe, originator of the title role in the *Harry Potter* film series, played the tortured Alan Strang, opposite Richard Griffiths as his psychiatrist. Directed by Thea Sharrock, the UK-originated production made great use of sound effects and a revolving stage to create the world of the strange boy who blinds a stable full of horses after building a religion around them. Gregory Clarke won a Tony Award for Sound Design, and production was near capacity for much of the show's 156-performance scheduled run.

A lionized London revival of Friedrich Schiller's drama *Mary Stuart* from the Donmar Warehouse Theatre enthroned itself at the Broadhurst April 19, 2009, with Janet McTeer and Harriet Walter recreating their roles as

Top: Richard Griffiths and Daniel Radcliffe in a 2008 revival of *Equus*.

Bottom: Janet McTeer enjoys a moment of freedom in a rainstorm in the title role of Schiller's *Mary Stuart* (2009)

rival queens (and cousins) Mary Queen of Scots and Mary I of England. Both star performances were cheered by New York critics, and set/costume designer Anthony Ward won a Tony Award for, among other things, a scene in which McTeer, on a few minutes' release from long imprisonment, danced in a very convincing rainstorm. April 19, 2009, was the opening and August 16, 2009, was the closing.

As the weather changed outside the Broadhurst, Jude Law brought his driven London *Hamlet* to the theatre beginning October 6, 2009, and delivered his great soliloquy in an onstage snowstorm. He was Broadway's sixty-sixth Hamlet on record, and he gave seventy-two performances in the role.

The disastrous collapse of the Enron energy company in the 1990s was the subject of a British import drama, Lucy Prebble's play with music, *Enron*, which debuted at the Broadhurst on April 27, 2010. Norbert Leo Butz was featured as Jeffrey Skilling, and the show was presented as a parable of human greed with considerable significance for events of the late 2000s.

BROADWAY
THEATRE

THE BROADWAY THEATRE AT BROADWAY and Fifty-third Street is at least the fifth New York playhouse to bear that name, others dating back to the nineteenth century in locations as varied as the corner with Canal Street, 326 Broadway, 485 Broadway, 1221 Broadway, and 1445 Broadway.

Today's Broadway Theatre (at 1681 Broadway) is also one of the few legitimate theatres originally built as a movie house. B. S. Moss, a mogul who operated a chain of movie houses that also featured vaudeville, built this theatre in 1924. Designed by architect Eugene DeRosa, the house had one of the largest seating capacities (1,765) of any theatre on Broadway, thus making it ideal, in later years, for the staging and performing of musical comedies.

Left: Irving Berlin and Ezra Stone in Berlin's all-soldier revue, *This Is the Army* (1942).

Center: Mark Baker in the title role of *Candide*, the musical that won five Tony Awards.

Right: Peter Arno's program sketch for the "sociological musical satire," *The New Yorkers* (1930). Harold K. Simon's cover sketch of showman Earl Carroll for the tenth edition of *The Earl Carroll Vanities* (1932).

It also served for many years as the northern outpost of the Times Square theatre district until a refurbished Studio 54 (formerly the Gallo Opera House), one block north, returned to legitimacy in 1998.

When this movie/vaudeville palace opened on Christmas Eve 1924 it was called B. F. Moss's Colony Theatre. By 1930 Moss realized that the talkies were killing vaudeville, and he converted his house to a legitimate theatre called the Broadway. At this time, he placed an ad in PLAYBILL in which he stated that his new playhouse "embodies an ideal not only for the theatrical profession, but equally for the public it serves. This ideal combines the magnitude, luxury and courtesy of the theatre with the comforts and charm of the drawing room. Every modern device for the production of greater entertainment has been incorporated into the physical perfection of the New Broadway. This insures not only more pretentious [sic] productions, but a price scale that is within the reach of every man's pocketbook. It is the aim of the management to make this theatre the last word in theatrical entertainment—the brightest spot on Broadway."

After that credo, Moss had to come up with something glittering for his first legitimate show. He chose *The New Yorkers*, a very sophisticated "sociological" musical by Cole Porter and Herbert Fields in which a Park Avenue woman (played by the true blueblood Hope Williams) dreams that she's in love with a bootlegger. The show opened on December 8, 1930, and the critics liked it, especially the outlandish clowning of Jimmy Durante. The gold-plated cast also included Fred Waring and his Pennsylvanians; Ann Pennington; Frances Williams; Charles King; and Rags Ragland, who sang a Porter song called "I Happen to Like New York" that Bobby Short popularized years later. Another song from this show, the sensuous "Love for Sale," was banned on the radio as obscene. Despite Moss's claim that his price scale would suit every man's pocketbook, he charged a $5.50 top, which was quite high in 1930. He soon had to lower his prices, but the Depression was on, and after twenty weeks *The New Yorkers* closed at a financial loss.

The Broadway's next show was a new edition of the *Earl Carroll Vanities* (1932), with the up-and-coming comic Milton Berle, deadpan comedienne Helen Broderick, and the beautiful ballerina Harriet Hoctor. Outstanding features of this revue were the spectacular neon effects by a young genius named Vincente Minnelli, plus a hit tune, "I've Got a Right to Sing the Blues," by Harold Arlen and Ted Koehler. But times were bad and the show ran for only eleven weeks.

After a dud called *The O'Flynn* in 1934, the Broadway went back to showing talkies. Then

Above: PLAYBILL for the Tony Award-winning musical *Les Misérables* (1987).

Center: Patti LuPone in her Tony Award-winning performance as Eva Peron in *Evita* (1979).

Right: Ethel Merman doing "Rose's Turn" in the memorable musical *Gypsy* (1959).

in 1940 it went legit again and began a policy that it was to pursue on and off during the rest of its history. It became the last stop for big, hit Broadway musicals that were nearing the end of their runs. They would move to the huge Broadway Theatre and offer seats at lower prices until their runs came to an end. This began with the Rodgers and Hart musical *Too Many Girls*, which moved here from the Imperial in 1940.

A great theatrical event occurred at the Broadway on July 4, 1942. America was at war, and Irving Berlin, who had written a famed World War I soldier show called *Yip, Yip, Yaphank*, now came up with another. It was *This Is the Army*, and its opening night at the Broadway was one of the greatest in the history of the theatre. All proceeds from the show went to Army Emergency Relief. Singer Kate Smith, who had immortalized Berlin's "God Bless America," paid $10,000 for two seats. Berlin himself appeared in the revue, repeating his world-famous number "Oh, How I Hate to Get Up in the Morning," from his earlier soldier show. The cast of *This Is the Army* consisted of professional actors who were in the armed services, and their wives. Many of these performers later became famous on stage and screen. Berlin's score had such standout numbers as "I Left My Heart at the Stage Door Canteen," "I'm Getting Tired So I Can Sleep," and the rousing title tune.

Later in 1942 the hit comedy *My Sister Eileen* moved in from the Biltmore, and in 1943 Gertrude Lawrence returned from a tour in her psychological musical *Lady in the Dark* and played for three months at the Broadway in this Moss Hart/Kurt Weill/Ira Gershwin classic. This was followed by a revival of *The Student Prince* and the San Carlo Opera

Company in repertory.

On December 2, 1943, Billy Rose brought his production of *Carmen Jones* to this theatre, and the critics flipped. Oscar Hammerstein II, who was back on top with *Oklahoma!*, conceived the offbeat notion of doing an all-black *Carmen* set in a parachute factory in America's South during World War II. The experiment worked, and the show ran for 503 performances.

The policy of moving hit shows to the Broadway continued with Mike Todd's *Up in Central Park*, which moved from the Century Theatre in 1945 and stayed for nine months. The operetta *Song of Norway* moved from the Imperial in 1946, and the propaganda play *A Flag Is Born* transferred from the Music Box.

Late in 1946 Duke Ellington collaborated with John LaTouche on a version of *The Beggar's Opera*, which he called *Beggar's Holiday*. It starred Alfred Drake and featured Avon Long and Zero Mostel (who got panned); it was not a success.

The year 1948 brought a revival of *The

Cradle Will Rock, also starring Alfred Drake, which moved from the Mansfield. Leonard Bernstein appeared in this as a clerk. The Habimah Players from Palestine (soon to be Israel) presented a repertory of *The Golem, The Dybbuk, Oedipus Rex*, and other plays in 1948.

In the summer of 1949, concert impresario Sol Hurok brought a dancing/singing show from Madrid called *Cabalgata* for a three-month engagement.

Olsen and Johnson of *Hellzapoppin'* and other zany revues tried out a new one here called *Pardon Our French* in 1950, but even with French beauty Denise Darcel in the show it managed to run for only 100 performances. *Where's Charley?*, the Ray Bolger smash from the St. James Theatre, ended its run here; then a revival of Marc Connelly's Pulitzer Prize play *The Green Pastures* arrived in 1951 but lasted only forty-four more performances. Mae West wiggled in with a revival of her play *Diamond Lil* (1951), which didn't fare too well; nor did revivals of the Gertrude Stein/Virgil Thompson opera *Four Saints in Three Acts* (1952) and the black revue *Shuffle Along* (1952). The Pulitzer Prize—winning musical *South Pacific* transferred from the Majestic and ended its run here, chalking up 1,925 performances.

Les Ballets de Paris and Spanish dancer José Greco played the Broadway in 1954, and there was the premiere engagement of Gian Carlo Menotti's opera *The Saint of Bleeker Street*, a powerful religious work that ran for ninety-two performances. More dance companies paid visits—Katherine Dunham, Azuma Kabuki Dancers and Musicians—before Sammy Davis Jr. opened in the popular musical *Mr. Wonderful* in 1956. With comic Jack Carter, Chita Rivera, and Pat Marshall in the cast, the musical recorded 383 performances.

Mel Brooks and Joe Darion made a musical of Don Marquis's *archy and mehitabel*, called *Shinbone Alley*, but Eartha Kitt, Eddie Bracken, and others could not turn it into gold. *The Most Happy Fella* dropped in from the Imperial to end its long run and stayed for three months. A boxing musical, *The Body Beautiful*, with a score by Jerry Bock and Sheldon Harnick, went nowhere and closed to make room for *Les Ballets de Paris*, the Beryozka Russian Dance Company, and the Old Vic, imported by Sol Hurok, doing *Henry V, Twelfth Night*, and *Hamlet*.

In May 1959 one of the Broadway Theatre's

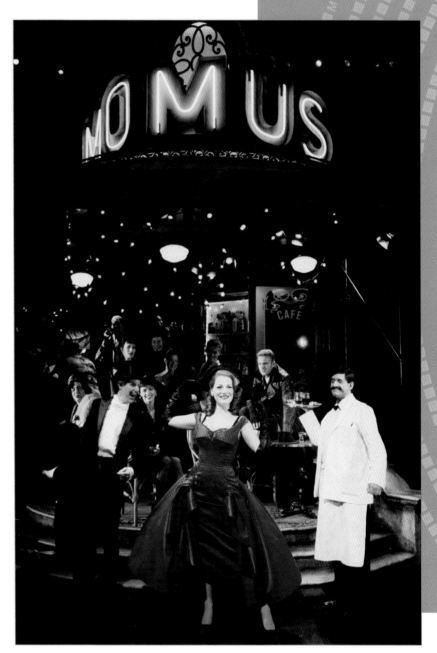

Chlöe Wright (center) as Musetta in Baz Luhrmann's staging of Puccini's opera *La Bohème* (2002). (Photo by Sue Adler)

milestones arrived. It was Ethel Merman in *Gypsy*, and it offered the great singer her most memorable part—Rose, the pushy mother of Gypsy Rose Lee and June Havoc. With a book by Arthur Laurents, a soaring score by Jule Styne and Stephen Sondheim, and choreography and direction by Jerome Robbins, this tough show about show business has become a classic of the American musical theatre. Merman's eleven-o'clock number—"Rose's Turn"—was electrifying, as was her belting of "Everything's Coming Up Roses." The Broadway Theatre was extensively renovated for this engagement, and the house had one of its most impressive and historic bookings.

In 1963 *Tovarich* was notable for offering Vivien Leigh in her musical-comedy debut,

Manu Narayan and Ayesha Dharker lead the company in a number from *Bombay Dreams* (2004). (Photo by Joan Marcus)

with Jean-Pierre Aumont as her costar. Leigh won a Tony for her delightful performance, and the show ran for 264 performances. Noël Coward's musical *The Girl Who Came to Supper* (1963) was almost as boring as the play from which it was adapted (*The Sleeping Prince*). It starred Florence Henderson and José Ferrer, but it was music hall singer Tessie O'Shea who woke up the audience and was awarded with a Tony for her efforts.

The Obratsov Puppets, the Folies Bergère, and a revue starring dancer Zizi Jeanmarie were booked in the early 1960s. Alexander H. Cohen opened his lavish musical *Baker Street* in 1965, with Fritz Weaver as Sherlock Holmes, Peter Sallis as Dr. Watson, Martin Gabel as the nefarious Professor Moriarty, and Inga Swenson as the love interest. Hal Prince directed the show, which had a rare (for the time) four-color PLAY-BILL cover and ran for nine months.

The Devils, a dramatization of Aldous

Huxley's nightmarish book about diabolism in seventeenth-century France, scared theatregoers away from the box office in 1966, although it starred Jason Robards Jr. and Anne Bancroft. A musical version of Richard Llewellyn's famed novel *How Green Was My Valley*, retitled *A Time for Singing*, was also unsuccessful that year. The Lincoln Center revival of Irving Berlin's *Annie Get Your Gun*, with its original star, Ethel Merman, and a new Berlin showstopper, "Old Fashioned Wedding," was so popular that it moved here in 1966, to be followed by the Winter Garden hit *Funny Girl*, which ended its long run here.

After the Harkness Ballet played an engagement, Kander and Ebb's new musical version of the hit comedy *The Happy Time* (1968) opened and offered a Tony Award—winning performance by Robert Goulet. It was brilliantly directed by Gower Champion and attracted much publicity because of an incident that occurred on opening night. Clive Barnes, the critic for the *New York Times*, was delayed on a plane, and the first-night curtain was held until he arrived. His critical colleagues disparaged excessive favoritism.

Cabaret and *Mame* moved in from other theatres to finish their long runs (1968—69), and a new musical, *Purlie*, based on the hit play *Purlie Victorious*, opened in 1970 and ran for 688 performances. Cleavon Little and Melba Moore won Tony Awards for their engaging performances. In 1972 *Fiddler on the Roof*, the multi-award-winning musical, moved here, and on the evening of June 17, 1972, it became the longest-running show in Broadway history up to that time (3,225 performances). By the time it ended its run shortly thereafter, it had reached 3,242 performances.

The creators of *Hair*, the enormously pop-

ular rock musical, opened their newest, *Dude* (1972), which required that the Broadway Theatre be drastically reconfigured, with tons and tons of dirt brought in to create a bare-earth playing area, and bleachers constructed to replace theatre seats. It was all for naught. The critics buried this disaster, and the Broadway had to be restored to normalcy.

In 1974 *Candide*, Leonard Bernstein's musical version of Voltaire's classic that had flopped on Broadway in 1956, came to the Broadway in a revised version. With additional lyrics by Stephen Sondheim and a new book by Hugh Wheeler, it was tried out first at the Chelsea Theatre Center of Brooklyn, with dynamic, arena-style staging by Harold Prince. It was so successful that it was transferred to the Broadway Theatre, where it triumphed for almost two years. The house was again recon-

Fantasia Barrino (center, in blue dress) in the finale of the 2005 musical *The Color Purple*. (Photo by Paul Kolnik)

Right: A scene from the acrobatic musical *Cirque Dreams: Jungle Fantasy* (2008). (Photo by Carol Rosegg)

figured, this time into a labyrinth, with the audience seated on many levels and the action occurring all over the theatre. Prince won a Tony Award for his galvanic staging, but so many seats were removed for the experimental arrangement that the show struggled to turn a profit.

An all-black revival of *Guys and Dolls*, with new orchestrations, proved popular in 1976—77. This was followed by another hit black musical, *The Wiz*, which transferred here from the Majestic and stayed for more than a year and a half. A new musical, *Saravà*, which moved from the Mark Hellinger, played for four months in early 1979 and was followed by the phenomenal *Evita*, by Andrew Lloyd Webber and Tim Rice, with revolutionary staging by Harold Prince. It won seven Tony Awards, including Best Musical.

After *Evita* ended its long run, a new production of the musical *Zorbá* moved in, starring Anthony Quinn. Lila Kedrova, a featured actress in the show, won a Tony Award for her performance. In 1984 Yul Brynner made his last Broadway appearance, in a revival of *The King and I*, which had earned him a Tony Award in 1952. On this occasion, he was accorded a Special Tony.

Another 1984 musical did not fare as well at this theatre. It was a new version of the old Ziegfeld show *The Three Musketeers* (with a revised book by Mark Bramble). It lasted only nine performances. Also ill-fated was *Big Deal* in 1986, Bob Fosse's last Broadway show. He wrote the book, directed, and choreographed the musical, which was based on the film *Big Deal on Madonna Street*. The score consisted of hit songs of the past by a battery of composer/lyricists. Although Fosse won a Tony Award for his choreography, the musical danced for only sixty-two performances.

In 1987 a blockbuster from London, *Les Misérables*, opened and won eight Tony Awards, including Best Musical of the season. The French songwriting team of Alain Boublil and Claude-Michel Schönberg (with Herbert Kretzmer) created this musical version of the Victor Hugo classic about a man, Jean Valjean, who steals a loaf of bread and spends the rest of his life on the run from single-minded police inspector Javert, across a terrain of poverty and revolution. This epic set the standard for the quasi-operatic "megamusicals" of the 1980s and 1990s.

Boublil and Schönberg also provided the next blockbuster at this theatre, *Miss Saigon* (with co-lyricist Richard Maltby Jr.), which retold the story of *Madame Butterfly*, but set in the context of the Vietnam War. It opened in April 1991 (*Les Misérables* moved to the Imperial Theatre and continued to flourish) and won Tony Awards for its leading actor (Jonathan Pryce), its leading actress (Lea Salonga), and its featured actor (Hinton Battle). When *Miss Saigon* finally closed on January 28, 2001, after 4,095 performances, it had become the longest-running show in the history of this theatre.

The north wall of the Broadway Theatre faces West Fifty-third Street, where, for most of the 1990s and into the 2000s, the CBS-TV program *The Late Show with David Letterman* frequently staged pranks. A wall of show posters soon appeared there, such as the ones in Shubert Alley. The Broadway's marquee was sometimes seen on the TV program, and the

Broadway Theatre casts sometimes took part in the skits.

The Broadway was quickly rebooked with an unusual attraction, *Blast!*, a revue of intricately choreographed marching-band performances. This halftime show on steroids marched for 180 performances. The next show at the Broadway had a shorter run but greater success: the solo standup comedy show *Robin Williams: Live on Broadway*, whose three July 2002 performances were taped for cable television by HBO and edited into a special that included his now classic Scotsman-explains-golf routine. It was nominated for and won five primetime Emmy Awards following its broadcast.

In December 2002, producers Jeffrey Seller and Kevin McCollum, who were enjoying the success of the show *Rent*, went back to the source material, collaborating with other producers and with director Baz Luhrmann on a Broadway mounting of the Giacomo Puccini/Gisuseppe Giacosa/Luigi Illica opera *La Bohéme*, about love and death in wintertime Paris. Luhrmann staged the tragedy more like a musical than an opera and attracted music lovers (along with curious *Rent* fans) for 228 performances.

Monologuist John Leguizamo played a four-week return engagement of his Tony-nominated solo show *Sexaholix*, starting November 11, 2003.

The Broadway Theatre undulated past her eightieth birthday in 2004 with *Bombay Dreams*, an original stage musical done in the style of India's popular "Bollywood" film musicals. Produced by Andrew Lloyd Webber and with a score by India's A. R. Rahman, the show told the fairy-tale story of a romance between a young man from the slums and his wealthy, high-caste dream girl. Highlights included exotic percussionists located in the boxes, and a traditional dance number in a fountain. *Bombay Dreams* lasted 284 performances.

Talk-show host and mistress-of-all-media Oprah Winfrey chose the Broadway Theatre as the site of her foray into Broadway producing, *The Color Purple*, a musical based on the Alice Walker novel and the film in which Winfrey had costarred. First-time Broadway songwriters Brenda Russell, Allcc Willis, and Stephen Bray collaborated with Pulitzer Prize—winner Marsha Norman (*'night, Mother*) on the inspirational show about a young woman who survives grueling emotional and physical abuse to build a happy and fulfilling life for herself. The musical opened December 1, 2005, and its eye-catching purple marquee reigned over Broadway for 910 performances, a run boosted by frequent mentions on Winfrey's widely watched TV show.

The wonders of circus-style acrobatics were brought to the legitimate stage from the arena and the big top on June 26, 2008, with *Cirque Dreams: Jungle Fantasy*, a family show that added the Broadway Theatre to its roster of touring stops. The show, with original music and lyrics by Jill Winters, stayed the summer before returning to the road.

Hollywood's DreamWorks company tried repeating Disney's success on the legitimate stage with *Shrek the Musical*, an adaptation of one of its own animated movie hits. The story of a grumpy and flatulent green ogre transformed by love for a beautiful princess replaced the purple theme of *The Color Purple* with a green theme that pervaded the theatre and its marquee. "Let Your Freak Flag Wave" and "Who I'd Be" were two of the songs from the lively score by composer Jeanine Tesori and another Pulitzer Prize—winning playwright, David Lindsay-Abaire (*Rabbit Hole*), who supplied both book and lyrics. Opening on December 14, 2008, *Shrek the Musical* provided a starring vehicle for Brian d'Arcy James (Shrek), Daniel Breaker (Donkey), and Sutton Foster (Princess Fiona), along with juicy character roles for some of the top comedic actors of their generation, including Christopher Sieber, John Tartaglia, and Jen Cody.

The ambitious spectacle won a Tony Award for its fractured-fairytale costumes by Tim Hatley and ran through January 2010.

On April 25, 2010, this theatre played host to the first Broadway revival of the Burt Bacharach/Hal David musical *Promises, Promises*, based on the Oscar-winning film *The Apartment*. Sean Hayes of TV's *Will & Grace* starred as Chuck Baxter opposite Kristin Chenoweth as Fran, with Katie Finneran stealing the show in her one-scene appearance at the top of Act II. This production interpolated two Bacharach/David pop hits, "I Say a Little Prayer" and "A House Is Not a Home," to beef up Chenoweth's role.

Despite its origin as a cinema, the Broadway Theatre possesses a theatrical grandeur that makes it ideal for sweeping musicals and special events.

Brian d'Arcy James as Shrek, Daniel Breaker as Donkey, and Sutton Foster as Princess Fiona in *Shrek The Musical* (2008). (Photo by Joan Marcus)

BROOKS ATKINSON
THEATRE

THE BROOKS ATKINSON THEATRE AT 256 West Forty-seventh Street opened in 1926 as the Mansfield Theatre, named in honor of the great classical American actor Richard Mansfield, who died in 1907. The theatre was another house built by the Chanin Brothers, construction tycoons, and it was designed by architect Herbert J. Krapp, who seemed to turn out a theatre a week in the Roaring Twenties. It followed the latest trends—only one balcony and an auditorium that was wide rather than deep. According to the *New York Times*, the attractive color scheme was old rose, gold, and light tan.

The opening bill at the Mansfield on the night of February 15, 1926, was a melodrama called *The Night Duel*, by Daniel Rubin and

Top left to right: Program cover for the immortal 1930 Pulitzer Prize play *The Green Pastures*. PLAYBILL covers for Albert Finney in *A Day in the Death of Joe Egg* (1968), Julian Barry's *Lenny* (1971), and Dustin Hoffman in *Jimmy Shine* (1968).

Far left: Hilda Simms (standing), Earle Hyman, and Georgia Burke in *Anna Lucasta* (1944).

Left: Antoinette Perry in *The Ladder*, which ran for 789 performances.

Edgar MacGregor, starring Marjorie Rambeau and Felix Krembs. The *Times* reported that there was an embarrassing bedroom scene in the second act but that it seemed to please the audience. The play lasted only seventeen performances. It was followed by three more failures: *The Masque of Venice*, with Arnold Daly, Osgood Perkins, Selena Royle, and Antoinette Perry (the Tony Awards were named in her honor); *Schweiger*, with Ann Harding as a wife who discovers that her husband (played by Jacob Ben-Ami) was a child murderer; and *Beau-Strings*, with Estelle Winwood as a flirt and Clarence Derwent (namesake of another

theatre award, the one specifically for actors) as one of her interests.

The first moderate hit at the Mansfield opened on September 2, 1926: William Anthony McGuire's *If I Was Rich*, starring vaudeville/musical comedy favorite Joe Laurie Jr. It ran for ninety-two performances.

Antoinette Perry again appeared at this theatre, in a long-running play with a curious history. *The Ladder*, a show about reincarnation, was disliked by the critics, but it was backed by a millionaire, Edgar B. Davis, who wanted the world to listen to the drama's message. So he kept the play running for 789 performances

Top left to right: PLAY-BILL cover for the Duke Ellington-Shakespeare musical, *Play On!* (1997). PLAYBILL cover for Neil Simon's *The Odd Couple*, Richard B. Harrison as "De Lawd" and Edna M. Harris as a "sinner" in the classic Marc Connelly play, *The Green Pastures* (1930). Barry Fitzgerald and Sara Allgood in a revival of *Juno and the Paycock* (1940).

Bottom left: Ellen Burstyn and Charles Grodin in the smash comedy about infidelity, *Same Time, Next Year* (1975).

Bottom right: Paul Rogers and Tom Courtenay in the British play *The Dresser* (1981).

(often allowing people in for free) and lost half a million pre-Depression dollars on it.

The Actors' Theatre revived Eugene O'Neill's Pulitzer Prize—winning play *Beyond the Horizon* (1926), and it ran for seventy-nine performances. This production starred Robert Keith, Thomas Chalmers, and Aline MacMahon. The year ended with a revival of *The Dybbuk.*

Minnie Maddern Fiske revived Ibsen's *Ghosts* for twenty-four performances in January 1927, but the rest of the year brought undistinguished productions.

The year 1928 began with something called *Mongolia*, which transferred here from the Greenwich Village Theatre but played for only three weeks. This was followed by *Atlas and Eva*, a comedy about a family called the Nebblepredders, which expired after twenty-four labored performances. Finally, on April 26, 1928, Rodgers and Hart came to the rescue with a sprightly musical about U.S. Marines stationed at Pearl Harbor. Called *Present Arms*, it

produced one Rodgers and Hart classic: "You Took Advantage of Me." This song was performed in the show by none other than Busby Berkeley (who also did the dances for the musical), and on the opening night he forgot the lyrics and made up some of the most foolish words ever sung on the American stage. Lew Fields, originally half of the vaudeville team Weber and Fields, produced this musical. He was the father of Herbert Fields, who wrote the show's book. For the next year or so, this theatre was known as Lew Fields' Mansfield Theatre. *Present Arms* ran for 147 performances.

The next Rodgers/Hart/Fields musical at this theatre was a disaster. Called *Chee-Chee*, it was inspired by a novel called "*The Son of the Grand Eunuch*," but critics did not find this musical comedy about castration amusing. St. John Ervine, critic for *The New York World*, snapped: "Nasty! Nasty! I did not believe that any act could possibly be duller than the first—until I saw the second."

Herbert and Dorothy Fields next provided a musical called *Hello, Daddy*, which was appropriate since their daddy, Lew Fields, again produced it and this time starred in it. It turned out to be the Mansfield's biggest hit so far, running for 198 performances. The catchy music was the work of Jimmy McHugh.

On February 26, 1930, a classic of the American theatre opened at the Mansfield and won the Pulitzer Prize for the season. It was Marc Connelly's magnificent adaptation of Roark Bradford's stories from the Old Testament, "Ol' Man Adam an' His Chillun." Connelly's adaptation was called *The Green Pastures* and it had an enormous cast, consisting entirely of black actors. Many Broadway producers turned the script down, saying that a play about Bible incidents as viewed by southern blacks would never make it on Broadway. They were wrong. Richard B. Harrison, a sixty-six-year-old man who had never acted before, gave an enthralling performance as de Lawd God Jehovah. *The Green Pastures* played for 640 performances and was also successful down South and wherever it was staged throughout the world.

During the Great Depression, the Chanin Brothers lost all six of the theatres they had built, including the Mansfield. From early March of 1932 until December of that year, the house was dark. Then, on December 26, it reopened with *Shuffle Along of 1933*, a successor to two former black musicals with similar titles. Once again the show was the work of Eubie Blake, Noble Sissle, and Flournoy Miller, who also appeared in the entertainment. Unfortunately, this edition ran for only seventeen performances.

The Mansfield's bookings in 1933—34 were sparse and undistinguished. A comedy called *Page Miss Glory*, directed by George Abbott, was a moderate hit in November 1934. The cast included James Stewart, Charles D. Brown, Jane Seymour, Royal Beal, and Dorothy Hall. Another moderate hit, *Moon Over Mulberry Street*, moved in from the Lyceum in 1935. It was followed by Osgood Perkins giving an excellent performance as a playwright who dreams that he is a character in his latest drama. The play was called *On Stage*, but it did not stay there for very long. It had a short run of forty-seven performances.

In January 1937, a lurid exposé of a Manhattan prostitution ring on Park Avenue

Above: Fredric March and Florence Eldridge in Ruth Gordon's auto-biographical play *Years Ago* (1946).

Left: Essie Davis rides the moon in a scene from Tom Stoppard's intellectual farce, *Jumpers* (2004). (Photo by Hugo Glendenning)

called *Behind Red Lights* opened and stayed for 176 performances.

In 1940 Barry Fitzgerald, Sara Allgood, and Effie Shannon appeared in a successful revival of O'Casey's *Juno and the Paycock*. This was followed by *Separate Rooms*, a popular comedy that moved here from Maxine Elliott's Theatre. A West Coast revue, *Meet the People*, was a welcome Christmas present in 1940 and stayed for 160 performances. The cast included such bright talents as Jack Gilford, Nanette Fabares (later, Fabray), Jack Williams, Jack Albertson, and Peggy Ryan.

The years 1942 and 1943 brought mostly failures to this theatre. A popular wartime comedy, *Janie*, which had already played at three other theatres, moved in for a few months in 1943—44. Then, on August 30, 1944, a bonanza arrived. *Anna Lucasta*, a play by Philip Yordan, was first done by the American Negro Theatre in Harlem (although the playwright had originally written it to be played by white actors. It was so successful that producer John Wildberg transferred it to the Mansfield Theatre with a few changes in the script. Harry Wagstaff Gribble directed the superb cast, featuring Hilda Simms as the prostitute Anna, plus Canada Lee, Earle Hyman, and Frederick O'Neal. The drama ran for 957 performances.

Another hit arrived at this theatre on December 3, 1946. Actress Ruth Gordon switched to playwriting, and her autobiographical play *Years Ago* was warmly received. It starred Fredric March as her father, Florence Eldridge as her mother, and Bethel Leslie as Ruth Gordon Jones. The play recaptured Gordon's high school days in Massachusetts when she startled her parents and friends by announcing that she was going to New York to be an actress. The nostalgic hit played for 206 performances.

A lively revival of Marc Blitzstein's proletarian musical *The Cradle Will Rock* opened during the famed blizzard of December 26, 1947. The cast included such luminaries as Alfred Drake, Will Geer, Vivian Vance, Dennis King Jr., Estelle Loring, Jack Albertson, and Leonard Bernstein, but it lasted for only two weeks at this theatre before it moved to another house. Charles Boyer gave a powerful performance in *Red Gloves* in December 1948, but the Jean-Paul Sartre play was too talky and full of messages for the public. The brilliant revue

Lend an Ear moved in from another theatre in 1949 and played for three months.

A mediocre play, *All You Need Is One Good Break*, was the last legitimate show to play the Mansfield. For the next decade, it functioned as a television playhouse.

When this theatre returned to legitimacy in 1960, producer Michael Myerberg was its

Suzanne Somers tells the story of her life in *The Blonde in the Thunderbird* (2005). (Photo by Paul Parks)

owner/manager. The house was renovated and renamed the Brooks Atkinson Theatre in honor of the drama critic of the *New York Times*, who had retired from reviewing the previous spring. According to the PLAYBILL for that occasion, Atkinson was the first critic in recorded history to have a theatre named for him.

The Brooks Atkinson opened on September 12, 1960, with a revue called *Vintage '60*. Although it was produced by David Merrick, with Zev Bufman, George Skaff, and Max Perkins, it lasted only eight performances. The next tenant, a comedy called *Send Me No Flowers*, with David Wayne and Nancy Olson, wilted after forty performances.

On February 22, 1961, Neil Simon's first play, *Come Blow Your Horn*, opened, and it flourished for 677 performances. The cast featured Hal March, Sarah Marshall, Warren Berlinger, Lou Jacobi, and Pert Kelton. In late 1962, Sidney Kingsley's play *Night Life*, with Neville Brand, Walter Abel, Carmen Matthews,

Carol Lawrence, Salomé Jens, and Bobby Short, presented a realistic nightclub onstage, but the drama lasted only 63 performances. Peter Ustinov's comedy, *Photo Finish*, offered Ustinov as a writer with alter egos played by Dennis King, Donald Davis, and John Horton. Eileen Herlie, Jessica Walters, and Paul Rogers were also in the cast of this charade, which ran for 160 performances in 1963.

The year 1964 started out disastrously at the Brooks Atkinson. Tennessee Williams decided to rewrite his unsuccessful play *The Milk Train Doesn't Stop Here Anymore*, and this time he turned it into, of all things, a Kabuki-style drama. The great Tallulah Bankhead made her last Broadway appearance in this error, and Tab Hunter, Ruth Ford, and Marian Seldes all went down the drain with her. It played only five times.

Josephine Baker made a dazzling personal appearance here in 1964, followed by a very controversial play, Rolf Hochhuth's *The*

Deputy, which accused Pope Pius XII of having failed to denounce the Nazi extermination of the Jews. Emlyn Williams played the pope. The drama was picketed by Catholic organizations, but it managed to run for 318 performances. Julie Harris, Estelle Parsons, and Lou Antonio were next in a comedy called *Ready When You Are, C. B.!* Harris was praised for her acting, but the show closed after 80 performances. A revival of *The Glass Menagerie*, with Maureen Stapleton, George Grizzard, Pat Hingle, and Piper Laurie, was well received and lasted 176 performances in 1965.

From November 1965 until November 1967 the Brooks Atkinson housed a series of undistinguished plays. Peter Ustinov's *Halfway Up the Tree*, a generation-gap comedy—with the younger generation winning out—was moderately amusing, with Eileen Herlie, Anthony Quayle, Sam Waterston, and Graham Jarvis.

Peter Nichols's macabre comedy *A Day in the Death of Joe Egg* had memorable performances by Albert Finney, Zena Walker, and Elizabeth Hubbard. Walker won a Tony Award as Best Supporting Actress in a Play.

Lovers and Other Strangers, a quartet of revue-style playlets by Renée Taylor and Joseph Bologna, in which they appeared, was amusing in 1968, as was *Jimmy Shine*, a Murray Schisgal comedy starring Dustin Hoffman that ran for 153 performances in 1968—69.

After a series of mishaps, the Brooks Atkinson booked *Lenny*, a play about the late Lenny Bruce. Written by Julian Barry, the stinging biographical study gave Cliff Gorman a part that won him a Tony Award for his tour de force performance. Brilliantly directed by Tom O'Horgan, who also wrote the play's music, *Lenny* presented a corrosive portrait of the drug-riddled, foulmouthed comic whose fame increased after he died. This "dynamite shtick of theatre," as critic Clive Barnes labeled it, played for 453 explosive performances and was made into a film with Dustin Hoffman, directed by Bob Fosse.

In 1973 the Negro Ensemble Company transferred its successful play *The River Niger* from Off-Broadway to the Brooks Atkinson, where it remained for 280 performances. Written by Joseph A. Walker and directed by Douglas Turner Ward, who also appeared in the play, it won a Tony Award as the best drama of the season. In January 1974 Michael Moriarty gave a stunning performance as a homosexual

hustler in *Find Your Way Home*, by John Hopkins, and was rewarded with a Tony. Jane Alexander costarred with him. The British comedy *My Fat Friend*, with Lynn Redgrave and George Rose, brought laughter to this theatre in 1974 and was followed by a revival of John Steinbeck's powerful play *Of Mice and Men*, with James Earl Jones as Lenny, Kevin Conway as George, and Pamela Blair as Curley's Wife.

On March 13, 1975, a comedy with only two performers—Ellen Burstyn and Charles Grodin—opened at the Brooks Atkinson and stayed for 1,453 performances, making it this theatre's record holder. It was Bernard Slade's *Same Time, Next Year*—a merry romp about a man and woman who meet every year in a motel for a sexual tryst, unknown to their respective spouses. Burstyn won a Tony Award for her beguiling performance.

Jack Lemmon returned to Broadway in another play by Slade—*Tribute*—in 1978, and his performance was rated better than the play. The British comedy *Bedroom Farce* had some hilarious moments and won Tony Awards for Michael Gough (Best Featured Actor in a Play) and Joan Hickson (Best Featured Actress in a Play).

Teibele and Her Demon, a drama by Isaac Bashevis Singer and Eve Friedman, did not succeed in 1979, despite Tovah Feldshuh in the starring role. But *Talley's Folly*, one of Lanford Wilson's cycle of plays about the Talley family, moved here from Off-Broadway's Circle Rep with its original cast—Judd Hirsch and Trish Hawkins—and scored a triumph. Directed by Marshall W. Mason, the play won the Pulitzer Prize and the Drama Critics Circle Award for best play.

Four unsuccessful shows followed: *Tricks of the Trade* (1980), with George C. Scott and his wife, Trish Van Devere; *Mixed Couples* (1980), with Julie Harris, Geraldine Page, and Rip Torn; Edward Albee's adaptation of *Lolita* (1981), with Blanche Baker as the nymphet and Donald Sutherland as Humbert Humbert; and *Wally's Cafe* (1981), with Rita Moreno, James Coco, and Sally Struthers.

The British play *The Dresser* (1981), by Ronald Harwood, starred Tom Courtenay as a dresser to an aging drunk actor, played by Paul Rogers, and the fascinating drama played for 200 performances. Christopher Durang's Off-Broadway hit *Beyond Therapy* did not repeat its success on Broadway in 1982. Liv Ullmann and John Neville appeared in a revival of Ibsen's *Ghosts* for a few weeks, and the British comedy *Steaming*, set in a women's steam room, won a Tony Award for Judith Ivey as Best Featured Actress in a Play. Patrick Meyers's thrilling *K2* was about two mountain climbers—Jeffrey DeMunn and Jay Patterson—trapped on an icy ledge on the second-highest mountain in the world. The incredible set for this drama won a Tony Award for its designer, Ming Cho Lee.

Ben Kingsley starred in a one-man performance of *Edmund Kean*, followed by an enormous British hit, *Noises Off*, with Dorothy Loudon, Brian Murray, and Victor Garber, which ran here from December 1983 to April 1985. Later that year, Rex Harrison, Claudette Colbert, Lynn Redgrave, and George Rose cavorted in a revival of Frederick Lonsdale's amusing trifle *Aren't We All?* In December 1985 the British hit *Benefactors*, by Michael Frayn, set up shop here, starring Sam Waterston, Glenn Close, Simon Jones, and Mary Beth Hurt. The following December, *Jackie Mason's The World According to Me!* had a highly successful engagement with the stand-up comic receiving a Special Tony Award for his galvanic comic performance. He played his trenchant political romp for more than a year. The show, which revitalized his career, was the first in a series of eight (so far) Mason comedy shows on Broadway.

In 1989 a revival of the 1942 play *Café Crown*, starring Eli Wallach and Anne Jackson, won a Tony Award for the best scenic design of the season (Santo Loquasto). That same year, *Peter, Paul & Mary: A Holiday Celebration* on Broadway and *Stephanie Mills Comes "Home" to Broadway* brightened the Atkinson with limited runs, as did *The Victor Borge Holiday Show on Broadway*.

The Cemetery Club by Ivan Menchell had a short run here in 1990, and later that year *Shadowlands*, by William Nicholson, starred Nigel Hawthorne as British author C. S. Lewis and Jane Alexander as American poetess Joy Davidman. Hawthorne won a Tony as Best Actor in a play.

In 1992 Glenn Close, Gene Hackman, and Richard Dreyfuss starred in *Death and the Maiden* by Ariel Dorfman, directed by Mike Nichols. Close won a Tony Award for her performance as a South American woman who captures and confronts the government agent who had once tortured her.

On October 7, 1993, the delightful Roundabout Theatre Company revival of Bock & Harnick's witty *She Loves Me* moved here from the Criterion Center/Stage Right Theatre and continued its run.

On December 8, 1994, *What's Wrong With This Picture?*, a new play by Donald Margulies, opened to mostly negative reviews, despite the presence of actress Faith Prince as a woman who returns to her family from beyond the grave. Jerry Stiller was in the cast and the offbeat comedy was directed by Joe Mantello. It closed after twelve performances.

In May 1995 a disastrous failure that seemed to be jinxed came to this theatre. It was a stage adaptation of the classic film *On the Waterfront* and bore the same title. Adapted by Budd Schulberg (who won an Academy Award for the film's screenplay) and Stan Silverman, the play had nothing but trouble during previews. The original director was replaced by Adrian Hall, one actor was fired, and another suffered a heart attack and had to be replaced. It closed after eight performances at a loss of $2.6 million.

On April 30, 1996, a revised version of Sam Shepard's 1979 Pulitzer Prize play *Buried Child* was presented by Chicago's Steppenwolf Theatre Company, directed by one of its leading actors, Gary Sinise. Most critics felt that the playwright had improved the play about a family with a terrible secret, and it ran for seventy-one performances.

Taking Sides, an engrossing play about Wilhelm Furtwängler, the famed orchestra leader who refused to leave Germany but conducted for the Nazis, opened on October 17, 1996, and was praised for the electric performances of Daniel Massey as the conductor and Ed Harris as the American denazification officer who confronts him. Taking place in the American sector of occupied Berlin, the play by Ronald Harwood was a bigger hit in London. On Broadway it closed after eighty-five performances. It was followed in March 1997 by the musical *Play On!*, which updated Shakespeare's *Twelfth Night* to 1940s Harlem with a score of Duke Ellington standards. Toplining the cast were André De Shields and Tonya Pinkins.

The next attraction at this theatre, in November 1997, was really more of a concert than a musical. Called *Street Corner Symphony*, it featured eight young singers/dancers performing pop and soul songs of the 1960s and

1970s under a streetlight in Gainesville, Florida. The show was performed without an intermission and with virtually no plot. It lasted seventy-nine performances.

A new production of Frederick Knott's 1966 thriller *Wait until Dark* arrived in 1998, starring the Hollywood director Quentin Tarantino and film actress Marisa Tomei, but it failed to achieve the success of the original, which ran for 373 performances. Lee Remick had thrilled audiences in 1966 as a blind victim stalked by drug dealers, but the acting in this production, especially by Tarantino, was severely criticized. It closed after sixty-five performances.

On April 8, 1999, a highly praised production of Eugene O'Neill's *The Iceman Cometh* arrived from London, where it had scored an enormous success, first at the Almeida, then at the Old Vic. Kevin Spacey, who was the acclaimed Hickey of the revival, repeated his performance on Broadway and was joined by four actors from the British cast. The production, scheduled for a limited engagement, received five Tony Award nominations: Best Actor (Spacey); Best Revival of a Play; Best Director (Howard Davies); Best Scenic Design (Bob Crowley); and Best Lighting Design (Mark Henderson).

Roundabout Theatre Company returned to the Atkinson in spring 2000 with a short-lived revival of *Uncle Vanya* starring Derek Jacobi. In December 2000 the Atkinson hosted a rare musical, *Jane Eyre*, with a sweeping score by Paul Gordon and a grand performance by Marla Schaffel as Charlotte Brontë's resolute heroine.

The Atkinson next hosted a starry November 1, 2001, revival of Michael Frayn's backstage farce *Noises Off*, with a cast that featured Patti LuPone, Faith Prince, Richard Easton, Peter Gallagher, Edward Hibbert, and, in a Tony-winning performance, Kate Finneran. Directed by Jeremy Sams, it drew laughs for 348 performances.

Even after 2,400 years, Greek playwright Euripides had another hit in December 2002 with a revival of his tragedy *Medea*, in a bloody production from the Abbey Theatre of Dublin starring Fiona Shaw as the murderous mom. It was a hot ticket for its limited run of seventy-eight performances.

The Look of Love, a May 2003 lackluster revue of pop tunes by Burt Bacharach and Hal David, did the songwriters no favors and lasted just forty-nine performances despite a cast that included Liz Callaway, Janine LaManna, Rachelle Rak, and Capathia Jenkins.

Jackie Mason, who had revived his career at the Atkinson in 1986 with the first in a series of hit stand-up comedy shows on Broadway, tried expanding the concept in November 2003, hosting his own mini vaudeville revue, titled *Jackie Mason's Laughing Room Only*, with original songs by Doug Katsaros. Critics shrugged and Mason departed after fourteen performances, his shortest Broadway run.

Tom Stoppard's complex, brilliant drama *Jumpers* got an April 25, 2004, revival (via London's Royal National Theatre) that thrilled and perplexed audiences for eighty-nine performances. David Leveaux directed a cast that included Simon Russell Beale and Essie Davis. The drama about philosophy, gymnastics, and the beauty of the moon completed a limited run of eighty-nine performances.

The Atkinson had enjoyed the work of playwright Michael Frayn in a playful mood in *Noises Off*. On November 18, 2004, the theatre hosted one of the ambidextrous author's serious works, *Democracy*, about a communist spy who infiltrated the office of West German Chancellor Willy Brandt in the 1960s. James Naughton played Brandt; Richard Thomas played his secretary and betrayer. Also in the cast were Robert Prosky, Michael Cumpsty, and John Dosset, and the production earned a Tony nomination as Best Play during its five-month run. In a sad coda, Broadway composer Cy Coleman collapsed and died after attending the opening-night performance of *Democracy*.

Hal Holbrook brought his touring-staple solo show *Mark Twain Tonight!* to the Atkinson beginning June 9, 2005, for its third and, as it turned out, last visit to Broadway, going back to the 1960s. The master actor impersonated the master storyteller for a limited run of fifteen performances.

Three's Company actress Suzanne Somers walked audiences through her tabloidy life story in her July 2005 solo show *The Blonde in the Thunderbird*, a reference to a career-making cameo in the film *American Graffiti*. In possibly a first for Broadway, she at one point displayed merchandise as she had on a cable TV shopping network. Critics were aghast and shot it down after nine performances.

Nathan Lane and Matthew Broderick, who had enjoyed a megahit with *The Producers* and who were friends offstage, reteamed for a revival of Neil Simon's *The Odd Couple* that earned mixed reviews but sold out virtually its entire extended limited run from October 27, 2005, to June 4, 2006.

Lightning failed to strike twice for director/choreographer Twyla Tharp, who had enjoyed tremendous success with her 2002 Billy Joel dance musical *Movin' Out* but who was unable to work the same magic with the oeuvre of another singer-songwriter, Bob Dylan, in 2006's *The Times They Are A-Changin'*. Audiences liked the music, though it was sometimes odd to hear the songs sung by someone other than Dylan. Tharp's story about an intergenerational uprising at a traveling circus left audiences perplexed. *Times* folded after twenty-eight performances.

Kevin Spacey was a plaintive James Tyrone Jr. in Howard Davies's April 9, 2007, revival of Eugene O'Neill's *A Moon for the Misbegotten*. His costar, English actress Eve Best, took the Drama Desk Award for her performance as Josie Hogan, and the show completed a limited run of seventy-one performances.

A revival of the rock-'n'-roll musical *Grease* chose its leads via an *American Idol—*style TV reality show titled *You're the One That I Want*. Winners Max Crumm and Laura Osnes opened a 554-performance run on August 19, 2007.

Big hair, spandex, and power chords abounded in *Rock of Ages*, an absurdly entertaining celebration of the excesses of 1980s rock music, which opened April 7, 2009. Librettist Chris D'Arienzo wrote a story about two aspiring rockers who get involved in saving a music club from a villainous German developer. Into every crack in this story D'Arienzo wedged a vintage hit song by groups including Journey, Bon Jovi, Styx, Twisted Sister, Poison, Asia, and other headbangers. The audience was allowed to order drinks from their seats, and ticket holders were given lighter-shaped mini flashlights to wave during favorite songs, rock-concert style. A transfer from Off-Broadway, the show was a surprise hit and was nominated for five Tony Awards including Best Musical and Best Actor in a Musical (*American Idol* finalist Constantine Maroulis).

The Brooks Atkinson is owned and operated by the Messrs. Nederlander. Its intimate ambience makes it ideally suited for dramas and comedies, though in recent years it has become the choice of rock musicals.

The original cast of the 1980s-tribute musical *Rock of Ages* (2009), including (front) Mitchell Jarvis and (fourth from right) Constantine Maroulis. (Photo by Joan Marcus)

CIRCLE IN THE SQUARE

THEATRE

THE NEW CIRCLE IN THE SQUARE
Theatre opened on November 15, 1972, with Theodore Mann as artistic director and Paul Libin as managing director. The nonprofit organization was the uptown successor to the legendary Circle in the Square company in Greenwich Village, which helped to define the Off-Broadway movement. The handsome new theatre, with its distinctive U-shaped seating area around a true thrust stage, was designed by architect Allen Sayles, with lighting by Jules Fisher.

Located in the Uris Building at Fiftieth Street, west of Broadway, the Circle in the Square is situated below the former Uris Theatre, now renamed the Gershwin Theatre. It has 650 seats, more than double the number

WiCKED

CIRCLE in the SQUARE

The 25th Annual Putnam County
**SPELLING
BEE**
A New Musical

AZALEA

Top left to right: PLAY-BILL cover sketch of George C. Scott in the scintillating revival of Noël Coward's *Present Laughter* (1982). PLAY-BILL for Lynn Redgrave's *Saint Joan* (1977). Philip Seymour Hoffman and John C. Reilly alternated in the two main roles of *True West* (2000). A revival of the sci-fi spoof, *The Rocky Horror Show* (2000).

Bottom left: Ellis Rabb (in wheelchair) berates Patricia O'Connell and Richard Woods in the 1980 revival of *The Man Who Came to Dinner*.

Bottom right: William Atherton, Michael Moriarty, and John Rubinstein hold court in the revival of Herman Wouk's *The Caine Mutiny Court-Martial* (1983).

of its Off-Broadway parent. At the time of the new theatre's opening, Mann told PLAYBILL: "Every seat here has a perfect view. Essentially, the design is based on the old the-atre—with almost exactly the same stage space. But we have the latest technical facili-ties—we can trap the stage, have enough height to fly the scenery—from an artistic and scenic point of view. And look at the ceiling in the audi-torium. I don't know of any other theatre like this that has a visible grid above the audience where electricians and stage hands can walk about. All our lighting will come from there. This is a whole new innovation in the Broadway area—the arrival of institutional theatres."

The new theatre was much more cheerful than its predecessor on Bleecker Street, with bright red seats and a red-and-gray checked carpet bearing the Circle in the Square cube symbol, which was repeated in the solid cube

lights in the handsome lobby. Audiences enter the theatre by walking down a flight of stairs or riding escalators to a lounge below street level.

"We owe a lot to [the late *New York Times* critic] Brooks Atkinson for the design of this theatre," Mann stated. "When we were building the first one, I asked Mr. Atkinson what the essential ingredient should be. He replied, 'When you walk in the door, you should see the stage—that should predominate—not the audi-ence.' So, when you walk into our theatre, the first thing you see is the stage—and it works."

Owing to the stature of Circle in the Square and its policy of offering a subscription season of short runs, the new theatre quickly amassed an impressive roll call of stars and produc-tions, photographs of which were used to deco-rate the lounge and bar area.

The new Circle in the Square opened auspi-ciously with a revival of an edited version of

Top left: The Circle In The Square Theatre when it opened in 1972.

Top right: The PLAYBILL for *Frozen* (2004).

Bottom left: Tom Hewitt and Jarrod Emick in the raucous revival of *The Rocky Horror Show* (2000). (Photo by Carol Rosegg)

Bottom right: Finbar Lynch and Dion Graham share a prison cell in Tennessee Williams's *Not About Nightingales* (1999). (Photo by Joan Marcus)

Eugene O'Neill's *Mourning Becomes Electra*, with Colleen Dewhurst. Critics praised the production and the new theatre, expressing satisfaction that although the house was larger and more modern, it preserved the intimacy and ambience of its downtown predecessor.

In 1973 the theatre presented Irene Papas in *Medea*; Siobhan McKenna in *Here Are Ladies*; Lillian Gish, George C. Scott, Nicol Williamson, Barnard Hughes, and Julie Christie in *Uncle Vanya*; Anne Jackson and Eli Wallach in *The Waltz of the Toreadors*; and James Earl Jones in *The Iceman Cometh*.

The year 1974 offered a new play, *An American Millionaire*, by Murray Schisgal; Jim Dale in *Scapino*, which transferred to a commercial run at the Ambassador; Rita Moreno in *The National Health*; and Raul Julia in the musical *Where's Charley?* During the course of the latter run, original star Ray Bolger attended a performance. Julia spotted him and invited him onto the stage for an impromptu dance.

In 1975 Circle in the Square staged Eugene O'Neill's *All God's Chillun Got Wings*, directed by George C. Scott; Arthur Miller's *Death of a Salesman*, starring Scott; *Ah, Wilderness!*, with Geraldine Fitzgerald; and Tennessee Williams's *The Glass Menagerie*, with Maureen Stapleton and Rip Torn.

The 1976 season highlighted Vanessa Redgrave in Ibsen's *The Lady from the Sea*; Rodgers and Hart's *Pal Joey*, with Christopher Chadman and Joan Copeland; Mildred Dunnock in *Days in the Trees*, by Marguerite Duras; and Tennessee Williams's *The Night of the Iguana*, starring Richard Chamberlain and Dorothy McGuire.

Four revivals were presented in 1977: Paul Rudd and Pamela Payton-Wright in *Romeo and Juliet*; Wilde's *The Importance of Being Earnest*; John Wood, Mildred Dunnock, and Tammy Grimes in Molière's *Tartuffe*; and Lynn Redgrave in Shaw's *Saint Joan*.

In 1978 Circle in the Square staged Feydeau's 13 *Rue de L'Amour*, with Louis Jourdan and Patricia Elliott; Kaufman and Hart's *Once in a Lifetime*, with John Lithgow, Treat Williams, Max Wright, and Jayne Meadows Allen; Gogol's *The Inspector General*, with Theodore Bikel; and Shaw's *Man and Superman*, with George Grizzard, Philip Bosco, and Laurie Kennedy.

The 1979 season included two new plays: *Spokesong*, by Stewart Parker, with John Lithgow, Virginia Vestoff, Joseph Maher, and Maria Tucci; and *Loose Ends*, by Michael Weller, with Kevin Kline and Roxanne Hart.

The 1980 productions included *Major Barbara*, with Philip Bosco and Laurie Kennedy; *Past Tense*, by Jack Zeman, with Barbara Feldon and Laurence Luckinbill; and Ellis Rabb in *The Man Who Came to Dinner*.

In 1981 Irene Papas returned in *The Bacchae*; E. G. Marshall, Irene Worth, and Rosemary Murphy appeared in *John Gabriel Borkman*; Ralph Waite and Frances Sternhagen headlined *The Father*; and a new American play, *Scenes and Revelations*, by Elan Garonzik, was presented.

The 1982 season opened with Joanne Woodward in *Candida*, followed by *Macbeth*, starring Nicol Williamson. Next came Percy Granger's new play, *Eminent Domain*, with Philip Bosco and Betty Miller.

In the summer of 1982 George C. Scott was hailed in a hilarious revival of Noël Coward's light comedy *Present Laughter*, which featured the twenty-six-year-old Nathan Lane making his Broadway debut.

The year 1983 began with a scintillating revival of Molière's *The Misanthrope*, with Brian Bedford, Carole Shelley, and Mary Beth

Clockwise from left: Linda Emond, Helen Hunt, Brent Spiner, and John Turturro on the circular set for Yasmina Reza's *Life (x) 3* (2003). (Photo by Joan Marcus)

Hurt. This was followed by an exciting revival of Herman Wouk's *The Caine Mutiny Court-Martial* with John Rubinstein, Michael Moriarty, and William Atherton. Later, football star Joe Namath joined the cast, making his Broadway debut. Next came a revival of Shaw's *Heartbreak House* starring Rex Harrison and Rosemary Harris, with Amy Irving.

The year 1984 brought a new production of Clifford Odets's *Awake and Sing!*; Noël Coward's *Design For Living*, starring Jill Clayburgh, Frank Langella, Raul Julia and Lisa Kirk; Shaw's *Arms and the Man* starring Kevin Kline and Julia, directed by John Malkovich; *The Marriage of Figaro*, starring Christopher Reeve, Anthony Heald, Dana Ivey, Mary Elizabeth Mastrantonio, and Louis Zorich; and a limited engagement of *The Robert Klein Show*, starring the popular comic. Malkovich directed a 1986 production of Pinter's *The Caretaker*. George C. Scott and John Cullum starred in *The Boys in Autumn*, a play about the reunion after fifty years of Tom Sawyer and Huck Finn.

In the fall of 1986, a revival of Shaw's *You Never Can Tell* had a sterling cast headed by Uta Hagen, Victor Garber, Philip Bosco, and Amanda Plummer. In March 1987 Tina Howe's play *Coastal Disturbances* opened and played for ten months. Next came a revival of *A Streetcar Named Desire* starring Blythe Danner, Aidan Quinn, Frank Converse, and Frances McDormand. *An Evening with Robert Klein* played here in June 1988 and was followed by revivals of *Juno and the Paycock* and *The Night of the Iguana*. A revival of Shaw's *The Devil's Disciple*, with Bosco, Garber, Rosemary Murphy, and Remak Ramsey, played for 113 performances; and *Ghetto*, by Joshua Sobol (English version

by David Lan), gave thirty-three performances.

Susan H. Schulman's new production of the Stephen Sondheim/Hugh Wheeler classic *Sweeney Todd*, which had previously been presented at the York Theatre in Manhattan, was brought to the Circle in the Square in September 1989 and played for 189 performances, starring Bob Gunton and Beth Fowler. Taking note of its dimensions (greatly reduced from the Broadway original), the parody revue *Forbidden Broadway* dubbed this production "Teeny Todd."

May 1990 brought a new play, *Zoya's Apartment*, by Mikhail Bulgakov (translated by Nicholas Saunders); the following October saw a lively revival of Molière's *The Miser*, with Philip Bosco, Mia Dillon, and Carole Shelley. *Taking Steps*, a British farce by Alan Ayckbourn, enjoyed seventy-eight performances in 1991.

On Borrowed Time, a loving 1991 revival of Paul Osborn's charming comedy about Death trapped up a tree, starred George C. Scott as Gramps and Matthew Poroc as Pud, his grandson, with Teresa Wright and Nathan Lane (as a dapper "Mr. Brink"). It received excellent notices. Nevertheless, after this point, increasing financial difficulties limited the number of shows presented by the Circle in the Square company at the uptown theatre.

Search and Destroy, a play by Howard Korder, ran for forty-six performances in 1992 and was followed by Al Pacino in an evening of two very different plays: the overripe *Salome* by Oscar Wilde and the spartan *Chinese Coffee*, a new play by Ira Lewis. Both received mixed reviews from the critics. In fall 1992 a musical version of Tolstoy's *Anna Karenina* by Peter Kellogg and Daniel Levine was also dismissed by the critics, with one of them rating it "One Czar." Better received was the 1993 *Wilder, Wilder, Wilder*, three one-act plays by Thornton Wilder, which received a Tony nomination as the season's Best Revival.

After standing dark for more than a year, the theatre relit in November 1994 for a revival of the Pulitzer-winning play *The Shadow Box* by Michael Cristofer, starring Marlo Thomas, Estelle Parsons, and Mercedes Ruehl. Ruehl received a Tony Award nomination as Featured Actress in a Play. The revival received lukewarm reviews and played for forty-eight performances. In February 1995 Chekhov's *Uncle Vanya*, in an English version by Jean-Claude van Itallie, opened with Tom Courtenay, Werner Klemperer, Elizabeth Franz, and others, and played for twen-

Swoosie Kurtz plays a woman who confronts her child's murderer, Brían F. O'Byrne (left) as Sam Kitchin watches in *Frozen* (2004). (Photo by Joan Marcus)

ty-nine performances. Another revival, Tennessee Williams's *The Rose Tattoo*, followed, with Ruehl and Anthony LaPaglia in the leads. It was nominated for the Best Revival of a Play Tony Award and ran for thirty-six performances.

The following season, Circle in the Square presented a revival of Tennessee Williams's *Garden District*, which consisted of two one-act plays: *Something Unspoken* and *Suddenly Last Summer*. The first, short play starred Myra Carter and Pamela Payton-Wright and was considered "slight" by critics. The second was judged a better play but marred by overacting. It starred Elizabeth Ashley, Jordan Baker, Celia Weston, and Victor Slezak, with critics singling out Baker for praise. The production was compared unfavorably with the movie version of *Suddenly Last Summer*, which starred Elizabeth Taylor, Katharine Hepburn, and Montgomery Clift. The unsavory theme of cannibalism soured some critics and theatregoers. It ran for thirty-one performances.

Philip Barry's delightful high comedy *Holiday* starred Laura Linney, Tony Goldwyn, Kim Raver, and Reg Rogers, whose performance as an alcoholic earned him a Tony Award nomination for Best Featured Actor in a Play. The comedy ran for forty-nine performances. Next came William Inge's *Bus Stop*, starring Mary-Louise Parker and Billy Crudup. The play received

mixed reviews, with some critics feeling that it was dated. Crudup received excellent reviews as the boisterous cowboy. The revival ran for twenty-nine performances. *Tartuffe: Born Again*, a new version of Molière's 1664 satire, starred John Glover as the archetypal religious hypocrite, with the action transposed from France to the American South. But the reviews were not encouraging. It opened in May 1996 and ran for twenty-nine performances.

In August 1996 this theatre presented Al Pacino in a revival of Eugene O'Neill's one-act *Hughie*, with only one other actor in the cast, Paul Benedict. It's primarily a monologue for Pacino's character, talking to a night clerk in a New York hotel lobby in 1928. The star's performance received favorable reviews, boosting the show to a fifty-six-performance run.

During that run an era ended at this theatre. Founders Theodore Mann and Paul Libin resigned, and Circle in the Square filed for bankruptcy protection.

The company seemed to be healing its financial wounds under their successors, Gregory Mosher and M. Edgar Rosenblum. On February 20, 1997, it hosted the Royal National Theater of London's production of *Stanley*, starring Anthony Sher as the artist Stanley Spencer. Publicity over a brief nude scene almost overshadowed author Pam Gems's study of whether

Top: Dan Fogler (center) demonstrates his "Magic Foot" to fellow spellers (clockwise from bottom left): Sarah Saltzberg, Derrick Baskin, Jesse Tyler Ferguson, Celia Keenan-Bolger (in headstand), Deborah S. Craig, Lisa Howard, and Jose Llana in the musical *The 25th Annual Putnam County Spelling Bee* (2005). (Photo by Joan Marcus)

Bottom: left to right: Andrew C. Call, Jesse J.P. Johnson, Adam Halpin, and Steven Booth in the one-performance musical *Glory Days* (2008). (Photo by Scott Suchman)

artists are subject to the same rules as the rest of society. The critics admired Sher's performance more than the play, and he received a Tony Award nomination as Best Actor in a Play. Other nominations: Best Play (Gems) and Best Director of a Play (John Caird). The production ran for seventy-four performances.

But financial difficulties persisted, and the theatre's leadership changed again. The Circle in the Square remained closed until 1999, when it reopened as a regular commercial rental theatre, one of a handful of remaining "independents." The Circle in the Square School continues to operate on its premises, as well. Several

notable dramas have made use of the theatre's flexible oblong performing space, which can be used in the round or as a thrust stage. The unorthodox arrangement of the theatre has tended to attract innovative and offbeat fare.

The first tenant after the reopening was *Not about Nightingales*, an early Tennessee Williams play, said to have been rediscovered among the author's papers by Vanessa Redgrave. Presented to considerable acclaim, it was the harrowing true story of a notorious incident at an American prison in 1938, in which a brutal warden punished some rebellious convicts by locking them in a section of the jail where radiators made the heat unbearable and scalded the men until they died.

The warden was played by Corin Redgrave (Vanessa's brother), who received a Tony Award nomination, as did Finbar Lynch as one of the inmates. The play received a Best Play Tony Award nomination and ran for 125 performances.

The Circle in the Square Theatre was leased to the HBO cable TV service in fall 1999. The theatre was used for taping the comedy-interview program *The Chris Rock Show*. It returned to legitimacy in spring 2000 with a revival of Sam Shepard's *True West*, in which actors Philip Seymour Hoffman and John C. Reilly alternated performances in the two primary roles.

The theatre had a hit starting in fall 2000. Christopher Ashley staged a stylish revival of Richard O'Brien's cult rock musical *The Rocky Horror Show*, with a cast that included rock star Joan Jett, plus Dick Cavett, Alice Ripley, Raúl Esparza, Jarrod Emick, and Tom Hewitt. The production, for which the interior of the theatre was redecorated with eerie casts of human figures hung on the walls, earned a Tony nomination as Best Revival of a Musical and ran 437 performances.

A huge pool of water became the new square in the circle of the Circle in the Square for *Metamorphoses*, Mary Zimmerman's adaptation and staging of Roman poet Ovid's classic, which she brought from Chicago and Off-Broadway. She won the 2002 Tony Award as Best Director of a Play for her entertaining reimagining of the two-thousand-year-old stories, which opened March 4, 2002, and ran 400 performances.

Things got drier but more contemporary on March 31, 2003, with the next offering, Yasmina Reza's *Life (x) 3*, in which two couples are shown at the same dinner party but the action is played three different times with slight character changes that result in three different outcomes. Linda Emond, Helen Hunt, Brent Spiner, and John Turturro played the couples for 104 performances.

In Bryony Lavery's drama *Frozen*, Swoosie Kurtz played an Englishwoman who tracks down and confronts the man (Brían F. O'Byrne) who kidnapped, sexually abused, and murdered her child. Laila Robbins played an American psychologist researching serial killers who tries to get to the heart of the crime. *Frozen* opened May 4, 2004, and ran 128 performances.

The Circle in the Square welcomed its greatest success in May 2005 with one of its most off-beat offerings, *The 25th Annual Putnam County Spelling Bee*. Composer William Finn and librettist Rachel Sheinkin fashioned a musical around the emotionally fraught final rounds of a small regional spelling bee. A sterling cast led by Dan Fogler, Celia Keenan-Bolger, Sarah Saltzberg, and Jesse Tyler Ferguson helped them walk the line between affection and parody for the nerdy but full-of-heart twelve-year-old characters. Sheinkin won the Tony Award for Best Book of a Musical, besting the authors of *Spamalot*, *Light in the Piazza*, and *Dirty Rotten Scoundrels*. *Spelling Bee* lasted 1,136 performances, making it the longest-running show in the Circle in the Square's history.

The theatre was next home to the 2008 musical *Glory Days*, the story of four high-school friends who reunite on their alma mater's football field to play a prank and tell some secrets. With a score by Nick Blaemire and a book by James Gardner, the show was a hit at Virginia's Signature Theatre but a one-performance flop on Broadway on May 6, 2008, earning it the snarky nickname "*Glory Day*."

Starting April 25, 2009, Kevin Spacey and the Old Vic Theatre of London brought over their acclaimed revival of Alan Ayckbourn's comedic triptych *The Norman Conquests* with its British ensemble intact. The project involved three full-length plays—*Living Together*, *Table Manners*, and *Round and Round the Garden*—which showed what happened at the same dinner party in three different parts of the same house. The play was presented for an aggregate 109 performances and won the 200 Tony Award for Best Revival of a Play.

Director Kate Whoriskey, who had earned critical accolades for staging the Off-Broadway production of the 2009 Pulitzer Prize—winning drama *Ruined*, made her Broadway debut March 3, 2010, with the first Broadway revival of William Gibson's drama *The Miracle Worker*, about the blind and deaf wunderkind Helen Keller (Abigail Breslin) and her determined teacher Annie Sullivan (Allison Pill). Critics felt this theatre's in-the-round stage was not right for the play, and it lasted just twenty-eight performances.

At this writing, the Circle in the Square was again under the direction of Theodore Mann and Paul Libin and was preparing for the fall 2010 debut of *Lombardi*, a solo show about noted football coach Vince Lombardi, starring Dan Lauria. The show will mark the producing debut of the National Football League.

CORT
THEATRE

RARELY HAS A BROADWAY LEGITIMATE
theatre opened with as resounding a hit as the
Cort had on the night of December 20, 1912.
The play was *Peg o' My Heart* by J. Hartley
Manners, and it starred his illustrious wife,
Laurette Taylor. The incandescent actress
scored a triumph. As critic Brooks Atkinson
reported years later: "J. Hartley Manners
wrote a part for Laurette Taylor in 1912 that
made her the most generally worshipped star
of her time. She opened the new Cort Theatre
on 48th Street as Peg and played it for 607 performances—the longest run of any dramatic
play up to that time."

The critics also had praise for the new playhouse, located east of Broadway. Built by John
Cort, a West Coast theatre impresario who came
east, it was designed by architect Edward B.

Top left to right: A program cover for the Cort Theatre 1915. Caricatures of José Ferrer and Judith Evelyn in *The Shrike* (1952). The PLAYBILL cover for Wendy Wasserstein's *An American Daughter* (1997).

Corey in the style of Louis XVI. It had a marble facade with four Corinthian columns, a lobby of Pavanozza marble with panels of Marie Antoinette plasterwork, and an auditorium with a seating capacity of 999 (later augmented to 1,084). According to the *New York Tribune*, "A distinctive feature of the interior is the proscenium arch, which is of perforated plaster work against a background of art glass capable of illumination during the performance. The sounding board has been decorated with a painting of a minuet during the period made famous in Watteau's drawings of French court life at Versailles."

The article added that instead of an orchestra (most theatres had live orchestras to entertain the patrons), the Cort had a "Wurlitzer Hope-Jones unit orchestra, an electrical instrument capable of operation by one musician."

The Cort's luck continued with its next occupant, *Under Cover*, a play about an undercover customs agent, starring Harry Crosby, Ralph Morgan, and George Stevens. It opened in August 1914 and ran for 349 performances. In 1915 the Cort went musical with Victor Herbert's *The Princess Pat*, which had a hit tune: "Neapolitan Love Song." It ran for 158 performances.

Other successes during this period were a Chinese play called *The Yellow Jacket* (1916); *Flo-Flo* (1917), a musical with some vaudeville headliners; and John Drinkwater's masterly *Abraham Lincoln*, starring Frank McGlyn in the title role. It ran for 244 performances.

The Cort housed a wide variety of fare during the 1920s. A musical comedy called *Jim Jam Jems* featured an incredible collection of comics: Joe E. Brown, Frank Fay, Harry Langdon, Ned Sparks, and Mr. Jokes himself, Joe E. Miller. They provided solid yocks for 105 performances in 1920. The following year brought a farcical comedy, *Captain Applejack*, produced by the estimable Sam H. Harris, and it was funny enough to continue for 366 performances. Then in 1922 came a classic American comedy: George S. Kaufman and Marc Connelly's *Merton of the Movies*. The critics were unanimous in their praise of this satire in which a shy, movie-crazy grocery clerk, splendidly played by Glenn Hunter, went to Hollywood and became a success because he was such a terrible actor. It was on Burns Mantle's ten-best list and ran for 398 performances.

In contrast to *Merton of the Movies* was the genteel high comedy of Ferenc Molnar's *The Swan* (1923), starring the lovely Eva Le Gallienne as a princess sought by a prince (Philip Merivale) and a humble tutor (Basil Rathbone). The Hungarian romance charmed audiences for 253 performances.

After a number of failures in 1924, the Cort presented Ethel Barrymore, who was praised for her performance in a revival of Sir Arthur Wing Pinero's *The Second Mrs. Tanqueray*, staged by Arthur Hopkins. A comedy called *White Collars* with Cornelia Otis Skinner also found favor in 1925. Six shows followed, none of them successful; then came *The Jazz Singer*, starring George Jessel, which moved here from the Fulton Theatre and ran for 315 performances. This Samson Raphaelson play later became the first commercially released talking picture, starring Al Jolson.

A comedy called *The Little Spitfire* played for 201 performances in 1926. A strange drama came to the Cort later that year. It was called *The Ladder*, and before it had run its course

Above: PLAYBILL covers for *The Male Animal* (1940), José Ferrer in *Charley's Aunt* (1940), and Wolcott Gibbs's comedy *Season in the Sun* (1950).

Top left to right: The magnificent Laurette Taylor in the Cort's famed opening show, *Peg o' My Heart* (1912).

Lillian Gish in the acclaimed Jed Harris production of *Uncle Vanya* (1930).

Laurence Olivier and Jill Esmond in the British shocker *The Green Bay Tree* (1933).

Grace Kelly, making her Broadway debut, with Mady Christians in *The Father* (1949).

Bottom: Katharine Cornell in Anouilh's treatment of *Antigone* (1946).

(789 performances) it had played in five different Broadway theatres—including two engagements at the Cort. The play was about reincarnation and had Antoinette Perry and Ross Alexander in the cast. The critics called it hokum, and the producer, Brock Pemberton, sometimes let people in for nothing.

George Kelly's *Behold the Bridegroom* (1927), starring Judith Anderson, Mary Servoss, and Lester Vail, was admired but lasted for only eighty-eight performances. On November 12, 1928, a drama called *These Days* opened with a large cast of young girls playing rich young students in a finishing school. Among them was an actress making her Broadway debut—her name was Katharine Hepburn. The play ran for only eight performances but launched a spectacular career.

Alice Brady appeared at the Cort in *A Most Immoral Lady* in late 1928 and helped the play to run for 160 performances. The Cort's last show of the 1920s was *Your Uncle Dudley*, a homespun comedy by Howard Lindsay and Bertrand Robinson, starring Walter Connolly. It rang out the Roaring Twenties with 96 performances.

In April 1930 producer Jed Harris, known as the boy wonder, returned from London and produced and directed an acclaimed revival of Chekhov's *Uncle Vanya*, adapted by Rose Caylor. Harris's direction and the acting of his sterling cast—Lillian Gish, Osgood Perkins, Walter Connolly, Eduardo Ciannelli, Joanna Roos, and others—made the occasion a theatrical event.

The end of 1930 brought a taut, cynical exposé of scandalmongering newspapers called *Five-Star Final*. It starred Arthur Byron, Frances Fuller, and Berton Churchill and featured Allen Jenkins. Theatregoers supported it for 176 showings.

Two enterprising producers—Alfred de

Liagre Jr. and Richard Aldrich—brought a screwball family to the Cort in 1933 in a comedy called *Three-Cornered Moon*, making an auspicious producing debut. The excellent cast included Ruth Gordon, Richard Whorf, Brian Donlevy, and Cecilia Loftus.

Later in 1933 a sensational drama arrived from Britain. It was Mordaunt Shairp's *The Green Bay Tree*, and it starred Laurence Olivier, James Dale, Jill Esmond (Mrs. Olivier at that time), O. P. Heggie, and Leo G. Carroll. Jed Harris's direction was highly praised for its subtlety in depicting a questionable relationship between a wealthy male hedonist and a poor, handsome young boy, played by Olivier.

From October 1935 to July 1938 the Cort had only two bookings, but they were both George Abbott smashes. The first one, the riotous *Boy Meets Girl*, by Bella and Samuel Spewack, was a hysterical spoof of Hollywood said to be inspired by the West Coast shenanigans of Ben Hecht and Charles MacArthur when they toiled there as scriptwriters. With Jerome Cowan and Allyn Joslyn as the madcap scribes, Joyce Arling as an unwed mother, and Abbott's famous "touch" in direction, *Boy Meets Girl* had Cort audiences in stitches for 669 performances.

On May 19, 1937, Abbott ushered in his production of another raucous farce, *Room Service*, by John P. Murray and Allen Boretz. With such expert farceurs as Sam Levene, Teddy Hart, Philip Loeb, Eddie Albert, and Betty Field, the comedy chronicled the plight of a group of hungry actors and some shoestring producers living in a seedy hotel while trying to get backing for the play they wish to put on. It was a Cort favorite for 500 performances and later was made into a film with the Marx Brothers.

The year 1939 witnessed memorable performances by Jessica Tandy and Barry Fitzgerald in Paul Vincent Carroll's *The White Steed*.

The 1940s brought exciting theatre to the Cort. Among the highlights: *The Male Animal* (1940), an intelligent comedy by James Thurber and Elliott Nugent, starring Nugent, Gene Tierney, Ruth Matteson, and Don DeFore; a lively revival of *Charley's Aunt* (1940), staged by Joshua Logan, with José Ferrer and Nedda Harrigan (Mrs. Logan); the warmhearted *Café Crown* (1942), starring Sam Jaffe and Morris Carnovsky as leading actors of the Yiddish Theatre who gather each evening in a popular Second Avenue cafe; Maxwell Anderson's moving war drama *The Eve of St. Mark* (1942), with William Prince as a farm boy who goes to war and Aline MacMahon as his mother.

Next came *A Bell for Adano* (1944), Paul Osborn's faithful adaptation of John Hersey's novel about the American occupation of Italy at war's end, starring Fredric March as an army major; the Theatre Guild Shakespearean Company in *The Winter's Tale* (1946); Katharine Cornell and Cedric Hardwicke in Anouilh's ver-

sion of *Antigone* (1946), alternating with Shaw's *Candida*, in which Marlon Brando played a rather prissy Marchbanks; Canada Lee in *On Whitman Avenue* (1946), a play about a black family moving into a white neighborhood; Cornelia Otis Skinner, Estelle Winwood, and Cecil Beaton in Wilde's *Lady Windermere's Fan* (1946—47), with sets, costumes, and lighting by Beaton; Meg Mundy's powerful performance in Sartre's *The Respectful Prostitute* (1948), which moved to the Cort from the New Stages Theatre on Bleecker Street; Melvyn Douglas and Jan Sterling in Sam Spewack's political satire *Two Blind Mice* (1949); and a revival of Strindberg's *The Father* (1949), with Raymond Massey, Mady Christians, and, making her Broadway debut, Grace Kelly.

The Cort continued to house hits in the 1950s, beginning with Katharine Hepburn in an engaging revival of *As You Like It*, with William Prince as Orlando and Cloris Leachman as Celia. Wolcott Gibbs, drama critic for *The New Yorker*, came up with a hit comedy, *Season in the Sun*, about the (straight) denizens of Fire Island (1950). Uta Hagen drew praise for her Joan in Shaw's *Saint Joan* (1951). Joseph Kramm won a Pulitzer Prize for his harrowing drama *The Shrike* (1952), about a husband (José Ferrer) who is committed to a mental institution by his odious wife (Judith Evelyn).

The decade continued with Menasha Skulnik entertaining in a garment-district spoof, *The Fifth Season* (1953). Geraldine Page, Albert Salmi, and Darren McGavin enhanced *The Rainmaker* (1954). Frances Goodrich and Albert Hackett won a Pulitzer Prize, New York Drama Critics Circle Award, and Tony Award for their moving play *The Diary of Anne Frank* (1955), about a Dutch-Jewish girl during World War II, struggling with puberty as she and her family spend months in hiding from Nazi terror. Susan

Top left: Katharine Hepburn and William Prince in the 1950 revival of *As You Like It*.

Top center: Ralph Bellamy as FDR in *Sunrise at Campobello* (1958).

Top right: Susan Strasberg and Joseph Schildkraut in *The Diary of Anne Frank* (1955).

Bottom: Zoe Caldwell and Dame Judith Anderson in the 1982 revival of *Medea*.

Top: left to right, Mark Linn-Baker and Jay Goede in the musical *A Year With Frog and Toad* (2003). (Photo by Rob Levine)

Right: The company in the spectacular fantasy, *The Green Bird* (2000). (Photo by Joan Marcus)

Strasberg starred as Anne, Joseph Schildkraut and Gusti Huber as her parents, and Lou Jacobi and Jack Gilford as others hidden in the attic.

Siobhan McKenna, Art Carney, and Joan Blondell scored in the tragic drama *The Rope Dancers* (1957). *Sunrise at Campobello*, Dore Schary's study of President Franklin Delano Roosevelt's early years, won four Tony Awards, including Best Play and Best Actor (Ralph Bellamy as Roosevelt), in 1958.

The 1960s brought Brendan Behan's rowdy play *The Hostage* (1960), with a cast largely drawn from Joan Littlewood's Theatre Workshop in London. Next came a dramatization of Allen Drury's popular political novel *Advise and Consent*, with a cast that included Richard Kiley, Ed Begley, Kevin McCarthy, and Barnard Hughes. It lasted for 212 performances. This was followed by the engaging *Purlie Victorious*, written by and starring Ossie Davis, with Ruby Dee, Alan Alda, and Godfrey Cambridge. In November 1961 a young Robert Redford held forth on the Cort stage in Norman Krasna's thin comedy *Sunday in New York*, produced by David Merrick, directed by

Garson Kanin—and not very successful.

From mid-1962 until mid-1969 the Cort booked many shows but few successes. Some of the more interesting exhibits were a brief visit by the Royal Dramatic Theatre of Sweden acting in *The Father*, *Long Day's Journey into Night*, and *Miss Julie* (1962); Kirk Douglas in an unsuccessful adaptation of *One Flew Over the Cuckoo's Nest* (1963), which later proved a major hit Off-Broadway and became an Oscar-winning film; and Louis Gossett and Menasha Skulnik in the musical *The Zulu and the Zayda* (1965).

The marquee of the Cort can be glimpsed momentarily in the classic film spoof of Broadway, *The Producers* (1968), which was shot at the since-demolished Playhouse Theatre directly across Forty-eighth Street.

In 1969 the Cort was leased to television for several years and served as another theatre from which *The Merv Griffin Show* emanated for a time.

On May 28, 1974, the Cort made a dazzling comeback. Owned for many years by the Shubert Organization, the theatre was beautifully restored for its return to the legitimate fold. It reopened with *The Magic Show*, a musical that would have died on its opening night if it had not had Doug Henning in the lead. Henning, one of the world's best and most amiable magicians, created such incredible magic on the Cort's stage that the show ran for 1,920 performances.

Al Pacino starred in a disastrous Brooklynese version of Shakespeare's *Richard III* (1979), and Tennessee Williams suffered critical arrows for his play about F. Scott and Zelda Fitzgerald, *Clothes for a Summer Hotel* (1980). An engaging black-themed play, *Home*, won favor that spring; and Glenda Jackson and Jessica Tandy acted grandly in the unsuccessful British play *Rose* (1981). In 1982 there was an engrossing revival of *Medea* starring Zoe Caldwell, whose passionate performance won her a Tony Award, and Judith Anderson, who put her stamp on the title role in 1947, playing the Nurse this time.

In 1983 Murray Schisgal's *Twice Around the Park*, two one-act plays, starred Eli Wallach and Anne Jackson, and it was followed by August Wilson's first Broadway drama, *Ma Rainey's Black Bottom* (1984) and a revival of O'Neill's *A Moon for the Misbegotten* (1984) that starred Kate Nelligan and Ian Bannen.

Sarafina! (1988), the South African drama with music, played here for over a year. The Steppenwolf Theatre's production of John Steinbeck's classic *The Grapes of Wrath* won a

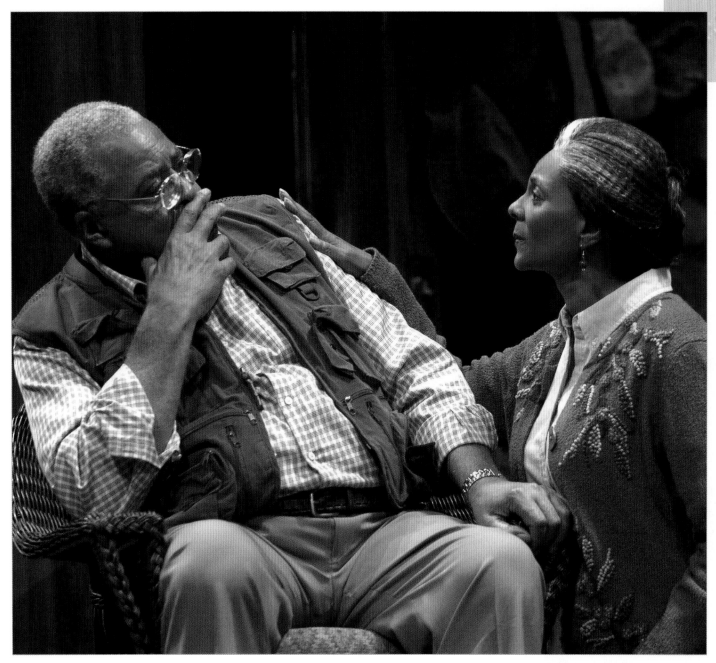

Tony Award as the season's Best Play (1990). *Two Shakespearean Actors*, by Richard Nelson, starred Victor Garber as Edwin Forrest and Brian Bedford as William Charles Macready, master thespians whose bitter rivalry caused the tragic Astor Place riots in 1847, in which twenty-two people were killed and more than one hundred wounded. The play was presented by the Lincoln Center Theater in 1992, but it ran for only twenty-nine performances.

On April 17, 1994, *Twilight: Los Angeles, 1992*, a new play conceived, written, and performed by the remarkable Anna Deavere Smith (who played more than forty characters with amazing skill), moved here from the New York Shakespeare Festival. Smith received a Tony nomination for her dazzling work embodying the people in and around a Los Angeles race riot.

In March 1995 Lincoln Center Theater presented a prestigious revival of *The Heiress*, the 1947 play by Ruth and Augustus Goetz, based on the Henry James novel *Washington Square*. The production received seven Tony Award nominations and won the following: Best Revival of a Play, Best Director of a Play (Gerald Gutierrez), Best Actress in a Play (Cherry Jones), and Best Featured Actress in a Play (Frances Sternhagen). It ran for 340 performances.

Lincoln Center Theatre booked the Cort for new works by two major playwrights, Christopher Durang and Wendy Wasserstein, in the 1996—97 season. They got very different

James Earl Jones and Leslie Uggams in a revival of *On Golden Pond* (2005). (Photo by Scott Suchman)

responses. Durang's vulgar 1996 comedy *Sex and Longing* repelled thirteen critics (as well as audiences) and lasted only forty-five performances. The cast included Sigourney Weaver, Dana Ivey, and Peter Michael Goetz. Wasserstein's 1997 play *An American Daughter* garnered three favorable reviews, three mixed, and four negative. It starred Kate Nelligan, Hal Holbrook, Peter Riegert, and Lynne Thigpen, with Thigpen winning a Tony Award as Best Featured Actress in a Play. Nelligan played a candidate for U.S. attorney general whose appointment runs into political trouble. The play ran for eighty-eight performances.

John Leguizamo brought his amusing one-man show (which he wrote and starred in) to the Cort in 1998. He called it *Freak*, and he outrageously spoofed his racy upbringing. Both his play and performance were nominated for Tonys, and he entertained audiences for 145 performances. Director Spike Lee adapted it as a film for the HBO cable TV network. Later that same year, there was much publicity about the nude appearance of Nicole Kidman in David Hare's play *The Blue Room*, freely adapted from Arthur Schnitzler's *La Ronde*. The two-character play, costarring Kidman and Iain Glen, was a huge financial success (although Kidman was bare only briefly), but it was not a critical success. It completed a limited run of eighty-one performances.

On August 19, 1999, an entertainment called *Kat and the Kings* brought an exuberant vocal/dancing group from South Africa (via London) in a musical about the rise and fall of a doo-wop group in 1950s Capetown. The critics were impressed by the youthful cast's energy but found the show's book weak. However, audiences were enthusiastic enough to attend the show for 157 performances.

On April 18, 2000, *The Lion King* director Julie Taymor returned to Broadway with *The Green Bird*, a spectacular satirical fable, featuring music by Elliot Goldenthal and a translation by Albert Bermel and Ted Emery from an Italian tale by Carlo Gozzi. Taymor directed the show and designed its masks and puppet

designs, as she had done for *The Lion King*. The production originated with Theatre for a New Audience in 1996 at the New Victory Theatre on Forty-second Street. This production had sets by Christine Jones, costumes by Constance Hoffman, and lighting by Donald Holder. Hoffman was nominated for a Tony Award for her dazzling costumes and Derek Smith for Best Featured Actor in a Play. The critics were more enchanted by the fable's visual splendors than with the play's foolish Venetian tale. The show closed after fifty-five performances.

The effects of the Holocaust on three generations of American Jews were examined in Arje Shaw's drama *The Gathering*, which starred Hal Linden and lasted twenty-four performances starting April 24, 2001.

The husband-and-wife team of Joseph Bologna and Renée Taylor turned the incidents of their showbiz marriage into an autobiographical comedy, *If you ever leave me . . . I'm going with you!*, in August 2001, but audiences just weren't that into them, and they left together after fifty-three performances.

Comedienne Carol Burnett turned playwright with *Hollywood Arms*, an autobiographical play about growing up funny with a tough grandmother and a flibbertigibbet mother; it opened on October 31, 2002. To complete the family scenario, Burnett wrote the play with her daughter, Carrie Hamilton. Donna Lynn Champlin starred with Linda Lavin and Michele Pawk, and Harold Prince directed, but *Hollywood Arms* folded after seventy-six performances.

As with 2000's *The Green Bird*, the New Victory Theatre supplied the Cort with another tenant, *A Year with Frog and Toad*. This tiny musical for children was based on a book about

Gareth Saxe, Raúl Esparza, and James Frain in the 2007 revival of Pinter's *The Homecoming*. (Photo by Scott Landis)

the friendship between the two titular cookie-loving amphibians, played by Mark Linn-Baker and Jay Goede. Despite the modest source material, the show had an engaging score by brothers Robert and Willie Reale, who earned Tony nominations for their work. The show, which also earned a Tony nomination as Best Musical, lasted seventy-three performances after its April 13, 2003, opening.

The next production at the Cort never actually opened. *Bobbi Boland*, Nancy Hasty's play about a clash of beauties in a Florida backwater, closed in previews despite the presence of its star, 1970s icon Farrah Fawcett. Its final performance was November 9, 2003. The strengths or weaknesses of the play were forgotten in an ongoing tabloid analysis of the star's alleged eccentric behavior backstage and onstage.

Perhaps inspired by the 1998 success of John Leguizamo's *Freak* at this theatre, another comedian, Mario Cantone, took audiences on a tour through *his* upbringing in a boisterous ethnic family (Italian-American this time) in the solo show *Laugh Whore*. It enjoyed a two-month run in fall 2004 and was taped for cable TV.

Tony-winning stars James Earl Jones and Leslie Uggams teamed up for a nontraditionally cast revival of Ernest Thompson's gentle family comedy *On Golden Pond*, which gave 93 performances starting April 7, 2005. The Cort followed it with another comedy revival, Neil Simon's *Barefoot in the Park*, in February 2006. Patrick Wilson and Amanda Peet played the newlyweds, with Jill Clayburgh and Tony Roberts handling the autumn romance. Scott Ellis staged the production, which lasted 109 performances.

Julie White gave the performance of her career at the Cort starting November 13, 2006, when the hit Off-Broadway comedy *The Little Dog Laughed* moved here from a sold-out engagement at Off-Broadway's Second Stage Theatre. White won the 2007 Tony Award as Best Actress in a Play for her performance as a relentless talent agent who sets out to salvage the career of a client, a closeted gay actor who falls in love with a male hooker. The play gave 112 performances on Broadway.

On May 8, 2007, the Cort hosted a distinguished and historic production: *Radio Golf*, the tenth and final installment in August Wilson's Pittsburgh Cycle of plays about African-American life in the twentieth century. Though the production wound up giving only sixty-four performances, one of Wilson's briefest

Broadway runs, it brought the cycle to a fascinating close with the story of a black politician in 1990s Pittsburgh who must help decide what to do with the rundown house that once belonged to Aunt Ester, the semi-supernatural matriarch who represents the legacy of Africa and slavery that underpins the entire ten-play epic. Kenny Leon directed a sterling cast including Anthony Chisholm, John Earl Jelks, Harry Lennix, Tonya Pinkins, and James A. Williams. *Radio Golf* was nominated for a Tony Award as Best Play of 2007, but Wilson didn't get to enjoy its success. He had died October 2, 2005, shortly after completing the script.

On December 16, 2007, Harold Pinter's *The Homecoming* got a first-class revival at the Cort directed by Daniel Sullivan and starring Raúl Esparza, Eve Best, Michael McKean, and Ian McShane. The game of sex and power among male members of a family after one of them marries lasted 137 performances.

From April 29, 2008, to January 4, 2009, the Cort hosted a transfer of *The 39 Steps*, the imaginatively staged adaptation of the Alfred Hitchcock film. The peripatetic London hit had debuted on Broadway at Roundabout Theatre Company's American Airlines Theatre; after the Cort it moved on to the Helen Hayes Theatre.

In January and February 2009 the Cort briefly housed the hottest ticket on Broadway. Comedian Will Ferrell, star of nutball film comedies including *Anchorman* and *Talladega Nights*, had honed his aggressive-dim-bulb impression of President George W. Bush on the late-night comedy show *Saturday Night Live*. He chose the Cort as the site of his full-length satirical send-off to the forty-third president, *You're Welcome America: A Final Night with George W. Bush*. The show opened the night Bush left the White House, and Ferrell opened the show by pretending to be the president parachuting onto the stage.

It was followed by two distinguished revivals featuring Hollywood stars. Live Schreiber played a Brooklyn dockworker who loves his grown niece perhaps a little too much in Arthur Miller's *A View from the Bridge*, which also featured Scarlett Johansson in her Broadway debut. It opened January 24, 2010, and gave eighty-one performances.

In April of that year, Denzel Washington took the role of retired Negro League baseball player Troy Maxson, opposite Viola Davis and Chris Chalk in August Wilson's *Fences*, directed by Kenny Leon.

Will Ferrell as the Commander-in-Chief in his comedy *You're Welcome America. A Final Night with George W. Bush* (2009). (Photo by Robert J. Saferstein)

DAVID T. NEDERLANDER

THEATRE

THE NEDERLANDER THEATRE HAS HAD
a long and distinguished history under several
different names: the National, the Billy Rose,
and the Trafalgar.

Walter C. Jordan, a theatrical agent of note,
built the National Theatre at 208 West Forty-
first Street. When it opened on September 1,
1921, the *New York Times* reported that the new
house cost $950,000 to build, was designed by
architect William Neil Smith, and contained
1,200 seats, making it capable of housing both
dramatic productions and musicals.

At the time of its opening there were still
plenty of other full-size theatres on the downtown side of Times Square. But with the demolition of the Casino, the Comedy, the Empire,
the old Broadway, and other vintage playhous-

es over the years, the National eventually became the southernmost outpost of the Broadway theatre district, a distinction it has held for more than half a century.

The theatre's original interior was done in burnished Italian walnut with gold embellishments. "The style is early Renaissance and the carved figures are of lyric and epic subjects, unobtrusive but attractive, and emerging in the half round from wood like Flemish carvings," wrote the *New York Times*. The paper went on to praise Jordan for providing actors with luxurious dressing rooms with baths and the audience with the latest in restrooms and lounges, making a trip to the new theatre a comfortable and pleasurable experience.

Unfortunately, the National's opening show was *Swords*, Sidney Howard's first play, which ran for only thirty-six performances. Howard, however, benefited from the experience. He married Clare Eames, who played the leading role.

In February 1922 the theatre had a stroke of luck in booking a thriller that would become a classic of its genre: *The Cat and the Canary*, written by actor John Willard. Critic Alexander Woollcott wrote in the *Times*, "He has turned out a creepy young thriller, nicely calculated to make every hair on your head rise and remain standing from 8:30 till nearly 11." The play, which took place in a spooky mansion on the Hudson, required an heiress (Florence Eldridge) to remain sane—while people were being snuffed out all around her—in order to win her inheritance. Henry Hull was the costar.

In 1923 Walter Hampden revived the Rostand classic *Cyrano de Bergerac* and was rewarded with great notices and a run of 250 performances. The blank-verse adaptation of the play was by Brian Hooker. Another hit followed in 1924 when H. B. Warner starred in *Silence*, a melodrama in which a crook (Warner) takes the

rap for a crime that his daughter has committed.

The popular movie actress Lila Lee appeared at the National in 1925 in *The Bride Retires*, one of those French farces about young people who are forced to marry by their parents and then discover that they really love each other. Movie fans bought it for 146 performances. Later in the year *The Gorilla*, a popular spoof of mystery plays, transferred here from the Selwyn Theatre. Walter Hampden next moved in from his own house, the Hampden Theatre, with his production of *Hamlet*, and this classic was followed early in 1926 by the great magician Houdini in a spectacular personal appearance.

Fredric March came to the National in 1926 in *The Half-Caste*, subtitled "A story of love and sacrifice in a Land of Forgotten Men," but the *Times* labeled it "a trite and loquacious drama." The National's next offering fared better. It was George M. Cohan's production of a play called *Yellow*, in which Chester Morris played a rotter. (There was a young actor in the supporting cast named Spencer Tracy.) Some first-nighters felt that the play's author, Margaret Vernon, was a pseudonym for Cohan. It ran for 132 performances.

John Willard, who had given the National the smash *The Cat and the Canary*, tried again with a melodrama called *Fog* in 1927, but the critics found it murky and it evaporated after 97 performances. Next came a huge hit and one of the National's most fondly remembered shows. It was A. H. Woods's production of Bayard Veiller's *The Trial of Mary Dugan*, and it starred Ann Harding in the role of a showgirl accused of murdering her millionaire lover. The court went into session 437 times.

The 1920s came to a dramatic close at the National with the opening of Martin Flavin's *The Criminal Code*, which jolted theatregoers with its realistic view of life in the big house.

Top left: Florence Eldridge as the menaced heiress in *The Cat and the Canary* (1922).

Top center: Henry Hull and Eugenie Leontovich in *Grand Hotel* (1930).

Top right: Ethel Barrymore and Richard Waring in *The Corn is Green* (1940).

Bottom: Program-cover art of British actress Elizabeth Simpson Inchbald.

Top left: Walter Hampden in the classic *Cyrano de Bergerac* (1923).

Top center: Gertrude Lawrence and Noël Coward in *Tonight at 8:30*.

Top right: Tallulah Bankhead in her biggest hit, *The Little Foxes* (1939).

Above: PLAYBILL covers for the British hit, *Whose Life Is It Anyway?* (1979), *Sherlock's Last Case* (1987) and *Our Country's Good* (1990).

Arthur Byron gave a powerful performance as an inmate who witnessed a murder in the warden's office but chose not to reveal which of his prison mates committed the crime. It thrilled audiences for 174 performances.

Peking's most illustrious actor, Mei Lan-Fang, played a highly successful Broadway engagement with his Chinese company of actors, singers, and musicians in 1930. He opened first at the Forty-ninth Street Theatre, then moved to the National for an additional three weeks. On November 13, 1930, a landmark theatrical event occurred at the National: Herman Shumlin opened his production of *Grand Hotel*, a swirling drama based on a play by Vicki Baum, translated from the German by William A. Drake. The opulent production was the first dramatic play on Broadway to use a revolving stage, and it captivated audiences with its portrayal of life in a luxury hotel in Berlin. Eugenie Leontovich played a weary Russian ballerina, Sam Jaffe played a clerk with only a few weeks to live, Henry Hull was a baron who gets murdered in the hotel, and the rest of the enormous cast played employees and guests of the Grand Hotel, with myriad problems. It ran for 459 performances and was adapted as a hit musical in 1988.

The National had a series of failures and quick bookings during 1932 and 1933 and was dark for more than a year during those gray Depression days. But on October 22, 1934, a distinguished drama opened at this theatre. It was Sean O'Casey's *Within the Gates*, directed by Melvyn Douglas and starring Lillian Gish as a prostitute, Bramwell Fletcher as a poet, and Moffat Johnston as a bishop. The play took place in London's Hyde Park, and the very large cast represented the great variety of humanity who spent their days in the park. There was music, dancing, and philosophizing, and Brooks Atkinson in the *Times* pronounced: "Nothing so

grand has risen in our impoverished theatre since this reporter first began writing of plays."

A charming, nostalgic play, *Remember the Day*, by Philip Dunning and Philo Higley, came to the National on September 25, 1935. It starred Frankie Thomas as a schoolboy who has a crush on his teacher (Francesca Bruning) until he sees her kissing the school's athletic coach (Russell Hardie). A novelty of the well-received play was that Frank M. Thomas Sr. played the father of Frankie Thomas.

Another fine drama, *Ethan Frome*, adapted by Owen and Donald Davis from the novel of the same name by Edith Wharton, opened in January 1936. Staged by Guthrie McClintic, the play had magnificent performances by Raymond Massey, Ruth Gordon, and Pauline Lord, but its depressing story and somber atmosphere resulted in a run of only 119 performances.

On November 24, 1936, New York's elite descended upon the National in their finest evening wear and jewels to welcome Noël Coward and Gertrude Lawrence back to the Broadway stage in Coward's collection of one-act plays under the umbrella title *Tonight at 8:30*. The nine playlets were performed in groups of three at three different performances. Coward and Lawrence had not been seen on Broadway together since 1931, when they triumphed in Coward's *Private Lives*, and their return was the social event of the 1936—37 season. On opening night, during the first intermission, a lady had her chinchilla coat stolen. At openings in those days, there was always a gray-haired detective stationed in the theatre to keep an eye on the audience. This super-sleuth apprehended the thieves and the lady had her coat back by the time the final curtain fell.

In 1938 Orson Welles and John Houseman's celebrated Mercury Theatre had such success with its revivals of Shakespeare's *Julius Caesar*

Top left: Souvenir program for Judith Anderson in *Medea* (1947).

Top center: Uta Hagen, Arthur Hill, and George Grizzard trade insults in *Who's Afraid of Virginia Woolf?* (1962).

Top right: Ethel Barrymore and Richard Waring in *The Corn is GREEN* (1940).

Bottom: Peter Brook's production of *A Midsummer Night's Dream* (1971).

and Thomas Dekker's *The Shoemaker's Holiday* that they moved these productions from the small Mercury Theatre to the larger National. The group was the sensation of the season. They played *Julius Caesar* in black shirts as an indictment of fascism, and *The Shoemaker's Holiday* was turned into a rowdy, lusty prank without an intermission. The Mercury Theatre company for these two productions included such actors as Welles, Joseph Cotten, Martin Gabel, Hiram Sherman, John Hoysradt, George Coulouris, Stefan Schnabel, Vincent Price, Ruth Ford, Edith Barrett, Elliott Reid, and Whitford Kane.

On February 15, 1939, the National housed one of its finest tenants. Lillian Hellman's vitriolic play about greed, *The Little Foxes*, starred Tallulah Bankhead as Regina Giddens. It was Tallulah's first superior role in the American theatre. Herman Shumlin's direction was praised, and so was the supporting cast:

Patricia Collinge, Frank Conroy, Dan Duryea, Carl Benton Reid, Charles Dingle, and Florence Williams. It ran for 410 performances.

During the 1940s the National housed some memorable productions. Ethel Barrymore had one of her greatest triumphs in Emlyn Williams's drama *The Corn Is Green*, in which she played a determined schoolteacher in Wales who discovers literary talent in one of the local miners and exerts all her power to make a success of him. The New York Drama Critics Circle named it the best foreign play of the year, and it ran for 477 performances during the 1940—41 season.

Another notable production came to this theatre in November 1941: Maurice Evans and Judith Anderson in Shakespeare's *Macbeth*. Staged by Margaret Webster, the revival was acclaimed as one of the finest productions of this classic ever mounted in the United States. It ran for 131 performances. In 1943 Sidney

Top left: PLAYBILL cover for *Rent*.

Top right: The happy military revue, *Call Me Mister* (1946).

Bottom left: Lillian Gish, Moffat Johnston, and Kathryn Collier in *Within the Gates* (1934).

Bottom right: Lena Horne in her sensational musical autobiography, *Lena Horne: The Lady and Her Music* (1981).

Kingsley's *The Patriots* opened and won the New York Drama Critics Award as best play of the season. The cast included Raymond E. Johnson as Thomas Jefferson, House Jameson as Alexander Hamilton, and Cecil Humphreys as George Washington. Mrs. Sidney Kingsley, Madge Evans, played a romantic role.

A failure of note was a musical called *What's Up?*, which happened to be Alan Jay Lerner and Frederick Loewe's first Broadway musical. Jimmy Savo had the lead, and the staging and choreography were by George Balanchine, but the critics declared that nothing was up and the show closed after 63 performances in 1943. Early in 1944 Eva Le Gallienne and Joseph Schildkraut acted brilliantly in a revival of Chekhov's *The Cherry Orchard*, staged by Le Gallienne and Margaret Webster. Later that year Ethel Barrymore returned to this theatre in an adaptation of the Franz Werfel novel *Embezzled Heaven*, but the play was not a success. Lerner and Loewe returned to the National in November 1945 with a delightful musical called *The Day Before Spring*, about a college reunion. Anthony Tudor created the ballets, and the cast included Irene Manning, John Archer, Bill Johnson, Estelle Loring, and dancer Hugh Laing. The pleasant musical lasted for 165 performances.

This was followed by one of the most entertaining revues ever produced on Broadway—*Call Me Mister*—satirizing the plight of the returning servicemen and -women from World War II. Produced by Melvyn Douglas and Herman Levin, the revue had a beguiling score by Harold Rome and sharp performances by Betty Garrett, Jules Munshin, Danny Scholl, Bill Callahan, Maria Karnilova, and many others and had a gratifying run of 734 performances.

In 1947 Judith Anderson returned to the National and gave a shattering performance in the title role of *Medea*. Assisted by John Gielgud as Jason and Florence Reed as the Nurse, she brought Robinson Jeffers's adaptation of Euripides' tragedy to painful life. It had a run of 214 performances, still a Broadway record for the classic. Gielgud was in the National's next production, as well, *Crime and Punishment*, costarring Lillian Gish, but the adaptation of Dostoyevsky's novel was not a success. Another failure followed in 1948: Gertrude Lawrence attempted to revive Noël Coward's *Tonight at 8:30*, with young Graham Payn, but it did not come off. That spring

The original cast of *Rent* performs "La Vie Boheme" (1996). (Photo by Joan Marcus)

Michael Redgrave and Flora Robeson revived *Macbeth*, but that, too, failed.

The string of flops was broken in December 1948, when a delirious revue, *Lend an Ear*, written entirely by Charles Gaynor, became an audience favorite. Carol Channing was an overnight success as a loony, wide-eyed blonde in such numbers as "The Gladiola Girl" and "Opera without Music"; and Yvonne Adair, William Eythe, Gene Nelson, and the rest of the cast made this one of the theatre's most fondly remembered revues.

John Garfield and Nancy Kelly starred in Clifford Odets's *The Big Knife*, an exposé of Hollywood, in 1949, but despite excellent per-

formances and expert direction by Lee Strasberg, the play was only a moderate success. The 1940s came to a scintillating end at the National with Sir Cedric Hardwicke and Lilli Palmer in a shimmering revival of Shaw's *Caesar and Cleopatra*, staged by Hardwicke.

Highlights of the 1950s included an appearance by Les Ballets de Paris and Louis Calhern in *King Lear*, both in 1950; Katharine Cornell, Grace George, and Brian Aherne in a highly successful revival of Somerset Maugham's *The Constant Wife* (1951); Tennessee Williams's fascinating but obscure play *Camino Real* (1953), with Eli Wallach as Kilroy; and Margaret

Sullavan, Luella Gear, John Cromwell, and Scott McKay in Samuel Taylor's sterling comedy of manners *Sabrina Fair* (1953).

In 1955 Paul Muni returned to the Broadway stage in one of his finest roles, in *Inherit the Wind*, the Jerome Lawrence/Robert E. Lee play about the sensational Scopes "Monkey Trial." Muni and his costar, Ed Begley, both won Tony Awards for their powerful performances in parts inspired by the great trial lawyer Clarence Darrow (Muni) and by William Jennings Bryan (Begley). The enormous cast also included Bethel Leslie, Muriel Kirkland, Staats Cotsworth, and Tony Randall (who, as artistic director of his own National Actors Theatre, gave the play a major Broadway revival in 1996). Directed by Herman Shumlin, it ran for 806 performances, the longest-running nonmusical in this theatre's history. Muni was succeeded by Melvyn Douglas during the run.

In 1958 Arlene Francis, Joseph Cotten, and Walter Matthau amused audiences for 263 performances in Harry Kurnitz's *Once More with Feeling*. This comedy was the last show to play the National Theatre before it was bought by Billy Rose, who renamed it after himself. A songwriter, producer, and millionaire art collector, Rose spent a fortune refurbishing his new theatre in lush red and gold and reopened it on October 18, 1959, with Maurice Evans, Sam Levene, Diane Cilento, Pamela Brown, Diane Wynyard, and Alan Webb in Shaw's *Heartbreak House*. The revival ran for 112 performances.

The Billy Rose greeted the 1960s with Katharine Cornell in her final play on Broadway before her retirement. It was *Dear Liar*, Jerome Kilty's comedy, with Cornell and Brian Aherne reading letters adapted for the stage from the correspondence of Mrs. Patrick Campbell and George Bernard Shaw. The play ran for only fifty-two performances.

In October 1960 *The Wall*, an adaptation of John Hersey's novel, presented a harrowing story about the Warsaw Ghetto. The cast included George C. Scott, Joseph Buloff, David Opatoshu, and Marian Seldes, and the drama ran for 167 performances.

Edward Albee's first full-length play, *Who's Afraid of Virginia Woolf?*, opened at the Billy Rose on October 14, 1962, and sent shockwaves through Times Square. The stinging drama about a self-destructive married couple, brilliantly played by Uta Hagen and Arthur Hill, and their unfortunate guests—George Grizzard and Melinda Dillon—was the sensation of the season and won Tony Awards for its author, director (Alan Schneider), stars (Hagen and Hill), and producers (Richard Barr and Clinton Wilder). It ran for 664 performances. Two years later Albee tried again at this theatre with a play called *Tiny Alice*, starring John Gielgud and Irene Worth, but not even the actors seemed to understand what this pretentious play was all about.

A series of short plays by Albee and Samuel Beckett was presented at the Billy Rose by the Playwrights Repertory Theatre in 1968, including *Box*, *Krapp's Last Tape*, *The Death of Bessie Smith*, and *Happy Days*, followed by the Minnesota Theatre Company's revivals of *The House of Atreus* and *The Resistible Rise of Arturo Ui*. The decade came to an end with a sleek revival of Noël Coward's *Private Lives*, costarring Brian Bedford and Tammy Grimes, who won a Tony Award for her hoydenish performance as Amanda.

In 1971 the Royal Shakespeare Company's production of *A Midsummer Night's Dream*, directed by Peter Brook, provided great fun; and later that year Harold Pinter's *Old Times*, with Robert Shaw, Rosemary Harris, and Mary Ure, was hailed. In 1974 Brian Bedford and Jill Clayburgh were delightful in Tom Stoppard's buoyant comedy *Jumpers*.

The theatre closed for a year in 1978 but then was bought by James and Joseph Nederlander and the British firm of Cooney-Marsh. It was beautifully refurbished and renamed the Trafalgar. It housed two British hits: *Whose Life Is It Anyway?*, starring Tom Conti, who won a Tony Award for his performance (later replaced in the gender-switched role by Mary Tyler Moore), and Pinter's *Betrayal*, starring Raul Julia, Blythe Danner, and Roy Scheider.

In late 1980 the Trafalgar became the Nederlander Theatre, named in honor of the late theatre owner David Tobias Nederlander, whose scions now operate the Nederlander Organization.

Beginning on May 12, 1981, this theatre housed one of its most distinguished attractions. The incomparable Lena Horne opened in a spectacular personal appearance called *Lena Horne: The Lady and Her Music*. The unforgettable concert program won her a special Tony Award and a special citation from the New York Drama Critics Circle for her singing and the way she recounted the highlights of her brilliant career as the top black star in 1940s Hollywood.

The Nederlander Theatre's subsequent tenants included the charming British import *84 Charing Cross Road*, by Helene Hanff, starring Ellen Burstyn and Joseph Maher; and a musical version of the James Baldwin play *The Amen Corner*.

In 1984 this theatre housed Peter Ustinov's *Beethoven's Tenth*, followed by Glenda Jackson in a revival of Eugene O'Neill's *Strange Interlude* (1985); the musical *Wind in the Willows* (1985), with pre-stardom Nathan Lane and David Carroll; another musical, *Raggedy Ann* (1986); Frank Langella and Donal Donnelly in *Sherlock's Last Case* (1987); Graciela Daniele's dance production *Dangerous Games* (1989); the Hartford Stage Company's production of *Our Country's Good*, under the auspices

Lauren Graham as Miss Adelaide in the 2009 revival of *Guys and Dolls*. (Photo by Carol Rosegg)

of the Broadway Alliance; and Stacy Keach in a dazzling one-man performance in *Solitary Confinement*, a thriller by Rupert Holmes.

On April 29, 1996, a spectacular musical success with a tragic history opened at this theatre. *Rent*, a rock opera inspired by Puccini's *La Bohème*, with music, lyrics, and book by young Jonathan Larson, transferred here from its successful Off-Broadway engagement at New York Theatre Workshop and received a tumultuous reception. Unfortunately, Larson was not alive to enjoy the theatrical triumph of his musical about the preciousness of life and friendship in the face of AIDS and greed. Larson had died January 25, 1996, of an aortic aneurysm after attending the final Off-Broadway dress rehearsal of the show. He was just thirty-five years old.

The Nederlander was a good choice for the anti-establishment *Rent*. Standing geographically apart from the rest of the Broadway theatre district on the far side of the pre-Disney Forty-second Street abutting the (then) seedy Port Authority neighborhood, the site reflected a modicum of the grungy East Village atmosphere that the musical sought to capture onstage. To enhance the environmental staging, the inside of the theatre was redecorated to resemble a downtown club, complete with crumbling, sickly green paint and inlaid shards of mirror. The marquee used only the outline of the word "Rent" over bare fluorescent bulbs. Long after the gentrification decried in *Rent* had transformed the actual Alphabet City and brought it fatally upscale, a facsimile of the original was preserved at the Nederlander like a tattered fly in amber.

Rent immediately became the hottest ticket in town and won the Pulitzer Prize, the Tony Award for Best Musical, and the New York Drama Critics Circle Award for Best Musical. It also won Tony Awards for Best Original Score, Best Book of a Musical, and Featured Actor in a Musical (Wilson Jermaine Heredia).

The producers' policy of setting aside the first two rows of the orchestra as the cheapest seats (not the last row of the mezzanine or balcony, as had been the usual case), made the daily lineup of students and workers on Forty-first Street into a signature Broadway experience of the late 1990s and was widely imitated by other shows. Fans were encouraged to scrawl graffiti on the front of the theatre, and many of them left their names and personal messages to the cast—and to Larson's memory—on the green facade. For many theatergoers who were young during this period (and for many who were young at heart), the Nederlander was the magical place where *Rent* came alive each night. It was more than a theatre; it was a kind of shrine.

Rent settled in for twelve years (1996 to 2008) at the Nederlander Theatre, becoming its longest-running production. One of the Broadway theatres that had been the hardest to book now boasted one of the steadiest rent payers on Broadway.

Rent's grand and bittersweet 5,123rd and final performance on September 8, 2008, was filmed by Sony Pictures as part of a planned series of special events collectively titled "The Hot Tickets." The film, which included documentary footage of the audience out front and the cast backstage, was shown later that same month around the United States.

Dumpsters full of broken lumber and glitter were carted out of the Nederlander during the bleak recession winter of 2008—9, and the theatre was classed up for Des McAnuff's short-lived revival of *Guys and Dolls*, starring Oliver Platt as Nathan Detroit, Craig Bierko as Sky Masterson, Kate Jennings Grant as Sarah Brown, and Lauren Graham as Miss Adelaide. The formerly scruffy flagship of the Nederlander Organization had been transformed with plush fittings including carved wooden panels on the mezzanine walls.

In fall 2009 the Nederlander was scheduled to host an unusual pair of revivals. Neil Simon's semi-autobiographical plays *Brighton Beach Memoirs* and *Broadway Bound* were to be presented in repertory, with much of the cast playing the same roles in the two plays, which were to be performed on alternating nights. Hot young director David Cromer was called up from Off-Broadway to stage the comedies, which were produced by Emanuel Azenberg, who envisioned the productions as "a victory lap" for the prolific eighty-two-year-old Simon. Sadly, the mixed-to-positive reviews did not bring out the ticket buyers, and *Brighton Beach Memoirs* closed abruptly after just nine performances; *Broadway Bound* never played at all, silencing lovely performances from Laurie Metcalf, Dennis Boutsikaris, Noah Robbins, and the rest of the fine ensemble.

On April 11, 2010, the Nederlander hosted the opening of *Million Dollar Quartet*, a transfer of the hit Chicago musical set on December 4, 1956, the night four future rock superstars gathered at the Sun Records studio in Memphis to hash out their differences and play some of their greatest tunes together. Original Chicago stars played the foursome: Eddie Clendening as Elvis Presley, Lance Guest as Johnny Cash, Rob Lyons as Carl Perkins, and Levi Kreis stealing the show as Jerry Lee Lewis. Broadway veteran Hunter Foster joined them in the nonsinging role of Sam Phillips, the record producer who discovered them all.

Beautifully restored and updated by the Nederlander Organization, the Nederlander Theatre is ideal for musicals, concert shows, and large-scale plays.

ETHEL BARRYMORE

THEATRE

IN 1927, WHEN ETHEL BARRYMORE was appearing at Maxine Elliott's Theatre in W. Somerset Maugham's hit play *The Constant Wife*, playwright Zoë Atkins came to her with an irresistible proposition. Atkins said that the Shuberts wanted Barrymore to star in a new play for them—and were willing to build a theatre in her name if she consented. Barrymore read the play, a religious drama called *The Kingdom of God*, liked it, and thereupon agreed to switch to Shubert management.

The Ethel Barrymore Theatre, designed by Herbert J. Krapp, opened on the night of December 20, 1928. The star played Sister Gracia, a character who aged from nineteen to seventy. Wrote Brooks Atkinson in the *New York Times*: "As the curtain raiser for a splen-

Right: PLAYBILL cover for *Lettice and Lovage*.

Left: Ethel Barrymore as Sister Gracia in *The Kingdom of God*, the play that opened the theatre built for her by the Shuberts (1928).

Center: Margalo Gillmore, Jane Seymour, Phyllis Povah, Ilka Chase (displaying her "Jungle Red" nail polish), and Adrienne Marden in Clare Boothe's witches' brew, *The Women* (1936).

did new theatre that fittingly bears her own name, Ethel Barrymore has chosen a quiet and elusive piece by that dexterous Spaniard, G. Martinez Sierra. For Miss Barrymore, it serves as a vehicle." Critic Heywood Broun was more enthusiastic. He wrote: "Miss Barrymore's performance is the most moving piece of acting I have ever seen in the theatre."

With more than one thousand seats, the Barrymore was ideal for dramas, comedies, and intimate musicals. Barrymore chose for her next appearance at her theatre one of those Hungarian romances in which the lovers are named He and She. *The Love Duel*, as it was called, starred Barrymore as She and Louis Calhern as He, and it was directed (as *The Kingdom of God* had been) by E. M. Blythe (who happened to be Ethel Barrymore). This Hungarian trifle ran for eighty-eight performances.

In 1929 John Drinkwater's hit comedy *Bird in Hand* moved to the Barrymore from the Morosco for three months. This was followed by a fascinating drama called *Death Takes a Holiday*, in which Philip Merivale played death on vacation, masquerading as Prince Sirki. Death falls in love with a young mortal named Grazia (Rose Hobart) and takes her with him (willingly) as he returns to "the other side." This fanciful play engrossed theatregoers for 181 performances.

Topaze, a popular comedy, moved here from the Music Box in 1930, with Frank Morgan, Catherine Willard, and Clarence Derwent. Miriam Hopkins appeared very fleetingly in

another of those Hungarian romances, *His Majesty's Car*. Ethel Barrymore returned in blackface to do a play about blacks called *Scarlet Sister Mary*. The critics felt that whites should not attempt to portray blacks when blacks did it so much better, and this curious drama ran for only twenty-three performances. It did, however, serve to introduce Barrymore's daughter, Ethel Barrymore Colt, in her Broadway debut.

The beautiful Billie Burke returned to the stage in Ivor Novello's 1930 play *The Truth* Game, in which the author also appeared. *The Times* labeled the work "a perfect matinee comedy," and audiences flocked to it for 105 performances. The following year brought Edna Best, Basil Rathbone, and Earl Larimore in a French triangle situation, *Melo*, but it was only moderately successful. Later in the year, Ethel Barrymore returned in Lee Shubert's revival of *The School for Scandal*, and this time the actress introduced her son, John Drew Colt, to Broadway.

Socialite/actress Hope Williams starred in something called *The Passing Present* in 1931, with Maria Ouspenskaya, but this made way after 16 performances for a more deserving production, *Whistling in the Dark*. Starring the amusing Ernest Truex as a detective story writer who is forced by a gang of gunmen to concoct a perfect crime, the comedy delighted Barrymore patrons for 144 performances.

Here Today, a "comedy of bad manners," by George Oppenheimer, directed by George S. Kaufman, amused first-nighters in September 1932 mainly because the acid-mouth character played by Ruth Gordon was supposed to be no less than acid-mouth Dorothy Parker. But the general public did not take to this evening of bitchiness and the play folded after thirty-nine performances. John Van Druten's more civilized comedy hit *There's Always Juliet* moved here next from Henry Miller's Theatre.

On November 29, 1932, the Barrymore Theatre housed its first musical, Cole Porter's *Gay Divorce*. Fred Astaire, without his sister

Above: PLAYBILL for Wendy Wasserstein's *The Sisters Rosensweig* (1993).

Center: Vivienne Segal and Gene Kelly in the "amoral" *Pal Joey* (1940).

Right: Marlon Brando rapes Jessica Tandy in *A Streetcar Named Desire* (1947).

Adele for the first time, danced with the blonde Claire Luce, who once rode a live ostrich in the *Ziegfeld Follies*. Astaire and Luce singing and dancing Porter's haunting "Night and Day" helped to turn this into a hit. The scintillating cast included the venomous Luella Gear and the wry Eric Blore and Erik Rhodes, who would repeat their roles when Astaire appeared in the movie version, slightly retitled *The Gay Divorcee*. The stage version had to move to the Shubert Theatre to make way for another event at the Barrymore but rang up a total of 248 performances.

On January 24, 1933, Alfred Lunt, Lynn Fontanne, and Noël Coward dazzled first-nighters in *Design for Living*, a comedy Coward had promised to write for them and himself as a starring vehicle. Coward, who did not relish long runs, limited this engagement to 135 performances, but it could have run all season. The play presented two men in love with the same woman but, when she was not available, in love with each other. One critic described this as the most amoral situation ever viewed on the Broadway stage. It proved an acting triumph for this gilded trio.

A mystery play, *Ten-Minute Alibi*, with Bramwell Fletcher, John Williams, and Joseph Spurin-Calleia, was a moderate success in the fall of 1933. This was succeeded by *Jezebel*, a southern drama by Owen Davis, originally written for Tallulah Bankhead. When she became ill, Miriam Hopkins stepped in, but the play was not a success. It later made an excellent film for Bette Davis.

The year 1934 was not a bountiful one for this theatre. No fewer than seven failures paraded across its stage. Theatregoers looked

forward to Noël Coward's *Point Valaine*, starring the Lunts, Osgood Perkins, Louis Hayward, and Broderick Crawford, in January 1935, but the play was sordid and overly melodramatic, with Lunt spitting in Fontanne's face in one scene. This turgid tale of tropical lust expired none too soon after fifty-six performances.

The hit play *The Distaff Side* moved here from the Longacre Theatre in March 1935. Later in the year, Philip Merivale and his wife, Gladys Cooper, brought their revivals of *Othello* and *Macbeth*, but they were not successful. A historical play, *Parnell*, with George Curzon as the Irish hero, fared better, playing for ninety-eight performances. Irwin Shaw provided excitement in 1936 with his one-act war play *Bury the Dead*, paired with another short work, *Prelude*, by J. Edward Shugrue and John O'Shaughnessy, which moved theatregoers for ninety-seven performances. In the fall of 1936, the British playwright/actor Emlyn Williams starred in his terrifying *Night Must Fall*, based on an actual case in the British courts. He played a charming psychopath who carries around the head of one of his victims in a hatbox. May Whitty (later Dame May Whitty) played his intended next victim.

On December 26, 1936, Clare Boothe Luce's play *The Women* opened at this theatre with about forty women in the cast and not one male. Critic Brooks Atkinson called it "a kettle of venom" in *The New York Times* and said he disliked it. It promptly became the Barrymore's longest running play to date, keeping that kettle bubbling for 657 performances, with such brittle actresses as Ilka Chase, Margalo Gillmore, Betty Lawford, Arlene Francis, Audrey Christie, and Marjorie Main.

In October 1938 the Playwrights' Company presented the Maxwell Anderson/Kurt Weill musical *Knickerbocker Holiday*, starring Walter Huston as Peter Stuyvesant. It is chiefly remembered today for Huston's magnificent rendition of the classic "September Song."

The spring of 1939 brought Katharine Cornell in a rarity—a modern comedy by S. N. Behrman called *No Time for Comedy*. Laurence Olivier costarred as her playwright husband who is swayed by his mistress (Margalo Gillmore) to switch from writing hit comedies and instead attempt a stuffy drama. The public took to Cornell in high-fashion gowns by Valentina, and the comedy ran for 185 performances, with Olivier turning into a matinee idol.

The last show to play this theatre in the 1930s was Maxwell Anderson's *Key Largo*, a moderate hit with Paul Muni, Uta Hagen, José Ferrer, and Carl (later Karl) Malden. It ran for 105 performances.

Highlights of the 1940s at the Barrymore included Ethel Barrymore's last appearance at her theatre, in a weak play by Vincent Sheean called *An International Incident*. On Christmas night 1940, Rodgers and Hart and John O'Hara

brought in a landmark musical that shocked some of the critics. It was *Pal Joey*, the tough chronicle of a Chicago heel (Gene Kelly) who is kept by a rich adulteress (Vivienne Segal). The memorable score contained "Bewitched, Bothered and Bewildered," "I Could Write a Book," and some great musical comedy numbers that stopped the show. The cast also included June Havoc, Van Johnson, Leila Ernst, and Jack Durant. It ran for 270 performances. When it was revived in the 1950s, it shocked no one and it played a triumphant 540 performances, the longest Broadway run of any Rodgers and Hart show.

George Abbott, who produced and staged *Pal Joey*, brought another musical hit here on October 1, 1941: the prep-school show *Best Foot Forward*, detailing what happens when a movie queen visits a campus as a publicity stunt. The star was Rosemary Lane, but the show was stolen by Nancy Walker, June Allyson, and Maureen Cannon as students. It ran for 326 performances.

This was followed by a musical failure, *Count Me In*, written by Walter Kerr (before he was a critic) and Leo Brady, with such talents as Charles Butterworth, Luella Gear, Hal LeRoy, Mary Healy, and Gower and Jeanne (Champion).

The early 1940s are remembered for Katharine Cornell's production of Chekhov's *The Three Sisters* (1942), in which she starred with Ruth Gordon and Judith Anderson. The distinguished cast also included Gertrude Musgrove, Dennis King, Edmund Gwenn, Alexander Knox, McKay Morris, Kirk Douglas, Tom Powers, and Marie Paxton. This splendid production was directed by Cornell's husband, Guthrie McClintic, and played for 123 performances. Ralph Bellamy and Shirley Booth appeared in an enormous success, *Tomorrow the World*, by James Gow and

Left: Gertrude Lawrence makes a fair lady in Shaw's *Pygmalion* (1945 revival).

Center: Alfred Lunt, Lynn Fontanne, and Noël Coward in Coward's ménage-a-trois comedy *Design for Living* (1933).

Right: Gertrude Musgrove, Judith Anderson, Katharine Cornell in *The Three Sisters* (1942).

Zoë Wanamaker had an unusual hit with Sophocles' *Electra* (1998).

Top left: Hume Cronyn marries Jessica Tandy in the long-running comedy *The Fourposter* (1951).

Top center: Katharine Hepburn at the ivories and Dorothy Loudon on the fiddle in *West Side Waltz* (1981).

Top right: Deborah Kerr is kind to John Kerr in *Tea and Sympathy* (1953).

Philip Merivale as the Grim Reaper prepares to take Rose Hobart with him to the "other side" in *Death Takes a Holiday* (1929).

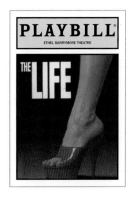

Cy Coleman and Ira Gasman's musical, *The Life* (1997).

Arnaud d'Usseau in 1943, which showed what happened to members of an American family who sheltered a twelve-year-old boy (Skippy Homeier) brought up in Germany as a Nazi.

A series of revivals played this theatre in the mid-1940s: Katharine Cornell and Brian Aherne in *The Barretts of Wimpole Street* (1945); Gertrude Lawrence, Raymond Massey and Melville Cooper in *Pygmalion* (1945); Elisabeth Bergner, John Carradine, and Canada Lee in *The Duchess of Malfi* (1946); and José Ferrer in his acclaimed revival of *Cyrano de Bergerac*, which moved here from the Alvin Theatre (1946).

Gian-Carlo Menotti's twin opera bill, *The Telephone* and *The Medium* (1947), received high praise, especially for Marie Powers's electrifying performance in the latter.

On December 3, 1947, the Barrymore Theatre presented its most distinguished offering, Tennessee Williams's *A Streetcar Named Desire*, one of the greatest plays of the twentieth century. Jessica Tandy won a Tony Award for her unforgettable performance as Blanche DuBois, and the inspired acting of Marlon Brando, Kim Hunter, and Karl Malden made this a historic night in the American theatre. The haunting drama won the Pulitzer Prize and the New York Drama Critics Circle Award for best play of the season and ran for 855 performances. During the run, Anthony Quinn and Uta Hagen succeeded Brando and Tandy.

Gian-Carlo Menotti returned in 1950 with another superb opera, *The Consul*, a harrowing work about postwar Europe, with magnificent performances by Patricia Neway and Marie Powers. Irene Mayer Selznick, who produced *A Streetcar Named Desire*, piloted another hit at this theatre in 1950 when she presented Rex Harrison and his then-wife, Lili Palmer, in John Van Druten's beguiling comedy about witchcraft, *Bell, Book and Candle*. The silken duo enchanted

audiences for 233 performances. Another huge hit opened on October 24, 1951, when Jessica Tandy and her husband, Hume Cronyn, starred in Jan de Hartog's two-character comedy *The Fourposter*, which won a Tony Award as the season's Best Play and another Tony for its director, José Ferrer. The play, about events in the thirty-five-year married life of a couple simply named Agnes and Michael, ran for 632 performances. It was later adapted as the musical *I Do! I Do!*

A spirited revival of Shaw's *Misalliance*, with William Redfield, Roddy McDowall, Richard Kiley, Tamara Geva, and Jerome Kilty, moved here from the New York City Center in 1953. Later that year, Robert Anderson's first Broadway play, *Tea and Sympathy*, with Deborah Kerr, John Kerr, and Leif Erickson, presented a poignant study of a young prep-school student who is suspected of being gay in an extremely closeted era. One of the first broadly popular plays to deal with this formerly taboo subject, the drama ran for 712 performances. John Kerr won a Tony Award for his performance.

In February 1955 Paul Newman returned to the stage in a thriller by Joseph Hayes called *The Desperate Hours*. It was one of those plays in which criminals hide out in a pleasant family's house and terrorize them. The excellent cast also included Karl Malden, Nancy Coleman, Patricia Peardon, George Grizzard, James Gregory, and Mary Orr. *The Desperate Hours* won a Tony Award as Best Play Production and also one for Robert Montgomery's direction.

Marcel Marceau played an engagement here in 1955, followed by another Irene Mayer Selznick production, the exquisite Enid Bagnold play *The Chalk Garden*, with sparkling performances by Gladys Cooper, Fritz Weaver, Siobhan McKenna, Betsy von Furstenberg, Percy Waram, and Marian Seldes. The unusual drama played for 182 performances.

Left: Rex Harrison seduces Lili Palmer in *Bell, Book and Candle* (1950).

Center: The cast of *The Life* (1997) recreated the underworld of 1970s Times Square.

Right: Judi Dench won a Tony Award for her performance in *Amy's View* (1999).

The British actress Maggie Smith made her Broadway debut at the Barrymore in June 1956 as one of Leonard Sillman's *New Faces of 1956*. But it was female impersonator T. C. Jones who drew raves for his embodiments of Tallulah Bankhead, Bette Davis, and other stars, and who kept the revue running for 220 performances.

The Barrymore's next hit was Ketti Frings's 1957 dramatization of Thomas Wolfe's *Look Homeward, Angel*, which was awarded the Pulitzer Prize and the New York Drama Critics Circle Award for Best Play. It starred Anthony Perkins, Jo Van Fleet, Arthur Hill, Hugh Griffith, Rosemary Murphy, and others, and ran for 564 performances. Another fine drama, *A Raisin in the Sun*, by Lorraine Hansberry, opened here in March 1959, starring Sidney Poitier, Claudia McNeil, Diana Sands, Ruby Dee, and Louis Gossett. This drama, about a black family's struggles to take its place in the middle class in white America, won the New York Drama Critics Circle Award for Best Play and had a run of 530 performances.

The smash hit comedy *A Majority of One*, starring Gertrude Berg and Cedric Hardwicke, moved here in 1959 from the Shubert Theatre and stayed for eight months. Some highlights of the 1960s included Henry Fonda and Mildred Natwick in Ira Levin's comedy *Critic's Choice* (1960); Michael Redgrave, Sandy Dennis, and Googie Withers in Graham Greene's comedy *The Complaisant Lover* (1961); Henry Fonda and Olivia de Havilland in Garson Kanin's play *A Gift of Time* (1962); James Baldwin's play *The Amen Corner* (1965); Lee Remick and Robert Duvall in Frederick Knott's thriller *Wait Until Dark* (1966); an engagement of *Les Ballets Africains* (1966); Peter Shaffer's offbeat twin bill—*Black Comedy* and *White Lies* (1967)—with Geraldine Page, Lynn Redgrave, Donald Madden, Michael Crawford, Peter Bull, and Camila Ashland; *Noël Coward's*

Sweet Potato (1968), a revue of Coward's songs with Dorothy Loudon, George Grizzard, Carole Shelley, and Arthur Mitchell; and a revival of *The Front Page* with Robert Ryan, Bert Convy, Doro Merande, Peggy Cass, and Julia Meade (Helen Hayes later joined the cast) in 1969.

The 1970s brought to this theatre *Conduct Unbecoming* (1970), the British thriller with Jeremy Clyde and Michael Barrington; Alec McCowen in *The Philanthropist* (1971); Melvin Van Peebles's vignettes of black life, titled *Ain't Supposed to Die a Natural Death* (1971); Pirandello's Emperor *Henry IV* (1973), with Rex Harrison; the New Phoenix Repertory Company with revivals of *The Visit, Chemin de Fer*, and *Holiday* (1973); Jessica Tandy, Hume Cronyn, and Anne Baxter in two plays by Noël Coward, *Noël Coward in Two Keys* (1974); John Wood's Tony Award performance in Tom Stoppard's *Travesties* (1975), which also won a Tony Award for Best Play; Robert Duvall in David Mamet's *American Buffalo* (1977), winner of the New York Drama Critics Circle Award for Best Play; the inventive musical *I Love My Wife* (1977), by Michael Stewart and Cy Coleman; Anthony Perkins and Mia Farrow in Bernard Slade's *Romantic Comedy* (1979); Jean Kerr's *Lunch Hour* (1980), with Sam Waterston and Gilda Radner; Katharine Hepburn and Dorothy Loudon in Ernest Thompson's *The West Side Waltz* (1981); and Jessica Tandy, Hume Cronyn, and Keith Carradine in *Foxfire*, by Cronyn and Susan Cooper. Tandy won a Tony Award for her performance in this play with music.

In December 1983 the musical *Baby* arrived, based on a story developed by Susan Yankowitz, with a book by Sybille Pearson, music by David Shire, and lyrics by Richard Maltby Jr. The interesting entertainment, about a group of expectant parents, received several Tony nominations and ran for 241 performances.

The following year, David Rabe's scabrous play about Hollywood vermin, *Hurlyburly*, transferred here from Off-Broadway and starred William Hurt, Harvey Keitel, Ron Silver, Jerry Stiller, Sigourney Weaver, Cynthia Nixon, and Judith Ivey. Directed by Mike Nichols, the play ran for 343 performances and won a Tony Award for Ivey as Best Featured Actress. During its run, the following stars succeeded members of the original cast: Candice Bergen, John Christopher Jones, John Rubinstein, Christine Baranski, Frank Langella, and Danny Aiello.

In January 1986 Zoe Caldwell starred in *Lillian*, a one-woman show by William Luce about writer Lillian Hellman. When the curtain rose on the opening night, there was a gasp in the audience at Caldwell's remarkable makeup, which made her the spitting image of the fiery authoress.

Social Security, a popular comedy by Andrew Bergman, arrived on April 17, 1986, with this interesting cast: Ron Silver, Marlo Thomas, Joanna Gleason, Kenneth Welsh, Olympia Dukakis, and Stefan Schnabel. Directed by Mike Nichols, the comedy, about a senior citizen who embarks on her last fling with an artist, played here for a year.

An arresting, mystical play, *Joe Turner's Come and Gone* by August Wilson, opened on March 27, 1988. Part of Wilson's epic cycle of plays about black life in America during the twentieth century, it was directed by Lloyd Richards and won a Tony Award for L. Scott Caldwell as Best Featured Actress in a Play. The following year, ballet superstar Mikhail Baryshnikov made his Broadway debut playing a giant insect in Kafka's *Metamorphosis* and was nominated for a Tony Award.

David Hare's play *The Secret Rapture* (October 26, 1989) caused a brouhaha, not as a play, but as an altercation between the playwright and *New York Times* critic Frank Rich, who wrote a devastating review of it. Hare wrote a scathing letter to the critic, which somehow got published in newspapers, and the result was much publicity for a play that ran for only ten performances.

On March 25, 1990, a delirious theatrical event occurred at the Barrymore Theatre. The volatile actress Maggie Smith arrived in her London hit *Lettice & Lovage* by the British playwright Peter Shaffer. The scintillating comedy, about a tour guide who embellishes history with fiction to make it more interesting, won Tony Awards for Smith and Margaret Tyzack (who had

appeared in the play in London with Smith). This sparkling theatrical experience ran here for a sold-out ten months and could have run longer if the two actresses had continued to be available.

On February 14, 1991, *Mule Bone* received its long-delayed Broadway debut. Written in 1930 by Langston Hughes and Zora Neale Hurston, it had never been performed because of a dispute between the authors. This production had a prologue and epilogue by George Houston Bass and music by Taj Mahal. It ran for sixty-seven performances.

In 1992 the classic *A Streetcar Named Desire* returned to the Barrymore, this time starring Alec Baldwin and Jessica Lange with Amy Madigan and Timothy Carhart. Directed by Gregory Mosher, it had a limited run of four months and garnered a Tony nomination for Baldwin.

Wendy Wasserstein's popular Off-Broadway play *The Sisters Rosensweig* moved here on March 18, 1993, from the Mitzi E. Newhouse Theatre at Lincoln Center with its original cast, including Jane Alexander, Madeline Kahn (Tony Award), and Robert Klein. It enjoyed a 556-performance run at the Barrymore.

A curious play opened here on April 27, 1995. Called *Indiscretions*, it was Jeremy Sams's translation of Jean Cocteau's play *Les Parents Terribles*. It had an impressive cast—Kathleen Turner, Eileen Atkins, Jude Law, Roger Rees and Cynthia Nixon—and was directed by Sean Mathias. According to *Variety*, the drama, which featured incest and male nudity (from future film star Law), received fifteen favorable reviews, two mixed and four unfavorable. It ran for 220 performances and received the following Tony Award nominations: Best Actor in a Play (Rees), Best Actress in a Play (Atkins), Best Featured Actor (Law), Best Featured Actress (Nixon), Best Play, Best Director of a Play (Mathias), Best Scenic Designer (Stephen Brimson Lewis), Best Costume Designer (also Lewis), and Best Lighting Designer (Mark Henderson).

The next tenant at the Barrymore was Oscar Wilde's *An Ideal Husband*, which had not been produced on Broadway since 1918. The 1895 play dealt with political blackmail in London's high society. This production found favor with critics and audiences for 309 performances. Martin Shaw, who played Lord Goring, was highly praised for his witty performance and was nominated for a Tony Award. Other Tony nominations went to Peter Hall for his direction and to Bill

Left to right, Cass Morgan, Lari White, and Beth Malone sing "Orleans Parish Prison" in the Johnny Cash musical revue, *Ring of Fire* (2006). (Photo by Joan Marcus)

Kenwright for producing a Best Revival of a Play.

A raucous musical exploded next at the Barrymore on April 26, 1997. *The Life*, with music by Cy Coleman, lyrics by Ira Gasman, and a book by Gasman, David Newman, and Coleman, had been previously produced Off-Off-Broadway at the Westbeth Theater Center. It was a seamy look at the sordid life led by hookers in the Times Square area before the Disney-led 1990s cleanup. *The Life* received what George S. Kaufman once called "mixed reviews—good and lousy." One critic called it a morality tale in which everyone pays for their sins. Coleman's songs were praised, and so was the gritty cast. The musical ran for 466 performances and won Tony Awards for two of its featured performers: Lillias White and Chuck Cooper. Other Tony nominations included Best Actress in a Musical (Pamela Isaacs), Best Featured Actor in Musical (Sam Harris), Best Musical Book (Gasman, Newman, and Coleman), Best Musical, Best Musical Director (Michael Blakemore), Best Costume Designer (Martin Pakledinaz), Best Lighting Designer (Richard Pilbrow), Best Choreographer (Joey McKneely), Best Score (Coleman and Gasman), and Best Orchestrations (Don Sebesky and Harold Wheeler).

From Forty-second Street mayhem, the Barrymore went to ancient Greek violence for its next attraction. On December 3, 1998, a splendid production of Sophocles' *Electra* opened with a magnificent cast including Zoë Wanamaker, Claire Bloom, Michael Cumpsty, Pat Carroll, and Stephen Spinella. Wanamaker, who had won an Olivier Award in London for her commanding performance as Electra, was nominated for a Tony Award, as was Bloom as her mother, Clytemnestra. With a new translation by Frank McGuinness, the play also received a nomination for Best Revival. Some critics found Wanamaker's costume—an oversized trench coat and a fright wig—somewhat bizarre, but her frenzied performance was praised, as were the startling, bloody stage effects. Due to overwhelming ticket demand, the limited engagement was extended an additional nine weeks. The 2,400-year-old play recouped its investment in six weeks, a modern record for a Greek classic.

Another London hit opened at the Barrymore on April 15, 1999: David Hare's *Amy's View*, starring a radiant Judi Dench as a veteran actress who has problems with a grown daughter and with the irritations of contemporary society. For her acclaimed performance, Dench won a Tony

Left to right, Nathan Lane as an embattled president and Dylan Baker as his chief of staff in David Mamet's 2008 comedy, *November*. (Photo by Scott Landis)

Award as Best Actress in a Play. Samantha Bond, who played her daughter, received a nomination as a Best Supporting Actress in a Play. The show ran for 103 performances.

The next show at the Barrymore Theatre had a complex history. Called *Putting It Together—A Musical Review* [sic], it showcased a rich collection of songs with words and music by Stephen Sondheim. The show originated in 1992 as a Cameron Mackintosh production in Oxford, England. He produced a revised version of the revue in 1993 at the Manhattan Theater Club Off-Broadway, starring Julie Andrews. In the fall of 1998 he produced still another version of the musical at the Mark Taper Forum in Los Angeles. Starring Carol Burnett, it broke every one of that theatre's box office records. On November 21, 1999, it opened at the Barrymore with Burnett, George Hearn, John Barrowman, Ruthie Henshall, Bronson Pinchot—and, at certain performances, talk-show hostess Kathie Lee Gifford, substituting for Burnett. It did not repeat the success it had enjoyed at the Mark Taper Forum. Some critics did not feel that Burnett was an ideal Sondheim singer, and they also disliked the show's frame for Sondheim's celebrated songs. It ran for 101 performances and was videotaped in the new high-definition format.

The highly anticipated engagement of the new Donmar Warehouse production of Tom Stoppard's *The Real Thing* opened here on April 17, 2000, and repeated the great success it had achieved in England. The play starred the lauded Donmar cast led by Stephen Dillane, Jennifer Ehle, Nigel Lindsay, and Sarah Woodward, all making their Broadway debuts, and was directed by David Leveaux. The play dealt with marriage and writing, emotional fidelity and intellectual integrity, high art and pop culture, and truth and acting, both onstage and in real life. *The Real Thing* won the following Tony Awards: Best Revival, Best Performance by a Leading Actor in a Play (Stephen Dillane), and Best Performance by a Leading Actress in a Play (Jennifer Ehle).

In late fall 2000 the Barrymore hosted the transfer of a more successful Manhattan Theatre Club show: *The Tale of the Allergist's Wife*, which featured Linda Lavin, Michele Lee, and Tony Roberts, and marked the Broadway playwriting debut of Charles Busch, previously known for his Off-Broadway campfests, including *Vampire Lesbians of Sodom*. *Tale* got told a lucky 777 times.

The rivalry between writers Lillian Hellman and Mary McCarthy inspired a December 2002 musical experiment called *Imaginary Friends*, a "play with music" by Nora Ephron, with original songs by Marvin Hamlisch and Craig Carnelia. Swoosie Kurtz and Cherry Jones played the literary lionesses in this ahead-of-its-time curiosity that turned to song and dance only when it wanted to. Unable to pigeonhole it, audiences stayed away, and the run ended after just seventy-six showings.

April 30, 2003, saw the return of Oscar Wilde's *Salome* in a version Al Pacino had been exploring in New York and regionally for a decade. With Dianne Wiest as Herodias, and

Marisa Tomei performing the Dance of the Seven Veils in the title role, this "Staged Reading" version lasted forty performances.

Sly Fox, Larry Gelbart's Americanized adaptation of Molière's *Volpone*, got a Broadway revival on April 1, 2004, with Richard Dreyfuss as con man Foxwell J. Sly, supported by a sparkling cast of New York and Hollywood character actors including Bob Dishy, René Auberjonois, Elizabeth Berkley, Professor Irwin Corey, Bronson Pinchot, and Rachel York. Audiences laughed for 173 performances.

Charm replaced laughter for the March 22, 2005, revival of Tennessee Williams's *The Glass Menagerie*, featuring Jessica Lange as Amanda, Christian Slater as her son, Sarah Paulson as Laura, and Josh Lucas as the Gentleman Caller. Directed by David Leveaux, it lasted four months.

Richard Maltby Jr. had enjoyed Tony-winning success with the Fats Waller revue *Ain't Misbehavin'*. On November 29, 2006, he attempted a similar tribute to country music icon Johnny Cash in the revue *Ring of Fire*. But producers discovered that the Man in Black just didn't have as big a following in the city as he did in the country. The cast shed "Bitter Tears" after just fifty-seven performances.

John Doyle had enjoyed Tony-winning success with a version of Stephen Sondheim's *Sweeney Todd* that made the actors double as the orchestra. He tried the formula again at the Barrymore on November 29, 2006, with a revival of Sondheim's *Company*, starring Raúl Esparza as uncertain bachelor Bobby. It was named Best Revival of a Musical and ran 246 performances.

The rock group Duran Duran hoped to kick off the release of its new album with the concert show *Duran Duran: Red Carpet Massacre* here in November 2007, but the show arrived just in time to be shuttered by a stagehands strike. *Massacre* did not resume after the strike was settled.

A rare David Mamet comedy arrived at the Barrymore January 17, 2008. Titled *November*, it parodied presidential politics. Running catastrophically behind in a race for reelection, President Charles Smith (Nathan Lane) tries to turn a ritual pardoning of a Thanksgiving turkey into a source of cash and publicity. Laurie Metcalf and Dylan Baker were among the bright supporting cast, and the show stayed through the summer of the real presidential race, totaling 205 performances.

Speed-the-Plow, Mamet's vivisection of

West Coast showbiz decision makers, got a creditable revival here on October 23, 2008, notable primarily for Raúl Esparza's performance as Charlie Fox, which went off like a string of firecrackers. But tabloids pulled back the curtain on a bit of East Coast showbiz, as well, when Esparza's costar Jeremy Piven abruptly quit the show. He claimed mercury poisoning from eating too much sushi. The departure was eventually blessed by an arbitrator after producers filed a complaint with the union. But for months that excuse was used as a punch line by late-night comedians and

Left to right, Susan Sarandon, William Sadler, Geoffrey Rush, Brian Hutchison, Lauren Ambrose, and Andrea Martin in the 2009 revival of the absurdist play *Exit the King*. (Photo by Joan Marcus)

even referenced at the following year's Tony Awards. Mamet himself cracked that Piven had left to take a job as a thermometer.

Absurdist master Eugene Ionesco found himself with a Broadway hit in March 2009, fifteen years after his death: *Exit the King*, about a group of courtiers trying to hasten the end of their sovereign as their unnamed country (and the palace itself) crumbles around them. Geoffrey Rush earned the 2009 Tony Award as Best Actor in a Play for his performance as spectral King Berenger, clad only in a crown and long underwear. The sterling supporting cast included

Susan Sarandon, Lauren Ambrose, and Andrea Martin, and they helped draw crowds through the ninety-three-performance limited run.

The third Mamet play in less than two years arrived at the Barrymore on December 6, 2009, and it was the most explosive of the three: *Race*, a drama about a multiracial law firm that takes on a white client involved in a crime against a black woman.

The Barrymore was the last of the pre-Depression playhouses to be built and remains one of the few Broadway theatres that has never changed name or owner.

EUGENE O'NEILL

THEATRE

THE EUGENE O'NEILL THEATRE AT 230 West Forty-ninth Street originated as the Forrest Theatre in 1925. It was named after one of America's greatest classical actors, Edwin Forrest, whose bitter feud with the classical British actor William Charles Macready ignited the tragic 1849 riot at the Astor Place Opera House in New York City. In the course of that event twenty-two persons were killed and more than one hundred wounded.

The Forrest Theatre was built by the Shuberts and designed in the Georgian style by architect Herbert J. Krapp. The capacity was 1,200, making it flexible for the staging of dramas or musical comedies. Unfortunately, the new theatre began with a string of flops. The theatre opened officially on November 25, 1925,

with a musical comedy called *Mayflowers*, starring Ivy Sawyer, Joseph Santley, and a newcomer named Nancy Carroll, who would later become a movie star. The *New York Times* labeled the show "attractive," but it lasted for only eighty-one performances.

After *Mayflowers*, the theatre housed such short-lived shows as *The Matinee Girl*, *Mama Loves Papa*, *Rainbow Rose*, and *My Country*.

After six more very short-lived plays in 1927, the Forrest finally had a hit with a drama called *Women Go On Forever*. Produced by William A. Brady Jr. and Dwight Deere Wiman, the play featured this impressive cast: Mary Boland, Osgood Perkins, Douglass Montgomery, and James Cagney. A seamy, realistic play that the *Times* found "cheap and malodorous," the show attracted the public for 118 performances.

After that, the Forrest reverted to potboilers whose very titles denoted their doom: *Bless You, Sister*; *Mirrors*; *It Is to Laugh*; *The Skull*; *Fast Life*; *The Common Sin*; *The Squealer*; and *Café de Danse*, all from December 1927 to December 1928. Ruth St. Denis and Ted Shawn brought some class to the house with their dancing in 1929, and things brightened a bit when the popular comedy *Bird in Hand*, by John Drinkwater, transferred here from the Masque Theatre in 1930.

The Blue Ghost, a mystery play, managed

to run for 112 performances in 1930, possibly because it was the only creepy show in town. Ushers at the Forrest Theatre wore blue hoods over their heads to get the audience in the proper shivery mood, but the *New York Times* declared that after that device they expected the worst—and got it.

A farce, *Stepping Sisters*, about three ex-queens of burlesque, moved to the Forrest from the Royale Theatre in August 1930 and stayed for two months. In October of that year, the theatre suddenly became Edgar Wallace's Forrest Theatre when Wallace's play *On the Spot* opened there. This gangster play, with Anna May Wong and Glenda Farrell, was the theatre's biggest hit thus far, running for 167 performances.

A terrible farce called *In the Best of Families* was pronounced dull and dirty by Brooks Atkinson of the *Times*, so it ran for 141 performances, moving to the Forrest from the Bijou in March 1931. From October of that year until November of 1932, this theatre housed seven plays of such mediocrity that none of them ran for more than thirty-six performances and four ran for fewer than twelve performances.

Things picked up a bit in 1932 when the Helen Hayes/Walter Connolly hit *The Good Fairy* moved here from Henry Miller's Theatre and stayed for two months. A revival of Rachel Crothers's comedy *As Husbands Go* chalked up 144 performances in 1933. The Ballets Jooss played a gratifying engagement from October to December of 1933.

From January through August 1934 the

Clockwise from top left: Betty Field and Wendell Corey in Elmer Rice's bewitching comedy *Dream Girl* (1945). A formal portrait of the turnip-eating Jeeter Lester family in *Tobacco Road*. Steve Cochran comes up to see Mae West in a revival of her *Diamond Lil* (1949). Arthur Miller outside the O'Neill for the opening of the fiftieth anniversary revival of *Death of a Salesman* (1999).

Top left: Standard program cover for the Forrest Theatre in the 1920s.

Top center: Ed Begley (seated) and Arthur Kennedy in Arthur Miller's first success, *All My Sons* (1947).

Top right: Van Heflin, Jack Warden (holding chair), Eileen Heckart, (in background:) Gloria Marlowe, and Richard Davalos, in Arthur Miller's *A View from the Bridge* (1955).

Far right, bottom: The male cast of the musical *The Full Monty* (2000). (Photo by Carol Rosegg)

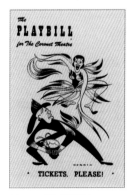

Above: PLAYBILL cover for Paul and Grace Hartman's hit revue, *Tickets, Please!* (1950).

Forrest had seven flops, including a lavish musical romance, *Caviar*, with dancer Jack Cole in the cast, and a musical revue, *Keep Moving*, starring Tom Howard. Then in September 1934 a bonanza finally arrived at this theatre. It was *Tobacco Road*, Jack Kirkland's shocking dramatization of Erskine Caldwell's novel of the same name, which had opened at the Masque Theatre on December 5, 1933. Starring Henry Hull as Jeeter Lester, Margaret Wycherly as Ada, and Dean Jagger as Lou, this seamy play, which many critics disliked, stayed at the Forrest from September 1934 until May 31, 1941. When it ended its marathon run at the Forrest, it had played for 3,182 performances, making it the longest-running play in the history of the American theatre up to that time. Today it is second only to *Life with Father* (3,224 performances) among nonmusicals. Henry Hull was succeeded by the following actors during *Tobacco Road*'s record run: James Barton, James Bell, Eddie Garr, and Will Geer. *Tobacco Road* came back to the Forrest in 1942 after a long road tour, and then John Barton, son of James, was playing Jeeter Lester. But the return engagement lasted only thirty-four performances. Audiences had had enough of squalor, sex, and turnips in this drama about Georgia "crackers." Meanwhile, the mayor of Chicago had deemed the play too dirty to be staged there, and Rhode Island and the

American South had made the same decision.

The 1940s at the Forrest reverted to the unfortunate booking of a series of flop shows. Occasionally, hits from another theatre, such as *Three Men on a Horse* and *Claudia*, played there, but usually they were clinkers like *Bright Lights of 1944*; *Manhattan Nocturne*; *Topical Revue*; *Listen, Professor*; *Dark Hammock*; and *Hand in Glove*. The last show to play the Forrest before it changed its name was a comedy called *The Overtons* (1945), which moved in from the Booth. It played for three months at the Forrest before the theatre closed for extensive renovations.

In 1945 City Playhouses, Inc., with Louis A. Lotito as managing director, bought the Forrest

In January 1947 Arthur Miller's first successful play, *All My Sons*, opened here and stayed for 328 performances. The cast featured Ed Begley, Arthur Kennedy, Karl Malden, and Lois Wheeler. Brooks Atkinson in the *New York Times* wrote: "With the production of *All My Sons* at the Coronet . . . the theatre has acquired a new talent . . . Arthur Miller."

For a change of pace, the Coronet next booked a revue, *Angel in the Wings* (1947), and it was one of the season's big hits. Starring the infectious dance satirists Paul and Grace Hartman, assisted by Hank Ladd, Elaine Stritch, Nadine Gae, Johnny Barnes, and others, the revue cheered audiences for 308 performances. Another bright revue, *Small Wonder* (1948), followed this, and its scintillating cast included Tom Ewell, Alice Pearce, Mary McCarthy, Jack Cassidy, Joan Diener, and Jonathan Lucas. Staged by Burt Shevelove and choreographed by Gower Champion, it pleased revue lovers for 134 performances.

The indestructible Mae West revived her play *Diamond Lil* with sumptuous sets and gaudy costumes in February 1949, and the public flocked to it for 181 performances.

Maurice Evans was featured in Terence Rattigan's double bill of *The Browning Version* and *A Harlequinade*, costarring with Edna Best, but the Peter Glenville production lasted only sixty-nine showings. After two unsuccessful plays (*Happy as Larry* and *The Bird Cage*) the Coronet had another hit revue with the Hartmans—*Tickets, Please!*—in the spring of 1950. Their cast this time included Jack Albertson, Tommy Wonder, Larry Kert, and Dorothy Jarnac. The Hartmans' formula paid off for 245 performances.

Other 1950s highlights at this theatre included Jessica Tandy, Beulah Bondi, Evelyn Varden, Eileen Heckart, and John Alexander in Samson

from the Select Operating Corporation, which was controlled by the Shuberts. The new owners completely renovated this theatre, turning it into a stunning space covered with silken gray fabrics. Renamed the Coronet, it became one of the handsomest playhouses in Manhattan. And with this new dressing and new management, its luck changed—though not immediately. The first show to play the Coronet, *Beggars Are Coming to Town*, opened on October 27, 1945. It had an impressive cast: Paul Kelly, Luther Adler, Dorothy Comingore, Herbert Berghof, E.G. Marshall, George Mathews, and Adrienne Ames. Despite excellent acting and expert direction by Harold Clurman, it ran for only twenty-five performances.

But the Coronet's second show turned out to be a winner. Elmer Rice's enchanting fantasy *Dream Girl* was written for his wife, Betty Field, and she gave a captivating performance as a woman who enlivened her dull life with vivid daydreams. She was ably supported by Wendell Corey, Evelyn Varden, and Edmon Ryan, and the cheerful comedy ran for 348 performances.

PLAYBILL from the original production of *Big River* (1985).

Tonya Pinkins in the title role of *Caroline, Or Change* (2004) with Adriane Lenox as The Moon. (Photo by Michal Daniel)

Raphaelson's *Hilda Crane* (1950), staged by Hume Cronyn; Lillian Hellman's fascinating play about the middle-age crisis, *The Autumn Garden* (1951), with Fredric March, Florence Eldridge, Jane Wyatt, Ethel Griffies, and others, directed by Harold Clurman; Edna Best giving a memorable performance in S. N. Behrman's *Jane* (1952), based on a W. Somerset Maugham story; and a revival of Miss Hellman's explosive play *The Children's Hour* (1952), with Patricia Neal, Kim Hunter, Robert Pastene, and Iris Mann.

More hits of the 1950s: Burgess Meredith, Martha Scott, Glenn Anders, and Una Merkel in Liam O'Brien's *The Remarkable Mr. Pennypacker* (1953); Robert Anderson's *All Summer Long* (1954), with John Kerr, Ed Begley, June Walker, and Carroll Baker; Noël Coward's *Quadrille* (1954), starring the Lunts, Brian Aherne, and Edna Best, directed by Lunt, with striking sets and costumes by Cecil Beaton. Maxwell Anderson's hit thriller about a sweet little murderess, *The Bad Seed* (1954), with Nancy Kelly, Patty McCormack, Eileen Heckart, Henry Jones, and Evelyn Varden, moved here from the 46th Street Theatre. Then came the original one-act version of Arthur Miller's *A View from the Bridge*, with Van Heflin, J. Carrol Naish, and Eileen Heckart, on a double bill with Miller's *A Memory of Two Mondays* (1955).

The Lunts returned in *The Great Sebastians* (1956), which transferred from the ANTA Theatre. Barbara Bel Geddes, Michael Redgrave, and Cathleen Nesbitt starred in Terence Rattigan's *The Sleeping Prince* (1956). Siobhan McKenna transferred her *St. Joan* (1956), from the Phoenix Theatre. Sir Ralph Richardson and Mildred Natwick had fun in Jean Anouilh's memorable play *The Waltz of the Toreadors* (1957), directed by Harold Clurman, followed by Katharine Cornell and Anthony Quayle in Christopher Fry's *The Firstborn* (1958), with songs by Leonard Bernstein.

Jason Robards Jr. gave a Tony Award—winning performance as a writer (said to be inspired by F. Scott Fitzgerald) in *The Disenchanted* (1958), with Jason Robards Sr. also in the cast, along with George Grizzard, Rosemary Harris, and Salomé Jens. The last show to play the Coronet before it had yet another change of name was a revival of Eugene O'Neill's *The Great God Brown* (1959), with Fritz Weaver, Robert Lansing, and Nan Martin, in a Phoenix Theatre production.

In November 1959 the Coronet was renamed the Eugene O'Neill Theatre, in honor of America's greatest playwright, who had died in 1953. The first play at the O'Neill was William Inge's *A Loss of Roses*, with Betty Field, Warren Beatty, Carol Haney, Robert Webber, and Michael J. Pollard, but the critics found the play dull and it closed after twenty-five performances.

After several quick failures, the theatre housed Carol Channing in Charles Gaynor's revue *Show Girl*, with Jules Munshin and Les Quat' Jeudis, a quartet of singing Frenchmen. It ran for 100 performances. John Mills starred in Terence Rattigan's *Ross* (1961), about Lawrence of Arabia; Jason Robards Jr. and Sandy Dennis enjoyed a long run in Herb Gardner's comedy *A Thousand Clowns* (1962), which perfectly captured the growing anti-establishment spirit of the time.

The 1960s brought Hal Prince's production of the charming musical *She Loves Me* (1963), by Joe Masteroff, Sheldon Harnick, and Jerry Bock, with Jack Cassidy, Daniel Massey, and Barbara Cook singing what became one of her signature tunes, "Ice Cream"; plus two hits from other theatres, *The Odd Couple* and *Rosencrantz and Guildenstern Are Dead* (1966—67); and the London musical version of *The Canterbury Tales* (1969), with George Rose, Sandy Duncan, Hermione Baddeley, Martyn Green, and Reid Shelton.

In the late 1960s, playwright Neil Simon bought this theatre but did not change its name. A series of Simon plays were then staged here, beginning with the successful comedy *Last of the Red Hot Lovers* (1969), with James Coco, Linda Lavin, Marcia Rodd, and Doris Roberts; *The Prisoner of Second Avenue* (1971), with Peter Falk, Lee Grant, and Vincent Gardenia, who won a Tony Award for his performance; *The Good Doctor* (1973), a series of sketches and songs that Simon adapted from Chekhov stories, starring Christopher Plummer, Marsha Mason, René Auberjonois, Barnard Hughes, and Frances Sternhagen; *God's Favorite* (1974), Simon's comedy version of the biblical story of Job, with

Sebastian Arcelus with the chorus of the Beach Boys musical, *Good Vibrations* (2005) sing "Surfin' USA." (Photo by Carol Rosegg)

Vincent Gardenia, Charles Nelson Reilly, and Rosetta LeNoire, staged by Michael Bennett.

The Simon parade was interrupted in 1975 by the arrival of *Yentl*, a play by Isaac Bashevis Singer and Leah Napolin, starring Tovah Feldshuh, which stayed for seven months and was later adapted as a film with Barbra Streisand. Simon returned with *California Suite* (1976), an evening of four short plays, with Tammy Grimes, Jack Weston, and George Grizzard, which ran for 445 performances. Simon's hit play *Chapter Two* moved here from the Imperial in 1979, followed by another of his comedies, *I Ought to Be in Pictures* (1980), with Ron Leibman, Joyce Van Patten, and Dinah Manoff, who won a Tony Award for her performance. Simon's play *Fools*, with John Rubinstein, had a brief run in 1981, followed by *Annie*, which moved in from another theatre. A revival of Simon's musical *Little Me*, starring James Coco and Victor Garber, did not succeed in 1982, and the hit musical *The Best Little Whorehouse in Texas* returned from its tour and played at this theatre for a month.

In 1982 Jujamcyn Theatres bought the Eugene O'Neill from Simon and has operated the theatre ever since. In October of that year Beth Henley's play *The Wake of Jamey Foster*, with Anthony Heald, played a short run here, followed by William Gibson's *Monday after the Miracle*, a sequel to his acclaimed play *The Miracle Worker*. Then came a legendary fiasco, *Moose Murders*, which closed on its opening night. Eve Arden, who had starred in it, wisely left the show after an early preview. Arthur Bicknell's dreadful comedy/thriller, about high

jinks at a hunting lodge decorated with mounted moose heads, became a touchstone for Broadway flopdom.

Jessica Tandy, Amanda Plummer, Bruce Davison, and John Heard starred in a 1983 revival of Tennessee Williams's *The Glass Menagerie*, directed by John Dexter. In 1985 a musical called *Big River*, based on Mark Twain's *The Adventures of Huckleberry Finn*, opened and won the following Tony Awards: Best Musical, Best Book (William Hauptman), Best Score (Roger Miller), Best Direction (Des McAnuff), Best Featured Actor (Ron Richardson), Best Scenic Design (Heidi Landesman), and Best Lighting (Richard Riddell). Two years later this hit was followed by *Tom Waits in Concert on Broadway* for a limited engagement.

Another hit arrived in 1988 when David Henry Hwang's controversial play *M. Butterfly* opened and won three Tony Awards: Best Play, Best Direction (John Dexter), and Best Supporting Actor (B. D. Wong). Kathleen Turner and Charles Durning opened in a revival of Tennessee Williams's *Cat on a Hot Tin Roof* in 1990, and Durning was rewarded with a Tony for his performance as Big Daddy.

David Hirson's verse drama *La Bête* was an interesting failure in 1991, followed by the New Vaudeville *Penn & Teller: The Refrigerator Tour*; the hit British revue *Five Guys Named Moe*; and a new production of the musical *Grease!* (exclamation point added for this production), which ran for 1,503 performances. Producers Fran and Barry Weissler opened *Grease!* with comedian/actress (and later talk show and Tony

The actors served as their own orchestra in John Doyle's 2005 revival of *Sweeney Todd*. Clockwise from top: Patti LuPone, Donna Lynn Champlin, Manoel Felciano, and Michael Cerveris. (Photo by Paul Kolnik)

Awards host) Rosie O'Donnell as Rizzo. This began what became a signature Weissler policy of bringing in stars from other media for brief stints to extend the runs of their shows. Among those who stepped into this production during its nearly four-year run: Brooke Shields, JoAnne Worley, Debby Boone, Sheena Easton, Jon Secada, Al Jarreau, Chubby Checker, and Darlene Love. Comedian Joe Piscopo was playing Vince Fontaine on January 8, 1996, when a blizzard shut down all of Broadway . . . except *Grease!* For that one night, Piscopo and *Grease!* had Broadway all to themselves.

The Herbal Bed, Peter Whelan's hit London drama about Shakespeare's daughter, was one of the most eagerly awaited events of spring 1998. Unfortunately, it did not repeat its success in New York and closed after thirteen performances. In October 1998 an even bigger disaster arrived. *More to Love*, by radio comic Rob Bartlett and also starring him, received brutal notices. Subtitled "A big fat comedy," the play about obesity was dubbed "A stand-up dramedy" by Peter Marks of the *New York Times*. It wasted away after four performances.

The fiftieth-anniversary production of Arthur Miller's *Death of a Salesman* (from Chicago's Goodman Theatre) opened on February 10, 1999, and was acclaimed. Brian Dennehy and Elizabeth Franz won Tony

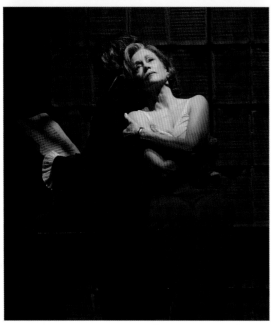

Awards for their performances as Willy and
Linda Loman. Robert Falls won a Tony as Best
Director of a Play, and the production received
a Tony as Best Revival of a Play. It ran for 276
performances and was taped for broadcast on
cable TV, where it won more awards.

Playwright David Hirson, who had endured
the twenty-five-performance run of his *La Bête* in
1991, returned to the O'Neill in January 2000 with
another intelligent comedy, *Wrong Mountain*,
which did better—twenty-eight performances.

A bonanza opened at the O'Neill Theatre on
October 26, 2000. *The Full Monty*, a musical
comedy based on the popular film of the same
name, with music and lyrics by David Yazbek
and a book by Terrence McNally, came to
Broadway from the Old Globe Theatre in San
Diego and proved an immediate hit. With its
appealing story of six men who lose their jobs
and decide to become male strippers to support
their families, the show quickly (though briefly)
established itself as Broadway's hottest ticket.
Not all theatregoers were impressed. Many
older playgoers felt the musical had a mediocre
score, but the general public embraced its
warmhearted comedy. Following twenty years
during which musical drama was king, *The Full
Monty* was hailed for heralding a rebirth of
musical *comedy*. The production also demonstrated what a fine showcase the O'Neill was for
small- to medium-sized musicals, which dominated its programming for the next few years.

A two-night benefit titled *Short Talks on the
Universe* attracted major names on November 17
and 18, 2002. Angela Lansbury, Matthew
Broderick, Bette Midler, Alec Baldwin, and Raúl
Esparza were among the stars who performed
original one-acts by Steve Martin, Tony Kushner,
Elaine May, Terrence McNally, Nora Ephron, and
Jon Robin Baitz. Proceeds went to the Friends in
Deed foundation and to Bay Street Theatre.

April 10, 2003, brought Roundabout
Theatre Company's stylish revival of the Maury
Yeston/Arthur Kopit musical *Nine*, directed by
David Leveaux, who at one point flooded the all-
white stage for a scene set in Venice. Antonio
Banderas played the charismatic Italian film

director Guido Contini, whose "body's nearing forty as his mind is nearing ten." His all-female supporting cast included Jane Krakowski (Tony Award), Laura Benanti, Mary Stuart Masterson, Nell Campbell, Mary Beth Peil, and, performing a showstopping "Folies Bergère" at a blooming age seventy, Chita Rivera. *Nine* won the 2003 Tony Award as Best Revival of a Musical and continued for 283 performances.

Playwright Tony Kushner, who had won back-to-back Tony Awards for the two parts of *Angels in America*, delved into his Georgia childhood for the libretto of an unusual musical, *Caroline, Or Change*, which debuted Off-Broadway at the Public Theatre, then moved to the O'Neill May 2, 2004, with the help of producers more interested in its message than its profit potential. Tonya Pinkins played Caroline, a black housekeeper who finds herself in conflict with her employers, a well-off and well-meaning Jewish family. Jeanine Tesori wrote the innovative score, while Kushner supplied book and lyrics. In place of a chorus, Kushner gave voices and personalities to inanimate objects, including a washing machine (Capathia Jenkins), a bus (Chuck Cooper), and even the moon (Aisha de Haas). *Caroline, Or Change* was nominated for Best Musical and ran 136 performances. Anika Noni Rose won the Tony Award as Best Featured Actress in a Play as Caroline's daughter Emmy.

An attractive young cast spent a good part of the evening in bathing suits in the February 2005 jukebox musical *Good Vibrations*, featuring the music of the rock group The Beach Boys. As part of the fun, the cast tossed large beach balls through the fourth wall and into the house for the audience to bat around. But the show was washed away in a tsunami of bad reviews after ninety-four performances.

Things got much more serious for the O'Neill's next show, John Doyle's fall 2005 revival of Stephen Sondheim and Hugh Wheeler's mass-murder musical *Sweeney Todd*, which was remarkable for merging the cast with the orchestra. The huge cast of the original was slashed to just ten actors for this production, and when those actors weren't performing a scene, they picked up instruments and played the skillfully shaved-down orchestrations by Sarah Travis, who earned a Tony Award for her work. The cast was led by Michael Cerveris (Sweeney/guitar and percussion) and Patti LuPone (Mrs. Lovett/tuba and triangle). Instead of spurting blood during the throat-cutting scenes, cast members slowly poured blood from one eerie white pail into another. Some critics found these innovations revelatory; others found them just stingy. But at Tony time Doyle was named Best Director of the season and the show dished up the meat pies for 349 performances.

Young audiences embraced the O'Neill's next presentation, *Spring Awakening*, a tragic musical about the catastrophic sexual awakening of a group of nineteenth-century German teens. Alt-rock composer Duncan Sheik worked with lyricist-librettist Steven Sater on the adaptation of Frank Wedekind's drama. An electrifying young ensemble led by future stars Lea Michele, Jonathan Groff, and John Gallagher Jr. performed the anachronistic rock score that had them pulling microphones from their clothes and singing rock-concert style. The R-rated staging included scenes of simulated flagellation, group masturbation, and a seduction aboard a swinging platform. The show opened on December 10, 2006, and struggled financially until it won the 2007 Tony Award as Best Musical, along with seven more Tonys: Best Score, Best Book, Best Featured Actor in a Musical (Gallagher), Best Director (Michael Mayer), Best Choreography (Bill T. Jones), Best Orchestrations (Sheik), and Best Lighting (Kevin Adams). *Spring Awakening* then cruised to a two-year, 859-performance run.

After a forty-six-year absence from Broadway, film actress and exercise guru Jane Fonda returned to the boards March 9, 2009 in *33 Variations*, Moisès Kaufman's intriguing drama about a music historian trying to crack a mystery in the career of composer Ludwig van Beethoven before she succumbs to a terminal illness. Fonda's was the main character, but actor Zach Grenier had a remarkable monologue that took audiences inside Beethoven's head as he composed one of the variations. Fans followed the show's progress on Fonda's thoughtful diary-like blog throughout the show's thirty-one previews and eighty-five-performance run.

Another fascinating musical transferred from Off-Broadway on November 23, 2009: *Fela!*, a biography of Nigerian musical/political activist Fela Anikulapo Kuti, with his own songs woven into a book by Jim Lewis and Bill T. Jones. The busy Jones also served as director and choreographer.

Known as the home of flops for much of its early existence under other names, the O'Neill is now considered one of the most desirable midsize Broadway theatres.

GERSHWIN
THEATRE

THE GERSHWIN THEATRE OPENED IN 1972 as the Uris, occupying six stories of the new Uris Building on the site of the old Capitol movie palace at Broadway and Fifty-first Street. The same complex houses the Circle in the Square Theatre below ground level, essentially in the Gershwin's basement. The two theatres have adjoining entrances in a drive-through passageway connecting Fiftieth and Fifty-first streets. With more than 1,900 seats—the most of any regularly used theatre on Broadway—the Gershwin was devised by set designer Ralph Alswang. It was the first large Broadway theatre to be built since the Earl Carroll in 1931.

At the time of the theatre's opening, Alswang told PLAYBILL: "The Uris represents what I think is the total philosophy of a modern

Gershwin
theatre

WICKED

222 W
51 ST

A New Musical
WICKED
THE UNTOLD STORY OF THE WITCHES OF OZ

PARK
←

QUIK
PARK

Gershwin
theatre

WICKED

1633
Broadway

224 W 51st

222 W
51 ST

AZALEA

AZALEA
RISTORANTE ITALIANO

BOX OFFICE

WICKED

WICKED

musical comedy house—seating, sight lines, acoustics—the economy and aesthetics of this kind of theatre. I was given a completely free hand by the Uris people and by the Nederlanders and Gerard Oestreicher."

The designer said that the whole theatre was done in a sensuous Art Nouveau style. The auditorium is on the second floor and is reached by escalators. "The bar, the plaster wall running 200 feet on a reverse curve and the Lalique lighting fixtures are all Art Nouveau shapes," Alswang stated. "Most people want to sit in the orchestra, so we have 1,280 seats downstairs and a very small balcony with 660 seats with projecting side sections to replace box seats. We have dark proscenium panels that serve as light towers and that are removable if the production demands it. The flexible stage floor can be taken apart like a Tinkertoy or be extended as a thrust stage. And for the first time in theatre history, there is a water curtain instead of an asbestos curtain in the event of an onstage fire."

Another first for a legitimate theatre was a revolutionary automatic rigging system called Hydra-Float. Alswang estimated that the building cost would amount to about $12.5 million.

The Gershwin is a Nederlander Organization theatre, under the direction of the Messrs. Nederlander. Its large seating capacity makes it ideal for lavish musicals and dance events.

A special feature of the theatre is the inclusion of a Theatre Hall of Fame with the names of stage greats inscribed in bas-relief on the walls of an impressive rotunda. Another rotunda on the theatre's other side may be used for theatrical exhibitions. The Hall of Fame rotunda was suggested to the Nederlanders by Earl Blackwell.

The Uris opened on November 28, 1972, with Galt MacDermot's spectacular rock musical *Via Galactica*, starring Raul Julia and Virginia Vestoff as space beings in the year 2972. Unfortunately, the special effects were more dazzling than the show, and it closed after only seven performances.

The theatre's next tenant was more successful. *Seesaw*, a musical version of William Gibson's hit comedy *Two for the Seesaw*, had music by Cy Coleman, lyrics by Dorothy Fields, a book credited to Michael Bennett, and Ken Howard and Michele Lee as its stars. Tommy Tune won a Tony Award as Best Supporting Actor in a Musical, and Bennett received another for his choreography. On March 23, 1973, Mayor John V. Lindsay replaced Ken Howard in the opening "My City" number for seven minutes. The musical ran for 296 performances.

In September 1973 the Uris presented a revival of the operetta *The Desert Song*, but its 1920s appeal was lost on 1970s audiences. It closed after fifteen performances. The next booking was unusual. The brilliant movie musical *Gigi* was converted to a stage show, not the usual order

Above: PLAYBILL covers for the opening production, *Via Galactica* (1972), and the musical *Seesaw* (1973).

Two scenes from the 2002 revival of *Oklahoma!* Left: Justin Bohon and dancers perform "Kansas City." Right: Josefina Gabrielle and Patrick Wilson reprise "People Will Say."

PLAYBILL cover for the popular revival of *The Pirates of Penzance* (1980).

The PLAYBILL for the 1997 revival of *Candide*.

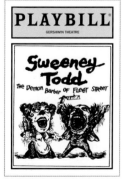

The opening night PLAYBILL for *Sweeney Todd: The Demon Barber of Fleet Street* (1979).

of creativity at that time, but one that would become increasingly frequent in ensuing years. Alan Jay Lerner and Frederick Loewe added some songs to the score, which won a Tony Award. The cast included Alfred Drake, Agnes Moorehead (later succeeded by Arlene Francis), Karin Wolfe, Daniel Massey, and Maria Karnilova. It ran for 103 performances.

During 1974 the Uris housed personal appearances by a series of celebrated artists, including Sammy Davis Jr.; the rock group Mott the Hoople; Enrico Macias and his La Fete Orientale Co.; Andy Williams and Michel Legrand; Anthony Newley and Henry Mancini; Johnny Mathis; The Fifth Dimension; Raphael in Concert; and Nureyev and Friends.

These concert bookings continued in 1975 with the Dance Theatre of Harlem, Count Basie, Ella Fitzgerald, and Frank Sinatra. The first New York production of Scott Joplin's opera *Treemonisha* opened here in October of that year. The Houston Grand Opera Association production of this work, which had been lost for many years, was conceived and directed by Frank Corsaro and ran for 64 performances. This was followed by the American Ballet Theatre, Margot Fonteyn and Rudolf Nureyev, Paul Anka, Dance Theatre of Harlem, D'Oyly Carte Opera Company, and Al Green.

The Houston Grand Opera and Sherwin M. Goldman presented an acclaimed revival of George Gershwin's opera *Porgy and Bess* in 1976, and the production received a Tony Award as the Most Innovative Production of a Revival, as the award was then called. Clamma Dale was especially praised for her singing and acting as Bess.

Bing Crosby made a rare appearance on Broadway at the Uris in 1976 with his wife,

Kathryn, and other members of his family, plus Rosemary Clooney, Joe Bushkin, and others. *Bing Crosby on Broadway* played a limited engagement of twelve performances during the Christmas holiday season. Nureyev appeared next in a dance concert, followed by the Ballet of the Twentieth Century.

A splendid revival of Rodgers and Hammerstein's *The King and I* opened here on May 2, 1977, starring Yul Brynner and Constance Towers. Produced by Lee Guber and Shelly Gross, it was an immediate hit and became the Uris's longest-running show to that time: 719 performances.

On March 1, 1979, a thrillingly ghoulish event occurred at this theatre. It was *Sweeney Todd: The Demon Barber of Fleet Street*, the grisly musical by Stephen Sondheim and Hugh Wheeler, based on a version of *Sweeney Todd* by Christopher Bond. The work received critical acclaim and won Tony Awards for Best Musical, Best Score (Sondheim), Best Book (Wheeler), Best Musical Actress (Angela Lansbury), Best Musical Actor (Len Cariou), Best Director (Hal Prince), Best Scenic Design (Eugene Lee), and Best Costume Design (Franne Lee). The Grand Guignol—style shocker about a London barber who slits his customers' throats in revenge for an injustice suffered by him was not everyone's cup of blood, but the highly imaginative production ran for 557 performances and is now considered Sondheim's masterpiece.

In 1980 the Uris presented Roland Petit's Ballet National de Marseille, Makarova and Company, and Nureyev and the Boston Ballet. On January 1, 1981, Joseph Papp presented the New York Shakespeare Festival production of *The Pirates of Penzance*, which had been a hit in Central Park the preceding summer. The cast included Kevin Kline (who received the Tony Award as Best Actor in a Musical), Linda Ronstadt, Estelle Parsons, Rex Smith, George Rose, and Tony Azito. The production received additional Tony Awards for Best Revival and Best Direction (Wilford Leach). It ran for 772 performances, a new record for the Uris and still a Broadway record for Gilbert and Sullivan.

On August 18, 1981, the Uris presented a revival of Lerner and Loewe's classic *My Fair Lady*, with its original star, Rex Harrison. Nancy Ringham played Eliza Doolittle, Milo O'Shea played her father, and Cathleen Nesbitt, also from the original cast, recreated her role as Mrs. Higgins. The revival ran for 124 performances.

The long-running musical *Annie* moved into the Uris from the Eugene O'Neill Theatre in January 1982 and stayed here for a year. It

ended its run at the Uris, having chalked up 2,377 performances.

Barry Manilow made a personal appearance here in February 1983, followed by a Houston Grand Opera revival of the Jerome Kern/Oscar Hammerstein II classic *Show Boat*, starring Donald O'Connor.

On the evening of June 5, 1983, during the annual Tony Award telecast, the name of the Uris was officially changed to the Gershwin Theatre, in honor of composer George Gershwin and his lyricist brother, Ira, who contributed many distinguished musicals and the opera *Porgy and Bess* to the Broadway theatre.

Idina Menzel, the original Elphaba (a.k.a. the Wicked Witch of the West) sings "Defying Gravity" in the long-running *Wicked* (2003). Inset: the opening night PLAYBILL. (Photo by Joan Marcus)

A month later Angela Lansbury returned in a revival of the hit musical *Mame*, in the title role, which she had originated. Other repeaters in the show: Jane Connell as Agnes Gooch, Anne Francine, Willard Waterman, and Sab Shimono.

In 1984 *Wayne Newton on Broadway* and *Twyla Tharp Dances on Broadway* were seen here, followed by the long-running *Beatlemania*, which moved here from another theatre. Later in the summer, singer Patti LaBelle took the stage.

In October 1984, the Royal Shakespeare Company arrived with two productions: *Much Ado about Nothing* and *Cyrano de Bergerac*. Among the players were Derek Jacobi and Sinead Cusack. Jacobi was awarded a Tony for his performance as Benedick in *Much Ado*. The actor reported at a PLAYBILL luncheon that on the opening night of *Cyrano*, José Ferrer, who won a Tony for playing that role in 1947, went backstage and said to the British Jacobi: "Your performance proves my point that only a Latin can play Cyrano."

Patti LaBelle returned to the Gershwin in January 1985. That summer, the lavish *Singin' in the Rain* opened here after many difficulties. It was a live incarnation of the classic MGM musical, with Comden and Green adapting their original screenplay about Hollywood's bumpy transition from silent films to talkies. The songs were mostly by the MGM team of Nacio Herb Brown and Arthur Freed. Don Correia played the Gene Kelly role and danced the title song in a heavy stage downpour created by a system of pipes above the stage. The choreography was by Twyla Tharp, who also directed the musical. It ran for ten months.

The next production at this theatre, the British spectacular *Starlight Express* (1987), required the theatre to be turned into a gigantic roller rink, with the cast roller-skating on ramps and bridges around the stage to give the impression of being railroad cars. One of the costliest productions ever staged on Broadway to that time, the Andrew Lloyd Webber/Richard Stilgoe musical ran for nearly two years and won a Tony Award for John Napier's elaborate costumes. However, it did not achieve the success of the London production, nor did it recoup its enormous investment.

In 1989 *Barry Manilow at the Gershwin* played for two months. That fall another MGM screen musical, *Meet Me in St. Louis*, took to the stage with some additional songs by Hugh Martin and Ralph Blane, who had written the famed movie score for this charming musical. The stage version starred George Hearn, Milo O'Shea, Charlotte Moore, and Betty Garrett (who was welcomed back by the critics) and featured Donna Kane in the Judy Garland role. The musical ran for seven months.

Bugs Bunny on Broadway played for several weeks in 1990, followed by a handsome revival of *Fiddler on the Roof*, starring Topol, recreating the role of Tevye, which he had played both onstage (in London) and in the highly praised film version of the musical. This production won the Tony Award for Best Revival of the season and ran for seven months. In 1991 and 1992 the Moscow Circus and *Tommy Tune Tonite!* played here, followed by a 1993 production of the Lerner/Loewe musical *Camelot*, starring Robert Goulet, the show's original Lancelot, who this time took the role of King Arthur.

In the fall of 1994 the highly anticipated Hal Prince production of *Show Boat* steamed in after a hugely successful run in Canada. The new production of this classic was rapturously received. A program note stated that this revival was based on the original 1927 Ziegfeld production, the London production, the 1936 film version, and the 1946 Broadway revival. Additional credit was given to musicologist John McGlinn and archivist Myles Kreuger, who had written an acclaimed book on the history of all productions of *Show Boat*.

Produced by Garth Drabinsky's Livent (US) Inc., the sumptuously mounted production made some interesting departures from other versions of the show. Prince restored six songs that had been dropped from other *Show Boat* productions, including "Mis'ry's Comin' Aroun'," which had been considered too depressing for a musical. He also ameliorated some racial stereotypes that were felt to be too "Uncle Tom."

The cast included John McMartin (Cap'n Andy), Elaine Stritch (Parthy), Rebecca Luker (Magnolia), Mark Jacoby (Ravenal), and Michel Bell (Joe), whose rendition of the classic "Ol' Man River" stopped the show at every performance. One change that irritated some purist playgoers was having Stritch sing the lovely "Why Do I Love You?," instead of the traditional trio of Magnolia, Ravenal, and Cap'n Andy. Stritch's voice at this time was particularly harsh.

Show Boat received ten Tony Award nominations and won the following five: Best Musical Revival, Best Director of a Musical (Prince), Best Costume Designer (Florence Klotz), Best Choreographer (Susan Stroman), and Best Featured Actress in a Musical (Gretha Boston). *Show Boat* ran for 949 performances, closing on January 5, 1997.

The next Livent production, also directed by Hal Prince, did not fare as well. It was a revival of the musical version of Voltaire's *Candide*, with a book by Hugh Wheeler; music by Leonard Bernstein; lyrics by Richard Wilbur, Stephen Sondheim, and John Latouche; and choreography by Patricia Birch.

This revival was based on three earlier versions of the musical, the most successful being the 1974 production, also directed by Prince, which ran for 740 performances. The 1997 cast starred Jim Dale, who played a variety of parts; Mal Z. Lawrence and Arte Johnson, who also played multiple roles; Harolyn Blackwell as Cunegonde (spelled by Glenda Balkan at some performances); Jason Danieley as Candide; Andrea Martin as the Old

Lady; and Stacey Logan as Paquette.

The musical traced the marvelous adventures and appalling tribulations of the innocent Westphalian hero Candide, who faces great hardships in his travels but remains loyal to the optimistic lesson of his teacher Dr. Pangloss: "All is for the best in this best of all possible worlds." Critics praised (as usual) the great score by Bernstein but disliked the show's book and the circusy staging that overwhelmed Voltaire's sharp-edged satire. Critic Howard Kissel wrote: "Bernstein's sublime score lacks the best of all books." Critic David Patrick Stearns' review stated: "New *Candide* low-voltage Voltaire." The musical received four Tony Award nominations—Best Musical Revival, Best Actor in a Musical (Dale), Best Featured Actress in a Musical (Martin), and Best Costumes (Judith Dolan)—but won none. The show ran for 103 performances.

The next booking at the Gershwin Theatre was the successful revival of the 1969 Tony Award—winning musical *1776*, about the events that swirled around the signing of the Declaration of Independence. This production by the Roundabout Theatre moved here on December 3, 1997, from the Criterion Center

Kristin Chenoweth, Idina Menzel, and the chorus enter the Emerald City of Oz with the song "One Fine Day" in *Wicked* (2003). (Photo by Joan Marcus)

Stage Right Theatre, where it had played from August 14, 1997, to November 16, 1997. It was directed by Scott Ellis. The cast included Pat Hingle as Benjamin Franklin, Michael Cumpsty as John Dickinson, Richard Poe as John Hancock, Brent Spiner as John Adams, Tom Aldredge as Stephen Hopkins, Paul Michael Valley as Thomas Jefferson, Gregg Edelman as Edward Rutledge, and Lauren Ward as Martha Jefferson. It ran for 333 performances.

On November 19, 1998, a new production of the celebrated 1944 musical *On the Town* opened here. George C. Wolfe staged the New York Shakespeare Festival production, which originated as an August 1997 Central Park revival. The musical, inspired by Jerome Robbins's ballet *Fancy Free,* had music by Leonard Bernstein and book and lyrics by Comden and Green. It depicted the joyous shore leave of three sailors in Manhattan, and their adventures with three girls they encounter.

The most imaginative feature of this revival was the set by Adrienne Lobel, which contained a replica of the Brooklyn Bridge overhead, on which the orchestra was placed. The Manhattan skyline loomed behind the bridge. Some critics objected to this scenic device, saying that it took up too much space and resulted in a cramped stage for the dancers. The new choreography by Keith Young was compared unfavorably with Jerome Robbins's original 1944 dances, and Wolfe's direction was considered bland. The cast received decent reviews, especially Lea DeLaria as the rowdy cab driver and Mary Testa as a tipsy singing instructor. The revival played only sixty-five performances and lost a lot of money for the New York Shakespeare Festival. It received only one Tony Award nomination: Testa for Best Featured Actress in a Musical.

The next tenant at the Gershwin was a return of the popular 1985 music and dance revue *Tango Argentino.* This entertainment, conceived by Claudio Segovia and Hector Orezzoli, featured Argentine artists interpreting the tango in song, story, and dance. It played for sixty-three performances.

On March 16, 2000, another dance showcase, the revue *Riverdance,* made its long-delayed Broadway debut, having originally proved a sensation at Radio City Music Hall in 1998 and having played around the world and even on PBS before returning to New York at last in a legitimate Broadway house. The extravaganza presented Irish step dances, and choral and solo songs by sparkling international performers. *Riverdance on Broadway* closed after a comparatively modest run of 605 performances.

Linda Eder at the Gershwin, featuring the eponymous singer whose main Broadway credit was the 1997 musical *Jekyll & Hyde,* played a concert show at the Gershwin during the 2001 holiday season.

The theatre's next major musical was a transfer of the hit London revival of *Oklahoma!,* which was imported with West End star Josefina Gabrielle as a toughened-up, overalls-clad Laurie, and Patrick Wilson replacing Hugh Jackman as Curly. However, the show's acting Tony Award went to Shuler Hensley, who played Judd. On June 28, 2002, the ensemble of *Oklahoma!* was joined by Barbara Cook, John Cullum, Lea Salonga, Laura Benanti, and other stellar performers for *Something Good,* a special concert celebrating the centenary of the show's composer, Richard Rodgers.

The Gershwin next welcomed the biggest hit of its history so far, *Wicked,* a special-effects-packed "prequel" to the beloved *The Wizard of Oz.* Based on the best-selling novel of the same title by Gregory Maguire, *Wicked* tells the story of the witches of Oz and their rise from girlhood to womanhood: Glinda, the Good Witch of the North, and Elphaba, the Wicked Witch of the West. Maguire fashioned the latter name from the initials of Oz creator L. Frank Baum. With music and lyrics by Stephen Schwartz and book by Winnie Holzman, *Wicked* helped cement the stardom of Tony-winner Idina Menzel (Elphaba) and Kristin Chenoweth (Glinda) and came to a rousing climax at the conclusion of Act I with the showstopper "Defying Gravity," in which Elphaba launched herself into flight for the first time.

The show also proved to be a favorite with prepubescent and teenage girls, who became (with their parents and other adult chaperones) an important segment of the Broadway audience in the first decade of the twenty-first century.

By virtue of so many people willing to pay full price at the city's largest legitimate theatre, *Wicked* quickly established itself as Broadway's highest-grossing show, regularly pulling in more than $1.5 million per week, whether it was the dog days of summer, the bitterly frosty days of winter, or the trough of the recession of 2008—10.

In 2010 *Wicked* was still selling out virtually every performance in the seventh year of its run at the Gershwin.

GERALD SCHOENFELD

THEATRE

BY THE TIME THE SHUBERTS BUILT THE theatre originally known as the Plymouth in 1917, the *New York Times* reported: "It is a dull week when no new theatre opens." The Shuberts now had a block of theatres—the Plymouth and Booth on West Forty-fifth Street and the Shubert and Broadhurst, back-to-back with these, on West Forty-fourth Street.

The Shuberts leased their new Plymouth Theatre to the distinguished producer/director Arthur Hopkins. It was designed by architect Herbert J. Krapp, and the *Times* reported that it was simple in décor; was decorated in shades of brown, blue, and gold; and had a seating capacity of about one thousand (since increased to 1,079), with only one balcony.

An unusual aspect of the opening bill on

Top left: Maude Hanaford, Lionel Barrymore, John Barrymore, and Arthur Forrest in *The Jest* (1919).

Top right: Zita Johann and Clark Gable as illicit lovers in the surrealistic *Machinal* (1928).

Bottom left: Leyla Georgie, Louis Wolheim, and William Boyd in the rousing *What Price Glory?* (1924).

the night of October 10, 1917, was that it was not a new show. Clare Kummer's comedy *A Successful Calamity*, starring William Gillette, had been a hit the previous year at the Booth next door, and it was revived with virtually the same cast at the Plymouth.

Producer Hopkins brought John Barrymore to the Plymouth in 1918 to play one of his most successful parts: Fedya in a dramatization of Tolstoy's *Redemption*. Hopkins directed the play, and Robert Edmond Jones designed a sumptuous production. Barrymore and the huge cast gave splendid performances. The producer even invited Tolstoy's son to attend a dress rehearsal, but the Russian's only comment afterward was, "Where's Fedya's beard?"

Later in 1918 Walter Hampden played Hamlet at the Plymouth in a revival of Shakespeare's tragedy. On April 9, 1919, Hopkins jolted the town with his superlative production of *The Jest*, an Italian play by Sem Benelli, starring John Barrymore as an effete painter and Lionel Barrymore as an odious Captain of the Mercenaries. The brilliant acting of the Barrymore brothers as deadly enemies, Robert Edmond Jones's magnificent Renaissance sets, and Hopkins's direction made this one of the early milestones in American theatre.

On December 22, 1919, Hopkins tried again with a Russian classic, Maxim Gorki's *The Lower Depths*, retitled *Night Lodging*. But despite excellent performances by Edward G. Robinson and Pauline Lord, it lasted only fourteen performances.

The Roaring Twenties started auspiciously at the Plymouth with *Little Old New York*, a hit comedy by Rida Johnson Young that took place in New York of 1810, when, as Burns Mantle noted, "John Jacob Astor spoke with a German

accent and Cornelius Vanderbilt ran a ferry." The play concerned an Irish girl, played by Genevieve Tobin, who masquerades as a boy in order to inherit a vast fortune. But she falls in love with the boy who is the rightful heir and gives up her inheritance to win him (and his inheritance). This bit of Irish blarney was good for 311 performances.

Other highlights of the 1920s included Zoe Akins's serious study of a marriage gone wrong, *Daddy's Gone A-Hunting* (1921), with fine acting by Marjorie Rambeau, Frank Conroy, and Lee Baker; and Arthur Hopkins's production of *The Old Soak* (1922), a lovable comedy about an alcoholic (Harry Beresford) and his wife, Matilda (Minnie Dupree), that was named one of the ten best plays of the season by Burns Mantle. Another family comedy, *The Potters*, by J. P. McEvoy, starred Donald Meek as Pa Potter, Catharine Calhoun Doucet as Ma, Raymond Guion (later Gene Raymond of the movies) as Bill Potter, and Mary Carroll as Mamie Potter. The Potters amused for 245 performances.

One of the American theatre's most significant plays, *What Price Glory?*, by Maxwell

Above: The PLAYBILL cover for *The Marriage-Go-Round* had to change weekly to satisfy the stars' egos (1958).

Top left: Paul Muni in Elmer Rice's *Counselor-at-Law* (1931).

Top right: Donald Ogden Stewart, Hope Williams, Ben Smith, and Barbara White in the charming Philip Barry comedy, *Holiday* (1928).

Bottom left: Gertrude Lawrence and Paul McGrath embrace the Oxford movement in *Susan and God* (1937).

Bottom right: Tallulah Bankhead and baby dinosaurs in Thornton Wilder's *The Skin of Our Teeth* (1942).

Above: PLAYBILL cover for the Pulitzer Prize play *Abe Lincoln in Illinois* (1938).

Anderson and Laurence Stallings, detonated at the Plymouth on September 5, 1924. The drama, produced and directed by Arthur Hopkins, was the first war play to use the profane speech of soldiers. The program carried this puzzling note by Hopkins: "I am presenting *What Price Glory?* exactly as it has been given at the Plymouth Theatre for every performance, except for the elimination of three expressions that are used in the best families and by our noblest public officials." The play focused on battling army buddies First Sergeant Quirt (William Boyd) and Captain Flagg (Louis Wolheim), and the characters became so memorable that a number of films were made about them. *What Price Glory?* ran for 435 performances.

Laurette Taylor, Frank Conroy and Louis Calhern tried to make a success of Philip Barry's metaphysical play *In a Garden* (1925), but it was a bit too murky for theatregoers.

Winthrop Ames presented several Gilbert and Sullivan operettas during 1927. On September 1 of that year, another huge hit came to this theatre: a lively comedy called *Burlesque*, by Arthur Hopkins and George

Manker Watters. It starred Hal Skelly as a burlesque comic and Barbara Stanwyck as his wife, who performs in a seedy act with him. Burns Mantle named it one of the year's ten best plays, and it had a healthy run of 372 performances.

The sensational Snyder—Gray murder case (Ruth Snyder was the first woman in America put to death by electrocution, for plotting to murder her husband) inspired an interesting surrealistic play, *Machinal* (1928), by Sophie Treadwell. Arthur Hopkins staged the drama, which was superbly played by Zita Johann in the Snyder role and by a young actor named Clark Gable as the lover who murders Snyder's husband.

On November 26, 1928, playwright Philip Barry returned to the Plymouth, this time in triumph. Arthur Hopkins produced and staged his felicitous comedy *Holiday*, and it became one of the theatre's most prized high comedies. Written specifically for Hope Williams, the socialite turned actress, the play dealt with a young man, Johnny Case (Ben Smith), who has made some money and wants to take a holiday and enjoy it while he is still young. His socialite fiancée and her stuffy father oppose this plan, so he takes his joyous holiday with his fiancée's rebellious sister, played by Williams. The star was understudied by Katharine Hepburn, who never got to play the role on Broadway but starred in the excellent movie version.

Hope Williams returned to the Plymouth in 1930 in *Rebound*, a comedy about divorce written especially for her by Donald Ogden Stewart, who had appeared with her at the Plymouth in *Holiday*. Burns Mantle selected it for his best-plays volume.

Highlights of the 1930s at the Plymouth included Paul Muni at his finest in Elmer Rice's *Counselor-at-Law* (1931); Roland Young, Laura Hope Crews, and Frances Fuller in Clare

Kummer's hilarious comedy *Her Master's Voice* (1933), voted one of the year's ten best plays by Burns Mantle; Tallulah Bankhead suffering a brain tumor in *Dark Victory* (1934); and Constance Cummings giving a memorable performance in Samson Raphaelson's comedy *Accent on Youth* (1934). Sidney Howard's *Paths of Glory* (1935), an impassioned play about a true, unjust incident in World War I, should have run longer than its twenty-four performances.

The second half of the 1930s saw Helen Jerome's faithful adaptation of Jane Austen's *Pride and Prejudice* (1935), which moved to the Plymouth from the Music Box; Robert E. Sherwood's deft adaptation of the French play *Tovarich* (1936), with the famed Italian actress Marta Abba making her Broadway debut, costarring with the suave John Halliday; and Gertrude Lawrence in one of her greatest roles, as a sappy society woman who finds God in the Oxford movement, in Rachel Crothers's scintillating *Susan and God* (1937). All three of these play made Mantle's best-of-the-year list.

Robert E. Sherwood's *Abe Lincoln in Illinois* (1938), winner of the Pulitzer Prize and the first production of the new Playwrights Company, starred Raymond Massey as an incredibly convincing Abe. Clare Boothe's anti-Nazi play *Margin for Error* (1939), directed by Otto Preminger, featured Sam Levene as a comic police officer and Preminger as an odious German consul.

The Plymouth was constantly operating during the 1940s, with new hits, transfers from other theatres, and a few revivals. William Saroyan's *Love's Old Sweet Song* (1940), a screwball comedy about the plight of mankind, with Walter Huston, Jessie Royce Landis and Alan Hewitt, was not as successful as his earlier plays. Alan Dinehart, Glenda Farrell, and Lyle Talbot ran seemingly forever in a sleazy come-

dy, *Separate Rooms* (1940). Mary Anderson was so nasty in *Guest in the House* (1942) that audiences hissed her, while critics raved.

Thornton Wilder won another Pulitzer Prize and rattled theatregoers with *The Skin of Our Teeth* (1942), a lunatic cartoon about the human race, starring Tallulah Bankhead as the eternal temptress; Fredric March as the inventor of the alphabet, the wheel, and adultery; Florence Eldridge as his homespun wife; and Montgomery Clift and Frances Heflin as his children.

Katharine Cornell, Raymond Massey, and Henry Daniell had a moderate success at the Plymouth in Dodie Smith's *Lovers and Friends* (1943). *Chicken Every Sunday* (1944), a homey comedy by Julius J. and Philip G. Epstein, was a wartime hit that transferred from Henry Miller's Theatre. Spencer Tracy returned to Broadway after many years in Hollywood to star in Robert E. Sherwood's drama *The Rugged Path* (1945), but the idealistic play, directed by Garson Kanin, ran for only eighty-one performances.

Mary Martin went Asian in a charming musical, *Lute Song* (1946), adapted from a Chinese classic by Sidney Howard and Will Irwin, with a score by Raymond Scott and two unknowns in the cast (Yul Brynner and Nancy Davis—later Mrs. Ronald Reagan). Clifton Webb returned to Broadway in Noël Coward's light comedy *Present Laughter* (1946), but it was too thin for critics and audiences. Tallulah Bankhead arrived in a dusty drama, *The Eagle Has Two Heads* (1947), by Jean Cocteau, with Helmut Dantine replacing Marlon Brando out of town because Bankhead claimed Brando was picking his nose and scratching his behind onstage—which would have helped this turkey considerably.

Alfred Drake and Marsha Hunt brought *Joy to the World* (1948), a play about the dangers of liberalism in Hollywood. Next at the

Top left to right:
Florence Eldridge and Fredric March in Wilder's Pulitzer Prize play, *The Skin of Our Teeth.*

Walter Matthau and Art Carney in *The Odd Couple* (1965).

George C. Scott and Maureen Stapleton in Neil Simon's *Plaza Suite* (1968).

Clive Reville, Elizabeth Seal, and Keith Michell in *Irma La Douce* (1960).

Above: Roger Rees and Emily Richard in the epic *The Life and Adventures of Nicholas Nickleby* (1981).

Top: Donald Cook and Tallulah Bankhead during the calm before the storm in *Private Lives* (1948).

Bottom: Jane Lapotaire gives a Tony Award performance in *Piaf* (1981).

Plymouth, Tallulah Bankhead and Donald Cook turned Noël Coward's *Private Lives* (1948) into a rough-house wrestling match, and they succeeded for 248 performances.

The 1950s started out with a huge hit for this theatre. Samuel Taylor's *The Happy Time*, a sentimental comedy about a French Canadian family, starred Claude Dauphin, Kurt Kasznar, Johnny Stewart, and Eva Gabor. The Rodgers and Hammerstein production ran for 614 performances. In April 1952 Paul Gregory's production of Shaw's *Don Juan in Hell*, which had previously played at Carnegie Hall and the Century Theatre, moved to the Plymouth for a two-month run. It starred Charles Boyer, Charles Laughton (who staged it), Cedric Hardwicke, and Agnes Moorehead. On October 29 of the same year, one of the Plymouth's biggest hits opened. It was Frederick Knott's *Dial 'M' for Murder*, a thriller about a husband hiring a hit man to kill his wife. It starred Maurice Evans, Gusti Huber, and Richard Derr, with John Williams as an impeccable inspector, and it ran for 552 performances.

Highlights of the remainder of the 1950s included *The Caine Mutiny Court-Martial* (1954), staged by Charles Laughton, starring Henry Fonda, Lloyd Nolan, and John Hodiak in Herman Wouk's powerful adaptation of his novel *The Caine Mutiny*; Marge and Gower Champion and Harry Belafonte in *3 For Tonight* (1955), a "diversion in song and dance"; Margaret Sullavan in her last Broadway appearance, Carolyn Green's bubbly comedy *Janus* (1955), with Robert Preston and Claude Dauphin; Maurice Evans, Claudia Morgan, and Signe Hasso in a revival of Shaw's *The Apple Cart* (1956); Arnold Schulman's amusing *A Hole in the Head* (1957), with an expert cast including Paul Douglas, David Burns, Kay Medford, Joyce Van Patten, Lee Grant, and Tom Pedi; Peter Ustinov's satiric *Romanoff and Juliet* (1957), starring Ustinov as a general who plays cupid to a Russian boy and an American girl; and Leslie Stevens's sexy comedy *The Marriage-Go-Round* (1958), starring Claudette Colbert, Charles Boyer, Julie Newmar, and Edmond Ryan, which ran into 1960.

The Plymouth greeted the 1960s with a smash musical, *Irma La Douce* (1960), that came by way of France and England. Directed by Peter Brook, it starred Elizabeth Seal, who won a Tony for her performance as a French hooker, and Keith Michell as her boyfriend, who disguises himself as her only patron to keep her to himself. Paddy Chayefsky's *Gideon* (1961) starred Fredric March as a debating angel, who is really God. Margaret Leighton and Anthony Quinn brought sparkle to a French/English play, *Tchin-Tchin* (1962).

Lillian Hellman had one of her rare failures with a satiric comedy about American materialism, *My Mother, My Father and Me* (1963), directed by Gower Champion and starring Ruth Gordon and Walter Matthau. Arnold Wesker's

Top: left to right, Brian Dennehy, Philip Seymour Hoffman, Vanessa Redgrave, and Robert Sean Leonard in the Tony award winning 2003 revival of *Long Day's Journey Into Night*. (Photo by Joan Marcus)

Bottom: Donna Murphy plays a homely young woman smitten with a handsome soldier (Jere Shea) in Stephen Sondheim's *Passion* (1994).

British hit *Chips with Everything* (1963) amused with the adventures of young recruits in an RAF training unit. Alec Guinness won a Tony Award for his memorable portrayal of the title role in *Dylan* (1964), with Kate Reid as his wife. William Hanley's *Slow Dance on the Killing Ground* (1964) was named one of the best plays of the year, but audiences avoided it.

In 1965 Neil Simon came up with his best and most immortal comedy, *The Odd Couple*, starring Walter Matthau as a sloppy sports announcer, recently divorced, who rooms with an incredibly neat friend (played to perfection by Art Carney), whose wife has just thrown him out of the house. It achieved a run of 965 performances. In 1966, however, Anthony Perkins, Connie Stevens, and Richard Benjamin starred in Simon's most insipid comedy, *The Star-Spangled Girl* (1966), a stultifying evening of vapidity. Edward Albee also came a cropper with his play *Everything in the Garden* (1967), based on a true incident involving Long Island wives who made extra money as hookers. Simon redeemed himself with a deft trio of playlets called *Plaza Suite* (1968), starring Maureen Stapleton and George C. Scott in vignettes set at New York's celebrated Plaza Hotel. It ran for 1,097 performances.

During the 1970s the Plymouth continued to reign as one of Broadway's top legitimate theatres. On December 13, 1970, Simon attempted his first serious drama with *The Gingerbread Lady*, a play supposedly inspired by Judy Garland's erratic career. It starred Maureen Stapleton, who won a Tony as the alcohol-drenched singer, but it ran only 193 performances. In 1973 Jean Kerr came up with *Finishing Touches*, a comedy about a college professor's middle-age problems, but even with Barbara Bel Geddes and James Woods in the leads, the play lingered for only five months.

Peter Cook and Dudley Moore assembled a sequel to their highly successful revue *Beyond the Fringe*, and the show, which they called *Good Evening* (1973), ran for 228 performances. The Plymouth then had another British invader, which turned out to be one of its most illustrious tenants: Peter Shaffer's *Equus*, a London hit based on a true, bizarre case about

Chita Rivera capped her six-decade Broadway career with the autobiographical musical *Chita Rivera: The Dancer's Life* (2005). (Photo by Paul Kolnik)

a young man who blinds a stable full of horses. It starred Anthony Hopkins as a psychiatrist and Peter Firth as the disturbed youth. As the run continued, Hopkins was succeeded by Anthony Perkins, Richard Burton, and other stars. *Equus*, which ran for 1,209 performances in New York, won the Tony Award as best play of the season and won another Tony for its director, John Dexter.

Another British import, *Otherwise Engaged* (1977), by Simon Gray, starred Tom

Courtenay as a British intellectual who tries to play a classical record and keeps getting interrupted by his scabrous friends. Elizabeth Swados's *Runaways* (1978) moved from the downtown New York Shakespeare Festival for 267 performances. *Ain't Misbehavin'* (1979), the Tony Award—winning revue based on Fats Waller's music, moved from the Longacre and played for two more years. Jane Lapotaire, repeating her triumph from Britain as Edith Piaf in *Piaf*, won a Tony for her interpretation of the famous street singer.

In the fall of 1981 the Royal Shakespeare Company brought its acclaimed production of Dickens's *The Life and Adventures of Nicholas Nickleby* (1981), and the Plymouth Theatre had to accommodate its complicated scenic design by constructing catwalks all over the house. The eight-hour play (performed over two nights, or on matinee days with a dinner intermission) caused a sensation for its staging (and $100 ticket price) and won a Tony for Best Play and for Best Performance by an Actor—Roger Rees. Directors Trevor Nunn and John Caird were also honored with a shared Tony Award for their inspired direction of this extremely complex production.

In 1982 the Circle in the Square offered Colleen Dewhurst in a revival of Ugo Betti's *The Queen and the Rebels*. In 1983 the New York Shakespeare Festival's production of the British play *Plenty* garnered raves. Written by David Hare, it offered memorable performances by Canadian actress Kate Nelligan and by American actor Edward Herrmann.

In 1983 this theatre housed an all-star revival of Kaufman and Hart's Pulitzer Prize comedy *You Can't Take It with You*, with Jason Robards, Elizabeth Wilson, Colleen Dewhurst, Maureen Anderman, James Coco, Meg Mundy, Bill McCutcheon, and many others. This was followed by Tom Stoppard's Tony Award—winning play *The Real Thing*, which also won Tony Awards for its stars, Jeremy Irons, Glenn Close and Christine Baranski, and for its director, Mike Nichols. The play ran for 566 performances.

Another bonanza opened here in 1985: Lily Tomlin in her virtuoso one-woman show *The Search for Signs of Intelligent Life in the Universe*, by Jane Wagner, which won Tomlin a Tony Award for her dazzling performance. Next came a revival of Shaw's *Pygmalion*, starring Peter O'Toole and Amanda Plummer; and Lanford Wilson's *Burn This*, with an explosive portrayal by John Malkovich and a Tony Award—winning performance by Joan Allen. Wendy Wasserstein's play *The Heidi Chronicles* won the Pulitzer Prize for its story of art historian Heidi Holland, whose life reflects the evolution of the feminist movement over twenty-five years. The play moved to the Plymouth from Off-Broadway's Playwrights Horizons.

The Plymouth's next tenants were Tracey Ullman in *The Big Love* (1991); and Brian Friel's Tony Award—winning drama *Dancing*

Hugh Jackman and Daniel Craig played Chicago cops tangling with corruption in *A Steady Rain* (2009). (Photo by Joan Marcus)

at Lughnasa, a portrait of small-town Irish life, with Dublin's famed Abbey Theatre players. *Dancing* won Tony Awards for Best Play (Brian Friel), Best Featured Actress (Brid Brennan), and Best Direction of a Play (Patrick Manson), and it ran for 421 performances.

Gypsy Passion, the Flamenco musical that had been a success at The Town Hall, played a return engagement in 1992 at this theatre. The following year *The Song of Jacob Zulu*, a Steppenwolf Theatre Company production, played here, followed by another Friel drama, *Wonderful Kentucky*, also from the Abbey Theatre. But this one received mixed reviews and closed after nine performances.

The next Plymouth tenant fared better: *Passion*, with music and lyrics by Stephen Sondheim, book and direction by James Lapine.

The rather depressing tale of an odd romance between an ugly Italian woman and a handsome Italian officer was performed without intermission. Although the musical received mixed reviews, reflecting the strongly mixed audience reaction, it ran for 280 performances and won the following Tony Awards: Best Musical, Best Book of a Musical (Lapine), Best Original Musical Score (Sondheim), and Best Actress in a Musical (Donna Murphy). It was additionally nominated for these Tony Awards: Best Actor in a Musical (Jere Shea), Best Featured Actor in a Musical (Tom Aldredge), Best Featured Actress in a Musical (Marin Mazzie), Best Director of a Musical (Lapine), Best Costume Designer (Jane Greenwood), and Best Lighting Designer (Beverly Emmons).

Brian Friel had his third opening at the Plymouth in four years on March 19, 1995, when Brian Dennehy and Donal Donnelly starred in a revival of his 1981 play *Translations*. It lasted only twenty-five performances.

The Lincoln Center Theater produced a splendid revival of Edward Albee's 1966 play *A Delicate Balance* on April 21, 1996, with Rosemary Harris, George Grizzard, Elaine Stritch, Elizabeth Wilson, Mary Beth Hurt, and John Carter. Highly praised by critics, the revival ran for 186 performances and won the following Tony Awards: Best Revival of a Play, Best Direction of a Play (Gerald Gutierrez), Best Actor (Grizzard). Rosemary Harris, and Elaine Stritch earned Tony nominations for Best Actress in a Play.

April 28, 1997, brought a long-running musical to this theatre: *Jekyll & Hyde*, with music by Frank Wildhorn and book and lyrics by Leslie Bricusse. It starred Robert Cuccioli (as Jekyll/Hyde), Christiane Noll, and Linda Eder. The show received the following Tony Award nominations: Actor in a Musical (Cuccioli), Musical Book (Bricusse), Costume Designer (Ann Curtis), and Lighting Designer (Beverly Emmons), but it won none. Despite very mixed reviews, the musical found its audience (many of whom christened themselves "Jekkies" and tracked the show through websites) and ran for 1,543 performances, the record for this theatre. It was Broadway's first true Internet hit.

In April 2001 Faith Prince starred in the first Broadway revival of the tuneful Jule Styne/Betty Comden/Adolph Green musical *Bells Are Ringing*. Prince played the role of the lovelorn answering-service operator originated by Judy Holliday, with Marc Kudisch as her secret love. The party was over after two months.

Closely following her Tony-winning blockbuster success with *The Producers* at the St. James Theatre, director-choreographer Susan Stroman returned to Broadway six months later with *Thou Shalt Not*, an original musical based on the 1867 novel *Thérèse Raquin*, with music and lyrics by Harry Connick Jr. and book by

David Thompson. Kate Levering and Craig Bierko starred as the two illicit lovers in this story of passion and murder, but Norbert Leo Butz got what good reviews were to be had as the ghost of the dead husband. Overall, however, it was as big a flop as *The Producers* was a hit, and it closed after eighty-five performances.

Kathleen Turner starred as Mrs. Robinson in Terry Johnson's April 2002 stage adaptation of the film classic *The Graduate*, including a nude scene that got more press attention than the drama.

One of the highlights of the 2002—3 season came in its closing days with a superbly acted revival of Eugene O'Neill's classic family drama *Long Day's Journey into Night*, starring Brian Dennehy and Vanessa Redgrave as James and Mary Tyrone. The pair were named Best Actor and Best Actress in a Play at the 2003 Tony Awards. Tony nominations went to Philip Seymour Hoffman and Robert Sean Leonard as their tortured sons. The production represented a high-water mark in the multiproduction collaboration between Dennehy and director Robert Falls that originated at the Goodman Theatre in Chicago. The play ran 117 performances.

Talk-show host and former Tony Awards host Rosie O'Donnell found out the hard way that Broadway producing was more difficult than it looked when critics savaged her November 2003 project *Taboo*, a musical about the drugs-and-sex-infused London club scene of the 1980s. Onetime punk rocker Boy George (real name George O'Dowd) supplied the score and also starred in the production as his real-life mentor, Leigh Bowery, while Euan Morton somewhat confusingly played the young Boy George. O'Donnell had fallen in love with *Taboo* (pronounced "tuh-BOO," British style) in its West End debut and struggled under a media microscope to get it on its feet in New York. But the show never found its audience and closed after a round 100 performances, losing its entire investment, much of it from O'Donnell's own pocket. Morton, Boy George, and costar Raúl Esparza all copped Tony nominations for their acting, and Boy George got a nomination for his score.

Frank Langella, Ray Liotta, and Jane Adams starred in Stephen Belber's short-lived April 2004 drama *Match*, about a comfortable and loquacious older bachelor who is suddenly confronted by a grown man claiming to be his son.

Brooklyn, listed on the poster as "Bklyn," was a self-described "sidewalk fairytale" about a singing prodigy who comes to America looking for her long-lost father, armed only with her name (after his hometown, Brooklyn) and an unfinished lullaby he wrote. The musical stayed for 284 performances starting October 21, 2004, and introduced future star Eden Espinoza, who blew the roof off with a power ballad, "Once upon a Time," by Mark Schoenfeld and Barri McPherson. The show is also remembered for Tobin Ost's costumes, supposedly designed by the show's street-people characters, composed of trash bags, police emergency tape, and other Dumpster jetsam.

On May 9, 2005, during the run of *Brooklyn*, the Plymouth Theatre was renamed the Gerald Schoenfeld Theatre after the chairman of the Shubert Organization.

The first show to open at the rechristened house was *Chita Rivera: The Dancer's Life*, a tour through the career of the dancing star of *Chicago*, *Bye Bye Birdie*, and *West Side Story*. Songs from these and other great shows were combined with several original songs by Stephen Flaherty and Lynn Ahrens. But the seventy-two-year-old Rivera, who recreated all her own dances, may have waited until too late in her career to do such a show. It folded after a two-month run.

March 2006 saw an underrated revival of Herman Wouk's *The Caine Mutiny Court-Martial*, starring David Schwimmer of TV's *Friends* as Lieutenant Greenwald and Îeljko Ivanek as Queeg. The jury of critics said that Jerry Zaks's production lacked the high dramatic tension of the courtroom drama's original and film productions, and the case was dismissed after seventeen performances.

On October 5, 2006, attorney John Breglio, trustee of the Michael Bennett estate, produced a revival of the classic musical *A Chorus Line*, which enlisted Bennett's original codirector Bob Avian as director and original dance captain Baayork Lee as choreographer. Dancer interest in the production was intense, and the audition process became the subject of a 2008 documentary film, *Every Little Step*. Rather than trying to find a far-fetched new concept for the show, Avian and Lee went the other direction and strove to present *A Chorus Line* almost exactly as it had been done originally in 1975. This approach earned them some critical finger wagging. But with a cast that included Charlotte d'Amboise as Cassie, Mara Davi as Maggie, Chrissie Whitehead as Kristine, and Tony Yazbeck as Al, the show was welcomed by audiences and kept the Schoenfeld stage lit up with "What I Did for Love" for 759 performances.

On October 16, 2008, John Lithgow, Katie Holmes, Dianne Wiest, and Patrick Wilson took to the Schoenfeld stage in a revival of Arthur Miller's drama *All My Sons*, about a wartime crime whose true perpetrator is finally revealed years after his partner is wrongly convicted and imprisoned. Simon McBurney staged the production with projections and sound effects to keep the war in the back of the minds of the characters and the audience.

A great disappointment of the 2008—9 season was Michael Jacobs's drama *Impressionism*, about a slow-blooming romance between an art gallery owner and a photographer. The script was strong enough to attract Joan Allen and Jeremy Irons in the main roles, with Marsha Mason, André De Shields, and Aaron Lazar among the powerhouse supporting cast. But critics and audiences just didn't see what the stars saw in it, and when the production received no Tony nominations, producers shuttered it after fifty-six performances.

One of the hottest tickets of fall 2009 was Keith Huff's two-hander, *A Steady Rain*, about a pair of buddy cops whose small professional compromises snowball into corruption, murder, and suicide. What made this production a sensation was the casting of Hugh Jackman and Daniel Craig as the cops, drawing mobs of cheering fans both inside and outside the Schoenfeld at each performance. The show shattered the record for highest weekly gross for any nonmusical Broadway production up to that point, pulling more than $1.1 million dollars a week over the course of its ten-week limited run.

Martin McDonagh's peculiar black comedy *A Behanding in Spokane* arrived March 4, 2010, with Christopher Walken adding to his rogues' gallery of eccentric characters as Carmichael, a man who has spent his whole life searching for his lost hand, which was lopped off by sadistic hillbillies . . . or perhaps not. He turns the tables on a young couple (Anthony Mackie and Zoe Kazan) who try to palm him off, so to speak, with a different hand. Sam Rockwell played a suspicious hotel clerk who finds himself wrapped up in their drama.

Operated by the Shubert Organization, the Schoenfeld remains one of Broadway's most sought-after theatres for dramas and modest-sized musicals.

HELEN HAYES
THEATRE

IN JULY 1983 THE FORMER LITTLE
Theatre at 240 West Forty-fourth Street was
officially renamed the Helen Hayes Theatre in
honor of one of America's most beloved actresses. The tribute was deemed fitting by the theatrical community, since the first theatre bearing the name of Helen Hayes, on West Forty-
sixth Street, had been torn down in 1982 to make
way for the Marriott Marquis Hotel.

The Little was built by producer Winthrop
Ames and opened on March 12, 1912. Ames, an
aristocratic New Englander, rebelled against
Broadway commercialism and built the Little,
then with only 299 seats, as an intimate house for
the production of noncommercial plays that were
too risky to stage in large Broadway theatres.

The *New York Times* admired the theatre's

Left: Program cover for the 1924 hit, *Pigs*.

Center: Program cover for Rachel Crothers's 1929 comedy, *Let Us Be Gay*.

Right: Aline MacMahon and Thomas Chalmers in Eugene O'Neill's Pulitzer Prize-winning play, *Beyond the Horizon* (1920).

red-brick, green-shuttered exterior, its Colonial-style lobby with a fireplace, and the auditorium, which had no balcony or boxes and was built on an incline that afforded an unobstructed view of the stage.

The opening play was John Galsworthy's *The Pigeon*, which critic Ward Morehouse described as "a thoughtfully written comedy that brought forth human and delightful characterizations from Frank Reicher and Russ Whytal."

Ames's policy—to produce "the clever, the unusual drama that had a chance of becoming a library classic"—continued to be reflected in the Little Theatre's fare. Among the early productions, all financed solely by Ames, were George Bernard Shaw's *The Philanderer* (1913); *Prunella*, a fantasy by Laurence Houseman and Harley Granville-Barker, starring Marguerite Clark and Ernest Glendinning (1913); and Cyril Harcourt's comedy *A Pair of Stockings* (1914).

By 1915 Ames was having financial problems with the Little. Because of his theatre's small seating capacity, the impresario was losing money, even with hits. On March 11, 1915, the *New York Times* reported that Ames was in danger of losing his house. To prevent this, Ames planned to increase the seating capacity to 1,000, add a balcony, and make the stage larger. In 1920 Burns Mantle reported that the Little had been remodeled and the seating capacity was now 450 seats.

Ames, whose money came from his family's manufacturing interests, began leasing the Little to outside producers such as the highly respected John Golden and Oliver Morosco.

During the 1918—19 season, Rachel Crothers directed her own comedy, *A Little Journey*, at the Little. It ran for 252 performances. This was followed by another hit, *Please*

Get Married, a farce starring Ernest Truex.

The true purpose of the Little Theatre, to present new playwrights and experimental dramas, was fulfilled by its next two bookings. In January 1920 Oliver Morosco presented *Mamma's Affair*, a first play by Rachel Barton Butler that won a prize as the best drama written by a student of Professor George Baker's famous "English 47" class at Harvard. Morosco presented a cash award to the author and mounted her play successfully with Effie Shannon. The other drama was Eugene O'Neill's first full-length play, *Beyond the Horizon*, which had been playing matinees at other theatres before it was moved to the Little. It starred Richard Bennett and won the Pulitzer Prize.

The Little next housed one of its gold mines. *The First Year*, by actor Frank Craven, who starred in it with Roberta Arnold, proved to be a sensation. It opened on October 20, 1920, was produced by John Golden and ran for 760 performances.

Producer Golden and playwright Craven thought that lightning might strike twice. In 1922 they tried again with Craven's *Spite Corner*, a small-town play about feuding families and lovers, but the comedy lasted only three months.

Guy Bolton, the prolific playwright who wrote many hit musicals and plays in his long career, had two comedies produced at the Little in 1923. The first, *Polly Preferred*, starring the vivacious blonde Genevieve Tobin and William Harrigan, was a daffy hit about a chorus girl who is sold to promoters like a product in a store window; the other, *Chicken Feed*, subtitled "Wages for Wives," was really ahead of its time. It would have delighted women's lib advocates a half-century later.

At this time Ames still owned the Little,

Above: Harvey Fierstein gives a Tony Award-winning performance in his Tony-winning play, *Torch Song Trilogy* (1982).

Center: Raphael Klackin (with balloons) and Aharon Meskin in *Children of the Shadows* (1964).

Right: Danny Aiello, Barbara Coggin, and Kathleen Turner in *Gemini* (1977).

but he leased it to John Golden, F. Ray Comstock, and L. Lawrence Weber, with Weber also managing the theatre.

Brooks Atkinson reported in his book *Broadway* that by 1922 Ames had lost $504,372 on the Little Theatre. His other theatre, the Booth, which he built with Lee Shubert in 1913, was a commercial house and is still successful today. When Ames died in 1937, his estate had dwindled to $77,000, and his widow was forced to move from the sprawling Ames mansion to a small cottage on their estate.

In 1924 a play with the odd title *Pigs* turned out to be one of the year's best. Produced by John Golden, it starred Wallace Ford as a speculator who bought fifty sick pigs, cured them, and sold them at an enormous profit. He was greatly helped by his girlfriend, played by the refreshing Nydia Westman, who garnered love letters from the critics. The hit ran for 347 performances.

Thomas Mitchell proved popular in a 1926 comedy, *The Wisdom Tooth*, by Marc Connelly; *2 Girls Wanted* was a smash in 1926; *The Grand Street Follies*, a popular annual revue that spoofed the season's plays and players, moved

here from the Neighborhood Playhouse in 1927; and Rachel Crothers returned to the Little with *Let Us Be Gay*, a 1929 hit starring Francine Larrimore and Warren William.

In 1930 Edward G. Robinson was praised for his acting in *Mr. Samuel*, and Elmer Rice's *The Left Bank* (1931), about Americans in Paris, entertained patrons for 241 performances. A spate of plays with "Honeymoon" in their titles moved in. *Honeymoon* and *One More Honeymoon* were short-lived, but *Pre-Honeymoon*, by Alford Van Ronkel and Anne Nichols (author of *Abie's Irish Rose*), was a big enough hit to move from the Lyceum to the Little and to cause the theatre's name to be changed to Anne Nichols' Little Theatre.

In 1936 Sir Cedric Hardwicke made his U.S. debut in *Promise*. In 1937, when Cornelia Otis Skinner opened her one-woman show, *Edna His Wife*, the house reverted to being called the Little. A sparkling revue, *Reunion in New York*, opened in 1940 and reunited a group of talented performers from Vienna who had been introduced to New Yorkers previously in another revue, *From Vienna* (1939).

The Little Theatre ceased being a legitimate Broadway theatre for the next two decades. During this hiatus, the house, located adjacent to the headquarters of the *New York Times*, was known as the New York Times Hall from 1942 until 1959, when it became an ABC Television studio.

The Little returned to the legitimate fold in 1963 with *Tambourines to Glory*, a gospel music play by Langston Hughes and Jobe Huntley. The Paul Taylor Dance Company appeared there in the same year. In 1964 Habimah, the national theatre of Israel, staged *The Dybbuk*, *Children of the Shadows* and *Each Had Six Wings*. Later that year Paul Newman, Joanne Woodward, and James Costigan appeared in the Actors Studio production of Costigan's comedy *Baby Want a Kiss*. The critics gave it the kiss of death. In 1964, when the Pulitzer Prize play *The*

Left: Claudia Shear as Mae West in her play *Dirty Blonde* (2000). (Photo by Joan Marcus)

Right: Peter Michael Goetz and Kelly Bishop in the Tony-winning play *The Last Night of Ballyhoo* (1997). (Photo by Carol Rosegg)

Subject Was Roses moved to this theatre from the Royale, the theatre's name was changed to the Winthrop Ames. In March 1965 the name went back to the Little, which it retained until 1983. From late 1964 to mid-1974 the theatre was leased to Westinghouse Broadcasting and hosted the David Frost and Merv Griffin TV shows. Fans of the latter program may remember announcer Arthur Treacher's cheery opening: "From the Little Theatre in Times Square, it's the *Merv Griffin Show!*"

In 1974 the Little went legit again and housed Ray Aranha's play *My Sister, My Sister*. *The Runner Stumbles* (1976) was a success, but *Unexpected Guests* (1977) was a failure. *Lamppost Reunion*, Louis LaRusso II's much-heralded play about a Frank Sinatra—like singer returning to his old haunts in Hoboken, New Jersey, managed a run of only seventy-seven performances.

In June 1977 Albert Innaurato's comedy *Gemini* moved in, and it epitomized the kind of show Winthrop Ames wanted in his theatre. The play was first done at Playwrights Horizons, then at the PAF Playhouse in Huntington, Long Island, followed by a production at the Circle Repertory Company. Finally, this production was moved to the Little, where it ran for an amazing 1,788 performances, making it the Little's longest-running show and the fourth-longest-

running straight play in Broadway history.

In 1979 the Helen Hayes Theatre was purchased by the Little Theatre Group—Martin Markinson and Donald Tick—with Ashton Springer serving as managing director. In 1981 this group spent a considerable amount to restore the house. Its interior was beautifully redesigned by ADCADESIGN: Wayne Adams, John Carlson, and Wolfgang H. Kurth.

The Little's next three shows did not fare well. They were *Ned and Jack* (1981); William Alfred's *The Curse of an Aching Heart* (1982), starring Faye Dunaway; and *Solomon's Child* (1982), an exposé of fanatical religious cults.

In June 1982 another ideal Little Theatre play came to the house. It was *Torch Song Trilogy* by Harvey Fierstein, who starred in his trio of bittersweet comedies about gay life, all with the same central character. The triptych originated at La MaMa E.T.C., was next done at the Richard Allen Center for Culture, and then appeared at the Actors' Playhouse before it moved to the Little. *Torch Song Trilogy* won the 1983 Tony Award for Best Play, and a Tony for Best Actor in a Play went to Fierstein.

Torch Song Trilogy was followed by such varied productions as *The News* (1985), a rock musical about sensational journalism; *Corpse!* (1985), a comedy thriller starring Keith Baxter and Milo O'Shea; *Oh Coward!* (1986), a revival of Roderick Cook's 1972 revue of Noël Coward songs and skits, starring Cook, Patrick Quinn, and Catherine Cox; *Mummenschanz/The New Show* (1986), a new edition of the popular mime show; *The Nerd* (1987), the late Larry Shue's amusing comedy about a man posing as a jerk to help out a friend; Scott Bakula and Alison Fraser in *Romance/Romance* (1988), two charming one-act musicals that moved here from Off-Broadway; *Mandy Patinkin in Concert: Dress Casual* (1989), the singing actor in a diverting program; *Artist Descending a Staircase* (1989), Tom Stoppard's complex com-

Frank Gorshin incarnated comedian George Burns in *Say Goodnight, Gracie* (2002). (Photo by Carol Rosegg)

edy about the art world; and *Miss Margarida's Way* (1990), Estelle Parsons in a return engagement of her acclaimed one-woman show about an explosive teacher and her unruly pupils.

Prelude to a Kiss (1990), Craig Lucas's fantasy that originally starred Alec Baldwin Off-Broadway, moved here with Timothy Hutton in Baldwin's role, plus Mary-Louise Parker, Barnard Hughes, and Debra Monk. The 1990s saw *The High Rollers Social and Pleasure Club* (1992), a musical revue set in New Orleans; *3 from Brooklyn* (1992), Roslyn Kind in a revue about Brooklyn; *Shakespeare for My Father* (1993), Lynn Redgrave in a highly praised one-woman show about her late father, actor Michael Redgrave; and Joan Rivers in *Sally Marr . . . and her escorts* (1994). Rivers not only starred in this play about Lenny Bruce's mother, but cowrote it with Ernie Sanders and Lonny Price. She was nominated for a Tony Award for her performance. The voice of young Lenny Bruce was supplied by Jason Woliner.

In November 1994, the popular Flying Karamazov Brothers juggling troupe opened here in their fourth Broadway appearance. They called their vaudeville show *The Flying Karamazov Brothers Do the Impossible*. They entertained for fifty performances.

The theatre's next tenant was *Defending the Caveman*, a comic monologue on the differences between men and women. It had a prosperous run of 671 performances, a record for a nonmusical solo show. It made way for another success: Alfred Uhry's *The Last Night of Ballyhoo* (1997), starring Paul Rudd and Dana Ivey, which ran for 557 performances. The play dealt with the conflicts within an Atlanta Jewish family at the time of the 1939 premiere of the film *Gone with the Wind* in that city. The play won the Tony Award as Best Play of the season, making Uhry the only playwright to win a Tony Award, a Pulitzer Prize (for *Driving Miss Daisy*), and an Academy Award (for the screenplay of *Driving Miss Daisy*). Tony Awards were also won by Dana Ivey and Terry Beaver for their performances in *The Last Night of Ballyhoo*.

This theatre's next two entries were not successful: *Getting and Spending* (1998), a play by Michael J. Chepiga, which originated at the Old Globe Theater in San Diego (forty-one performances); and *Band in Berlin*, a musical about the Comedian Harmonists, a real-life troupe of singers popular in Germany in the 1920s but banned by Hitler in the 1930s because it com-

bined Jewish and non-Jewish performers.

In 1999 *Night Must Fall*, a revival of Emlyn Williams's 1936 thriller about a psychotic killer, moved here from the Lyceum Theater. Based on an actual London murder case, it starred Matthew Broderick, Judy Parfitt, and Pamela J. Gray and was produced by Tony Randall's National Arts Theater. It ran ninety-six performances.

Night Must Fall was followed by a comedy called *Epic Proportions*, by Larry Coen and David Crane, which spoofed the absurdities of filming a Hollywood biblical spectacle with thousands of extras—all played by a cast of just eight. It starred Kristin Chenoweth and Richard B. Shull. Unfortunately, Shull died during the play's run. He was replaced by Lewis J. Stadlen. The play ran for eighty-four performances.

On May 1, 2000, *Dirty Blonde*, a hit Off-Broadway play, moved here from the New York Theatre Workshop. The comedy dealt with the famed actress/playwright Mae West. It was written by Claudia Shear, who also starred in a dual role as West and one of her fans. The play was conceived by Shear and James Lapine, who directed it. Kevin Chamberlin and Bob Stillman costarred in a variety of roles. The play proved an instant hit and was nominated for five Tony Awards.

Hershey Felder wrote, acted in, and played piano in *George Gershwin Alone*, his solo tribute to the great Broadway composer. It opened April

30, 2001, and shared its fascinatin' rhythm with audiences for ninety-six-man performances.

Composer Andrew Lloyd Webber and prolific British playwright Alan Ayckbourn shared an interest in P. G. Wodehouse's stories about dim-witted aristocrat Bertie Wooster and his super-humanly capable butler, Jeeves. In the 1970s, between Lloyd Webber's hits *Jesus Christ Superstar* and *Evita*, they collaborated on a flop musical adaptation called *Jeeves*. In the late 1990s the two writers returned to this project, determined to whack it into shape. The result was *By Jeeves*, a scaled-down version of the story (including the lovely takeout song "Half a Moment"), which had a modest run in London. It moved to the Hayes October 28, 2001, just weeks after the September 11 attacks, and Lloyd Webber himself attended box office opening day, greeting ticket buyers on the sidewalk out front and congratulating New Yorkers on their stiff upper lip. The generous gesture didn't help the slightly twee and very British musical, which lasted only seventy-three performances, the composer's shortest Broadway run to date.

Michele Lowe's black-comedy wish-fulfill-ment play *The Smell of the Kill* showed a group of women who are so sick of their loutish husbands that they concoct a plan to murder them all. The play opened March 26, 2002, and closed after forty performances.

Rupert Holmes, better known as a composer, lyricist, and mystery writer for shows such as *The Mystery of Edwin Drood*, earned a Tony nomination for his gentle solo show *Say Goodnight, Gracie*, a portrait of comedian George Burns. Frank Gorshin embodied Burns for 364 performances, starting October 10, 2002.

It was followed by another Tony-nominated solo show, William Gibson's *Golda's Balcony*, in which Tovah Feldshuh played Israeli founding mother Golda Meir. Feldshuh was also Tony-nominated as Best Actress in a Play and incarnated the prime minister for 493 performances, from October 15, 2003, to January 2, 2005.

Jackie Mason returned to Broadway with his eighth comedy show, this one titled *Jackie Mason: Freshly Squeezed*, filled with his patented takes on politics, culture, and the modern woild. It stayed at the Hayes for 172 performances.

Cheech Marin, half of the comedy team of Cheech and Chong, made his Broadway directorial debut with *Latinologues*, a showcase for Latino comedians. The bill featured Rick Najera, Eugenio Derbez, Rene Lavan, and Shirley A. Rumierk. It played ninety-three performances starting October 13, 2005.

Sarah Jones, daughter of a United Nations diplomat, put her observations to work in *Bridge & Tunnel*, a solo show in which she embodied a whole rainbow of recent immigrants to New York. It opened January 26, 2006, and occupied the Hayes for 213 performances, winning the 2006 Tony Award for Best Special Theatrical Event.

On April 27, 2006, during the run of *Bridge & Tunnel*, Hayes co-owner Donald Tick passed away. His name continued to appear as a principal of the Little Theatre Group.

The popular downtown comedy musical club act known as Kiki and Herb (actually Justin Bond and Kenny Mellman), came uptown to the Hayes for a twenty-seven-performance late-summer 2006 limited run titled *Kiki & Herb: Alive on Broadway*.

From a semi-drag act, the Hayes next turned itself over to a puppet show—but a distinguished one. *Jay Johnson: The Two and Only* (September 28, 2006) was also an autobiography. In addition to more traditional puppet high jinks, Johnson and his "costar" Bob narrated Johnson's life story as a ventriloquist, notably his relationship with his mentor. Though the show ran only two months and didn't survive until the June Tony Awards, it won the 2007 Tony for Best Theatrical Event.

On July 10, 2007, the Hayes got one of the great sleeper hits of modern times, a full-scale musical called *Xanadu*, which was based on a spectacular flop disco-era film musical of the same name but reconceived as a tongue-in-cheek campfest by librettist Douglas Carter Beane. Cheyenne Jackson (replacing James Carpinello, who injured himself during previews) played a man whose life dream is to open . . . a roller disco. Kerry Butler played one of the Greek muses who decides to help him, and Mary Testa and Jackie Hoffman played her sister muses, who plot her failure. Also featuring Tony Roberts as Zeus(!), the musical fantasy drew incredulous reviews from critics who couldn't believe how much they liked it, and *Xanadu* roller-skated its way to a 512-performance run.

With the thirtieth anniversary of the Little Theatre Group approaching, Markinson and Tick's family announced in summer 2008 that they had entered into an agreement with Off-Broadway's Second Stage Theatre to transfer ownership of the Helen Hayes Theatre. Second

Mary Testa and Jackie Hoffman with their fellow Muses in the musical *Xanadu* (2007). Photo by Paul Kolnik

Stage, whose flagship 296-seat stage was a converted bank building about a block away at the corner of Forty-third Street and Eighth Avenue, was planning to create a Broadway pied-à-terre like Manhattan Theatre Club's Friedman Theatre and Roundabout's American Airlines Theatre and Studio 54. Second Stage was hoping to take ownership sometime in 2010. The *New York Times* reported that the 597-seat Hayes would be "dedicated exclusively to the development and presentation of contemporary American theatrical productions."

In the meantime, New Vaudeville clown Slava Polunin transferred his *Slava's Snowshow* to the Hayes in December 2008 after giving more than a thousand performanc-

es Off-Broadway. It played out the holidays and prepared to tour.

In January 2009 the Hayes became the third Broadway stop for the long-running hit *The 39 Steps*, which had opened at the American Airlines Theatre, then moved to the Cort for several months. In early 2010 *The 39 Steps* took its fourth New York step and moved Off-Broadway.

In its place came *Next Fall*, Geoffrey Nauffts's play about religion and gay relationships, which had been developed by the Naked Angels company Off-Broadway.

The Helen Hayes remains Broadway smallest theatre and fiercely independent in both its management and programming.

HILTON
THEATRE

THE HILTON THEATRE, NOW UNDER
the direction of Clear Channel corporation,
opened in 1998 as the Ford Center for the
Performing Arts after a miraculous restoration that combined elements of two adjacent,
historic Forty-second Street theatres on the
site—the Lyric and the Apollo.

In 1995 the Toronto-based Livent company
announced that the Ford Motor Company would
grant its name and financial support to a new
1,839-seat theatre, combining features of the
Lyric (built in 1903) and the Apollo (1910).
Although the two vintage theatres were largely
demolished, landmark elements of their build-
ings, both interior and exterior, were retained
and combined in the new structure by architects
Richard Blinder and Peter Kofman. This includ-

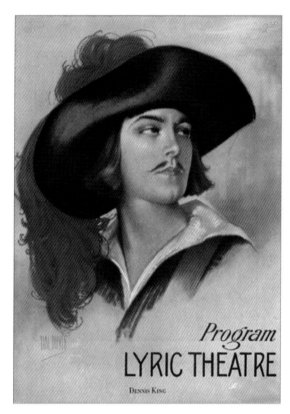

Program LYRIC THEATRE

DENNIS KING

ed ceiling domes and the proscenium arch, sail vault, and side boxes, all of which were expanded to fit the scale of the new, larger theatre. An elliptical dome from the Lyric Theatre was reproduced and now forms the centerpiece of a magnificent two-story atrium design with a majestic limestone staircase. In the atrium's floor there is a spectacular mosaic design featuring masks of comedy and tragedy inspired by similar designs that adorn the Forty-third Street facade retained from the Lyric Theatre. At the top of the stair is a medallion with the head of Zeus, also taken from the Lyric Theatre.

The Ford Center was baptized in starlight at a special December 18, 1997, ceremony, attended by stars and writers from previous Livent shows, including Chita Rivera, Christopher Plummer, Colm Wilkinson, Elaine Stritch, Harold Prince, Terrence McNally, Marvin Hamlisch, E. L. Doctorow, Vanessa Williams, John Guare, Stephen Flaherty, Lynn Ahrens, James Hammerstein, and many more. Marin Mazzie and Brian Stokes Mitchell sang "Wheels of a Dream" from the forthcoming inaugural production, *Ragtime*, and Mazzie alone sang the hymn "Bless This House" with new lyrics by Marty Bell and Ahrens. Led by Livent's Garth Drabinsky, the assembled stars used multiple sets of scissors to cut a red ribbon across the stage and declared the house christened.

The opening of the new theatre on January 18, 1998, was a gala event afforded much media attention. Fortunately, *Ragtime* equaled the splendor of the theatre. Based on the novel by Doctorow and the film of the same title, adapted by McNally with a score by Flaherty and Ahrens, the musical boasted a stellar cast that included Mazzie, Mitchell, Audra McDonald, Mark Jacoby, and Judy Kaye. Graciela Daniele staged the musical segments and Frank Galati directed the book, which featured personages of the past (Booker T. Washington, Harry Houdini, J. P. Morgan, Henry Ford, Evelyn Nesbit,

Stanford White, Harry K. Thaw, Emma Goldman, and others) in a fictional story.

Racial discrimination was a strong element of the plot, and some critics and theatregoers felt that the musical's second act was too long and depressing. *Ragtime* lost to *The Lion King* for the 1998 Best Musical Tony Award, but it won the following Tonys: Best Musical Book (McNally), Best Score (Flaherty and Ahrens), Best Featured Musical Actress (McDonald), and Best Orchestrations (William David Brohn). It also received seven other Tony Award nominations. The musical ran for 861 performances and was hailed by the Drama League as "one of the 20 greatest musicals of the 20th Century." It got the Ford Center off to a flying start.

In 1999, after operating the theatre for a little over a year, the financially troubled Livent included the Ford Center among assets sold to the SFX Theatrical Group. Parent company SFX Entertainment was the largest diversified promoter, producer, and venue operator for live entertainment events in the United States at that time. SFX also bought the Ford Center for the Performing Arts in Chicago. SFX was subsequently purchased by Live Nation, Inc., which thereby gained control of the theatre. The company is now called Clear Channel.

Andrew Lloyd Webber's Really Useful Group was behind the April 16, 2000, revival of his rock opera *Jesus Christ Superstar*. Glenn

Top left: PLAYBILL from the 2006 Earth, Wind & Fire musical *Hot Feet*.

Top center: Program cover for *Her Family Tree* (1921)

Top right: PLAYBILL cover for *Take a Chance* (1932).

Above: PLAYBILL cover for George White's *Scandals of 1931*, starring Ethel Merman, Ray Bolger, Rudy Vallee, Willie and Eugene Howard, and, in the chorus, Alice Faye.

Carter and Maya Days were featured as Jesus of Nazareth and Mary Magdalene, and the show continued for 161 performances.

It was followed on May 2, 2001, by a no-expenses-spared revival of *42nd Street*, which enjoyed the publicity value of putting the show of that name on the street of that name. It won the 2001 Tony Award as Best Revival of a Musical and earned Christine Ebersole the Tony as Best Featured Actress in a Musical for her performance as diva Dorothy Brock. The standard "I Only Have Eyes for You" was added to the score especially for her. *42nd Street* continued for an impressive 1,524 performances, one of the longest runs ever for a Broadway revival.

During its run, a special September 24, 2001, concert performance of the musical *Dreamgirls* featured performances by Audra McDonald, Heather Headley, Norm Lewis, and Lillias White to benefit the Actors Fund of America.

Just over seven years after opening as the Ford Center, the theatre got a new name for a new sponsor, the Hilton Hotel chain, which purchased the right to rechristen the playhouse. On April 28, 2005, the new Hilton Theatre welcomed Jeremy Sams's stage adaptation of the musical film *Chitty Chitty Bang Bang*, based on Ian Fleming's children's book about an inventor's adventures in his flying car. The show featured a tuneful score by the team of Richard M. Sherman and Robert B. Sherman, and warm-hearted performances by Raúl Esparza as Caractacus Potts, Philip Bosco as Grandpa Potts, Erin Dilly as Truly Scrumptious, plus Marc Kudisch as the Baron, Jan Maxwell as the Baroness, and Kevin Cahoon as the nightmarish Childcatcher. Nevertheless, the true star was the shiny flying car of the title, designed by Anthony Ward, which looked more fun than a carnival ride. *Chitty* flew 285 times.

To the growing roster of "jukebox musicals" was added *Hot Feet* on April 30, 2006, using the music of the funk group Earth, Wind and Fire (EWF) to tell a *Red Shoes*—like story about how the devil uses a pair of magical dancing shoes to ensnare the soul of a talented young dancer. Heru Ptah supplied a book that wove together songs by EWF principal Maurice White and more than a dozen others. Conceived, directed and choreographed by Maurice Hines, the show ran ninety-seven performances.

Children's author Dr. Seuss came to Broadway on November 8, 2006, with the debut of *Dr. Seuss' How the Grinch Stole Christmas!* The holiday show starred resonant-voiced Patrick Page as the misanthropic title character, who hopes to ruin Christmas for the quaint town of Whoville by stealing their holiday decorations, gifts, and food. Timothy Mason adapted the book and wove songs from a popular animated TV version of the story with new songs by himself and Mel Marvin. The Grinch filched the Roast Beast for 107 performances and did well enough to return to Broadway the following year, though at the St. James Theatre.

The mighty songwriting team that gave Broadway the megahits *Les Misérables* and *Miss Saigon* struck out in their third Broadway production, *The Pirate Queen*, based on the true story of an Irishwoman who defied Queen Elizabeth I and harried the British royal navy in the sixteenth century. "I'll Be There" was an attractive and stirring anthem, but the consensus was that the score by Claude-Michel Schönberg, Alain Boublil, John Dempsey, and Richard Maltby Jr. did not measure up to the previous Schönberg-Boublil efforts. The show opened April 5, 2007, and hung on for eighty-five performances, though leading lady Stephanie J. Block attracted a cadre of devoted fans.

Hopes were high for *Young Frankenstein*, a stage musical adaptation of Mel Brooks's movie comedy classic of the same title. To musicalize his spoof of classic Hollywood horror movies, Brooks reassembled most of the team that helped make his 2001 adaptation of *The Producers* one of the biggest hits of the decade, including director/choreographer Susan Stroman and co-librettist Thomas Meehan. Brooks and the rest of the producers set their premium seat top price at a whopping $450—a new record. After the November 8, 2007, opening, critics found it hard to talk about the merits of the show without doing so in light of that expense. *Young Frankenstein* showcased the raucous performances by Roger Bart as Dr. Frederick Frankenstein,

Christopher Fitzgerald as Igor, Sutton Foster as Inga, Shuler Hensley as the Monster, Andrea Martin as Frau Blucher, and Megan Mullally as Elizabeth. Despite brand-new Brooks songs, including the pell-mell patter song "The Brain" for Bart, the torch song "He Vas My Boyfriend" for Martin, and the bouncy "Roll in the Hay" for Foster, the show found itself shut out of the Tony Awards. It ran 485 performances and toured with Bart and Hensley recreating their Broadway roles.

The Hilton put up a marquee for the musical *Spider-Man: Turn Off the Dark* in summer 2009 and began selling tickets to the promised spectacular, to be directed by Julie Taymor, with a score by Bono and The Edge from the rock group U2. But uncertainty about the show's financing arose, and the production was postponed until later in 2010. The Hilton was dark for most of 2009 and 2010.

Since the Hilton Theatre/Ford Center in New York combined elements of both the Lyric

Dancers from the musical *The Pirate Queen* (2007). (Photo by Joan Marcus)

Theatre and the Apollo, brief histories of both are in order. The Lyric Theatre at 213 West Forty-second Street was built in 1903 by the Shuberts and composer Reginald De Koven to house the type of operettas De Koven composed. The Lyric was noted for its magnificent turn-of-the-century Forty-second Street and Forty-third Street facades, which have been splendidly restored as part of the Hilton Theatre. The Lyric was one of the few Broadway theatres that had two entrances—one on Forty-second Street and one on Forty-third Street. The theatre was designed by Victor Hugo Koehler and was criticized because posts supporting the two balconies obstructed the view from some seats. Also, there were too many boxes (eighteen) for a theatre this size.

The Lyric opened on October 12, 1903, with a play called *Old Heidelberg*, starring the distinguished actor Richard Mansfield.

The Shubert brothers established their first New York producing headquarters above the theatre. In 1905 Douglas Fairbanks Sr. starred there in the hit musical *Fantana*, whose producer and co-librettist was Sam S. Shubert. Oscar Straus's *The Chocolate Soldier*, a musical version of Shaw's play *Arms and the Man*, proved to be a huge hit in 1909. Another operetta hit was Rudolf Friml's *The Firefly* (1912). In 1911 Henrik Ibsen's *The Lady From the Sea* had its New York premiere here.

In its heyday, the Lyric enjoyed such delights as Fred and Adele Astaire in the 1922 musical *For Goodness Sake*. Bedlam ensued in 1925 when the four Marx Brothers (Harpo, Groucho, Chico, and Zeppo) wreaked havoc on the Lyric in their lunatic musical *The Cocoanuts*, with a book by George S. Kaufman and a score by Irving Berlin. In the cast was also the stately dowager Margaret Dumont, who was to become the victim of Groucho's insults in many of their

shows and films. There is an amusing anecdote about Berlin's score. Kaufman, who hated love songs, forced Berlin to take his song "Always" out of the musical. The lyric, which stated, "I'll be loving you always," bothered Kaufman, who insisted that you can't love someone always. He argued that if the lyric was "I'll be loving you, Thursday," he might accept it. The song was dropped, but it soon swept the country and was the only song from the score that became a huge hit. *The Cocoanuts* ran for 375 performances—spectacular for the 1920s.

In 1926 the popular comedy team of Bobby Clark and Paul McCullough romped successfully in a musical called *The Ramblers*. In 1928 Florenz Ziegfeld produced a hit musical version of *The Three Musketeers* with a score by Rudolf Friml, P. G. Wodehouse, and Clifford Grey, and a book by Anthony Maguire. The stellar cast included Dennis King, Vivienne Segal, dancer Harriet Hoctor, Reginald Owen, and Clarence Derwent. It was one of Ziegfeld's last hits.

The following year, Cole Porter enjoyed an early hit with the musical *Fifty Million Frenchmen*, starring William Gaxton, Helen Broderick, Genevieve Tobin, and Evelyn Hoey. "You Do Something to Me" was the show's hit song, and the score also contained several numbers that are still heard in nightclubs: "You've Got That Thing," "Find Me a Primitive Man," "I Worship You," and the clever "The Tale of an Oyster," which, unfortunately, was cut from the show after the opening night.

The book, by Herbert Fields, dealt with Americans in Paris and in particular with wealthy playboy Peter Forbes (Gaxton) pursuing a beautiful American blonde named Looloo Carroll (Tobin) in such exotic locales as Longchamps, the Ritz Bar, Café de la Paix, and the American Express Company—all brilliantly designed by Norman Bel Geddes. Helen Broderick amused with her perusal of "feelthy French postcards." Despite the stock market's crash just a month before this show opened, the musical ran for a healthy 254 performances.

Sadly, after a series of flops in the early 1930s, the Lyric became one of Forty-second Street's notorious movie houses and showed films until 1992, when it closed for good.

The adjacent Apollo Theatre began its life in 1910 as a movie and vaudeville house. In 1920 the Selwyns, notable Broadway producers, took it over, renamed it the Apollo, and converted it to a legitimate theatre. Its first production, on

Shuler Hensley as The Monster and Roger Bart as Dr. Frederick Frankenstein sing "Puttin' on the Ritz" in Mel Brooks' *Young Frankenstein* (2007). (Photo by Paul Kolnik)

November 17, 1920, was the unsuccessful musical *Jimmie* by Oscar Hammerstein II and Herbert Stothart. The following year, Lionel Barrymore also failed, as Macbeth. First-nighters had their eyes on Lionel's sister, Ethel, seated in a box, and wondered what she thought of her brother acting Shakespeare.

The house's first big hit was a musical called *Poppy* (1923), starring the great comic W. C. Fields. The book was by Howard Dietz and Dorothy Donnelly, the lyrics by Donnelly, and the music by Stephen Jones and Arthur Samuels. Fields played a traveling showman named Professor Eustace McGargle who tarries long enough in a Connecticut town to install his daughter (Madge Kennedy) as a long-lost heiress. Also in the cast was Robert Woolsey, later to become half of the popular comedy team known as Wheeler and Woolsey.

Fields was hailed by critics for his skillful juggling, his bouts with inanimate objects, and his verbal acrobatics. The *New York Times* proclaimed that it was the best performance he ever gave. The musical ran for 346 performances and was later made into a movie, also starring Fields.

Beginning in 1924 the Apollo became famous as the home of six editions of the glittering *George White's Scandals* revues, starring such luminaries as Jimmy Durante, Ethel Merman, Rudy Vallee, Ray Bolger, Eugene and Willie Howard, and, in the chorus, Alice Faye. The *Scandals* were noted for their dazzling dances performed by Ann Pennington and White, who was a gifted tap dancer, and by Tom Patricola. George Gershwin contributed hits to the Scandals, including "Somebody Loves Me" and "I'll Build a Stairway to Paradise." The two biggest *Scandals* editions were produced in 1926 and 1931. During the 1920s this theatre occasionally showed silent films.

In 1930 Bert Lahr and Kate Smith had a huge hit in the musical *Flying High*. One of that era's most successful musical comedy writing teams—DeSylva, Brown, and Henderson—collaborated with John McGowan. With aviation much in the news (Charles Lindbergh and Amelia Earhart), Broadway embraced the flying theme. Lahr played a goofy plane mechanic who establishes an all-time endurance record in the air because he doesn't know how to land the plane. The show's most fondly remembered scene was one in which Lahr must give a doctor his urine specimen and he pours scotch into the container. Asked what nationality he is, he replied, "Scotch—by absorption."

Two popular songs were sung in the show—"Thank Your Father" and "Red Hot Chicago," the latter a showstopper belted by Smith. This laugh fest ran for 355 performances.

Another big hit opened at the Apollo on November 26, 1932. With a book by B. G. DeSylva and Laurence Schwab, music by Nacio Herb Brown and Richard A. Whiting, and lyrics by DeSylva, the show had flopped in Pittsburgh, where it was called *Humpty Dumpty*. It was rewritten as *Take a Chance*, with five new songs by Vincent Youmans, and had this superlative cast: Ethel Merman, Jack Haley, Sid Silvers, Jack Whiting, Mitzi Mayfair, and "Rags" Ragland. The plot dealt with the production of a revue called *Humpty Dumpty*, scenes and songs from which were incorporated into the story. Merman and Haley stopped the show with the catchy song "You're an Old Smoothie." In fact, they sang it in a saloon setting with a swinging door. Sid Silvers was supposed to come in via these doors when they finished singing, but the opening-night audience demanded four encores and the singers were forced to push Silvers offstage through the doors to sing another encore. It was one of the evening's biggest laughs. Merman had another showstopper with "Eadie Was a Lady," which became one of her standards. She also sang two Youmans numbers that critics loved: "Rise 'n' Shine" and "I Got Religion." This rowdy musical was an enormous audience pleaser for 243 performances. The last legit show at the Apollo was the short-lived revue *Blackbirds of 1934* with Bill Robinson.

From 1934 to 1938 the Apollo housed burlesque. Then, for forty years, it became a movie house. In the late 1970s the Brandt Organization, which owned the theatre, closed it and beautifully restored it to legitimacy. It reopened in 1979 with the warmly received play *On Golden Pond*, with Tom Aldredge and Frances Sternhagen, followed by two hits, *The Fifth of July* with Christopher Reeve and *Bent* with Richard Gere, plus the flop *The Guys in the Truck*.

After a period as the Academy Theatre for rock and jazz concerts, the theatre closed in 1992. In 1995 the Livent company announced that the Lyric and Apollo would be razed and transformed into one state-of-the-art theatre, which brings us to the present incarnation. The Hilton Theatre is one of the most beautiful theatres in Manhattan and is gracing its splendors with impressive bookings.

IMPERIAL
THEATRE

IN 1923 THE NEW YORK TIMES REPORTED
that the new theatre being built at 249 West
Forty-fifth Street by the Shuberts was the fiftieth playhouse that the theatrical brothers from
Syracuse had built in the New York City area.
Herbert J. Krapp designed the Imperial obviously as a musical comedy house, with a large
seating capacity of 1,650 (since reduced to
1,421). The main body of the playhouse is situated on the Forty-sixth Street side of the block
but is reached by a long, opulent gallery from
its entrance on Forty-fifth Street. The Imperial
has been the Shuberts' pride since it opened,
housing some of Broadway's most notable and
successful musicals.

The theatre's first show set the pace: a hit
musical called *Mary Jane McKane*, with Mary

Hay in the title role and a jaunty score by Vincent Youmans. It opened on Christmas night 1923 and ran for a then-impressive 151 performances. In September 1924 this theatre housed one of its most celebrated shows, the Rudolf Friml operetta *Rose-Marie*, with a book by Otto Harbach and Oscar Hammerstein II. According to Gerald Bordman in *American Musical Theatre*, this musical was "not only the biggest hit of the season, but the biggest grosser of the decade." Mary Ellis played Rose-Marie, a singer in a hotel located in the Canadian Rockies, and Dennis King was Jim Kenyon, the man she loved, who was unjustly accused of murder. The score included the lilting title song, the sonorous "Indian Love Call" ("When I'm calling you-oo-oo-ooh-oo-oo-ooh"), and "The Song of the Mounties." *Rose-Marie* ran for 557 performances on Broadway, and at one point there were four road companies of the show touring America at the same time.

The Imperial's next show was a musical called *Sweetheart Time*, with Eddie Buzzell and Mary Milburn, but it was only a moderate hit. The theatre's next bonanza occurred on November 8, 1926, with the opening of *Oh, Kay!*, a musical with a score by George and Ira Gershwin and a book by Guy Bolton and P. G. Wodehouse. Gertrude Lawrence was the star, and her singing of "Someone to Watch Over Me" to a rag doll is one of the musical theatre's most cherished moments. Victor Moore and Oscar Shaw were Lawrence's costars in this merry musical about Long Island bootleggers. Other hit tunes from the score were "Maybe," "Do Do Do," and "Clap Yo' Hands." When Ira Gershwin became ill during the creation of this hit, Howard Dietz wrote some of the lyrics for the show.

On September 19, 1928, another blockbuster came to this house: Sigmund Romberg's glorious operetta *The New Moon*, with a libretto by Oscar Hammerstein II, Frank Mandel, and Laurence Schwab. Set in New Orleans at the time of the French Revolution, the operetta was studded with such gems as "Wanting You," "Lover, Come Back to Me," "Softly as in a Morning Sunrise," "Stouthearted Men," and "One Kiss." It was the only show of that otherwise bountiful season to run for more than five hundred performances.

A snappy World War I musical, *Sons o' Guns*, starring Jack Donahue, Lily Damita, and William Frawley, exploded at the Imperial in November 1929 and, despite the stock market crash, spread mirth for 297 performances. Two hit songs—"Why?" and "Cross Your Fingers"—emerged from the lively score by J. Fred Coots, Arthur Swanstrom, and Benny Davis.

Highlights of the 1930s at the Imperial included Ed Wynn in his joyous vaudeville-type show *The Laugh Parade* (1931), in which he introduced some of his latest zany inventions and interrupted other people's acts with lisping comments. An elaborate revue, *Flying Colors* (1932), boasted modernistic sets by Norman Bel Geddes, hit songs by Howard Dietz and Arthur Schwartz ("Louisiana Hayride," "Alone Together," "A Shine on Your Shoes"), and a dream cast consisting of Clifton Webb, Tamara Geva, Patsy Kelly, Charles Butterworth, Imogene Coca, Larry Adler, and Vilma and Buddy Ebsen. *Let 'Em Eat Cake* (1933), a sequel to *Of Thee I Sing* (by the same creators), reunited William Gaxton, Victor Moore, and Lois Moran, the stars of the first show, but was not successful. Bob Hope, Harry Richman, Lillian Emerson, and "Prince" Michael Romanoff starred in a saucy musical, *Say When* (1934).

Despite the Depression, some 1930s opening nights on Broadway were the pinnacles of glamour, and such was the case at the glittery opening of the Cole Porter/Moss Hart musical *Jubilee* on October 12, 1935. An opulent satire about the royal holiday of the king and queen of a mythical country (splendidly played by Mary Boland and

Imperial program cover for 1926

Sheet music for the title song of the operetta *Rose Marie* (1924).

PLAYBILL cover for the British hit *Oliver!* (1961).

Top: Desi Arnaz pounds the conga as the chorus sings in Rodgers and Hart's college musical, *Too Many Girls* (1939).

Center left: Mary Martin and behind her, at left, Gene Kelly in Cole Porter's *Leave It to Me* (1938).

Center right: Ben Vereen and chorus have "Magic To Do" in the long running *Pippin* (1972).

Imperial program cover for 1930.

Souvenir program for Sigmund Romberg's *The New Moon* (1928).

PLAYBILL cover sketch of Mrs. Hartley of Covent Garden during run of *Jubilee* (1935).

Melville Cooper), the show drew a bejeweled audience who had heard that some of the characters depicted were really spoofs of Noël Coward, Johnny Weissmuller, Elsa Maxwell, and Britain's royal family. Burns Mantle of the *Daily News* gave the musical his rare four-star rating, and two of its Porter songs have become classics: "Begin the Beguine" and "Just One of Those Things."

Another memorable musical followed *Jubilee* into the Imperial: *On Your Toes*, the Rodgers/Hart/George Abbott spoof of the Russian ballet craze. It starred Ray Bolger, Tamara Geva, Luella Gear, and Monty Woolley, and it broke the mold of American musical comedies by using two extended George Balanchine ballets as an integral part of the plot. One of these, "Slaughter on Tenth Avenue," is one of the few ballet scores from a musical to become popular, and the ballet itself has joined the repertoire of the New York City Ballet.

The battle of the *Hamlets* raged on Broadway in the fall of 1936. John Gielgud opened first as the Melancholy Dane at the Empire Theatre in October and triumphed. Leslie Howard played the same part at the Imperial in November and came in a poor second. Howard's last Broadway play had been *The Petrified Forest*. When reviewing Howard's *Hamlet*, critic Robert Benchley wrote in *The New Yorker* that it was "the petrified Hamlet." Gielgud's production ran for 132 performances, Howard's only 39.

The Shuberts brought an elaborate operetta, *Frederika*, to the Imperial in February 1937, but despite lilting music by Franz Lehar it ran for only ninety-four performances. The excellent cast included Dennis King, Ernest Truex, Helen Gleason, and Edith King, but as Brooks Atkinson noted in the *Times*, operetta had become passé on Broadway. At the end of 1937 Dietz and Schwartz returned with a glossy musical about a bigamist who had one wife in London and another in Paris. *Between the Devil* showcased three bright British stars, Jack Buchanan, Evelyn Laye, and Adele Dixon, and featured dancers Vilma Ebsen and Charles Walters. But the bigamy theme was distasteful to some, and the musical called it quits after ninety-three performances.

The Cole Porter show *Leave It to Me!*, which sailed smartly into the Imperial in the fall of 1938, starred Victor Moore, William Gaxton, Sophie Tucker, and Tamara, but it made Broadway history by introducing a Texas singer named Mary Martin doing a polite striptease in a Siberian railway station while singing "My Heart Belongs to Daddy." The musical, based on Sam and Bella Spewack's play *Clear All Wires*, was a huge hit and featured some Porter winners, such as "Get Out of Town" and "Most Gentlemen Don't Like Love." One of the chorus boys was future film star Gene Kelly.

The last musical of the 1930s at this theatre was also a hit. Rodgers and Hart and George

Marion Jr. collaborated on a college campus show, *Too Many Girls*, which was set at Pottawatomie College in Stop Gap, New Mexico, where the female students wore "beanies" if they were virgins. The only hatless female onstage was Mary Jane Walsh, who played a divorcée. George Abbott directed the show with lightning speed; Robert Alton was highly praised for his swirling dances. Eddie Bracken, Richard Kollmar, Marcy Wescott, Hal Le Roy, Desi Arnaz (pre—*I Love Lucy*), and Walsh sang and danced such Rodgers and Hart delights as "I Didn't Know What Time It Was," "I'd Like to Recognize the Tune," "She Could Shake the Maracas," and "Give It Back to the Indians." One of the chorus boys with a few spoken lines was a newcomer named Van Johnson.

Smash hit musicals continued to populate the Imperial in the 1940s. Irving Berlin and Morrie Ryskind rang the bell with *Louisiana Purchase*, a political musical set in New Orleans, starring Victor Moore, William Gaxton, Vera Zorina, and Irene Bordoni. Balanchine provided the choreography and Berlin some fetching

Above: Jennifer Holliday, Sheryl Lee Ralph, and Loretta Devine in *Dreamgirls* (1981).

songs, such as "It's a Lovely Day Tomorrow," the title song, and some spirited numbers for Carol Bruce. It ran for 444 performances.

Cole Porter returned to the Imperial in 1941 with a rousing wartime musical, *Let's Face It!* Based on the hit 1920s comedy *Cradle Snatchers*, the show focused on three married women (Eve Arden, Edith Meiser, and Vivian Vance) who took up with young soldiers to get even with their philandering husbands. One of the soldiers was Danny Kaye, who stopped the show with specialty numbers, some written by his wife, Sylvia Fine. Porter provided such hits as "Everything I Love," "Farming," "Let's Not Talk about Love," "Ace in the Hole," and "I Hate You, Darling."

The enormous success of the operetta *Rosalinda* (1943), Max Reinhardt's version of *Die Fledermaus*, caused it to be moved to the Imperial from the Forty-fourth Street Theatre. Starring Dorothy Sarnoff and Oscar Karlweis, the comic show also featured Shelley Winters and ran for 521 performances.

Mary Martin, who made her debut as an unknown at the Imperial in *Leave It to Me*, returned as a star in *One Touch of Venus* (1943), a musical fantasy with a haunting score by Kurt Weill and a witty book by S. J. Perelman and Ogden Nash. Martin played a statue of Venus that comes to life and is pursued by an art gallery owner (John Boles) and a barber (Kenny Baker). Martin scored a triumph singing "Speak Low," "I'm a Stranger Here Myself," and "That's Him." Paula Lawrence sang the amusing title song and "Very, Very, Very." The show had a smashing run of 567 performances, but not all at the Imperial.

Another successful musical that moved to the Imperial from the Winter Garden was the

Ziegfeld Follies of 1943. It starred Milton Berle (who stuck his two cents into everybody's act), the film beauty Ilona Massey, Arthur Treacher, and Jack Cole. The critics praised Berle's high jinks, and this *Follies* still holds the record—553 performances—for the longest run of any *Ziegfeld Follies*.

On May 16, 1946, one of the Imperial's hallmark shows arrived. Ethel Merman opened in Irving Berlin's *Annie Get Your Gun* and made it one of her most memorable portraits. Jerome Kern was slated to write the score for this show, but he died before he could start it. His successor, Berlin, wrote what many consider his greatest score, with such hits as "They Say It's Wonderful," "There's No Business Like Show Business," "The Girl That I Marry," "Doin' What Comes Natur'lly," and "I Got the Sun in the Morning." Few Broadway musicals have produced as many song hits as this one. It was Merman's longest-running show: 1,147 performances.

The last two shows at the Imperial during the 1940s were minor successes. A revue called *Along Fifth Avenue* moved from the Broadhurst and starred Nancy Walker, Jackie Gleason, Carol Bruce, and Hank Ladd, but it lasted only seven months. Irving Berlin's *Miss Liberty* had a book by Robert E. Sherwood and starred Eddie Albert, Mary McCarty, and Allyn McLerie, but the critics felt that the project fell flat. It managed to run for 308 performances.

During the 1950s musicals continued to be the major fare at this theatre. In 1950 there was a successful adaptation of *Peter Pan*, with new music by Leonard Bernstein. Jean Arthur made a perfect Peter, and Boris Karloff doubled as Mr. Darling and the evil Captain Hook. This was followed by Ethel Merman in another Irving Berlin winner, *Call Me Madam*, in which she played a Perle Mesta—type Washington, D.C., hostess. Howard Lindsay and Russel Crouse wrote the amusing book, Paul Lukas was Merman's romantic costar, and Merman and a newcomer, Russell Nype, stopped the show with their singing of the contrapuntal melody "You're Just in Love." It ran for 644 performances. In June 1952 *Wish You Were Here*, a fair musical version of Arthur Kober's delightful play *Having Wonderful Time*, opened and managed to run for 598 performances, mainly because Eddie Fisher (who was not in the show) recorded the title song and it became a Hit Parade favorite. The show also had a real pool onstage, which garnered much publicity. In

December 1953 one of Broadway's last opulent revues—*John Murray Anderson's Almanac*—arrived, with Hermione Gingold, Billy De Wolfe, Harry Belafonte, Polly Bergen, Orson Bean, Kay Medford, and Carleton Carpenter, but despite some funny sketches and good songs it was a financial failure, proving that TV was killing the revue form on Broadway.

Cole Porter's last musical, *Silk Stockings*, an adaptation of Greta Garbo's famous film *Ninotchka*, was a hit in 1955, with Don Ameche, Hildegarde, Neff and Gretchen Wyler. Frank Loesser was acclaimed for his operatic musical *The Most Happy Fella* (1956), based on Sidney Howard's play *They Knew What They Wanted*. Lena Horne was a popular success in the Harold Arlen/E. Y. Harburg musical *Jamaica* (1957), with Ricardo Montalban. Dolores Gray and Andy Griffith had a hit in *Destry Rides Again* (1959), a musical version of the James Stewart/Marlene Dietrich film, aided by dazzling Michael Kidd choreography, although a feud between Gray and Kidd made all the newspapers.

During the 1960s the Imperial housed more long-running musicals. Ethel Merman in her triumphant *Gypsy* moved here from the Broadway Theatre in 1960 and was followed by David Merrick's smash *Carnival* (1961), a musical adapted from the film *Lili*, starring Jerry Orbach (fresh from his Off-Broadway success in *The Fantasticks*) and Anna Maria Alberghetti, with excellent choreography and staging by Gower Champion. A British import, Lionel Bart's *Oliver!*, based on Dickens's *Oliver Twist*, starred Clive Revill and Georgia Brown and had two song hits: "As Long as He Needs Me" and "Consider Yourself." It played at the Imperial for eighteen months.

On September 22, 1964, *Fiddler on the Roof* opened and stayed at this theatre for more than two years before moving to the Majestic. The multi-award-winning musical, written by Joseph Stein, Jerry Bock, and Sheldon Harnick, was based on Sholem Aleichem's tales of life in the impoverished Jewish *shtetls* of early twentieth-century Russia. Zero Mostel gave the greatest performance of his career as the milkman Tevye, who talks to God and tries to find good husbands for his daughters in tumultuous times. Directed and choreographed by Jerome Robbins, the musical filled the Imperial with tunes that became part of people's lives: "Sunrise, Sunset," "If I Were a Rich Man," "Tradition." The show won numerous Tony Awards, including Best

Musical. It eventually became, for a time, the longest-running musical in Broadway history, and it was produced around the world.

Another landmark musical, *Cabaret*, came to the Imperial from the Broadhurst Theatre and continued for a year and half in 1967—68. Kander and Ebb, who wrote the memorable score for *Cabaret*, also wrote the score for the next Imperial tenant, *Zorba* (1968), a musical based on the film *Zorba the Greek*. But the stage version did not have the distinction of the film, and it ran for a moderately successful nine months. *Minnie's Boys*, a musical about the early career of the Marx Brothers, had a short run in 1970. Richard Rodgers and Martin Charnin had a minor success with their musical *Two by Two* (1970), a biblical story about Noah and his family based on Clifford Odets's play *The Flowering Peach*. It starred Danny Kaye as Noah, and the comic took to ad-libbing during the show's run, which some in the audience found unprofessional. Even a torn ligament in his leg didn't slow Kaye down. He continued his shenanigans wearing a cast and riding across the ark in a wheelchair. Two revivals—*On the Town* (1971) and *Lost in the Stars* (1972)—struck out before the next home run was hit from this theatre.

On October 23, 1972, *Pippin* opened, and it stayed for 1,944 performances, making it the longest-running show to open at the Imperial. With a score by Stephen Schwartz, this unorthodox musical about Charlemagne's irresolute son was boosted to success by Bob Fosse's inventive choreography, by Ben Vereen's animated dancing, and by one of the most successful TV commercials ever produced for a Broadway show, "One Minute from *Pippin*."

Drama returned to the Imperial with a revival of Eugene O'Neill's *Anna Christie* (1977), starring Liv Ullmann, and Victor Borge returned in a short run of his show *Comedy with Music* (1977). Two Neil Simon shows next occupied the Imperial, and both were long-running hits. *Chapter Two* (1977), a drama about Simon's personal experience after losing his first wife to cancer, starred Judd Hirsch, Anita Gillette, and Cliff Gorman and ran for 857 performances, the longest-running nonmusical in this theatre's history. The other Simon show, *They're Playing Our Song* (1979), was a musical with a score by Marvin Hamlisch and Carole Bayer Sager, about a songwriter (Robert Klein) and his kooky romance with his lyricist (Lucie Arnaz). This ran for a hefty 1,082 performances.

Above: Opening night PLAYBILLs from musicals *Chess* (1988) and *Jerome Robbins' Broadway* (1989).

Left to right, Norbert Leo Butz, John Lithgow, and Sherie Rene Scott in *Dirty Rotten Scoundrels* (2005). (Photo by Carol Rosegg)

In 1981 Michael Bennett's blockbuster musical *Dreamgirls* opened here and stayed until 1985. With a score by Henry Krieger and Tom Eyen and a book by Eyen, the musical about a singing trio patterned after The Supremes won six Tony Awards, including Best Actor and Actress in a Musical: Ben Harney and Jennifer Holliday. Holliday raised the roof with her Act I finale, "And I Am Telling You I'm Not Going."

The Mystery of Edwin Drood (a title later shortened to *Drood*) by Rupert Holmes, a musical first done by the New York Shakespeare Festival at Central Park's Delacorte Theatre, transferred here in 1985 and promptly won Five Tony Awards, including Best Musical, Best Book of a Musical (Holmes), Best Original Score (Holmes), Best Leading Actor in a Musical (George Rose), and Best Direction of a Musical (Wilford Leach). Based on an unfinished mystery novel by Charles Dickens, the show was notable for allowing the audience to vote on which of several endings would be played that night. Actors (in character) would "campaign" during intermission to be chosen as the murderer. It played here until May 1987.

The British hit *Chess* opened in 1988 in a

revised version, but the pop opera by Benny Andersson, Björn Ulvaeus/Tim Rice/Richard Nelson about politics and romance colliding in the world of international chess championships did not repeat its London success in New York. *Jerome Robbins' Broadway* came next; a compilation of musical numbers from the master choreographer's musicals, it won Tony Awards for Best Musical, Best Actor in a Musical (pre-*Seinfeld* Jason Alexander), Best Featured Actor in a Musical (Scott Wise), Best Featured Actress in a Musical (Debbie Shapiro), Best Direction of a Musical (Robbins), and Best Lighting Designer (Jennifer Tipton).

In October 1990 *Les Misérables* moved from the Broadway Theatre and continued its epic run here for more than twelve years, eventually breaking the Imperial record held by *Pippin*. It closed May 18, 2003, after 6,680 performances—more than five thousand of them at the Imperial.

Hugh Jackman made his Broadway debut in *The Boy from Oz* at the very top of his game, riding this star vehicle about the gaudy, brief life of late composer/singer Peter Allen and winning the 2004 Tony as Best Actor in a Musical. Charismatic, gentlemanly, energetic, and appealing to members of both sexes, Jackman had begun his career on the stage in Australia and Great Britain and had won stardom playing the cowboy Curly in a London revival of *Oklahoma!* Since then, he had taken several macho film roles and earned an international

fandom. His tour de force in the Allen musical led to a lauded gig hosting the Tony Awards. *The Boy From Oz* also showcased future stars Stephanie J. Block and Isabel Keating, who supplied impressions of showbiz legends Liza Minnelli and Judy Garland, Allen's real-life wife and mother-in-law. The show opened October 16, 2003, and drew fans for 364 performances.

One of the most underrated shows of this period opened here March 3, 2005: *Dirty Rotten Scoundrels*, based on the film of the same name about two con men who themselves become the victims of a masterful con. John Lithgow played the suave older crook, while Norbert Leo Butz played his gauche younger partner in one of the great bad-guy hats of modern Broadway millinery history. They were supported by a cast of some of Broadway's bright musical comedians of the period: Sherie Rene Scott, Gregory Jbara, Joanna Gleason, and Sara Gettelfinger.

Jeffrey Lane wrote the book and David Yazbek (*The Full Monty*) supplied *Dirty Rotten Scoundrels* with a classic musical comedy score that would have easily won the Tony Award in most other seasons this decade, but the show had the misfortune to open in the era's most bountiful season, opposite the extraordinary *The Light in the Piazza* and the hilarious *Monty Python's Spamalot*. Songs included "Great Big Stuff,"

Left: Jan Maxwell in a scene from the epic but short-lived British drama, *Coram Boy* (2007). (Photo by Joan Marcus)

Center: Tony winner Deanna Dunagan eviscerates her family in the Pulitzer and Tony-winning drama *August: Osage County*. (Photo by Michael Brosilow)

Right: Billy (Kiril Kulish) flies in his imagination with his grown-up self (Stephen Hanna) during the number "Electricity" in the Tony-winning musical *Billy Elliot* (2008). (Photo by David Scheinmann)

"Here I Am," and "Nothing Is Too Wonderful to Be True," which featured one lovely poetic verse and one nutty comedic verse. In the end *Dirty Rotten Scoundrels* brought home just one Tony Award, but a big one: Best Actor in a Musical for Butz. The show ran 627 performances.

The music-loving owner of a slowly dying record store tries to win back the girl he loves in *High Fidelity*, a musical based on the film of the same title. A lot of top talent was involved in the show, but it somehow struck the wrong chord and expired after just thirteen performances. Pulitzer Prize—winner David Lindsay-Abaire supplied the book. Amanda Green rhymed the lyrics. Young composer Tom Kitt, who would go on to a Tony Award three years later with *Next to Normal*, demonstrated his ability to write music in virtually any pop style.

Coram Boy, an epic drama about the crimes and passions surrounding an eighteenth-century foundling home, had the scale and opulence of a musical and booked the Imperial in spring 2007 in anticipation of a musical-sized audience. But the show did not stir passions in New York the way it had in two runs at the National Theatre in London, and it closed after just thirty showings.

The Imperial got another drama on December 4, 2007, but one that actually did fill the house: Tracy Letts's *August: Osage County*, the story of an extended Oklahoma family that gathers after the mysterious disappearance of their patriarch. This remarkable modern take on the American family drama earned the 2008 Pulitzer Prize for Drama and won five Tony Awards: Best Play, Best Lead Actress in a Play (Deanna Dunagan), Best Director of a Play (Anna D. Shapiro), Best Featured Actress in a Play (Rondi Reed), and, for his three-story house set, Todd Rosenthal. In April 2008, after five months at the Imperial, the show moved next door to the more intimate Music Box Theatre.

The Imperial returned to melody with *Billy Elliot: The Musical*, an SRO hit that originated in London, based on the Lee Hall film about a blue-collar boy in a northern English mining community who dreams of becoming a classical dancer. The show had a score by Elton John and Hall, highlighted by the song "Electricity" and a moment when Billy takes flight in his imagination as he dances. The heart-grabbing show opened November 13, 2008, and won ten Tony Awards including Best Musical, Best Directing (Stephen Daldry), and Best Choreography (Peter Darling). The three young men who alternated in the role of Billy collectively won the Tony as Best Actor in a Musical, the fourth time a top performing honor had come home to the Imperial in six years. It might be the last for a while; *Billy Elliot* appeared ready to keep flying around the stage of this theatre for years to come.

The Imperial, which was completely refurbished by the Shubert Organization, is one of the finest musical-comedy houses ever built and has been one of Broadway's most consistently successful houses.

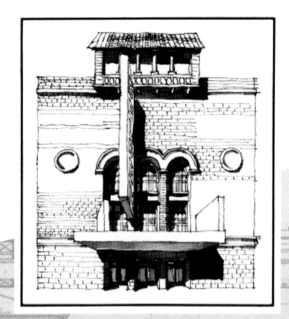

JOHN GOLDEN
THEATRE

THE JOHN GOLDEN THEATRE AT 252
West Forty-fifth Street was originally named
the Theatre Masque. It was the fifth theatre
built by the Chanin Brothers, and once again
they chose Herbert J. Krapp as their architect.
This house was their smallest, with 800 seats,
and the Chanins announced that it aimed to be
"the home of fine plays of the 'artistic' or 'intimate' type." They also reiterated their philosophy that their theatres were built to afford ease
and comfort to actors as well as playgoers.

The *New York Times* reviewed the first production at the Theatre Masque, an Italian play
called *Puppets of Passion,* which opened on
February 24, 1927, and the paper liked the new
playhouse more than the new play. "Like all the
Chanin houses," wrote critic Brooks Atkinson,

Top left: Sketch of Victor Borge in *Comedy in Music* on the souvenir program (1953).

Top center: Osgood Perkins as a best-selling novelist besieged by female fans in *Goodbye Again* (1932).

Top right: Vincent Price and Judith Evelyn in the celebrated thriller, *Angel Street* (1941).

Bottom: Jessica Tandy and Hume Cronyn in *The Gin Game* (1977).

"the Theatre Masque is pleasing and comfortable. The architecture is modern Spanish in character, and the interior of the house is decorated in pastel shades, trimmed in grayish blues and reds." Of the play, which had Frank Morgan in the cast, Atkinson wrote that it moved along at a funereal pace. It expired after twelve performances, though its title would become ironic in light of the theatre's longest-running show some seventy-five years later, *Avenue Q*.

The theatre's next attraction fared better. It ran for fifteen performances. This was a play called *The Comic*, with J. C. Nugent, Patricia Collinge, and Rex O'Malley. The program stated that the author was one Lajos Luria, a pseudonym for a famous serious European dramatist, who wouldn't use his real name on a comedy.

During the remainder of 1927 this theatre housed a revival of the Gilbert and Sullivan operetta *Patience*; a play about the corruption of the Harding administration in Washington, *Revelry*; Lionel Atwill in a sorry swashbuckler, *The King Can Do No Wrong*; and, finally, a misguided comedy called *Venus*, by the usually skillful Rachel Crothers, who, this time out, wrote a futuristic play about man's first flight to the planet Venus. Her play was visible for only eight performances.

Things did not improve much in 1928. There were eight productions here, and only one ran more than a hundred performances. This was an ethnic comedy called *Relations*, written by and starring Edward Clark. *The Scarlet Fox*, written by and starring Willard Mack, ran for seventy-nine performances. *Young Love*, by Samson Raphaelson, starring Dorothy Gish and James Rennie, lasted for eighty-seven performances.

Theatre Masque's biggest hit in 1929 was a

macabre drama called *Rope's End*, by British playwright Patrick Hamilton. The play detailed the grisly murder of an Oxford undergraduate by two upperclassmen, just for kicks. Although the playwright denied it, he was obviously influenced by the similar murder of a young boy in Chicago by Leopold and Loeb, two intellectuals who also committed a thrill kill. In *Rope's End*, the murderers put their victim's body in a chest, then invite his father and aunt to dinner. The meal is served on the chest. Alfred Hitchcock made a rarely shown film of this play and called it *Rope*.

In early 1930 the hit play *Broken Dishes*, with Bette Davis and Donald Meek, moved here from the Ritz and played for three months. A comedy about life in Greenwich Village, *Up Pops the Devil*, with Roger Pryor, Sally Bates, Brian Donlevy, and Albert Hackett (who coauthored the play with Frances Goodrich), ran for 146 performances that year. An interesting but unsuccessful drama, *Brass Ankle*, by DuBose Heyward (who later wrote *Porgy and Bess* with the Gershwins), starred Alice Brady in 1931.

A Norman Krasna farce about Hollywood,

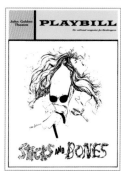

Above: PLAYBILL covers for *An Evening with Mike Nichols and Elaine May* (1960) and David Rabe's *Sticks and Bones* (1972).

Louder, Please!, was a moderate success in 1931. It starred Lee Tracy as a loudmouth publicity man, and it was directed at top speed by George Abbott. A much bigger hit was Goodbye Again, a comedy in which Osgood Perkins felicitously played a novelist who tries to renew an old affair while on a publicity tour for his latest book. This romantic trifle kept the Theatre Masque full for 212 performances in 1932—33.

Post Road, a hit 1934 play about kidnapping, featured delirious performances by Lucile Watson and Percy Kilbride. The following year brought J. B. Priestley's Laburnum Grove, starring Edmund Gwenn, Elizabeth Risdon, and Melville Cooper, which moved here from the Booth. In 1936 Russet Mantle, a pleasant play about Santa Fe characters by Lynn Riggs, moved in and stayed for 116 performances. There was much praise for the actors—Evelyn Varden, John Beal, Martha Sleeper, Margaret Douglass, Jay Fassett, and others.

The last show to play the Masque before it changed its name was The Holmeses of Baker Street, in which Sherlock's daughter (Helen Chandler) proved that she was as good a sleuth as her old man. Cyril Scott played Sherlock, Conway Wingfield was Dr. Watson, and the wonderful mimic Cecilia Loftus was Mrs. Watson.

On February 2, 1937, the Masque became the John Golden Theatre, making it the third house named after the illustrious theatrical producer. Its first play was And Now Good-bye, a drama based on a James Hilton novel, starring Philip Merivale as a reverend who falls in love with a parishioner. It was not successful.

A radiant play, Shadow and Substance, by Paul Vincent Carroll, arrived in January 1938 and was acclaimed by the drama critics. It had shining performances by the ethereal Julie Haydon as the servant to an intellectual snob, and by Sir

Cedric Hardwicke, who played her employer. The spiritual play found favor and stayed for 206 performances. The following year, another memorable play by Paul Vincent Carroll, The White Steed, moved here from the Cort. It starred Jessica Tandy and Barry Fitzgerald.

On December 5, 1941, a Victorian thriller called Angel Street opened here, with Judith Evelyn, Vincent Price, and Leo G. Carroll. Produced by Shepard Traube, in association with Alexander H. Cohen, it was not expected to succeed, and consequently, only a three-day supply of PLAYBILL magazines was ordered. The producers underestimated their show. It most unforget-table performanc-es as Estragon in Samuel Beckett's parable of perpet-ual anticipation, *Waiting for Godot.* It was a radical departure for this famed clown of revues and musi-cal comedies, and the critics hailed him, though few at the time recognized the play as one of the masterpieces of twentieth-century drama. Also in the cast were E. G. Marshall, Kurt Kasznar, and Alvin Epstein.

played 1,295 times (the last two months at the Bijou Theatre), making it the longest-running nonmusical in this theatre's history.

Rose Franken's comedy *Soldier's Wife* found an audience in 1944 and ran for 255 performanc-es. The play, which had a star-studded cast—Martha Scott, Frieda Inescort, Lili Darvas, Glenn Anders, and Myron McCormick—was not a war play. It was about a woman who wrote a best-seller and the problems it engendered for her family.

The remainder of the 1940s brought a num-ber of shows to this theatre, but none was out-standing. Among them were *The Rich Full Life* (1945), with Judith Evelyn and Virginia Weidler; S. N. Behrman's *Dunnigan's Daughter* (1945), with June Havoc, Dennis King, Richard Widmark, Jan Sterling, and Luther Adler; *January Thaw* (1946), with Robert Keith and Lulu Mae Hubbard; and *I Like It Here* (1946), with Oscar Karlweis and Bert Lytell.

From mid-1946 until February 1948 the John Golden was leased as a motion picture theatre. It returned to legitimacy on February 29, 1948, with Maurice Chevalier in a one-man show of songs and impressions.

Highlights of the 1950s at the John Golden included Grace George and Walter Hampden in *The Velvet Glove* (1950), which moved here from the Booth; Emlyn Williams in a solo per-formance of six scenes from the works of Charles Dickens (1952); Cornelia Otis Skinner in *Paris '90* (1952), a monodrama that moved here from the Booth; and the long-running comedy *The Fourposter* (1952), which moved here from the Ethel Barrymore.

On October 2, 1953, the witty Victor Borge opened at this theatre in a one-man show called *Comedy in Music.* Borge played the piano and indulged in deadpan patter and lampoons that kept audiences in stitches for 849 performances.

In 1956 comic Bert Lahr gave one of his

In late 1956 Menasha Skulnik appeared in a comedy, *Uncle Willie*, that stayed for 141 per-formances. The play was a variant of *Abie's Irish Rose*, focusing on two neighboring fami-lies, one Irish, the other Jewish.

John Osborn's vitriolic hit *Look Back in Anger* moved here from the Lyceum in 1958 and stayed for six months. *A Party with Betty Comden and Adolph Green*, with the popular duo singing their witty lyrics from Broadway musi-cals and Hollywood films, was welcomed in 1958—59, as was the *Billy Barnes Revue* from the West Coast. The British duo of Michael Flanders and Donald Swann scored a hit in their two-man revue *At the Drop of a Hat* (1959).

One of the John Golden's most cherished entertainments was the brilliant Alexander H. Cohen production of *An Evening with Mike Nichols and Elaine May.* Even their PLAYBILL biographies, which they wrote themselves, were hilarious. The duo presented some of their classic comedy sketches that satirized everyday foibles, and they kept the John Golden Theatre quaking with laughter for 306 performances in 1960—61.

An Evening with Yves Montand (1961) also proved a hit, with the French actor/singer charming audiences in a one-man show. Robert Redford appeared here in *Sunday in New York*, a fair comedy by Norman Krasna that moved to the Golden from the Cort Theatre in 1962. On October 27, 1962, a tornado of mirth called *Beyond the Fringe* arrived from England and fractured audiences for 667 performances. This Alexander H. Cohen import was a deliri-ous revue written and performed by Alan Bennett, Peter Cook, Jonathan Miller, and

Left: David Loud accompanies Zoë Caldwell in her Tony-winning performance as Maria Callas in *Master Class* (1995).

Right: Geraldine McEwan and Richard Briers in Ionesco's *The Chairs* (1998). (Photo by Joan Marcus)

Dudley Moore; Cohen staged the uproar.

In 1964 Victor Borge returned to the Golden with *Comedy in Music, Opus 2*, which was good enough for 192 performances. Another hit revue, *Wait a Minim!*, opened here in 1966, bringing eight extremely personable and talented performers from South Africa. Their zany entertainment delighted theatregoers for 457 performances. The remainder of the 1960s brought seven shows, but only two of them were of much interest: John Bowen's British play *After the Rain* (1967) with Alec McCowen; and the British actor Roy Dotrice in his one-man show, *Brief Lives*, about an English antiquarian named John Aubrey.

Highlights of the 1970s included *Bob and Ray—The Two and Only* (1970), a two-man show featuring the popular radio comics Bob Elliott and Ray Goulding; David Rabe's Vietnam War drama *Sticks and Bones* (1972), which won a Tony Award for best play of the season; *Words and Music* (1974), a revue featuring the songs of Sammy Cahn, who appeared in the show with Kelly Garrett, Jon Peck, and Shirley Lemmon; Robert Patrick's *Kennedy's Children* (1975), with Shirley Knight, who won a Tony Award as Best Featured Actress of the season; and Tom Stoppard's *Dirty Linen* and *New-Found-Land* (1977), two plays in one, performed without intermission.

D. L. Coburn's Pulitzer Prize—winning *The Gin Game* (1977) starred husband—wife team Hume Cronyn and Jessica Tandy as two residents of a nursing home whose relationship is reflected in the games of cards they try to play. Tandy won a Tony Award for her performance.

The 1980s began with a revival of Lillian Hellman's *Watch on the Rhine*, soon followed by *A Day in Hollywood/A Night in the Ukraine* (1980), which transferred to the larger Royale Theatre; *Tintypes* (1980), a diverting revue of turn-of-the-century songs, which moved to the

John Golden from the Off-Broadway Theatre at St. Peter's Church; Beth Henley's Pulitzer-winning play *Crimes of the Heart* (1981), which transferred from Off-Broadway's Manhattan Theatre Club; and Marsha Norman's Pulitzer Prize play *'night, Mother*, with Kathy Bates as a daughter who announces to her mother (Anne Pitoniak) that she intends to commit suicide.

In 1984 another Pulitzer-winning play opened here: David Mamet's *Glengarry Glen Ross*, making it three Pulitzer Prize plays in a row—four in seven years—a record for any Broadway theatre. Gregory Mosher won a Tony Award for his direction of the Mamet play about ruthless real-estate salesmen, which starred Ron Silver, Joe Mantegna (Tony Award), and Robert Prosky.

This was followed by a revival of Athol Fugard's play *Blood Knot*, starring the playwright and Zakes Mokae. Tandy and Cronyn returned in *The Petition*, a British play having its world premiere on Broadway. Another British production, *Stepping Out*, directed by Tommy Tune, arrived for a brief run in 1987; then came a revival of Arthur Miller's *All My Sons*; the Gate Theatre Dublin production of O'Casey's *Juno and the Paycock*, presented in a limited engagement by the Circle in the Square Theatre as part of the first New York International Festival of the Arts; *Paul Robeson*, starring Avery Brooks; Richard Greenberg's Broadway debut, *Eastern Standard*, with Peter Frechette, Anne Meara, and others; *Sid Caesar & Company: Does Anyone Know What I'm Talking About?*; and *Michael Feinstein in Concert—Piano and Voice*.

In 1992 the Golden hosted an unusual musical: *Falsettos*, an amalgam of William Finn's and James Lapine's two earlier Off-Broadway musicals, *March of the Falsettos* and *Falsettoland*. The combined show chronicled the misadventures of Marvin, a married man who comes out es in which she tutored aspiring opera singers. In the play, Zoë Caldwell, who played Callas, dramatically coached three would-be singers with volcanic fury, commanding them, "You've got to get a *look!*" Caldwell and Audra McDonald, who played one of her badgered students, both won Tony Awards for their dynamic performances. Their offstage friendship was so warm that McDonald named her daughter after the star. *Master Class* won the Best Play Tony Award for the season. During its 601-performance run, Caldwell was succeeded by Patti LuPone and Dixie Carter. McDonald was succeeded by Helen Goldsby and Alaine Rodin-Lo.

On April 1, 1998, a revival of Eugene Ionesco's play *The Chairs*, translated by Martin Crimp, opened at this theatre. A production of Théâtre de Complicité and Royal Court Theater, the acclaimed absurdist play starred Geraldine McEwan and Richard Briers and filled the Golden's chairs for a twelve-week limited engagement. The two stars played a very eccentric old couple who entertain a growing number of invisible guests, each of whom needs a chair. Both stars made their Broadway debuts in this production, directed by Simon McBurney. *The Chairs* received six Tony Award nominations: Best Actor (Briers), Best Actress (McEwan), Best Revival of a Play, Best Director (McBurney), Best Scenic Designer (Quay Brothers), and Best Lighting Designer (Paul Anderson).

Side Man, a memory play by Warren Leight, had a fortunate career. It opened Off-Broadway in March of 1998 and earned such glowing reviews that it moved to the uptown Roundabout Theater Company's Criterion Center Stage Right, where it again received rave notices. From there it moved to the Golden

Dutch actor Jochem ten Haaf played the painter Vincent Van Gogh as a young man in the 2003 import *Vincent in Brixon*. (Photo by Joan Marcus)

as gay and tries to build a family that includes his son, his ex-wife, her new husband, and Marvin's lover, Whizzer. The combined show won Tony Awards for Best Musical Book and Score and ran 487 performances.

In 1993 a play called *Mixed Emotions* by Richard Baer, with Katherine Helmond, ran for 55 performances. It depicted a romance between a widow and a widower. This was followed by an evening of political comedy by Jackie Mason called *Politically Incorrect*. Hilariously performed by Mason, it ran for 347 performances.

The next tenant at this theatre scored a resounding hit. It was Terrence McNally's fascinating *Master Class*, which opened to rave reviews on November 5, 1995. McNally, who was a friend and great admirer of opera superstar Maria Callas, attended some of her master class-

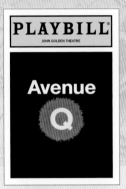

Top: Stephanie D'Abruzzo and John Tartaglia with their respective alter egos Kate Monster and Princeton in the long-running musical *Avenue Q* (2003). (Photo by Carol Rosegg)

Bottom: The opening night PLAYBILL.

Theatre on November 8, 1998, and critics again hailed it. It was a deft examination of the troubled family life of a professional jazz trumpet player who is married to his music, with little emotion left for his wife and son. The son is the play's narrator, reviewing his life with father and mother in vivid flashbacks. One of the play's attributes was the use of the recordings of jazz greats in the background. In music circles, a side man is a musician who plays alongside the star performer, an anonymous artist to the audience. The autobiographical play won the Best Play Tony Award. Frank Wood, who played the father, won a Tony Award as Best Featured Actor in a Play. *Side Man* ran at the Golden until October 31, 1999. During the run, Robert Sella, who played Clifford, was succeeded by Christian Slater. Sella returned to the role in March 1999 and was succeeded by Scott Wolf in May of that year. The cast also included a group of actors who played musicians and who enlivened the play with jazz slang.

Comedian Jackie Mason returned to the Golden in December 1999 to share his views on race, politics, and the state of coffee in America in his solo show *Much Ado about Everything*.

Marie Jones's April 1, 2001, play *Stones in His Pockets* told what happens when a Hollywood film company virtually takes over a small Irish town to shoot a movie. Seán Campion and Conleth Hill impersonated the whole town for 198 performances.

Edward Albee painted another of his savage portraits of toxic marriages in *The Goat, or Who Is Sylvia?*, about a married woman (Mercedes Ruehl) who discovers that the "other woman" is literally a goat, whom her husband (Bill Pullman) has named Sylvia. The titillating drama opened March 10, 2002, and won the Tony Award as Best Play, en route to a 309-performance run. The Golden was occupied for nine weeks in spring 2003 with a British drama, Nicholas Wright's *Vincent in Brixton*, which imagined a powerfully formative love affair early in the life of painter Vincent Van Gogh (played by Dutch actor Jochem Haaf).

Though the Golden had been occupied for more than a decade by nonmusicals, it enjoyed the greatest success in its history starting July 31, 2003, with the transfer of the hit Off-Broadway musical *Avenue Q*. The show, which was designed for the generation raised on PBS's *Sesame Street*, used songs, puppets, and politically incorrect comedy to guide a young man on his voyage from college into a cold, hard world filled with unemployment, drugs, racism, and broken romance. The songs "Everyone's a Little Bit Racist" and "The Internet Is for Porn" were popular with ticket buyers, and with Internet users who created animations and viral videos riffing on the songs.

Robert Lopez and Jeff Marx won the Tony Award for Best Score, Jeff Whitty won the Tony for Best Book, and *Avenue Q* won the Tony as Best Musical of 2004, beating pundits' favorite, *Wicked*, after *Avenue Q* mounted an imaginative Tony campaign in which the show's puppets urged voters to "Vote your heart." The puppets became mainstays of Broadway benefits and other special gatherings.

During *Avenue Q*'s house-record 2,534-performance run, many young puppeteers worked on the show, following in the footsteps of John Tartaglia, Stephanie D'Abruzzo, Ann Harada, and others in the lively cast. The show was scheduled to close September 13, 2009, but at its final performance producers dramatically revealed that the show would be moving to the Off-Broadway New World Stages instead.

The Goat leading man Bill Pullman returned to his old dressing room at the Golden in fall 2009 for a revival of David Mamet's teacher/student, man/woman power-battle drama *Oleanna*, costarring Julia Stiles.

It was followed in April 2010 by John Logan's drama *Red*, in which Alfred Molina gave a dramatic portrait of artist Mark Rothko.

The John Golden is a Shubert Organization Theatre. It has been very successful as a house for intimate revues, one- and two-person shows, dramatic plays with small casts, and one tiny, long-running musical.

LONGACRE
THEATRE

A COLORFUL CHARACTER NAMED H. H.
Frazee built the Longacre Theatre at 220 West
Forty-eighth Street, between Broadway and
Eighth Avenue. It was named after nearby
Longacre Square, the crossroads long since
rechristened as Times Square. Frazee hired
architect Henry Herts to create a theatre that
would specialize in the staging of musical comedies. Herts, who designed some of Broadway's
finest theatres, turned out a lovely playhouse
that managed to look intimate while having two
balconies and seating more than 1,400 patrons
(subsequently reduced to 1,091).

The Longacre opened on the night of May
1, 1913, with an unfunny farce called *Are You a
Crook?*, starring Marguerite Clark. It perished
after a dozen showings. Frazee did much better

Top left: **The Group Theatre's stirring production of Clifford Odets's *Waiting for Lefty* (1935).**

Bottom left: Jo Mielziner's enchanting setting for Paul Osborn's *Morning's at Seven* (1939).

Top right: Standard Longacre program cover in the 1920s.

with a musical show. On August 28 of that year his theatre housed a French entertainment called *Adele*, and it was the most successful import of the season. It delighted theatregoers for 196 performances.

A. H. Woods, a producer who thrived on melodramas, presented a play called *Kick In* in 1914. The interesting cast included John Barrymore, Katherine Harris (who became the first Mrs. Barrymore), Jane Gray, and Forrest Winant. The "crook" melodrama stole its way into playgoers' hearts for 188 performances. That year a farce called *A Pair of Sixes* also won favor and ran for 207 mirthful performances.

A number of shows played in 1915, including Lewis Stone in *Inside the Lines* and May Vokes in *A Full House*. But the most successful was a comedy called *The Great Lover*, starring Leo Ditrichstein, which focused on love among the egocentric temperaments of the opera world.

The Longacre welcomed its biggest hit to that date when *Nothing but the Truth* opened on September 14, 1916. Written by James Montgomery, the comedy starred the deadpan William Collier, who convulsed audiences as a man who vowed not to tell lies for one day. He managed to do this for 332 performances.

The kind of intimate, charming musical that Frazee envisioned for his house came to the Longacre in 1917. It was the Jerome Kern/P. G. Wodehouse/Guy Bolton winner *Leave It to Jane*, about a football-crazy college campus. Among the Kern gems were "The Siren's Song," "The Crickets Are Calling," "Cleopatterer," and the lilting title song. The Longacre had full houses for 167 performances.

Guy Bolton and George Middleton provided a palpable hit for the house with *Adam and Eva*, starring Otto Kruger and Ruth Shepley, in 1919.

Some highlights of the 1920s included a musical called *Pitter Patter* (1920), starring William Kent; *The Champion* (1920), with Grant Mitchell; and *Little Jesse James* (1923), an intimate musical with only one set, eight chorus girls, a modest cast that included future movie star Miriam Hopkins, one hit song—"I

Left: The Longacre's first show, *Are You A Crook?*, with Marguerite Clark and Elizabeth Nelson (1913).

Center: Dudley Diggs, Peter Holden, and Dorothy Stickney in *On Borrowed Time* (1938).

Right: Sam Jaffe and Julie Harris in Lillian Hellman's adaptation of Anouilh's *The Lark* (1955).

Love You"—and a smash run of 385 performances. This was followed by *Moonlight* (1924), another intimate musical with tuneful Con Conrad music; *The Dark Angel* (1925), a poignant drama about a woman whose lover returns blind from World War I and pretends that he is dead; *Mercenary Mary* (1925), another Con Conrad musical, with a jazz band and a star-and-garter chorus; George S. Kaufman's *The Butter and Egg Man* (1925), a hit "inside" comedy about a hick (memorably played by Gregory Kelly) who comes to Broadway with $20,000 to invest in a show and, after many tribulations, succeeds; and a thrilling adaptation of Theodore Dreiser's novel *An American Tragedy* (1926), starring Morgan Farley as the murderer, Katherine Wilson as his victim, and Miriam Hopkins as his rich girlfriend.

Later in the decade the Longacre hosted *The Command to Love* (1927), a surprisingly delightful German high comedy starring Basil Rathbone, Mary Nash, Violet Kemble Cooper, and Anthony Kemble Cooper that lasted for 236 performances; Richard Bennett and his attractive daughter Joan in a shocker about Hollywood lowlife called *Jarnegan* (1928); Clark Gable in an interesting murder mystery, *Hawk Island* (1929), that ran for only three weeks; and its final play of the 1920s, *A Primer for Lovers*, a sex farce with the delightful Alison Skipworth.

After a series of unsuccessful plays in 1930 and 1931, the Longacre finally had a hit in *Blessed Event* (1932), starring Roger Pryor in a thinly disguised impersonation of the egotistical Broadway columnist Walter Winchell, with Isabel Jewell and Allen Jenkins in support. A

dramatization of the infamous Lizzie Borden ax murders, *Nine Pine Street*, had a fine performance by Lillian Gish as the neurotic killer, but it ran only a few weeks in 1933. The same fate was accorded *Wednesday's Child* (1934), a study of a young boy (Frank M. Thomas Jr.) whose life is ruined when his parents divorce.

During the height of the Depression, the Longacre was dark for months on end. Most of the shows that played there were quick flops. A bright spot in 1935, however, was the arrival of the revolutionary Group Theatre company with two of Clifford Odets's inflammatory plays, *Waiting for Lefty* and *Till the Day I Die*. Odets appeared in *Waiting for Lefty*, and both plays had such Group stalwarts as Elia Kazan, Lee J. Cobb, Roman Bohnen, Russell Collins, and Alexander Kirkland. Later in 1935 another Odets play, *Paradise Lost*, with many of the same actors, played the theatre.

Late in 1936 the great actress Alla Nazimova played Ibsen's *Hedda Gabler* for a month; and Vincent Price and the beautiful Elissa Landi starred in a romantic Hungarian play about royal affairs, *The Lady Has a Heart* (1937).

Things took a better turn on February 3, 1938, when an enchanting play came to the Longacre: Paul Osborn's loving adaptation of a novel called *On Borrowed Time*. Said Brooks Atkinson in the *Times*: "Nothing so original and jovial has turned up on our stages for a long time." The fantasy concerned a grandfather (Dudley Digges) who chases Death (called Mr. Brink) up a tree so that he can have some more time to spend with his lovable grandson (Peter Holden). Grandma was played by Dorothy Stickney. Directed by Joshua Logan, the play brought bittersweet magic to the Longacre for 321 performances.

In late 1939 Paul Osborn returned to this theatre with another endearing play about small-town people—*Morning's at Seven*. Despite Joshua Logan's direction and a superb cast that included Dorothy Gish, Russell Collins, Enid Markey, Effie Shannon, and Jean Adair, this gentle comedy about life among the elderly lasted only forty-four performances. It was clearly ahead of its time. When it was revived on Broadway in 1980 it ran for 564 performances, was hailed as an American classic, and won a Tony Award as the season's best revival.

The critics may have turned up their noses at a comedy called *Three's a Family* (1943), but audiences loved this play about the raising of babies and the care of expectant mothers. It was perfect escapist comedy for World War II theatergoers, and it amused them for close to five hundred performances. It was to be the Longacre's last legitimate show for a decade. From the spring of 1944 to the fall of 1953 the theatre was leased as a radio and television studio.

In November 1953 the Longacre reopened as a legitimate theatre with a promising play, *The Ladies of the Corridor*, by Dorothy Parker and Arnaud d'Usseau. Harold Clurman directed a cast that featured Edna Best, Betty Field, June Walker, Walter Matthau, and Shepperd Strudwick. Unfortunately, its depressing plot about lonely old women who live in hotels did not find a public.

The Longacre's best plays in the 1950s were Lillian Hellman's adaptation of Jean Anouilh's *The Lark* (1955), with Julie Harris as a radiant Saint Joan, also starring Boris Karloff and Christopher Plummer; and a silken comedy of manners, *The Pleasure of His Company* (1958), by Samuel Taylor, starring Cornelia Otis Skinner, Walter Abel, Cyril Ritchard, George Peppard, Charlie Ruggles, and Dolores Hart. In between these two hits there was an amiable comedy about the Seventh Avenue garment district, *Fair Game* (1957), starring the expert

comic Sam Levene and a new actress named Ellen McRae, who later changed her name to Ellen Burstyn and became a star.

In 1961 Zero Mostel's powerful performance in *Rhinoceros*, the antic play by Ionesco, won him a Tony Award. The excellent cast also included Eli Wallach, Anne Jackson, Morris Carnovsky, and Jean Stapleton. At the end of the year the popular *Purlie Victorious* moved to the Longacre from the Cort and stayed for six months.

Highlights of the 1960s included Henry Denker's courtroom drama *A Case of Libel* (1963), based on Quentin Reynolds's suit against Westbrook Pegler and starring Van Heflin, Sidney Blackmer, and Larry Gates; Gabriel Dell and Rita Moreno in Lorraine Hansberry's *The Sign in Sidney Brustein's Window* (1964); Margaret Leighton, Zoe Caldwell, and Kate Reid in Tennessee Williams's lunatic *Slapstick Tragedy* (1966); Hal Holbrook in his dazzling one-man show *Mark Twain Tonight!* (1966); Holbrook again in Robert Anderson's somber autobiographical drama *I Never Sang for My Father* (1968), also starring Teresa Wright (then Mrs. Robert Anderson) and Lillian Gish; and a visit by the National Theatre of the Deaf (1969).

It was during this period that William Goldman, in his landmark 1969 survey of Broadway, *The Season*, used the Longacre as an example of a "bad" theatre—that is, one avoided by producers for a variety of reasons. Goldman took readers through the "doublethink" and circular logic of producers who refused to put likely hits into the Longacre, leading to few hits opening there, in turn reinforcing the notion that no hits open there.

Breaking the cycle in 1975 was a rollicking hit, *The Ritz*, by Terrence McNally, with Rita Moreno and Jack Weston, which caused hysterics for a year, followed by a Tony Award—winning performance by Julie Harris in her one-woman show *The Belle of Amherst*, in which she impersonated the poet Emily Dickinson. John

Left: Armelia McQueen. Nell Carter. and Charlayne Woodard in *Ain't Misbehavin'* (1978).

Right: John Rubinstein and Phyllis Frelich in *Children of a Lesser God* (1980).

Left to right: The opening night PLAYBILL for the 2005 revival of Edward Albee's *Who's Afraid of Virginia Woolf?*

Albee (top) with *Virginia Woolf* stars Kathleen Turner and Bill Irwin. (Photo by Carol Rosegg)

Russell Simmons, producer of *Def Poetry Jam* (2002).

Gielgud and Ralph Richardson were hypnotic in Pinter's *No Man's Land* (1976); Al Pacino garnered raves in a revival of David Rabe's *The Basic Training of Pavlo Hummel* (1977).

On May 9, 1978, *Ain't Misbehavin'* moved in and proved to be this theatre's biggest hit, eventually running 1,604 performances. This revue of Thomas "Fats" Waller's music was named Best Musical of the season by the Tony Awards, New York Drama Critics Circle Awards, Drama Desk Awards, and Outer Critics Circle Awards. The brilliant performers were Ken Page, Nell Carter, Charlayne Woodard, Andre De Shields, Armelia McQueen, and pianist Luther Henderson. Director Richard Maltby Jr. won a Tony.

The Longacre's longest-running nonmusical, *Children of a Lesser God*, came to the theatre from the Mark Taper Forum in Los Angeles in 1980. A sensitive study of a woman with impaired hearing and speech, it won Tony Awards for Best Play (by Mark Medoff) and Outstanding Performances by a Lead Actress (Phyllis Frelich) and Actor (John Rubinstein). It ran for 887 performances.

The 1980s saw Lanford Wilson's fascinating *Angels Fall* (1983), followed by Peter Nichols's British play *Passion*, starring Frank Langella, Cathryn Damon, Bob Gunton, E. Katherine Kerr, Roxanne Hart, and Stephanie Gordon. The decade continued with *Play Memory* (1984); the musical *Harrigan 'n Hart* (1985); a splendid revival of *Joe Egg* starring Jim Dale and Stockard Channing, for which

Channing won a Tony Award (1985); *Precious Sons*, George Furth's play starring Ed Harris and Judith Ivey (1986); the hilarious *Musical Comedy Murders of 1940*, which transferred here from Off-Broadway (1987); *Don't Get God Started*, a gospel musical (1987); *Hizzoner*, a solo show about New York Mayor Fiorello H. LaGuardia, which transferred here from Off-Broadway (1989); *Truly Blessed* (1990), a musical celebration of Mahalia Jackson; and the dance musical *Tango Pasión* (1993).

That same year *Any Given Day*, a play by Frank D. Gilroy starring Sada Thompson, lasted only thirty-two performances. In 1994 Diana Rigg scored a personal triumph in a new adaptation of the classic *Medea* and won a Tony Award for her performance. The following year Avery Brooks starred in the title role of *Paul Robeson*, a revival of Philip Hayes Dean's 1978 play with music about the life of the controversial actor/singer. The play included songs made famous by Robeson, including "Ol' Man River." Ernie Scott played Lawrence Brown. The play had a short run of eleven performances. Another revival came to the Longacre in 1996: Horton Foote's 1995 Off-Off-Broadway play *The Young Man from Atlanta*, which had won the Pulitzer Prize. Rip Torn and Shirley Knight starred in the Broadway production, which ran for seventy-nine performances.

A revised version of David Henry Hwang's play *Golden Child* opened in 1998, directed by James Lapine. The story of a Chinese man who must choose which of his three wives to keep when he embraces Christianity, *Golden Child* received the following Tony Award nominations: Featured Actress in a Play (Julyana Soelistyo) and Best Play and Costume Designer

(Martin Pakledinaz). The play ran for sixty-nine performances.

In April 1999 *The Gershwins' Fascinating Rhythm*, a revue with ten singers and dancers, presented twenty-seven songs by the Gershwin brothers in ninety minutes, without an intermission. Most of the critics loathed it, objecting to the incongruous musical arrangements and the vulgarity of some of the staging. The show was gone after seventeen performances.

In August 1999 a thriller called *Voices in the Dark*, by John Pielmeier, opened here. It starred Judith Ivey as a popular radio talk-show host who finds herself menaced by a sinister caller. The suspense play won the Edgar Award (Best Play) from the Mystery Writers of America, but New York's drama critics were less kind. Critic John Simon called it worthless garbage and reported that the cottage set's walls displayed enough antlered heads to staff a revival of *Moose Murders* (see Eugene O'Neill Theatre).

Throughout the early and mid 2000s the

Longacre housed an almost unbroken series of financial failures, though not all without interest. The managers booked a promising play in March 2000: Elaine May's comedy *Taller Than a Dwarf*, with Matthew Broderick, Parker Posey, Joyce Van Patten, and others, directed by Alan Arkin. Unfortunately, this power team was defeated by a script that was called tasteless, unfunny, and derivative. It had a short run.

Abby Mann directed George Grizzard, Maximilian Schell, and Michael Hayden in a brief revival of *Judgment at Nuremberg* starting in March 2001. TV star Tom Selleck was judged to be miscast in a similarly evanescent run of the Herb Gardner favorite *A Thousand Clowns* in July 2001.

The 1979 Off-Broadway revue *One Mo' Time* had offered a glimpse of backstage life at a 1920s New Orleans blues club and drew fans for three years. Creator Vernel Bagneris tried to reanimate the show at the Longacre in spring 2002, but its magic didn't translate to

Kathryn Hahn greets Mark Rylance in the Tony-winning 2008 revival of the sex farce *Boeing-Boeing*. (Photo by Joan Marcus)

Giselle Peacock and Robin Windsor in one of the athletic dance encounters from *Burn the Floor* (2009). (Photo by Kevin Berne)

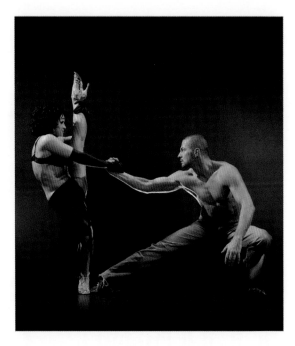

the larger stage, and it lasted just three weeks.

The pure power of the spoken word was demonstrated in fall 2002 when cable TV phenomenon Russell Simmons brought a talented group of young rap-style poets to this theatre for a musical-without-music called *Def Poetry Jam*. Among the wordsmiths showcased over the six-month run were Beau Sia, Black Ice, Staceyann Chin, Steve Colman, Mayda del Valle, Suheir Hammad, Lemon, Georgia Me, and the appropriately named Poetri.

The estimable actress Ellen Burstyn had a rare modern-day one-performance flop the night of November 17, 2003, with the solo show *The Oldest Living Confederate Widow Tells All*, based on a best-selling book. All that remained on November 18 was a highly collectible PLAYBILL.

A low of another sort was reached May 5, 2004, with the opening of *Prymate*, Mark Medoff's controversial drama about a group of researchers who teach an ape to "speak" with sign language and then have to deal with the things he communicates. Audiences were scandalized by the use of a black actor, the fine André de Shields, as the ape. Prymate fell out of the tree after five performances.

The Longacre recovered some of its luster March 20, 2005, with a well-received revival of Edward Albee's modern classic *Who's Afraid of Virginia Woolf?*, with a swaggering, whiskey-voiced Kathleen Turner as Martha, hurling verbal thunderbolts around like a drunken Zeus. Holding his own against the storm was onetime New Vaudevillian and MacArthur "Genius" Grant recipient Bill Irwin, taking his career

path on a highly successful swerve into the world of drama. His performance as George earned him the Tony Award as Best Actor in a Play. The run totaled 177 performances.

In late March 2006 Lisa Kron brought her hit Off-Broadway play *Well* to this theatre for fifty-two performances, narrating the story of the mystery ailment that was just one of the many comic (in retrospect) trials of her childhood. Jayne Houdyshell attracted universal thumbs-up as her domineering mom.

The Longacre was dark for most of the next year until the March 2007 arrival of Liev Schreiber playing a radio shock jock who goes over the line, in the Broadway debut of Eric Bogosian's drama *Talk Radio* for 121 performances.

In 2007 the Shubert Organization took the Longacre off the market and spent the better part of the next year repairing, refurbishing, and refitting the theatre to bring it up to twenty-first-century standards. Sure enough, after the renovation the Longacre housed two hits in a row.

It reopened May 4, 2008, with a sparkling revival of Marc Camoletti's retro 1960s sex farce *Boeing-Boeing*, about an American in Paris who juggles three stewardess girlfriends in a single apartment. Bradley Whitford was the putative lead, with delicious performances turned in by Gina Gershon, Kathry Hahn, and Mary McCormack (Tony nomination) as the three color-coded sweethearts. But Mark Rylance won the Tony Award as Best Actor in a Play for his dizzy performance as Whitford's visiting friend, a rare example of that honor going to a comic actor. The comedy flew for 279 performances, the longest run at the Longacre since *Children of a Lesser God* in 1980.

Next in was *Burn the Floor*, a revue of ballroom dance with a curious history. Originated as entertainment at a birthday bash for singer-songwriter Elton John in 1999, the hot, high-energy couples dancing inspired Australian Jason Gilkison and Harley Medcalf to mount it as a full-scale stage show, and it spent the next decade touring the world and the United States before it finally got up the nerve to hit Broadway August 2, 2009, where it was embraced and extended its original twelve-week engagement into 2010.

At this writing, the Longacre was preparing to host a revival of *La Cage aux Folles* via London in April 2010, starring Kelsey Grammer, Douglas Hodge, and Christine Andreas.

LUNT-FONTANNE
THEATRE

THIS BEAUTIFUL THEATRE OPENED ON
January 10, 1910, as the Globe, named after
Shakespeare's theatre in England. It was built by
the illustrious producer Charles B. Dillingham
and originally had its entrance on Broadway
between Forty-sixth and Forty-seventh streets.
Dillingham, who spared no expense on his projects, hired the famed architects Carrère and
Hastings to design his theatre. According to a
report in the *New York Dramatic Mirror* on
January 22, 1910, the new theatre had a large
stage, a compact auditorium, Italian
Renaissance decor with draperies of Rose du
Barry and walls of old gold, blue, and ivory
white. One feature of the theatre that attracted
much attention was a large oval panel in the ceiling that could be opened when the weather per-

Left: Raymond Hitchcock and Betty Carsdale in the *Ziegfeld Follies of 1921*.

Center: Standard program cover for Globe Theatre shows in the 1920s.

Right: Sheet-music cover for the Jerome Kern hit *The Stepping Stones*, starring Fred Stone (1923).

mitted. The *Mirror* called this "a complete novelty in American theatrical design."

Another unusual feature was the theatre's principal facade on West Forty-sixth Street (which today is used as the entrance). The Globe used this side entrance for its carriage patrons. Above the entrance was an outdoor balcony that theatregoers could visit during intermissions, weather permitting.

For his premiere attraction, Dillingham wisely chose a lavish musical for two of that era's most popular musical-comedy stars, Dave Montgomery and Fred Stone. The show was called *The Old Town* and had a book by George Ade and music by Gustav Luders. The two comics won raves, and the hit show got the new Globe theatre off to a rousing start.

In 1911 the popular Elsie Janis amused audiences in a sappy musical called *The Slim Princess*, in which she played a princess too slim to attract suitors, often stepping out of character to do her famous impersonations of Sarah Bernhardt, Ethel Barrymore, Eddie Foy, and George M. Cohan. In recent years it has been discovered that Victor Herbert wrote some of the music for this show.

Elsie Janis teamed up with Montgomery and Stone in *The Lady of the Slipper* (1912), and the Victor Herbert musical proved to be a smash.

Montgomery and Stone scored still another triumph in 1914 when they opened in *Chin-Chin*,

a Chinese fantasy about Aladdin and his two slaves, played by the comedy team. The musical was a sellout and ran for 295 performances.

Irving Berlin's *Stop! Look! Listen!* brought ragtime to the Globe in 1915, plus *Ziegfeld Follies* beauty Justine Johnstone, comic Joseph Santley, and Harland Dixon in a popular show.

In 1916 the Globe had a dramatic change of pace. The great American actress Laurette Taylor, who had been acting in England, returned to Broadway in a play called *The Harp of Life*, written by her husband, J. Hartley Manners. The *New York Dramatic Mirror* reported that Taylor "has made a triumphant return to her native stage." Also in the cast: young Lynn Fontanne, a name later to have great significance for this theatre.

One of the Globe's favorite performers, Dave Montgomery, died in the spring of 1917, but his partner, Fred Stone, returned to the theatre on his own and scored a triumph in the musical *Jack o' Lantern* in October of that year. Written by the same team that had created *Chin-Chin*, and produced by Dillingham, the show had sumptuous sets by Joseph Urban of *Ziegfeld Follies* fame and a perfect role for Stone as a loving man who saves two children from a wicked uncle.

The most interesting thing about *The Canary* (1918) was that it had songs by Irving Berlin, Jerome Kern, Harry Tierney, and Ivan Caryll. It starred the beautiful Julia Sanderson and comic Joseph Cawthorn, and it was about a man who swallowed a diamond.

Kern had his own show, *She's a Good Fellow*, written with Anne Caldwell, in 1919, with Joseph Santley playing in drag and the Duncan Sisters doing their vaudeville act. The musical ran for 120 performances and would have continued except for the famed actors' strike, which forced it to close.

The Roaring Twenties at the Globe brought a very mixed bag of material. In June 1920

Above: PLAYBILL cover for the long-running revue *Sophisticated Ladies* (1981).

Above: The opening night program for Tony-winner *Titanic* (1997).

Top left: Ona Munson in the 1925 smash *No, No, Nanette*.

Top center: Alfred Lunt and Lynn Fontanne in *The Visit*, their last Broadway appearance (1958).

Top right: Georges Metaxa and Bettina Hall in the memorable musical *The Cat and the Fiddle* (1931).

Bottom: Mary Martin in Rodgers and Hammerstein's last show, *The Sound of Music* (1959).

Above: *The Best Little Whorehouse Goes Public* (1994), an unsuccessful sequel to *The Best Little Whorehouse in Texas*, issued PLAYBILLs that resembled stock certificates for the namesake brothel.

George White presented his second edition of *George White's Scandals*. It had a score by George Gershwin, lyrics by Arthur Jackson, and sketches by George White and Andy Rice. The headliners were White, tapping furiously; Ann Pennington as a mechanical piano doll; and Lou Holtz providing the low comedy.

In sharp contrast to the worldly outlook of the *Scandals* was the return of Fred Stone in still another innocent musical involving children, a fantasy fairyland, and "family" entertainment. This one was called *Tip Top* (October 5, 1920), and it was written by Globe veterans Anne Caldwell and composer Ivan Caryll. Fred Stone's popularity triggered the musical's run of 241 performances.

Since Ziegfeld's New Amsterdam Theatre was occupied by one of his greatest hits, *Sally*, he presented his *Ziegfeld Follies of 1921* at the Globe. It had much to recommend it. Joseph Urban's sets and James Reynolds's costumes were so extravagant that this was Flo's most expensive *Follies*, costing over a quarter of a million dollars. The cast was stupendous. Fanny

Brice sang two of her most memorable numbers: "Second Hand Rose" and "My Man," a radical departure for her. And the great comics W. C. Fields, Raymond Hitchcock, and Ray Dooley joined Brice in sketches that became immortal.

The end of 1921 brought an endearing Jerome Kern show to the Globe, *Good Morning, Dearie*, starring Louise Groody and Oscar Shaw.

George White staged his 1922 *Scandals* at the Globe, and it is still remembered today for George Gershwin's "I'll Build a Stairway to Paradise" and for "Blue Monday Blues," a twenty-five-minute jazz opera that was cut after the opening. It was a work that would influence Gershwin to write his full-scale opera *Porgy and Bess*. W. C. Fields and Paul Whiteman and his orchestra were among the luminaries in the cast. In June of 1923 another *Scandals* with a Gershwin score opened at the Globe, but it was one of the least successful in the series.

In 1923 Fred Stone returned to the Globe in

Stepping Stones, and this time he brought his stunning, dancing daughter Dorothy along to make her Broadway debut (hence the title). Dad and daughter were a hit. The memorable score was by Jerome Kern and Anne Caldwell, and the plot was an adaptation of *Little Red Riding Hood*, allowing Fred Stone to play his usual role of a good man, who this time saves a little girl from the big bad wolf.

Ed Wynn, the lisping comic billed as "The Perfect Fool," brought one of his ingenious shows—*The Grab Bag*—to the Globe in 1924. The Wynn formula was to present a revue in which he would barge in on other acts and amuse the audience with his ludicrous comments and insane inventions, such as a typewriter-like device for eating corn on the cob without getting his fingers full of butter. The revue was a hit and ran for 184 performances.

On the evening of September 16, 1925, the audience attending the opening night of a new musical at the Globe entered the theatre humming two of the show's hits—"Tea for Two" and "I Want to Be Happy"—before they even heard the overture. The show was *No, No, Nanette*, and it had a curious history. It had already played in London (although it was strictly an American musical), had played for one year in Chicago, and had several road companies touring the country before the Broadway opening. The musical was a 321-performance hit.

The Globe's next tenant also had a strange history. It was supposed to be the *Ziegfeld Follies of 1926*, but because Flo had ended his partnership with Klaw and Erlanger, he was temporarily not permitted, by court decision, to use the *Follies* name. Therefore, he called this edition *No Foolin'* for its Globe opening but very quickly changed the title to *Ziegfeld's American Revue of 1926*. It was not one of his best revues, but it had young Paulette Goddard and Louise Brooks in the chorus and featured the beautiful Claire Luce (the dancer, not the playwright).

Fred Stone and his daughter Dorothy appeared in *Criss Cross* at the Globe in 1926, and the musical had practically the same plot as Stone's 1917 musical *Jack O'Lantern*. In this one he saves a child (his daughter) from being swindled out of her inheritance. It was another Jerome Kern/Anne Caldwell show, with Otto Harbach collaborating on book and lyrics. This was to be Fred Stone's last show at the Globe. He and his daughter were supposed to appear in another Globe musical in 1928, called *Three Cheers*, but he was not well and was replaced by Will Rogers. At the opening-night performance, Rogers said to the audience: "I don't know one thing that Fred does that I can do." Dorothy Stone was featured in the cast, and she drew raves for her singing and dancing.

In December 1926 Beatrice Lillie starred in Vincent Youmans's musical *Oh, Please!*, but it failed. The only thing that survived was the hit song "I Know That You Know."

Top left: Elizabeth Taylor and Richard Burton in the 1983 revival of Noël Coward's durable drawing room comedy *Private Lives*.

Top center: Sandy Duncan flying high in the 1979 revival of the musical *Peter Pan*.

Left to right, Sierra Boggess as Ariel gives up her voice to Tyler Maynard as Flotsam and Sherie Rene Scott as Ursula in Disney's *The Little Mermaid* (2007). (Photo by Joan Marcus)

The last legitimate show to play at this theatre under the Globe name was the memorable musical *The Cat and the Fiddle*. Jerome Kern provided one of his best scores (including "The Night Was Made for Love," "Try to Forget," and "She Didn't Say Yes"). Book and lyrics were by Otto Harbach. The leads in this Brussels operetta were played by Georges Metaxa, Odette Myrtil, Bettina Hall, and Eddie Foy Jr. It ran for 395 performances.

The stock market crash in 1929, which caused some Broadway theatres to remain dark during the Depression years, had a tragic effect on producer Charles B. Dillingham. He was wiped out financially and lost the Globe Theatre. When *The Cat and the Fiddle* closed in mid-1932, his theatre, like so many elsewhere in the theatre district, was converted to a movie house. It continued to show films until 1957.

Fortunately, Roger Stevens and Robert W.

Dowling of the City Investing Company rescued the old house by buying it and spending a fortune to reconstruct it. Dowling chose to redo the theatre in an elegant eighteenth-century style. A new stage was built, the second balcony removed, and a cantilevered mezzanine added. Blue damask walls, crystal chandeliers, and a hundred-foot ceiling mural depicting the theatrical muses added to the house's new opulence, and, most impressive of all, the theatre was renamed the Lunt-Fontanne in honor of America's foremost husband/wife acting couple, Alfred Lunt and Lynn Fontanne.

Appropriately, on May 5, 1958, the Lunts opened their new house with one of their best plays, *The Visit*, a stark, harrowing drama of revenge by Friedrich Duerrenmatt. Tickets were printed in gold for the gala opening night, and the celebrity-studded audience gave the Lunt-Fontanne Theatre and the Lunts a clamorous welcome. The critics also loved the new house and the new play (189 performances), which, unfortunately, proved to be the Lunts' Broadway swan song.

After 1958 the Lunt-Fontanne enjoyed a parade of hits. Some highlights: John Gielgud and Margaret Leighton in *Much Ado about Nothing* (1959); the last Rodgers and Hammerstein musical, *The Sound of Music*, starring Mary Martin, which played for 1,443 performances (including some at the Mark Hellinger) and won six Tony Awards, including Best Musical, Best Score, and Best Performance in a Musical (Martin). Classic songs "Do-Re-Mi," "My Favorite Things," "Climb Every Mountain," and the team's final collaboration, "Edelweiss," were introduced from the Lunt-Fontanne stage at this time.

The 1960s brought Sid Caesar in Cy Coleman and Carolyn Leigh's marvelous musical *Little Me* (1962), which should have run longer but was hampered by a newspaper strike; Martha Graham and her Dance Company (1963); Richard Burton in a commendable *Hamlet*, attended at each performance by his then wife, Elizabeth Taylor (1964); Julie Harris in her first musical, *Skyscraper* (1965); the British comic Norman Wisdom in *Walking Happy* (1966), a musical version of the novel *Hobson's Choice*; Marlene Dietrich making her Broadway debut in dazzling fashion, singing her famous songs and backed by Burt Bacharach and his huge orchestra (1967); a musical about Wall Street called *How Now,*

Dow Jones (1967); and Nicol Williamson in another *Hamlet* (1969).

The Rothschilds (1970) was a musical success about the famed Jewish banking family by the *Fiddler on the Roof* team of Jerry Bock and Sheldon Harnick. It was the team's last full collaboration. Hal Linden won a Tony as Best Actor in a Musical, and Keene Curtis won the same award as Best Featured Actor.

Several famous musicals were revived at the Lunt-Fontanne during the 1970s, including *A Funny Thing Happened on the Way to the Forum* (1972), starring Phil Silvers (who won a Tony Award); an interracial production of *The Pajama Game* (1973) with Hal Linden, Barbara McNair, and Cab Calloway; the lavish twentieth-anniversary production of *My Fair Lady*, which moved to the Lunt-Fontanne from the St. James in December 1976; and Carol Channing in a revival of her signature show, Jerry Herman's *Hello, Dolly!* (1978). In the middle of all these revivals, a Richard Rodgers/Sheldon Harnick/Sherman Yellen musical about King Henry VIII, called *Rex* (1976), was beheaded by the critics. Nicol Williamson starred as the king.

In 1979 Sandy Duncan brightened the Lunt-Fontanne by flying all over the house in *Peter Pan*. In 1981 the elegant Duke Ellington revue *Sophisticated Ladies* moved into the Lunt-Fontanne, starring Gregory Hines and Judith Jamison, and thrilled theatregoers for 767 performances with its silken Ellington melodies and sparkling choreography.

In 1983 Zev Bufman produced two revivals at this theatre: Noël Coward's *Private Lives*, starring real-life feuding couple Richard Burton and Elizabeth Taylor, and *The Corn Is Green*, starring Cicely Tyson. These were followed by Peggy Lee in her autobiographical musical *Peg*, a one-woman show backed by a large band.

The remainder of the 1980s brought revivals of *The Wiz*, O'Neill's *The Iceman Cometh*, and rock star Sting in *The 3 Penny Opera*. There were also the short-lived new musicals *Uptown . . . It's Hot*, *Smile* and *The Gospel at Colonus*; and such entertainments as *Doug Henning & His World of Magic*; *Jerry Garcia on Broadway*; *Joan Jett and the Blackhearts on Broadway*; and *Freddie Jackson: Up Close and Personal*.

Cathy Rigby starred in another successful revival of *Peter Pan* in 1990; *An Evening With Harry Connick, Jr.*, proved popular that same year; and in 1991 the hilarious *Catskills on Broadway* played to enthusiastic audiences.

In 1993 *Ain't Broadway Grand*, a musical about showman Mike Todd, opened here. Mike Burstyn played Todd, with Debbie Shapiro Gravitte as Gypsy Rose Lee, Maureen McNamara as actress Joan Blondell (one of Todd's wives), and Gerry Vichi as comic Bobby Clark. The musical had a score by Mitch Leigh, lyrics by Lee Adams, and a book by Adams and Thomas Meehan. The show managed only twenty-five performances.

In 1994 *The Best Little Whorehouse Goes Public* (a sequel to the hit musical *The Best Little Whorehouse in Texas*) went nowhere, running for only fifteen performances despite the presence in the cast of classy Dee Hoty. This was followed by another flop—*Comedy Tonight*—a vaudeville-type show with Mort Sahl, Dorothy Loudon, Joy Behar, and Michael Davis, which lasted for only eight performances.

In 1995 Carol Channing returned to this theatre in still another revival of *Hello, Dolly!* Once again the critics raved, and the musical had a run of 188 performances. The Royal Shakespeare Company's production of *A Midsummer Night's Dream*, directed by Adrian Noble, opened at the Lunt-Fontanne in March 1996, and it received eight positive reviews, which helped it to run for 65 performances. In November of that year the Moscow Theatre Sovremennik presented Chekhov's *The Three Sisters* and *The Whirlwind*, by Eugenia Ginsburg, performed in Russian, with simultaneous English translation via headphones. The company gave eight performances.

The musical *Titanic* opened to mixed reviews after severe technical mishaps during previews, with a set that recreated the tipping of the decks on the doomed oceanliner. Nevertheless, Peter Stone's story and the choral score by Maury Yeston struck a chord with audiences, and the show went on to win five Tony Awards, including Best Musical of the season. It sailed on for 804 performances.

After *Titanic* disembarked for the last time, the theatre was closed from spring through fall 1999 for extensive renovations made by the theatre's owner, the Nederlander Organization, and executed by the Sachs Morgan Studio (SMS). The aim was to make the elongated orchestra section seem more intimate and to brighten the house's decor. Improved restroom facilities were installed, and the second floor lobby was completely redone.

On November 12, 1999, the Disney superhit *Beauty and the Beast* moved from the Palace and, over the next eight years through July 29, 2007, completed a long run of 5,461 performances—the second-longest of any show of the 1990s, after *Rent.* The Nederlander Organization then took the house out of circulation for the rest of that year for another comprehensive renovation that included modernized electronics and a handsome mini museum in the lower lounge area dedicated to the theatre's namesakes, with photos of Lunt and Fontanne from throughout their illustrious careers. A grand portrait of the acting couple also greets playgoers as they pass upward from the main lobby to the mezzanine.

The Lunt-Fontanne proved to be a favorite of Disney Theatricals, which booked it for its next musical spectacular, *The Little Mermaid*, an adaptation of another Disney animated film, based on the Hans Christian Andersen tale. Like *Beauty and the Beast*, *The Little Mermaid* had music and lyrics by Alan Menken and Howard Ashman (with additional lyrics by Glenn Slater and a book by Doug Wright).

Several of the film's original voice actors attended the glittering opening night on January 10, 2008, to watch Sierra Boggess, Sean Palmer, and Sherie Rene Scott cavort in the imaginative undersea environment designed by a team that included George Tyspin (sets), Tatiana Noginova (costumes), and Natasha Katz (lighting) and was led by director Francesca Zambello, who created the illusion of swimming by putting the actors in Heelys—shoes with small built-in wheels that were popular with children of the period. *The Little Mermaid* closed August 30, 2009, after 685 performances.

Things got creepy and kooky at the Lunt-Fontanne on April 4, 2010, when it welcomed *The Addams Family*, a musical adaptation of the Charles Addams cartoons (and popular TV series) with Nathan Lane as Gomez and Bebe Neuwirth as Morticia. The show had music and lyrics by Andrew Lippa and a libretto by the *Jersey Boys* team of Marshall Brickman and Rick Elice. Despite mixed reviews, including a vehement pan from the *New York Times* ("Like going to a Halloween party in a strait-jacket"), the gothic show proved popular with ticket buyers in its early weeks and seemed ready for life after a critical death.

LYCEUM
THEATRE

WHEN THE FAMED IMPRESARIO DANIEL
Frohman opened the Lyceum Theatre on
November 2, 1903, on West Forty-fifth Street,
east of Broadway, he called it the New Lyceum
to distinguish it from the old Lyceum, which he
formerly owned on Fourth Avenue. The opening of his new theatre brought much publicity,
and the day before its premiere the *New York
Tribune* ran a feature article on the splendors
of the new house. One of the unusual features
was a ten-story tower at its rear section con-
taining such departments as a carpenter shop,
scene-building and painting studios, wardrobe
sections, and extra dressing rooms.

The paper praised the theatre's decorative
scheme by architects Herts and Tallant; its gray
limestone facade with Roman columns; the marble staircases in the lobby; the width of the audi-

torium, which brought seats closer to the stage; the absence of posts, giving all theatregoers an unobstructed view of the stage; and Frohman's elegant quarters above the theatre, with a concealed window that permitted him to supervise rehearsals from above and to telephone directions to his stage manager below. The window can be glimpsed from the front of the orchestra by looking into the highest section of the ceiling vault above the topmost balcony on the side nearest the back of the house. A small ladder can be spotted leading to a doorlike shutter, which is now kept shut. Today Frohman's quarters are part of the private museum known as the Shubert Archive.

Ideal for dramas and comedies, the New Lyceum opened with *The Proud Prince*, starring the distinguished American actor E. H. Sothern, who had appeared in many fine plays at the downtown Lyceum. Later in 1903 another illustrious star, William Gillette, sparkled in James M. Barrie's *The Admirable Crichton*.

In 1905 a tremendous hit came to the Lyceum. Charles Klein's *The Lion and the Mouse* was an attack on big business and in particular on John D. Rockefeller. The drama was about a judge whose career was unjustly ruined by a tycoon named John Burkett Ryder (the Rockefeller character, played by Edmund Breese). The judge's daughter, who exposes the injustice (a character based on the real-life Ida Tarbell), was acted by Grace Elliston. Her boyfriend was played by Richard Bennett, father of the future stars Constance and Joan Bennett. The play caused a sensation and ran for 686 performances.

In 1907 Daniel Frohman presented his wife, Margaret Illington, and Kyrle Bellew in Henri Bernstein's play *The Thief*. During the run of this hit, Frohman and his wife discovered a way to control her performance in the explosive second act. Margaret would look up, and if she was overacting Frohman would wave

his handkerchief frantically from his secret window above the stage.

During the early years of the Lyceum, the theatre presented a parade of ravishing stars in plays that were regarded more as star vehicles than as great dramas. Billie Burke, a Virginia beauty, soon became a Lyceum fixture in a series of these productions, many produced by Daniel Frohman's celebrated brother, Charles Frohman. Among these plays were *Love Watches* (1908); *Mrs. Dot* (1910); *Suzanne* (1910); *The Runaway* (1911), with C. Aubrey Smith and Henry Miller Jr.; and *The "Mind the Paint" Girl* (1912). The beautiful young Ethel Barrymore starred in *Our Mrs. McChesney* (1915), by Edna Ferber and George Hobart; the steamy Lenore Ulric heated the house with Pedro de Cordoba in David Belasco's *Tiger Rose* (1917); and the coruscating Ina Claire made sparks in *The Gold Diggers* (1919), another hit Belasco production. It ran for 720 performances.

The Roaring Twenties continued to bring hits to the Lyceum. In September 1921 Belasco revived Eugene Walter's shocker *The Easiest Way*, starring the revered actress Frances Starr. In his autobiography, *Present Indicative*,

Top left: E.H Sothern in the *Proud Prince* (1903).

Top center: Lenore Ulric in the sultry hit *Tiger Rose* (1917).

Top right: Sketch of the Lyceum Theatre in 1909 from *The Wanamaker Diary*.

Bottom left: Patricia Peardon, Lenore Lonergan, and their boyfriends in *Junior Miss* (1941).

Bottom right: Alan Bates, Mary Ure, and Kenneth Haigh clash in *Look Back in Anger* (1957).

Top left: Shelly Winters and her junkie husband (Ben Gazzara) in *A Hatful of Rain* (1955).

Top center: Sir Edward Lutyens' set for *Berkeley Square*.

Top right: Nancy Marchand, Elizabeth Wilson, Maureen O'Sullivan, and Teresa Wright in *Morning's at Seven* (1980).

Bottom: *Your Arms Too Short to Box With God* (1976).

Above: Leslie Howard travels back in time in the memorable *Berkeley Square* (1929).

Above: Billie Burke, a Lyceum favorite, in *Mrs. Dot* (1910).

Noël Coward relates how he attended this opening night while on his first visit to New York. He was introduced to the acerbic critic Alexander Woollcott, and Coward confessed to the critic that he found the performance of one of the actresses in the cast "vexing." Woollcott thought the remark hysterically funny, and he and Coward became lifelong friends.

David Belasco continued to provide the Lyceum with hits. In November 1921 he presented actor Lionel Atwill and popular Lina Abarbanell in one of Sacha Guitry's romantic comedies, *The Grand Duke*, about royalty mingling with peasantry. It worked for 131 performances. In the summer of 1922 Belasco produced a naval comedy, *Shore Leave*, starring James Rennie as a romantic gob and Frances Starr as his girl in a New England port. This amusing comedy later was turned into the smash musical *Hit the Deck*, and still later into the enchanting Rogers/Astaire film musical *Follow the Fleet*.

Belasco's 1924 hit was *Ladies of the Evening*, a Pygmalion tale about a man (James Kirkwood) who makes a lady out of a prostitute

(Beth Merrill) and then falls in love with her.

Charles Frohman returned to producing at the Lyceum in 1925 and presented *The Grand Duchess and the Waiter*, with Elsie Ferguson as the royal dame who falls for a waiter (Basil Rathbone) who turns out to be the son of the president of the Swiss Republic. Later in the year, Frohman produced another continental comedy, *Naughty Cinderella*, with the vivacious French star Irene Bordoni as an amorous secretary.

In 1926 revue genius Fanny Brice starred in a comedy called *Fanny* with Warren William, but despite the Belasco production and Brice's clowning, it lasted only sixty-three performances. In 1928 Walter Huston gave a comical performance as baseball pitcher Elmer Kane in Ring Lardner's *Elmer the Great*, produced by George M. Cohan, but the unpopularity of baseball as a stage topic resulted in only forty performances.

One of 1929's ten best plays (as chosen by critic Burns Mantle for his annual *Best Plays* volumes) opened at the Lyceum and became one of its most fondly remembered experiences. The prestigious producer Gilbert Miller and

Top left: Paul Douglas and Judy Holliday battle over gin rummy in *Born Yesterday* (1946).

Bottom left: left to right, Zane Lasky, Jack Klugman, Jerry Stiller, Joey Faye, and Tony Randall in the National Actors Theatre revival of the gambling comedy *Three Men on a Horse* (1992). (Photo by Joan Marcus)

Right: Sean Foley and Hamish McColl in the British entertainment, *The Play What I Wrote* (2002). (Photo by Joan Marcus)

actor Leslie Howard co-produced a fantasy called *Berkeley Square* by John L. Balderston. It starred Howard as a contemporary American whose spirit is transported back to his ancestors' home in London in 1784, where he engages in a fateful romance with a lovely British woman (Margalo Gillmore). The enchanting play ran for 227 performances and was made into a successful film with Howard.

The Depression had its effect on the Lyceum as Daniel Frohman's career declined, and he was threatened with eviction in the early 1930s. In 1939 the Lyceum was in danger of being demolished, but a group of theatre titans, who loved the old playhouse, banded together and bought it the following year. They were playwrights George S. Kaufman and Moss Hart, producer Max Gordon, and others. They assumed ownership of the Lyceum with the stipulation that Daniel Frohman be permitted to live in his quarters above the house for one dollar a year. It was a fitting gesture for the aged impresario, who died on December 16, 1940. The Kaufman/Hart group sold the Lyceum at a profit in 1945, and it is currently owned by the Shubert Organization.

Highlights of the 1930s at this theatre includ-ed the American debut of Charles Laughton with his wife, Elsa Lanchester, in a murder thriller, *Payment Deferred* (1931). Laughton was hailed for his performance. In 1933 a raucous naval comedy called *Sailor, Beware!* made critics blush and ran for 500 laugh-provoking performances. The glittering Ina Claire returned to the Lyceum in 1934 with Walter Slezak in *Ode to Liberty*; Jessie Royce Landis had a hit in *Pre-Honeymoon* (1936); Maurice Evans was an admired Napoleon in *St. Helena* (1936); Arthur Kober's charmingly ethnic *Having Wonderful Time*, starring Jules Garfield (later, John) and Katherine Locke, was a huge hit in 1937; a British hit, *Bachelor Born*, moved here from the Morosco and played for many months in 1938; and the decade ended with J. B. Priestley's *When We Are Married*.

Kaufman and Hart's *George Washington Slept Here* was one of their lesser hits, in 1940; William Saroyan had a fanciful fling with *The Beautiful People* (1941); and a marvelous comedy called *Junior Miss*, about adolescence, was expertly staged by Moss Hart and romped for 710 performances.

The authors of *Junior Miss*—Jerome Chodorov and Joseph Fields—came up with another winner for the Lyceum in 1942 when their wartime comedy *The Doughgirls* opened. Arlene Francis was the hit of the show as a Russian guerrilla fighter sharing a Washington apartment with two other women. It was good for 671 performances, thanks to George S. Kaufman's dazzling direction.

Kaufman also co-wrote, with John P. Marquand, and directed *The Late George Apley*, based on Marquand's Pulitzer Prize novel of the same name. The play, a warm chronicle about a Boston Brahmin (brilliantly played by Leo G. Carroll) and his family, opened on November 21, 1944, and stayed for 384 performances.

A Sound of Hunting (1945) was not a hit, but it served as the Broadway debut of Burt Lancaster (billed as "Burton"), who promptly went to Hollywood and made a fortune. In 1946 the Lyceum housed Garson Kanin's comedy *Born Yesterday*, about a dumb blonde and her uncouth keeper, a loudmouth junk dealer. The morning after it opened, the blonde (Judy Holliday) and the junk dealer (Paul Douglas) were famous. It was the Lyceum's longest-running show, chalking up 1,642 performances.

The Lyceum's next hit occurred in 1950 when Clifford Odets returned to Broadway with *The Country Girl*, starring Uta Hagen as the courageous wife of an alcoholic actor (Paul Kelly) who has to contend with a tough stage director (Steven Hill). Odets directed his successful drama.

Melvyn Douglas starred in two fluffy

comedies at this theatre: *Glad Tidings* (1951), with Signe Hasso, and *Time Out for Ginger* (1952), with Nancy Malone as his daughter, Ginger, who tries out for her high school's football team. Another light comedy, *King of Hearts* (1954)—by Jean Kerr and Eleanor Brooke and directed by Kerr's husband, critic Walter Kerr—starred Jackie Cooper and Donald Cook and featured Cloris Leachman.

Anastasia (1954), a fascinating drama about a woman who claims to be the daughter of the last Russian czar and to have survived the family's massacre, was brilliantly acted by Viveca Lindfors as the claimant and by Eugenie Leontovich as the dowager empress.

Another powerful drama, *A Hatful of Rain* (1955), by actor Michael V. Gazzo, dramatized the anguish of a wife (Shelley Winters) married to a drug addict (Ben Gazzara). Harry Guardino and Anthony Franciosa were also in the cast.

Comedy returned to the Lyceum in 1956 when Walter Pidgeon arrived as *The Happiest Millionaire*, based on the life of millionaire Anthony J. Drexel Biddle. In sharp contrast to this high-society romp was a 1957 drama from England, John Osborne's *Look Back in Anger*, starring Kenneth Haigh, Alan Bates, and Mary Ure. This lashing protest against the genteel Britain of yesteryear started a new school of playwriting called "kitchen sink drama." Its vitriolic antihero, Jimmy Porter (Mr. Haigh), became the dramatic symbol for the "angry young man."

Another fine drama from Britain, *A Taste of Honey*, by young playwright Shelagh Delaney, started the Lyceum off with a hit in 1960. It starred Angela Lansbury as the mother of a pregnant, unmarried daughter, and it was written in the "kitchen sink" style. Britain sent still another excellent play in 1961, *The Caretaker* by Harold Pinter, starring Alan Bates and Robert Shaw as brothers who make the charitable error of taking in a homeless, ominous stranger (Donald Pleasence).

After a number of short runs, the Lyceum

had a mild hit in *Nobody Loves an Albatross* (1963), a comedy about an overpowering TV personality (said to be inspired by Lucille Ball) and her coworkers. It starred Robert Preston and Constance Ford.

From 1965 to 1969 the Lyceum became the home for the Phoenix Theatre and the APA Repertory Company with Ellis Rabb as artistic director. During these years the combined companies staged a rich variety of theatre, including a highly successful revival of *You Can't Take It with You*, *War and Peace*, Helen Hayes in George Kelly's *The Show-off*, *The Cherry Orchard*, *The Cocktail Party*, *The Misanthrope*, and *Hamlet*.

In the 1970s the Lyceum housed a number of productions, none of which ran very long, except for the gospel musical *Your Arms Too Short to Box with God*. Worthy of mention is *Borstal Boy*, Frank McMahon's adaptation of Brendan Behan's book about his early years in prison. Although the play ran only a few months, it won a Tony Award and a New York Drama Critics Circle Award. Also admired in the 1970s was *Cold Storage*, with Len Cariou and Martin Balsam as patients in a hospital terminal ward, and Arthur Kopit's *Wings*, a harrowing study of a woman who suffered a stroke. Constance Cummings's performance won her a Tony Award.

In 1980 a play called *Morning's at Seven*, by Paul Osborn, which had flopped on Broadway in 1939, was beautifully revived with an all-star cast and turned into a belated hit. It won a Tony as the season's best revival and additional Tonys for its director, Vivian Matalon, and David Rounds for best featured actor.

This was followed by Jules Feiffer's *Grown Ups* (1981), with Bob Dishy, Frances Sternhagen, and Harold Gould; Athol Fugard's powerful racial drama "MASTER HAROLD". . . *and the boys* (1982); Edward Albee's *The Man Who Had Three Arms* (1983); Whoopi Goldberg in a one-woman show that won her a Theatre World Award and a Drama Desk citation (1984); *As Is*, William M. Hoffman's powerful play about AIDS (1985); *A Little Like Magic*, the Canadian life-size puppet theatre presented by Famous People Players (1986); *Safe Sex*, three one-act plays by Harvey Fierstein on gay themes (1987); *Michael Feinstein in Concert* (1988); and the Lincoln Center Theater's revival of Thornton Wilder's classic *Our Town*, which won a Tony as the season's Best Revival (1988).

As it had housed the APA-Phoenix Rep in the 1960s, the Lyceum spent most of the 1990s as home to Tony Randall's National Actors Theatre. NAT inaugurated its tenancy in 1992 with three revivals: *The Seagull*, with Tyne Daly, Jon Voight, Maryann Plunkett, Tony Roberts, and John Beal; *Saint Joan*, with Plunkett in the title role; and *Three Men on a Horse*, with Randall, Jack Klugman, and Joey Faye.

The National Actors Theatre returned to the Lyceum in 1994 with revivals of Shakespeare's *Timon of Athens* and of *The Government Inspector* and *The Flowering Peach*, the last of these starring Eli Wallach and Anne Jackson. In 1995 the company presented revivals of *Gentlemen Prefer Blondes* and Sheridan's *School for Scandal*. The company scored two hits with revivals in 1997: *The Gin Game*, starring Julie Harris and Charles Durning, and *The Sunshine Boys*, starring Randall and Klugman. In March of that year *Mandy Patinkin in Concert* played a limited engagement.

In 1999 Randall's troupe scored another hit with a revival of the suspense play *Night Must Fall*, starring Matthew Broderick and Judy Parfitt, which moved to the Helen Hayes Theatre to make way for Irish playwright Martin McDonagh's *The Lonesome West*, an unsuccessful follow-up to his 1998 hit *The Beauty Queen of Leenane*.

Lincoln Center Theater's production of Martin Sherman's one-woman play *Rose*, starring Olympia Dukakis, allowed her to recreate her London success with this drama about a woman recalling the Holocaust. Produced by arrangement with the Royal National Theatre, the play ran for a limited engagement.

Poet A. E. Houseman's lifelong unrequited homosexual love for a college classmate was the subject of Tom Stoppard's drama *The Invention of Love*, which arrived at the Lyceum from the Royal National Theatre in London and earned Tony Awards for both Richard Easton and Robert Sean Leonard, who played elder and younger versions of Houseman. Heavily reliant on literary allusions that bewildered some audience members, the production opened March 29, 2001, and closed three months later.

In the spring of 2002, Lincoln Center Theater booked the Lyceum for another revival of Paul Osborn's unsettling play *Morning's at Seven*, which earned a raft of Tony nominations (but no wins) for its distinguished cast. The production supplied three of the four nominees in the category Best Featured Actress in a Play: Elizabeth Franz, Frances Sternhagen, and Estelle Parsons;

Norbert Leo Butz in drag to fool Jenn Gambatese in the long-lost Mark Twain drama *Is He Dead?* (2007). (Photo by Joan Marcus)

and two of the four nominees for Best Featured Actor in a Play: William Biff McGuire and Stephen Tobolowsky. It ran 112 performances.

The antics of the 1950s British comedy team Morecambe and Wise was were recreated in *The Play What I Wrote*, a comedy revue written by Hamish McColl, Sean Foley, and Eddie Braben and performed by McColl and Foley under the direction of Kenneth Branagh. The transferred London hit was notable for having a different celebrity "Mystery Guest" each night, including Roger Moore, Glenn Close, Nathan Lane, and Liam Neeson. It gave eighty-nine performances, starting March 30, 2003.

Actor Jefferson Mays got the role—or, more accurately, "roles"—of his career in Doug Wright's drama *I Am My Own Wife*, the story of real-life East German transvestite Charlotte von Mahlsdorf, who somehow managed to survive the brutalities of both the Nazi and Communist regimes while keeping his/her antiquarian business intact. Mays played not only the title roles, but everyone von Mahlsdorf met along the way, including interviewer Wright. The play gave 360 performances and won the 2004 Pulitzer Prize for Drama and three Tony Awards, including Best Play and Best Performance by an Actor.

The demands of playing three dozen different characters required that Mays cut back to six performances a week. In an unusual arrangement, the other two performance slots each week (starting May 24, 2004) were handed off to a New Vaudeville solo show by mentalist Marc Salem, called *Marc Salem's Mind Games on Broadway*. During his ninety-minute show, the unprepossessing Salem demonstrated his prodigious memory and his ability to deduce intimate details of people's lives simply from their appearance. He gave a total of thirty performances through November 22, 2004.

Twenty years after the hit Broadway solo show that launched her career, comedian Whoopi Goldberg returned to the Lyceum November 17, 2004, with a new set of observations on life, culture, and politics. Audiences, who by now had seen her extensively in movies and TV shows, did not return in the hoped-for droves, and *Whoopi* departed after seventy-two performances.

Another blast from the 1980s, *Steel Magnolias*, arrived at the Lyceum April 4, 2005, bringing a bouquet of female stars—Delta Burke, Christine Ebersole, Marsha Mason, Lily Rabe, and Rebecca Gayheart—for nearly four months.

It takes a great singer to perfectly embody a terrible singer, as actress Judy Kaye proved in *Souvenir*, her homage to musical curiosity Florence Foster Jenkins (1868—1944). Jenkins imagined herself one of the premier operatic singers of her day—apparently unaware of the tuneless bray she was actually emitting. Such was the entertainment value of her performances that she attracted an amazed and devoted following despite the cacophony. Stephen Temperley's play with music transferred to the Lyceum from a successful Off-Broadway run, stayed for two months starting November 10, 2005, and earned Kaye a Tony Nomination as Best Actress in a Play.

Gunshot blindings, mutilated corpses, and a character hanging bloody from a rope are just a sampling of the repellent violence presented May 3, 2006, in Martin McDonagh's Irish "comedy" *The Lieutenant of Inishmore*. This tale of revenge for the death of a cat named Wee Thomas spun out for 142 performances, earning a Tony nomination as Best Play. Cast members David Wilmot, Domhnall Gleeson, and Alison Pill all got Tony nominations, as did director Wilson Milam.

Creationists in America had Darwin's theory of evolution under serious attack in spring 2007 when *Inherit the Wind* got a major Broadway revival. The drama was based on the 1925 so-called Scopes Monkey Trial, in which a Tennessee teacher was charged with teaching evolution in a state where the theory was banned. Christopher Plummer starred as defense attorney Henry Drummond, with Brian Dennehy as his demagogue opponent, Matthew Harrison Brady. The production lasted an even 100 performances.

The next show at the Lyceum was a very funny comedy with a superb pedigree—but a business-killer of a title. It turns out that that great American humorist Mark Twain, after completing his classics including *Tom Sawyer* and *The Adventures of Huckleberry Finn*, managed to scratch out a stage comedy, a raucous farce and a satire on the art world, called *Is He Dead?* Rejected by Broadway producers of the 1890s, the script languished in a drawer until rediscovered by researchers. With some updating by playwright David Ives, the production had its Broadway debut December 9, 2007. Norbert Leo Butz played an artist who fakes his own death to drive up the popularity of his paintings, but things soon get out of hand. Also in the sterling cast were Jenn Gambatese, David Pittu, John McMartin, Byron Jennings, and Michael McGrath. *Is He Dead?* lived for 105 performances.

Patrick Stewart brought Broadway its forty-

Left: The self-referencing PLAYBILL cover for [title of show].

Right: Clockwise from top left: Heidi Blickenstaff, Susan Blackwell, Hunter Bell, and Jeff Bowen in the musical about the writing of itself, [title of show] (2009). (Photo by Joan Marcus)

sixth recorded mounting of Shakespeare's *Macbeth* on April 8, 2008, in a production that arrived from England's Chichester Festival Theatre via the Brooklyn Academy of Music. Kate Fleetwood played Lady Macbeth in the starkly designed revival, which played out a fifty-two-performance limited run.

Things brightened considerably April 2, 2009, with the arrival of a musical that told the story of its own creation: [title of show], starring its own creators, who played themselves. Composer/lyricist Jeff Bowen and book writer Hunter Bell began with the tale of how they constructed the show for the New York Musical Theatre Festival. But they then added an account of how they moved the show Off-Broadway, and then how they (with costars Heidi Blickenstaff and Susan Blackwell) launched an Internet campaign called "The [title of show] Show" to get the production to Broadway. Life imitated art in a big way. Despite a gag on the original cast album in which they argue about whether to include a song about wanting to win a Tony Award for the show, Bell went on to win the real-life Tony Award for Best Book of a Musical. The problem was that [title of show]'s fan base proved to be a mile deep but only an inch wide, and it struggled to reach 100 performances.

Neil LaBute, author of a series of provocative Off-Broadway dramas about modern male—female relationships, made his Broadway debut with a transfer of his play *reasons to be pretty*, the last play in his trilogy about people's obsession with looks (along with *The Shape of Things*

and *Fat Pig*). *Reasons* was about a relationship that goes messily on the rocks when the man (Thomas Sadoski) impolitically refers to the woman's appearance as "regular." Thus damned with faint praise, she (Marin Ireland) opens the show with a verbal reaming likely to become a staple of acting classes for years to come. An underrated play along the lines of *Is He Dead?*, *reasons to be pretty* ran just eighty-five performances, though it was nominated for three Tony Awards, including Best Play of 2009.

No less a subject than the liberation of the female orgasm was explored in Sarah Ruhl's play *In the Next Room (or The Vibrator Play)*. Set in the late nineteenth century, when scientists and inventors were discovering so many marvelous uses for electricity, *In the Next Room* tells the story (based on actual incidents) of a doctor who uses a primitive vibrator to relieve female patients of their pent-up nervousness and "melancholy." The provocative subject attracted stars Laura Benanti and Michael Cerveris and ran sixty performances, starting November 19, 2009.

Valerie Harper gave an uncanny impersonation of stage and film star Tallulah Bankhead in Matthew Lombardo's comedy *Looped*, set in 1965, when the heartily profane Bankhead needed to re-record a single line in a minor film near the end of her career. The production stayed a brief thirty-three performances.

Though it is among Broadway's smallest and oldest theatres, the Lyceum has found its place as a home for small-cast dramas, comedies, and musicals.

MAJESTIC
THEATRE

THE MAJESTIC THEATRE AT 245 WEST
Forty-forth Street, right off the corner of Eighth
Avenue, was the sixth and last of the houses
built by the Chanin Brothers. With a seating
capacity of 1,800 (1,655 today), it was for
decades the largest legitimate theatre in the
Times Square district, suited primarily for the
staging of lavish musical comedies and revues.

Architect Herbert J. Krapp used the same
stadium-style design for this house as he had for
the Chanins' first theatre, the 46th Street. The
orchestra was built on a steep slope, and patrons
had to climb stairs to reach the rear section of the
orchestra. There was only one balcony. The *New
York Times* described the architecture and decoration of the interior as being in the Louis XV
style, with a color scheme of gold and ivory. "The

next but didn't tarry more than eighty-eight performances. An extremely elaborate 1928 Gilbert Miller production, *The Patriot*, had John Gielgud in the cast and, considering the reviews, should have run longer than twelve performances. George Kelly's play *Behold the Bridegroom*, which critic Burns Mantle named one of the year's ten best, moved to the Majestic from the Cort Theatre in February 1928. It starred Judith Anderson, Jean Dixon, Mary Servoss, Thurston Hall, and Lester Vail, but it ran only eighty-eight performances.

Ziegfeld's enormous hit *Rio Rita* (1928) moved to the Majestic after playing some months at the splendid new Ziegfeld Theatre. Champion boxer Jack Dempsey made his Broadway debut at the Majestic September 18, 1928, in a drama called, aptly, *The Big Fight*, in which he had to knock out another boxer to win the hand of a manicurist named Shirley. The critics rated his boxing better than his acting and the novelty wore off after thirty-one rounds.

The Majestic's biggest hit thus far was a revue called *Pleasure Bound*, with Phil Baker, Jack Pearl, Grace Brinkley, and others. The young Busby Berkeley created the dances, and the show made it to 136 performances. The Shuberts produced a new version of *Die Fledermaus* called *A Wonderful Night*, and the star was a young stilt walker from England called Archie Leach, who became better known in Hollywood as Cary Grant. This Johann Strauss bauble played 125 performances.

In February 1930 *The International Revue* opened here and should have been a triumph. It cost $200,000 to mount (an exorbitant amount for the Depression), and it had such luminaries in the cast as Gertrude Lawrence, Harry Richman, Jack Pearl, ballet star Anton Dolin, the great Spanish dancer Argentinita, Moss and Fontana, and the

house curtain, the valence, the box drapes and panels on the side walls are of gold and rose silk damask," the paper reported. "As in other Chanin houses, the seats are said to be three inches wider than the ordinary theatre chair."

The Majestic Theatre opened on March 28, 1927, with a revue curiously called *Rufus LeMaire's Affairs*, after the show's producer, Rufus LeMaire. Despite such talents as Ted Lewis, Charlotte Greenwood, and Peggy Fears, the show was a dud and played only fifty-six times. This was succeeded by a black revue, *Rang Tang*, that moved here from the Royale Theatre and stayed for two months. A Sigmund Romberg musical play called *The Love Call* was

Above: Program cover sketch for the musical *Fanny* (1954).

Julie Andrews charms Richard Burton in the Lerner and Loewe musical *Camelot* (1960).

Right: Tiger Haynes, James Wigfall, Stephanie Mills, and Hinton Battle in the long-running hit *The Wiz* (1975).

Above: Liza Minnelli gives a Tony Award-winning performance in *The Act* (1977).

Chester Hale Girls. It also had two song hits by Dorothy Fields and Jimmy McHugh that have become standards: "On the Sunny Side of the Street" and "Exactly Like You." But the revue was earthbound. On the opening night, it was so long that the second act did not begin until 11:00 p.m., and the highly touted Argentinita laid an egg.

The Shuberts' next venture, an operetta called *Nina Rosa*, by Sigmund Romberg, Otto Harbach, and Irving Caesar, ran 137 times. It starred Ethelind Terry (the famed star of *Rio Rita*) and Guy Robertson, and it had a novel setting—the Peruvian Andes. A revival of Romberg's *The Student Prince* in 1931 fared less well, running for 45 performances. The Depression was felt by this theatre in 1932, when it was dark for many months.

In January 1933 much was expected of *Pardon My English*, a musical with a score by George and Ira Gershwin and book by Herbert

Fields. The producers were Alex Aarons and Vinton Freedley, who had mounted a series of highly successful Gershwin shows. The stars were Jack Pearl, Lyda Roberti ("the Polish bombshell"), Josephine Huston, and the dance team of Carl Randall and Barbara Newberry. The net result was one of the Gershwins' biggest flops. It ran for only forty-three performances. According to Gerald Bordman in his book *American Musical Theatre*, the fact that this musical was set in Germany disturbed many theatregoers, since Hitler was coming to power there.

The successful team of Ray Henderson and Lew Brown decided to give the Depression a kick in the slats by writing and producing an opulent revue, *Strike Me Pink*, at the Majestic in March 1933. The show, backed by gangster Waxey Gordon, smacked of the Roaring Twenties. Opening-night top was $25 (outrageous for those dark days), and the tickets were printed on gold stock. The stars included the ebullient Jimmy Durante, the vivacious Lupe Velez (then married to Tarzan, Johnny Weissmuller), and that cool socialite Hope Williams. The result was neither a flop nor a smash, but a pleasant run of 122 performances.

An ingenious musical, *Murder at the Vanities*, moved to the Majestic from the New Amsterdam in November 1933 and stayed for four months. It focused on backstage murders during a performance of *Earl Carroll's Vanities* and thus combined thrills with lush scenes from a typical Carroll revue. Bela Lugosi was in the cast, but he wasn't the one who "dunnit." Since producers are constantly promising to revive this novelty, we shall not divulge the killer's identity.

An impresario named S. M. Chartock took over the Majestic in the spring of 1934 and staged a festival of five Gilbert and Sullivan operettas. During 1935 a series of quick failures played at this theatre. The only show to stay longer than a few weeks was the *Earl Carroll Sketch Book*, described as a "Hysterical Historical Revue," or American history as seen through the eyes of a chorus girl. This amusing show, starring Ken Murray and the usual near-nude Carroll girls, moved here from the Winter Garden and stayed for almost three months.

Beginning in 1936 the Majestic booked more and more successful musicals that had opened in other theatres and would end their Broadway runs here, usually at reduced prices. In 1937 there was an unsuccessful attempt to magazine photographed. But despite a rave review in the *New York Times*, it ran for only 127 performances. Producer Dwight Deere Wiman blamed the comparatively short run on the fact that the highly publicized World's Fair opened in Flushing Meadows that spring and presumably siphoned away audiences. Perhaps the most remarkable aspect of *Stars in Your Eyes* was its chorus line, which numbered such future ballet and Broadway luminaries as Alicia Alonso, Jerome Robbins, Nora Kaye, and Maria Karnilova.

The next musical at the Majestic, *Yokel Boy*, was not as good as *Stars in Your Eyes* but ran longer. It also dealt with Hollywood studios—and not very kindly. Buddy Ebsen, Judy Canova, Lois January, and Phil Silvers led the cast, and one hit tune emerged: "Comes Love."

Clare Boothe's hit anti-Nazi play *Margin for Error* moved here from the Plymouth in 1940; and Olsen and Johnson's *Hellzapoppin'* transferred from the Winter Garden in 1941. In January 1942 producer Cheryl Crawford presented the first Broadway revival of the Gershwins' *Porgy and Bess*, and this production proved to be an artistic and a commercial success. Crawford removed the operatic recitatives and made the work more of a Broadway musical than an opera, and the public flocked to it for thirty-five weeks. Many members of the original cast (Todd Duncan, Anne Brown, Warren Coleman, Ruby Elzy, and J. Rosamond Johnson) were in this revival, and they brought luster to a work that had failed in its premiere engagement in 1935.

Paul Green and Richard Wright's powerful drama *Native Son*, directed by Orson Welles, played a return engagement at the Majestic in 1942, followed by the frothy hit comedy *Junior Miss*, which moved here from the Lyceum Theatre in 1943.

One of the Majestic's biggest hits to this time opened on August 4, 1943: a new version

On January 9, 2006 *The Phantom of the Opera* (1988) surpassed *Cats* to become the longest-running show in Broadway history.

Top: The cast gathers on the Majestic stage to celebrate the milestone.

Bottom: That same night, Abby Simon, costumed as Victoria, one of the Jellicle Cats from *Cats*, performed a symbolic passing of the torch to Howard McGillin, as The Phantom. (Photos by Joan Marcus)

revive two old thrillers, *The Bat* and *The Cat and the Canary*. A new operetta, *Three Waltzes*, employing the music of Johann Strauss Sr. and Jr., was a moderate success that year. It starred Kitty Carlisle, Glenn Anders, and Michael Bartlett and ran for 122 performances.

At the end of 1938 Gertrude Lawrence moved into this theatre from the Plymouth with her hit *Susan and God*, and this was followed in February 1939 by the lively musical *Stars in Your Eyes*, with such personalities as Ethel Merman, Jimmy Durante, Richard Carlson, Mildred Natwick, and the Russian ballerina Tamara Toumanova. With a bright score by Arthur Schwartz and Dorothy Fields, a witty book about a lusty Hollywood star (Merman) trying to seduce her innocent leading man (Carlson), and direction by Joshua Logan, the show had a glittering opening night, which *Life* of that favorite Franz Lehár/Victor Leon/Leo Stein operetta *The Merry Widow*. The cast included Marta Eggerth and her husband, Jan Kiepura, along with David Wayne, Gene Barry, Melville Cooper, and Ruth Matteson. It waltzed for 321 performances.

Cole Porter's *Mexican Hayride*, with Bobby Clark and June Havoc, moved here from the Winter Garden in 1945. But it soon made way for one of the treasures of the American Musical Theatre: Rodgers and Hammerstein's lilting *Carousel*. A musical adaptation of Molnar's play *Liliom*, the work opened to rapturous reviews in April 1945. Critic John Chapman in the *Daily News* stated that it was one of the finest musical plays he had ever seen, and Richard Rodgers later confessed that of all the musicals he had written, this was his favorite. John Raitt was memorable singing his "Soliloquy," and he and Jan Clayton shared the lovely ballad "If I Loved You." The musical ran 890 performances, and the Majestic established itself (with the St. James across the street) as one of the preferred theatres for Rodgers and Hammerstein musicals.

The hit soldier revue *Call Me Mister* moved to this theatre in 1947 from the National, followed by another Rodgers and Hammerstein musical, *Allegro*, a rather pretentious chronicle of a man named Joseph Taylor Jr., which critic Woollcott Gibbs described in *The New Yorker* as "a shocking disappointment." It ran for 315 performances.

On April 7, 1949, Rodgers and Hammerstein's *South Pacific* opened here, starring Mary Martin and Ezio Pinza, and immediately became the hottest ticket in town. Based on James A. Michener's Pulitzer-winning book *Tales of the South Pacific*, this parable of conflicting love and racial prejudice between American military and Polynesian locals during World War II also won the Pulitzer Prize for drama in 1950, plus the Tony Award, the New York Drama Critics Circle Award, and the Donaldson Award for best musical of the season. With direction by Joshua Logan (who coauthored the book with Oscar Hammerstein II) and with some of Richard Rodgers's most inspired melodies, the musical ran for 1,925 performances and won Tony Awards for Martin; Pinza; supporting performers Juanita Hall and Myron McCormick; director Logan; and Rodgers, Hammerstein, and Logan for their music, lyrics, and book.

The remainder of the 1950s at this theatre saw the production of some musicals of varying merit that enjoyed respectable runs. Rodgers and Hammerstein's backstage musical *Me and Juliet* was second-rate R&H but ran for 358 performances in 1953—54; *By the Beautiful Sea*, a musical by Arthur Schwartz and Herbert and Dorothy Fields, starring Shirley Booth, ran a moderate 268 performances in 1954.

Fanny (1954), a musical adaptation of Marcel Pagnol's trilogy (*Marius*, *César*, and *Fanny*) by S. N. Behrman, Joshua Logan, and Harold Rome, ran for 888 performances. It starred Walter Slezak (who won a Tony Award for his performance) and Ezio Pinza.

The Majestic next hosted another musical theatre landmark, Meredith Willson's phenomenal *The Music Man* (1957), which won Tony Awards for Best Musical, Best Actor (Robert Preston), Best Supporting Players (Barbara Cook and David Burns), Best Book (Willson and Franklin Lacey), Best Composer and Lyricist (Willson), Best Musical Director (Herbert Greene), and Best Producers (Kermit Bloomgarden, Herbert Greene, and Frank Productions). This bonanza about a charismatic con man who tries to sell a small Iowa town on the fraudulent idea of a boys' band—but winds up falling in love with the place—ran for 1,375 performances.

Much was expected of *Camelot*, the Majestic's next musical, in late 1960. Written by Alan Jay Lerner and Frederick Loewe, directed by Moss Hart, whose previous show had been the sensational *My Fair Lady*, it costarred Julie Andrews of that show, plus movie star Richard Burton and newcomer Robert Goulet. The critics gave it very mixed reviews, and after a few weeks it appeared that the expensive musical was not long for Broadway. Then a miracle happened. Ed Sullivan presented four musical numbers from the show on his popular TV variety show, and the following morning there was a long line of ticket buyers at the Majestic Theatre. Burton won a Tony Award for his performance as King Arthur, and the musical played for 873 performances.

The remainder of the early 1960s was devoted to a revival of *The School for Scandal* (1963), starring Ralph Richardson and John Gielgud (who also directed it), plus a remarkable series of flops with notable names attached: Judy Holliday in her last Broadway show, the lamentable musical *Hot Spot* (1963); *Tovarich* (1963), the musical version of the play of the same name, which moved here from the Broadway

Theatre with Tony Award—winner Vivien Leigh and Jean Pierre Aumont; and Mary Martin in the flop musical *Jennie* (1963), supposedly based on the early career of actress Laurette Taylor.

The misguided musical *Anyone Can Whistle* (1964) had a beguiling score by Stephen Sondheim, a murky book by Arthur Laurents, and good performances by Angela Lansbury, Lee Remick, and Harry Guardino. It lasted only nine performances but developed something of a cult following. Sammy Davis Jr. starred in Strouse and Adams's unsuccessful musical version of Clifford Odets's *Golden Boy* (1964), followed by a transfer of the hit *Funny Girl* (1966) from the Winter Garden; and then the long-running classic *Fiddler on the Roof*, which moved here from the Imperial in 1967 and stayed until December 1970.

The 1970s saw a flop musical version of *The Teahouse of the August Moon* called *Lovely Ladies, Kind Gentlemen* (1970); the Tony Award-winning musical *1776* (1971), here from the St. James Theatre; and a fairly successful musical version of the popular movie *Some Like It Hot*, retitled *Sugar* (1972), with Robert Morse and Tony Roberts as the musicians who must masquerade as women to hide from gangsters, and Cyril Ritchard as the old tycoon who falls for one of them. *A Little Night Music* (1973), the Tony Award—winning musical, moved here from the Shubert Theatre.

Mack and Mabel (1974), the eagerly anticipated Jerry Herman/Michael Stewart musical about silent film icons Mack Sennett and Mabel Normand, ran only 65 performances despite the presence of Robert Preston and Bernadette Peters in the lead roles. *The Wiz*, an all-black take on *The Wizard of Oz*, won Tony Awards for Best Musical, Best Score (Charlie Smalls), Best Director (Geoffrey Holder), Best Supporting Performers (Ted Ross, Dee Dee Bridgewater), Best Costume Designer (Geoffrey Holder), and Best Choreographer (George Faison) and ran for 1,672 performances.

In the late 1970s Liza Minnelli and Barry Nelson starred in a pallid musical, *The Act* (1977), for which Minnelli won a Tony Award. Henry Fonda and Jane Alexander played Supreme Court Justices in *First Monday in October* (1978). Michael Bennett directed and choreographed *Ballroom* (1978). And Richard Rodgers presented his last show, *I Remember Mama*, a 1979 musical version of a John Van Druten play that Rodgers and Hammerstein had produced in 1944. Liv Ullmann starred.

The next few years saw a series of short runs: a revival of *The Most Happy Fella* (1979); a personal appearance by Bette Midler (1979—80); the final performances of *Grease* (1980), from the Royale Theatre; *Blackstone!* (1980), a magic show; and a revival of the 1947 musical *Brigadoon* with Agnes de Mille recreating her dances that won a Tony Award in 1947.

In 1981 David Merrick's sumptuous production of the musical *42nd Street* (based on the classic movie musical of the same name) moved here from the Winter Garden, where it had won Tony Awards for Best Musical and Best Choreography.

The lavish production stayed at this theatre until 1988, then moved across the street to the St. James to make way for the biggest hit in the distinguished history of the Majestic, *The Phantom of the Opera*, the pinnacle of the pop opera movement of the 1980s. The Broadway production imported three of its London stars, Michael Crawford, Sarah Brightman, and Steve Barton. This phenomenal success by Andrew Lloyd Webber, Charles Hart, and Richard Stilgoe won Tony Awards for Best Musical, Best Direction (Harold Prince), Best Actor in a Musical (Crawford), Best Featured Actress (Judy Kaye), Best Scenic and Costume Designer (Maria Bjornson), and Best Lighting Designer (Andrew Bridges).

The great popularity of this spectacular musical was due in part to its grand score flavored by rock, opera, and Broadway, and partly owing to director Prince's dictum that each scene have some sort of spectacular surprise or special effect. Most memorable was a huge chandelier that came crashing to the stage at the climax of Act I.

Phantom ran and ran, climbing its way up the lists of Broadway long runs until finally, on January 22, 2006, it passed Lloyd Webber's *Cats* to become the longest-running show in Broadway history. It logged its 9,000th performance in September 2009. The production also claims to be the highest-grossing show in history, earning more than $5 billion worldwide as of 2010.

A share of that money was used to update the theatre's sound system and lighting system, and *Phantom*'s orchestrations around the time of the show's twentieth anniversary in 2008. *The Phantom of the Opera* was still turning a weekly profit as it began its third decade at the Majestic.

The Majestic Theatre is owned by the Shubert Organization and is one of the world's finest musical-comedy houses.

Howard McGillin as The Phantom of the Opera. (Photo by Joan Marcus)

MARQUIS THEATRE

THE MARQUIS THEATRE OPENED IN
July 1986 as part of the new Marriott Marquis
Hotel on Broadway between Forty-fifth and
Forty-sixth streets. Just before its unveiling,
John C. Portman Jr., the theatre's architect and
designer, told PLAYBILL: "Our dream was to
create a new theatre for the Broadway of today
that could handle any type of production, any
kind of light and sound equipment, provide
maximum comfort for audience and actors and
still convey a feeling of intimacy."

Three working Broadway theatres—the
Morosco, Hayes, and Bijou—along with the
shells of the old Astor and Gaiety theatres, were
demolished to make way for the hotel, which
occasioned protests and pickets. In return,
Broadwayites got a second walk-through arcade

a block north of Shubert Alley, and this splendid new musical-size state-of-the-art theatre that has quickly become a favorite with actors and audiences. It is also one of the few Broadway theatres that actually fronts on Broadway, and in the center of Times Square, to boot.

Leased by the Nederlander Organization, the Marquis boasts many unique features. It is Broadway's only legitimate theatre built specifically as part of a new hotel; it has an extraordinary ceiling that masks lighting and sound equipment (with no ugly pipes in view of the audience); the orchestra floor is steeply raked, with three separate aisles that offer perfect viewing from all seats; and there's a ramp for wheelchair patrons and a special seating area for the disabled.

The auditorium can be reached by escalator from the Broadway box office, or by escalators or elevators inside the hotel. The hotel's enclosed portico is ideal for arriving by car or cab or for catching a cab after the performance, especially in cold and inclement weather. The theatre is on the hotel's third floor, and two stunning spiral stairways lead to the mezzanine.

The theatre's lobby has a magnificent marble bar with a brass rail. The wall above the entryway has been decorated with window cards from the many show that have played there. As theatergoers entered the new house, the stage was (and is) directly in front of them, offering a splendid view of the dazzling main curtain of many colors designed by artist Bjorn Wimblad. There are 1,000 seats in the orchestra and 600 in the mezzanine, with no seat farther than eighty feet from the stage.

"The theatre's interior is very straightforward, very understated and simplified," Portman said. "There are no chandeliers. The lighting emanates essentially from the walls. The house's color scheme is rose and different shades of burgundy." The architect's designs were executed by the project architect, Bob Jones.

Roger Morgan, the Tony Award—winning lighting designer, was retained as theatre design consultant, and Chris Jaffe of Jaffe Acoustics was the acoustical consultant, assisted by Abe Jacob, one of Broadway's leading sound designers. "The Marquis," said Morgan, "rates very high with other musical theatres in terms of backstage area. The first show there— the British musical *Me and My Girl*—had eight huge sets, which meant we could do anything. There are seventy-five dressing-room stations and three greenrooms for the actors, musicians,

and stagehands. Chris Jaffe and Abe Jacob have been able to integrate the latest technology in acoustical system and we know that audiences will be happy with the sound in this theatre. My firm added the lighting."

A concert appearance by Shirley Bassey and George Kirby inaugurated the theatre on July 8, 1986. But the legitimate opening came on August 10, 1986, with the spectacular debut of *Me and My Girl*. Robert Lindsay recreated his award-winning London performance in the role of Bill Snibson, adding a Tony Award for his effort. Tonys were also bestowed on his costar Mary Ann Plunkett and on Gillian Gregory for her choreography.

Me and My Girl was a new production of a 1937 Noel Gay musical, and it delighted 1986 audiences with its broad humor, music-hall turns, glamorous sets and costumes, and rousing musical score, including the 1930s dance craze "the Lambeth Walk," which spilled out into the audience and raised the roof. The jubilant import ran for 1,420 performances and got the beautiful new theatre off to a flying start.

Next came a spirited Brazilian song-and-dance revue called *Oba Oba '90*. The near-nude dancing by a large cast enlivened the extravaganza.

The scenic resources of the Marquis were tested to their fullest by *Shogun: The Musical*, which opened in November 1990. Based on the best-selling novel by James Clavell, the musical had book and lyrics by John Driver and music by Paul Chihara. But scenic effects were not enough, and the show played here for only two months.

Tyne Daly, who had won a Tony Award the previous season for her starring role in a revival of the celebrated musical *Gypsy*, by Jule Styne, Stephen Sondheim, and Arthur Laurents, brought the show back in 1991 at the Marquis, repeating her acclaimed performance as Rose, with Crista Moore again playing the title role.

Laurents was back at the Marquis later that year as librettist and director of the musical *Nick & Nora*, with a score by Charles Strouse and Richard Maltby Jr. Based on the beloved characters Nick and Nora Charles, created by Dashiell Hammett in the Thin Man series, the musical murder spoof cast Barry Bostwick and Joanna Gleason as the husband/wife sleuths and Faith Prince as a very comical murder victim. Unfortunately, the musical did not recapture the charm of the old MGM Thin Man films and ran for only nine performances.

On April 24, 1992, a new production of *Man*

Top: Neil Simon adapted his film *The Goodbye Girl* as a musical (1993).

Center: *Damn Yankees* (1994) opened with Victor Garber as the Devil, but then brought Jerry Lewis into the role.

Bottom: Julie Andrews returned to Broadway after a thirty-five year absence to star in *Victor/Victoria* (1995).

Top: **Bernadette Peters** won a Tony in the 1999 revival of *Annie Get Your Gun*.

Center: Paul Simon and Derek Walcott collaborated on the interesting failure, *The Capeman* (1998).

Bottom: The PLAYBILL for Andrew Lloyd Webber's musical *The Woman in White* (2005).

of La Mancha opened here, starring Raul Julia as Cervantes/Don Quixote and pop singer Sheena Easton as Aldonza/Dulcinea. The revival ran for three months.

The next musical here was *The Goodbye Girl*, based on Neil Simon's film of the same name. With a book by Simon and a score by Marvin Hamlisch and David Zippel, the show starred Bernadette Peters and TV comic Martin Short, with Carol Woods, Scott Wise, and Cynthia Onrubia. The critics were unenthusiastic about most aspects of the show, except for Short's hilarious antics, and the musical managed a six-month run.

A splendid revival of the 1955 musical *Damn Yankees*, by George Abbott and Douglas Wallop, with a score by Richard Adler and Jerry Ross, opened here on March 3, 1994. One of the delights of the opening night was that Abbott (106 years old) attended. The new production, starring Bebe Neuwirth and Victor Garber, with Jarrod Emick, Dennis Kelly, Dick Latessa, Vicki Lewis, Linda Stephens, and Scott Wise, pleased most of the critics, especially the crusty John Simon, who gave it a surprisingly glowing review. Emick won a Tony for his performance. The Faustian baseball musical also garnered the following Tony Award nominations: Best Musical Revival, Leading Musical Actor (Garber), and Best Choreographer (Rob Marshall).

On March 12, 1995, comedian Jerry Lewis made his Broadway debut when he succeeded Garber as Applegate. His excellent tomfoolery and good reviews helped to prolong the show's run to 533 performances.

On October 25, 1995, the red carpet was rolled out at the Marquis Theatre for the return of Julie Andrews to Broadway in a stage adaptation of her hit 1982 film *Victor/Victoria*. Before the curtain rose, Mayor Rudolph Giuliani appeared onstage to make a welcoming speech for the star, who was making her first Broadway appearance since *Camelot* in 1960.

Andrews's husband, Blake Edwards, had written and directed the film, and he repeated these services for the stage version. Henry Mancini's songs from the movie were retained, with new tunes added by Frank Wildhorn. The critics were happy to have Andrews back but compared the show unfavorably with the film, and the lyrics by Leslie Bricusse were declared inept. The supporting cast included Tony Roberts, Rachel York, Michael Nouri, and Gregory Jbara.

The show earned a niche in Broadway history for the controversy that erupted when the Tony Awards failed to nominate anything about the production for an award, with the notable exception of Andrews's performance. She responded with a vehement curtain speech from the Marquis stage following a May 1996 matinee of the show, denouncing the snub, renouncing her nomination, and declaring solidarity with the rest of her cast and company, whom she said had been "egregiously overlooked." The phrase became a favorite in ensuing years whenever the Tonys ignored a favorite actor or show. Andrews also boycotted the Tony Awards ceremony—where the award for Best Actress in a Musical went to Donna Murphy of *The King and I*.

During Andrews's vacation and frequent illnesses, her replacements included Ann Runolfsson and Liza Minnelli. Andrews was eventually succeeded in the role by Raquel Welch. The stormy run ended after 734 performances.

The next musical to arrive was controversial in a very different way. Pop composer Paul Simon made his Broadway debut with *The Capeman*, the story of Salvador Agron, the Puerto Rican—born real-life killer who made headlines for wearing a cape during his murder of two young men in 1950s New York. Simon said the musical was about the need for "forgiveness," but families and friends of his victims resented the depiction of Agron as a product of poverty and environment. They picketed the theatre on opening night, January 29, 1998. Much had been expected of this musical, since it had music by Grammy-winner Simon and book and lyrics co-written by Nobel laureate Derek Walcott. Three actors portrayed the murderer at different stages of his life, including Latin pop stars Marc Anthony and Ruben Blades. But critics were not impressed, and the musical played for only sixty-eight performances. *The Capeman* received no Tony Awards but was nominated for the following: Best Score, Best Orchestrations, and Best Scenic Designer. Simon was bitter about the failure of his first Broadway musical and vowed someday to rewrite the show and bring it back.

A concert performance by seventy-four-year-old French singer Charles Aznavour was next at this theatre and had a pleasant engagement of twenty-four performances.

Cathy Rigby brought her revival of *Peter Pan*, in which she played the flying sprite, from November 1998 to January 1999. She reopened it at the Gershwin Theatre in April and it ran until August, totaling 214 performances. This was the popular 1954 musical version of *Peter Pan* with a score by Jule Styne, Comden and Green, "Moose" Charlap, and Carolyn Leigh, and choreography by Jerome Robbins.

Another musical classic had even greater success at the Marquis starting March 4, 1999, with the revival of Irving Berlin's beloved *Annie Get Your Gun*, starring Bernadette Peters as sharpshooter Annie Oakley. The original book by Herbert and Dorothy Fields was revised by Peter Stone to remove material deemed offensive, including the song "I'm An Indian, Too." Ethel Merman, who immortalized the role in the 1946 original production and in the 1966 revival, proved a tough act to follow. Peters's singing was excellent, as usual, but some critics felt that she wasn't "country" enough for the part and that her accent varied. Still, she won a Tony Award as Best Leading Actress in a Musical for her performance. Also nominated was her costar Tom Wopat, who played rival marksman (and love interest) Frank Butler. The show won the Tony as Best Musical Revival. Some critics were disappointed with the directorial concept of staging it as a play-within-a-play being presented by Buffalo Bill's Wild West Show, and felt that the production it lacked visual splendor. The Berlin score, however, remained his best. The musical had a 1,045-performance run, with Peters succeeded by Susan Lucci, Cheryl Ladd, and country singer Reba McEntire, the latter of whom received the best reviews of all as Annie Oakley.

Patrick Stewart drew crowds for his week-long solo performance of Charles Dickens's *A Christmas Carol* at holiday time 2001.

Sutton Foster, who had spent more than a decade in supporting, replacement, and understudy roles, got her crack at a starring part when she was chosen to take over the title character in a new musical adaptation of the 1960s film comedy *Thoroughly Modern Millie*. Her indefatigable spunk helped put the show over top, ably supported by Marc Kudisch and Harriet Harris in the story of a 1920s flapper with her eye on a star. Around the familiar title song, Jeanine Tesori and Dick Scanlan built a full Broadway score to Richard Morris's book. The production opened April 18, 2002, and ran 903 performances, winning six Tony Awards including Best Actress (Foster), Best Featured Actress (Harris), and Best Musical.

A wan December 2004 revival of Jerry Herman's *La Cage aux Folles* closed just weeks after winning the 2005 Tony Award for Best Revival. Directed by Jerry Zaks and choreographed by Jerry Mitchell, the production is remembered as much for its backstage drama between co—leading man Daniel Davis and the cast as for the action onstage.

Composer Andrew Lloyd Webber returned

Top: The "notorious and dangerous" Cagelles from the 2004 revival of *La Cage aux Folles*. (Photo by Carol Rosegg)

Bottom: Danny Burstein works his charm on Tony-winner Beth Leavel in the title role of The Drowsy Chaperone (2006) with the song "I Am Aldolpho." (Photo by Joan Marcus)

to Broadway November 17, 2005, with *The Woman in White*, "freely adapted from the classic novel by Wilkie Collins," about a young woman who disappears under mysterious circumstances. Charlotte Jones wrote the book and David Zippel the lyrics. Maria Friedman and Jill Paice played the central roles, but Michael Ball stopped the show as the villainous Count Fosco in a huge fat suit, oiling his way through the comedy waltz "You Can Get Away with Anything" as his pet white rat scurried around his shoulders. One of the most remarkable attributes of this briefly seen musical (109 performances, one of Lloyd Webber's shortest runs) was William Dudley's set design—curved white panels on which he projected a variety of three-dimensional landscapes that had the ability to shift perspective as the characters did, making the actors look like characters in a giant video game.

Fans of bubbly 1920s musical comedies got a real treat with the May 2006 arrival of *The Drowsy Chaperone*, billed as "a musical within a comedy" and narrated by show-tune-lover Man in Chair (played by librettist Bob Martin), whose favorite old show comes to life around him as he plays the cast album and narrates the story to the audience. Sutton Foster returned to the Marquis stage in triumph as about-to-retire diva Janet Van De Graaff, performing one of the great show-stoppers of recent years, "Show Off," in which she demonstrated all the stunts she wouldn't be doing anymore, including cartwheels, splits, high notes, quick change, ventriloquism, playing the jug, and even spinning plates. Tonys also were won for Best Book (Martin and Don McKellar), Score (Lisa Lambert and Greg Morrison), Sets (David Gallo), and Costumes (Gregg Barnes). Over the course of the show's 674 performances, Mara Davi replaced Foster.

Around the time of *Drowsy Chaperone*'s opening, the familiar red-and-white TKTS discount ticket booth located diagonally across Times Square from the Marquis closed so that a more permanent structure could be built. During the twenty-eight-month project, TKTS operated out of a street-level space in the same building as the Marquis. Producers put up a blockwide mural of scenes from *Drowsy Chaperone* opposite the queue to entice ticket buyers to consider choosing the show upstairs. The *Drowsy Chaperone* mural replaced a previous mural of photos from classic Broadway shows.

The multiyear success of *Hairspray* helped inspire an April 2008 musical adaptation of another John Waters film, *Cry-Baby*, with a libretto by the *Hairspray* team of Thomas Meehan and Mark O'Donnell, and a score by Adam Schlesinger and David Javerbaum. Though similarly set in the world of Baltimore teens, *Cry-Baby* did not repeat *Hairspray*'s success, running just two months.

The 1954 Danny Kaye/Bing Crosby film *White Christmas* told the story of a pair of army buddies—turned-entertainers who help their old sarge keep his hotel afloat with a Christmas show. Librettists Paul Blake and David Ives raided composer Irving Berlin's songbook to beef up the film's score for an acceptable holiday-time stage musical, which opened at the Marquis November 23, 2008. A cast led by Stephen Bogardus, Jeffry Denman, Kerry O'Malley, and Meredith Patterson loaned some melody and sparkle to a city weighed down with economic worries. The show completed a limited run through January 2009 and returned the following November, with a different cast, to spread a little more cheer.

In the meantime, January 2009 saw an interim limited-run booking of the acrobatic Chinese martial arts show *Soul of Shaolin*, which marked the Communist Chinese government's debut as a Broadway producer.

It was followed April 30, 2009, by an all-American debut: country star Dolly Parton's bow as a Broadway composer. As her maiden project, she and librettist Patricia Resnick adapted their hit film *9 to 5*, about three put-upon working women who get revenge on their male chauvinist pig of a boss. Critics said the story seemed dated and that Parton had merely inserted songs into the story rather than rebuild the tale as a creature of the stage. In any case, *9 to 5* continued for 148 performances before making way for the return of *White Christmas*.

Director-choreographer Twyla Tharp saluted the music of crooner Frank Sinatra with the dance show *Come Fly Away*, which opened March 25, 2010. A series of couples flirted, squabbled, uncoupled, and recoupled as a live orchestra played under Ol' Blue Eyes's original vocal tracks.

Though some theatergoers have a little trouble wending their way from the street-level box office to the third-floor auditorium, the Marquis Theatre remains one of Broadway's most sought-after legitimate houses for its size, modern amenities, and central location. The theatre has achieved its goal of providing maximum comfort for audiences and actors while conveying a feeling of intimacy.

THE MINSKOFF
THEATRE

THE MINSKOFF THEATRE, WHICH occupies several floors of One Astor Plaza, the fifty-five-story office tower on the site of Broadway's old Astor Hotel, derives its name from Sam Minskoff and Sons, builders and owners of the high-rise. The modern theatre, with a very large 1,621-seat capacity, was designed by the architectural firm of Kahn and Jacobs and offers a spectacular view of the Great White Way from the glass front of the building on all levels of the theatre.

The theatre features a pedestrian arcade that runs from Forty-fourth to Forty-fifth streets, parallel to Shubert Alley. Inside the spacious lobby, dual escalators take playgoers to the Grand Foyer of the house. Here there are coat-check concessions and bars. Additional

FIRST

MIN

Top left: Debbie Reynolds parades her "Alice Blue Gown" for the ensemble in a revival of the 1919 hit *Irene* (1973), the inaugural production at the Minskoff. Note her daughter, future *Star Wars* star Carrie Fisher, to her left, on floor,

Top right: Opening night PLAYBILL from the short-lived Polish musical, *Metro* (1992).

Bottom left: Pearl Bailey in a revival of *Hello, Dolly!* (1975).

Bottom right: The ensemble from Broadway production of Andrew Lloyd Webber's *Sunset Boulevard* (1994).

we've created one of the most exciting, three-dimensional processional routes for the theatre-goers—a series of forms, changes in ceiling heights, and spatial explosions. The whole processional, from the moment you enter and rise thirty-five feet to the theatre level, is a theatrical event in itself. Our forms are purely architectural, beautifully proportioned in relation to the processional drama you're going through."

Jacobs stated that his firm had kept everything simple in the theatre's decor, without hiring what he called "exotic interior desecraters." The theatre was done primarily in white and gold, with roomy charcoal-gray seats that offer an excellent view. The orchestra floor rakes steeply up from the stage. Hundreds of small clear bulbs sparkle in the lobbies, and crystal-basket lights glow in the auditorium. The ceiling is broken into two sections with a narrow grid between them for the stage lights. The proscenium has removable mesh panels on both sides, and the mezzanine, with 590 seats, has narrow side projections

escalators rise to the orchestra level and above.

At the time of the theatre's opening in 1973, Robert A. Jacobs, partner-in-charge of Kahn and Jacobs, told PLAYBILL: "A theatre that is thirty-five feet in the air is quite an innovation. According to the old building code in Manhattan, a theatre's orchestra floor had to be within three feet of the sidewalk. We think

Top: *The Scarlet Pimpernel* (1997).

Center: Special PLAY-BILL given out at the 1995 Tony Awards ceremony, which was held at the Minskoff.

Bottom: The PLAYBILL for the 2004 revival of *Fiddler on the Roof*.

instead of box seats. The stage has an innovation: all the flies are on the upstage wall instead of on the side wall. Part of the stage is trapped and can be extended out over the orchestra pit. The dressing rooms are comparatively sumptuous, and the restrooms are large, cheerful, and comfortable.

The Minskoff Theatre opened on March 13, 1973, with a lavish revival of the 1919 musical *Irene*. Debbie Reynolds played the title role and sang the show's classic, "Alice Blue Gown." The cast also included Patsy Kelly, Monte Markham, Janie Sell, Ruth Warrick, Carmen Alvarez, and George S. Irving, who won a Tony Award for his performance. The musical ran until the fall of 1974. It was succeeded by two concert shows: *Charles Aznavour on Broadway* and *Tony Bennett and Lena Horne Sing*.

The 1975 offerings at the Minskoff were extremely varied. The year began on a sober note with Henry Fonda in his one-man show *Clarence Darrow*. The raucous Bette Midler was next in her salty *Clams on the Half Shell Revue*. In the fall of that year, Pearl Bailey and Billy Daniels brought their version of *Hello, Dolly!* to the theatre. The 1976 attractions included a short-lived rock version of *Hamlet* called *Rockabye Hamlet*, with Meat Loaf playing a priest, and an Ophelia who commits suicide by wrapping her microphone cord around her neck. This was followed by the Dutch National Ballet and the Chinese Acrobats of Taiwan.

The 1977 season brought the Merce Cunningham Dance Company, followed by the long-running musical *Pippin*, which moved here from the Imperial. The year ended with engagements of Cleo Laine and *Star Wars Concert Live*.

Rudolf Nureyev made a dance appearance at the Minskoff in 1978 with the Murray Lewis Dance Company. Next came a musical version of the play *Look Homeward, Angel*, called simply *Angel*. Its cast included Fred Gwynne, Frances Sternhagen, Don Scardino, Leslie Ann Ray, Patti Allison, and Joel Higgins, but the Thomas Wolfe classic did not succeed as a musical and it closed after five performances. Another unsuccessful musical opened in 1978: *King of Hearts*, adapted from the cult film of the same name, about a group of sweet-natured mental patients who escape into a small town during World War I. The cast included Don Scardino, Millicent Martin, Pamela Blair, Gary Morgan, Timothy Scott, and Michael McCarty. It expired after forty-eight performances.

In late 1978 an elaborate spectacle, *Ice Dancing*, opened here. It was followed by *Béjart—Ballet of the Twentieth Century*. A musical called *Got Tu Go Disco* tried to capitalize on the disco dance craze but was a quick failure in 1979. Appearances by Shirley Bassey and the *Chinese Acrobats & Magicians of Taiwan* followed.

A revival of *West Side Story* in 1980 was moderately successful, running for 341 performances. A revival of Cole Porter's *Can-Can*, however, proved a disaster in 1981, despite the dancing of Zizi Jeanmaire and the choreography of Roland Petit. It folded after 5 showings.

In the fall of 1981 the successful revival of *The Pirates of Penzance* moved here from the Uris Theatre and stayed for more than a year.

In the spring of 1983 *Dance a Little Closer*, an ill-advised musicalization of Robert E. Sherwood's Pulitzer-winning play *Idiot's Delight*, closed on its opening night, despite the fact that the book and lyrics were by Alan Jay Lerner and the music by Charles Strouse. The title song was especially lilting, but that didn't stop wags from dubbing the production *Close a Little Faster*. Starring Len Cariou and Liz Robertson, and featuring George Rose, the updated musical sadly was Lerner's last show.

Next came *Marilyn: An American Fable*, another fiasco. It purported to be a musical biography of the late sex goddess Marilyn Monroe, but the critics were not kindly disposed toward the enterprise. It vanished after two weeks.

The Tap Dance Kid moved here from the Broadhurst on March 27, 1984, and stayed until August 11, 1985, winning Tony Awards for Best Featured Actor in a Musical (Hinton Battle) and Best Choreography (Danny Daniels). Late in its run, the title role was assumed by an amazing child dancer named Savion Glover, who went on to help redefine tap a decade later in *Bring in 'da Noise, Bring in 'da Funk*.

In early 1986, personal appearances were made here by Patti LaBelle, TNT, and Peter, Paul and Mary. In April of that year a new production of Cy Coleman's *Sweet Charity* opened with Debbie Allen, Bebe Neuwirth, and Michael Rupert. The revival won the following Tony Awards: Best Revival, Best Featured Actor in a Musical (Rupert), Best Featured Actress (Neuwirth), and Best Costumes (Patricia Zipprodt). It ran for 368 performances.

On February 9, 1988, a new production of *Cabaret* moved here from the Imperial Theatre with Joel Grey recreating his Tony Award—winning role as the Emcee, and with Alyson Reed, Gregg Edelman, Regina Resnik, and Werner Klemperer in other leading roles. It had a run of 262 performances. The next musical at this theatre was an elaborate patriotic spectacle called *Teddy & Alice*, set to tunes by John Philip Sousa, with book by Jerome Alden and lyrics by Hal Hackaday. Original songs were provided by Richard Kapp. Len Cariou played Teddy Roosevelt, Nancy Hume was Alice Roosevelt, and Ron Raines was Nick Longworth. It had a short run of 77 performances.

More successful was the next Minskoff musical, *Black and Blue*, a lavish revue using standard blues and hit songs of the past. It won Tony Awards for Ruth Brown (Best Actress in a Musical), Claudio Segovia and Hector Orezzoli (Best Costume Design), and the four choreographers. It played here until January 20, 1991, achieving 829 performances. In November 1991 Cathy Rigby played a return engagement in the title role of *Peter Pan*, which she had played at the Lunt-Fontanne Theatre the previous season.

A spectacular multimedia production from Poland, *Metro*, did not repeat its success on Broadway. The youthful cast included a former miner and other blue-collar workers who had been scouted by the director at open auditions around Poland. A year later they found themselves opening on Broadway in a blaze of laser effects. But Frank Rich of the *New York Times* opened his review, "What's the Polish word for fiasco?" And they stayed only thirteen performances.

On November 10, 1993, a sumptuous new production of the Andrew Lloyd Webber/Tim Rice musical *Joseph and the Amazing Technicolor Dreamcoat* opened and had a successful run, starring Michael Damian in the title role.

Another Lloyd Webber musical arrived next: the highly anticipated London production of *Sunset Boulevard*. Controversy surrounded the production. Patti LuPone starred in it in London and was supposed to repeat her performance on Broadway. Unfortunately, a *New York Times* critic was unenthusiastic about her London performance, and Glenn Close was hired to replace her. (Since LuPone had a contract to star in it on Broadway, she was paid a handsome sum for her dismissal.) The musical, based on the famous 1950 Billy Wilder film, was a dark look at Hollywood that infuriated the movie colony when the movie was released. It depicted a has-been actress (Norma Desmond) vainly trying to

make a movie comeback via a penniless screenwriter who becomes her gigolo.

The settings by John Napier were staggering. The palatial Hollywood villa Norma occupied was a gigantic set that resembled the lobby of the old Roxy theatre in Manhattan. At one point the entire set was elevated and another set rose into place below it. Projections were used to simulate a car chase. The physical production received better reviews than the show, which had music by Lloyd Webber, book and lyrics by Don Black and Christopher Hampton, and direction by Trevor Nunn. Also in the cast were Alan Campbell, George Hearn, and Alice Ripley.

Two of Lloyd Webber's songs enjoyed popularity: "With One Look" and "As If We Never Said Goodbye," both of which were recorded by Barbra Streisand. The musical won the following Tony Awards: Best Musical, Leading Actress/Musical (Close), Best Supporting Actor (Hearn), Best Musical Book (Black and Hampton), Best Score (Lloyd Webber, Black, Hampton), Scenic Design (Napier), and Lighting Design (Andrew Bridge), though book and score were won by default, as there were no other eligible nominees in those categories in a very lean Broadway season. *Sunset Boulevard* ran for 977 performances—the house record at the time. During its long run Close was succeeded by Betty Buckley, who was followed by British musical comedy star Elaine Paige, making her Broadway debut.

The next musical to open here had a complex history. *The Scarlet Pimpernel*, a spectacular production with music by Frank Wildhorn and book and lyrics by Nan Knighton, opened on November 9, 1997. Based on Baroness Orczy's popular novel, which Leslie Howard had glorified in a 1935 film, the musical followed the adventures of a British nobleman who poses as a fop in order to rescue French aristocrats from the guillotine. Unfortunately, the musical received mostly negative reviews, with most critics branding it boring. The charismatic Douglas Sills was praised as the Scarlet Pimpernel, and he received a Tony Award nomination as Leading Actor in a Musical. Other Tony nominations: Best Musical and Best Musical Book (Knighton). The producers decided to make changes, and the musical went on hiatus for several months of rewriting and restaging that reduced the scope of the production. When it reopened at the Minskoff Theatre, critics felt the show had been improved—but not enough, and it closed after 643 performances. Surprisingly, yet a

Alfred Molina embraces his five daughters in the 2004 revival of *Fiddler on the Roof*. Note Laura Michelle Kelly, just visible second from right, who would later create the title role of *Mary Poppins* for the London stage adaptation. (Photo by Carol Rosegg)

further revised version, nicknamed *"The Scarlet Pimpernel* Version 3.0," opened at the Neil Simon Theatre on September 10, 1999, and ran another 129 performances, for a total of 772 in all.

In fall of 1999 the producer of the 1977 disco film *Saturday Night Fever* brought over the hit London stage adaptation, with extra songs by the Bee Gees and a book by *The Scarlet Pimpernel's* Nan Knighton. It ran for 500 performances, with James Carpinello and Paige Price in the leads.

Perhaps inspired by the Tony-winning success that fellow country music composer Roger Miller had with his Huckleberry Finn musical *Big River*, Don Schlitz adapted another Mark Twain classic as the musical *The Adventures of Tom Sawyer*, which did not repeat the previous show's success. It ran just twenty-one performance, starting April 16, 2001.

The Minskoff next housed the first of three unsuccessful vampire-related Broadway musicals of the 2000s, *Dance of the Vampires*, based on the Roman Polanski film *The Fearless Vampire Killers*. A marked success in its Vienna debut, the musical bowed at the Minskoff December 9, 2002, but ran just fifty-six performances. It had a score by Jim Steinman, and a book by David Ives, based on the Austrian original by Michael Kunze.

Director David Leveaux took some critical heat for casting the gentile Alfred Molina in the leading role of Tevye in the February 26, 2004, revival of traditional favorite *Fiddler on the Roof*. But the production, which also featured Nancy Opel as Yente, Randy Graff as Golde, and John Cariani as Motel, proved popular with ticket buyers and gratefully got to sing "L'Chaim" 781 times.

Around this time, superstitious theatre folk began to note that the Minskoff had rarely housed a show that turned a profit. Even such long runs as *Irene* and *Sunset Boulevard* had closed in the red. All that changed on June 13, 2006, when Disney Theatricals moved its blockbuster *The Lion King* to the Minskoff from its original home at the New Amsterdam Theatre to make way for the long-awaited stage adaptation of *Mary Poppins*. Comfortably converted to a little corner of Africa, the Minskoff has happily hosted the family favorite for more than a thousand extra performances so far, with no end in sight.

The Minskoff Theatre is under the direction of the Nederlander Organization. It is an ideal house for large-scale musicals, dance companies, and personal-appearance shows.

THE MUSIC BOX

THEATRE

THIS LOVELY PLAYHOUSE ON WEST
Forty-fifth Street, which Moss Hart described
as everyone's dream of a theatre, celebrated its
seventy-fifth birthday on September 22, 1996.
Never once in its many decades was its elegant
limestone facade marred by a movie or burlesque marquee.

The Music Box was built by the late producer Sam H. Harris and composer Irving
Berlin to house a series of lavish revues to be
composed by Berlin. The composer's estate co-
owned the theatre with the Shubert
Organization until 2007, when the Shuberts
assumed full ownership.

On September 22, 1921, the resplendent
theatre, designed by C. Howard Crane, opened
with the first *Music Box Revue*, starring

Berlin, Sam Bernard, Florence Moore, Joseph Santley, and—in the chorus—young Miriam Hopkins. The critics raved about the production and the new theatre, but it was the show's comic, Sam Bernard, who best described the opulent new house: "It stinks from class."

Four editions of the *Music Box Revue*, starring such luminaries as Fanny Brice, Grace Moore, Bobby Clark, Robert Benchley, and Charlotte Greenwood, brought fame to Berlin and the Music Box. In 1925 the theatre departed from its revues-only policy to present a smash hit comedy called *Cradle Snatchers*, starring Mary Boland, Humphrey Bogart, Edna May Oliver, and Raymond Guion (later Gene Raymond of the movies).

Other big Music Box hits in the 1920s include *Chicago* (1926), later made into a successful musical; *The Spider* (1927), a clever thriller that moved here from the 46th Street Theatre; Philip Barry's charming comedy *Paris Bound* (1927); Cole Porter's *Paris* (1928), which introduced the song "Let's Do It (Let's Fall in Love)"; and the last Music Box show of the 1920s, the historic intimate revue *The Little Show* (1929), starring Clifton Webb, Fred Allen, and Libby Holman.

The Music Box faced the Depression with élan. *Topaze*, a French comedy starring Frank Morgan, was a hit in early 1930, followed by the famed satire *Once in a Lifetime*, the first collaboration of George S. Kaufman and Moss Hart. In 1931 Beatrice Lillie graced the Music Box in *The Third Little Show*, in which she introduced Noël Coward's celebrated song "Mad Dogs and Englishmen" to American audiences.

On December 26, 1931, *Of Thee I Sing* marched into the Music Box and became the first musical comedy to win a Pulitzer Prize. The musical had a biting book by George S. Kaufman and Morrie Ryskind, memorable music by George Gershwin, and stinging lyrics by his brother Ira. William Gaxton played President John P. Wintergreen, Victor Moore was mousy

vice president Alexander Throttlebottom, and George Murphy played a featured role. At 441 performances, the show became the longest-running book musical of the 1930s.

Kaufman (with Edna Ferber) brought another hit to the Music Box in 1932. *Dinner at Eight* was a fascinating comedy about a socialite's problems in arranging a dinner for British royalty, who cancel their appearance at the last moment. The play examined the lives of all those invited to the dinner. During its run, the rising star Margaret Sullavan joined the cast as a replacement. The comedy ran for 232 performances and was later made into a hit MGM film with an all-star cast.

The Music Box really struck it rich with its next tenant. Irving Berlin and Moss Hart teamed to create a topical revue that would use newspaper headlines to satirize celebrities of that era. The show was called *As Thousands Cheer*, and it starred Marilyn Miller, Clifton Webb, Helen Broderick, and Ethel Waters, who stopped the show at every performance with

Top left: Souvenir book for the second *Music Box Revue* (1922).

Top center: Lois Moran and William Gaxton sing the Gershwins's title song on election night in the Pulitzer Prize-winning musical, *Of Thee I Sing* (1931).

Top right: Irene Bordoni glitters in Cole Porter's 1928 musical, *Paris*.

Bottom: Marilyn Miller, Clifton Webb, and Helen Broderick in the "Easter Parade" finale of the famed revue, *As Thousands Cheer* (1933).

Top left: Herald for Mike Todd's rowdy burlesque revue, *Star and Garter* (1942).

Top center: Beatrice Lillie sings "I Went to a Marvelous Party" in Noël Coward's revue *Set to Music* (1939).

Top right: Paul Rogers and Vivien Merchant (in foreground) under family scrutiny in Harold Pinter's sinister puzzle, *The Homecoming* (1967).

Bottom left: Ralph Meeker and Janice Rule smolder in William Inge's *Picnic* (1953).

Bottom right: Keith Baxter (in disguise) and Anthony Quayle play Anthony Shaffer's complex games in *Sleuth* (1970).

Above: A radiant Margaret Sullavan returns from Hollywood stardom to appear in the theatrical comedy *Stage Door* (1936).

"Heat Wave," "Harlem on My Mind," and "Supper Time." The revue ran for 400 performances at the Music Box and was one of the biggest hits of Depression-era Broadway.

Kaufman and Hart once again joined forces to write the next Music Box show: *Merrily We Roll Along* (1934). This unusual comedy started in the present and went backward in time. It served as the basis for a 1981 musical of the same title by Stephen Sondheim and George Furth.

Five shows played the Music Box in 1935: Tallulah Bankhead in a revival of *Rain*; a hit melodrama about pilots, *Ceiling Zero*, starring Osgood Perkins (Anthony's illustrious father); a prophetic drama, *If This Be Treason*, in which the United States and Japan almost engage in war; a successful adaptation of Jane Austen's *Pride and Prejudice*; and George S. Kaufman

and Katherine Dayton's political comedy *First Lady*, starring the noted actress Jane Cowl playing a role said to be inspired by Alice Longworth Roosevelt.

Margaret Sullavan, now a big Hollywood star, returned to the Music Box in 1936 in *Stage Door*, by Kaufman and Ferber. Set in the Foot-Lights Club (modeled on the actual Rehearsal Club in Manhattan), the play presented a group of aspiring actresses who live in a popular boardinghouse for young theatricals. One of the characters—a radical playwright named Keith Burgess—was said to be based on the Group Theatre's Clifford Odets.

Young Madam Conti (1937), starring Constance Cummings, was one of the theatre's lesser tenants, but this melodrama was followed by John Steinbeck's *Of Mice and Men* in 1937, starring Wallace Ford and Broderick

Top left: Monty Woolley needles Edith Atwater, Carol Goodner, and Theodore Newton in the classic comedy of insults, *The Man Who Came to Dinner* (1939).

Top right: Mady Christians (far left) and a young Marlon Brando with members of the cast of *I Remember Mama* (1944).

Bottom: Geraldine Page and Amanda Plummer anguish over a baby's murder in the tense drama, *Agnes of God* (1982).

Crawford, and directed by George S. Kaufman. It won the New York Drama Critics Circle Award as best play of the season.

George M. Cohan played President Franklin D. Roosevelt in *I'd Rather Be Right*, which opened at the Alvin Theatre in 1937 but ended its successful run at the Music Box. The satirical political musical by Kaufman and Hart, with a score by Richard Rodgers and Lorenz Hart, dared to portray a living president who was still in the White House when the show opened. Cohan garnered raves for his good-natured performance, and the show was one of the season's top tickets.

In September 1938 Kaufman and Hart came to the Music Box in a new guise. In association with Max Gordon, they presented a topical musical revue called *Sing Out the News*, by

Harold Rome and Charles Friedman. The revue perfectly suited the Music Box tradition of topical satire but was only moderately successful.

In 1939 two more revues graced the house. One of them, *Set to Music*, by Noël Coward and starring Beatrice Lillie, was the type of sophisticated revue for which the Music Box was built—and a genre of entertainment that would become almost obsolete after World War II. The celebrity-studded opening was the kind of glittering first night that would become rare in years to come. *Set to Music* was followed by a charming entertainment called *From Vienna* (1939), a revue featuring performers who were Viennese refugees.

It is fitting that the last show to play the Music Box in the 1930s was another satire by Kaufman and Hart. Both were close friends of the obese, waspish, self-promoting critic, author, and radio celebrity Alexander Woollcott, and they wrote a classic comedy about what would happen if someone like him (called Sheridan Whiteside in the play) slipped on the ice while visiting a middle-class Midwestern family and had to stay with them while recovering from a fractured hip. Called *The Man Who Came to Dinner*, this comedy of outrages and insults starred Monty Woolley as Whiteside and also caricatured such luminaries as Noël Coward, Gertrude Lawrence, and Harpo Marx. The comedy proved to be the Music Box's longest-running show to that time, playing for 739 performances.

World War II brought a change in audience tastes on Broadway. The revue form and plays that satirized celebrities soon began to vanish. The last revue to play the Music Box for many years to come was Mike Todd's rowdy *Star and Garter*, starring strippers Gypsy Rose Lee and Georgia Southern and low comics Bobby Clark, Pat Harrington, and Professor Lamberti. The critics were not overjoyed with the burlesque, but audiences loved the show and it ran for 609 performances.

After *Star and Garter* closed at the Music Box, there was a definite change in the house's fare. For the next four decades, only three musicals were housed there: *Lost in the Stars* (1949), *Rainbow Jones* (1974), and *Side by Side by Sondheim* (1977). One of the reasons for the lack of musical bookings was that the theatre's 1,010-seat capacity was no longer considered adequate to support an expensive musical show.

During the ensuing four decades, the Music Box thrived on romantic comedies, usually with small casts, and dramas. *I Remember Mama* (1944) starred Mady Christians and Oscar Homolka, with a young Marlon Brando making his Broadway debut. This was followed by Tennessee Williams's *Summer and Smoke* (1948); *Lost in the Stars*, by Kurt Weill and Maxwell Anderson (1949); and *Affairs of State*, a light comedy starring Celeste Holm that moved from the Royale to the Music Box.

Playwright William Inge inaugurated his happy association with this theatre in 1953. Over the next five years he was to have three solid hits in the house: *Picnic* (1953) (Pulitzer Prize, New York Drama Critics Circle Award); *Bus Stop* (1955); and *The Dark at the Top of the Stairs* (1957).

Other 1950s hits included a revival of *The Male Animal*; Josephine Hull in *The Solid Gold Cadillac* (moved from the Belasco); *Separate Tables* (1956), starring Margaret Leighton and Eric Portman; Rod Steiger and Claire Bloom in *Rashomon* (1959); Cornelia Otis Skinner, Cyril Ritchard, Walter Abel, Charlie Ruggles, and George Peppard in *The Pleasure of His Company* (from the Longacre Theatre); and *Five Finger Exercise* (1959), with Jessica Tandy and Brian Bedford.

In 1961 *A Far Country* presented Steven Hill as Sigmund Freud and Kim Stanley as his patient in Henry Denker's case study. In 1962 Bert Lahr convulsed theatregoers by playing numerous roles in S. J. Perelman's *The Beauty Part*. More laughter followed in 1963 when Gertrude Berg starred in *Dear Me, the Sky is Falling*. Sandy Dennis, Gene Hackman, Rosemary Murphy, and Don Porter came to the Music Box in February 1964 in *Any Wednesday*, and the comedy stayed for 983 performances, a new record holder for this theatre.

Harold Pinter's *The Homecoming* chilled

patrons in 1967, followed by Gig Young in the warm British comedy *There's a Girl in My Soup*. On November 12, 1970, Anthony Shaffer's *Sleuth* opened with Anthony Quayle and Keith Baxter and played for a record-breaking 1,222 performances. The following year the Music Box celebrated its fiftieth anniversary, and Irving Berlin was photographed by the *New York Times* proudly standing before the theatre. Berlin stated that he and the Shubert Organization were constantly refurbishing the theatre.

Absurd Person Singular, a British import, amused capacity audiences in 1974 with stars Geraldine Page, Richard Kiley, Larry Blyden, Carole Shelley, Sandy Dennis, and Tony Roberts. Colleen Dewhurst and Ben Gazzara starred in a 1976 revival of *Who's Afraid of Virginia Woolf?*, followed by the British play *Comedians*, and the delightful portfolio of Sondheim songs *Side by Side by Sondheim* (1977). Then in 1978 came John Wood and Marian Seldes in Ira Levin's thriller *Deathtrap*. The comedy murder mystery had such an original plot that theatregoers attended it for 1,793 performances, making it the Music Box's champion attraction and the longest-running such thriller in Broadway history. In 1982 stark drama returned to the Music Box with *Agnes of God*, starring Geraldine Page, Elizabeth Ashley, and Amanda Plummer, who won a Tony Award for her performance. The religious drama played for 599 performances.

Left: Stephen Lang and Tom Hulce in Aaron Sorkin's military court-room drama, *A Few Good Men*. (Photo by Joan Marcus)

Center: John Ritter and Henry Winkler in *The Dinner Party* (2000). (Photo by Carol Rosegg)

Right: PLAYBILL from *State Fair* (1996).

In 1985 a delightful revival of Noël Coward's amusing trifle *Hay Fever* won approval for its sterling cast headed by Rosemary Harris, Roy Dotrice, Mia Dillon, and Charles Kimbrough. The following year another revival, *Loot*, by Joe Orton, also gained applause for hilarious performances by Joseph Maher, Îeljko Ivanek, Zoe Caldwell, and Alec Baldwin in his Broadway debut. Mary Tyler Moore starred here in A. R. Gurney Jr.'s comedy *Sweet Sue* (1987). This was followed by a British hit, *Les Liaisons Dangereuses*, by Christopher Hampton, given a stunning production by the Royal Shakespeare Company. In 1988 this theatre housed an offbeat musical, *Mail*, followed by Kate Nelligan in a play by Michael Weller, *Spoils of War*. Cy Coleman's divorce-court musical *Welcome to the Club* came here in 1989, and later that year *A Few Good Men*, an explosive military drama by Aaron Sorkin, enjoyed a long run. Julie Harris starred in *Lucifer's Child*, a one-woman show about the Danish author Isak Dinesen (1991); Jason Robards and Judith Ivey starred in *Park Your Car in Harvard Yard* (1991), followed by Alan Ayckbourn's *A Small Family Business* (1992).

The British musical *Blood Brothers* (1993) told of fraternal twins who are separated at birth. One is raised in wealth, the other in poverty, and they meet later in life to become violent rivals, neither realizing the other is his brother until the final moments of the play. A long-running hit in London, *Blood Brothers* received mostly negative reviews on Broadway but caught on with playgoers and ran for 839 performances.

Swinging on a Star, a songbook revue of the lyrics of Johnny Burke, came to Broadway in October 1995 from its production at the Goodspeed-at-Chester–/Norma Terris Theatre in Connecticut, with virtually the same cast. It received mixed reviews but managed to run for ninety-seven performances and earn a Tony nomination as Best Musical.

Master impresario David Merrick's last Broadway production opened at this theatre on March 27, 1996. The musical was a stage adaptation of Rodgers and Hammerstein's film *State Fair*—both the 1945 and 1962 versions—including some previously unused Rodgers and Hammerstein songs. The show had a glittering cast: Andrea McArdle, Kathryn Crosby, John Davidson, Scott Wise, Donna McKechnie, and others. It received mixed reviews and played for 118 performances. Merrick's final publicity stunt, suing the Tony Awards when only part of the score was nominated for Best Score, ended in dismissal.

Christopher Plummer scored a triumph in the play *Barrymore* in March 1997. His splendid portrayal of actor John Barrymore, one month before his death in 1942, won him a Tony Award for Leading Actor in a Play. The show, which starred Plummer onstage and Michael Mastro as an offstage voice, received rave reviews and ran for 238 performances.

Above: The PLAYBILL for Joseph Brooks' Tourette's syndrome musical *In My Life* (2005)

Right: Malcolm Gets and Melissa Errico in the musical fantasy *Amour* (2002), about a man who can walk through walls. (Photo by Jean-Marie Guyaux)

December 4, 1997, brought a new production of Frances Goodrich and Albert Hackett's play *The Diary of Anne Frank*, newly adapted by Wendy Kesselman. It starred Natalie Portman as Anne Frank, and the cast included George Hearn (Otto Frank), Sophie Hayden (Edith Frank), Linda Lavin (Mrs. Van Daan), and Austin Pendleton (Dussel). Some critics objected to changes in this revised version that made the drama more sexually explicit, among other alterations, but the play ran for more than six months. The production received two Tony Award nominations: Best Revival of a Play and Best Featured Actress (Lavin).

The next play to open at the Music Box was a controversial London drama, *Closer*, by

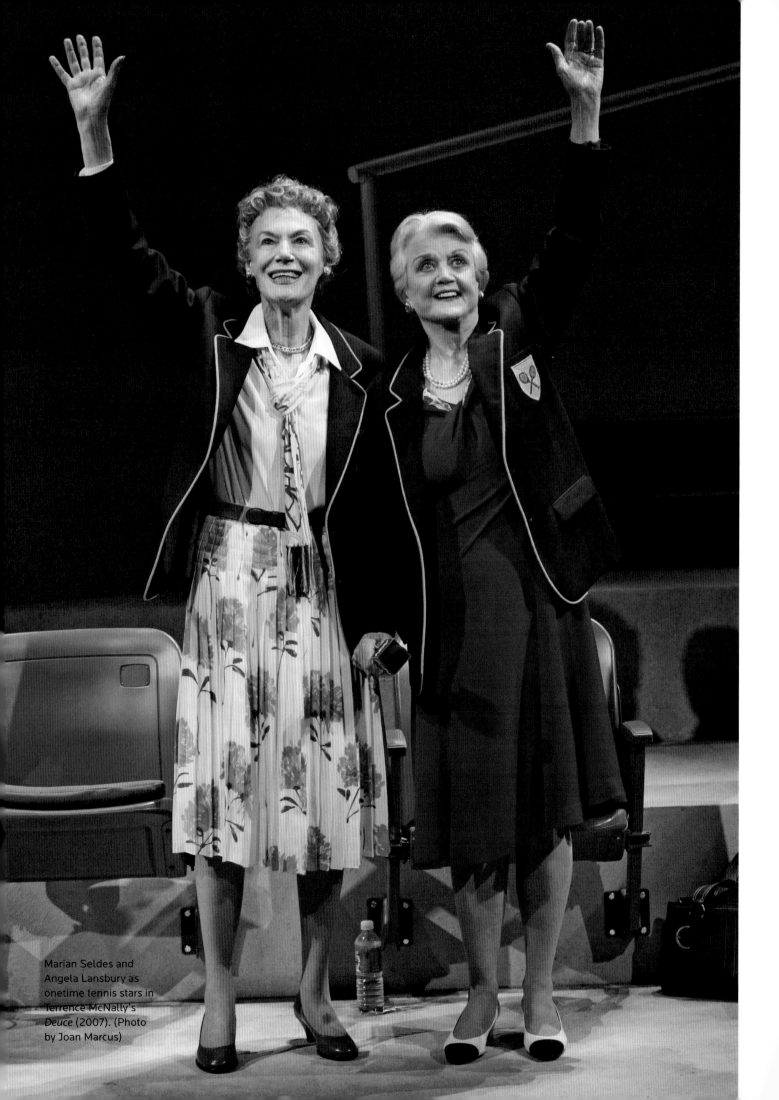

Marian Seldes and Angela Lansbury as onetime tennis stars in Terrence McNally's *Deuce* (2007). (Photo by Joan Marcus)

Patrick Marber. It starred Natasha Richardson, Ciaran Hinds, Rupert Graves, and Anna Friel, and it followed the sexual shenanigans of two couples. The language and situations were graphic and offended some playgoers, but the play won the season's Best Foreign Play Award bestowed by the New York Drama Critics Circle and was nominated for the Best Play Tony Award. It ran for 173 performances.

TV's Kelsey Grammer starred (briefly) in a darkly lit and lamentable production of *Macbeth* in June 2000. But October 19, 2000, brought Neil Simon's *The Dinner Party* with a stellar cast: Len Cariou, John Ritter, Henry Winkler, Jan Maxwell, Veanne Cox, and Penny Fuller. The scene was a chic restaurant in Paris, but, as some critics complained, the characters sounded more like people from the Bronx. Nevertheless, it proved a solid 364-performance hit for the seventy-three-year-old Simon, the first in nearly a decade for one of the most durable comedy writers in Broadway history.

For the next several years the Music Box became a revolving door. It attracted high-profile and interesting plays and small musicals, but none proved to be a long-running hit.

Talk about a long-delayed opening: Ivan Turgenev's influential 1848 drama *Fortune's Fool* got its first Broadway production on April 2, 2002, in a production that starred Frank Langella, Alan Bates, George Morfogen, and Ridiculous Theatrical Company stalwart Lola Pashalinski (in her first and so far only Broadway appearance). Despite the fact that the play had been written 154 years earlier, the Tony Awards committee pronounced it eligible for the Best Play category, in which it was then duly nominated. It lost to Edward Albee's *The Goat, or Who Is Sylvia?* and ran 127 performances.

French composer Michel Legrand enjoyed great success in his homeland; somewhat less so in the United States, where he had pop hits with "The Windmills of Your Mind" and "The Summer Knows." In 1997 he enjoyed a Parisian stage hit with *Le Passe-Muraille*, a musical about a timid man who discovers a magical ability to walk through walls. He uses his power superhero-like to champion the powerless and to win the heart of a girl who is trapped in a loveless marriage. It won the Prix Molière for Best Musical. Retitled *Amour*, the Broadway version opened at the Music Box October 20, 2002, with multitalented Melissa Errico and Malcolm Gets as the leads. It got a full-court press from its lead producer, the Shubert Organization. But American critics were not impressed, especially with the insubstantial book by Didier van Cauwelaert, and Amour lasted only fourteen performances, though an original cast album was released.

Anthony Page directed a revival of Tennessee Williams's *Cat on a Hot Tin Roof* here in November 2003, starring Ashley Judd as Maggie and Jason Patric as Brick. While the production got some respectful reviews, it didn't help when Ned Beatty (as "Big Daddy") criticized his costars' acting ability in a *New York Times* interview. They had to work together for only 145 performances. Margo Martindale ("Big Mama") earned a Tony nomination.

Australian "housewife megastar" Dame Edna (alter ego of actor Barry Humphries) followed up her hit Broadway debut with a second engagement on November 21, 2004, *Dame Edna: Back with a Vengeance*, in which she again bestowed gladiolas and saintly smiles on the audience while grossly insulting everyone and everything that crossed her path, for 163 performances.

British actor Antony Sher brought his one-man show *Primo* to the Music Box on July 11, 2005, telling the story of Italian-Jewish chemist Primo Levi, who survived a year in the Auschwitz concentration camp and lived to write a memoir about it. The acclaimed show completed a limited run of thirty-five performances,

Songwriter Joseph ("You Light Up My Life") Brooks presented Broadway with a head-scratcher of a musical, *In My Life*, on October 20, 2005. Brooks provided book, music, and lyrics for this story of J. T. (Christopher J. Hanke), a young man with Tourette's syndrome who turns out to be the unwitting lead in a "reality opera" supervised by a pudgy, bike-riding individual named Al (Michael J. Farina), who turns out to be God. For some reason the proceedings were illustrated with pervasive images of lemons, which provided good fun for the critics who put the squeeze on the show. Despite a vigorous advertising campaign, the show could not overcome cataclysmic reviews and closed after sixty-one performances.

The award-winning London drama *Festen* got a less welcoming reception on Broadway in April 2006. Larry Bryggman, Michael Hayden, Julianna Margulies, and Ali MacGraw starred in David Eldridge's drama (based on a Danish cult film) about a family gathered to celebrate

Hank Azaria (left) as broadcast pioneer David Sarnoff with a group awaiting the demonstration of the first working television in *The Farnsworth Invention* (2007). (Photo by Joan Marcus)

their patriarch's birthday, only to turn the event into a *Walpurgisnacht* of recrimination as they reveal the abuse to which he subjected them when they were growing up. The unpleasant party disbanded after forty-nine performances.

Film actress Julianne Moore braved the waters of Broadway with *The Vertical Hour* (not to be confused with 2003's *The Violet Hour*), about an American foreign correspondent who gets into a debate with her fiancé's English father (Bill Nighy) about the American invasion of Iraq. David Hare's November 2006 drama struck some critics as smug and one-sided, and it lasted only 117 performances.

For decades the Shubert Organization's total number of theatres always ended with a fraction: sixteen and a *half* theatres. They owned only half of the Music Box. The other half, Irving Berlin's half, passed to the hands of his three daughters, Mary Ellin Barrett, Linda Emmett, and Elizabeth Peters. In July 2007 an era ended when it was reported that the three women had sold their portion of the Music Box to the Shuberts.

Broadway was delighted in May 2007 at the

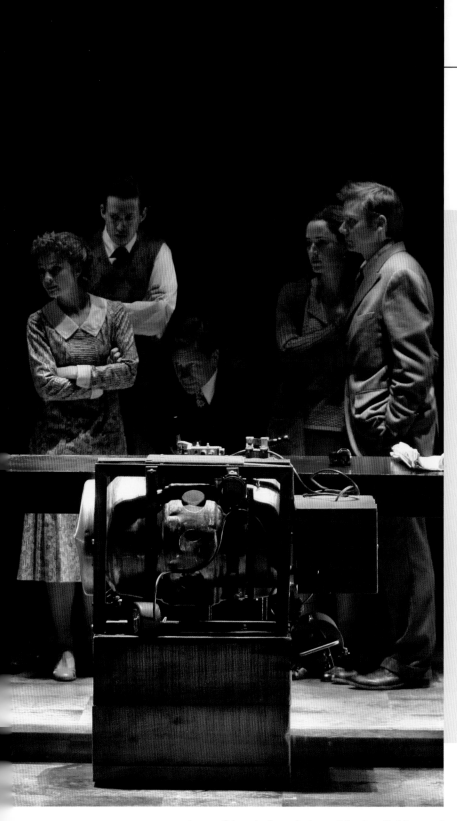

Men, 1989) who had enjoyed great success with the TV series *The West Wing*, returned to Broadway with the drama *The Farnsworth Invention*, which purported to tell the story of the invention of television. The dramatic story of how radio magnate David Sarnoff (Hank Azaria) "stole" the patent from brilliant small-time inventor Philo T. Farnsworth (Jimmi Simpson) was very dramatic, but the script came under fire for allegedly fudging the facts, and the play wobbled through a disappointing 104 performances.

One of the most distinguished American plays of the early twenty-first century was *August: Osage County*, Tracy Letts's drama about the tangled relationships of an Oklahoma family thrown together as it becomes apparent that their patriarch has committed suicide. In December 2007 *August: Osage County* moved from the Steppenwolf Theatre in Chicago to a temporary berth next door at the musical-sized Imperial. Even while enjoying the flush of initial rave reviews, awards, and strong box office, producers decided to move it to the Music Box, which was thought to be more congenial for a family drama. The show opened with Deanna Dunagan in the role of the snarling matriarch. She was named Best Actress in a Play by the Tony Awards, one of five Tonys earned by the show, including Best Play of 2008. The play also won the Pulitzer Prize for Drama.

August: Osage County transferred to the Music Box on April 29, 2008, and stayed more than a year, with Estelle Parsons and then Phylicia Rashad taking over the role of Violet. Dunagan took the role to London; Parsons took it on a North American tour. The Broadway production closed June 28, 2009, after 648 performances.

The Music Box welcomed Letts's subsequent play, *Superior Donuts*, about a Vietnam draft evader (Michael McKean), long settled as a doughnut shop operator, who finally finds something to fight for when a young employee (Jon Michael Hill) is threatened by the mob. It ran 109 performances.

Comic actor Stanley Tucci made his Broadway directing debut with a lauded spring 2010 revival of Ken Ludwig's farce Lend Me a Tenor, starring Tony Shalhoub, Anthony LaPaglia, and Jan Maxwell. It seemed perfectly at home in the cozy Music Box.

Despite its early history and melodic name, the theatre's scale and seating capacity have made it ideal not for musicals, but for plays.

return of two beloved stars, Marian Seldes and Angela Lansbury in Terrence McNally's play *Deuce*, in which they played two retired tennis stars looking back on their lives and careers. It was Lansbury's first return to the Broadway stage in a full-scale production since a *Mame* revival in 1983. The production was McNally's personal salute to the two *grandes dames* and included a scene in which one character observed, "We will never see their like again." It ran 121 performances.

Aaron Sorkin, a playwright (*A Few Good*

NEIL SIMON
THEATRE

ONE OF MANHATTAN'S MOST ILLUSTRIOUS musical comedy houses, the Neil Simon Theatre was known for most of its history as the Alvin. The theatre was named after the men who built it and produced shows there—Alex Aarons and Vinton Freedley. Having made considerable money producing musicals, Aarons and Freedley built their own playhouse at 250 West Fifty-second Street, facing the stately Guild Theatre (now the August Wilson Theatre).

Critic Brooks Atkinson of the *New York Times* wrote: "The new Alvin Theatre, set defiantly across the street from the scholarly Theatre Guild, seems to have all the best features of the modern playhouse—even an old English lounge where refreshments may be had. The auditorium is decorated with pastel

Left: Standard program cover for the Alvin Theatre in the 1920s.

Center: Opening night PLAYBILL cover for the paired booking of O'Neill's *Long Day's Journey Into Night* and *Ah! Wilderness* (1988).

Right: Neil Simon's comedy *Jake's Women* (1992)

shades of blue and gray, with ivory and gold decorations. The Alvin can serve 1,400 drama gluttons at one sitting."

Designed by Herbert J. Krapp, the new house had three floors of offices above it where Aarons and Freedley had their headquarters. The theatre contained a spacious lobby in black marble and an inner lobby of simple design. There was only one balcony. The ample orchestra pit could accommodate forty-eight musicians, and the stage was spacious enough to allow for the production and staging of the most elaborate musicals.

The Alvin opened auspiciously on November 22, 1927, with the Aarons/Freedley *Funny Face*, a hit musical by George and Ira Gershwin, Paul Gerard Smith, and Fred Thompson. The cast included Fred and Adele Astaire, Victor Moore, Allen Kearns, Betty Compton, William Kent, and the duo pianists Phil Ohman and Victor Arden. The memorable score featured such gems as "He Loves and She Loves," "'S Wonderful," "My One and Only," "The Babbitt and the Bromide," and the title song. The Astaires captivated theatregoers for 250 performances.

The following November, Aarons and Freedley tried again with another Gershwin musical, *Treasure Girl*, but this time they failed. The star was Gertrude Lawrence, and

her supporting cast included Paul Frawley, Walter Catlett, Clifton Webb, and Mary Hay, with Ohman and Arden again at the ivories. But the show's book was uninspired, and the critics complained that Lawrence had to play a disagreeable liar. Clifton Webb and Mary Hay's dancing was applauded, and the Gershwin tunes included "I Don't Think I'll Fall in Love Today," "Feeling I'm Falling," and "I've Got a Crush on You." The musical expired after sixty-nine performances.

In 1929 the Theatre Guild production of *Wings Over Europe*, a startling drama that speculated about the destructive power of atomic energy, moved here from the Martin Beck Theatre. This was followed by two Rodgers and Hart musicals in succession. The first was *Spring Is Here*, with a book by Owen Davis from his play *Shotgun Wedding*. It was not one of Rodgers and Hart's triumphs, but a pleasant show with two songs that lasted: "With a Song in My Heart" and "Yours Sincerely." In the cast were Inez Courtney, Glenn Hunter, Charles Ruggles, and Joyce Barbour. *Spring Is Here* lasted 104 performances. *Heads Up!*, the next Rodgers and Hart musical, had a book by John McGowan and Paul Gerard Smith and contained a lovely song that is sometimes heard in supper clubs—"A Ship without a Sail." The cast included Ray Bolger, Victor Moore,

Above: Matthew Bourne's *Swan Lake* (1998).

Top left: Polo-playing convict Jimmy Durante taps Ethel Merman's wire in *Red, Hot and Blue!* (1936).

Top center: George M. Cohan as F.D.R. gives a fireside chat in *I'd Rather Be Right* (1937).

Top right: Helen Hayes loses her head in Maxwell Anderson's *Mary of Scotland* (1933).

Bottom: Ingrid Bergman plays Saint Joan in Maxwell Anderson's play-within-a-play *Joan of Lorraine* (1946).

Betty Starbuck, Jack Whiting, Barbara Newberry, and Lewis (later, Lew) Parker. Victor Moore won raves for his comedy routines. The musical ran for 144 performances.

In 1930 the Theatre Guild's production of Shaw's *The Apple Cart*, with Claude Rains and Violet Kemble Cooper, moved here from the Martin Beck. Then, on October 14, 1930, one of this theatre's historic musicals opened. It was the Aarons/Freedley production of George and Ira Gershwin's *Girl Crazy*, with a book by Guy Bolton and John McGowan. The cast included

Ginger Rogers, Willie Howard, Allen Kearns, William Kent, and the Foursome. But it was Ethel Merman, making her Broadway debut, who shook the Alvin with her electrifying rendition of the classic "I Got Rhythm." The musical, which also introduced the standards "But Not for Me" and "Embraceable You," ran 272 performances.

Eugene O'Neill's great trilogy *Mourning Becomes Electra* moved here from the Guild Theatre across the street in 1932.

Jerome Kern's *Music in the Air* was an enormous hit in 1932 at this theatre, which did not have another theatrical booking until May 29, 1933, when The Players chose it as the house for their twelfth annual revival of a classic play. They scheduled a revival of *Uncle Tom's Cabin* for a week, but it was so popular that it stayed for three. The distinguished cast included Otis Skinner as Uncle Tom, Fay Bainter as Topsy, Thomas Chalmers as Simon Legree, Elizabeth Risdon as Eliza, Minnie Dupree as Aunt Ophelia, Cecilia Loftus as Aunt Chloe, and Gene Lockhart as Gumption Cute.

The Alvin housed a distinguished drama in

Top left: Ethel Merman and chorus belt out Cole Porter's rousing "Blow, Gabriel, Blow" in *Anything Goes* (1934).

Top right: Lynn Fontanne, Montgomery Clift, and Alfred Lunt in the Pulitzer-winning play *There Shall Be No Night* (1940).

Bottom: David Wayne, Henry Fonda and Robert Keith sample some homemade Scotch in *Mister Roberts* (1948).

the fall of 1933. It was the Theatre Guild production of Maxwell Anderson's verse play *Mary of Scotland*, starring Helen Hayes in the title role, Helen Menken as Queen Elizabeth, and Philip Merivale as the Earl of Bothwell.

On the night of November 21, 1934, one of the Depression's most glittering first-night audiences gathered at the Alvin to roar its approval of Cole Porter's felicitous musical *Anything Goes*. This show had a very shaky history. The original libretto by Guy Bolton and P. G. Wodehouse involved a group of zany characters on a luxury liner that is shipwrecked. Just as the musical was about to go into rehearsal, the luxury liner SS *Morro Castle* burned off the coast of Asbury Park and the musical's plot seemed very unfunny. As the story goes, with Bolton and Wodehouse out of the country, producer Vinton Freedley turned in desperation to the show's director, Howard Lindsay, who hired press agent Russel Crouse to help him quickly write a new libretto. The show went into rehearsal with only a portion of the first act on paper. They kept the action on a luxury liner but dropped the shipwreck notion. The result was a triumph of mirth and melody, with Ethel Merman as Reno Sweeney (a parody of Aimee Semple MacPherson) traveling with her band of singers, called "Angels." Victor Moore was Public Enemy No. 13, gangster Moonface Martin, disguised as Reverend Dr. Moon (with a machine gun in his violin case), and William Gaxton was a playboy in pursuit of Hope Harcourt (Bettina Hall). Porter wrote his greatest score to that time, including "I Get a Kick Out of You," "You're the Top," "All Through the Night," "Blow, Gabriel, Blow," and the infectious title song. The musical became the most representative show of the 1930s—glamorous, screwball, slightly risqué, very topical, and very sophisticated. It ran for 420 performances.

In October 1935 the Gershwins and DuBose Heyward brought their magnificent opera *Porgy and Bess* to the Alvin. The reception was mixed, and it played only 124 times. George Gershwin went to his grave two years later thinking it was a failure, but revivals have helped audiences recognize it as his masterpiece and the capstone of his career.

In October of 1936 Vinton Freedley hoped to strike gold again with another Ethel Merman/Cole Porter show. This one was called *Red, Hot and Blue*, and there was trouble from the very start. Both Ethel and her costar, Jimmy Durante, wanted top billing. After much haggling, Mrs. Porter came up with a solution: a crisscross arrangement of the two names so that each could be construed as having top billing. The other star, Bob Hope, took to lying down and mugging during one of Ethel's song numbers, and she threatened "to sit on the son of a bitch" if he didn't stop. He stopped. The show was not another *Anything Goes*. The plot, by Howard Lindsay and Russel Crouse, was about a national lottery. The winner was the person who could find one "Peaches Le Fleur," who had a distinctive mark on her behind because she once sat on a hot waffle iron. The Supreme Court got into the lottery and began examining showgirls in cellophane skirts to see if they had the winning mark. The dippy show ran for 181 performances, and the most memorable moments were provided by Durante, as a polo-playing convict, and three great Porter songs: "It's De-Lovely," "Ridin' High," and

"Down in the Depths (on the Ninetieth Floor)."

On November 2, 1937, George M. Cohan returned to this theatre as President Franklin D. Roosevelt in the satirical musical *I'd Rather Be Right*, and the occasion turned into one of Broadway's most flamboyant opening nights. The fact that no sitting U.S. president had ever been portrayed onstage (and in a satire, no less), and the added lure that the show was the creation of Richard Rodgers and Lorenz Hart, George S. Kaufman, and Moss Hart made this a must-see event. Reported Lucius Beebe in *Stage* magazine: "Probably no theatrical event has occasioned such civic tumult since the Astor Place Riots. All New York wanted in, as the phrase has it. New York seemed completely overwhelmed by the return of Cohan, and popular rejoicing and Morris dancing in Longacre Square complemented the most insufferable crush, confusion, and amiable uproar Fifty-second Street has ever known."

Although *I'd Rather Be Right* was not as biting as *Of Thee I Sing*, Cohan's affectionate portrayal of FDR and his delightful tap dancing made the show one of the season's sold-out delights. Only one Rodgers and Hart song was played beyond the show: "Have You Met Miss Jones?" The musical ran for 289 performances.

In November 1938 Rodgers and Hart and George Abbott brought to the Alvin their memorable musical *The Boys from Syracuse*, based on Shakespeare's *The Comedy of Errors*, with Eddie Albert and Ronald Graham as one set of twins, Jimmy Savo and Teddy Hart (brother of lyricist Lorenz) as the other set, plus Muriel Angelus, Marcy Wescott, Wynn Murray, Betty Bruce, and Burl Ives. With choreography by George Balanchine and such lilting songs as "This Can't Be Love," "Falling in Love with Love," and "Sing for Your Supper," the exuberant musical ran for 235 performances.

In February 1940, to aid the Finnish Relief Fund, the Lunts brought back their 1935 revival of *The Taming of the Shrew*. It was a short engagement but a notable one for a worthy war cause. In April of that year, they returned to this theatre in Robert E. Sherwood's *There Shall Be No Night*, which was awarded the Pulitzer Prize. It was a powerful denunciation of war and, in particular, Russia's invasion of Finland. The play showed the devastating effects on a Finnish family. The supporting cast included Montgomery Clift, Richard Whorf, Sydney Greenstreet, Elizabeth Praser, and Phyllis Thaxter. It ran for 115 performances, took a vacation, then resumed for 66 additional performances.

On January 23, 1941, the Alvin housed one of the American Musical Theatre's finest works: *Lady in the Dark*, by Moss Hart, Kurt Weill, and Ira Gershwin. Gertrude Lawrence scored one of her greatest triumphs in it, bumping and grinding to one of the musical's greatest tunes, "The Saga of Jenny." Danny Kaye also stopped the show with his tongue twister "Tchaikowsky." The supporting cast included Bert Lytell, Macdonald Carey, Victor Mature, and Margaret Dale. The choreography by Albertina Rasch and the opulent sets and costumes made it one of the most memorable musicals ever seen on Broadway. Brooks Atkinson in the *New York Times* called it "a work of theatre art." It ran for 467 performances.

On January 7, 1943, there was a unique opening night at the Alvin for the latest Cole Porter/Ethel Merman musical, *Something for the Boys*. This was the date that a new government ruling went into effect because of the war. Private automobiles could not be driven to places of entertainment; therefore, Fifty-second Street was jammed with taxicabs, all honking to get through the crush. The musical, with Paula Laurence, Allen Jenkins, Betty Garrett, Bill Johnson, Jed Prouty, Betty Bruce, and—in the chorus—Dody Goodman, was a smash hit. Its plot, by Herbert and Dorothy Fields, was even more foolish than that of *Red, Hot and Blue*. Merman played a defense worker who got Carborundum in her teeth fillings, which turned her into a radio receiving set. At the show's climax, she saved an army plane from crashing by receiving landing instructions via her teeth. Wartime audiences ate this up for 422 performances.

A series of failures played this theatre during 1944 and 1945. They were a musical called *Jackpot*, with Nanette Fabray, Benny Baker, Allan Jones, Wendell Corey, and Betty Garrett; *Helen Goes to Troy*, a new musical version of Offenbach's operetta *La Belle Hélène*, with Ernest Truex and Jarmila Novotna; *The Firebrand of Florence*, a musical version of the play *The Firebrand*, by Kurt Weill, Ira Gershwin, and Edwin Justus Mayer, with Lotte Lenya; and *Hollywood Pinafore*, George S. Kaufman's modern interpretation of Gilbert and Sullivan's *H.M.S. Pinafore*, with Victor Moore, William Gaxton, and Shirley Booth. More successful was a revival of *The Tempest*, as interpreted by Margaret Webster and Eva Le Gallienne and starring Vera Zorina, Arnold Moss, Canada Lee, and Frances Heflin.

Betty Comden, Adolph Green, and Morton Gould combined talents on *Billion Dollar Baby*, an interesting musical about the Roaring Twenties. Mitzi Green, Joan McCracken, Helen Gallagher,

Danny Daniels, William Tabbert, and David Burns gave vivid performances, and the show amused postwar audiences for 220 performances.

Ingrid Bergman scored a triumph in Maxwell Anderson's *Joan of Lorraine* (1946), with Sam Wanamaker and Romney Brent also giving memorable performances in this unconventional interpretation of the story of Joan of Arc.

In 1947 *Life with Father* moved to the Alvin from the Bijou Theatre and here ended its record run of 3,224 performances, making it the longest-running straight play in the history of the American theatre—a record that it still holds.

On October 8, 1947, Maurice Evans opened his highly successful revival of Shaw's *Man and Superman* and starred in it for 294 performances. This was followed by one of the Alvin's most fondly remembered bookings: *Mister Roberts*, the navy comedy, which opened on February 18, 1948, and stayed in port at the Alvin until January 6, 1951, for a total of 1,157 performances. The Thomas Heggen/Joshua Logan play starred Henry Fonda, who won a Tony Award for his performance in the title role. Other Tony Awards went to the play, to its producer, and to its authors.

Highlights of the 1950s at this theatre included Sidney Kingsley's adaptation of Arthur Koestler's novel *Darkness at Noon* (1951), which won a Tony Award for its star, Claude Rains; the musical version of Betty Smith's novel *A Tree Grows in Brooklyn* (1951), by Smith, George Abbott, Arthur Schwartz, and Dorothy Fields, starring Shirley Booth, Johnny Johnston, Marcia Van Dyke, and Nathaniel Frey; and Henry Fonda again in *Point of No Return* (1951), Paul Osborn's dramatization of John P. Marquand's novel of the same name, with Leora Dana, Frank Conroy, and John Cromwell.

In 1952 Bette Davis chose to star in a

Vernon Duke revue called *Two's Company*, but the decision was ill-advised. The show closed after 90 performances. Mary Martin and Charles Boyer starred in a humdrum comedy, *Kind Sir*, by Norman Krasna, in 1953. The spring of 1954 brought the Phoenix Theatre production of *The Golden Apple*, based on Homer's *Iliad* and *Odyssey*, and it won the New York Drama Critics Circle Award for best musical of the season, though it continued for only 173 performances. This was followed in December 1954 by *House of Flowers*, a musical created by Truman Capote and Harold Arlen, directed by Peter Brook, and starring Pearl Bailey, Diahann Carroll, Ray Walston, Juanita Hall, and dancers Alvin Ailey, Geoffrey Holder, and Carmen de Lavallade. Although the score, sets, costumes, and cast were praised, the musical had a weak book, and it did not recoup its large investment despite a run of 165 performances.

On October 20, 1955, *No Time for Sergeants* opened and convulsed theatregoers for 796 performances. Ira Levin's comedy, based on Mac Hyman's novel, starred Andy Griffith as an amiable southerner who throws the army into an uproar with his friendly simplicity; Roddy McDowall played his army buddy.

In the late 1950s this theatre hosted some musicals that were only moderately successful: *Oh, Captain!* (1958), with Tony Randall, Abbe Lane, Susan Johnson, and Alexandra Danilova; and *First Impressions*, a musical version of *Pride and Prejudice* (1959), starring Hermione Gingold, Farley Granger, Polly Bergen, Phyllis Newman, and Ellen Hanley. During these years there were also engagements of Jerome Robbins's *Ballet U.S.A.* and of *Bells Are Ringing*, a musical that moved here from the Shubert.

The 1960s brought Frank Loesser's unsuccessful musical *Greenwillow* (1960), starring Anthony Perkins, Ellen McCown, Pert Kelton, and Cecil Kellaway; the *Ballets Africains and West Side Story*, from the Winter Garden (1960); Lucille Ball in a moderately entertaining musical (and Cy Coleman's Broadway debut), *Wildcat* (1961); *Irma La Douce* (1961), the hit musical from the Plymouth Theatre; an unsuccessful revue, *New Faces of 1962*; and a huge hit, *A Funny Thing Happened on the Way to the Forum*, the Stephen Sondheim/Burt Shevelove/Larry Gelbart musical based on several plays by Roman playwright Plautus, directed by George Abbott, and starring Zero Mostel, David Burns, Jack Gilford, John Carradine, and Raymond

Walburn. This antic production tickled theatregoers for 964 performances.

Beatrice Lillie made her final Broadway appearance at the Alvin in 1964 in *High Spirits*, an uproarious musical version of Noël Coward's comedy *Blithe Spirit*, by Hugh Martin and Timothy Gray, staged by Coward. Lillie was brilliant as the medium, Madame Arcati, and she was splendidly assisted by Tammy Grimes, Edward Woodward, and Louise Troy. The musical ran for 376 performances.

Maurice Chevalier at 77, a personal appearance by the French singer, came to the Alvin in 1965, as did Broadway debutante Liza Minnelli in an unsuccessful musical, *Flora, the Red Menace*, which also marked the Broadway debut of John Kander and Fred Ebb as a team. Other unsuccessful shows followed: a musical version of the best-selling book *The Yearling* (1965); a musical adaptation of the *Superman* comic strip called *It's a Bird . . . It's a Plane . . . It's Superman* (1966); an all-star revival of *Dinner at Eight* (1966); and a musical version of *The Man Who Came to Dinner*, called *Sherry!* (1967), with book and lyrics by James Lipton, later host of TV's *Inside the Actors Studio*.

A palpable hit arrived in October 1967, when Tom Stoppard's coruscating play *Rosencrantz and Guildenstern Are Dead* opened. The dazzling work, which offered *Hamlet* as seen through the eyes of two of its minor characters, won a Tony Award as the best drama of the season. It was brilliantly acted by John Wood, Paul Hecht, and Brian Murray, and it played for 421 performances.

Another powerful drama, *The Great White Hope*, by Howard Sackler, opened here in 1968 and won the Pulitzer Prize, New York Drama Critics Circle Award, and Tony Award for Best Play. James Earl Jones and Jane Alexander won Tony Awards for their memorable performances as the first black heavyweight champion of the world and his tragic girlfriend. The play ran for 557 performances.

In the spring of 1970 Harold Prince arrived with an exciting, groundbreaking musical, *Company*, by Stephen Sondheim and George Furth. A popular bachelor (played by Dean Jones briefly, then succeeded by Larry Kert) takes a tour through the imperfect marriages of his demanding friends in a series of musical sketches. *Company* won seven Tony Awards, including Best Musical, Best Book, Best Music, Best Lyrics, and Best Direction. Boris Aronson's magnificent set—a skeletal apartment house with running elevators—also won a Tony.

Shenandoah, a musical that arrived from the Goodspeed Opera House in Connecticut in 1975, starred John Cullum, who won a Tony Award for his performance in this Civil War musical. Next came a veritable gold mine for this theatre, another winner from the Goodspeed Opera House, called *Annie*. Martin Charnin, Thomas Meehan, and Charles Strouse's musical adaptation of the popular comic strip "Little Orphan Annie" played at the Alvin for almost five years before moving to another theatre. It received Tony Awards for Best Musical, Best Book, Best Score, Best Sets, Best Costumes, Best Choreography, and Best Actress (Dorothy Loudon, as the villainous Miss Hannigan). Young Andrea McArdle was highly praised for her performance as Annie and the beguiling orphans also received raves. It was a great family show and ran for 2,377 performances.

After *Annie* left the Alvin, the theatre had five musical failures in succession: *Merrily We Roll Along*, *The Little Prince and the Aviator* (which closed during previews), *Little Johnny Jones*, *Do Black Patent Leather Shoes Really Reflect Up?* and *Seven Brides for Seven Brothers*.

Next came a revival of the gospel musical *Your Arms Too Short to Box with God*, starring Al Green and Patti LaBelle. It was followed by Neil Simon's *Brighton Beach Memoirs*, the first play of an autobiographical trilogy about his youth with his family, which won the New York Drama Critics Circle Award for the season's best play. Matthew Broderick won a Tony Award for his performance, and Îeljko Ivanek, Elizabeth Franz, Peter Michael Goetz, Joyce Van Patten, and Mindy Ingber also sparkled.

On June 29, 1983, the Alvin was officially renamed the Neil Simon Theatre in honor of one of America's most prolific playwrights.

In 1985 the second play of Simon's trilogy—*Biloxi Blues*—opened here and won the following Tony Awards: Best Play (Simon's first such honor), Best Featured Actor (Barry Miller), and Best Director of a Play (Gene Saks). The play ran here for more than a year. Next came an unlikely musical called *Into the Light*, about scientists testing the authenticity of the Shroud of Turin. Starring Dean Jones, the show had a brief run of six performances.

In March 1987 a revival of Noël Coward's *Blithe Spirit* starred Richard Chamberlain, Blythe Danner, Judith Ivey, and the admired actress Geraldine Page. Tragically, on June 13, 1987, in the midst of its run, Page died. Patricia Conolly succeeded her in the plum role of Madame Arcati. Page was nominated for a Tony Award for her performance.

In October 1987 *Mort Sahl on Broadway* played a limited engagement, followed by a London success, *Breaking the Code*, by Hugh Whitmore, a playwright who liked to use real-life situations in his scripts (*Stevie* and *Pack of Lies*). Based on the book *Alan Turing: The Enigma*, by Andrew Hodges, the play dealt with the brilliant but eccentric British mathematician who broke Nazi Germany's "Enigma" code during World War II, saving millions of Allied lives. The play's title had two meanings: Turing not only broke the mathematical code, but the moral code, because he was a homosexual at a time when that was a criminal offense and branded him a security risk. Turing was brilliantly played by Derek Jacobi. He was nominated for a Tony Award for Best Actor in a Play, and his costar Michael Gough was nominated as Best Featured Actor in a play. The drama ran for 161 performances and was later televised.

In June 1988, as part of the First New York International Festival of the Arts, two Eugene O'Neill plays were revived: *Long Day's Journey into Night* and *Ah, Wilderness!* both starring Colleen Dewhurst and Jason Robards. Elizabeth Wilson and George Hearn also appeared in the latter play, O'Neill's only comedy. *Long Day's Journey into Night* played for twenty-eight performances. *Ah, Wilderness!* ran for twelve and was nominated for a Best Play Revival Tony Award.

In the fall of 1988 *Kenny Loggins on Broadway* presented the singer-composer in a program of folk and rock songs. The engagement ran for eight performances. In January 1989 two musicals with music by Tom O'Horgan were announced to open at this theatre. One of them, *Senator Joe*, a rock opera about red-baiting senator Joseph McCarthy, played only three days of previews, then closed before the official opening. The other one, *The Tower of Babel*, never even had a preview.

From the Theatre Royal Haymarket in London came Peter Hall's revival of Tennessee Williams's *Orpheus Descending* in September 1989. It starred Vanessa Redgrave and Kevin Anderson, with Tammy Grimes and Anne Twomey in the supporting cast. Redgrave's performance was admired by some and

Top: The PLAYBILL from the 2000 revival of *The Music Man*.

Bottom: The PLAYBILL from *Hairspray* (2002).

Tony winner Harvey Fierstein in drag as Edna Turnblad sings "Welcome to the '60s" in *Hairspray* (2002). (Photo by Paul Kolnik)

deemed "wrong-headed" by others. The revival lasted ninety-seven performances.

There was a limited engagement by the *Don Cossacks, the State Academic Ensemble of Rostov, USSR* in January 1990. Later in the year *Jackie Mason: Brand New*, another of his hysterical one-man shows of topical barbs, played from October 1990 to 1991.

On March 24, 1992, Neil Simon's *Jake's Women* opened with an impressive cast: Alan Alda, Helen Shaver, Kate Burton, Joyce Van Patten, and Brenda Vaccaro. Directed by Gene Saks, the play dealt with the women in the life of Jake (Simon's alter ego), acted by Alda. His relationships with six women were depicted both in actuality and in fantasy—in Jake's mind. The play received mixed reviews, and it reminded one critic of the musical *Company*, which examines the relationships of the leading male character with his friends. Some critics felt that the play's philosophies were rather

shallow. It ran for 245 performances.

Cyrano: The Musical, based on the classic play by Edmond Rostand, arrived here from the Netherlands on November 21, 1993. It did not receive enthusiastic reviews, but it ran for 137 performances and was praised for its sets, lights, and costumes. It received the following Tony Award nominations: Best Musical, Best Original Score, Best Book of a Musical, and Best Costumes.

An odd play from London, *The Rise and Fall of Little Voice*, arrived on May 1, 1994, and lasted only until May 8. It depicted a shy girl (Hynden Walch) with a talent for impersonating famous singers (Judy Garland, Edith Piaf, etc.). The critics judged it to be a tasteless minor English comedy, but it was later filmed.

A short run was achieved by another vocal acrobat, impressionist Danny Gans, who called himself "The Man of Many Voices." He claimed that he could impersonate more than two hundred famous voices, and one critic wrote that it seemed as if he did all of them in his intermissionless show, which ran for only six performances in 1995.

A welcome hit opened on April 11, 1996: a handsome revival of Rodgers and Hammerstein's beloved *The King and I*. Donna Murphy played Anna, and Lou Diamond Phillips played the King of Siam. Both received excellent reviews. It was a sumptuous production, and it won Tony Awards for Murphy (Best Actress in a Musical), for Best Musical Revival, for Brian Thomson (Best Scenic Designer), and for Roger Kirk (Best Costume Designer). It also received the following Tony Award nominations: Best Actor in a Musical (Phillips), Best Featured Actress in a Musical (Joohee Choi), Best Musical Director (Christopher Renshaw), and Best Lighting Designer (Nigel Levings). During its long run (807 performances), Murphy was succeeded as Mrs. Anna by Faith Prince and Marie Osmond; Phillips was succeeded as the King by Kevin Gray.

An unusual and critically acclaimed dance entertainment came to this theatre from London and Los Angeles on October 8, 1998. It was Matthew Bourne's trendy version of *Swan Lake*, featuring a bevy of hirsute male swans. The plot featured a Prince with a smothering mother, who searches for love among the gay swans. Tony Awards were garnered by Matthew Bourne for Direction and Choreography, and by Lez Brotherston for Costumes. Adam Cooper was nominated as Leading Actor in a Musical. The popular spectacle had a limited engagement of 124 performances.

The last show at the Neil Simon Theatre before the celebration of the millennium was *The Scarlet Pimpernel*, nicknamed Version 3.0 because it was the third version of this musical by Frank Wildhorn and Nan Knighton. The first, in 1997, played 373 performances at the Minskoff Theatre; the second, in 1998, played for 239 performances; and the last, at this theatre, lasted for 129 performances.

In spring 2000 Susan Stroman directed a warmhearted revival of Meredith Willson's classic *The Music Man*, starring Rebecca Luker and Craig Bierko. The production was memorable for its finale, in which the entire cast appeared dressed as a marching band, toting trombones, and were led by Bierko in playing the show's signature tune, "Seventy-six Trombones." Professor Harold Hill worked his

magic for 699 performances.

Tony-winner Mandy Patinkin took over the Neil Simon stage for a single performance of *Mandy Patinkin in Concert*, in support of his solo CD *Kidults*. Despite the playful tone of much of the concert, the finale turned political, predicting a dire outcome if problems in the Middle East were not resolved. The date was September 10, 2001, and, coincidentally, the next morning came the terror attacks at the World Trade Center and Pentagon that colored the rest of the decade.

One of the most remarkable solo shows in recent years came next at the Neil Simon. *The New Yorker* theatre critic John Lahr worked with director George C. Wolfe and brash Broadway grande dame Elaine Stritch to fashion a no-holds-barred evening of songs and salty autobiographical stores titled *Elaine Stritch: At Liberty*. Transferring from Off-Broadway's Public Theater on February 21, 2002, the show won the inaugural Tony Award for Best Special Theatrical Event and stayed for sixty-nine performances.

August 15, 2002, brought the biggest hit in the long and glittering history of the Neil Simon Theatre: *Hairspray*, a high-energy musical based on the cult John Waters film of the same name, about a plus-size Baltimore girl who believes in her own beauty and who is determined to win a place on the local TV teen dance show. Full of great tunes, campy humor, bright sets and costumes, and an athletic supporting cast, the show trounced the competition, winning eight Tony Awards including Best Musical, Best Score (Marc Shaiman and Scott Wittman), Best Book (Tom Meehan and Mark O'Donnell), Best Director (Jack O'Brien), and Best Actor and Actress for the leads: gravel-voiced Harvey Fierstein (in colossal drag as mom Edna Turnblad) and Marissa Jaret Winokur (as the resolute leading lady). The two stars returned to the show for its final weeks in late 2008 and early 2009. It closed January 4, 2009, after 2,642 performances.

The Neil Simon stood empty for most of 2009, preparing for a major revival of the musical *Ragtime*, which opened November 15 of that year, starring Quentin Earl Darrington, Christiane Noll, Stephanie P. Umoh, and Robert Petkoff. It ran a disappointingly brief sixty-five performances.

The theatre is currently owned by the Nederlander Organization and remains in the top tier of Broadway's most sought-after musical houses.

NEW AMSTERDAM THEATRE

WHEN THIS MAGNIFICENT THEATRE
was opened in 1903 by producers Klaw and
Erlanger, it was described as "the house beautiful." The entire building, which also held
offices, was designed and decorated in lush Art
Nouveau style by architects Herts and Tallant.

The opening production on October 26,
1903, was an appropriately lavish staging of
Shakespeare's *A Midsummer Night's Dream*,
featuring music by Mendelssohn and star turns
by popular performers of that day, Nat C.
Goodwin and William Farnum. The production
was only a moderate success, with the best
reviews going to the theatre itself, for its classic splendor.

The eleven-story building contained two
theatres, including one on the roof, and the

most elaborate lobby, staircases, murals, lounges, and even elevator doors seen in any Broadway theatre. The media devoted unprecedented space to its glories. The predominant color scheme of the theatre was green, mother of pearl, and mauve. The seating capacity was 1,750 in the orchestra, two balconies, and twelve boxes.

Among the great stars of that era who appeared on the New Amsterdam stage were James O'Neill (Eugene O'Neill's father), Lillian Russell, comics Weber and Fields, Grace George, Mrs. Patrick Campbell, and Richard Mansfield.

Musicals and classic repertory were the staples of this theatre in its early years. George M. Cohan wrote book, music, and lyrics for his 1906 musical *Forty-five Minutes from Broadway*, which starred Fay Templeton, Victor Moore, and Donald Brian. Shaw's *Caesar and Cleopatra* had its world premiere in 1906 and starred Johnston Forbes-Robertson and

Gertrude Elliott. Winchell Smith and Byron Ongley's comedy *Brewster's Millions* arrived on New Year's Eve 1906 and ran for just sixty-four performances but was constantly revived.

The New Amsterdam's first real megahit arrived on October 21, 1907, when Franz Lehar's beloved operetta *The Merry Widow* opened, starring Ethel Jackson and Donald Brian. With its enchanting waltz, *The Merry Widow* played here for 416 performances in an age when any show that played more than a hundred performances was considered a hit.

In 1910 a melodrama called *Madame X* opened here and became a favorite for revivals and movie versions.

Another popular operetta, *Madame Sherry*, was booked here in 1910, starring Lina Abarbanell, and ran for 231 performances. It was followed by an even bigger hit, *The Pink Lady*, starring Hazel Dawn and William Elliott, which delighted audiences for 312 performances.

A spectacular adaptation by William Young of Lew Wallace's epic novel *Ben Hur* opened in 1911, starring Richard Buhler and Edward H. Robbins. There were many productions of this classic at different theatres at this time. Treadmills were used for the exciting chariot-race scene.

Two operettas were popular here in 1912: Reginald De Koven's *Robin Hood* and the American premiere of Lehar's *The Count of Luxembourg*.

On June 16, 1913, an event occurred that came to define the New Amsterdam, and, indeed, an entire era. Florenz Ziegfeld began producing his annual *Ziegfeld Follies* revues at this theatre. He had produced six of them before at other theatres, but the jewel-like New Amsterdam seemed to have been custom-made for these superlative revues, which showcased the funniest comedians, the sweetest singers,

Top left: Images from "souvenir postal cards" reproducing murals from the New Amsterdam's smoking room. "Governor Andrus Takes the City for the English." : "Landing of Stuyvesant."

Top center: program from the *Midnight Frolic* atop the New Amsterdam Roof (1929).

Top right: View of West 42nd Street, looking west from Seventh Avenue toward Eighth Avenue in 1931 near the end of its heyday. The New Amsterdam marquee is visible at left, above trolley.

Bottom left: Marilyn Miller and friends in *Sunny* (1925).

Top left: Marilyn Miller autographed the dancing shoes she used in the show.

Top right: Bob Hope, Ray Middleton, Lyda Roberti, and Sydney Greenstreet in *Roberta* (1933).

Above: Sheet music from the Irving Berlin hit "Shaking the Blues Away," introduced by Eddie Cantor in the *Ziegfeld Follies of 1927*.

Above: Sheet music for "My Baby Just Cares for Me" by Walter Donaldson and Gus Kahn "with ukelele accompaniment," from *Whoopee* (1928).

Above: William Gillette's perennial favorite, *Sherlock Holmes* (1929).

the most sparkling of melodies by the era's top songwriters, and the most stunning American beauties in the most gorgeous and scanty gowns on the most opulent sets. The annual editions were the last word in class and talent, and their magic resonated years after the lights went out on the series, in shows like Stephen Sondheim's *Follies* and Cy Coleman's *The Will Rogers Follies*. The New Amsterdam was the natural home of the *Ziegfeld Follies*. The 1913 *Follies* had Leon Errol, dancer Ann Pennington, and Frank Tinney in the cast and played for ninety-six performances.

The Roof Theatre of the New Amsterdam was first called Aerial Gardens, but when Ziegfeld started presenting his *Midnight Frolic* there in 1915, it was changed to Dance de Follies. The space was successively rechristened the Dresden Theatre and the Frolic Theatre in later years. This theatre featured a glass promenade on its second level, overhanging the first, and Peeping Toms got their thrills looking up for an intimate view of the girls sashaying above. The Roof Theatre was renovated in 2008 as offices for Disney Theatricals, but Disney restored and retained both the proscenium and the glass promenade, though the latter now uses demurely clouded glass.

Victor Herbert's *Sweethearts* was a hit in 1913, and so was Hazel Dawn in a musical adapted from the French, called *The Little Cafe*. The *Ziegfeld Follies of 1914* starred Ed Wynn, Bert Williams, Leon Errol, and the dynamic dancer Ann Pennington and played for 112 performances.

On December 8, 1914, a dance sensation opened at the New Amsterdam. It was Irving Berlin's first complete score for Broadway, in a ragtime musical called *Watch Your Step*, subtitled "A Syncopated Musical Show." The program stated: "plot—if any—by Harry B.

Smith." The show, which was really a revue, starred that great dance team of this era, Vernon and Irene Castle. One of the songs from the score, the counterpoint number "Play a Simple Melody," eventually became a standard. Frank Tinney and a *Follies* beauty, Justine Johnson, were also in the cast. The jazzy musical played for 175 performances.

The *Ziegfeld Follies of 1915* boasted a number of outstanding attributes. It was the first *Follies* with sets by the famed European designer Joseph Urban (who would later design the glorious Ziegfeld Theatre, the Central Park Casino, and the St. Regis Hotel Roof). The revue starred W. C. Fields, Ina Claire, Ed Wynn, Bert Williams, Leon Errol, and Billie Burke (Ziegfeld's second wife).

In 1916 Sir Herbert Tree and Company played Shakespeare's *Henry VIII*, *The Merchant of Venice*, and *The Merry Wives of Windsor* at this theatre. The company included Constance Collier, Henrietta Crosman, and Elsie Ferguson. This was followed by the *Ziegfeld Follies of 1916*, which had Fanny Brice (in her third *Follies* appearance), surrounded by the revue's usual beauties. Among the Ziegfeld glorified girls: the actress Marion Davies, who also gained fame as the mistress of William Randolph Hearst.

Miss Springtime, a 1916 musical by Guy Bolton and Emmerich Kálmán, starring Ada Mae Weeks and Charles Meakins, delighted audiences for 224 performances. The *Ziegfeld Follies of 1917* was distinguished by the first appearance of Will Rogers in the series, surrounded by Eddie Cantor, Fanny Brice, W. C. Fields, Peggy Hopkins, Lilyan Tashman, and Ann Pennington.

The Cohan Revue of 1918 had book, music, and lyrics by George M. Cohan, with additional songs by Irving Berlin. Starring Nora Bayes,

Charles Winninger, and Frederic Santley, it ran for ninety-six performances. Sydney Greenstreet and Laura Hamilton appeared next in a musical called *The Rainbow Girl*, by Rennold Wolf and Louis A. Hirsch, which played for eighty-seven performances.

Will Rogers's monologues, which he delivered while displaying his agility with a lasso, were so topical and popular that he appeared again in the *Follies of 1918* and in many succeeding editions. Another bright star to grace this revue was the lovely dancer/singer Marilyn Miller. Two musical hits followed the *Follies*. *The Girl Behind the Gun*, with book and lyrics by the popular team of Guy Bolton and P. G. Wodehouse, and music by Ivan Caryll, played for 160 performances. *The Velvet Lady*, with music by Victor Herbert, book by Frederick Jackson, and lyrics by Henry Blossom, lasted for 136 performances.

The *Follies of 1919* was considered by critics to be the finest of the series. It introduced an Irving Berlin song that was to become the signature number not only for the *Follies*, but also for countless beauty pageants: "A Pretty Girl Is Like a Melody." The show's other hits included "Mandy," "You'd Be Surprised," and "You Cannot Make Your Shimmy Shake on Tea." It was the last *Follies* in which the popular comic Bert Williams and Marilyn Miller (soon to become Broadway's greatest musical comedy star) appeared. It ran for 171 performances.

In 1919 a musical version of Booth Tarkington's short story *Monsieur Beaucaire* played for 143 performances, followed by *Ed Wynn's Carnival*, a revue that starred Wynn and Marion Davies. Wynn not only starred in it, but also wrote the dialogue and songs. It ran for sixty-four performances. The 1920 *Follies* starred Fannie Brice and comedienne Ray Dooley, who really originated the baby-talk character later immortalized by Brice both in the *Follies* and on the radio as Baby Snooks. Joseph Urban's elaborate settings were becoming works of art, and Ben Ali Haggin's tableaux (featuring near-nude showgirls in historic settings) were the talk of Broadway.

On December 21, 1920, one of the New Amsterdam's most illustrious hits arrived. It was *Sally*, with music by Jerome Kern and Victor Herbert, book by Clifford Grey, and the luminous Marilyn Miller starring in her greatest success. It made her the queen of Broadway musicals in the 1920s. She played a poor girl who worked as a waitress, and while she washed dishes she sang one of Kern's most enduring songs: "Look for the Silver Lining." Since Ziegfeld was the producer, the waitress ended up as a glamorous *Follies* girl. This gem ran for 570 performances—just two fewer than Ziegfeld's masterpiece, *Show Boat*.

The 1922 *Follies* introduced the comedy team of Gallagher and Shean, who stopped the revue with their comic routine of smart-aleck questions and answers in thick accents. Dancer Gilda Gray and Will Rogers also starred in this edition. The 1923 *Follies* was considered one of the weakest by the critics, but, surprisingly, it ran for 333 performances. (Tallies of the performance totals for *Follies* editions vary.) Perhaps the fact that Paul Whiteman and His Orchestra were in the pit hyped its popularity.

In 1924 the popular singer Vivienne Segal joined the *Follies*. Strangely, although it was neither a critical nor artistic success, it enjoyed the longest run (401 performances) of any *Follies* produced by Ziegfeld himself. (In 1943 the *Follies* produced by the Shuberts at the Winter Garden broke all records for this revue series, running 553 performances. It starred Milton Berle, Ilona Massey, Jack Cole, and Arthur Treacher.)

In 1925 singer Ethel Shutta joined the revue. (She would stop Sondheim's 1971 *Follies* with her rendition of the song "Broadway Baby.") Also in this production was the exotic Louise Brooks, who was to become a ravishing cult movie star. On September 22, 1925, Marilyn Miller returned to this theatre in another Jerome Kern/Otto Harbach/Oscar Hammerstein II triumph. Produced by Charles Dillingham, the musical was titled *Sunny*—obviously trading on the success of *Sally*. This time Miss Miller played a British circus rider who stows away on a United States—bound boat to be with her lover. Others in the cast: Jack Donahue, Paul Frawley, and the dance team of Clifton Webb and Mary Hay. The show's hit song was Kern's "Who?" sung by Miller. The musical was the season's hot ticket and ran for 517 performances.

A curious musical opened in 1926. Called *Betsy*, it had a book by Irving Caesar and David Freedman and a score by Rodgers and Hart (with an interpolated number by Irving Berlin, "Blue Skies," that turned out to be the show's only hit.) In fact, one critic was so tone-deaf that he recommended Hart get a new composer, since

Above: Walter Huston and Brian Aherne as Othello and Iago in *Othello* (1937), the final legitimate production at the New Amsterdam for 60 years.

Above: Sheet music for Schwartz and Dietz's "Love Louisa," a hit from *The Band Wagon* (1931).

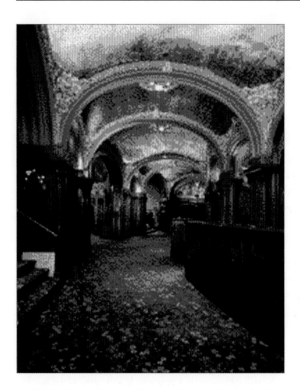

Rodgers's music wasn't as fine as Hart's lyrics. The show starred Belle Baker and Al Shean and closed after only thirty-nine performances.

Another curiosity was a 1927 musical called *Lucky*, by Otto Harbach, Bert Kalmar, and Harry Ruby, with a score by Jerome Kern. Ruby Keeler and Walter Catlett starred in it, and the program lists a song sung by Miss Keeler with the eyebrow-raising title "The Man in the Moon Is a Coon." In later years Keeler denied singing this politically incorrect number. The show ran for just seventy-one performances.

The *Ziegfeld Follies of 1927* was the last of this revue series to play at the New Amsterdam Theatre. Eddie Cantor not only starred in it, but also wrote most of the script, while Irving Berlin composed the score. It cost a then-staggering $289,000 to mount. Chiefly remembered about the spectacle was the sight of dancer Claire Luce making her startling entrance riding a live ostrich with a bejeweled collar across a jungle setting. Ruth Etting sang the catchy "Shaking the Blues Away," and Cantor did his customary numbers in black-face. Since he was doing so many numbers in the revue and had written much of it, he felt he should be paid more. He quit the show, was hauled before Actors' Equity, and lost his case. The show closed after 167 performances. He and Ziegfeld later made up.

Marilyn Miller returned to the New Amsterdam in the new musical *Rosalie*, with a score by George and Ira Gershwin, Sigmund Romberg, and P. G. Wodehouse. The book was by Guy Bolton and William Anthony McGuire. Miss Miller played a princess studying at an American college, who falls in love with a West Point lieutenant. Since it was a Ziegfeld production, the musical was opulently produced. Frank Morgan played her father, a comic king, a role he repeated in the movie version with a score by Cole Porter. Two Gershwin songs are remembered from the score: "How Long Has This Been Going On?" and "Oh, Gee! Oh, Joy!" It ran for 327 performances.

One of the most cherished 1920s musicals came to this theatre on December 4, 1928: *Whoopee!*, which proved to be Eddie Cantor's greatest success. The show was based on a hit play, *The Nervous Wreck*, by Owen Davis. The hero (Cantor's role) was an extreme hypochondriac who got into all sorts of comic situations because of his imaginary affliction. The book was by one of Ziegfeld's favorite writers, William Anthony McGuire, and the great score was by Walter Donaldson and Gus Kahn. Supporting Cantor were Ruth Etting, Ethel Shutta, and, in a small role, Buddy Ebsen. The title song, "Makin' Whoopee!" became Cantor's signature tune. Other hits from the show: "Love Me or Leave Me" and "I'm Bringing a Red Red Rose." The show's Wild West locale inspired Ziegfeld to have his glorified girls ride real horses and to have Joseph Urban to design memorable sets, including one of the Grand Canyon. John Harkrider's costumes also stunned the audience. This musical-comedy gem ran for 379 performances. Ziegfeld teamed with Sam Goldwyn to make a Technicolor movie (one of the first) of the show—also a big hit.

The next tenant at the New Amsterdam was a revival of *Sherlock Holmes* written by and starring William Gillette. Gillette made this play a perennial of his, just as James O'Neill (Eugene's father) made *The Count of Monte Cristo* his annuity.

The popular Stone family—Fred, his wife, and his daughter Dorothy—starred next in a musical called *Ripples*. Fred played the great-great-grandson of Rip Van Winkle, who is an alcoholic. The book was written by William Anthony McGuire, and the score was by Oscar Levant and Albert Sirmay, with lyrics by Irving Caesar and Graham John. There were interpolated songs by Jerome Kern, Fred Coots, Howard Dietz, and Arthur Schwartz. Despite all these noteworthy contributors, the musical died after fifty-five performances.

In July 1930 one of Ziegfeld's archrivals, Earl Carroll, opened one of his celebrated *Vanities* revues at the New Amsterdam. (Ziegfeld had meanwhile erected his magnificent Ziegfeld Theater on Sixth Avenue and Fifty-fourth Street in 1927 and was producing his shows there, including his last *Follies* in 1931.)

Stars in the *Vanities* included Jack Benny, Jimmy Savo, and Patsy Kelly. The songs were written by Harold Arlen, E. Y. Harburg, Jay Gorney, and Ted Koehler, and the sketches were by Eddie Welch and Eugene Conrad. The costumes were by Vincente Minnelli and Charles Le Maire and the scenery by Hugh Willoughby. The revue was extremely vulgar and ran into censorship problems. The first-act finale featured a huge glass swimming tank in which a male swimmer pursued two showgirls who appeared to be nude. Carroll was forced to launder this scene and some of the blue sketches, but the revue benefitted from all the publicity and ran for 215 performances.

Next at this theatre was a revival of J. M. Barrie's popular play *The Admirable Crichton* with a sterling cast: Walter Hampden, Fay Bainter, Estelle Winwood, and Effie Shannon. It played for fifty-six performances.

On June 3, 1931, a great event occurred at the New Amsterdam: the opening of *The Band Wagon*. To this day it is considered one of the two greatest revues produced on Broadway. (The other was the Moss Hart/Irving Berlin production *As Thousands Cheer* in 1933.) The brilliant score by Dietz and Schwartz and hilarious sketches by George S. Kaufman—and the stellar cast headed by Fred and Adele Astaire (her last Broadway appearance), Frank Morgan, Helen Broderick, and the enchanting Austrian dancer Tilly Losch—thrilled critics and audiences with their artistry and intelligence. Albert Johnson's magnificent sets (two revolving stages and a carousel) garnered raves, as did Hassard Short's staging and Albertina Rasch's choreography. The memorable score included "Dancing in the Dark," "I Love Louisa" (sung by the principals on a revolving carousel), "New Sun in the Sky," and "High and Low." The Astaires performed a witty song called "Hoops" while rolling hoops on the revolving stage, and Fred and Tilly Losch dazzled in a ballet called "The Beggar's Waltz." Kaufman's sketches were models of hilarity, and the entire production was a theatrical highlight of the 1930s. It ran for 260

performances.

Next came Irving Berlin and Moss Hart's musical *Face the Music*, their first collaboration. It was a political satire with Mary Boland as the filthy-rich Mrs. Meshbesher, married to a policeman whose wealth was achieved by graft. In one scene, Boland arrived onstage riding a gigantic papier-mâché elephant. A clever scene showed social figures burned by the Wall Street crash, eating at an automat and singing one of the show's hit songs, "Let's Have Another Cup of Coffee." Another hit was "Soft Lights and Sweet Music." Staged by Hassard Short and George S. Kaufman, the musical ran for 165 performances.

Walter Hampden, who had played *Cyrano de Bergerac* for years in New York and on tour, revived it once again at this theatre in 1932. Another revival, Eva Le Gallienne's Civic Repertory Theatre production of *Alice in Wonderland*, moved here from downtown and played for sixty-four performances. In addition to Le Gallienne, the outstanding cast included Alla Nazimova, Burgess Meredith, Joseph Schildkraut, and Josephine Hutchinson. This same company appeared in a revival of *The Cherry Orchard*, which followed *Alice in Wonderland*. Both these productions had sets by the famed designer Aline Bernstein.

Earl Carroll returned to the New Amsterdam in 1933 with a novelty. Called *Murder at the Vanities*, it depicted a series of murders backstage at the opening night of a *Vanities* revue. The book was by Carroll and Rufus King, and the score by no fewer than nine writers. In the cast were future movie star Robert Cummings, James Rennie, Jean Adair, and horror-film idol Bela Lugosi. One of the songs—"Weep No More My Baby," by John W. Green and Edward Heyman—became popular. The show ran for 298 performances.

The next musical at this theatre proved that a hit song can turn a lukewarm show into a hit. This was the case for *Roberta*, with Jerome Kern and Otto Harbach's immortal "Smoke Gets in Your Eyes," radiantly sung by Tamara. Kern supplied other gems: "The Touch of Your Hand," "Yesterdays," and "You're Devastating." The superlative cast in addition to Tamara included Bob Hope, George Murphy, Fred MacMurray, Fay Templeton, Ray Middleton, Alan Jones, and Sydney Greenstreet. The plot by Otto Harbach was considered weak. It was based on Alice Duer Miller's novel *Gowns by Roberta* and told of an American halfback (Ray Middleton) who inherits his Aunt Minnie's haute couture shop in Paris and goes there with his friends (including comic Bob Hope) to run it. He falls in love with his aunt's assistant, a Russian princess (Tamara), and starts to run the shop with her until complications set in. On the musical's opening night, Noël Coward walked up the aisle and spotted Max Gordon, its producer. Coward, with his usual bitchiness, shouted, "It stinks, Max." The show cost a staggering $115,000 in Depression dollars to mount and featured an elaborate fashion show that helped the box office. It ran for 295 performances.

The next musical at the New Amsterdam arrived with a touch of scandal. It was called *Revenge with Music* by Howard Dietz and Arthur Schwartz. It starred torch singer Libby Holman, who had been accused of fatally shooting her wealthy husband, a Reynolds tobacco heir, but was acquitted. This was to be her Broadway comeback after having scored in such lauded revues as *The Little Show* and

Three's a Crowd. Although the score included such hits as "You and the Night and the Music" and "If There Is Someone Lovelier Than You," the book's libretto was criticized. Holman was supported by Charles Winninger, George Metaxa, and Ilka Chase.

The spicy tale told of Winninger trying to woo Holman away from her new husband on their wedding night, and the groom (Metaxa) seeking revenge by having a romance with Winninger's wife (Chase). The musical played for 158 performances and, despite its cost, recouped its investment.

Another Ziegfeld rival—George White—came to the New Amsterdam with one of his *Scandals* series in 1935. This one starred Rudy Vallee, Bert Lahr, and Willie and Eugene Howard. The revue format was beginning to wane, and the critics were not enchanted with this latest example. There were no hit songs, and much of the comic material had been seen before in other revues. It nevertheless had a run of 110 performances.

Ashley Brown as Mary Poppins, Alexander Scheitinger as Michael, Katherine Leigh Doherty as Jane, and Gavin Lee as Bert in the stage adaptation of *Mary Poppins* (2007). (Photo by Joan Marcus)

Walter Hampden once again brought his production of *Cyrano de Bergerac* to the New Amsterdam in 1936. This time it ran for forty performances.

Unfortunately, the last two legitimate shows to play the New Amsterdam before it became a movie theatre were not successful. On November 2, 1936, *Forbidden Melody*, an operetta by Sigmund Romberg and Otto Harbach, limped into the theatre and was judged old-fashioned and maudlin by the critics. Operettas, like revues, were becoming passé.

The last production at this theatre for many years should have been outstanding. It was *Othello*, with Walter Huston as the Moor of Venice, his wife Nan Sunderland as Desdemona, and Brian Aherne as Iago. Despite the fact that the eminent scenic designer Robert Edmond Jones designed and directed the production, it was not well received. Huston's Othello was considered weak. Aherne's Iago received better notices—but not good enough to save the show. The revival opened January 6, 1937, and closed after just twenty-one performances.

The Depression took a heavy toll on the once-glittering acropolis of theatres on West Forty-second Street. Most had switched to burlesque or movies. By 1937 the New Amsterdam was the last legitimate house on the block—and then it, too, succumbed, and its bright history as a Broadway theatre seemed to come to an end. The Abe Erlanger estate, probably for financial reasons, turned the theatre over to the Dry Dock Savings Bank, which sold it to Max A. Cohen, with the proviso that the theatre was never to house burlesque. It never did. After extensive renovations and a new marquee, the theatre's first film booking was ironic. In 1903 the New Amsterdam had opened with a live production of *A Midsummer Night's Dream*. Its first film was Max Reinhardt's movie of the Shakespeare comedy. It had an all-star Warner Brothers cast: Mickey Rooney, James Cagney, Joe E. Brown, Olivia De Havilland, and countless others, along with Mendelssohn's familiar score.

The deterioration of the New Amsterdam over the ensuing half-century was one of Forty-second Street's greatest tragedies. In 1979, after decades of showing action films (but no pornography), the interior and exterior of the theatre were declared New York City landmarks, but the decline continued. In 1982 the Nederlander Organization bought the the-

Tony Award nominee Tsidii Le Loka as Rafiki in *The Lion King* (1997).

atre, hoping to restore it and stage lavish musicals there. Meanwhile, the rooftop theatre was being used to rehearse Broadway plays. There were plans to restore the theatre, and producer Alexander H. Cohen stated that his production of *La Tragédie de Carmen* would open there. However, it was discovered that the rooftop theatre had structural flaws, and Cohen had to move his production to Lincoln Center. It looked like only a miracle would ever save the New Amsterdam and its neighbors.

With the redevelopment of the Times Square area, the miracle happened. The New Amsterdam had decayed miserably and was closed for ten years. But in 1992 the 42nd Street Development Project bought the theatre, and Hardy Holzman Pfeiffer Associates was hired to restore the house to soundness. The Walt Disney Company began to eye the theatre as a possible venue for its planned spectacular Broadway musicals. Walt Disney CEO Michael Eisner took a now-legendary tour of the New Amsterdam and was so impressed (and saddened) by what he saw that he resolved that the former "House Beautiful" must be restored. Combining with the 42nd Street Development Project (which contributed a loan of $26 million), Disney kicked in with $36 million. Disney also received a forty-nine-year lease on the theatre. Famed architect Hugh Hardy was engaged to achieve the restoration, and a large crew of workers was assembled. For a complete report on this epic restoration, read Mary C. Henderson's magnificent book *The New Amsterdam: The Biography of a Broadway Theatre* (Hyperion), the most beautiful book on a Broadway theatre ever published.

On May 18, 1997, with much media hoopla, the House Beautiful, restored to its original splendor, reopened for nine performances of *King David* (a concert) by Alan Menken and Tim Rice. The high praise in the press was for the stupendous restoration of the theatre, but not for *King David*. This was followed by a short debut engagement of the animated Disney film *Hercules*.

On November 13, 1997, Disney's magnificent production of *The Lion King* opened to jubilant reviews. Ziegfeld would have been proud. Brilliantly directed by Julie Taymor, with costumes, masks, and puppet designs by her, the production was a magical adaptation of the popular Disney animated film of the same name about trouble in a realm of talking African animals. The book was by Roger Allers and Irene Mecchi, and the score was by Elton John and Tim Rice. The highest praise went to Taymor for the enchanting parade of faux animals down the aisles at the show's opening, a sight never before seen in a Broadway theatre.

For her artistic triumph, Taymor won two Tony Awards: one for her direction and another for her costumes. *The Lion King* also won the Best Musical Tony Award; Best Scenic Designer (Richard Hudson); Best Lighting (Donald Holder); and Best Choreographer (Garth Fagan). The musical also received these Tony Award nominations: Featured Musical Actor (Samuel E. Wright), Featured Musical Actress (Tsidii Le Loka), Musical Book (Allers and Mecchi), and Best Score (Elton John, Tim Rice, Lebo M, Mark Mancina, Jay Rifkin, Julie Taymor, and Hans Zimmer).

The Lion King immediately became the hottest ticket in town and was still selling out nightly in 2006 when Disney transferred it to the Minskoff Theatre to make way for a British adaptation of the P. L. Travers books and Disney musical film of *Mary Poppins*. It's the tale of a magical English nanny who helps the family of a stuffy banker rediscover what's really important in life. Ashley Brown played the "practically perfect" governess who thrilled audiences young and old when she opened her umbrella and made one of Broadway's great exits, flying over the heads of the orchestra and even the balcony as the east wind swept her away. Songs from the original film score by brothers Richard M. Sherman and Robert B. Sherman (such as Oscar winner "Chim Chim Cheree") were joined by several new songs by composer George Stiles and lyricist Anthony Drewe.

Mary Poppins opened November 16, 2006, and was still running as this edition of *At This Theatre* went to press.

And the House Beautiful, having risen from its ashes like the proverbial phoenix, will continue to dazzle playgoers for decades to come.

Two postscripts to the history of this theatre must be added. First is the legend that it is a haunted house. In his book *Ziegfeld*, Charles Higham reported that in 1952 a handyman at the theatre was alarmed by the appearance of a beautiful, ghostly showgirl in a white dress with a gold sash on which appeared the name "Olive." When he followed her, she vanished. Two weeks later, the apparition returned. Another worker identified her as Olive Thomas, a statuesque Follies girl whom he knew and adored. She had committed suicide in Paris, reportedly after discovering that her husband, Jack Pickford (Mary's brother), had given her syphilis. During the restoration of the New Amsterdam in the 1990s, a crewman on the project called PLAYBILL and stated that there had been spooky incidents in the theatre while he worked. Things moved mysteriously backstage, and a woman's voice behind him asked, "Hey—how're you doin'?" He turned around and no one was there.

Olive remains active at the theatre through the publication of this edition, appearing regularly to performers and backstage workers (generally males) and making her occasional displeasure known to staff with acts of mischief. As a result, house manager Dana Amendola posted framed photographs of Olive Thomas inside each of the theatre's entrances so employees can greet her with a daily "Good evening" to stay in her good graces.

Reports of ghosts in theatres are not unusual. The ghost of David Belasco is still often spotted in the Belasco Theatre, and the ghost of Enrico Caruso has been seen in the Brooklyn Academy of Music. Fortunately, they generally do not disrupt performances.

A much happier reappearance of *Follies* alumnae will bring the history of the New Amsterdam full circle. On April 13 and 14, 1998, five original Follies showgirls, Nona Otero Friedman, Yvonne Arden Hyde, Lucile Layton Zinman, Eleanor Dana O'Connell, and Doris Eaton Travis, some in their nineties, returned to the New Amsterdam stage as special guests of that year's Broadway Cares/Equity Fights AIDS Easter Bonnet Competition. Travis led a company of young gypsies in performing the original choreography from "Mandy" and became a fixture of the event in succeeding annual editions well past her one hundredth birthday.

PALACE
THEATRE

"PLAYING THE PALACE"—IT WAS THE dream of every vaudeville performer. In its heyday, from 1913 until the 1930s, the "mecca of migrating minstrels" at Forty-seventh Street and Times Square booked everyone who was anyone—from Sarah Bernhardt to Trixie Friganza and her bag of Trix, from Ethel Barrymore to Dr. Rockwell ("Quack! Quack! Quack!").

The Palace was the dream house of impresario Martin Beck, but by the time it opened he held only 25 percent interest in the theatre. By complex wheeling and dealing, vaudeville circuit mogul B. F. Keith and E. F. Albee (playwright Edward Albee's adoptive grandfather) stormed the Palace and gained control.

In her book *The Palace*, Marian Spitzer describes the opening of the theatre on Easter Monday, March 24, 1913: "The theatre itself, liv-

ing up to advance publicity, was spacious, handsome and lavishly decorated in crimson and gold. But nothing happened that afternoon to suggest the birth of a great theatrical tradition."

On the Palace's opening vaudeville bill, presented twice daily with a $1.50 top at matinees and $2.00 at night, were such acts as Ota Gygi ("the court violinist of Spain"), McIntyre and Harty ("a comedy team"), La Napierkowska ("pantomimist and interpretive dancer"), *The Eternal Walk* ("a condensed Viennese operetta with a cast of 30"), and Ed Wynn ("The King's Jester"). It was the hope of the Palace Theatre management to give competition to its chief rival, Oscar Hammerstein's Victoria Theatre at Broadway and Forty-second Street, but it did not achieve this goal during its opening week. The show was negatively received, especially by *Variety*, the show business Bible, which lamented the poor quality of the acts and the outrageous $2.00 top.

It took the prestige of two major legitimate theatre actresses to put the Palace on the map. In its sixth week, the theatre presented "the First Lady of the American Theatre"—Ethel Barrymore—in a one-act play by Richard Harding Davis, *Miss Civilization*, and business began to improve. But the turning point came on May 5, when the Divine Sarah Bernhardt brought her French company of actors and her repertoire to the Palace and caused a sensation for almost a month. It was her first appearance in vaudeville in New York. She saved the Palace from disaster and helped turn it into the foremost vaudeville theatre in the world.

B.F. KEITH'S PALACE THEATRE

NEXT WEEK
COMMENCING MONDAY MATINEE, JULY 9, 1923

QUEEN PARAMOUNT OF THE AMERICAN STAGE
THE FIRST LADY OF THE THEATRE

ETHEL BARRYMORE

In Sir James Matthew Barrie's One-Act Play

"THE TWELVE POUND ($60) LOOK"

Most Distinguished Engagement of the Season

PROGRAM

In the golden era of vaudeville, the Palace stage saw the likes of such great headliners as Harry Houdini, Will Rogers, W. C. Fields, Fanny Brice, Sophie Tucker, Ethel Merman, William Gaxton, Eddie Cantor, Jack Benny, Milton Berle, Smith and Dale, the Marx Brothers, Kate Smith, and countless others. Burns and Allen arrived with a new act every season. And then there were other acts, like Fink's Mules and Power's Elephants.

The Palace was the queen of Broadway in

Above: PLAYBILL covers for Christopher Plummer in the musical *Cyrano* (1973) and Bette Midler in concert (1973).

Left: Gwen Verdon in her hit *Sweet Charity*, which made the Palace "legitimate" (1966);

Right: Lauren Bacall played a Tony Award recipient in *Applause* (1970).

Above: PLAYBILL covers for the 1977 revival of *Man of La Mancha* and the huge success *La Cage aux Folles* (1983).

1927 when a talking picture called *The Jazz Singer* opened a few blocks uptown. Once the silver screen began to talk, vaudeville was on its way out.

From the 1930s on, it was a constant struggle for survival. The Palace tried a little of everything—combination bills of movies and vaudeville shows, then just movies, and finally, in the 1950s, personal appearances by select

superstars. The first arrived on the night of October 16, 1951, and her name was Judy Garland. She scored a triumph and played the Palace for nineteen weeks. Next came Betty Hutton, then Danny Kaye (fourteen weeks), followed by return engagements of Hutton and Garland. Jerry Lewis was a hit with his personal-appearance show, but Liberace failed to draw crowds.

On August 13, 1957, the Palace reverted to showing movies, with no vaudeville, and interrupted this policy only once, starting December 15, 1959, when Harry Belafonte made a sensational appearance for more than three months. During this period the building was allowed to deteriorate.

On August 19, 1965, a miracle happened. James Nederlander, acting for the Nederlander family, who owned legitimate theatres in Detroit and Chicago, bought the Palace. At great expense, he had it beautifully restored to its original crimson and gold. Crystal chandeliers were removed from storage and rehung in the theatre, stage boxes that had been concealed for decades by false fronts were restored, and the lobby was refurbished and embellished with portraits of Palace greats, loaned by the Museum of the City of New York. The restoration of the Palace was achieved by the famed scene designer Ralph Alswang. When he and his workers were through, the Palace was ready for its first legitimate show.

The reopening of the Palace as a legitimate theatre on January 29, 1966, was a major news event covered by television cameras and print media. Fortunately, the opening show was *Sweet Charity*, starring the great Gwen Verdon. Both the musical and the restored Palace were huge hits. With a book by Neil Simon, a jaunty score by Cy Coleman and Dorothy Fields, and spectacular choreography by Verdon's husband, Bob Fosse, the musical, based on Fellini's film *Nights of Cabiria*,

brightened the Messrs. Nederlanders' Palace for 608 performances.

In July 1967 Judy Garland returned in a production called *At Home at the Palace*, followed later that summer by a double bill of Eddie Fisher and Buddy Hackett.

Don Ameche and Carol Bruce, aided by three talented young girls—Alice Playten, Neva Small, and Robin Wilson—were engaging

Left: Beth Fowler as Mrs. Potts in one of the fanciful costumes for *Beauty and the Beast* (1994). (Photo by Joan Marcus)

Right: Adam Pascal and Heather Headley (Tony Award) in *Aida* (2000). (Photo by Joan Marcus)

Hugh Panaro (center) as Lestat leads the cast in "Welcome To The New World" from the vampire musical *Lestat* (2006). (Photo by Paul Kolnik)

Left to right: Special PLAYBILL cover for George Abbott's centennial celebration in June 1987.

PLAYBILL covers for *The Will Rogers Follies* (1992) and *Beauty and the Beast* (1994).

Susan Egan, as Belle, begins to tame the Beast (Terrence Mann) in *Beauty and the Beast*. (Photo by Joan Marcus)

in a musical called *Henry, Sweet Henry* (1967), but the show lasted only 80 performances. The Grand Music Hall of Israel paid a visit in the early months of 1968. Then, on April 10, *George M!* took over. It is ironic that George M. Cohan was one of the few headliners who never played the Palace. (Al Jolson was another.) But Cohan was skillfully impersonated by Joel Grey in *George M!* He strutted the Palace stage for 433 performances.

Lauren Bacall gave such a cyclonic performance in *Applause* (1970), her first Broadway musical, that she was awarded a Tony for her tour de force. It was a case of life imitating art, as the show included a scene of her character accepting a Tony Award. The musical, with a book by Betty Comden and Adolph Green and a score by Charles Strouse and Lee Adams, was based on the celebrated Bette Davis film *All About Eve*. Supported by Len Cariou, Bonnie Franklin, Penny Fuller, and Lee Roy Reams, Bacall flourished at the Palace for eighteen months, and the show continued for eight months more.

During the 1970s, superstars such as Bette Midler, Josephine Baker, Shirley MacLaine, and Diana Ross made splashy Palace appearances. Legitimate attractions included Christopher Plummer in his Tony Award—winning performance in the title role of the musical *Cyrano* (1973); Carol Channing in a revised version of *Gentlemen Prefer Blondes*, called *Lorelei* (1974); Richard Kiley in a return engagement of *Man of La Mancha* (1977); Joel Grey in *The Grand Tour* (1979), a musical version of *Jacobowsky and the Colonel*; a lively revival of *Oklahoma!* (1979); and a colossal production of *Frankenstein* (1981), starring John Carradine, that closed on its opening night.

Lauren Bacall returned to the Palace in *Woman of the Year*, a musical version of the

popular 1942 film of the same name starring Spencer Tracy and Katharine Hepburn. Bacall's costar in the musical was Harry Guardino. The show won four Tonys: Outstanding Actress in a Musical (Bacall), Outstanding Featured Actress in a Musical (Marilyn Cooper), Best Musical Book (Peter Stone), and Best Musical Score (John Kander and Fred Ebb).

On August 21, 1983, the Palace welcomed *La Cage aux Folles*, with a score by Jerry Herman and a book by Harvey Fierstein. A musical version of the popular French film of the same name, it starred George Hearn and Gene Barry as gay lovers and ran for 1,761 performances. It won the following Tony Awards: Best Musical, Best Score, Best Book, Best Direction of a Musical (Arthur Laurents), Best Actor in a Musical (Hearn), and Best Costume Designer (Theoni V. Aldredge).

After being closed for four years for extensive renovations, this historic theatre was beautifully renovated for the opening of the Tony Award—winning musical *The Will Rogers Follies*, starring Keith Carradine as the Hoosier Philosopher and featuring Tony-winning staging by Tommy Tune; a Tony-winning score by Coleman, Comden, and Green; and a Tony Award—winning book by Peter Stone. The show used the format of the *Ziegfeld Follies* (Ziegfeld himself was a character) to tell the story of Rogers's marriage, career, and dramatic demise in a plane crash. The musical ran for 983 performances.

This was followed by the spectacular musical *Beauty and the Beast* (1994), which broke box-office records at this theatre and introduced children of all ages to the wonders of live Broadway entertainment. Adapted from the animated Disney film of the same title, the show marked composer Alan Menken's Broadway debut and the inaugural presentation of Walt Disney Theatrical Productions, soon to become a powerhouse producer on Broadway. Susan Egan was the first of many Belles. As the Beast, Terrence Mann appeared to make a magical full-body transformation in full view of the audience each night. The show transferred in 1999 to the Lunt-Fontanne Theatre.

From December 1, 1999, to January 2, 2000, Liza Minnelli returned to the scene of her mother, Judy Garland's, triumph. However, her show, *Minnelli On Minnelli*, paid tribute to her father, Vincente Minnelli, the celebrated Broadway and Hollywood director. Supported

by six male singer/dancers, Minnelli performed memorable songs from her father's famed film musicals—*Meet Me in St. Louis*, *An American in Paris*, *The Bandwagon*, *Gigi*, and others. The revue was directed by her friend the lyricist Fred Ebb and had costumes by Bob Mackie and musical arrangements by Marvin Hamlisch.

On March 23, 2000, Hyperion Theatricals (a division of Walt Disney Theatrical Productions) presented a lavish new musical, *Aida*, with music by Elton John and lyrics by Tim Rice. Suggested by Verdi's classic opera about a fatal love triangle involving two princesses and a handsome

Above: left to right, Kate Shindle, Richard H. Blake, Laura Bell Bundy, and Michael Rupert confront each other in the courtroom in *Legally Blonde* (2007). (Photo by Paul Kolnik)

Bottom: Cody Green (center, as Riff) and the Jets perform "Cool" in the 2009 revival of *West Side Story*. (Photo by Joan Marcus)

army general in ancient Egypt, the spectacle starred Heather Headley, Adam Pascal, and Sherie René Scott. The musical received five Tony Award nominations and won the following four: Best Original Score (Elton John, Tim Rice); Best Scenic Design (Bob Crowley); Best Lighting Design (Natasha Katz); and Best Leading Actress in a Musical (Headley). It settled in for a run of 1,852 performances.

What do Elvis Presley and William Shakespeare have in common? *All Shook Up*, the musical very roughly based on *Twelfth Night* that raided the Elvis songbook for a score. The unlikely combination had a book by Joe DiPietro and featured heartthrob Cheyenne Jackson in his first starring role. *All Shook Up* opened March 2, 2005, and stayed at the Palace for 213 performances.

In April 2006, composer Elton John had his first and (to date) only Broadway flop with *Lestat*, based on Anne Rice's best-selling *The Vampire Chronicles*. Despite powerful performances from Hugh Panaro and Carolee Carmello, as well as some impressive special effects, the critics pounded in their hawthorn stakes and the show withered after only thirty-nine performances. *Lestat* was the second of three unsuccessful vampire musicals that haunted Broadway in this decade.

Husband-and-wife Off-Broadway songwriters Laurence O'Keefe and Nell Benjamin made their Broadway splash on April 27, 2007, with *Legally Blonde*, a musical adaptation of the hit film comedy about a seemingly dim-bulb, clothes-obsessed party girl who sets herself the goal of getting into Harvard Law School in order to win back her ex-boyfriend, who found her too shallow. With a book by Heather Hach, *Legally Blonde* attracted a devoted following, especially among teenaged girls, and ran 595 performances. Laura Bell Bundy led a cast that included Christian Borle, Michael Rupert, and Orfeh. Late in the run, fans helped choose Bundy's successor via a TV reality show, and winner Bailey Hanks got to play the "Omigod you guys!" role for the last three months of the run. During its run the show took the unusual step of allowing itself to be taped for broadcast on cable TV.

Just as Liza Minnelli's 2000 Palace show saluted her father, her December 2008 concert show, *Liza's at the Palace . . .*, was a bouquet of roses to her godmother, polymath Hollywood favorite Kaye Thompson, known for singing, dancing, arranging music, designing clothes, and even writing the "Eloise" series of classic children's books. For this show Minnelli reminisced about Thompson and, for Act II, recreated highlights of Thompson's nightclub show, to the delight of Minnelli's legion of fans. Though it stayed for only twenty-two performances, *Liza's at the Palace . . .* won the 2009 Tony Award as Best Theatrical Event. A subsequent Las Vegas production was taped for broadcast on cable TV and release on DVD.

As Broadway librettist Arthur Laurents approached his ninetieth birthday in 2008, he went into a frenzy of activity, first directing a revival of his classic *Gypsy* at "Encores!" and the St. James Theatre, and then following it by directing his other great classic, *West Side Story*, at the Palace. The Leonard Bernstein score was performed intact, but lyricist Stephen Sondheim granted Laurents permission to make an unusual change in the lyrics. The verses sung in many places by the Puerto Rican characters were translated into Spanish by Lin-Manuel Miranda, a Tony winner for *In the Heights*. (Most of the English lyrics were restored several months into the run.) Despite mixed reviews upon its March 19, 2009, opening, the production quickly became one of the top-grossing shows on Broadway, and Karen Olivo, another graduate of *In the Heights*, won the Tony Award for Best Featured Actress in a Musical, for her performance as Anita.

Dressed grandly in crimson and gold with marble trimmings, and ruling over the northeast corner of Times Square, the Palace has regained a measure of its vaudeville-era hauteur and is very much in demand for big musicals and concert shows.

RICHARD RODGERS

THEATRE

THROUGH THE EFFORTS OF PRODUCER
Alexander H. Cohen and the Nederlander Organization, the former 46th Street Theatre was renamed the Richard Rodgers in 1990, in honor of the late composer whose music brightened more than three dozen Broadway musicals.

During the 1920s, brothers Irwin S. and Harry I. Chanin, who ran a lucrative construction firm, became interested in show business. They built six legitimate theatres in the short span of five years. One of these was called Chanin's 46th Street Theatre, located at 226 West Forty-sixth Street, and spent many years known simply as the 46th Street Theatre.

The architect was the very busy Herbert J. Krapp, and this time he came up with a novel notion. Instead of building the orchestra level

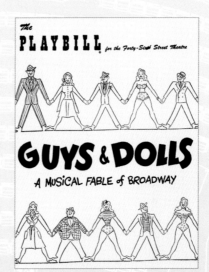

in the style of other theatres, he had the seats—from Row L on—slope upward so that theatregoers in the rear of the orchestra had an excellent view of the stage. The rear section of the orchestra was really as high as a mezzanine, and patrons in that section had to climb stairs to reach their orchestra seats.

According to Brooks Atkinson in his book *Broadway*, the Chanins made critics feel welcome by putting nameplates on the seats they occupied on opening nights. For their opening attraction on Christmas Eve 1924, the brothers chose the 1924 edition of the *Greenwich Village Follies*, which was not new. It had already played at the Shubert and Winter Garden theatres, and it stayed only briefly at the new house.

This theatre was to have a curious history in its early years. It had a policy of booking shows that had played in other theatres first, and, on occasion, these shows had interrupted runs. This was the case with the 46th Street Theatre's second booking. *Is Zat So?*, the long-running comedy about boxing, moved in from the 39th Street Theatre in February 1925 and played until mid-December. On Christmas Eve the latest edition of the *Greenwich Village Follies* opened here and ran until March. Then, on March 15, 1926, *Is Zat So?* reopened at the theatre and stayed until the end of July.

In September 1926 the lurid melodrama *The Shanghai Gesture* moved here from the Shubert and stayed for three months. This was followed by the eminent French team of Sacha Guitry and his wife, Yvonne Printemps, in two plays by Guitry: *Mozart* and a short piece, *Deburau*. The stars alternated these plays with another comedy by Guitry, *L'Illusioniste*. The French company of actors was highly praised.

In March 1927 a tingling thriller called *The*

Spider excited audiences with a novel device. The scene of the play was a vaudeville house, and the murders took place in the audience, with policemen, detectives, and nurses running up and down the aisles during the performance. A theatregoer could attend this play with the wonderful apprehension that he might be seated next to the murderer.

The 46th Street's next tenant, *Baby Mine* (1927), lasted only twelve performances, but it attracted publicity because it marked the return to the stage of Roscoe ("Fatty") Arbuckle, a famed movie comic whose film career was ruined by a notorious sex murder case. The *New York Times* reported that the actor was given "an extremely cordial reception."

September 6, 1927, saw the opening of this theatre's biggest hit to that date—and one of the 1920s' most famous musicals. It was the spirited *Good News*, by the rah-rah team of DeSylva, Brown, Henderson, and Laurence Schwab. To get the audience in the mood for this youthful football scrimmage, the ushers wore college jerseys, and the musicians in George Olsen's nifty jazz orchestra delivered school cheers before the overture. The sappy plot about a dumb football player who has to be tutored in order to pass an exam and be allowed to play in the season's biggest game was enlivened by such durable musical comedy songs as "The Best Things in Life Are Free," "Lucky in Love," "Just Imagine," and two rousing showstoppers, "Good News" and "The Varsity Drag," both sung by a fabulous flapper named Zelma O'Neal.

The four creators of *Good News* scored again in 1929 when they brought *Follow Thru* to this theatre. This time the subject was golf, and they paired Zelma O'Neal with the likable comic Jack Haley, later to achieve immortality as the Tin Man in the film *The Wizard of Oz.*

Above: Henry Fonda and June Walker in *The Farmer Takes a Wife* (1934), the play that won Fonda a Hollywood contract.

Above: Souvenir programs for Gwen Verdon in *Damn Yankees* (1955) and *Redhead* (1959.)

Their big number was the infectious "Button Up Your Overcoat." *Good News* ran for 551 performances; *Follow Thru* for 401. The latter show had a sensational tap dancer in the cast: the young Eleanor Powell.

Christmas night 1929 brought a platinum gift to the 46th Street Theatre: the Broadway debut of Ginger Rogers as Babs Green, a wealthy young thing who stopped the show with a song called "Hot and Bothered." The musical was called *Top Speed*, and it ran for 104 performances.

The enterprising songwriter Billy Rose became a producer in November 1930 by putting his illustrious wife, Fannie Brice, into a revue, *Sweet and Low*, to which he also contributed some excellent lyrics. Brice was a standout, assisted by George Jessel and James Barton.

Another college musical, *You Said It*, breezed into the 46th Street Theatre on January 19, 1931, bringing Lou Holtz, Benny Baker, and the Polish sexpot Lyda Roberti. Roberti stopped the proceedings with her torrid singing of Harold Arlen's "Sweet and Hot."

In 1932 the Chanins lost the 46th Street Theatre and their name no longer graced the marquee. The radiant Margaret Sullavan appeared briefly that year in a drama called *Happy Landing*

and was praised by critic Brooks Atkinson as having fine possibilities as an actress. Two shows from other theatres—*Of Thee I Sing* and *Autumn Crocus* (Richard Nixon's favorite play)—were next, followed by a hit comedy, *She Loves Me Not*, by Howard Lindsay, which took place at Princeton. The lunatic plot involved a nightclub singer (Polly Walters) who hides out in a Princeton dorm because she is wanted as a witness to a murder. Burgess Meredith and John Beal played two students, and the merry campus lark sang for 367 performances.

In October 1934 young actor Henry Fonda finally played a part that attracted attention—Dan Harrow in *The Farmer Takes a Wife*—and his performance got him whisked off to Hollywood to repeat his role in the film version of this play about the Erie Canal. Another future *Oz* star, Margaret Hamilton, went with him to repeat her performance as Lucy Gurget.

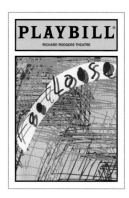

Above: PLAYBILL covers from *Chicago* (1996), *Steel Pier* (1997), and *Footloose* (1998).

Above left: Elizabeth Parkinson and the corps of dancers in Twyla Tharp's *Movin' Out* (2002), based on the music of Billy Joel. (Photo by Joan Marcus)

Cole Porter's smash musical *Anything Goes* moved here in the summer of 1935 from the Alvin (minus Ethel Merman). For several years after this, the 46th Street Theatre had a series of undistinguished plays.

In September 1938 Olsen and Johnson brought their insane show *Hellzapoppin'* to this theatre. The critics hated this rowdy vaudeville revue, but Walter Winchell kept plugging it and turned it into a hit. It was quickly moved to the Winter Garden, where it became Broadway's longest-running musical (1,404 performances) until its record was surpassed by *Oklahoma!*

The 1930s went out in style at this theatre with a ribald Cole Porter triumph called *DuBarry Was a Lady* (1939). The trumpet-voiced Ethel Merman and the baggy-pants clown Bert Lahr played dual roles in this royal fantasy: She was a nightclub singer, May Daly, and DuBarry in the dream sequences; Lahr was Louis Blore, a washroom attendant, and Louis XV, king of France, in the dream scenes. The cast also included Betty Grable, Benny Baker, Ronald Graham, and Charles Walters. Porter's hit songs were "Do I Love You?" and "Friendship."

Porter and Merman struck another lucky vein with their next musical, *Panama Hattie*, at this theatre. It opened in October 1940 and ran for 501 performances. For the first time in her fabulous career, Merman received solo star billing. Her supporting cast included Arthur

Treacher, James Dunn, Betty Hutton, Rags Ragland, and little Joan Carroll, who stopped the show with Merman in their charming duet "Let's Be Buddies." The chorus line for this musical featured such up-and-coming talents as June Allyson, Betsy Blair, Lucille Bremer, Vera-Ellen, Constance Dowling, and Doris Dowling.

In March 1945 an unusual play, *Dark of the Moon*, called "a legend with music," opened to some negative reviews, but the public found this sexual drama—about a witch boy (Richard Hart) who wants to be human so he can marry Barbara (Carol Stone)—fascinating, and it ran for 318 performances.

In 1945 the successful revival of Victor Herbert's *The Red Mill* moved here from the Ziegfeld Theatre and remained for a year. On January 10, 1947, the joyful *Finian's Rainbow* opened and played for 725 performances. This entrancing fantasy about a leprechaun (David Wayne), an Irishman (Albert Sharpe), and his daughter (Ella Logan) was the work of Burton Lane, E. Y. "Yip" Harburg, and Fred Saidy. The memorable score included such delights as "How Are Things in Glocca Morra?," "If This Isn't Love," "Old Devil Moon," "Look to the Rainbow," "When I'm Not Near the Girl I Love," and "Something Sort of Grandish."

Alan Jay Lerner and Kurt Weill supplied the next musical at this theatre, but *Love Life* (1948), starring Nanette Fabray and Ray Middleton, was

Disney's 2006 stage adaptation of *Tarzan* starred Jenn Gambatese as Jane and Josh Strickland as the king of the apes. (Photo by Joan Marcus)

only a moderate success. An opera version of Lillian Hellman's *The Little Foxes*, called *Regina*, by Marc Blitzstein, starring Jane Pickens, Brenda Lewis, William Warfield, and Priscilla Gillette, could muster only 56 performances in 1949. *Arms and the Girl* (1950), a musical version of the play The *Pursuit of Happiness*, was more successful, running for 134 performances. It had a score by Morton Gould and Dorothy Fields, and a book by Herbert and Dorothy Fields; it starred Nanette Fabray, Pearl Bailey, and Georges Guetary.

A landmark musical, *Guys and Dolls*, opened here on November 24, 1950, and stayed put for three years. Earning some of the most vociferous (and unanimous) raves in the history of Broadway, the show escorted audiences into Damon Runyon's urban Neverland of gamblers, gangsters, nightclub singers, and Salvation Army soul-savers who supplied the heartbeat of

old Times Square. Based on a story and characters by Damon Runyon, with a book by Jo Swerling and Abe Burrows, a superb score by Frank Loesser, and witty direction by George S. Kaufman, the show won eight Tony Awards, was named Best Musical by the New York Drama Critics Circle, and ran for 1,200 performances.

In 1954 the lovely Audrey Hepburn illuminated the theatre as a water sprite in Giraudoux's *Ondine*, staged by Alfred Lunt and costarring Hepburn's husband, Mel Ferrer. The play won four Tony Awards, including Best Actress (Hepburn), Best Director (Lunt), Best Costume Designer (Richard Whorf), and Best Set Designer (Peter Larkin).

A revival of the 1936 Rodgers and Hart musical *On Your Toes*, starring Vera Zorina, Bobby Van, and Elaine Stritch, did not wear well in 1954, but Maxwell Anderson's frightening play *The Bad Seed* fascinated audiences for

Kevin Kline played the tragic poet title character in *Cyrano de Bergerac* (2007). (Photo by Carol Rosegg)

334 performances. Little Patty McCormack, as a sweet-as-taffy murderess, got rid of some of the cast. Nancy Kelly, who played her mother, won a Tony Award for her bravery.

From May 5, 1955, until mid-March 1960, this theatre might as well have been renamed the Gwen Verdon Theatre. The great singer/dancer reigned here in three musicals: *Damn Yankees*, *New Girl in Town*, and, after a break for three short-run plays, *Redhead*. Verdon was rewarded for her bravura talents by winning Tony Awards as Best Actress in a Musical in all three shows. The hit musicals also won Tonys for the other creative talents involved.

Highlights of the 1960s at the 46th Street Theatre included Maurice Evans in the musical *Tenderloin* (1960), and the Pulitzer Prize—winning musical *How to Succeed in Business without Really Trying* (1961), by Frank Loesser, Abe Burrows, Jack Weinstock, and Willie Gilbert. Starring Robert Morse and Rudy Vallee, the parody of corporate life played for 1,417 performances.

Do I Hear a Waltz? (1965), the moderately successful musical version of *The Time of the Cuckoo*, was the sole collaboration between songwriting legends of two generations: Richard Rodgers (music) and Stephen Sondheim (lyrics). Arthur Laurents supplied the book, and the musical starred Sergio Franchi, Elizabeth Allen, and Carol Bruce. It ran 220 performances, but there

was no love lost between the two tunesmiths, who rubbed each other the wrong way.

Mary Martin and Robert Preston teamed for the two-character musical *I Do! I Do!* (1966), based on the hit play *The Fourposter*, with a libretto by Tom Jones and music by Harvey Schmidt. The last musical of the 1960s at this theatre, *1776*, the Sherman Edwards/Peter Stone depiction of events leading up to the signing of the Declaration of Independence, was awarded a Tony for Best Musical and ran for 1,217 performances.

The happy 1971 revival of the 1925 musical *No, No, Nanette* brought Ruby Keeler back to the stage in triumph. It ran for 861 performances, far surpassing its first Broadway production, which registered only 329 showings. Keeler sang and tapped and won many accolades for her comeback. Also in the cast was her old friend Patsy Kelly, plus Helen Gallagher, Bobby Van, Jack Gilford, and Susan Watson.

A 1973 revival of *The Women* did not win favor, but *Raisin*, a musical adaptation of Lorraine Hansberry's play *A Raisin in the Sun*, fared better, running for 847 performances and being named Best Musical in the Tony Awards. Virginia Capers also won a Tony for her performance as the family's matriarch. The 1975 revival of *Private Lives*, starring Maggie Smith and John Standing, directed by John Gielgud, won raves and stayed for three months.

A musical version of the 1920s play *Chicago*

Above: PLAYBILL cover for the conjoined twins musical, *Side Show* (1997).

proved a solid hit in 1975, with dazzling choreography and staging by Bob Fosse and an evocative score by John Kander and Fred Ebb. Starring the sensational Gwen Verdon (in a return to the scene of her 1950s triumphs), Chita Rivera, and Jerry Orbach, it ran for 898 performances. It was nominated for eleven Tony Awards but lost them all, mainly to that year's juggernaut, *A Chorus Line. Chicago* would do much better in a 1996 revival, which became one of Broadway's longest-running shows.

The blockbuster *The Best Little Whorehouse in Texas* moved to this theatre in July 1978 from the Entermedia Theatre and stayed for 1,584 performances, making it the 46th Street Theatre's longest-running show. Carlin Glynn and Henderson Forsythe won Tony Awards for their performances.

On May 9, 1982, the offbeat musical *Nine* opened and promptly won Tony Awards for Best Musical, Best Score, Best Direction, Best Costumes, and Best Featured Actress (Liliane Montevecchi). An adaptation of the Fellini film *8½*, this unusual musical had an arresting score by Maury Yeston, an adaptation from the Italian by Mario Fratti, a book by Arthur Kopit, and direction by Tommy Tune. Raul Julia played the Italian film director and lover Guido Contini, a young boy played Guido as a child, and the rest of the cast was composed mainly of the many women in this Don Juan's life. Anita Morris stopped the show with her torrid number "A Call from the Vatican," and Karen Akers, Shelly Burch, Taina Elg, Camille Saviola, and Kathi Moss all had spectacular supporting roles.

From 1983 to 1986 *Brighton Beach Memoirs*, the first part of Neil Simon's trilogy based on his own family, enjoyed a huge success here and won Tony Awards for Matthew Broderick (Best Featured Actor in a Play) and Gene Saks (Direction).

In June 1986 Jean Stapleton and an all-star cast brought hilarity in a revival of the celebrated homicidal comedy *Arsenic and Old Lace*. The following year, August Wilson's powerful play *Fences* won the Pulitzer Prize and Tony Award for Best Play, along with additional Tonys for James Earl Jones (Best Actor in a Play), Mary Alice (Best Featured Actress), and Lloyd Richards (Best Director). In August 1988 *Checkmates* arrived, with Denzel Washington, Marsha Jackson, Ruby Dee, and Paul Winfield. This was followed by a revival of Garson Kanin's classic comedy *Born Yesterday*, starring Madeline Kahn,

Ed Asner, and Daniel Hugh Kelly. In the fall of 1989 Dustin Hoffman starred in a revival of *The Merchant of Venice*, in which he played Shylock for a limited run of eighty-one performances.

When this theatre was rechristened the Richard Rodgers in 1990, the inaugural production was Rupert Holmes's short-lived thriller *Accomplice*, produced by Alexander H. Cohen and his wife Hildy Parks. David Merrick returned to Broadway in 1990 with a revival of the Gershwins' musical *Oh, Kay!*, but it ran for only seventy-seven performances. This theatre had an enormous success when Neil Simon's *Lost in Yonkers* opened in 1991 and won the Pulitzer Prize, plus the following Tony Awards: Best Play, Leading Actress (Mercedes Ruehl), Featured Actress (Irene Worth), and Featured Actor (Kevin Spacey).

In 1993 *The Boys Choir of Harlem and Friends* performed here; later that year the delightful *Fool Moon*, starring pantomimists Bill Irwin and David Shiner, amused for 109 performances. Additional hilarity was triggered by Neil Simon's *Laughter on the 23rd Floor*, a zany memoir of his early years as a comedy writer for Sid Caesar's seminal TV series *Your Show of Shows*. The stage comedy was brightened by the antics of Nathan Lane, Randy Graff, Mark Linn-Baker, Lewis J. Stadlen, John Slattery, Ron Orbach, J. K. Simmons, Stephen Mailer, and Bitty Schram. It ran for 320 performances.

On March 23, 1995, the 1961 Pulitzer-winning musical *How to Succeed in Business without Really Trying* returned to this theatre. The famed show was favorably received and won a Tony Award for its star, Matthew Broderick, his second at this theatre. This new *How to Succeed* ran for 548 performances—respectable but less than the original, which ran for 1,417.

Another hit of the past returned to the 46th Street the following year, but with far greater success. The 1975 musical *Chicago*, with a score by John Kander and Fred Ebb and book by Ebb, Bob Fosse, and script adaptation by David Thompson, had been acclaimed as a staged concert presented by City Center's "Encores!" series in the spring 1996 season. On November 14, 1996, it transferred to the Richard Rodgers Theatre (where the 1975 original opened) with great success. It played here until May 1997, then continued its long run at the Shubert Theatre and subsequently at the Ambassador Theatre. It starred Bebe Neuwirth, Ann Reinking, Joel Grey, James Naughton, and Marcia Lewis, and it won the following Tony

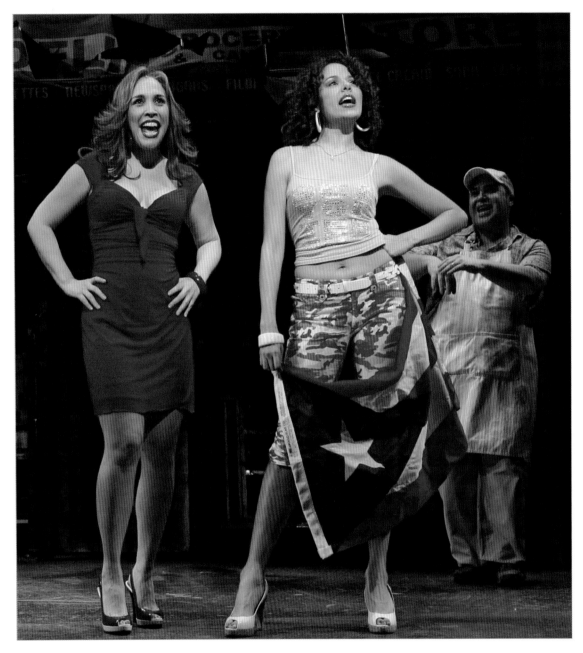

Left to right, Andrea Burns, Janet Dacal and Eliseo Roman in the Tony-winning celebration of New York's diverse Latino culture, Lyn-Manuel Miranda's *In the Heights* (2008). (Photo by Joan Marcus)

Awards: Best Revival of a Musical, Best Actor in a Musical (Naughton), Best Actress in a Musical (Neuwirth), Best Director of a Musical (Walter Bobbie), Best Choreographer (Reinking), and Best Lighting (Ken Billington). As of this writing, the revival is still running at the Ambassador.

Another Kander/Ebb musical, *Steel Pier*, opened at the Rodgers in 1997, with a book by David Thompson, but it did not enjoy the success of *Chicago*. Depicting the dance marathon craze of the 1920s in Atlantic City, it starred Daniel McDonald, Karen Ziemba, Debra Monk, and Gregory Harrison, and it closed after seventy-six performances. The following cast members were nominated for Tony Awards: McDonald, Ziemba, Monk, and Joel Blum. Other Tony nominations included Best Musical

Book (David Thompson), Best Musical, Best Musical Director (Scott Ellis), Best Scenic Designer (Tony Walton), Best Choreographer (Susan Stroman), Best Score (Kander and Ebb), and Best Orchestrations (Michael Gibson).

October 16, 1997, brought a most unusual musical to this theatre. Called *Side Show*, it depicted the show-business careers of real-life Siamese twins Daisy and Violet Hilton, brilliantly acted by Emily Skinner and Alice Ripley. With book and lyrics by Bill Russell and music by Henry Krieger, the production had many admirers, but the public resisted attending a musical about sisters who were literally joined at the hip. It received the following Tony Award nominations: Best Musical Actress (shared by Ripley and Skinner); Best Musical Book (Russell), Best

Above: The Cat in the Hat arrives in New York in this poster image from *Seussical* (2000).

Musical, and Best Score (Krieger and Russell). It closed after only ninety-one performances but ran long enough to become a pet show of disabled theatre fans. The cast chipped in to pay for a ticket so one especially devoted wheelchair-bound fan could see the show one last time on closing night.

Footloose, a musical based on a popular film of the same name, arrived on October 22, 1998, and enjoyed a long run of 709 performances, despite several negative reviews. It dealt with a small-town minister battling the "evil" effect of rock and roll on the town's young people. It received several Tony nominations but did not win any awards.

The characters of the whimsically rhymed Dr. Seuss children's books took to the stage in a musical called *Seussical* in 2000. With a score by the *Ragtime* team of Stephen Flaherty and Lynn Ahrens and a book by Ahrens (conceived by Monty Python alumnus Eric Idle), the show wove several of the Seuss stories into a single narrative, with the mischievous Cat in the Hat serving as emcee. After a difficult tryout in Boston, the show opened on Broadway in the fall and tried to build an audience on the charm of songs like "Anything's Possible" and "Alone in the Universe," and on the appeal of leads David Shiner, Kevin Chamberlin, and Janine LaManna. Talk-show host Rosie O'Donnell briefly joined the cast as the Cat in the Hat, but *Seussical* managed a run of only 198 performances.

In fall 2001 comedy master Neil Simon added a late-career entry to his resume: *45 Seconds from Broadway*, an affectionate portrait of life at the bustling old-Times-Square shrine to corned beef, Café Edison. Lewis J. Stadlen, Marian Seldes, Louis Zorich, Judith Blazer, Alix Korey, and other prime New York character actors played versions of the real-life owners and regulars for seventy-three performances—all just one block from the real thing on Forty-seventh Street.

Alan Rickman, then enjoying international fame as the glowering Professor Snape in the *Harry Potter* films, displayed his stage chops in a lauded April 2002 revival of Noël Coward's *Private Lives*, playing Elyot opposite Lindsay Duncan as Amanda. Duncan won the Tony Award as Best Actress in a Play, and the production was named Best Revival of a Play. The "damned moonlight" shone for 127 performances.

On October 24, 2002, choreographer Twyla Tharp opened a very different kind of jukebox show, *Movin' Out*. She fashioned hits of 1970s songsmith Billy Joel into a musical about three friends whose lives are torn apart by the Vietnam War—but she told their stories entirely through dance. Joel soundalike Michael Cavanaugh acted as narrator, singing the lyrics in front of a top-drawer band, while the saga was enacted by the buff John Selya, Elizabeth Parkinson, Ashley Tuttle, Benjamin G. Bowman, Scott Wise, and a talented ensemble of ballet-trained dancers. It stayed for 1,303 performances, Tharp's longest Broadway run to date.

With hits running at the New Amsterdam and the Lunt-Fontanne, Disney Theatricals turned, on May 10, 2006, to the Rodgers to house its latest family musical, *Tarzan*, also adapted from a hit Disney film. David Henry Hwang adapted the script, and composer Phil Collins, who had provided the film with its hit theme song, "You'll Be in My Heart," was asked to create a full Broadway score. Though visually sumptuous (especially in the opening shipwreck sequence), the show was criticized as overstuffed and its songs were deemed not up to the standard set by the film. Nevertheless, Disney marketing and a likeable cast—including Josh Strickland as Tarzan, Jenn Gambatese as Jane, and Shuler Hensley as Kerchak—kept the classic story of a man raised by apes swinging for 486 performances.

Another classic arrived at the Rodgers on November 1, 2007: *Cyrano de Bergerac*, featuring Kevin Kline as the hypertrophied poet/swordsman, Jennifer Garner as his beloved Roxane, Daniel Sunjata as his noble rival Christian, and Chris Sarandon as the villainous de Guiche.

One of the most joyous hits in Rodgers history opened March 9, 2008: *In the Heights*, a labor of love by young author Lin-Manuel Miranda, who had grown up listening to show tunes and salsa in the Latino-immigrant Manhattan neighborhood of Washington Heights. All those influences flowered in this musical about a group of neighbors and friends whose commitment to the Heights is tested when one of them wins $96,000 in the lottery. Miranda wrote music and lyrics and starred as convenience-store owner Usnavi (his parents named him after an American warship with "U.S. Navy" on the side), and the show had a book by Quiara Alegría Hudes. *In the Heights* won four Tony Awards, including Best Choreography (Andy Blankenbuehler), Best Score (Miranda), and Best Musical of 2008.

Today the Richard Rodgers Theatre is owned by the Nederlander Organization and is still one of Broadway's prime musical-comedy houses.

SAM S. SHUBERT
THEATRE

THE SHUBERT THEATRE OCCUPIES A special niche in theatrical history. It was built by the Shubert brothers (Lee and J. J.) in tribute to their brother Sam S. Shubert, who got them started in the theatrical business before he died in a railroad accident when he was just twenty-nine years old.

Occupying a choice location in the heart of the theatre district, on West Forty-fourth Street between Broadway and Eighth Avenue, the Shubert Theatre opened on October 2, 1913. It was enhanced by an alleyway that separated it from the Hotel Astor and served as a private thoroughfare for the Shuberts. But because it also provided a shortcut to Forty-fifth Street for Broadway crowds, the passage later became famous as Shubert Alley. It was notable for

Left: Shubert program covers for 1927, 1928, And 1929.

Above: Lionel Barrymore in the stirring Civil War drama *The Copperhead* (1918).

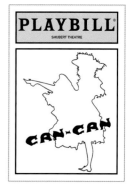

Above: PLAYBILL covers for two original hit musicals and one revival at the Shubert.

being lined with posters of current Broadway shows and for the Shubert limousines parked between its gates, which were locked at night. The alley continues today as a pedestrian passageway (with no gates), still lined with posters on the west side, and contains a small theatrical gift shop, One Shubert Alley.

During the Depression years, a long fence divided the passageway in two, lengthwise. The east side was used as part of the terminal for a New Jersey bus line; the west side provided access to the stage doors of the Shubert and Booth theatres. To improve the view, show posters were hung on the fence. This happy tradition soon became a fixture of Shubert Alley and remained even after the bus terminal was removed and the fence came down. Showcases for the posters were provided on the common wall of the Booth and Shubert. During intermissions, the casts of shows playing at these two theatres would congregate in Shubert Alley for fresh air (theatres were not air-conditioned yet), and the audiences could see them buying popsicles and soda pop.

Above the auditorium were the offices of the Shubert empire and an apartment where Lee Shubert lived. According to the *New York Tribune* for September 28, 1913, the new theatre had 1,400 seats, making it ideal for housing musicals. (The total has since been increased to 1,521. The architect was Henry B. Harris, and the elaborate interiors, in a Venetian Renaissance style, were by O. H. Bauer, with mural paintings by Lichtenauer. A portrait of Sam S. Shubert adorned the attractive lobby, overseeing the new house.

The opening attraction, surprisingly, was not a Shubert operetta nor musical but the eminent British actor Johnston Forbes-Robertson in his farewell performance as *Hamlet*. He and his repertory company also acted in several other plays, including *Othello* and *The Merchant of Venice*.

The Shubert's first musical, *The Belle of Bond Street*, opened on March 18, 1914, starring the stunning Gaby Deslys and the popular Sam Bernard. But it was not a success. Several other musical failures followed. Then there was a well-received revival of George Du Maurier's haunting play *Trilby* (1915), about the hypnotic influence of the sinister Svengali over the singer Trilby O'Ferrell. Even the acerbic critic Alexander Woollcott, who had been barred from Shubert theatres for panning a Shubert show called *Taking Chances*, praised *Trilby*.

The Shubert's first musical success was *Alone at Last* (1915), a Franz Lehar show starring John Charles Thomas. Jerome Kern had a hit in *Love o' Mike* (1917), with Clifton Webb dancing suavely with Gloria Goodwin. But both these shows were topped by Sigmund Romberg's lushly romantic operetta *Maytime*, which was so successful that the Shuberts had to open a second company of it right across the street from the Shubert Theatre at the (now vanished) Forty-fourth Street Theatre. The stars at the Shubert were Peggy Wood, Charles Purcell, and Douglas J. Ward, who sang their hearts out for almost 500 performances (1917).

On February 18, 1918, Lionel Barrymore scored one of his greatest successes in *The Copperhead*, a Civil War drama in which Barrymore had to pretend to be a Dixie sympathizer while supplying military secrets to the Yanks. Despised by his family and friends, he could not reveal his true sympathies until twenty years later.

On October 4, 1918, Mae West and Ed Wynn convulsed Shubert audiences in Rudolf Friml's musical *Sometime*. Mae played a vamp who compromised Ed Wynn and caused his fiancée (Francine Larrimore) to drop him for five years in protest. The musical played only a month at the Shubert, then was transferred to another house where it completed its run of 283 performances.

Two 1919 musicals were moderately successful. *Good Morning, Judge*, a British import, wisely interpolated two George Gershwin numbers: "There's More to the Kiss Than XXX" and "I Was So Young." Sigmund Romberg's *The Magic Melody* was too reminiscent of his *Maytime* plot, even to the employment of its same leading man, Charles Purcell.

Some class returned to the Shubert in the fall of 1919 when E. H. Sothern and Julia Marlowe played their classical repertory here.

Highlights of the 1920s at this theatre included an appearance by the silent-screen siren Theda Bara in a preposterous drama called *The Blue Flame* (1920), in which her dead body is brought back to life by a mad scientist; Margaret Anglin in *The Trial of Joan of Arc* (1921), translated from the French play by Emil Moreau; the luxurious *Greenwich Village Follies* revues, staged by John Murray Anderson; and the *Artists and Models* revues (1921—26), notorious for their nudity, starring period favorites such as Joe E. Brown, female impersonator Bert Savoy and Jay Brennan (his partner), Ted Lewis, Moran and Mack, and Vincent Lopez and his orchestra. Expert comics Jimmy Savo and Fred Allen starred in a revue called *Vogues of 1924*. An interesting failure, *The Magnolia Lady*, starred Ruth Chatterton and Ralph Forbes, performers usually associated with dramas and comedies rather than musicals.

For a change of pace, the Shubert presented Walter Hampden in *Othello* in January 1925,

and the actor set a record for that time by playing the role for eight consecutive weeks. In 1943, at the same theatre, Paul Robeson would also break records with his magnificent portrayal of Shakespeare's tragic Moor.

The homespun comic Chic Sale had a hit with a revue called *Gay Paree* (1925) that had nothing to do with Paris; *Countess Maritza* (1926), an operetta by Emmerich Kálmán, with the popular song "Play Gypsies—Dance Gypsies," was an enormous success; "rubber legs" Leon Errol had some hilarious drunk scenes in the hit musical *Yours Truly* (1927); the noisy nightclub hostess Texas Guinan, who coined the phrase "Hello, suckers," attracted customers in a revue called *Padlocks of 1927*, supported by Lillian Roth and J. C. Flippen singing some clever lyrics by Billy Rose. Not even Laurette Taylor could save Zoe Akins's murder mystery *The Furies* (1928) from rigor mortis. *Ups-a-Daisy* (1928) is a musical worth mentioning only because its cast included a comic butler played by a young man named Bob Hope. *A Night in Venice*, starring Ted Healy and His Stooges (later The Three Stooges), was a minor musical that brought the 1920s to a close at the Shubert.

The 1930s began with sobriety. The Chicago Civic Shakespeare Society, headed by Fritz Leiber, staged nine of Shakespeare's greatest plays in repertory. Nonsense returned with Walter Slezak making his debut in a musical, *Meet My Sister* (1930). Ann Pennington, Oscar Shaw, Frances Williams, and a newcomer named Harriette Lake (later Ann Sothern of films) played for 127 performances in a musical called *Everybody's Welcome* (1931), which boasted an immortal song by Herman Hupfeld: "As Time Goes By." Another celebrated tune, the theme

Top left: Al Jolson in his last Broadway show, *Hold On To Your Hats* (1940).

Top center: Alan Alda and Barbara Harris as Adam and Eve in *The Apple Tree* (1966).

Top right: Katharine Hepburn in her greatest hit, *The Philadelphia Story* (1939).

Bottom left: Judy Holliday and Sydney Chaplin in the popular *Bells Are Ringing* (1956).

Bottom right: Ray Heatherton and Mitzi Green in *Babes in Arms* (1937).

song of the Depression—"Brother, Can You Spare a Dime?"—was first heard in *Americana*, a revue that played the Shubert in 1932.

In January 1933 Fred Astaire's last Broadway musical, *Gay Divorce*, moved from the Barrymore to the Shubert, and Fred danced "Night and Day" with Claire Luce for six more months. Walter Huston, Fay Bainter, Maria Ouspenskaya, and Nan Sunderland (Mrs. Huston) were the hit of the season in Sidney Howard's *Dodsworth*, a skillful adaptation of the Sinclair Lewis novel of the same name.

The Shubert housed its first Pulitzer Prize play in March 1936. Robert E. Sherwood's antiwar drama *Idiot's Delight*, with glittering performances by Alfred Lunt as a seedy hoofer and Lynn Fontanne as the mysterious mistress of a munitions maker, took Broadway by storm and was one of the finest plays that the prestigious Theatre Guild produced in its distinguished history.

In 1937 Maxwell Anderson's *The Masque of Kings*, a retelling of the Mayerling tragedy, ran only eighty-nine performances despite the brilliant acting of Dudley Digges (as Emperor Franz Joseph) and Margo, Henry Hull, and Leo G. Carroll in other roles. The gloom of this drama was dispelled in April of that year when Rodgers and Hart's *Babes in Arms* opened with a young, largely unknown cast singing such gems as "Where or When," "The Lady Is a Tramp," "My Funny Valentine," "I Wish I Were in Love Again," and "Johnny One-Note." George Balanchine supplied the fantastic choreography.

The Lunts returned to the Shubert in S. N. Behrman's elegant adaptation of Jean Giraudoux's *Amphitryon 38* (1937), in which Lunt

Above: Playbill for the
Broadway run of *A
Chorus Line*.

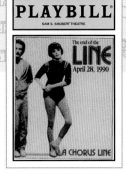

Bottom: PLAYBILL for
the final performance
of *A Chorus Line*.

impersonated Jupiter, who in turn masquerades as Amphitryon in order to woo Amphitryon's wife, Alkmena, blissfully played by Lynn Fontanne. They were excellently supported by Richard Whorf and Sydney Greenstreet. This Olympian frolic was followed by a heavenly musical, *I Married an Angel* (1938), with felicitous Rodgers and Hart songs, angelic dancing by Vera Zorina to Balanchine choreography, glorious singing by Dennis King and Vivienne Segal, clowning by Walter Slezak and Audrey Christie, and lovely Jo Mielziner sets that were whisked on and off on treadmills.

On March 28, 1939, a landmark event occurred at the Shubert: Philip Barry's enchanting high comedy *The Philadelphia Story* opened. It proved a lifesaver for Katharine Hepburn (who had been branded "box office poison" in Hollywood); for Barry, who hadn't had a hit in years; and for the Theatre Guild, which was on the verge of bankruptcy. Hepburn's company included Shirley Booth, Joseph Cotten, and Van Heflin, and their radiant acting kept the show selling out for most of its 417 performances.

During the 1940s Rodgers and Hart suffered one of their rare flops, *Higher and Higher* (1940), at the Shubert; Al Jolson and Martha Raye drew raves in the musical *Hold On to Your Hats* (1940), with an entrancing score by Burton Lane and E. Y. Harburg; Katharine Cornell was hailed in her revival of Shaw's *The Doctor's Dilemma* (1941), with Raymond Massey, Bramwell Fletcher, Ralph Forbes, and Clarence Derwent; Mary Boland, Bobby Clark, Walter Hampden, and

Helen Ford romped through a revival of Sheridan's *The Rivals* (1942); Rodgers and Hart provided Ray Bolger with one of his best musicals, *By Jupiter* (1942), based on the play *The Warrior's Husband*; Paul Robeson, Uta Hagen, and José Ferrer were cheered in *Othello* (1943), brilliantly directed by Margaret Webster and designed by Robert Edmond Jones.

Mae West wiggled her hips in Mike Todd's production of her play *Catherine Was Great* (1944), with Gene Barry as one of Mae's lovers; Celeste Holm clinched her star status as a suffragette in the tuneful musical *Bloomer Girl* (1944); and Bobby Clark enlivened Victor Herbert's *Sweethearts* (1947) with Marjorie Gateson for 288 performances.

High Button Shoes (1947), a charming musical with Jerome Robbins's dances, Nanette Fabray's singing, and Phil Silvers's comedy, moved to the Shubert from the Century Theatre and stayed for almost a year; Maxwell Anderson's *Anne of the Thousand Days* (1948) won Rex Harrison a Tony Award as outstanding lead actor; the Lunts celebrated their twenty-fifth anniversary as America's foremost acting couple, in S. N. Behrman's family chronicle play *I Know My Love* (1949); and Cole Porter's phenomenal *Kiss Me, Kate* moved from the Century Theatre to the Shubert in 1950 and thrilled musical-comedy buffs for a full year.

During the 1950s the Shubert continued its policy of alternating between musicals and straight fare. The Lerner and Loewe show *Paint Your Wagon* (1951), starring James Barton, stayed for 289 performances; Katharine Hepburn and Cyril Ritchard sparkled in Shaw's *The Millionairess* (1952); and Rex Harrison and Lili Palmer were their usual urbane selves in Peter Ustinov's *The Love of Four Colonels* (1953).

Cole Porter's *Can-Can* was a huge hit for two years (1953—55); Rodgers and Hammerstein's *Pipe Dream* (1955), based on John Steinbeck's novel *Sweet Thursday*, was one of their lesser efforts; Judy Holliday scored one of her major coups in the Comden/Green/Jule Styne musical *Bells Are Ringing* (1956), with Sydney Chaplin; and Gertrude Berg and Cedric Hardwicke had a hit in *A Majority of One* (1959).

The last hit of the 1950s at this theatre was *Take Me Along* (1959), a musical adaptation of Eugene O'Neill's comedy *Ah, Wilderness!* starring Jackie Gleason (who feuded with the show's producer, David Merrick, all through the run), Walter Pidgeon, Eileen Herlie, Robert Morse, and Una Merkel.

Highlights of the 1960s included Barbra Streisand's Broadway debut in a small but noticeable part in the musical *I Can Get It for You Wholesale* (1962), starring her future husband, Elliott Gould; Anthony Newley starring in *Stop the World—I Want to Get Off* (1962), which he wrote with Leslie Bricusse; and its follow-up, *The Roar of the Greasepaint—The Smell of the Crowd* (1965), from the same team.

Craig Stevens and Janis Paige starred in Meredith Willson's *Here's Love* (1963), adapted from the popular movie *Miracle on 34th Street*, but it did not enjoy the success of his *The Music Man* or *The Unsinkable Molly Brown* and proved to be his final Broadway musical.

On Oct. 2, 1963, the Shuberts celebrated the fiftieth anniversary of their eponymous theatre by unveiling a plaque dedicating Shubert Alley to "all those who glorify the theatre" and use the short thoroughfare. Attached to the exterior wall of the theatre overlooking Shubert Alley, it confirmed the passageway as the heart of the Broadway theatre district, as it remains today.

The Shubert Theatre hosted Barbara Harris, Alan Alda, Larry Blyden, and Robert Klein in an offbeat three-part musical, *The Apple Tree* (1966), by Jerry Bock and Sheldon Harnick. Steve Lawrence, Eydie Gorme, and Marilyn Cooper starred in *Golden Rainbow* (1968), a musical version of the play *A Hole in the Head*. The last show of the decade was the smash musical *Promises, Promises*, Neil Simon's adaptation of the film *The Apartment*, with a jaunty score by Burt Bacharach and Hal David, starring Jerry Orbach. Running 1,281 performances, it set a new record at the Shubert, but one that would last for less than a decade.

The demolition of the Astor Hotel on the east side of Shubert Alley and its replacement by an office tower with a windowed restaurant at ground level changed the ambience of the alley.

Some of the shows that played the Shubert Theatre in the 1970s were Hal Prince's elegant production of *A Little Night Music* (1973), with a book by Hugh Wheeler and a score by Stephen Sondheim, based on the Ingmar Bergman film *Smiles of a Summer Night*, starring Glynis Johns, Len Cariou, and Hermione Gingold; and *Over Here!* (1974), a nostalgic World War II musical with two of the Andrews Sisters—Maxene and Patty—and, in smaller roles, John Travolta and Treat Williams.

Above: Jon Cypher and Dan Jenkins perform the number "Fun" while dancing on a giant keyboard in the musical *Big* (1996).

The Shubert's second Pulitzer Prize play, Edward Albee's *Seascape* (1975), starred Deborah Kerr and Barry Nelson and won a Tony Award for supporting actor Frank Langella in the unlikely role of a giant, talking sea lizard. Ingrid Bergman made her last Broadway appearance in a revival of Maugham's *The Constant Wife* in April 1975.

On July 25, 1975, Joseph Papp and the New York Shakespeare Festival hosted the Broadway opening of their sensational Off-Broadway hit *A Chorus Line*. Directed by Michael Bennett, with choreography by Bennett and Bob Avian, the musical introduced twenty-four dancers auditioning for an unnamed Broadway show, then took audiences inside their hearts and heads to learn their secret dreams and desires as the moment approached when all but eight of them would be eliminated. The gold-leaf and glass *A Chorus Line* logo became a fixture of the theatre and of Shubert Alley for the next fifteen years. In September 1983 this Pulitzer Prize—winning musical, with a book by James Kirkwood and Nicholas Dante and a score by Marvin Hamlisch and Edward Kleban, became Broadway's longest-running musical to that date, and the Shubert Theatre, still owned by the Shubert Organization,

celebrated the longest-running show ever to play in the seventy-year-old house. A plaque memorializing the latter achievement (still unsurpassed in 2010) is affixed to the lobby wall.

The record-setting 6,137-performance run of *A Chorus Line* ended April 28, 1990. After a summerlong renovation, the Shubert reopened in November 1990 with *Buddy: The Buddy Holly Story*, a musical about the late rock star who died in a 1959 plane crash. The show, one of the first of the genre that came to be known as "jukebox musicals," was an enormous success in London—where it ran from 1989 to 2002—but failed to repeat its success on Broadway, running for only 225 performances.

Next, on February 19, 1992, the Shubert welcomed another big hit, *Crazy for You*, a revised version of the 1930 Gershwin musical *Girl Crazy*, with interpolated songs from many of the George and Ira Gershwin Broadway and film musicals. Starring Jodi Benson and Harry Groener, the show had a hilarious new book by Ken Ludwig and brilliant direction by Mike Ockrent. It won three Tony Awards: Best Musical, Best Choreography (Susan Stroman), and Best Costume Design (William Ivey Long). It closed in 1996 after 1,622 performances.

Angela Lansbury in her Tony-winning turn as Madame Arcati in the 2009 revival of *Blithe Spirit*. (Photo by Robert J. Saferstein)

The husband/wife team of director Ockrent and choreographer Stroman returned to the Shubert on April 28, 1996, with *Big*, a musical version of the hit 1988 film of the same name about a boy who is magically granted his wish to become "big"—that is, a grown-up. The stage adaptation, with a book by John Weidman, music by David Shire, and lyrics by Richard Maltby Jr., lacked the charm of the movie and ran for only 192 performances.

In 1996 the City Center's "Encores! Great American Musicals in Concert" series produced a sensational concert version of the 1975 musical *Chicago*, with music by John Kander, lyrics by Fred Ebb, and a book by Ebb and Bob Fosse. It was so successful (despite the virtual absence of sets, the buff dancers providing the only needed visual element) that it transferred to Broadway, first to the Richard Rodgers Theatre (November 14, 1996) and then to the Shubert Theatre (February 11, 1997). The concert cast was retained: Bebe Neuwirth, Ann Reinking, James Naughton, Joel Grey, Marcia Lewis, and many others. The megahit won the following 1997 Tony Awards: Best Revival of a Musical, Best Leading Actor in a Musical (Naughton), Best Leading Actress in a Musical (Neuwirth), Best Direction of a Musical (Walter Bobbie), Best Choreography (Reinking), and Best Lighting (Ken Billington). It stayed at the Shubert until January 26, 2003, when it transferred once again, this time to the Ambassador Theatre.

The front of the Shubert appeared as the set for the opening number of *The Producers* (2001) on the stage of the St. James Theatre just down the block. The Shubert is where Max Bialystock's doomed fictional musical *Funny Boy* (based on *Hamlet*) opens and closes in a single night. The dance number "The King of Broadway" is shown taking place in Shubert Alley just outside the theatre. It was one of the rare shows (with *Guys and Dolls*, *42nd Street*, and a handful of others) that actually used a Times Square location as a setting.

Replacing *Chicago* at the Shubert May 1, 2003, was a revival of the classic musical *Gypsy*, directed by Britain's Sam Mendes and starring Bernadette Peters as Rose, Tammy Blanchard as Louise, and John Dossett as Herbie. Everything came up roses for 451 performances.

After a brief summer 2004 revival of the dance revue *Forever Tango*, the Shubert got its biggest hit of the decade, *Monty Python's Spamalot*. Eric Idle, an original member of the British comedy troupe, teamed up with composer John Du Prez and director Mike Nichols to make a Broadway musical "lovingly ripped off from" the cult comedy film *Monty Python and the Holy Grail*, a spoof of the Round Table legend. The production featured a top-drawer cast of comedy talent, including Tim Curry as King Arthur, Hank Azaria as Sir Lancelot, David Hyde Pierce as Sir Robin, Christopher Sieber as Sir (Dennis) Galahad, and Sara Ramirez as the Lady of the Lake. Nichols and Ramirez won Tony Awards, and the production

Top: left to right, David Hyde Pierce, Hank Azaria, Christopher Siebert, Steve Rosen, and Tim Curry (as King Arthur) sing "All for One" in the Tony award-winning musical *Monty Python's Spamalot* (2005). (Photo by Joan Marcus)

Bottom left: Monty Python alumnus and *Spamalot* adapter Eric Idle on the stage of the Shubert in 2005 with the house behind him. (Photo by Larry Mah)

Bottom right: The exterior of the Shubert from 44th Street during the run of *Spamalot*. (Photo by David Gewirtzman)

as a whole was named Best Musical in one of the most fruitful seasons in recent years.

The Pythonesque sense of humor spilled onto the exterior of the Shubert, which featured pictures of comely "Laker Girls" and a marquee that promised "cows, cocoanuts, killer rabbits, witches," and other delights, with the word "witches" crossed out and the phrase "too expensive" scribbled above it. A cutout of the show's French Guards became a fixture in Shubert Alley throughout the run, so fans could pose with them for photos.

During the long tenure of *Spamalot*, there was a major changing of the guard upstairs at the Shubert Theatre in the offices of the august Shubert Organization. Chairman Bernard B. Jacobs, who had served the company since the 1960s, died in 2006. He was followed by his longtime partner Gerald Schoenfeld in 2008. The Shubert Organization renamed two of

their Broadway houses after these knights of the theatre. They were succeeded by Robert E. Wankel and Philip J. Smith.

Spamalot closed January 11, 2009, after 1,575 performances. It was quickly replaced in February 2009 by a limited-run revival of Noël Coward's sparkling comedy *Blithe Spirit*, which starred Christine Ebersole as a ghost who comes back to make trouble for her husband and his new wife. The production was stolen by veteran Angela Lansbury as dotty medium Madame Arcati. Dancing herself into a trance nightly, the eighty-three-year-old earned a miraculous fifth career Tony Award for her performance (her first in a supporting role).

In fall 2009 the Shubert hosted another major musical, *Memphis*, Joe DiPietro and David Bryan's story about an interracial romance set against the backdrop of the segregated 1950s southern music scene.

SAMUEL J. FRIEDMAN
THEATRE

THE CHANIN BROTHERS, CONSTRUCTION moguls who were bitten by the showbiz bug in the 1920s, built six legitimate theatres. The Biltmore Theatre at 261 West Forty-seventh Street (renamed the Samuel J. Friedman Theatre in 2008) was their second project. When this theatre opened on December 7, 1925, the *New York Times* reported that it was the first theatre to be built on the north side of Forty-seventh Street, just east of Eighth Avenue. The theatre was designed by the busiest theatre architect in town, Herbert J. Krapp, with a single balcony, just under a thousand seats, and a color scheme of cerise and brown.

The opening show at the Biltmore was not new. It was an Owen Davis farce called *Easy Come, Easy Go*, which moved here from the

Program cover for *Tin Pan Alley*, a 1928 play with Claudette Colbert and Norman Foster.

George M. Cohan Theatre on Broadway. Otto Kruger and Victor Moore played bank robbers, with Edward Arnold also involved in the fracas. It had a run of 180 performances.

Next came a very steamy drama, *Kongo* (1926), with Walter Huston as "Deadleg Flint," a bitter man in the Belgian "Kongo" who gets even with a man who not only stole his wife, but caused his legs to be paralyzed. This jungle rot lasted for

135 performances. A comedy called *Loose Ankles* (1926) followed, with Osgood Perkins, and it was sufficiently foolish to run for 161 performances. Walter Huston returned to the Biltmore in a solid hit, *The Barker* (1927), Kenyon Nicholson's play about carnival life. Huston played a tent-show barker; Claudette Colbert played a snake charmer who vamps Huston's son, acted by Norman Foster. Colbert vamped Foster so well that they got married, for real, offstage. The critics admired Colbert's legs, and this lively show ran for 225 performances.

A comedy called *Jimmie's Women* was a hit in 1927 but moved to another theatre after a month. Noël Coward's *The Marquise* was chichi nonsense about an errant society woman (Billie Burke) who returns to her family years after abandoning them, just in time to save her daughter (Madge Evans) from mistakenly marrying her half-brother (Rex O'Malley). Coward's fans supported this fluff for eighty-two performances.

There were several flops in 1928, including the play *Tin Pan Alley*, with Colbert and Foster returning to the scene of their first romance. There was also a cause célèbre at this theatre on October 1, 1928, when the incomparable Mae West opened her new play *The Pleasure Man*. This time Mae did not appear in her show, but her plot was sufficiently lurid to shock the populace, and the police closed the play after its

Top left: Program cover for *Tin Pan Alley*, a 1928 play with Claudette Colbert and Norman Foster.

Top center: Shirley Booth and Jo Ann Sayers in the rollicking hit *My Sister Eileen* (1940).

Top right: Critics pronounced Claudette Colbert's gams one of the highlights of the 1927 hit *The Barker*.

Bottom: George Abbot's hilarious production of *Brother Rat* with Richard Clark, Mary Mason, and Eddie Albert (1936).

Left: Ezra Stone, Vaughan Glaser, and James Corner in another George Abbot winner, *What A Life* (1937).

Center: Richard Widmark and Joan Caulfield in the wartime comedy hit *Kiss and Tell* (1943).

Right: Basil Rathbone and Wendy Hiller in the Jed Harris production of *The Heiress* (1947).

second performance. *The Pleasure Man* was about an actor who has impregnated so many women that the brother of one of them decides to perform a brutal operation on him that will permanently curtail his love life. The operation is performed at a party attended largely by transvestites, and the lover dies under the knife.

Wall Street laid an egg in 1929, and so did the Biltmore Theatre. It housed seven flops, including *Man's Estate*, a Theatre Guild production with Dudley Digges, Elizabeth Patterson, Earle Larimore, Armina Marshall, and Margalo Gillmore.

The 1930s began with an interesting but depressing play by Edwin Justus Mayer called *Children of Darkness*. Set in the notorious debtors' prison of Newgate in London, the drama dealt with the last days of the infamous criminal Jonathan Wild. The seamy play starred Basil Sydney, Mary Ellis, and Eugene Powers and lasted ten weeks.

George Kelly's play *Philip Goes Forth* was a near-hit in 1931, playing for ninety-eight performances. Madge Evans, Thurston Hall, Dorothy Stickney, Cora Witherspoon, and Harry Ellerbe were in the comedy about a young man who fails as a playwright and ends up in his father's business. From May 1931 until January 1934 the Biltmore housed a number of mediocre plays, such as *Her Supporting Cast*, *Zombie*, *Border-land*, and *The Scorpion*. One drama, a biographical study called *Carry Nation*, was unsuccessful but featured this interesting cast: James Stewart, Joshua Logan, Mildred Natwick, Esther Dale, and Katherine Emery.

New Year's Day 1934 brought a comedy hit at last to the Biltmore. It was called *Big Hearted Herbert* and starred J. C. Nugent as a mean miser who upsets all his family's plans until they turn the tables on him. It amused theatregoers for 154 performances. Emmet Lavery's religious play *The First Legion*, with Bert Lytell, John Litel, Charles Coburn, and Frankie Thomas,

moved in from the 46th Street Theatre in October and stayed through December.

The Chanin Brothers lost all six of their Broadway theatres, including the Biltmore, during the Depression. In 1936 the Federal Theatre Project took over the theatre and presented some of its "Living Newspaper" productions. These consisted of a series of news sketches written by a staff of seventy reporters and writers and about sixteen dramatists. A cast of a hundred actors appeared in such striking productions as *Triple A Plowed Under* and *1935*. In June 1936 the Federal Theatre presented *Stars on Strings*, a marionette show, at this theatre.

The Biltmore was next taken over by the Warner Brothers film studio to serve as a showcase for the work of famed producer/playwright/director George Abbott. PLAYBILL magazines for the Biltmore, beginning in 1937 and continuing into the 1940s, stated that the theatre was managed by Bernard Klawans.

Mr. Abbott's production of *Brother Rat*, a comedy about life at the Virginia Military Institute, by John Monks Jr. and Fred F. Finklehoffe, was a huge hit in 1936. The sprightly cast included Eddie Albert, José Ferrer, Frank Albertson, and Ezra Stone. It turned out to be the

Biltmore's longest-running show to that time, registering 577 performances. Abbott's next two shows, *Brown Sugar* and *All That Glitters*, were not successful, but his production of Clifford Goldsmith's *What a Life*, a hilarious comedy about a squeaky-voiced high schooler who is always in trouble (perfectly played by Ezra Stone), turned into a gold mine. Henry Aldrich became such a popular character that he ended up on a successful radio series (with its distinctive opening "Hen-REEE!") and, years later, on TV. Eddie Bracken, Betty Field, Joyce Arling, Edith Van Cleve, and Butterfly McQueen were also in the cast of the play, which ran for 538 performances.

George Abbott's 1939 show was a shocker and quite unlike the type of farce comedy at which he excelled. Called *The Primrose Path*, it was based on Victoria Lincoln's sultry novel *February Hill*. The language was salty and the morals very loose in this saga of a slattern and her family. Helen Westley, Betty Field, Betty Garde, and Russell Hardie were in the cast of this moderate success.

In 1940 Warner Brothers and Bernard Klawans produced a play called *Jupiter Laughs*, by A. J. Cronin, starring Jessica Tandy, Alexander Knox, Mary Orr, Edith Meiser, and Philip Tonge. This drama about doctors ran for only twenty-four performances. But on December 26, 1940, the Biltmore welcomed a comedy that would bring it distinction. It was the fabulous *My Sister Eileen*, by Joseph A. Fields and Jerome Chodorov, based on *The New Yorker* stories by Ruth McKenney. McKenney had written charming vignettes about her adventures with her wacky blond sister Eileen when they moved from Ohio to Manhattan's Greenwich Village. This uproarious comedy, skillfully staged by George S. Kaufman, played for 864 performances. The cast included

Shirley Booth as Ruth, Jo Ann Sayers as Eileen, and Morris Carnovsky as their Greek landlord. One tragic note marred this joyous production. The real Eileen was driving to attend the opening night of her sister's play when she was killed in an auto accident.

Another enormously successful comedy, *Janie*, moved here from another theatre for two months in 1942. On March 17, 1943, a play called *Kiss and Tell*, by F. Hugh Herbert, opened and broke all records at this theatre, running for 956 performances. The comedy about teenage pregnancy had in its cast Richard Widmark, Jessie Royce Landis, Joan Caulfield, and Robert Keith. It was produced and directed by the prolific George Abbott and was made into a hit movie and a successful radio series.

Bernard Klawans, who continued as manager of the Biltmore, presented (with Victor Payne-Jennings) an adaptation of Émile Zola's *Thérèse Raquin* by Thomas Job, called simply *Thérèse*, in 1945. Starring Dame May Whitty, Eva Le Gallienne, and Victor Jory, it played for 96 performances. In February 1946 Walter Huston returned once again to this theatre in *Apple of His Eye*, written by Charles Robinson and Kenyon Nicholson (who wrote Huston's big hit *The Barker*, performed at this theatre in 1927). Jed Harris directed the comedy, which played for 118 performances, and co-produced it with Huston.

Harris produced another comedy here, *Loco*, with Jean Parker, Elaine Stritch, and Jay Fassett in 1946, but it ran for only thirty-seven performances. Paul Bowles's adaptation of Sartre's play about three characters trapped in a room in hell, *No Exit*, played for only a month, but it was memorable for performances given by Claude Dauphin, Annabella, and Ruth Ford. One of the drama critics complained that movie star Annabella's performance gave him a stomachache, and she promptly sent him a laxative.

In March 1947 Russian playwright

Jere Burns and J. Smith Cameron find themselves unable to go through with a planned romantic encounter in "Swing Time" from *After the Night and the Music* (2005). (Photo by Joan Marcus)

Konstantine Simonov's comedy *The Whole World Over*, with Uta Hagen, Sanford Meisner, and Jo Van Fleet, opened and managed to stay for 100 performances. It was directed by Harold Clurman. On September 29, 1947, Jed Harris returned to this theatre with a fine play—Ruth and Augustus Goetz's excellent adaptation of Henry James's novel *Washington Square*. The play, called *The Heiress*, starred Basil Rathbone, Wendy Hiller, Patricia Collinge, and Peter Cookson and ran for 410 performances. It was directed by Jed Harris and produced by Fred F. Finklehoffe. Rathbone won a Tony Award for his chilling performance as Hiller's father.

More hits arrived at the Biltmore in the 1940s: José Ferrer, George Mathews, and Doro Merande in *The Silver Whistle* (1948), a comedy set in an old-people's home, which ran for

219 performances; and *Clutterbuck* (1949), a British comedy by Benn W. Levy about a Don Juan named "Clutterbuck," which was one of David Merrick's earliest Broadway productions (in association with Irving L. Jacobs).

The 1950s brought a dramatic adaptation of Herman Melville's novel *Billy Budd*. This excellent play, with Charles Nolte in the title role and Dennis King, James Daly, and Lee Marvin in the cast, had an unfortunate opening-night incident. A critic for a major newspaper arrived at the theatre intoxicated. The management called the newspaper, and the editor quickly sent another staff critic without telling the inebriated reviewer. Both critics wrote their reviews; the drunk raved, and the sober critic panned it. Unfortunately, the pan appeared in the paper, which helped to shorten the run to 105 performances for this superb drama.

From 1952 to 1961 the Biltmore suspended its legitimate-theatre policy. It was leased to the Columbia Broadcasting System. On December 21, 1961, it reverted to being a legitimate house with Harold Prince's production of the hit comedy *Take Her, She's Mine*, directed by the old Biltmore genius George Abbott. Art Carney, Phyllis Thaxter, and Elizabeth Ashley starred in this play about a father's concern when his daughter is ready to go to college. It ran for 404 performances. Ashley won a Tony for her performance. The actress returned to this theatre in October 1963 in an even bigger hit comedy, *Barefoot in the Park*. Neil Simon's play about the problems of newlyweds (attractively portrayed by Ashley and Robert Redford, with brilliant support by Mildred Natwick and Kurt Kasznar) became the longest-running play at the Biltmore up to this time (1,530 performances). It played from October 1963 to June 1967. Mike Nichols won a Tony Award for his direction.

Several short-lived plays followed—Dyan Cannon and Martin Milner in *The Ninety-Day Mistress* (1967); Milo O'Shea and Eli Wallach as homosexuals in the British play *Staircase* (1968); and Joe Orton's black comedy *Loot* (1968).

Perhaps the most famous production to play the Biltmore, the seminal rock musical *Hair*, opened there on April 29, 1968. This freewheeling look at the Flower Power Generation had been an Off-Broadway hit at the downtown New York Shakespeare Festival, produced by Joseph Papp. It then moved to an uptown disco called Cheetah, but it failed, until a producer named Michael Butler took it over and hired director Tom

David Pittu as Bertolt Brecht in the biographical musical *LoveMusik* (2007) with left to right Rachel Ulanet, Ann Morrison, and Judith Blazer. (Photo by Carol Rosegg)

O'Horgan. A very salable commodity was added to this show—total nudity, something that had not been seen on Broadway since some of the 1920s revues—and the show became the biggest hit in town, running a record four years and two months (1,750 performances), still a record at the Biltmore. With book and lyrics by Gerome Ragni and James Rado, and music by Galt MacDermot, Hair became an icon of the 1960s. Among the many performers the musical introduced were Melba Moore and Diane Keaton.

Some highlights of the 1970s at this theatre included Michael Moriarty in his Tony Award—winning performance as a homosexual in *Find Your Way Home* (1974); Jules Feiffer's farce *Knock, Knock* (1976), with Lynn Redgrave and Leonard Frey; Barry Bostwick winning a Tony Award in the musical *The Robber Bridegroom* (1976); Lily Tomlin in her dazzling one-woman show *Appearing Nitely*; an unsuccessful return engagement of *Hair* (1977); a revival of *The Effect of Gamma Rays on Man-in-the-Moon Marigolds* (1978), starting Shelley Winters; Claudette Colbert in her third appearance at this theatre, in *The Kingfisher* (1978), with Rex Harrison and George Rose; and Peter Allen in a spectacular

personal appearance called *Up in One*.

The 1980s brought such divergent fare as an exciting courtroom drama, *Nuts* (1980), with Anne Twomey; Arthur Miller's play *The American Clock* (1980), which failed; Eva Le Gallienne and Shepperd Strudwick in *To Grandmother's House We Go* (1981); and Claudette Colbert one last time, in *A Talent for Murder* (1981), with Jean-Pierre Aumont.

The Biltmore wasn't done with murder yet, however. Next came a transfer of the longest-running thriller in the American theatre, *Deathtrap* (1982), from the Music Box; and Anthony Shaffer's spoof of mystery plays, *Whodunnit* (1983).

Later in 1983 Pulitzer Prize—winning cartoonist Garry Trudeau turned his famous comic strip "Doonesbury" into a musical of the same name. He wrote the book and lyrics, and Elizabeth Swados supplied the music. In 1984 film actress Barbara Rush appeared in a one-woman show, *A Woman of Independent Means*, and the following year John Pielmeier's play *The Boys of Winter*, starring Matt Dillon, opened here and shocked some with its realistic scenes of the Vietnam War. A musical called *Honky Tonk Nights*, about black vaudeville, arrived here in 1986. In 1987 a musical revue, *Stardust*, celebrated the famed songs of Mitchell Parish. This was the last production of the twentieth century at the Biltmore.

Several factors made the Biltmore difficult to book or to sell—or to demolish. Its relatively small size for a Broadway house made it uneconomical. Standing dark for several years, it soon was vandalized. With part of the interior open to weather and pigeons, it soon began to mildew and crumble. However, the interior design of the theatre's auditorium had been landmarked—but not its exterior or even its stage, which made repairs difficult and expensive. Unable to find a bidder, the theatre's owner defaulted on the mortgage and the theatre was seized by a bank. The Biltmore was purchased by James Nederlander and Stewart Lane in 1993 for $550,000. With the late 1990s Times Square boom, several plans for refurbishment were considered, but these became tangled in legal and union conflicts.

The Biltmore enjoyed a momentary return to glory in 1999 when its marquee, festooned with 1930s-era posters, was used as a backdrop for the Oscar-nominated film *The Cradle Will Rock*.

On November 22, 2000, it was announced that the prestigious Manhattan Theatre Club (MTC), one of Manhattan's most prominent nonprofit theatres and producer of many successful Broadway transfers, would take part in a renovation of the Biltmore and occupy it as MTC's new mainstage. The restoration was part of the plan to build a fifty-one-story apartment tower next door to the theatre by Biltmore 47 Associates, a partnership of the Jack Parker Corporation and the Moinian Group, which owned the Biltmore. Ground was broken for the $27 million renovation in a starry ceremony December 12, 2001, amid bare concrete and plaster. The seating capacity of the house was reduced from 950 to 650, but in return the entire orchestra section was raked to create clearer sight lines. This was accomplished by digging out the front of the orchestra to lower the front rows and raising the back of the house so that ticket holders now must climb several steps to reach the back rows after entering the lobby. The renovation also included a downstairs shop and mini museum for MTC, plus an upstairs lounge for subscribers.

Work was completed in time for an October 15, 2003, relighting ceremony hosted by New York mayor Michael Bloomberg, MTC artistic director Lynne Meadow, and executive producer Barry Grove on a platform erected in front of the theatre.

Manhattan Theatre Club was founded Off-Broadway in 1970 with the stated aim of nurturing new American plays. During its first decade at the Biltmore/Friedman, MTC offered a mixture of new plays, Broadway debuts of recent plays that had been produced elsewhere, and revivals of rarely seen twentieth-century classics. Though the Biltmore served as its main Broadway production space, MTC produced some of its biggest hits, including *Proof* and *Doubt*, at other Broadway theatres. It also continued to produce Off-Broadway at the City Center Stage I and Stage II. Under MTC administration the Biltmore has housed a subscription series of three plays per season. All productions had preset limited runs, which meant that for the rest of its existence the Biltmore gave birth to many shows, but none for a long run—or for an excessively short run, for that matter. Shows generally ran forty to ninety performances, with the final production of each season usually staying the longest.

The renovated Biltmore opened officially on November 6, 2003, with Richard Greenberg's drama *The Violet Hour*, a *Twilight Zone*—like story about a book publisher who mysteriously receives a manuscript from the future, narrating the course of his life. Robert Sean Leonard and Mario Cantone starred, but critics were generally disappointed.

Anton Chekhov's *The Seagull* served as the template for Regina Taylor's *Drowning Crow*, about a veteran performer and the family, friends, and hangers-on who gather around her at her summer home. The production featured Anthony Mackie, Aunjanue Ellis, Ebony Jo-Ann, and Alfre Woodard. Critics felt that transferring the action from Russia to the Gullah islands off South Carolina did not quite work.

May 2004 brought Donald Margulies's *Sight Unseen*, a Pulitzer-finalist play that MTC had debuted Off-Broadway in 1992 with Laura Linney in the cast. Linney returned for this production (in a new role) opposite Ben Shenkman as a celebrated painter who returns to a woman he had dropped years before. Critics and audiences were happy, as nearly always, to see Linney.

MTC's second season at the Biltmore opened promisingly in October 2004 with the Broadway debut of Craig Lucas's black comedy *Reckless*, about a woman who escapes out the window of her home on Christmas Eve, beginning a multiyear odyssey of misadventures that always seem to involve the death of someone close to her on that normally joyful holiday. Mary-Louise Parker played the fleeing woman, with a fine cast of current and future notables: Debra Monk, Michael O'Keefe, Rosie Perez, Olga Merediz, and Thomas Sadoski.

After that dip into the past, MTC offered in February 2005 a new play by Pulitzer Prize winner Donald Margulies. *Brooklyn Boy* was the story of a novelist who sees his personal life fall apart just as his career is blasting off. The fine production starred Adam Arkin, with a supporting cast that included Dana Reeve, Allan Miller, and Ari Graynor.

The season wrapped that June with an unusual presentation, *After the Night and the Music*, comprising a short one-act called *Curtain Raiser*, plus two longer one-acts, *Giving Up Smoking* and *Swing Time*, all by cerebral-comedienne-turned-director Elaine May. The first featured Eddie Korbich and J. Smith-Cameron, as two people who develop an unusual relationship while they dance. The last featured Jeannie Berlin, Brian Kerwin, Jere Burns, and Smith-Cameron as a group of would-be swingers.

Echoing the *Reckless* theme of problematic Yuletides, *Absurd Person Singular*, the 2005—6 season opener, was a revival of Alan Ayckbourn's comedy about the change in relative social standing among three English couples over a series of Christmas parties. The cast consisted of Mireille Enos, Clea Lewis, Sam Robards, Alan Ruck, Deborah Rush, and Paxton Whitehead.

It was followed by a distinguished play, *Rabbit Hole* (February 2, 2006), by David Lindsay-Abaire, about a couple coming to terms with the death of their child. Cynthia Nixon and John Slattery played the parents, with Tyne Daly as the grandmother. The scene of anguish when they realize they have accidentally taped over a treasured VHS of the lost child playing helped loft this drama to the 2007 Pulitzer Prize.

Irish author Conor McPherson supplied another of his modern ghost plays in *Shining City* (March 9, 2006), starring Oliver Platt as a man who comes to a psychologist, Brían F. O'Byrne, claiming he is haunted by the ghost of his deceased wife. Her appearance is accompanied by the sound of an ice-cream-truck jingle. The shrink spends the bulk of the play helping his patient work through the possible causes of this "delusion," but the audience is treated to a disturbingly real-looking surprise before the final curtain falls.

Two brothers reuniting for the funeral of their father bring up a range of past issues and a fifty-year-old family mystery in *Losing Louie*, Simon Mendes da Costa's comedy that was a hit in the UK but got mixed reviews on Broadway. The October 2006 production starred Matthew Arkin, Scott Cohen, Mark Linn-Baker, and Michele Pawk.

In January 2007 MTC engaged Garry Hynes to stage a revival of Brian Friel's *Translations*, about a doomed romance between an Irish girl and an English soldier who is overseeing a project to anglicize the local Irish place names on military maps. Niall Buggy, Chandler Williams, and Susan Lynch were featured.

Director Harold Prince made an increasingly rare visit to Broadway on May 3, 2007, with *LoveMusik*, a musical biography of composer Kurt Weill and his muse/wife Lotte Lenya, using Weill's music and an original script by Alfred Uhry. Michael Cerveris and Donna Murphy starred in this underrated work, in which Lenya, not Weill, seemed to emerge as the central character. David Pittu made a strong impression is his supporting role as Bertolt Brecht. But the musical got shut out of the 2007 Tony Awards and did not make a hoped-for transfer to a commercial run, though it was recorded. It was the first musical at the Biltmore in more than thirty years.

Playwright Theresa Rebeck made her Broadway debut October 4, 2007, with *Mauritius*, a drama about how the bequest of a rare and valuable stamp rips apart the relationship between two sisters and brings out the worst in a collector and a dealer. F. Murray Abraham, Dylan Baker, Bobby Cannavale, Katie Finneran, and Alison Pill were featured in this interesting play, whose cryptic and hard-to-pronounce title (maw-RISH-us) comes from the name of the small country that issued the stamp.

Come Back, Little Sheba, William Inge's 1950 drama about a marriage hammered by alcoholism, got a beautiful and heartbreaking revival beginning January 24, 2008, starring Kevin Anderson as the sot, S. Epatha Merkerson as the long-suffering wife, and Zoe Kazan as the beautiful young border whose arrival sets off the action of the play.

Caryl Churchill's disjointed drama *Top Girls* got a starry production featuring Martha Plimpton, Mary Beth Hurt, Marisa Tomei, and Elizabeth Marvel, but critics and audiences were left scratching their heads after the May 7, 2008, opening.

On September 4, 2008, the theatre got its

Left to right, Rufus Collins, Rosemary Harris, and Reg Rogers in the 2009 revival of *The Royal Family*. (Photo by Joan Marcus)

first new name since it was built. Thanks to a generous donation from the Dr. Gerald J. and Dorothy R. Friedman Foundation, the Biltmore was rechristened for the pioneering press agent Samuel J. Friedman, the first of his profession so honored on Broadway.

The initial production at the new Friedman Theatre might have challenged even the skills of its namesake. *To Be or Not to Be* was an adaptation of the classic 1942 Ernst Lubitsch film comedy about a Polish acting troupe trying to escape the clutches of the Nazis during World War II. The project seemed to have great promise, but it suffered from friction between its director, Casey Nicholaw, and its British adapter, Nick Whitby. When it became clear that the production was not working and Whitby declined to adjust his script any further, cast members including Jan Maxwell and David Rasche were left to their own devices after a critical clobbering in October 2008.

Mercedes Ruehl, Lily Rabe, and Kieran Campion starred in the January 2009 Broadway debut of Richard Greenberg's drama *The American Plan*, about a handsome and charming liar who preys upon a mentally fragile young woman at her summer home. The play had debuted at MTC's Off-Broadway Stage II in 1990.

In his first return to Broadway after his Tony-winning performance in *Curtains*, David Hyde Pierce chose to play the role of a middle-aged playwright whose greatest work may be a fiction he cooks up to test the affections of his much younger fiancée in an April 2009 revival of Samson Raphaelson's *Accent on Youth*.

Manhattan Theatre Club opened its fall 2009 season with a grand revival of George S. Kaufman and Edna Ferber's classic *The Royal Family*, with Rosemary Harris as Fanny Cavendish, matriarch of the acting Cavendish clan, and Jan Maxwell having a triumph as leading lady Julie Cavendish on John Lee Beatty's sumptuous two-level set. Word of mouth was so positive, the production got a rare extension even before it opened.

MTC reaffirmed its commitment to playwright Donald Margulies by producing two of his plays in succession in early 2010. Laura Linney and Brian d'Arcy James starred in the January 28 debut of *Time Stands Still*, playing a married photographer and journalist adjusting to stateside life after she is injured covering the Iraq War. On April 28 audiences got to see the Broadway debut of Margulies's *Collected Stories*, which had been a finalist for the Pulitzer Prize in its 1996 Off-Broadway debut. Linda Lavin played an older woman writer who takes a younger writer (Sarah Paulson) under her wing.

The Biltmore stood as a crumbling hulk on Forty-seventh Street for the better part of a generation—a symbol of the city's decay. Its restoration, including a contemporary marquee and an exterior TV screen looping news and information about Manhattan Theatre Club's offerings, seemed to light up the entire neighborhood.

ST. JAMES
THEATRE

THE ST. JAMES THEATRE AT 246 WEST
Forty-fourth Street was built by Broadway booking agent Abraham Erlanger and opened as Erlanger's Theatre in the fall of 1927. The theatre was designed by the architectural firm of Warren and Wetmore, with interiors by John Singraldi.

With an ample capacity of 1,600 seats, Erlanger's Theatre was aimed primarily at the production of musicals. According to the *New York Times*, it cost $1.5 million to build and was the least ornate of all the theatres constructed in the Times Square district at the time. "In the auditorium," reported the paper, "there has been a studied attempt to create an intimate rather than a theatrical atmosphere. The interior design is Georgian, the color scheme coral and antique gold. Murals decorate the side walls

and the proscenium arch. Two large boxes on either side of the proscenium are known as the President's and the Governor's boxes. The main entrance is through wide doors to a spacious marble lobby extending all the way across the building. The facade, stretching along West Forty-fourth Street, is of marble, stone and stucco on a granite base and is also said to be representative of Georgian architecture."

The opening attraction at Erlanger's on the night of September 26, 1927, was George M. Cohan's musical *The Merry Malones*, which, Cohan, with his typical modesty, wrote, produced, and starred in. It was a hit and got the new theatre off to a good start. It played for 192 performances, strangely interrupted by a short engagement of a flop play called *The Behavior of Mrs. Crane*, then returned for 16 additional performances.

Erlanger's housed the last musical Cohan wrote. It was called *Billie* and was based on his 1912 play *Broadway Jones*. He did not appear in it, but it managed to run for 112 performances in 1928—29. This was followed by the popular musical *Hello, Daddy!* which moved here from the Mansfield Theatre. Herbert and Dorothy Fields wrote it for their father, vaudevillian Lew Fields, who starred in it. The remaining shows of 1929 were an unsuccessful revue, *John Murray Anderson's Almanac*, starring Jimmy Savo and Trixie Friganza, with Noël

Coward as one of the contributors; and a moderately successful comedy, *Ladies of the Jury*, with Mrs. Fiske as an opinionated juror who sways the other jurors to her way of thinking.

Mrs. Fiske appeared again at Erlanger's in 1930 in a brief revival of Sheridan's comedy *The Rivals*, in which she played Mrs. Malaprop. Next came this theatre's biggest hit thus far, the infectious musical *Fine and Dandy*, with a funny book by Donald Ogden Stewart and a score by Kay Swift and Paul James that included two standards: "Can This Be Love?" and the rousing title tune. Comedian Joe Cook fractured theatregoers with his acrobatics, juggling, daffy gadgets, and inane patter. The hit thrived for 246 performances.

From May 1931 until March 1932 this theatre was taken over by the Civic Light Opera Company, which presented a successful repertory of Gilbert and Sullivan operettas and other musical entertainments. Then a dark period followed, during which it was decided to rename the theatre the St. James, inspired by the St. James Theatre in London. On December 7, 1932, the theatre reopened with this new name. The

Above: Twiggy in the "new" Gershwin musical, *My One and Only* (1983).

Center: Yul Brynner dances with Gertrude Lawrence in *The King and I* (1951), her last show.

Right: Lillian Gish and John Gielgud in *Hamlet*, which moved to the St. James in 1937.

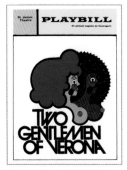

Above: The PLAYBILL cover for the Tony Award-winning musical, *Two Gentlemen of Verona* (1971).

star, appropriately, was London's favorite revue comedienne, Beatrice Lillie, in a new show called *Walk a Little Faster*. Her costars were the famed comedy team of Bobby Clark and Paul McCullough, and the score was by Vernon Duke and E. Y. Harburg. The show was staged by Monty Woolley and Albertina Rasch, the production was designed and conceived by Boris Aronson, and the orchestrations were by the fabulous Robert Russell Bennett and Conrad Salinger. So what went wrong? Who knows, but the revue was only a moderate success, running for 121 performances. One gem has survived from this show: the beautiful Duke/Harburg song "April in Paris," which the notoriously tone-deaf drama critics didn't even mention.

After this sophisticated revue, the St. James reverted to Gilbert and Sullivan for several months. An event more balletic than theatrical occurred at this theatre in January 1934. Concert impresario Sol Hurok brought over the Ballets Russe of Monte Carlo, and the famed company presented its repertoire from January through April. The lead dancers included Leonide Massine, Irina Baronova, David Lichine, André Eglevesky, Tamara Toumanova, and Sono Osato. It was the beginning of America's ballet craze and helped lay the groundwork for a more balletic style of Broadway choreography.

Bobby Clark and Paul McCullough returned to the St. James in another gilded revue, *Thumbs Up*, produced by Eddie Dowling, who also starred in the show with his comical wife, Ray Dooley. Two great dancers—Hal Le Roy and Jack Cole—were also in the show, as well as the popular Pickens sisters. It ran for 156 performances and introduced two song hits: James Hanley's "Zing Went the Strings of My Heart" and Vernon Duke's haunting "Autumn in New York."

On December 5, 1935, *May Wine*, a Sigmund Romberg, Oscar Hammerstein II, and Frank Mandel operetta that disguised itself as "a musical play," waltzed into the St. James for 212 performances. Among the large cast were Walter Slezak, Walter Woolf King, Leo G. Carroll, and Jack Cole.

John Gielgud moved his highly successful abridged *Hamlet* from the Empire Theatre to the St. James in January 1937, and Maurice Evans followed him in the title role of the highly praised revival of Shakespeare's *Richard II*, staged by Margaret Webster. The production was the first revival of this tragedy in America since Edwin Booth played it in 1878, and it was a triumph. It ran for 132 performances.

A truly delightful fantasy called *Father Malachy's Miracle* opened here on November 17, 1937. The beloved comic Al Shean (of Gallagher and Shean fame) played Father Malachy, a kindly priest who tires of a noisy dance hall across the way from his church and prays for it to be trans-

Left: Maurice Evans and Henry Edwards in the uncut revival of *Hamlet* (1938).

Right: Jane Lawrence and Ray Bolger in Frank Loesser's delightful musical, *Where's Charley?*

ported to an island far away. It happens, and he gets into a lot of trouble because he has not consulted the church hierarchy before working a miracle. Shean was hailed for his acting, and the fantasy ran for 125 performances.

On October 12, 1938, another dramatic milestone occurred at this theatre. The first full-length production of *Hamlet* to be presented in America was offered by Maurice Evans, Joseph Verner Reed, and Boris Said. Staged by the Shakespearean expert Margaret Webster, it ran from 6:45 to 8:15 p.m., with a dinner intermission, then resumed from 8:45 until 11:15. Later the dinner intermission was extended from a half-hour to an hour, bringing the final curtain down at 11:45. The production was a success, running for ninety-six performances. Ophelia was played by Katherine Locke, Gertrude by Mady Christians, and Rosencrantz by Alexander Scourby. Evans, of course, played Hamlet. In January 1939 Evans switched to playing the rotund Sir John Falstaff in a revival of Shakespeare's *Henry IV, Part 1*, with Edmond O'Brien as Henry, Prince of Wales. It was another success, running for seventy-four performances.

Shakespeare was interrupted for a brief moment by the arrival from the West Coast of the last *Earl Carroll Vanities*, a sorry revue with Jerry Lester and, worst of all, microphones onstage! According to Gerald Bordman in *American Musical Theatre*, this was really the beginning of that monster of our present-day musical theatre: electronic amplification.

Shakespeare returned to the St. James in the fall of 1940 with a splendid production of *Twelfth Night*, copresented by the Theatre Guild and Gilbert Miller. The cast included Helen Hayes (Viola), Maurice Evans (Malvolio), June Walker (Maria), Wesley Addy (Orsino), and Sophie Stewart (Olivia) in this delightful revival staged by Margaret Webster. In March 1941 a dramatic thunderbolt hit this theatre. It was *Native Son*, the dramatization of Richard Wright's novel of the same name by Wright and Paul Green. Produced by John Houseman and Orson Welles and directed by Welles, this powerful drama stunned theatregoers with its story of a black man who accidentally kills a white woman. It ran for 114 performances and was chosen one of the season's ten best plays by critic Burns Mantle.

The Boston Comic Opera Company and the Jooss Ballet Dance Theatre presented an exciting season of their works (including Kurt Jooss's brilliant dance drama *The Green Table*) at the St. James from January to March 1942. This event was followed by the hit play *Claudia*, transferred from the Booth, which stayed at this theatre until November. The Theatre Guild then moved in with Philip Barry's comedy *Without Love*, starring Katharine Hepburn, Elliott Nugent, and Audrey Christie. It was definitely not another winner like *The Philadelphia Story*, being a flimsy notion about a platonic marriage. After 110 performances, it departed. The best thing about the show was the stunning wardrobe designed for Hepburn by that supreme couturier Valentina.

On March 31, 1943, a musical play opened at the St. James that was rumored to be hopeless. In fact, the opening night was not sold out, and that was astounding, considering that it was a Theatre Guild production and the first fruit of a new collaboration between Richard Rodgers and Oscar Hammerstein II, with choreography by Agnes de Mille and staging by Rouben Mamoulian. The show was *Oklahoma!*, and after the opening night you needed powerful friends

Left: Carol Channing sings the title song of *Hello, Dolly!* and wins a Tony Award for her performance (1964).

Right: Joan Roberts, Joseph Buloff, Betty Garde, and Celeste Holm in the Rodgers and Hammerstein blockbuster *Oklahoma!* (1943).

or powerful ticket brokers to get you into the St. James. It became the hottest ticket since *Show Boat* in 1927. At the first matinee the following day, the St. James lobby was jammed with blue-haired ladies and rabid musical-comedy lovers all trying to get seats for the show that revolutionized the American musical theatre. Enough has been written about the significance of this musical—-integrated book and musical numbers, ballets woven into the plot—not to warrant repetition. Notably, the show launched the great team of Rodgers and Hammerstein, saved the Theatre Guild from bankruptcy and directed the course of musicals for decades to come. It ran for 2,212 performances.

Although the musical that followed *Oklahoma!* into this theatre—-Frank Loesser's *Where's Charley?*—-did not match the artistry of its predecessor, it featured a winning performance by Ray Bolger, who stopped the show at every performance with his engaging sing-along number "Once in Love with Amy." George Abbott wrote the libretto and directed the show, which ran for 792 performances. The choreography was by George Balanchine.

A successful revival of *Peter Pan*, starring Jean Arthur and Boris Karloff, with some songs by Leonard Bernstein, moved here from the Imperial Theatre in October 1950 and stayed until mid-January 1951. On March 29, 1951, Rodgers and Hammerstein presented their lat-

est creation, *The King and I*, directed by playwright John Van Druten and choreographed by Jerome Robbins. With Gertrude Lawrence and a practically unknown actor, Yul Brynner, in the leads, the romantic musical based on the popular novel *Anna and the King of Siam* proved an immediate hit and played for 1,246 performances. It also proved to be Gertrude Lawrence's last Broadway show. She passed away while it was still running and was succeeded by Constance Carpenter. In tribute to the great British star, all theatre marquee lights were dimmed for one minute on the night after her death.

Two more successful musicals followed *The King and I* at this theatre. The tuneful and high-energy *The Pajama Game* opened in May 1954 and stayed for 1,061 performances; *Li'l Abner*, based on Al Capp's hillbilly comic strip of the same name, opened in November 1956 and ran for 693 performances.

In 1957 the Shuberts, who owned the St. James at this point, sold the theatre to Scarborough House Inc., which leased it to Jujamcyn Amusement Corporation. It was the first Broadway theatre owned and operated by Jujamcyn Theatres. In 1987 it was granted landmark status by the New York City Landmarks Preservation Commission.

When *Li'l Abner* closed in 1958, the theatre was dark for almost six months and stripped to its skeleton. The noted stage and interior designer Frederick Fox was engaged to rebuild the house and redecorate it from its original shell. He designed a new marquee and houseboards; a new box office and lobby; new foyer walls and floors; a brand-new smoking loggia; a new lighting system and chandelier; a sculpture; murals; specially woven fabrics for seats, walls, and carpeting; new house and asbestos curtains; new stairs; and an improved stage and updated dressing rooms. The latest equipment was installed, including a closed-circuit TV system so that technicians backstage could follow the action onstage. The new St. James was hailed as one of the most beautiful theatres in America.

Above: Souvenir program cover for *Barnum* (Australian production).

Above: PLAYBILL cover for *The Secret Garden* (1991).

The first production in the renovated theatre was Rodgers and Hammerstein's *Flower Drum Song*, one of their lesser efforts, which ran from December 1, 1958, until May 7, 1960. It was succeeded by *Once Upon a Mattress*, the popular musical based on "The Princess and the Pea," starring Carol Burnett as Princess Winnifred. The show started at the Off-Broadway Phoenix Theatre and moved to Broadway when it turned into a hit. The show played in four different Broadway theatres, the last of which was the St. James, over the course of its 244 performance run. The score was written by Richard Rodgers's daughter, Mary Rodgers, in collaboration with Marshall Barer. Burnett was praised for her zany performance.

Highlights of the 1960s at this theatre included Laurence Olivier and Anthony Quinn in Jean Anouilh's *Becket* (1960); the Comden and Green, Jule Styne, Garson Kanin musical *Do Re Mi* (1960), starring Nancy Walker and Phil Silvers; *Subways Are for Sleeping*, another Comden/Green/Styne collaboration, with Sydney Chaplin, Carol Lawrence, Orson Bean, and Phyllis Newman (who won a Tony for her performance) in 1961; an uninspired Irving Berlin musical, *Mr. President* (1962), also his last Broadway show,

starring Robert Ryan and Nanette Fabray; and the exciting John Osborne play *Luther* (1963), which won the Tony Award for Best Play of the season and starred Albert Finney.

On January 16, 1964, *Hello, Dolly!* exploded at this theatre, and by the time it closed on December 27, 1970, it had chalked up 2,844 performances, making it the longest-running Broadway musical up to that time (and still the record holder at the St. James). The David Merrick production, with a score by Jerry Herman, a book by Michael Stewart (based on Thornton Wilder's *The Matchmaker*), and direction and choreography by Gower Champion, won a then-record ten Tony Awards. During its run at the St. James, Carol Channing was succeeded in the title role by the following stars: Ginger Rogers, Martha Raye, Betty Grable, Bibi Osterwald, Pearl Bailey, Thelma Carpenter, Phyllis Diller, and Ethel Merman.

In 1971 Joseph Papp then brought his free-wheeling musical adaptation of Shakespeare's *Two Gentlemen of Verona* from Central Park to this theatre, where it stayed for 613 performances, winning a Tony Award for Best Musical. It was the second (and last) hit for *Hair* composer Galt MacDermot. The cast included Raul

Above: The cast of *The Civil War* takes a curtain call (1999). (Photo by Joan Marcus)

Above: The stage adaptation of Cole Porter's film *High Society* (1998).

Above: PLAYBILL from *The Producers* with original stars Nathan Lane and Matthew Broderick (2001).

Julia, Clifton Davis, and Jonelle Allen, and all three received Tony nominations.

A revival of *A Streetcar Named Desire* in 1973, with Lois Nettleton, Alan Feinstein, Barbara Eda-Young, and Biff McGuire, was well received but lasted only 53 performances. A revival of the 1920s musical *Good News* (1974), with Alice Faye and John Payne (who was replaced by Gene Nelson during previews), fared even worse, with only 16 repetitions. A revival of Molière's *The Misanthrope*, starring Alec McCowen, Diana Rigg, and others, played 94 performances in 1975, and *A Musical Jubilee*, a revue of popular American songs, ran for just 92 performances. A twentieth-anniversary revival of *My Fair Lady* opened in March 1976, with Christine Andreas, Ian Richardson, Brenda Forbes, and George Rose, who won a Tony for his performance as Alfred P. Doolittle. It had a run of 384 performances.

In February 1978 Comden and Green and Cy Coleman brought in their musical version of the farce *Twentieth Century* and called it *On the Twentieth Century*. John Cullum and Kevin Kline won Tony Awards for their performances. The musical, about a broke Broadway producer trying to sign a movie star for his last-chance production while on a train ride from Chicago to New York, played 453 times.

From the spring of 1979 to the following spring, this theatre booked four unsuccessful productions. They were the Alan Jay Lerner/Burton Lane musical *Carmelina* (with a plot virtually identical to the later hit *Mamma Mia!*), *Broadway Opry '79*, *The 1940's Radio Hour*, and the British import *Filumena*, directed by Laurence Olivier and starring his wife Joan Plowright, along with Frank Finlay.

On April 30, 1980, the hit musical *Barnum* arrived and won a Tony Award for its star, Jim Dale, as well as for its sets (David Mitchell) and costumes (Theoni V. Aldredge). Cy Coleman and Michael Stewart wrote the score for this fanciful musical about the mighty circus impresario P. T. Barnum. It won three Tonys, including Best Actor in a Musical for Jim Dale, and ran for 854 performances.

In 1982 *Rock 'n Roll! The First 5,000 Years*, a tribute to that genre of music, had a very short run, but it was followed by a solid-gold hit in *My*

One and Only, a new version of the old Gershwin musical *Funny Face*. After many troubles on the road, this production opened on May 1, 1983, to some very enthusiastic notices, especially for its two stars, Twiggy and Tommy Tune, and for tap dancer Charles ("Honi") Coles. Tune won a Tony for his performance and another for his choreography with Thommie Walsh. The musical played here until March 3, 1985 (767 performances).

The next show at the St. James was a revue called *Jerry's Girls*, a tribute to the women who had starred in the musicals of Jerry Herman. It starred Dorothy Loudon, Chita Rivera, and Leslie Uggams and had choreography by Wayne Cilento. During the run of this revue, Rivera injured her leg in a serious auto accident and her numbers were taken over by a series of her understudies. Fortunately, after years of therapy, Rivera recovered and was able to resume her career.

The hit musical *42nd Street* moved here in 1987 and stayed until 1989. It was followed by *Largely New York*, starring the brilliant silent comedian Bill Irwin. Then came Tyne Daly in a well-received new production of the classic *Gypsy*, for which the TV star won a Tony Award. The musical also won a Tony for Best Revival. In 1991 a musical version of the children's classic *The Secret Garden* opened here and won Tony Awards for Best Book of a Musical (Marsha Norman), Best Featured Actress (Daisy Eagan), and Best Scenic Designer (Heidi Landesman). The popular musical played for 706 performances.

On April 22, 1993, this theatre saw the Broadway premiere of *The Who's Tommy*, the legendary rock opera by Pete Townshend (with additional music and lyrics by fellow Who rockers John Entwistle and Keith Moon), directed by Des McAnuff. The show dazzled critics and audiences with its multimedia effects and driving force. It garnered the following Tony Awards: Best Direction of a Musical (McAnuff), Best Original Music Score (Townshend, tied with Kander and Ebb for *Kiss of the Spider Woman*), Best Scenic Design (John Arnone), Best Lighting Design (Chris Parry), and Best Choreography (Wayne Cilento). The musical ran for 900 performances.

On April 18, 1996, another hit opened at this theatre. It was the revival of the 1962 Tony Award—winning musical *A Funny Thing Happened on the Way to the Forum*. The leading role of Pseudolus has been a lucky one for actors; it won the Tony Award for Zero Mostel in the original, Phil Silvers in the 1972 revival, and Nathan Lane in this revival. He was assisted by skillful farceurs Lewis J. Stadlen, Mary Testa, Mark Linn Baker, and Ernie Sabella. Stadlen was nominated for a Tony for his featured performance and Jerry Zaks for his choreography. The musical also received a Tony nomination for Best Revival of a Musical.

The production had a novel cast change on February 11, 1997, when Whoopi Goldberg succeeded Lane as Pseudolus. Cleverly, she left it unclear whether her Pseudolus was supposed to be a man or a woman but garnered much laughter with her raucous antics and ad libs. Later in the run she was succeeded by David Alan Grier. The show ran for 715 performances.

Pop singer Patti LaBelle played a brief engagement at this theatre in January 1998 in an entertainment called *Patti LaBelle on Broadway*.

The next tenant at the St. James seemed promising, but it proved a disappointment. It was a musical version of Philip Barry's classic high comedy *The Philadelphia Story*, using Cole Porter songs from the film-musical version of the property called *High Society*, the latter title being retained for this stage adaptation. Some other Cole Porter songs from various of his vintage musicals were thrown in, but it was not enough. The production was doomed by the golden memories of the 1939 stage version and the 1940 film version, both starring Katharine Hepburn, and the 1956 movie musical starring Grace Kelly, Frank Sinatra, and Bing Crosby. The musical was directed by Christopher Renshaw, had a book by Arthur Kopit, and featured a cast that included Melissa Errico, John McMartin, Daniel McDonald, Stephen Bogardus, Randy Graff, Marc Kudisch, and precocious youngster Anna Kendrick. Kendrick garnered the best reviews as Dinah Lord and was nominated for a Tony Award, as was stage veteran McMartin. The musical had a short run of ninety-eight performances. When it closed, Jujamcyn shuttered the St. James for eight months and embarked on a $3 million restoration that harmoniously incorporated recreations of Beaux Arts style architectural and design elements recovered from extensive research to return this illustrious house to its original 1927 splendor.

On April 22, 1999, *The Civil War* opened at the newly restored St. James. Frank Wildhorn wrote the music and lyrics and coauthored the book with Gregory Boyd and Jack Murphy. Adding it to his *Jekyll & Hyde* and *The Scarlet Pimpernel*,

Wildhorn became the first American composer in twenty years—since Jerry Herman—to have three musicals on Broadway simultaneously. The moment was marked by a tribute to the composer that put all three casts on the St. James stage at one time. Unfortunately, although his first two musicals ran a long time, *The Civil War* received adverse reviews and lasted only sixty-one performances. Originally commissioned and produced by Houston's Alley Theatre, it was a song cycle that eschewed plot and dialogue to depict the experiences of Civil War soldiers in song, with occasional spoken lines taken from history. The musical was directed by Jerry Zaks.

The next tenant at this theatre had a run of 461 performances. It was the popular musical *Swing!*, an all-singing, all-dancing entertainment with Ann Hampton Callaway, Everett Bradley, Jennifer Shrader, and J. C. Montgomery. The explosive show showcased more than thirty numbers directed and choreographed by Lynne Taylor-Corbett, supervised by Jerry Zaks, including such classic songs as "Boogie-Woogie Bugle Boy," "It Don't Mean a Thing (If It Ain't Got That Swing)," "Sing, Sing, Sing," "Stompin' at the Savoy," and "Blues in the Night." The musical received six Tony Award nominations.

Swing! ran through winter 2001, then closed to make way for Mel Brooks's stage adaptation of his film comedy *The Producers*, which had been a cult favorite with theatre fans (and Wall Streeters) since its release in 1968. It tells the zany story of a down-on-his-luck Broadway producer who, working with a mousy accountant, concocts a scheme that will allow them to make more money with a flop than with a hit. They then set out to produce the biggest flop Broadway has ever seen: *Springtime for Hitler*, subtitled "A Gay Romp with Adolf and Eva at Berchtesgaden." Along with insulting numerous ethnic groups, the story broadly satirized the personalities and practices of Broadway. The movie contained a handful of songs, including the title tune of the show-within-a-show. Working with arranger Glen Kelly, director Susan Stroman, and librettist Thomas Meehan, Brooks composed a complete stage score, including audience favorites "The King of Broadway" for star Nathan Lane, "I Want to Be a Producer" for costar Matthew Broderick, and a one-man tour de force for Lane, "Betrayed."

Once-in-a-generation reviews brought back to Broadway a sight rarely seen in the era of telephone and Internet ticket sales: a line of tick-

Tony-winner Patti LuPone puts her stamp on the role of Madame Rose, and the song "Rose's Turn," in the 2008 revival of *Gypsy*. (Photo by Joan Marcus)

et buyers down Forty-fourth Street. At one point shortly after the April 19, 2001, opening of *The Producers*, the Shubert Organization, which shared a ticket-selling service with Jujamcyn, allowed ticket buyers to use the box office of the Majestic Theatre across the street to keep up with demand. The show was nominated for a record fifteen Tony Awards and won a record twelve, including Best Musical, Best Score (Brooks), Best Actor in a Musical (Lane), and both Best Direction and Best Choreography for Stroman. The show soon set a record top ticket price of $100 for regular seats and a whopping $480 for something new: VIP seats. A segment of the audience was happy to pay that much for the hot-ticket musical comedy. Responding to criticism, Brooks defended the practice, saying audiences were paying that and more to ticket scalpers who returned nothing to the show's creators. Soon, other shows followed suit.

The Producers continued to sell out as long as Lane and Broderick were in the cast, but the

Left to right, Pablo Schreiber, Brian Dennehy, and Carla Gugino on their way to forming a deadly love triangle in the 2009 revival of O'Neill's *Desire Under the Elms.* Note the unusual set consisting of a stage full of boulders. (Photo by Liz Lauren)

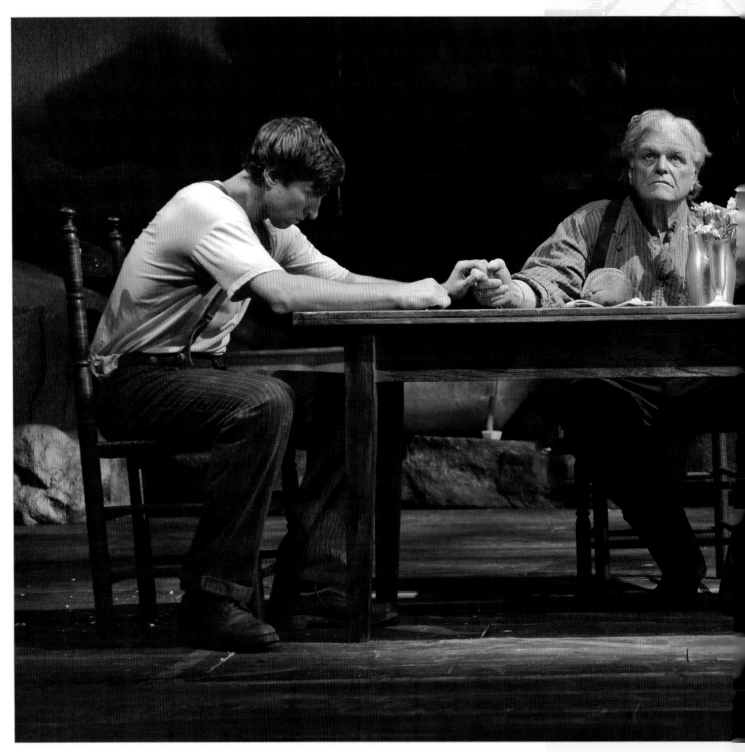

producers of *The Producers* had trouble finding replacements who could still draw a crowd. The HBO television series *Curb Your Enthusiasm* built its fourth-season finale around star Larry David's fictional decision to join the cast in Lane's role of Max Bialystock. Expected to run a decade, *The Producers* managed "only" 2,502 performances (second only to *Hello, Dolly!* at this theatre), closing on April 22, 2007.

The St. James next saw a fall 2007 holiday musical adaptation of a classic children's book,

Dr. Seuss' How the Grinch Stole Christmas! The St. James was among the theatres targeted by a stagehands' strike that eventually closed down most of Broadway for nineteen days around Thanksgiving. Owing to the Grinch's 11:00 a.m. matinee on the first day of the strike, it was the first show to get a picket line—just as families were showing up to take their seats. One of the memorable images of the strike's early days was *Grinch* star Patrick Page out on the sidewalk in front of the St. James doing something very un-Grinchlike: hugging disappointed children.

On March 27, 2008, Patti LuPone escorted her "Encores!" revival of the Jule Styne/Stephen Sondheim/Arthur Laurents classic *Gypsy* to the St. James, and she brought the house down nightly with her volcanic rendition of "Rose's Turn." She won the 2008 Tony Award as Best Actress in a Musical, with Laura Benanti (Louise) and Boyd Gaines (Herbie) taking home Tonys as Best Featured Performers in a Musical.

LuPone made a bit of Internet history at the show's second-to-last performance when she stopped in mid—"Rose's Turn" to upbraid an audience member for taking photographs, which is forbidden by law. At least one other audience member captured audio of the tirade and posted it as a YouTube clip, which drew more than fifty thousand views.

The Goodman Theatre of Chicago sent the St. James an April 27, 2009, revival of Eugene O'Neill's early masterpiece *Desire under the Elms*, starring Brian Dennehy, Carla Gugino, and Pablo Schreiber, directed by Robert Falls. One of the notable aspects of the production was Walt Spangler's set, overflowing with stones and boulders to represent the unforgiving nature of the soil the family fights over so desperately.

Fall 2009 saw a bright revival, via the City Center Encores! series, of *Finian's Rainbow*, starring Kate Baldwin and Cheyenne Jackson. It was the first time this socially conscious Burton Lane/ E. Y. "Yip" Harburg/ Fred Saidy classic had been seen on Broadway in nearly half a century, but adverse reviews limited its run to ninety-two performances.

The St. James was quickly rebooked with *American Idiot*, a rock musical that tracks the odyssey of a young man named Johnny (John Gallagher Jr.) on a quest to the big city. The show was based on songs from two Grammy-winning albums by the rock group Green Day: "American idiot" and "21st Century Breakdown." It opened April 20, 2010.

STEPHEN SONDHEIM
THEATRE

NEWLY RENAMED THE STEPHEN Sondheim Theatre in summer 2010, the old Henry Miller's Theatre is the first and so far only Broadway playhouse designed and built in the twenty-first century. It boasts of being Broadway's first thoroughly "green" theatre, designed to minimize its energy use and contribution to environmental pollution. But it stands on the site and incorporates elements of a far older theatre (which also bore the name Henry Miller's) with a rich history that leaves it with one foot in the past and one in the future.

The distinctive possessive in the "Henry Miller's" name reflects the philosophy of its namesake. The London-born Miller, who had originated the lead role of John Worthing in the 1895 U.S. premiere of Oscar Wilde's *The Importance of Being Earnest*, was not just an

HENRY MILLER'S
THEATRE

ONE-TWENTY-FOUR-WEST
FORTY-THIRD-STREET-NEW-YORK

actor and producer of the old school. He was a philosopher of theatre design. He believed the ideal theatre was not too large or too small, that its stage would be just wide enough to encompass the action while occupying a wide range of the viewers' field of vision, so they could all the better immerse themselves in the illusion being presented on the stage. On the other hand, while second balconies were beginning to go out of fashion, Miller opted to include one.

He was part of the generation of "personality" managers like David Belasco, Martin Beck, George Howells Broadhurst, John Cort, and Winthrop Ames, who built theatres, named them after themselves, and programmed them like a later generation would do with their personal websites. Miller's vision was bankrolled by philanthropist Elizabeth Milbank Anderson, who owned the land on which the theatre was built. Miller worked in partnership with the producing team of Klaw and Erlanger.

Architects Allen, Ingalls, and Hoffman incorporated Miller's theories in the 950-seat gem of a playhouse, which rose at 125 West Forty-third Street, half a block east of Times Square. It opened on April Fool's Day 1918, just as Germany was preparing to assault the allies at Ypres, Belgium, in one of its final offensives of World War I, and the day Britain merged her various airborne fighting forces into the Royal Air Force.

Henry Miller inaugurated his namesake playhouse with Louis Evan Shipman's romantic comedy *The Fountain of Youth*, starring none other than himself. Wartime audiences were not impressed with the play, but the playhouse itself was another matter. In the coming decades many distinguished American dramas and comedies would debut here, along with a bumper crop of flops, and many great careers would get their starts here. In all, more than 150 shows would open at Henry Miller's, which managed to sur-

vive the Depression, wars, numerous recessions, and even a long stint as a discotheque.

In fact, Henry Miller's theatre survived more or less intact until 2006, when everything but its landmarked facade was demolished, right down (and into) the Manhattan schist that underlies much of the island. But owing to a remarkable effort by owners the Durst family (notably the developer's granddaughter, theatre lover Anita Durst), a brand-new, state-of-the-art, 1,055-seat theatre rose on the same site behind the original facade, incorporating many of Henry Miller's original theories and—significantly, in an age of corporate branding of theatres—restoring Henry Miller's name (at least for a few months).

Miller played *The Fountain of Youth* for thirty-two performances, then appeared in the fifty-three-performance revival of the 1897 John Drew vehicle *A Marriage of Convenience*, which opened on May 1, 1918. In the years to come, the theatre hosted many dramas and comedies but only rarely a musical. Miller produced and/or starred in many of the early productions and hired his favorites, like Lillian Kemble-Cooper, who appeared in *The Fountain of Youth* and then again in Douglas Murray's flop *Perkins* (October 22, 1918), and Frances Goodrich Ames, who also appeared in *Perkins* and then returned less than a month later in Jean Webster's *Daddy Long Legs*, also with Miller (and also a failure, at fifteen performances).

Miller seemed to be searching for the kind of audience-pleasing melodrama that had been his bread and butter before World War I, but also trying to provide a showcase for writers who might earn the respect of a new generation, like Eugene O'Neill. Thus, in the early 1920s, Miller was both slightly behind and ahead of the times and suffered a series of short runs like *Back to Earth* (1918, sixteen performances) and *Tillie* (1919, thirty-two performances) as a result.

Left to right: Builder of the theatre that bore his name for more than ninety years, producer and actor Henry Miller. (Photo courtesy Cook + Fox).

A 1920s era PLAYBILL cover for shows at Henry Miller's Theatre.

The landmarked façade of the theatre during its original incarnation, circa 1929. (Photo courtesy Cook + Fox)

Miller turned over producing responsibilities to the team of George M. Cohan and Jed Harris in February 1919 with Laurence Eyre's "comedy of moonshine, madness and make-believe," *Mis' Nelly of N'Orleans*, which was performed by name star Mrs. Fiske (aka Minnie Maddern Fiske) in a thick Creole accent for 127 performances.

One of Broadway's all-time greatest talents marked a milestone at Henry Miller's Theatre: composer George Gershwin wrote his first complete score to a musical, *La, La, Lucille*, which bowed here May 26, 1919, with lyrics by B. G. "Buddy" DeSylva. It ran 104 performances, interrupted by the late-summer actors' strike that helped establish the power of Actors' Equity Association, the actors' union. After the strike, the show tried to come back at the Criterion Theatre but managed only a few extra performances, leaving behind the Gershwin rag "Tee Oodle Um Bum Bo."

Eva Le Gallienne starred in Grace Heyer and Rita Olcott's *Lusmore* (September 9, 1919, twenty-three performances), an Irish fancy about a poet hunchback who is suspected of having a supernatural birth.

With the women's suffrage movement gaining steam before women were granted the right to vote in 1920, playwright James Forbes brought to Henry Miller's Theatre a reactionary woman's-place-is-in-the-home drama, *The Famous Mrs. Fair*, which gave the theatre its longest run so far, 183 performances, beginning December 1919. Blanche Bates starred as Nancy Fair, a female war hero who returns home with a feminist agenda but decides to set it aside it when she realizes her husband (Henry Miller) and daughter (Margalo Gillmore) are drifting away.

A. E. Thomas welcomed the 1920s with a fantasy called *Just Suppose*, about a European royal much like the Prince of Wales coming to the United States and falling in love with an American girl. Fred Kerr, Patricia Collinge, and Leslie Howard starred in the play. The royal lead was changed to the "Prince of Koronia" for the subsequent film version after Brits objected to the very notion that their sovereign might consider anything so vulgar. (Ironically, the then-current Prince of Wales, the future King Edward VIII, would indeed fall for an American and renounce his throne to be with her.)

Long before *Avenue Q*, Mrs. Fiske got advice from puppets in *Wake Up, Jonathan!*, an early Elmer Rice play (co-written with Hatcher Hughes) described by the *New York Times* as a "fair to middling whimsy" about a woman trying to choose between a businessman and a poet. It opened January 7, 1921, and ran for 105 performances.

The Irish Players from the Abbey Theatre in Dublin brought over Lennox Robinson's hit London play *The White-Headed Boy*, on September 15, 1921. It was the story of a spoiled young man who blarneys his whole town into believing he's headed for an adventure in Canada, when actually he's just flunked out of college. The show did not repeat its London success, and by November 7, 1921, Henry Miller's Theatre was ready for its fifth show in less than a year: *The Intimate Stranger*. Alfred Lunt and Billie Burke starred in Booth Tarkington's comedy about a woman who tests her suitor by pretending to be much older than she is. This was Tarkington's first return to Broadway after his success with *Clarence*, and the new play suffered by comparison.

Three plays had short runs in 1922 before the Selwyn brothers brought in a hit revival of *Romeo and Juliet* on January 24, 1923, starring Jane Cowl and Rollo Peters as the star-crossed lovers. The lovers were united in death 157 times.

The state of modern marriage was explored in *The Changelings* by two mismatched couples and a daughter who elopes with an unsuitable husband. Lee Wilson Dodd's comedy opened September 17, 1923, with Blanche Bates, Ruth Chatterton, and Henry Miller, and it marched down the aisle 128 times. It was chosen by Burns Mantle as one of the ten best plays of the season.

Six undistinguished plays flitted across Henry Miller's boards in 1924, leaving barely a memory. But April 1925 brought an influential (if short-lived) comedy, *The Poor Nut*, by the father—son writing team of Elliott Nugent and J. C. Nugent. It told the story of a nerdy college student who writes love letters to a beauty contest winner, proclaiming his love and bragging about his looks and sports prowess. But when she shows up on campus to claim her superman, he has to find a way to live up to his self-created image. The play ran only thirty-two performances on Broadway but found greater success in several film versions, including one with Joe E. Brown. The plot device was recycled by plays, movies, and TV sitcoms for generations.

Noël Coward chose Henry Miller's Theatre for the September 16, 1925, U.S. premiere of his London hit *The Vortex*, which painted a portrait of the British upper class occupied with drugs, nymphomania, and a hint of homosexuality. The play had created a scandal, so naturally proved to be popular everywhere. Coward starred in his own play with Lillian Braithewaite and Leo G. Carroll and earned his first success in New York, as well.

Henry Miller's theatre was hung with black April 9, 1926, to mark the passing of its owner and namesake. Miller's son Gilbert took over the management of the playhouse, and it remained in the family until 1968. Gilbert Miller had an emphatic production philosophy of his own, and under his guidance his father's theatre reached even greater heights, hosting New York premieres of works by Eugene O'Neill, George Bernard Shaw, Thornton Wilder, T. S. Eliot, W. Somerset Maugham, Terence Rattigan, S. N. Behrman, Horton Foote, and many other of the leading lights of the eras through which it passed.

Gilbert Miller found his first hit in November 1926 with Hungarian author Ferenc Molnár's sophisticated backstage farce *The Play's the Thing*, in a translation by P. G. Wodehouse. Holbrook Blynn was featured in the story of a young playwright who is in love with an older actress but unable to write a word after he overhears her being wooed by another man. His desperate producer concocts an elaborate ruse to convince the author that all he heard was the actress rehearsing another play, one much inferior to his own. At 326 performances, *The Play's the Thing* was the theatre's greatest success so far. Even greater things were to come.

Pre-Hollywood Spencer Tracy was showcased by his mentor, George M. Cohan, in the 1927 farce *The Baby Cyclone*, about two women battling over the title character, a pet Pekinese. It ran five months. W. Somerset Maugham exposed the immorality of the British upper classes in the sarcastically titled *Our Betters*, which starred Ina Claire and Constance Collier, for 128 performances starting February 20, 1928.

Set in the city room of a big-city daily newspaper, *Gentlemen of the Press* (August 27, 1928) was notable for having been written by a real-life press gentleman, theatrical columnist Ward Morehouse, whose son, Ward Morehouse III, later served as theatrical columnist of the *New York Post*.

This theatre's next hit was one of the most heartbreaking plays of the 1920s, R. C. Sherriff's wartime drama *Journey's End*. Set in a trench on the front lines of World War I, the play painted a lifelike portrait of a group of British soldiers who are preparing for a major offensive against the Germans. The play introduced each man as an individual, full of hopes and fears and plans for what he might do after the war. The play let the audience understand that their unit was to be sacrificed as a diversionary action in the coming battle, and that all were doomed. Many in the audience were World War veterans themselves, and grown men were seen to weep during performances. The production opened March 22, 1929, and had a healthy run of 485 performances despite the fall 1929 stock market crash.

Molnár returned to Henry Miller's Theatre September 29, 1930, with a pair of one-act plays, *The Violet* and *One, Two, Three*, but they did not repeat the success of *The Play's the Thing*. The dark curtain of Depression was closing around Broadway, eventually leading to the shuttering and demolition of nearly half of Broadway's theatres. Henry Miller's Theatre, however, had the good fortune to stay steadily booked throughout the Depression, World War II, and the postwar boom with numerous short and medium runs, and it even enjoyed the occasional long-running hit.

In *Tomorrow and Tomorrow* (January 13, 1931), playwright Philip Barry presented the predicament of a man who raises a child he thinks is his own but who was really fathered by his wife's lover. It stayed for six months. Helen Hayes starred in Molnár's November 1931 comedy *The Good Fairy*, about an innocent movie usherette who embarks on a campaign of doing good deeds for strangers—but winds up creating a chaos of lust and greed for all concerned. After a run of 151 performances it was adapted for film by Preston Sturges, and it later returned to the stage as a Broadway musical called *Make a Wish*.

Eugene O'Neill presented one of his lesser works, *Days without End*, on January 8, 1924. In this experimental Jekyll-and-Hyde-like story, Earle Larimore and Stanley Ridges played the good and bad sides, respectively, of a single character named John Loving. It lasted fifty-seven performances. October 1934 brought Lawrence Riley's hit comedy *Personal Appearance*, starring Gladys George as a Hollywood glamour girl who finds herself smitten with a hunky salt-of-the-earth mechanic while on a PR tour for her new movie. The Broadway version ran 501 performances and was snatched up by real-life movie star Mae West, who adapted it as her classic *Go West, Young Man*.

A reputed war hero is denounced as a fake and a murderer in Edward Wooll's drama *Libel*,

Top: The original lobby (looking toward the 43rd Street doors) during renovation. (Photo courtesy the Museum of the City of New York)

Bottom: Exterior of the theatre during its long decline. (Photo courtesy Cook + Fox)

which opened in December 1935 and played 159 performances. Playwright Terence Rattigan made his Broadway debut September 28, 1937, with the lighter-than-air London comedy *French without Tears*, about romantic high jinks among English students taking a crash course in French. The production lasted 111 performances and opened the door to Rattigan's successful career on Broadway.

On February 4, 1938, Henry Miller's Theatre hosted the most distinguished play in its long history, and one of the greatest of all American plays: *Our Town*. Thornton Wilder's deceptively simple drama about a few days in the ordinary lives of two neighboring families in Grover's Corners, New Hampshire, somehow managed to capture the profoundest joy and sorrow of human life in its masterfully chosen tiny details. The drama was notable at the time for being performed on a virtually empty stage, narrated by an omniscient Stage Manager who could start and stop the action and cause the story to jump in time. *Our Town* earned the Pulitzer Prize for Drama, and while its reputation has waxed and waned over the years, its fascination has lasted and it continues to be produced around the world. Frank Craven originated the role of the Stage Manager, with Martha Scott as Emily.

Ironically, owing to doleful reports from the play's out-of-town tryout, the Henry Miller's management assumed that they had a flop on

their hands with *Our Town* and had already rebooked the house by the time it opened. As a result, Wilder's classic stayed just a few days at this theatre before transferring to the Morosco and completing a run of 336 performances.

The show for which *Our Town* was evicted, Frederick Lonsdale's old-fashioned comedy *Once Is Enough*, opened February 15, 1938, and struggled through three months of performances. *Time* magazine said the play "seemed even more dated than deft [and] appeared at times to be celebrating the love life of ice cubes."

The theatre had better luck with *Kiss the Boys Good-bye* (September 28, 1938), Clare Boothe Luce's scalding sendup of the much-publicized search for an actress to play Scarlett O'Hara in the film *Gone with the Wind*. Helen Claire played the southern belle determined to land the role of Violet O'Toole. Brock Pemberton's production ran 286 performances and was made into a film with Mary Martin in the central role.

The 1940s got off to a rocky start with nine failures in a row, including George Bernard Shaw's *Geneva* (January 1940), Molnár's *Delicate Story* (December 1940), and S. N. Behrman's *The Talley Method* (February 1941).

The popular wartime comedy Janie opened a 642-performance run here on September 10, 1942. Gwen Anderson played the seventeen-year-old Janie Coburn, who invites a handsome serviceman and his friends to use her parents' house for a party, only to have things get out of control. Antoinette Perry directed the script by Herschel Williams and Josephine Bentham.

Flare Path, the U.S. premiere of Terence Rattigan's play about RAF pilots and the sweethearts who waited for them, flew only fourteen times but was made into a popular film. Helen Hayes returned to Henry Miller's Theatre in March 1943 for Colin Clements's and Florence Ryerson's *Harriet* and stayed for 377 performances.

Twin-brother playwrights Julius J. Epstein and Philip Epstein, best known as Oscar-winning scriptwriters for the film classic *Casablanca*, debuted their play *Chicken Every Sunday* here on April 5, 1944. It told the entertaining story of a long-suffering woman who runs a boardinghouse while her husband pursues a series of wacky get-rich-quick schemes. The show moved to the Plymouth Theatre, where it completed a nine-month run.

After several more brief tenancies, Henry Miller's Theatre hosted Norma Krasna's hit comedy *Dear Ruth*, whose plot was not all that different from 1925's *The Poor Nut*, but with the genders reversed. Trying to impress her soldier pen-pal, a teenage girl (Virginia Gilmore) sends a photo of her prettier older sister. When the soldier shows up on leave, a comedy of mistaken identities ensues. Moss Hart directed the play, which ran 680 performances. The next production of note was F. Hugh Herbert's *For Love or Money*, a May—September romance between a naive young woman (June Lockhart) and an older man. The November 1947 production stayed for 263 performances.

On November 9, 1948, Henry Miller's Theatre welcomed a transfer of Garson Kanin's hit comedy *Born Yesterday*, which moved here from the Lyceum and played out its 1,642-peformance run, with its star-making lead performance by Judy Holliday. *Born Yesterday* was the first of three satisfying hits in a row at this theatre.

The musical *Urinetown* (2001) gave Henry Miller's Theatre a late-life hit.

Top: Jeff McCarthy and the cast sing the title number.

Bottom: John Cullum as the wealthy Caldwell B. Cladwell warns, "Don't Be the Bunny." (Photos by Joan Marcus)

Next up, on January 21, 1950, was T. S. Eliot's London drama *The Cocktail Party*, about a couple who separate just before they plan to host the party of the title. But a mysterious Uninvited Guest (who may be an angel) winds up convincing them that they would be better off staying together. Alec Guinness and Cathleen Nesbitt costarred in the production, which ran 409 performances and won the 1950 Tony Award as Best Play. Another European import, *The Moon Is Blue*, was the story of two men who try, over the course of a dinner party, to seduce a young actress but wind up earning some valuable wisdom instead. F. Hugh Herbert's comedy opened May 8, 1951, and ran an enviable 924 performances. Future film director Otto Preminger staged the production, which featured Barbara Bel Geddes, Donald Cook, and Barry Nelson.

Future Pulitzer Prize winner Horton Foote wrote the next production, *The Trip to Bountiful*, the story of an elderly woman who travels back to her girlhood home. Audiences had only thirty-nine chances to see Lillian Gish, Jo Van Fleet (Tony Award), and Eva Marie Saint in this touching November 1953 play. But Geraldine Page won an Oscar as Best Actress when she played the leading role in the 1985 film version.

Things got personal for a psychiatrist when he discovered that one of his patients is the ex-boyfriend of his fiancée in Edward Chodorov's December 1953 comedy *Oh, Men! Oh, Women!*, which starred Gig Young, Franchot Tone, Betsy Von Furstenberg, and Larry Blyden. It lasted 382 performances. Another psychiatrist contended with a disabled priest for the soul of a young woman (Barbara Bel Geddes) in a relationship with an older man in *The Living Room* (November 17, 1954). Novelist Graham Greene's first play had proved a sensation in London but seemed more like a sermon in New York and survived only 22 performances.

With her thriller *The Mousetrap* having settled into its world-record run in London, Agatha Christie sent another of her hit murder mysteries to Broadway on December 16, 1954. Based on one of her own short stories, *Witness for the Prosecution* was the story of a dying attorney who believes in his client's innocence even when the client's own wife agrees to testify against him. Tony Awards went to actors Francis L. Sullivan and Patricia Jessel, and the play kept Henry Miller's audiences at the edge of their seats for 645 performances. It was later filmed and won numerous Oscars, including Best Picture.

An English society girl scandalizes her upper-crusty parents when she falls in love with a common musician in William Douglas Home's October 1956 play *The Reluctant Debutante*, which starred Adrianne Allen, Wilfred Hyde White, and Brenda Forbes. Master clown Bert Lahr returned to Broadway April 11, 1957, in Georges Feydeau's bedroom farce *Hotel Paradiso*, which set some sort of Broadway record for slamming doors. The superb supporting cast included Angela Lansbury, James Coco, and Sondra Lee, but the production titillated for only 108 performances.

After a decade-long golden age full of hits, things began to thin out for Henry Miller's Theatre in the late 1950s. Still gamely programmed by the aging Gilbert Miller, the theatre rarely had trouble finding plays to book—but actual hits came more and more seldom. Dylan Thomas's elegiac portrait of Welsh village life, *Under Milk Wood*, had been a success as a radio play, but the October 15, 1957, Broadway adaptation lasted only thirty-nine performances.

The Playwright's Company brought in a January 1958 production of *The Rope Dancers* that lasted nearly six months with a cast that included Art Carney, Siobhán McKenna, Joan Blondell, and Theodore Bikel. But the theatre suffered five quick folds in 1959 alone. The wreckage included Noël Coward's ill-advised March 1959 adaptation of Georges Feydeu's comedy *Look After Lulu!*, starring Tammy Grimes as a prostitute. She hung out her red light just thirty-nine times. May of that year saw the Broadway transfer of *The Nervous Set*, a musical about life among Greenwich Village beatniks. The show had proved a sensation in St. Louis, where it was written, but it flopped after just twenty-three performances on Broadway. The cast album, which became a cult favorite, captured the score by Tommy Wolf and Fran Landesman, and performances by Larry Hagman, Gerald Hiken, and Tom Aldredge.

The sixth show of 1959 proved to be the charm, however. George C. Scott earned a Tony nomination as Best Actor in a Play for his performance in the Civil War atrocity drama *The Andersonville Trial*, by Saul Levitt. It opened December 29, 1959, and ran 173 performances through June 1960.

The November 1960 attraction *Under the Yum-Yum Tree* was presented as a swinging sex comedy about a playboy landlord who rents apartments to attractive young women he intends to seduce. Lawrence Roman's play ran a respectable 173 performances.

Alan Arkin (Tony Award as Best Featured Actor in a Play), Vivian Blaine, and Sylvia Sidney starred in *Enter Laughing*, Joseph Stein's comedy about a stagestruck young man trying to break into the smallest of small-time theatre. Based on the semi-autobiographical novel by Carl Reiner, the play bowed March 13, 1963, and ran 419 performances.

After the triumph of Lorraine Hansberry's *A Raisin in the Sun* at another theatre, fans eagerly awaited the "young, gifted and black" author's next play, despite its unpromising title, *The Sign in Sidney Brustein's Window*. It turned out to be the story of a progressive Greenwich Village neighborhood that must face up to the fact that the reformist candidate for public office isn't as honest as he seemed to be. Starring Gabriel Dell, Alice Ghostley, and Rita Moreno, the production opened October 15, 1964 at the Longacre Theatre, moved to the Henry Miller's on December 29, 1964, and closed on January 10, 1965, after ninety-nine performances. Sadly it was the final Broadway production for the talented young playwright. She died of cancer at age thirty-four on January 12, 1965, two days after the show closed.

Three more flops came and went in five performances or fewer that year. But on December 22, 1965, the theatre recaptured something of its glory days with a transfer of the hit *The Subject Was Roses*, Frank D. Gilroy's portrait of a dysfunctional family, which had won both the Tony Award as Best Play and the Pulitzer Prize for Drama. It stayed at Henry Miller's Theatre for a year.

As Gilbert Miller passed his eightieth birthday in 1965, his family tried to help him keep the theatre going but found it increasingly difficult to find quality material. Nine more shows followed in quick succession in the mid-1960s, some by distinguished writers, including Jerome Chodorov's *3 Bags Full* (March 1966), Maria Irene Fornes's *The Office* (April 1966), Aleksei Arbuzov's *The Promise* (November 1967), Lawrence Holofcener's *Before You Go* (January 1968) with Marian Seldes, and the Theatre of Genoa's staging of Goldoni's *The Venetian Twins* (May 1968). But none found an audience.

In 1968, tired of struggling to book the theatre in a Times Square that was sliding steadily downhill, the Miller family sold the playhouse to a rising theatrical family, the Nederlanders. Henry Miller's Theatre survived as a legitimate house under Nederlander ownership for less than a year. During that time it had some historic firsts, though they didn't seem so at the time. Off-Broadway favorite Jack Gelber (*The Connection*) made an inauspicious Broadway debut September 24, 1968, with the pro—Fidel Castro drama *The Cuban Thing*, which provoked a near-riot on Forty-third Street as opponents of the communist dictator tried to storm the theatre and disrupt the show. *New York Post* critic Richard Watts Jr. wrote the next day, "Perhaps as a salute to Fidel, the play seems as long as one of his speeches." Despite a cast that included Rip Torn, Jane White, and Raul Julia, there was no second performance.

Future multiple-Tony-winning playwright and librettist Terrence McNally made only his third Broadway appearance beginning November 28, 1968, with *Noon*, one of three one-acts on a triple bill called *Morning, Noon and Night*. The other two plays were written by rising Off-Broadway stars Israel Horovitz and Leonard Melfi, who made their Broadway debuts with this production.

On February 27, 1969, the theatre made one last stab at legitimacy with Julius J. Epstein's *But, Seriously . . .* , which featured Tom Poston, Dick Van Patten, and a young Richard Dreyfuss, but it lasted only four performances.

The Nederlanders then sold the theatre to developer Seymour Durst, who had a long-range plan to buy up all the properties on the block bounded by Forty-second Street, Seventh Avenue, Forty-third Street, and Avenue of the Americas. Durst wanted to build office towers on the site. As it turned out, it took more than three decades before the last holdout succumbed to Durst's

The theatre's interior as it looked just before reopening in 2009. (Photo courtesy Cook + Fox)

offers. Durst didn't live to see his plans realized; his theatre and his master plan were inherited by his son Douglas on Seymour's death in 1995.

In the meantime, there was the question of what to do with Henry Miller's Theatre. The house left live theatre behind in 1970, the year of Gilbert Miller's death, and began to screen feature films as the Park-Miller Theatre. But even that level of respectability did not last long. This was the period when the drug and pornography industries began to battle live theatre for the soul of Times Square. In 1972, one of the bleakest years for the neighborhood, this theatre was leased to the Avon chain of triple-X cinemas, and under the name Avon-at-the-Hudson it hosted hardcore for the next five years.

Then redemption appeared from an unexpected direction. The success of the Studio 54 discotheque in the old Gallo Theatre on Fifty-fourth Street encouraged the Henry Miller's next transformation. In 1978 the seats were removed from the orchestra section to make room for a dance floor, and the building was converted into a disco, christened Xenon. Operated by impresario Matt Johnson, Xenon quickly rose into the second tier of New York discos for the next two decades, long past the end of the actual disco era.

Even as the name on the marquee changed, the theatre's original appellation, "Henry Miller's Theatre," remained etched into the top of the landmark-protected facade and was visible from the street throughout this period, as if to say that it never really forgot its legitimate

origins. And the building did revert to a kind of legitimacy for a single performance on May 2, 1983, when the managers experimented with a variation on dinner theatre that might have been called "disco theatre." They presented a production of Terrence McNally's farce *The Ritz*, which is set in a gay bathhouse and includes a wild floor show. Ticket holders were allowed to stay after the performance and dance the night away. The experiment was not judged a success. Xenon went back to an all-music-and-dancing policy and stuck with it into the 1990s.

The rebirth of Henry Miller's Theatre as a Broadway house was set in motion in 1993 in London at the Donmar Warehouse Theatre, which hosted Sam Mendes's unusual revival of the 1966 Kander and Ebb musical *Cabaret*. Codirected by Mendes and Rob Marshall and choreographed by Marshall, it was set in a sleazy Berlin nightclub in the early 1930s twilight of the Weimar Republic. To recreate that atmosphere in London, Mendes staged an "environmental" production that spilled across the footlights to give the audience the sensation not only that they were watching a show about a Berlin cabaret, but that they could imagine themselves actually in such a place.

Rights to recreate the show in New York were awarded to Roundabout Theatre Company, an institutional theatre that had begun performing in an Off-Broadway space below a supermarket in 1965 and had grown into progressively better spaces downtown, then moved to Broadway in 1991, under the direction of Todd Haimes, with its headquarters in the center of Times Square at the Criterion Center (now the site of a Toys "R"Us store). In granting permission to stage the show in New York in spring 1998, Mendes required that Roundabout also recreate the seedy environment. The sleekly corporate environs of the Criterion Center didn't fit the bill. But Haimes and Mendes found the right spot just two blocks south and around the corner.

By 1998, Henry Miller's Theatre looked just as decadent as anyone could wish. You still entered through the neo-Georgian brick facade, but inside, the once-beautiful oval foyer had been nearly filled with a makeshift plywood box office. After you entered, you made a sharp left over cracked black and white tiles around the box office, then a right to enter the rundown performing space. Circular club tables were arrayed around the empty orchestra floor, which was pitted where seat bolts had been shorn off or ripped out. Threadbare leopard-print carpet on the stairs took you to the balcony.

And it was left just that way for the opening and run of *Cabaret*. "Henry Miller's Theatre" seemed too top-hat a name for such a dive, so, just in time for the start of previews, the building was rechristened the Kit Kat Klub, after the fictional cabaret where *Cabaret* takes place. Mendes even tried to do away with the tradition of handing out PLAYBILLS as patrons entered. He felt it was yet another reminder to audiences that they were indeed on Broadway and not in Berlin. In the end a compromise was reached and the PLAYBILL was distributed at the end.

The Broadway production of this revival was codirected by Mendes and Rob Marshall and choreographed by Marhall. It starred Natasha Richardson as Sally Bowles and Alan Cumming, leering and flaunting rouged nipples at the audience, as the creepy Emcee. Both actors won Tony Awards for their performances, as did Ron Rifkin as Herr Schultz.

Ben Brantley of the *New York Times* wrote, "the production pushes hard to remind us that the decadence of Weimar Berlin was far from divine. This *Cabaret* is seedier, raunchier and more sinister than either the original groundbreaking Broadway version, directed by Harold Prince, or the 1970 movie by Bob Fosse."

The revival proved to be a bonanza for Roundabout, eventually running 2,377 performances, more than double the 1,165-performances of the original production. However, most of those performances were given at Studio 54, to which *Cabaret* transferred in November 1998. The status of the Kit Kat Klub as a Broadway theatre was in limbo for a time.

Cabaret was considered a Broadway production for the Tony Awards, but the next planned production in the space was to have been *Rollin' on the T.O.B.A.*, a tribute to the all-black touring circuit in the 1920s South. However, when the Tony committee announced somewhat arbitrarily that the space would be considered an Off-Broadway theatre for that production, its planned March 1999 transfer from the Forty-Seventh Street Theatre went on the rocks.

After a legal wrangle with promoter Matt Johnson, Durst took back control of the eighty-one-year-old playhouse and restored its designation as Henry Miller's Theatre. Anita Durst, landlord Douglas Durst's theatre-loving daughter, hosted *The Bitter Tears of Petra Von Kant*, based on Rainer Werner Fassbinder's play and film about a lesbian couple in the world of high fashion. The production starred Rebecca Wisocky as Petra and Durst as Marlene. It opened November 30, 2000, and ran seventy-nine performances. Anita Durst, an avant-garde theatre artist behind the floating Chashama Theatre (it pops up here and there around Times Square in vacant storefronts), would prove instrumental in the playhouse's future.

Henry Miller's Theatre returned to the Broadway fold September 20, 2001, with the opening of an unusual new musical comedy, *Urinetown*, which had music by Mark Hollmann, book by Greg Kotis and lyrics by both. Originally developed at the New York Music Theatre Festival, *Urinetown* was not intended for Broadway. Alternately bleak and funny, the show was set in a dystopic future when water is so scarce that private toilets are outlawed and people must pay to relieve themselves. Written in the style of the 1920s German political musicals like *Happy End* and *The Threepenny Opera* by Kurt Weill and Bertolt Brecht, *Urinetown* is the story of a group who rise up against the capitalist head of the local water monopoly (the "Urine Good Company"), only to find that things are not as rosy afterward as they expected. With Hunter Foster as Bobby Strong, John Cullum as Caldwell B. Cladwell, Jeff McCarthy as Officer Lockstock, and Spencer Kayden as the grimly adorable Little Sally, the show, whose previews had been delayed by the September 11 terrorist attacks, captured the blackly comic spirit of the moment and ran 965 performances.

The final performance on the well-trod Henry Miller's stage came on January 18, 2004, after which the building was demolished, with only its landmark brick facade preserved. The wall was stabilized by steel and wood bracing and scaffolding that were maintained throughout the construction period. Hundreds of thousands of dollars were spent to equip the four-story edifice with motion sensors that would automatically shut off construction equipment if the vibrations threatened its stability.

The new Henry Miller's Theatre was designed as part of the fifty-seven-story Bank of America Tower at One Bryant Park, which, along with 4 Times Square, headquarters of the Condé Nast publishing empire, at last fulfilled Seymour Durst's dream of owning and rebuilding the entire city block on which they stand.

Designed by the firm of Cook + Fox, the 1,055-seat Henry Miller's Theatre 2.0 is unusual for several reasons. Where most classic theatres were built with their orchestra sections opening on the street, Henry Miller's descends four stories below the pavement, with the topmost rear of the balcony at street level, and the orchestra section and stage a level below that, accessible by elevator and staircase. The trap beneath the stage occupies a third underground level, along with dressing rooms and an air-filtration room. The bottommost level is used for ice storage.

Ice storage? The theatre/office complex is also notable for employing some of the latest "green" technology, including systems that capture, filter, and recycle heat, water, and fresh air, plus walls made of recycled paper, men's washrooms that employ waterless urinals (Caldwell B. Cladwell would approve), and a women's room with nearly two dozen stalls. Though most seats are reachable only by stairs or an elevator, the seats are wider and have more generous legroom than in nearly any other New York playhouse. Fragments of the old theatre were preserved, including sculptural friezes, old doors, and the house-right upper corner of the proscenium, and are used as decoration in the new theatre. New wood was used in construction is North American cherry harvested from a Forest Stewardship Council (FSC)—certified forest.

But Henry Miller's Theatre 2.0 might as well be called Anita Durst's Theatre. Her dedication to its preservation is remembered in Anita's Way, the midblock Shubert Alley—like pedestrian passageway that runs along the west wall of the theatre between Forty-second and Forty-third streets, providing outdoor seating, a stagelike raised wooden platform, and access to the Henry Miller's stage door, which is dominated by an electric sign, rescued from the demolition, which bears the theatre's name.

In 2007 it was announced that the Dursts would welcome back their old tenant, Roundabout Theatre Company, to run Henry Miller's Theatre as their third Times Square—area stage, along with the American Airlines Theatre, Studio 54, and the Off-Broadway Laura Pels Theatre. Their lease runs twenty years.

The first production in the new theatre was the supposedly can't-miss teen musical *Bye Bye Birdie* (October 15, 2009), having its first Broadway revival since its debut in 1960. The show starred John Stamos as Albert, Gina Gershon as Rosie, Nolan Gerard Funk as Conrad, and Bill Irwin as Mr. MacAfee. Unfortunately, the production was judged a letdown. Director Robert Longbottom was unable to accomplish what middle schools across the United States had been doing for the previous half-century: have a hit with this feel-good show about an Elvis-like rock star who kisses one of his fans on the Ed Sullivan show as a publicity stunt before being drafted into the army. Critics blamed miscasting in several key roles, and the show closed in January 2010 after a disappointing ninety-two-performance run.

As happened with the opening of the original playhouse in 1918, the best reviews went to the theatre itself, which Ben Brantley of the *New York Times* described as "handsomely renovated. It seems ready to embark on a second fruitful life as a desirable up-to-date medium-size theatre." At this printing, singer Michael Feinstein and Australian comic Dame Edna were planning to join forces for an evening of allied music and laughs titled *All About Me*.

On March 22, 2010, Roundabout Theatre Company announced that Henry Miller's Theatre would be renamed the Stephen Sondheim Theatre after the preeminent theatre composer of the late twentieth century. Sondheim wept publicly at the surprise announcement, which came from his longtime writing partners James Lapine and John Weidman at a Studio 54 concert marking the composer's eightieth birthday. The rechristening was secured by an anonymous group of Sondheim devotees who donated an undisclosed sum to Roundabout's Musical Production Fund. Roundabout artistic director Todd Haimes called Sondheim "an artistic genius."

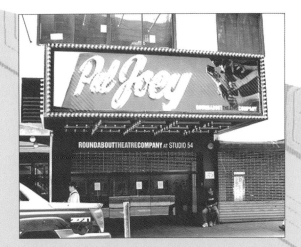

STUDIO 54

IT'S A SPECIAL BROADWAY MIRACLE that live theatre is seen on the stage of Studio 54 in the twenty-first century. That's because few theatres looked as far gone as Studio 54.

Built in 1927 as the Gallo Opera House, Studio 54 is possibly the most famous of the Broadway theatres to be returned to legitimate use in the late twentieth and early twenty-first centuries after many years standing empty or employed for other purposes. For the brief time that it was the most famous/notorious club of the disco era, few imagined that it could ever be a legitimate theatre again; indeed, few recognized it as the shell of a theatre at all. Nevertheless, despite all its sins, Studio 54 was never demolished and rebuilt like other "saved" playhouses. When you sit in Studio 54, you're inside the actual original auditorium space.

Top, left to right:
Standard PLAYBILL cover for the Gallo during its brief time with that name in the late 1920s.

Libby Holman, circa 1928 when she was featured in the 29-performance musical *Rainbow*. (1928). (Photofest).

Composer Vincent Youmans teamed with Oscar Hammerstein to write *Rainbow*, but they didn't get along. (Photofest).

Jackie "Moms" Mabley was featured in the 1931 revue *Fast and Furious*. (Photofest)

Bottom: Alfred Ryder and Dorothy McGuire in *Medicine Show* (1940).

The house was built by Italian-born opera entrepreneur Fortune Gallo to house a complement to his traveling San Carlo Opera Company, which he dreamed would someday take its place alongside the mighty Metropolitan Opera. The architect was Eugene DeRosa, designer of the Apollo Theatre on 42nd Street. The auditorium was located on the Fifty-third Street side of the block, but visitors entered through a doorway on Fifty-fourth Street that led down a hundred-foot marble and mirror promenade to their seats. There was a single balcony, but it was divided into forward mezzanine and rearward "balcony" sections. The Gallo arrived near the end of the classic Times Square theatre-building boom of 1904—28 and thus had little time to find its footing before the tsunami of the Great Depression swept over Broadway.

The Gallo Opera House began its assault on the Met on November 7, 1927, with a grand production of *La Bohème* that failed to attract an audience and closed after less than three weeks. This was a profound blow to Gallo, who had built his reputation as someone who knew how to attract general audiences to opera performances. With supreme irony, in view of the Gallo's aspirations and the theatre's original name, it has never again presented an opera. The closest was a revival of the musical *The Threepenny Opera* in 2006.

Before the end of 1927 the space's name had been adjusted to "Gallo Theatre," and it had endured two further high-toned flops. The first was Sophocles' *Electra*, with Margaret Anglin in the title role, recreating a performance she had given elsewhere earlier in the year. The production also featured two actors who would later have theatre awards named after them: Antoinette Perry as Clytemnestra and Clarence Derwent as Guardian. Despite their presence, the production opened Dec. 1, 1927, and gave only twelve performances.

The Irish Players followed quickly on December 19, with Sara Allgood in a revival of Sean O'Casey's *Juno and the Paycock*, which expired before the end of January 1928. It went on like this. Things never really improved for the Gallo Theatre, which hosted fourteen Broadway openings in the ensuing five years, all failures.

Perhaps the best-known and most regrettable of these was *Rainbow* (November 11, 1928), Oscar Hammerstein's eagerly anticipated follow-up to the classic *Show Boat*, which had opened the previous December at the Ziegfeld Theatre.

Kristin Chenoweth played three different roles in a revival of the triptych musical *The Apple Tree* (2006) including (left) Eve (with Mark Kudisch as the Snake) in *The Diary of Adam and Eve*, and the title role of *Passionella*. (Photos by Joan Marcus)

Set in the Gold Rush—era West, the musical featured Charles Ruggles and Libby Holman, the latter of whom introduced the torch song "I Want a Man." But the Phillip Goodman production was plagued with disharmony among composer Vincent Youmans, librettist Laurence Stallings, and producer Phillip Goodman. Hammerstein, who also functioned as director, was ill during part of the tryout, and the result that opened at the Gallo Theatre was a mess. Literally so: a donkey named Fanny who was included in the production for verisimilitude relieved itself during a love scene on opening night, thus summarizing Fate's entire attitude toward the Gallo during this period. *Rainbow*, called an "unfortunate debacle" by the *New York Times*, closed after twenty-nine performances. Youmans never again had a hit, and Hammerstein fled back to his songwriting partner Jerome Kern. Choreographer Busby Berkeley later abandoned Broadway for Hollywood, where he made film-musical history.

The Gallo Theatre lineup for the rest of the Depression continued the litany of failure. Paul Frank's "continental comedy" *Ladies Don't Lie* was offered to the public October 10, 1929, as the first in a series of twelve "popularly priced plays" by Radiant Productions, but with the stock market slide that month, the public didn't feel like paying even the discount price, and plans for the other eleven Radiant productions evaporated.

The Gallo was hastily rebooked with a revival of Harry James Smith's comedy *A Tailor-Made Man*, which had the misfortune of opening October 21, 1929, just three days before Black Thursday, when panic selling caused financial markets to collapse, beginning the Depression. Ironically, Grant Mitchell was playing a tailor who winds up saving a ship-building company. Unfortunately, he wasn't able to save his little theatre company, which went out of business after eight performances.

And that was enough for the ironically named Fortune Gallo. Unable to find a viable tenant for his pretty theatre, and unable to pay its mortgage like so many others living in that calamitous time, Gallo lost his playhouse to foreclosure just a few weeks later. He took the San Carlo Opera back on the road until 1950, and Gallo himself lived to age eighty-one, dying in 1970. The new owner renamed the space the New Yorker Theatre and reopened it on May 12, 1930, but Fate wasn't fooled. The inaugural production of Henrik Ibsen's rarely produced drama *The Vikings* met the same fate as all of Gallo's offerings and closed after eight performances.

The turkey parade continued under the

Left to right, Alexander Gemignani, Becky Ann Baker, Jeffrey Kuhn, Michael Cerveris, Neil Patrick Harris, Mario Cantone, Mary Catherine Garrison, Denis O'Hare, and James Barbour as a gallery of presidential killers in the 2004 musical *Assassins*. (Photo by Joan Marcus)

new name. An all-Greek revival of Sophocles' *Electra* flopped after eight performances, just after Christmas 1930. Roger Wheeler's melo-dramatic thriller *Gray Shadow* limped through thirty-nine performances starting March 10, 1931, with the *Times* quoting an opening-night audience member saying that the proceedings became so tedious that he had begun to wish his own throat was being cut. It was followed quickly by *Young Sinners* in April 1931 and

Harry Chapman Ford's *Ebb Tide* in June 1931.

Forbes Randolph produced, directed, and co-wrote an all-black musical revue called (appar-ently inaccurately) *Fast and Furious*, with music by Harry Revel, lyrics by Mack Gordon, and sketches by a variety of writers—including Clinton Fletcher, Zora Neale Hurston, Jackie "Moms" Mabley, and Clinton "Dusty" Fletcher—that barely kept audiences coming back for seven performances following the September 5, run even by Gallo standards. For the record, the show had music and lyrics by Alexander Hill and a book by Eileen Nutter.

In the superstitious world of the theatre, the Gallo/New Yorker was now firmly established as cursed and became unbookable. However, in the long run, the theatre actually proved to be very, very lucky. Many other playhouses on the fringe of the Times Square theatre district were demolished in the mid-twentieth century. But over the next seventy years the old Gallo managed to evade the ever-swinging wrecking ball like the hero of a video game. The first lucky leap came in 1933 when the building temporarily passed out of the world of legitimate theatre and became a nightclub and restaurant, gaudily rechristened the Casino de Paris and operated by ambitious songwriter/impresario Billy Rose, husband of Fanny Brice. Rows of seats were ripped out and tables installed, and whatever remained of New York's nightlife finally deigned to pass down the long mirrored arcade into its welcoming precincts. The club became known also for its "Green Carnation Boys"—male taxi dancers identified by a flower in their lapels—who were paid to dance with unaccompanied women. It wouldn't be the last time there was dancing in the theatre's former orchestra section. But even Rose, with his flair for showmanship, wasn't able to make the theatre pay. Persistent labor problems eventually led him to wash his hands of the place.

The owners tried to take another crack at legitimacy in 1936, briefly renaming the theatre the Palladium, possibly hoping to duplicate the success of the London emporium of the same name. That hope was quickly extinguished, and the building was rented to the WPA's Federal Theatre Project in 1937 and renamed the Federal Music Theatre. Under director Dr. Nikolai Sokoloff, the theatre hosted dance, singing, and instrumental concerts at "popular prices" of fifty or twenty-five cents. There was also a weekly Composer's Forum, showcasing the works of various songwriters. Like the rest of President Franklin Roosevelt's WPA, the theatre depended on federal subsidy for its existence, and the entire Federal Theatre Project was defunded in 1939.

Returning to legitimacy in 1939 again under the name the New Yorker Theatre, this house hosted a notable production, *The Swing Mikado*, the Gilbert and Sullivan operetta in an all-black adaptation that had originated at the Chicago Federal Theatre Project. Dr. Harry Minturn and arranger Gentry Warden staged the production

1931, opening. The Spanish Theatre of Madrid occupied the New Yorker for several weeks in spring 1932, but the result was more *mala suerte*.

Elusive scat singer Gertrude Cox, known to the jazz world as "Baby Cox," starred in a notable disaster that brought to a thundering close the first chapter of the theatre's life. Titled *Hummin' Sam*, this musical about life at a Kentucky racing stable opened and closed in a single performance on April 8, 1933—a bad in Chicago and later transferred it to Broadway with Maurice Cooper as Nanki-Poo and Herman Greene as Ko-Ko. After two months at the New Yorker starting March 1, 1939, this production transferred to the 44th Street Theatre, where it completed its run. Its success inspired an imitator, Billy Rose's *The Hot Mikado*.

The final legitimate stage production at the New Yorker came and went in spring 1940: *Medicine Show*, by Oscar Saul and H. R. Hayes. When the show closed on May 11, 1940, after a dismal thirty-five performances, the building stood empty until 1943 when it was leased by CBS-TV, which renamed it yet again. The great lady now had to put up with being called CBS Radio Playhouse No. 4, and then, after World War II, as CBS Studio No. 52.

Under that name it hosted several TV classics from the 1940s through the 1960s, including *The Jack Benny Show*, *Ted Mack's Original Amateur Hour*, and even part of the run of children's classic *Captain Kangaroo*. Several pioneering TV game shows were taped here for a time, including *Password*, *What's My Line?*, and *The $64,000 Question*. Among other Broadway theatres that spent some time as radio and/or TV studios: the Ambassador, the Belasco, the Cort, the Helen Hayes, the Bernard B. Jacobs, the Eugene O'Neill, and even the Broadway.

In a sense, the broadcast era saved many of these theatres. Nicolas Van Hoogstratten, author of the indispensable book *Lost Broadway Theatres*, said he doesn't mind so much when Broadway houses are temporarily sequestered for other uses, as long as they're not destroyed.

By the 1970s much television production once based in New York had moved west to Burbank and surrounding towns in Southern California. CBS found it had less and less use for Manhattan studios and put many of them up for sale. A soap opera called *Love of Life* was produced at CBS Studio No. 52 until 1974, when CBS decided to concentrate production elsewhere. The theatre was put on the market.

In late 1976 a pair of restaurateurs named Steve Rubell and Ian Schrager got the idea to open a nightclub that would use only recorded music (to keep expenses down) and serve expensive drinks (to maximize profits). They found the ideal space in the old TV studio on Fifty-fourth Street, its Broadway roots all but forgotten. And that is how they gave it the name by which the whole world came to know it: Studio 54. They pulled out the boxes, painted

over the murals, covered the architectural details with plywood and plaster, and installed high-tech lighting and sound equipment that required considerable modification of the old theatre's amenities. The exterior marquee was encased in metal panels, leaving only the Art Deco numerals "54."

Studio 54 opened April 16, 1977, with a star-studded guest list including future regulars from the showbiz, clothing-design, and art worlds, including Liza Minnelli, Andy Warhol, Halston, Mikhail Baryshnikov, Deborah Harry, and Brooke Shields. These and many more sashayed down the long promenade onto the dance floor, which made everyone feel like a movie star on the red carpet at the Oscars. The following week the disco hosted a birthday party for celebrity Bianca Jagger, at which the birthday girl made her entrance astride a white horse. The stunt helped establish the club as the last word in hedonistic excess, and it began its ascent to become the nightlife capitol of the world.

Schrager was the money man and stayed in the background. Rubell became the face of Studio 54. He wasn't the first to employ a velvet rope and snooty doormen to keep out the unhip, but he raised it to a ruthless art. Only the hottest stars and the most beautiful of the beautiful people were permitted entrance. Wannabes would line up along 54th Street hoping to convince doorman Marc Benecke (often aided by Rubell himself) that they made the grade. A lucky few were permitted entrance. As for the rest, Rubell would cut them off at the knees, often with grotesque insults. Fortune Gallo must have been spinning in his grave at the treatment given to potential paying customers in 1979, when they had been so scarce in 1929.

What drew them? A simple combination of sex, drugs, and extremely loud music. This was the era when the baby boomers were at their physical peak, *A Chorus Line*, which opened in 1975, had shown just how good people could look while dancing, and *Saturday Night Fever*, which opened on December 19, 1977, reinforced the notion. And it was a place where straight and gay people could boogie side by side.

Its legendary exclusivity made Studio 54 even more popular, but there was a practical reason to restrict occupancy, as well. The club wasn't all that big. It had a capacity of only seven hundred people. The orchestra section, which had once held rows of seats, now became the main dance floor, bathed in pulsating lights

Ana Gasteyer and Jim Dale as the corrupt Mrs. and Mr. Peachum in *The Threepenny Opera* (2006). (Photo by Joan Marcus)

from a half-dozen towers of red and orange bulbs, and from strobe units distributed around the periphery. The scene came to be imitated by discos around the world. The dee-jay was located in the mezzanine, overlooking the dance floor. The proscenium was still there, though covered. Hung with a Mylar-tin-sel curtain, the stage was sometimes used for live performances but sometimes also became another level of the dancing floor.

A large hanging sculpture of a leering cres-cent moon presided over the Studio 54 saturna-lia. A mechanical spoon would swing up to the moon's nose and deliver a line of sparkling, cocaine-like white bulbs, which would cause the moon to light up with delight. It mirrored the action in the private VIP lounge located on the second level, also known as the sex room. Whole books and films could be made about this period, and indeed they have been, notably *The Last Party*, by Anthony Haden-Guest, and the 1999 film *54*, with Mike Myers as Steve Rubell.

In the end, despite their fortune and fame, Schrager and Rubell operated Studio 54 for a scant thirty-three months. Rubell's profligate spending (including on his own drug habits) and Schrager's haphazard accounting brought the IRS down on them. Both men were arrested and each wound up spending more than a year in prison each. Studio 54 closed February 4, 1980, with—what else—a huge party. A second incarnation of the club opened in 1982. Long after disco music died, the disco ball spun here, with a new genera-tion of celebrities and dance lovers trying to recapture a wisp of the old craziness. Studio 54's "last dance" was danced in March 1986.

New owners offered the space as a nightclub and occasional concert hall under the names The Ritz and the Cabaret Royale. A 1994 renovation only drove the site deeper into debt, and once again, the wolf of demolition was at the door.

In 1998 the space got reinvented once again. It was leased by Roundabout Theatre Company, which had started in 1965 as an Off-Broadway institutional theatre and had eventu-ally moved to Broadway, first at the Criterion Center in Times Square in 1991. Later (2000) it would move into its own renovated small

Broadway theatre on Forty-second Street (named for sponsor American Airlines). In 1998 Roundabout rented Henry Miller's Theatre on Forty-third Street for a revival of Kander and Ebb's *Cabaret*.

They liked Henry Miller's partly because it had become run-down and shabby, which made an ideal setting for Sam Mendes's "environmental" production of the musical, set in a seedy Berlin nightclub in the 1930s. Henry Miller's had even served time as a disco called Xenon. However, the owners of Henry Miller's wanted to tear it down and build a new theatre on the site, meaning *Cabaret* had to find a new home, or close.

Studio 54 had a biography almost identical to Henry Miller's and was in similar crumbling shape. Roundabout and Mendes took one look at the mess and fell in love. The tawdry, deteriorated glory of the old theatre seemed tailor-made, to cite the title of its last legitimate show, for the likes of *Cabaret*. After nearly sixty years in the wilderness, Studio 54 was born again as a legitimate theatre. Aside from removing some of the plywood, turning the VIP lounge back into a mezzanine, and repairing the restrooms, Roundabout and Mendes left the squalor more or less as they found it. *Cabaret* reopened at Studio 54 on November 12, 1998. Among those who followed Natasha Richardson into the role of Sally Bowles was the now grown-up disco baby Brooke Shields.

The long run of *Cabaret* ended January 4, 2004, after 2,377 performances, more than twice that of the original. In 2003 Roundabout struck a deal to buy Studio 54 for $25 million, with the help of a city-backed bond issue, according to the New York *Daily News*. Starting April 22, 2004, with the Broadway debut of Stephen Sondheim and John Weidman's *Assassins*,

Roundabout began offering limited runs of larger shows than its American Airlines Theatre space on Forty-second Street allowed. The menu contained a mixture of plays, musicals, and even one solo show—two per season, fall and spring. It was a rare season that failed to include at least one Sondheim revival.

The third time proved to be the charm for *Assassins*, Sondheim and Weidman's musical about the sensitive subject of people who have attempted to assassinate U.S. presidents. The original 1991 Off-Broadway version at Playwrights Horizons couldn't get backing for a Broadway transfer, and then an aborted 2001 production was withdrawn by the writers after the September 11, 2001, terrorist attacks.

Roundabout got *Assassins* a seat at the Broadway table on April 22, 2004. Michael Cerveris played John Wilkes Booth, Neil Patrick Harris played the Balladeer. Various other killers and aspirants were played by Marc Kudisch, James Barbour, Denis O'Hare, Alexander Gemignani, and Mary Catherine Garrison on a carnival set by Robert Brill. The "cursed" theatre and the "cursed" musical now found blessed success together. The show ran more than a hundred performances and won a handsome five Tony Awards, including Best Revival of a Musical, Best Direction of a Musical (Joe Mantello), and Best Featured

Actor in a Musical (Cerveris).

Another Sondheim/Weidman revival followed on December 2, 2004: *Pacific Overtures*, the story of the opening of Japan to the West in the mid-nineteenth century after two centuries of self-imposed isolation from the rest of the world. Roundabout's revival was notable for being staged by Japanese director Amon Miyamoto, billed as the first Asian to direct a Broadway musical. B. D. Wong (*M. Butterfly*) and original 1976 cast member Sab Shimono (*Mame*) were featured. The "Next" sequence at the end, in which Japan is shown quickly building into its modern self, explicitly referenced the atomic bombing that ended World War II. The production was nominated for four Tony Awards, including, for the second year in a row, Best Revival of a Musical. The Gallo/New Yorker/et cetera/Studio 54 had finally fully been welcomed into the Broadway family nearly eighty years after Fortune Gallo first dreamed of it.

At this time Roundabout finally dispensed with the nightclub tables that it had been using since *Cabaret* and installed rows of seats on stepped risers to create the kind of raked seating that twenty-first-century audiences prefer. The renovation left Studio 54 with 944 seats. The swanky promenade, which is broken into three segments by doorways, was repurposed

Left to right: Nathan Lane and Bill Irwin as Estragon and Vladimir in a 2009 revival of *Waiting for Godot*. (Photo by Nigel Parry).

PLAYBILL cover for the Audra McDonald production of the musical *110 in the Shade* (2007). (Photo by Joan Marcus).

Audra McDonald and John Cullum as daughter and father in *110 in the Shade*. (Photo by Joan Marcus)

as a mini museum, offering background on the current production as well as on Roundabout Theatre Company itself. A concession stand also was added to the promenade for the sale of T-shirts, mugs, and other merchandise related to the show and the company.

The year 2005 at Studio 54 was dominated by dramas from two twentieth-century American masters, Tennessee Williams and Eugene O'Neill. In April, Williams's *A Streetcar Named Desire* got its eighth Broadway production in the half century since its 1947 debut. Director Edward Hall cast the role of Stanley Kowalski against type, employing doughy actor John C. Reilly instead of the ripped Marlon Brando type audiences had come to expect. Dreamy Blanche DuBois was played by Natasha Richardson in what no one would have guessed was her final Broadway appearance; she would die in a skiing accident the following March 18 at age forty-five. She had played several doomed heroines (Anna in *Anna Christie*, Sally Bowles in *Cabaret*) for Roundabout, so audiences didn't perceive any-

thing unusually foreboding about this one. Amy Ryan earned a Tony nomination for her performances as Stella.

Gabriel Byrne played the punctilious Cornelius Melody, who gradually sheds the cloak of civilization, in the December 8, 2005, revival of O'Neill's *A Touch of the Poet*, directed by Doug Hughes.

Writer Bertolt Brecht didn't flinch from the world's horrors, and in his work he often seemed to seek out the ugliest sides of his characters. Director Scott Elliott's April 20, 2006, production of Brecht's musical with Kurt Weill, *The Threepenny Opera*, tried perhaps a little too hard to show not just the dark side of the piece, but the even darker side. The in-period static staging didn't help, and performances from stars Alan Cumming, Cyndi Lauper, Ana Gasteyer, and Jim Dale showed the strain. Actually written during the time period of *Cabaret*, and in the style pastiched by *Cabaret*, this *Threepenny Opera* didn't go down nearly as well with Roundabout audiences and remains on many subscribers' "least favorite" list. Nevertheless, Tony nominations were forthcoming for Dale and for the production as a whole for Best Revival of a Musical; it lost to *The Pajama Game*. It was the closest thing to opera at the theatre since *La Bohéme* back in 1927 and gave Roundabout a little taste of the old Gallo luck.

The December 14, 2006, revival of Bock and Harnick's triptych musical *The Apple Tree* starred Brian d'Arcy James as a sturdy Adam, Kristin Chenoweth as a sparkling Eve, and Marc Kudisch in yet another of his gleeful villain roles, this time as the Serpent.

Major stars of two generations were featured in the May 9, 2007, revival of the 1963 Tom Jones and Harvey Schmidt musical *110 in the Shade*, adapted by N. Richard Nash from his own play *The Rainmaker*. Audra McDonald played the buttoned-up Lizzie, and John Cullum played her father, who tries to help her come out of her shell with the arrival of Starbuck, a man claiming the ability to bring rain to their drought-stricken Texas town. It was a tribute to everyone's performance that the nontraditional casting of the African-American McDonald was barely noticed. A gorgeous poster of McDonald's rain-spattered, smiling face became a favorite with collectors. Paul Gemignani conducted with a glorious delicacy that was captured on the cast album.

Matthew Risch, who stepped into the title role of *Pal Joey* opposite Stockard Channing during previews. (Photo by Joan Marcus)

October 2007 saw a full-scale revival of Terrence McNally's gay-bathhouse farce *The Ritz*, starring Kevin Chamberlin (*Seussical*) as Gaetano Proclo, who hides out from his murderous mafia family in the aforementioned bathhouse; Brooks Ashmanskas as Chris; and Rosie Perez as the irrepressible Googie Gomez, who performed an off-key, off-color, and off-kilter medley of show tunes, losing a shoe in the process.

For its February 2008 offering, Roundabout imported London's Donmar Warehouse Theatre production of Sondheim's *Sunday in the Park with George*, starring Daniel Evans as George and Jena Russell as Dot, both of whom earned Tony nominations.

Top left: "Three Maids" from the Federal Theatre Project's 1939 adaptation of The Mikado, titled *The Swing Mikado*. (Photofest)

Top right: left to right, Halson, Margaret Trudeau, Mark Gero, Liza Minnelli, and Steve Rubell in 1979 during the theatre's golden age as a disco. (Photofest)

Bottom left: left to right, Andy Warhol, Calvin Klein, Brooke Shields and Rubell at the disco in 1981. (Photofest)

The production used a drastically stripped-down five-musician orchestra and minimal sets but will be remembered for the animated drawings designed by Timothy Bird and the Knifedge Creative Network to show George Seurat's progress on his masterpiece *A Sunday Afternoon on the Island of La Grande Jatte* in Act I and his fictional grandson's computerized "chromolumes" in Act II.

From the minute it was announced that *Jersey Boys'* Tony-winning tough guy Christian Hoff would incarnate the title role of consummate "playa" Joey Evans in *Pal Joey*, all of Broadway believed it to be inspired casting. Excitement increased when Roundabout announced Stockard Channing would be play-ing sugar mama Vera Simpson. Previews were already under way in December 2008 when director Joe Mantello and the producers announced that Hoff had injured himself and the role would be assumed by understudy Matthew Risch. Hoff insisted he was fine. Channing and costar Martha Plimpton (as Gladys Bumps) earned Tony nominations, as did set designer Scott Pask (who set the story beneath a curving el track) and the production as a whole. But there was a strong sense of unfulfilled promise about the proceedings.

Two of the greatest comic masters of their generation, Bill Irwin and Nathan Lane, tackled Samuel Beckett's masterpiece *Waiting for Godot* in a wrenching April 30, 2009, production set on an arid, boulder-strewn set by Santo Loquasto. Their comic interplay with John Goodman as Pozzo was among the highlights of the production, but the sole Tony nomination went to John Glover as the infinitely abused Lucky.

Actress Carrie Fisher, best known as Princess Leia in the *Star Wars* films, laid bare the tawdry details of her life in the comically self-deprecating October 2009 solo show *Wishful Drinking*, which she had been developing in theatres across the United States over several years. Filled with anecdotes about her calamitous romances and experiments with drugs and alcohol, the wry litany proved so popular it extended into early 2010.

At this writing, Studio 54 was being readied for the April 22, 2010, opening of *Sondheim on Sondheim*, James Lapine's multimedia salute to his collaborator, the composer of many great musicals of the late twentieth century—not to mention one of the mainstays of Studio 54's miraculous renaissance.

VIVIAN BEAUMONT

THEATER

THE VIVIAN BEAUMONT THEATER AT Lincoln Center, built at a cost of $9.7 million, opened on October 21, 1965. It was named for the philanthropist who donated half of its construction cost. A smaller performing space downstairs in the same building was first called the Forum, then later changed to the Mitzi E. Newhouse Theater, for another donor.

The Beaumont was designed by the distinguished set designer Jo Mielziner and the noted architect Eero Saarinen. It had 1,140 seats when proscenium staging was used and 1,083 when the thrust stage was employed. The color scheme was a pleasing red and brown.

When the Beaumont opened it was designated as the home of the Repertory Theater of Lincoln Center. Codirected by Elia Kazan and

Robert Whitehead, this company had been operating for two seasons downtown at the ANTA Washington Square Theater while the Beaumont was under construction. The troupe moved to the Beaumont under the management of Herbert Blau and Jules Irving. Their plan for the Beaumont was to create a "theatre of loud involvement" with plays that would fill the large stage with modern social and emotional significance. Among the actors who regularly appeared in productions during those early years were Philip Bosco, Nancy Marchand, Aline MacMahon, and Robert Symonds.

The first production was Georg Büchner's *Danton's Death*—certainly a large and loud play—about the French Revolution. It was directed by Blau, had magnificent sets by Mielziner, and had a cast that included James Earl Jones, Stacy Keach, and Symonds. The physical production was praised, but the play was considered dull. (Orson Welles had also failed when his Mercury Theatre had produced the work.)

The three other plays produced that first season were Wycherley's *The Country Wife* with Elizabeth Huddle and Symonds (who also directed); the American premiere of Jean-Paul Sartre's *The Condemned of Altona* with George Coulouris; and the New York premiere of Brecht's *The Caucasian Chalk Circle*, adapted by Eric Bentley, in which actors wore masks. This surrealistic play, directed by Irving, was considered the best production offered by the company that season.

The first season was a financial success, with most subscribers signing up for the next year, but it was not an artistic success. Otis L. Guernsey Jr., editor of the "Best Plays" annual, complained that the company hadn't found itself yet and criticized the fact that they presented no American plays.

For its second season, the company began with a revival of Ben Johnson's *The Alchemist* with Michael O'Sullivan, Marchand, Bosco, MacMahon, and Symonds. Next came Lorca's *Yerma* with Frank Langella, Maria Tucci, MacMahon, and Marchand. The third offering was the group's first American play—*The East Wind* by Leo Lehman—with Estelle Parsons, George Voskovec, Bosco, and MacMahon. This satisfied the critics who complained that the company was not doing new or even old American plays. The fourth subscription play was a revival of Bertolt Brecht's *Galileo*, adapted by Charles Laughton. Anthony Quayle played the title character, supported by Parsons and others of the rep company. The play dramatized 1600s astronomer Galileo's battle for intellectual freedom against the Church, which forced him to recant his theory of the movement of the planets around the sun.

On January 13, 1967, Herbert Blau resigned as codirector of the Lincoln Center Repertory Theater of Lincoln Center and Irving remained as its sole director. During 1967 the Beaumont was rented twice. On July 8, 1967, Alexander H. Cohen presented Peter Ustinov's *The Unknown Soldier and His Wife*, directed by John Dexter. The cast of this war drama included Brian Bedford, Christopher Walken, Melissa C. Murphy, Howard Da Silva, Bob Dishy, and many others. It played at the Beaumont for eighty-four performances, then moved to the George Abbott Theatre for an additional sixty-four.

On October 26, 1987, the Beaumont presented a special invitational production of Lillian Hellman's *The Little Foxes*. The all-star cast—Anne Bancroft, E. G. Marshall, George C. Scott, Margaret Leighton, Maria Tucci, Austin Pendleton, and Richard A. Dysart—was directed brilliantly by Mike Nichols. The production was so successful that it moved to a commercial run at the Ethel Barrymore Theatre. Critics were beginning to have more faith in the Beaumont.

On January 4, 1968, with Irving still the company's director, the Beaumont presented Shaw's *Saint Joan* with Diana Sands in the title role. It played for forty-four performances. This was followed by Christopher Fry's adaptation of Jean

Top left: Victor Garber and Blair Brown in Tom Stoppard's *Arcadia* (1995).

Bottom left: Michael Hayden and Sally Murphy on Bob Crowley's Tony-winning set for *Carousel* (1994).

Above: Souvenir program for *The Little Foxes* (1967) with Anne Bancroft, Margaret Leighton, E.G. Marshall, George C. Scott, Austin Pendleton, William Prince, and Maria Tucci.

Above: Souvenir program for *The Time of Your Life* (1969) with James Broderick, Susan Tyrrel, and Skip Hinnant.

Above: PLAYBILL for Julie Taymor's *Juan Darién: A Carnival Mass* (1996).

Above: Jim McMullen's beautiful poster designs on the opening night PLAYBILLs for *The Little Foxes* (1997) and *Twelfth Night* (1998).

Giraudoux's *Tiger at the Gates*, directed by Anthony Quayle and starring Diana Sands, M'el Dowd, Bosco, and Symonds. It also played for forty-four performances. Symonds next starred played the title role in *Cyrano de Bergerac*, with Suzanne Grossman as Roxane.

In June 1968 the Lincoln Center Festival '68 presented Paris's Compagnie de Théâtre de la Cité de Villeurbanne in three plays: *The Three Musketeers*, *George Dandin*, and *Tartuffe* for a limited engagement of 24 performances. Also part of the festival was Brian Friel's *Lovers*, starring Art Carney, which ran for 149 performances. Lee J. Cobb starred next as *King Lear*, playing in repertory with William Gibson's *A Cry of Players*. The double bill stayed for 72 performances.

In April 1969 Heinar Kipphardt's *In the Matter of J. Robert Oppenheimer* opened with Joseph Wiseman in the title role. It closed that month but returned in June with Paul Sparer as Oppenheimer. During the play's absence, Robert Symonds, Blythe Danner, and Philip Bosco cavorted in Moliere's *The Miser* for fifty-two performances.

On November 6, 1969, William Saroyan's whimsical comedy *The Time of Your Life* was revived with James Broderick, Philip Bosco, and Susan Tyrrell in lead roles. It played for fifty-two performances. It was followed by Tennessee Williams's curious play *Camino Real*, with Jessica Tandy and Al Pacino in the lead roles, which mystified the subscribers for fifty-two performances. Next was a new play by Sam

Shepard called *Operation Sidewinder*, and it was staged with dazzling surrealism. The story involved a deadly military device—a large mechanical rattlesnake—and there was much violence and loud rock music onstage. George S. Kaufman and Marc Connelly's 1924 fantasy *Beggar on Horseback* arrived next, with Leonard Frey as a struggling artist about to be trapped in a loveless marriage to a wealthy woman. Much of the action occurred in the hero's dreams. Critics saluted the Repertory Theater of Lincoln Center for presenting an all-American season of plays—both new and old. The Sam Shepard play was judged to be the most interesting.

Four plays were presented in the 1970—71 season. Colleen Dewhurst starred in *The Good Woman of Setzuan* by Bertolt Brecht. David Birney, Frances Sternhagen, Philip Bosco, and Tandy Cronyn were in Synge's *The Playboy of the Western World*. Arthur Miller's adaptation of Ibsen's *An Enemy of the People* was revived with Stephen Elliott, Bosco, David Birney, and Barbara Cason. The final production of the season was Sophocles's *Antigone*, adapted by Dudley Fitts and Robert Fitzgerald, with Martha Henry as Antigone, Cronyn as Ismene, and Bosco as Creon. The critics pronounced it to be a distinguished season for the Beaumont.

The 1971—72 season brought a revival of Schiller's *Mary Stuart*, with Salomé Jens in the title role and Nancy Marchand as Queen Elizabeth. A very promising actor, Andy Robinson (later to chill audiences as the sniper in the film

Left: Martha Plimpton
in the title role of
Shakespeare's
Cymbeline (2007).
(Photo by Paul Kolnik)

Right: Tony-winner
Victoria Clark and Kelli
O'Hara as a mother and
daughter with a secret,
in the 2005 musical
The Light in the Piazza.
(Photo by Joan Marcus)

Above: PLAYBILLS for
The Light in the Piazza
(2005), *My Favorite
Year* (1992) and *Parade*
(1998).

Dirty Harry), appeared in this play as Sir William Davison and in many other productions of the Repertory Theater of Lincoln Center. This production also marked the American premiere of Stephen Spender's translation of the play.

Next came *Narrow Road to the Deep North* by Edward Bond, a boring, symbolic play set in Japan. It was followed by a revival of Shakespeare's *Twelfth Night* starring Blythe Danner as Viola, René Auberjonois as Malvolio, Leonard Frey as Sir Andrew Aguecheek, and Moses Gunn as Orsino.

The last production of the season was a revival of Arthur Miller's 1953 play *The Crucible*. This production, with Robert Foxworth as John Proctor, was enthusiastically received but somewhat dampened by Arthur Miller's denunciation of the Lincoln Center Board of Directors as being ignorant of how to run a repertory company. This attack appeared in several publications, including the *New York Times*. Wrote Miller: "The first order of business now is to get clear in our own minds what a repertory theater is, what it can do and what is financially needed to do it. Then, if we are convinced of its value, a considered serious attempt must be made to transform Lincoln Center into such a theater."

The 1972—73 season brought Gorky's *Enemies*, O'Casey's *The Plough and the Stars*, Shakespeare's *The Merchant of Venice*, and Tennessee Williams's *A Streetcar Named Desire*.

A dramatic event occurred during this sea-

son. Artistic Director Jules Irving announced he was leaving the Repertory Theater of Lincoln Center. He was displeased with the board of directors managed the company. The Forum Theater had been reduced to showing films; the board nearly permitted the destruction of the company's storage space for scenery and, most seriously, failed to provide the necessary financing for a true repertory company—a staple of British theatre, but an elusive ideal in American theatre to the time of this writing. A meeting was held and the board considered renting the Beaumont to outside productions. A touring company of *Man of La Mancha* had done very well the previous summer as an extra attraction at the Beaumont. (After all, it had started at the downtown ANTA Theater, the original home of the company.)

But no, something else was proposed and sanctioned. Joseph Papp, head of the New York Shakespeare Festival, would take over with his own board. Papp immediately began raising financing for his project, and when the Rockefeller Foundation granted $350,000 and Mrs. Samuel I. Newhouse donated $1 million, the name of the Forum Theater was changed to the Mitzi E. Newhouse.

Papp announced that he would continue to produce experimental plays downtown at his Public Theatre stages, and his Shakespeare summer productions at Central Park's Delacorte Theater, but he would present more finished plays at the Beaumont. His company was in resi-

Above: PLAYBILL from *Carousel*.

Above: Boyd Gaines is haunted by Deborah Yates on the PLAYBILL for the Tony Award-winning dance musical *Contact*.

dence at the Beaumont from 1973 to 1977, presenting only new plays at first, rather than classics. During this time he also staged productions in the Newhouse. Among his offerings were David Rabe's *In the Boom Boom Room*, an expensive failure with Madeline Kahn; *The Au Pair Man* by Hugh Leonard, with Julie Harris and Charles Durning; *What the Wine Sellers Buy* by Ron Miller; a revival of Strindberg's *The Dance of Death* with Zoe Caldwell, Robert Shaw, and Hector Elizondo; and a powerful prison drama called *Short Eyes* by Miguel Piñero, which transferred to the Beaumont from the downtown Public Theater. *Short Eyes* was judged the strongest entry of Papp's inaugural season at this theatre. Otis L. Guernsey Jr. wrote in *The Best Plays of 1972—1973*: "Joseph Papp's first season at the Vivian Beaumont was one of adventure for the Lincoln Center subscription audiences (and audiences who aren't adventurous don't belong at Papp productions)."

In 1974—75 Papp presented *Mert & Phil* by Anne Burr, *Black Picture Show* by Bill Gunn, Ibsen's *A Doll's House* with Liv Ullmann and Sam Waterston, and *Little Black Sheep* by Anthony Scully. Papp was upset by the public's lack of response to his new-play schedule at the Beaumont and announced that in the future he would mainly do revivals there.

His next season included *Trelawny of the "Wells"* by Arthur Wing Piñero, with a cast full of future stars: Meryl Streep, John Lithgow, Walter Abel, Mary Beth Hurt, and Mandy Patinkin. The production received the following Tony Award nominations: Featured Actress in a Play (Hurt), Scenic Designer (David Mitchell), and Lighting Designer (Ian Calderon). Hamlet followed with Sam Waterston, Jane Alexander, Maureen Anderman, George Hearn, Larry Gates, and Patinkin. Shaw's *Mrs. Warren's Profession* was revived with Lynn Redgrave, Ruth Gordon, Edward Herrmann, and Milo O'Shea. Herrmann won a Tony Award (Featured Actor in a Play), and Redgrave was nominated for Best Actress in a Play. *The Threepenny Opera* was next with Raul Julia as Mack the Knife, plus Elizabeth Wilson and Blair Brown, performing a controversial new translation by Ralph Manheim and John Willett, replacing the familiar one by Marc Blitzstein. This production was highly successful, as was David Rabe's powerful army play *Streamers*, which was nominated for a Best Play Tony Award.

In 1977 Papp presented a new adaptation of Chekhov's *The Cherry Orchard* by Jean-Claude van Itallie with Raul Julia, Meryl Streep, Irene Worth, Mary Beth Hurt, Max Wright, and Cathryn Damon. This was followed by a revival of *Agamemnon* by Aeschylus, as conceived by

Brían F. O'Byrne cradles August Gladstone (foreground) while members of the company of *Shipwreck* look on in part two of Tom Stoppard's Tony-winning *The Coast of Utopia* trilogy (2006-07). (Photo by Paul Kolnik)

Andrei Serban and Elizabeth Swados, using fragments of the original Greek and Edith Hamilton's translation. Both revivals were judged to be outstanding. Despite this record, Papp's productions downtown at his theatre on Astor Place were judged to be superior to his uptown output, and he decided to withdraw from the Beaumont. Plagued by complaints about poor acoustics and its unwieldy thrust stage, the Beaumont remained closed for eighteen months.

From 1979 to 1984 producer Richmond Crinkley was executive director of the Beaumont, which presented only one full season, in 1980—81, including an unsuccessful revival of Philip Barry's celebrated high comedy *The Philadelphia Story*, starring Blythe Danner as Tracy Lord, Meg Mundy as her mother, Frank Converse as C. K. Dexter Haven, Edward Herrmann as Mike Connor, Mary Louise Wilson as Liz Imbrie, Douglas Watson as Seth Lord, and George Ede as the lecherous Uncle Willie. The play was lost in a gigantic set that resembled Pennsylvania Station, and the charm of the 1939 original with Katharine Hepburn was missing.

Crinkley next presented *Macbeth*, with Philip Anglim, Maureen Anderman, Dana Ivey, and Kelsey Grammer, for sixty-one performances. The third offering that season was an inferior comedy by Woody Allen called *The Floating Light Bulb*, with Danny Aiello, Beatrice Arthur, Jack

Weston, and Brian Backer, who received a Featured Actor Tony Award for his performance. Jack Weston was nominated for a Leading Actor Tony Award. This memory play was compared unfavorably to *The Glass Menagerie*.

In 1983 a memorable event occurred at the Beaumont. The theatre was rented to producer Alexander H. Cohen for Peter Brook's magnificent production of *La Tragédie de Carmen*, an eighty-minute distillation of Bizet's opera *Carmen*. This production was originally aimed for the New Amsterdam Roof but had to be switched to the Beaumont when the Roof was declared unsafe. The drama critics were jubilant at Brook's dynamic staging of the condensed opera on a thrust stage, but the music critics weren't. One of the fascinating aspects of the production was that the performance area was covered with dirt, like a bull ring. Not all the Bizet music was used, and three singers alternated in the lead roles. The work was subtitled *A Full Length Musical in One Act*. It was a triumph and thrilled playgoers for 187 performances. It received a Special Tony Award for its brilliance.

In 1985 management was reorganized once again, this time as the Lincoln Center Theater, and at last began to shed its aura of unfulfilled promise. The Beaumont, which had come to be considered a white elephant, gradually transformed into the home of hits under the wise stewardship of

Left: PLAYBILL from *South Pacific* (2008).

Right: Li Jun Li as Liat and Loretta Ables Sayre as Bloody Mary in *South Pacific*. (Photo by Joan Marcus)

Gregory Mosher and Public Theater alumnus Bernard Gersten, and later Gersten and André Bishop. From 1985 to 1991 Mosher was director and Gersten was executive producer of LCT. In 1986 they produced *Juggling and Cheap Theatrics*, a variety revue devised by the incredible New Vaudeville troupe the Flying Karamazov Brothers. In April they came up with a real winner: a revival of *The House of Blue Leaves* by John Guare, which had been a 1971 Off-Broadway delight. The revival starred John Mahoney, Stockard Channing, Swoosie Kurtz, Christine Baranski, and Danny Aiello. The comedy, about bedlam in the New York borough of Queens when the Pope pays a visit, won the following Tony Awards: Best Featured Actor (Mahoney), Best Featured Actress (Kurtz), Best Play Director (Jerry Zaks), and Best Scenic Designer (Tony Walton). It also received the following Tony Award nominations: Best Featured Actress (Channing), Best Play, Best Costume Design (Ann Roth), and Best Lighting Design (Paul Gallo).

In November 1986 the Beaumont had another hit revival: the Hecht/MacArthur classic *The Front Page* with Richard Thomas, John Lithgow, and Bill McCutcheon. It received two Tony Award nominations: Best Revival and Best Scenic Designer (Tony Walton).

In 1987 the theatre presented Earle Hyman in *Death and the King's Horseman*, a Nigerian drama by Wole Soyinka; *The Regard of Flight* and *The Clown Bagatelles*, entertainment by the superb mime Bill Irwin; and an antic version of *The Comedy of Errors* conceived by the Flying Karamazov Brothers and Robert Woodruff, which played for 148 performances.

On November 19, 1987, the Beaumont welcomed a jubilant revival of the 1934 Cole Porter musical *Anything Goes*. Patti LuPone had the famous Ethel Merman role of Reno Sweeney, Howard McGillin took the William Gaxton role, and Bill McCutcheon expertly acted the Victor Moore Public Enemy No. 13 part. The original Porter score was beefed up with interpolated numbers such as "Easy to Love" and "It's De-Lovely," and Tony Walton designed a deluxe shipboard set on which the show's band was perched. The stunning revival ran for 804 performances and won the following Tony Awards: Best Featured Actor in a Musical (McCutcheon), Best Choreography (Michael Smuin), and Best Musical Revival. It also received these Tony nominations: Best Musical Actress (LuPone), Best Musical Actor (McGillin), Best Musical Featured Actor

(Anthony Heald), Best Musical Director (Jerry Zaks), Best Scenic Designer and Best Costume Designer (both for Tony Walton), and Best Lighting Designer (Paul Gallo). This bonanza ran 784 performances, through September 3, 1989.

The last production of the 1980s was a revival of Paddy Chayefsky's *The Tenth Man* with Phoebe Cates. This was followed by a play transferred from Off-Broadway called *Some Americans Abroad* by Richard Nelson, with Nathan Lane and Kate Burton. The play concerned a group of Anglophile American professors on a London theatre tour. In November 1990 another winner came to the Beaumont from Lincoln Center's smaller theatre, the Newhouse. It was John Guare's fascinating *Six Degrees of Separation*, based on a true-life incident in which an imposter passed himself off as the son of actor Sidney Poitier and was able to gain access to the apartments of rich Manhattanites. The play was stylishly directed by Jerry Zaks, who won a Tony Award, and was voted the Best Play of the year by the New York Drama Critics Circle. It also earned these Tony Award nominations: Best Actress (Stockard Channing), Best Actor (Courtney B. Vance), and Best Play. It had a healthy run of 485 performances.

Another John Guare drama arrived next, but it was only fair. *Four Baboons Adoring the Sun* was an odd play, which the *New York Times* called the most controversial of the season. Channing and James Naughton headed the cast.

André Bishop, who had successfully piloted Playwrights Horizons for many years, then succeeded Gregory Mosher in January 1992 and joined Bernard Gersten as artistic director of the Lincoln Center Theater. Over the next few years the Gersten/Bishop team was to elevate this theatre to its pinnacle of artistic achievement. In addition to choosing scripts astutely and forming strong bonds with some of the period's top theatre talent, they also programmed the Beaumont with canny flexibility. They would announce a season at the Beaumont and would produce a series of limited runs of shows like *King Lear* or *The Rivals*, which were generally well received. But if a show proved to be a hit, like *Contact* (2000, 1010 performances), *The Light in the Piazza* (2005, 504 performances) or *South Pacific* (2007, still running), they would simply move the rest of the season elsewhere, booking commercial productions at houses like the Atkinson or Cort and leaving the hit to fill LCT coffers as long as it made money. Such hits allowed LCT to continue to produce fascinating noncommercial works like *Juan Darién* and *The Coast of Utopia* on Broadway, plus continue to program works like *Dessa Rose, Hello Again,* and *Pride's Crossing* at the Off-Broadway Newhouse Theatre from de facto artists-in-residence like Susan Stroman, Ahrens and Flaherty, Michael John LaChiusa, and Wendy Wasserstein.

Another of LCT's innovations was to book the Beaumont's "dark" nights (Sunday and/or Monday, when the main production was not performing) with interesting solo shows or concerts by theatre stars. The first was Spalding Gray's *Monster in a Box* (1991), a monologue about his long-aborning novel. Gray returned in 1993 and 1994 with engagements of his *Gray's Anatomy,* about how an eye affliction literally changed his view of the world.

Over the next few years the Beaumont hosted special adjunct bookings of Gray's *It's a Slippery Slope* (1996) and *Morning, Noon and Night* (1999); Patti LuPone's concert show *Matters of the Heart* (2000); Alan Alda's portrait of Renaissance man Richard Feynman, *QED* (2001); Barbara Cook's *Mostly Sondheim* (2002) and *Barbara Cook's Broadway!* (2004); and Brian Stokes Mitchell's *Love/Life* (2005), plus several onetime concerts, including a November 2002 reunion concert version of *Anything Goes.*

During the 1992—93 season on the mainstage, a musical version of the film *My Favorite Year* proved a failure, despite a score by Lynn Ahrens and Stephen Flaherty. It was based on a film about a real-life incident. In 1954 Errol Flynn arrived in New York to do a guest stint on Sid Caesar's *Your Show of Shows* and wound up wreaking havoc with his outrageous behavior. Although the musical didn't work, it won a Tony Award for Andrea Martin as Best Featured Actress in a Musical. Other Tony nominees: Tim Curry (Best Actor in a Musical) and Lainie Kazan (Best Featured Actress in a Musical).

On November 29, 1993, a huge cast performed in a revival of Robert E. Sherwood's 1938 Pulitzer Prize play *Abe Lincoln in Illinois.* Sam Waterston was praised for his performance as Lincoln, and Lizbeth Mackay played Mary Todd. The production received the following Tony Award nominations: Best Actor in a Play (Waterston), Best Play Director (Gerald Gutierrez), and Best Revival.

Jane Bowles's pretentious drama *In the Summer House* was next, and it received mostly negative reviews. Dianne Wiest, Liev Schreiber, and Frances Conroy appeared in this misty fantasy, which was soon gone.

On March 24, 1994, London's Royal National Theatre sent New York its hit revival of *Carousel,* the Rodgers and Hammerstein classic. The cast included Audra Ann McDonald (who later dropped the "Ann"), Sally Murphy, and Michael Hayden. Bob Crowley's sets were outstanding, as was Nicholas Hytner's staging, especially the way the eponymous carousel assembled itself as if by magic in the opening scene. The voices of McDonald and the other singers were superlative, giving new grandeur to the haunting score. The musical won the following Tony Awards: Best Musical Revival, Best Featured Musical Actress (McDonald), Best Musical Director (Hytner), Best Scenic Designer (Crowley), and Best Choreographer (Sir Kenneth MacMillan). *Carousel* revolved for 322 performances.

On March 30, 1995, a play arrived that was a masterpiece to some (especially critics) and a colossal bore to others. It was Tom Stoppard's play *Arcadia,* which had been an enormous success in London. The action in the play kept shifting from the present to 1809, which some found confusing. One critic wrote: "The night I saw it, large portions of the audience stood and cheered but others left looking wan and defeated. Stoppard's intellectual plays are like caviar—you either love it or loathe it." *Arcadia* won the New York Drama Critics Circle Award for Best Play. The cast included Billy Crudup, Jennifer Dundas, Lisa Banes, Victor Garber, Blair Brown, Robert Sean Leonard, and David Manis. It won no Tony Awards but was nominated in the following categories: Best Play, Best Scenic Designer (Mark Thompson), and Best Lighting Designer (Paul Pyant). The play ran for 173 performances.

David Hare, one of Britain's most prolific playwrights, supplied the next Beaumont attraction, *Racing Demon,* which attacked the politics of the Church of England. *Variety* felt it was an "unsettling, deeply pessimistic play." The cast included Josef Sommer, Michael Cumpsty, Brian Murray, and Kathleen Chalfant. It ran for forty-eight performances and received a Best Play Tony Award nomination.

November 24, 1996, brought an imaginative novelty to the Beaumont: *Juan Darién,* subtitled *A Carnival Mass,* written and directed by the distinguished artist Julie Taymor, with composer Elliot Goldenthal. Taymor also designed the brilliant puppets and masks, and some of the sets and costumes, that made this a stunning visual experience. Set in a South American jungle, this

Paulo Szot and Kelli O'Hara as Emile de Becque and Nelly Forbush in *South Pacific*. (Photo by Joan Marcus)

"music theatre" piece about a jaguar cub who transforms into a boy was praised more for its spectacular beauty than for its content.

Another revival of Hellman's *The Little Foxes* opened at the Beaumont in April 1997. It starred Stockard Channing in the Tallulah Bankhead role. *New York Times* drama critic Ben Brantley pronounced the revival "miscast and misconceived."

Chekhov's *Ivanov* was revived in November 1997 with Kevin Kline, Jayne Atkinson, Hope Davis, and Robert Foxworth. It received mixed reviews, but Kline's performance was praised. It ran for fifty-one performances. Eugene O'Neill's comedy *Ah, Wilderness!* was given a loving revival in March 1998 with Craig T.

Nelson, Leo Burmester, Sam Trammell, and Jean Thompson in lead roles. It garnered mostly favorable reviews and received two Tony Award nominations: Best Play Revival and Best Featured Actor in a play (Trammell).

An eagerly awaited musical in 1998 proved to be a letdown. *Parade*, a musical treatment of a very tragic real-life incident, turned out to be too grim for the musical stage. Co-conceived by Harold Prince, who directed it, the show had a book by Alfred Uhry and a score by Broadway first-timer Jason Robert Brown. The show recounted the harrowing lynching of the northern-born Jew Leo Frank, wrongly accused of murdering a thirteen-year-old girl in a pencil factory in Atlanta. This tragedy had been made into a superlative 1937 film, *They Won't Forget*, as well as an acclaimed TV movie, *The Murder of Mary Phagan*, but it did not work as a musical, despite the splendid performances of Brent Carver and Carolee Carmello and an excellent score by Brown, captured on a superb RCA Victor cast album. The musical received the following Tony Awards: Best Musical Book (Uhry) and Best Musical Score (Brown). It also received the following Tony nominations: Best Musical, Best Choreography (Patricia Birch), Best Musical Direction (Harold Prince), and Best Scenic Design (Ricardo Hernandez). *Parade* closed after eighty-five performances.

Next, Lincoln Center Theater coproduced a musical revue called *It Ain't Nothin' but the Blues*, as created by the Crossroads Theater Company of New Jersey. Music by various composers was used to trace the history of the blues. The show transferred to the Beaumont after a stint at the New Victory Theatre on Forty-second Street, and it was nominated for the 1999 Tony Award as Best Musical.

The last new Broadway musical of the 1900s, *Marie Christine*, opened at the Beaumont on December 2, 1999. It was an odd work, a musical based on Euripides' *Medea* about a woman who murders her children rather than let her estranged husband take them from her. Michael John LaChiusa, who wrote the book and composed the score, set his version in New Orleans and Chicago. Audra McDonald gave a thrilling dramatic and singing performance as Marie Christine, the Medea character, who dabbled in voodoo. Anthony Crivello played the charismatic sailor for whose sake she killed her brother, abandoned her home and fortune, and took off for Chicago. The music was dissonant and the libretto disjointed. Critics and audiences found the show cold, depressing, unmoving, and devoid of humor. It received the following Tony Award nominations: Best Musical Book (LaChiusa), Best Orchestrations (Jonathan Tunick), Best Lighting Design (Jules Fisher and Peggy Eisenhauer), and Best Performance by the Lead Actress in a Musical (McDonald).

The Beaumont greeted 2000, however, with a great hit: Susan Stroman's triptych of one-act dance plays, collectively titled *Contact*, starring Boyd Gaines, Karen Ziemba, and Deborah Yates (as the mysterious Woman in the Yellow Dress). The show prompted much debate over whether it fit the definition of a musical. It had just scraps

of dialogue and no singing whatever. All dancing was done to prerecorded pop and classical music. Nevertheless, the production won the 2000 Tony Award as Best Musical and settled in at the Beaumont for a 1,010-performance run.

Modern audiences got a taste of the desperation people were suffering in the Great Depression with a December 19, 2002, revival of Edna Ferber and George S. Kaufman's *Dinner at Eight*, with a top-drawer cast featuring Christine Ebersole, Marian Seldes, John Dossett, James Rebhorn, and Emily Skinner. John Lee Beatty's posh set (which won the Tony Award for Best Set Design of a Play) reflected the strained elegance of the characters, who are all putting up a false front of wealth while planning to hit each other up for jobs or money.

The 2003—4 season was given over to two major Shakespeare revivals. In the fall, Kevin Kline starred as Falstaff in a production that combined *Henry IV, Part 1* and *Henry IV, Part 2*. The consolidated *Henry IV* also featured Michael Hayden as Prince Hal and Ethan Hawke as Hotspur. The spring brought Christopher Plummer as a majestic yet pitiable title character in *King Lear*. Both Lincoln Center Theater Bard productions were nominated for Tony Awards as Best Revival (*Henry IV* won), and both leading men were nominated for Tony Awards as Best Actor in a Play.

On July 22, 2004, Lincoln Center Theater presented an unusual project by some of the top musical talents of the period: *The Frogs*, Stephen Sondheim's first (mostly) new Broadway musical since *Passion* ten years earlier. Sondheim had worked with his *A Funny Thing Happened on the Way to the Forum* collaborator Burt Shevelove on a "freely adapted" musical version of Aristophanes' 405 B.C. comedy in 1974, when it got its world premiere in a swimming pool at Yale University. Nathan Lane, who had made a 2001 recording of the score, conceived an "even more freely adapted" full Broadway evening, complete with added Sondheim songs and an expanded book by none other than himself. In the story, the god Dionysus feels that the playwrights of Athens have become too complacent, so he travels with his slave Xanthias to the underworld to bring back a great poet of the past. In the musical, Dionysus (Lane) goes to fetch George Bernard Shaw and winds up coming back with Shakespeare. Lane and director/choreographer Susan Stroman sparked the interest of the seventy-four-year-old Sondheim when they showed how the story could apply to an America then in the grip of a conservative ascendancy represented by President George W. Bush, who was up for reelection that fall.

The production, which opened July 22, 2004, and ran ninety-two performances, used virtually all the songs from the 1974 original, notably the hilarious opening number "Invocation and Instructions to the Audience" and the beautiful "Fear No More," possibly the only Sondheim song for which the composer suffered someone else (Shakespeare) to write the lyrics. The score added new Sondheim songs including the funny "Dress Big" and the touching "Ariadne." Besides Lane, the show featured Roger Bart (replacing Chris Kattan in previews) as Xanthias, Peter Bartlett as Pluto, Burke Moses as Herakles, and Michael Siberry as Shakespeare.

LCT chose its next production from the more recent past: Richard Brinsley Sheridan's 18th-century comedy of young (and not-so-young) romance, *The Rivals*, which opened December 16, 2004, with Dana Ivey as Mrs. Malaprop, Richard Easton as Sir Anthony Absolute, and Brian Murray as Sir Lucius O'Trigger. Directed by Mark Lamos, the production boasted sumptuous period costumes by Jess Goldstein, who won a 2005 Tony Award for his work.

The Beaumont was occupied for more than a year, starting April 18, 2005, with the beautiful and romantic musical *The Light in the Piazza*. Based on a novella of the same name, the musical tells the story of a young woman (Kelli O'Hara) and her mother (Victoria Clark) on a sightseeing trip to Florence, Italy, when a chance breeze sends the girl's hat flying into the hands of the man who will change her life. The show had a lambent Tony-winning score by Adam Guettel (grandson of Richard Rodgers and son of Mary Rodgers) and a book by Craig Lucas, and it was directed with great delicacy by Bartlett Sher. It proved to be a favorite with LCT subscribers and won Tony Awards for Clark and Guettel, and in all the design categories.

The entire 2006—7 season was given over to Tom Stoppard's three-part epic *The Coast of Utopia*, charting the rise and fall of a group of failed nineteenth-century Russian revolutionaries, who prepared the way for the brutal success of Trotsky and Lenin but who didn't get to share in it, living out their lives in exile. Part one, *Voyage*, opened November 27, 2006. Part two, *Shipwreck*, opened December 21, 2006. Part three, *Salvage*, opened February 18, 2007, and then all three played in repertory through late May 2007. The sprawling production starred Brían F. O'Byrne, Martha Plimpton, Ethan Hawke, Billy Crudup, and Jennifer Ehle, representing a considerable commitment of time, money, and artistry by all concerned. The Tony committee rewarded their boldness with seven Tony Awards, including Best Play of 2007.

During the 2006—7 season Lincoln Center began to undergo a multiyear facelift, including a renovation of the plaza, plantings, and reflecting pool outside the Beaumont. For the next few seasons theatergoers had to thread their way down a long plywood passageway to get to the theatre's entrance aboveground, or to access it through the Newhouse entrance from the underground parking garage. Management decorated the barriers with posters from some of the theatre's past and current hits, and at holiday time the workers softened the harsh construction lights by having them blink cheerfully on and off.

Cymbeline, Shakespeare's drama about a test of love in pre-Roman Britain, got its first Broadway revival since 1923 on December 2, 2007, starring John Cullum as Cymbeline, Michael Cerveris as Posthumus Leonatus, Phylicia Rashad as the Queen, and Martha Plimpton as Imogen. It played a limited run of forty performances.

Starting on April 3, 2008, the rest of the decade at the Beaumont was occupied with a glorious revival of Rodgers and Hammerstein's *South Pacific*—unbelievably the first Broadway revival since its 1949 debut. Starring Kelli O'Hara as Nellie Forbush and Brazilian opera singer Paulo Szot as Emile de Becque, Bartlett Sher's production was hailed as not only one of Lincoln Center Theater's best revivals, but as one of the most sterling revivals of a musical ever. The production won Tony Awards for Best Revival of a Musical, Best Actor in a Musical (Szot), Best Director (Sher), and all three technical design awards, Best Costumes, Sets, and Lighting. But no Tony was given for one of the most outstanding aspects of this production: its full thirty-piece orchestra (rare in the age of synthesizers) conducted by Ted Sperling, with Robert Russell Bennett's orchestrations reconstructed by researcher Bruce Pomahac.

The record of Bernard Gersten and André Bishop at the helm of Lincoln Center has been outstanding and has fulfilled many of the original hopes for an exemplary institutional theatre in Manhattan.

WALTER KERR
THEATRE

FORMERLY THE RITZ, THIS THEATRE
at 219 West Forty-eighth Street was renamed
the Walter Kerr in 1990, in honor of the
Pulitzer-winning drama critic for the *New York
Times* and the *Herald Tribune*.

Jujamcyn Theatres, which acquired this
intimate house in 1981, has spent millions to
restore the theatre to its original splendor. A
1983 refurbishment returned the house to legitimacy after years as a cinema. A fuller refurbishment in 1990, the work of the Roger Morgan
Studio, Inc., has made this one of Broadway's
most impressive smaller playhouses.

The Ritz was built by the Shuberts as a sister
theatre to their Ambassador Theatre on West
Forty-ninth Street. It was built in a record sixty-
six days in 1921. The architect was Herbert J.

Krapp, the eminent theatre designer of that era, and the interior was done in Italian Renaissance style, with much gold leaf and Italian scrollwork.

On March 21, 1921, the intimate (under one thousand seats) new house opened with Clare Eames in John Drinkwater's *Mary Stuart*, preceded by a pantomime called *A Man About Town* that included in its cast the future opera composer Deems Taylor.

The Ritz flourished in the 1920s with some distinguished plays and players. A 1921 highlight was an ebullient performance by Ina Claire in *Bluebeard's Eighth Wife*. Roland Young appeared in *Madame Pierre* the following year, and in 1923 Katharine Cornell was admired in *The Enchanted Cottage*, as was Lynn Fontanne in *In Love with Love*. Audiences in 1924 were spellbound by Sutton Vane's eerie *Outward Bound*, starring Alfred Lunt, Leslie Howard, and Margalo Gillmore as dead passengers on a boat that is sailing to the "other world." The same year unveiled Hassard Short's *Ritz Revue*, hailed for its scenic splendors, and John Galsworthy's *Old English*, starring the noted character actor George Arliss.

A saucy Claudette Colbert graced *The Kiss in the Taxi* in 1925, followed by Helen Hayes in *Young Blood*, and Frank Morgan, Ralph Morgan, and Estelle Winwood in *A Weak Woman*. The next year found a young Ruby Keeler tapping in *Bye, Bye, Bonnie*; the beautiful Grace George in *The Legend of Leonora*; and Alice Brady and Lionel Atwill in *The Thief*.

On the day after Christmas 1927, bubbly

Miriam Hopkins and Frank McHugh cheered first-nighters in *Excess Baggage*, followed by another winner, Janet Beecher in *Courage*, which ran until May 1929. The decade came to an end with the successful *Broken Dishes*, with Donald Meek and a young actress named Bette Davis, who was immediately snapped up by Hollywood.

Highlights of the 1930s at the Ritz included the famed comedy team of Smith and Dale in a hit play called *Mendel, Inc.*; noted monologist Ruth Draper in some of her celebrated character sketches; the thriller *Double Door*; Frank Lawton and Mildred Natwick in *The Wind and the Rain*; Dennis King and Leo G. Carroll in Mark Reed's delightful *Petticoat Fever*; Ilka Chase and Peggy Conklin in *Co-Respondent Unknown*; the Surry Players (including Shepperd Strudwick, Anne Revere, and Katherine Emery) in a revival of *As You Like It*; and Jessica Tandy and Dame Sybil Thorndike in J. B. Priestly's *Time and the Conways*.

During the late 1930s the Federal Theatre Project (also known as the WPA Theatre) staged some exciting productions at the Ritz. Among them were T. S. Eliot's verse drama *Murder in the Cathedral*; the stirring *Power*, staged by the WPA's Living Newspaper unit, which ran for five months; and a lavish production of *Pinocchio* that ran for 197 performances.

In 1939 the Ritz became the CBS Theatre No. 4, from which live radio shows were broadcast, including the programs of the Town Crier, drama critic Alexander Woollcott. On

Top left to right: Standard Ritz program cover in the 1920s.

Herald for Sutton Vane's mystical play *Outward Bound* (1924).

PLAYBILL cover for the rock musical *Soon* (1971).

PLAYBILL for *The Flying Karamazov Brothers*, which restored the Ritz to legitimacy in 1983.

Bottom: Pixie children in *The Enchanted Cottage* peer out of a window seat (1923).

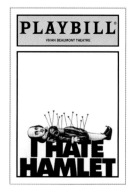

Above: PLAYBILL cover for *I Hate Hamlet* (1991).

Top left: PLAYBILL cover for *The Weir* (1999).

Top center: PLAYBILL cover for Pulitzer-winner *Proof* (2000).

Far right, top: Bette David and Duncan Penwarden in *Broken Dishes* (1929).

Far right, bottom: Claudete Colbert vamps John William in *The Kiss in the Taxi* (1925).

December 22, 1942, the theatre went legit again with Leonard Sillman's *New Faces of 1943*, with the producer onstage to introduce fresh talent, including John Lund and Alice Pearce. After that, the long-running *Tobacco Road* moved in from the Forrest Theatre. Toward the end of 1943 NBC took the theatre over for use as a radio and TV studio; later, so did ABC.

It was not until December 1970 that the Ritz returned to legitimacy, with previews for a new rock opera called *Soon*. The show, which opened on January 12, 1971, marked the Broadway debuts of Peter Allen, Nell Carter, and Richard Gere. Also featured in the cast were Barry Bostwick, Marta Heflin, and Leata Galloway. Unfortunately, it closed after three performances. Later that year, Rip Torn and Viveca Lindfors played a brief run in Strindberg's *Dance of Death*.

Following a renovation in late 1971, the Ritz reopened on March 7, 1972, with the short-lived thriller *Children, Children*, starring Gwen Verdon in a rare nonmusical role. It had only a single performance, but it was succeeded later that year by a show that ran twice as long—two performances—*Hurry, Harry*. In 1973 the Ritz housed a brief run of the English farce *No Sex, Please, We're British*. Shortly thereafter, the theatre was christened the Robert F. Kennedy Children's Theatre and, for a while, showed films.

The Ritz reopened under Jujamcyn ownership on May 10, 1983, with an entertaining troupe of New Vaudeville jugglers who named their show after themselves: *The Flying Karamazov Brothers*.

This was followed by the acclaimed *Ian McKellen Acting Shakespeare*, a one-man show of brilliance (1984); *Dancing in the End Zone*, a play with Pat Carroll and Laurence Luckinbill (1984); *Doubles*, a hit comedy about four tennis players, starring John Cullum, Ron Leibman,

Above: PLAYBILL cover for *Angels in America: Millennium Approaches* (1993).

Austin Pendleton, and Tony Roberts (1985); *Jerome Kern Goes to Hollywood*, a revue of Kern melodies that brought back Elisabeth Welch, an American singer of fame in the 1930s who scored a huge success in London musicals (1986); a new play called *A Month of Sundays* (1987); the musical *Late Nite Comic*, with music and lyrics by Brian Gari and a book by Allan Knee (1987); the comedy team of Penn & Teller (1987); and a revival of the musical *Chu Chem* (1989).

Left: The cast of *New Faces of 1943*.

Right: Frank Lawton in *The Wind and the Rain* (1934).

In 1990 Jujamcyn spent $1.5 million to restore the Ritz to its original legitimate splendour. According to *Interior Design* magazine, the total interior renovation of the Ritz was achieved by Karen Rosen of KMR Designs, Ltd., Manhattan. Her client, Richard Wolff, then president of the Jujamcyn Theatre Corp., requested that the Ritz be made elegant by restoring its classical feeling of the 1920s. Rosen chose a color scheme of pink/mauve/gray touched with black to reflect the 1920s look while appealing to current tastes. She restored ceiling decorations and murals and designed Art Deco—type sconces, chandeliers, balcony, and ceiling lights to achieve illumination without jarring glare. The theatre also acquired one of the most colorful marquees on Broadway, framing the tenant's title with a rainbow of hundreds of tiny lightbulbs.

The refurbished 947-seat Ritz Theatre was rechristened the Walter Kerr in 1990. The renovation and rechristening proved a boon for the theatre. In the following twenty years, the Walter Kerr housed a remarkable four Pulitzer-winning dramas and six Tony Award winners as Best Play, plus many career-defining performances by rising stars of the period.

The inaugural production under the new name was August Wilson's *The Piano Lesson*, which won both the Pulitzer Prize and the New York Drama Critics Award for the season's best play. Part of his Pittsburgh Cycle of dramas about black life in America during the twentieth century, *The Piano Lesson* involved a haunted piano that represented a black family's legacy.

After that came Paul Rudnick's amusing *I Hate Hamlet*, with Nicol Williamson playing the ghost of John Barrymore and sparkling performances by Celeste Holm, Adam Arkin, Jane Adams, and Evan Handler. *Crazy He Calls Me* ran briefly in 1991, and then came *Two Trains Running*, another chapter in August Wilson's Pittsburgh Cycle. It won a Tony Award for Larry Fishburne as Best Featured Actor in a Play.

Tony Kushner's *Angels in America: Millennium Approaches* caused a sensation here in 1993. The first half of this epic drama about AIDS, loyalty, and war in heaven during the Reagan era won the Pulitzer Prize, the Tony Award, and the New York Drama Critics Circle Award for the best play of the season. Additional Tony Awards went to Ron Leibman (Best Leading Actor), Stephen Spinella (Best Featured Actor), and George C. Wolfe (Best Direction of a Play). The show continued for 367 performances.

In 1994, Part II of the play, *Angels in America: Perestroika*, joined it in repertory and was critically acclaimed. *Perestroika* again won the Tony Award as Best Play, and Spinella won a second Tony for his acting in the role of Prior Walter, this time for Best Leading Actor. The Best Featured Actor award went to Jeffrey Wright. *Perestroika* continued for 216 performances, closing December 4, 1994, just two weeks after *Millennium Approaches* ended its run.

In February 1995 Terrence McNally's play *Love! Valour! Compassion!* moved here from its successful Off-Broadway run at the Manhattan Theatre Club. The play dealt with three weekends spent by a group of gay friends in Dutchess County, New York, and it received glowing reviews. It won Tony Awards for Best Play (McNally) and Best Featured Actor (John Glover). The play ran for 249 performances.

Patti LuPone on Broadway starred the popular diva backed by four men. Act I featured a variety of show tunes; Act II offered songs from LuPone's Broadway career. The entertainment ran for forty-six performances.

Above: Standard Ritz program-cover sketch in the 1930s of British actors Mr. and Mrs. John Wood in *As You Like It*.

Above: Program art of Ruth Draper in her character sketches (1932).

Ruben Santiago-Hudson and Lisa Gay Hamilton in August Wilson's *Gem of the Ocean* (2004). (Photo by Craig Schwartz)

On March 28, 1996, the August Wilson play cycle added yet another chapter at the Walter Kerr with the opening of *Seven Guitars*, which received a dozen favorable reviews. The play, about a Pittsburgh musician who dreams of going to Chicago to record a hit song, won the 1996 New York Drama Critics Circle Award for Best Play and a Tony Award for Featured Actor in a Play (Ruben Santiago-Hudson). Other Tony Award nominations included Featured Actor (Roger Robinson), Featured Actresses (Viola Davis and Michele Shay), Best Play (August Wilson), Best Director (Lloyd Richards), Best Scenic Designer (Scott Bradley), and Best Lighting (Christopher Akerlind). It had 187 performances.

A new production of Noël Coward's comedy *Present Laughter* (first seen on Broadway in 1946 with Clifton Webb) arrived on November 18, 1996. This time Frank Langella acted the role of Garry Essendine, said to be patterned on Coward himself. The new production included full-frontal male nudity, which some critics and theatregoers found gratuitous. The comedy ran for 175 performances and was nominated for the Tony Award as Best Revival of a Play.

The Beauty Queen of Leenane, an Irish play by Martin McDonagh, transferred from Off-Broadway to the Walter Kerr on April 23, 1998, to much acclaim. Concerning the thorny relationship between a repressed Irishwoman and

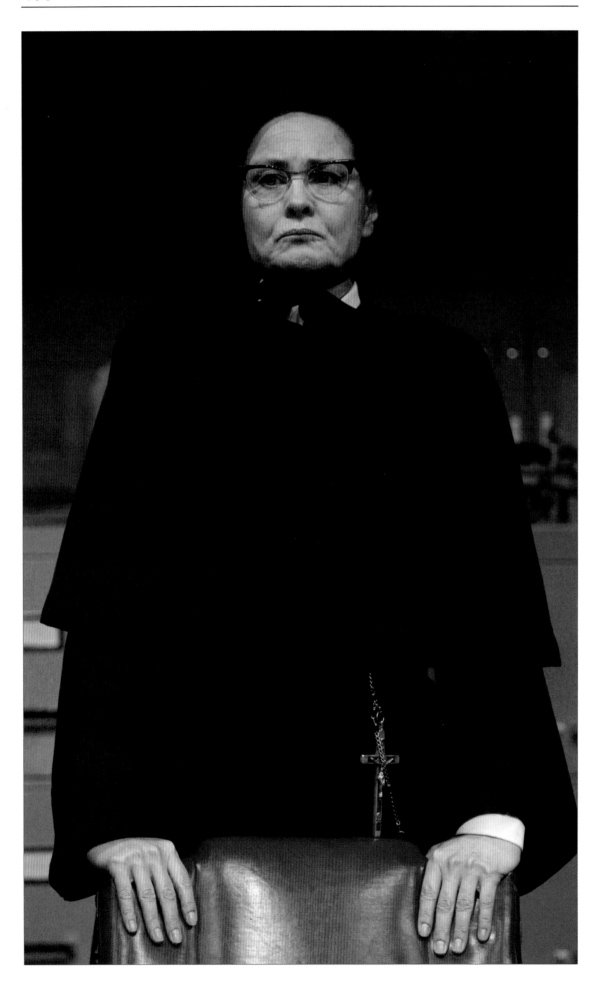

Cherry Jones as Sister Aloysius in the Tony- and Pulitzer Prize-winning drama, *Doubt* (2005). (Photo by Joan Marcus)

her manipulative mother with whom she lives, the drama was hailed for its writing and acting and won the following Tony Awards: Best Actress (Marie Mullen), Best Featured Actress (Anna Manahan), Best Featured Actor (Tom Murphy), and Best Director (Garry Hynes). It was also nominated for Best Featured Actor (Brían F. O'Byrne) and Best Play (Martin McDonagh). It played for 372 performances.

April 1, 1999, brought another Irish play to this theatre: *The Weir*, by Conor McPherson. The play took place in an Irish pub, where several local men and a female visitor exchange increasingly chilling ghost stories. The play was moderately successful and ran until the end of November.

The next tenant was *Waiting in the Wings*, a 1960 play by Noël Coward that had never been produced on Broadway. Timed to the centenary of Coward's birth, the play starred Lauren Bacall and Rosemary Harris as rival actresses in an English retirement home, with many vintage stars in supporting roles. The play was updated by Jeremy Sams. It received two Tony Award nominations: Rosemary Harris (Best Actress) and Helen Stenborg (Best Supporting Actress). It ran at the Walter Kerr Theatre for three months starting in December 1999, then moved to the Eugene O'Neill Theatre. Sadly, it was the last Broadway show produced by Alexander H. Cohen, who passed away in spring 2000.

Fall 2000 saw Mary Louise Parker starring in David Auburn's *Proof*, a drama about a mathematician's daughter who may be the one actually responsible for her father's greatest work. *Proof* won the Pulitzer Prize and the Tony Award for Best Play. It ran 917 performances, making it the longest-running nonmusical drama of the decade. *Proof* was produced here by the Manhattan Theatre Club, which would bring another Pulitzer/Tony winner to the Kerr before the decade was out.

But first Off-Broadway's The Public Theatre/New York Shakespeare Festival and London's Donmar Warehouse Theatre cooperated on another Tony winner for Best Play, the Broadway transfer of Richard Greenberg's *Take Me Out*. Daniel Sunjata played a Major League baseball champion who comes out of the closet as gay. But the show was stolen by a secondary character (Denis O'Hare), who becomes smitten with the game of baseball while working on the player's case. *Take Me Out* opened February 27, 2003, and ran 355 per-

formances. Tony Awards were won by O'Hare and by director Joe Mantello.

Another issue drama arrived April 15, 2004, with *Sixteen Wounded*, Eliam Kraiem's drama about the conflict that arises when a Jewish baker in Amsterdam hires a young Palestinian man as his assistant. The play treated the Palestinian and Israeli sides of the Mideast conflict as equally legitimate, but critics and audiences did not respond, and the drama, starring Judd Hirsch and Omar Metwally, lasted only twelve performances.

Gem of the Ocean was the third and last of August Wilson's Pittsburgh Cycle to have its Broadway debut at the Walter Kerr Theatre. Chronologically the first in the ten-decade epic, *Gem* introduced the anchor character of Aunt Ester, played by Phylicia Rashad. Lisa Gay Hamilton, Ruben Santiago-Hudson, and Eugene Lee were also featured in the production, which lasted seventy-two performances.

Starting March 31, 2005, the Kerr housed one of the most distinguished and honored dramas of the early twenty-first century, John Patrick Shanley's *Doubt*. Brían F. O'Byrne and Cherry Jones squared off as a Catholic priest who may or may not have molested a schoolboy, and the single-minded nun who is determined that he is guilty and should be brought to justice. The production was memorable for the groups of people who would gather under the colorful Kerr marquee after performances to debate whether the priest did it or not. Another production from Manhattan Theatre Club, *Doubt*, like *Proof*, won both the Pulitzer Prize and Tony Award as Best Play. The production won the following Tony Awards: Best Play, Best Actress (Cherry Jones), Best Featured Actress (Adriane Lenox), and Best Direction of a Play (Doug Hughes). *Doubt* ran for 525 performances.

The Kerr next housed a musical, *Grey Gardens*, that developed a fervent following. The show was based on the true story and subsequent documentary film about two benighted members of the extended Kennedy clan: Edith Bouvier Beale and her daughter, "Little Edie" Beale. Born to be debutantes in a glamorous world of glittering wealth, the two dysfunctional women end up as "cat ladies" wandering their filthy and empty mansion halls together. *Grey Gardens* had a book by Doug Wright, music by Scott Frankel, and lyrics by Michael Korie. The show proved to be a bonanza for its two stars, Christine Ebersole and Mary Louise

Wilson, who took the Tony Awards for Best Actress and Best Featured Actress in a Musical, respectively. Ebersole had the special assignment of playing the elder Edie in Act I, then her own grown daughter in Act II, with many juicy solos, notably "Will You," "The Revolutionary Costume for Today," "Around the World," and "Another Winter in a Summer Town." *Grey Gardens* opened November 2, 2006, and stayed for 307 performances.

Actor Chazz Palminteri brought his one-man show *A Bronx Tale* to the Kerr on October 25, 2007. The play followed an unusual path to Broadway. Palminteri said he had originally conceived the show (about growing up among Mafiosi) for the stage, but it had been bought and produced as a film first. Taking the lead role himself, he now finally performed it the way it had been conceived. It ran 111 performances and went on tour.

Fans of Off-Broadway concert and club composer John Bucchino eagerly looked forward to his first full Broadway score, for the musical *A Catered Affair*, which opened here April 17, 2008. Based on a film of the same name, the show starred Tom Wopat and Faith Prince as a blue-collar couple split between his desire to spend their life savings on a taxicab, and her desire to spend it on a fancy wedding for their daughter, played by Leslie Kritzer. Harvey Fierstein wrote the book and costarred as the gay uncle who is not invited to the event. The beautiful ballad "Don't Ever Stop Saying 'I Love You'" was not enough to overcome unfavorable reviews, and the show lasted just three months.

An acclaimed London revival of Anton Chekhov's *The Seagull* came to the Kerr for ninety-four performances starting October 2, 2008. The story of a grande dame actress (Kristin Scott Thomas) and the group that gathers around her at her country home was presented in a new translation by Christopher Hampton and directed by Ian Rickson.

Tovah Feldshuh told a true story of World War II heroism in Dan Gordon's drama *Irena's Vow*, about Irena Gut Opdyke, a Polish woman who hid a group of Jews in the basement of a Nazi official's home. It opened March 29, 2009, and ran 105 performances.

In December 2009 the Kerr hosted a revival of the Stephen Sondheim—Hugh Wheeler musical *A Little Night Music*, headlined by film star Catherine Zeta-Jones and the beloved Angela Lansbury.

Christine Ebersole in her Tony-winning twin performances Edith Bouvier Beale and "Little" Edie Beale in the musical *Grey Gardens* (2006). (Photo by Joan Marcus)

WINTER GARDEN

ON THE BLUSTERY EVENING OF MARCH
20, 1911, the Messrs. Shubert unveiled on
Broadway at Fiftieth Street the Winter Garden, a
lavish music hall "devoted to novel, international, spectacular and musical entertainments."

Built on the site of the former American
Horse Exchange, owned by W. K. Vanderbilt,
the theatre was designed by architect William
Albert Swasey to resemble an English garden,
with latticework on the walls and a trellised
ceiling. Roof gardens were a popular motif on
Broadway at this time, especially on top of
such theatres as the Casino, the Olympia, the
American, the Victoria, the Century, and the
New Amsterdam. Despite the Winter Garden's
ambience of an outdoor roof garden, some
unkind critics claimed they could still smell
the horses whenever a flop show opened there.

Unmarred by a marquee, the original Winter Garden had a classical facade with Palladian arches and columns, and it contained, besides the auditorium, a "promenoir" in the rear of the house, extending from Broadway to Seventh Avenue for intermission processions "which are joined in by everyone of prominence," an early program proclaimed.

The Winter Garden's opening production, *La Belle Paree* (1911), was composed of two parts. Part one was a one-act "Chinese opera" called *Bow Sing*; part two was a lively vaudeville, *Jumble of Jollity*, with songs by Frank Tours and Jerome Kern. The hit of this segment was singer Al Jolson, who for many years would be the Winter Garden's biggest star.

The Winter Garden was an instant hit ("New York's latest plaything, a very flashy toy, full of life and go and color and with no end of jingle to it!" wrote one critic). Two of the theatre's most talked-about features in its early days were a series of Sunday-night concerts, in which new talent such as Jolson and Marilynn (later shortened to Marilyn) Miller were brilliantly promoted, and a structural innovation that became a Winter Garden trademark: the "runway." On a European trip, Lee Shubert had met the great German producer/director Max Reinhardt, who broke down the invisible wall between actors and audience with a thrust stage that jutted out into the orchestra section of the theatre. The Shuberts borrowed this idea and built a bridge over the tops of orchestra seats from the stage to the rear of the house. On this bridge Jolson pranced into the audience, belting his songs and communicating with his delirious fans. Eighty near-nude showgirls also paraded on the runway, which soon became known as "the bridge of thighs."

Though it was subsequently removed, the "bridge" would return to the Winter Garden some sixty years later when director Hal Prince installed a Japanese Kabuki-style hanamichi runway through the Winter Garden (sans thighs) for the musical *Pacific Overtures*.

Just as the New Amsterdam Theatre became identified with the *Follies* and the Apollo with the *Scandals*, the Winter Garden became the home of a rowdy revue series called *The Passing Show*. From 1912 through 1924 there was an annual edition, except in 1920. Among the luminous stars who appeared in these shows were Fred and Adele Astaire, Marilyn Miller, Willie and Eugene Howard, Charlotte Greenwood, Ed Wynn, Frank Fay, John Charles

Thomas, Marie Dressler, the Avon Comedy Four, Fred Allen, George Jessel, and James Barton.

The major song contributors were Sigmund Romberg and Jean Schwartz; the gilded sets were mostly by Watson Barratt, and the silken costumes mostly by Cora McGeachey and Homer Conant.

The *Passing Show* revues were less subtle than those produced by the Shuberts' archrival, Florenz Ziegfeld. One wonders what women's lib would have said to a bizarre "Rotisserie" scene in which showgirls were roasted on a spit and then placed on tables like well-done chickens. In *The Passing Show* of 1924 (the last of the series), a chorus cutie named Lucille LeSueur portrayed a "Beaded Bag" and "Miss Labor Day." The chorine went to Hollywood and became better known as Joan Crawford.

Al Jolson never appeared in a *Passing Show*, but he headlined some of the Winter Garden's biggest hits. He first appeared in blackface (which became his specialty) in *Vera Violetta*, a 1911 musical in which he costarred with the French singer Gaby Deslys and a sexy newcomer named Mae West. He again appeared with Deslys in *The Honeymoon Express* (1913), with a funny girl in the cast named Fanny Brice. In 1918 Jolson took Broadway by storm in *Sinbad*, a fantastic musical in which he belted out some interpolated numbers that were forever identified with him: "My Mammy" (sung on the runway in blackface and white gloves), "Rock-a-Bye Your Baby with a Dixie Melody," and "Chloe." When the show went on tour, Jolson added a song called "Swanee," which made George Gershwin famous overnight. In many of his shows, Jolson played the same character, a smart-aleck blackface servant named Gus. In his last Winter Garden show, *Big Boy* (1925), the singer made Gus a stableboy who suddenly finds himself riding as a jockey in the Kentucky Derby.

After the *Passing Show* series was through, the Winter Garden staged other revues, such as

Top left: A sextet of chorines from one of the Greenwich Village *Follies* revues in the 1920s.

Top right: Al Jolson, who serenaded Winter Garden audiences from a specially-built runway.

Bottom: Eddie Cantor appeared in two Winter Garden shows.

Top: Standard Winter Garden program cover before 1930.

Center: Bert Lahr, Luella Gear, and Ray Bolger clown in the 1934 revue hit *Life Begins at 8:40*.

Bottom: Terrence V. Mann as Rum Tum Tugger with fellow Jellicle Cats in the spectacular success *Cats* (1982).

Artists and Models and *The Greenwich Village Follies*, studded with tall, medium, and "pony"-size showgirls and low comics. Eddie Cantor appeared in two Winter Garden shows, *Broadway Brevities of 1920* and *Make It Snappy*, and Martha Graham danced in the 1923 edition of *The Greenwich Village Follies*.

During the 1920s the Winter Garden was redesigned as it appears today by architect Herbert J. Krapp, and an enormous marquee was added. But to Broadway's dismay, from 1928 to 1933 the theatre was leased by Warner Brothers and converted into a Vitaphone (talking pictures) temple. Aptly, the first movie shown there was Al Jolson in *The Singing Fool*.

After a shaky return to legitimacy with Joe Cook in a mediocre musical, *Hold Your Horses* (1933), the Winter Garden embarked on its golden era of glittering revues, noted for their beauty and sophistication. It all began when the Shuberts and Billie Burke (Ziegfeld's widow) combined to present a posthumous *Ziegfeld Follies* (1934), starring Fanny Brice, Willie and Eugene Howard, Vilma and Buddy Ebsen (who stopped the show with their dancing), and Jane Froman.

In 1934 Ray Bolger, Bert Lahr, Luella Gear, and Frances Williams brightened the house in *Life Begins at 8:40*, a breathtaking revue with mechanical sets and a hit tune, "Let's Take a Walk Around the Block." This was followed by the racy *Earl Carroll Sketch Book*, starring Ken Murray.

In 1935 Vincente Minnelli began his splashy tenure as revue master of the Winter Garden and he came up with *At Home Abroad*, a travelogue starring Beatrice Lillie, Ethel Waters, Eleanor Powell, and Reginald Gardiner. Minnelli designed eye-filling sets of foreign ports, Lillie did her hilarious "Dozen Double Damask Dinner Napkins" sketch, Gardiner imitated wallpaper and trains, Powell tapped up a storm, and Waters sang Dietz and Schwartz gems.

Another *Ziegfeld Follies* arrived in 1936 with Minnelli sets and costumes, Fanny Brice doing Baby Snooks, Bob Hope singing "I Can't Get Started" to Eve Arden, and Josephine Baker singing and dancing dressed in strings of bananas.

Late 1936 brought perhaps the Winter Garden's best revue of all time—Vincente Minnelli's *The Show Is On*, a tribute to show business through the ages, with Bea Lillie swinging out over the audience on a huge half-moon and dropping garters on bald-headed men, Bert Lahr immortalizing "Song of the Woodman," the

Gershwins providing "By Strauss," and Hoagy Carmichael contributing "Little Old Lady."

In late 1937 Ed Wynn moved in with the marvelous antiwar musical *Hooray for What!* by Harold Arlen and E. Y. Harburg, Howard Lindsay, and Russel Crouse. Wynn played a zany inventor of gases who is pursued by nations that want his concoctions for their wars.

A phenomenon called *Hellzapoppin'* opened at the Forty-sixth Street Theatre in 1938 and proved so successful that it was moved to the Winter Garden, where it became the longest-running Broadway musical up to that time (1,404 performances). Starring Olsen and Johnson, the revue was a lunatic uproar, with all sorts of practical jokes played on the audience. It sparked two more Winter Garden revues: *Sons o' Fun* (1941) and *Laffing Room Only* (1944).

In between the last two Olsen and Johnson shows came two hits: Milton Berle, Ilona Massey, Arthur Treacher, and Jack Cole in the *Ziegfeld Follies of 1943*, and Cole Porter's *Mexican Hayride*, starring Bobby Clark and June Havoc, lavishly produced by Mike Todd.

In the summer of 1945 an operetta called *Marinka* opened at the Winter Garden and proved to be the last legitimate show to play there for several years. Once again, the theatre reverted to a movie house.

In November 1948 the rowdy Bobby Clark brought live theatre back to the Winter Garden in Michael Todd's funny *As the Girls Go*, a fast-paced musical in which Clark played the husband of the first female president of the United States (Irene Rich). Todd's production was so lush and expensive that he charged a $7.20 top, a record price at that time. Todd continued his association with this theatre by presenting a high-class burlesque, *Michael Todd's Peep Show* (1950).

Phil Silvers, another raucous comic, scored at the Winter Garden in a noisy musical, *Top Banana* (1951), about television, with Silvers impersonating a TV comic said to be inspired by Milton Berle. Then in 1953 Rosalind Russell triumphed in *Wonderful Town*, a brilliant musical by Leonard Bernstein, Betty Comden, and Adolph Green.

A rarely performed classic, *Tamburlaine the Great*, by Christopher Marlowe, was given a spectacular production in 1956, with Anthony Quayle in the title role and a newcomer named Colleen Dewhurst listed in the cast as "A Virgin of Memphis" in Act I and "A Turkish Concubine" in Act II. Her fall occurred during the intermission. Also making his Broadway debut in this play: William Shatner, the future Captain Kirk of TV's Star Trek, who played a character named "Usumcasane." During the same year, the Old Vic Company from England performed *Richard II*, *Romeo and Juliet*, *Macbeth*, and other plays.

The last *Ziegfeld Follies* opened at the Winter Garden in March 1957 and starred the illustrious Beatrice Lillie and Billy De Wolfe, but the critics were not enthusiastic and the show closed after 123 performances. On September 26, 1957, the landmark musical *West Side Story* blazed across the Winter Garden stage with its jazzy, violent treatment of *Romeo and Juliet* set in the rumble-ridden slums of Manhattan. The unusual musical was conceived, choreographed, and directed by Jerome Robbins; had a book by Arthur Laurents and music by Leonard Bernstein; and introduced twenty-seven-year-old Stephen Sondheim to Broadway as a lyricist. *West Side Story* moved to the Broadway Theatre in March 1959. After a brief hiatus for the 16-performance debut of Marc Blitzstein's musical *Juno*, based on *Juno and the Paycock*, *West Side Story* returned to the Winter Garden for the final two months of its run.

The offbeat actress Tammy Grimes proved a sensation in *The Unsinkable Molly Brown* in 1960, playing an actual character from the early 1900s. Harve Presnell was her costar in this popular Meredith Willson musical. Act II included a depiction of the sinking of the *Titanic*. It would not be the last musical to do so.

Fanny Brice, who had been a Winter Garden favorite for many decades, was memorably impersonated by Barbra Streisand in the 1964 bonanza *Funny Girl*. The show had a striking score by Jule Styne and Bob Merrill that included the standard "People," which became Streisand's signature tune. *Funny Girl* ran for 1,348 performances.

Another musical triumph was scored by Angela Lansbury in the title role of *Mame*, Jerry Herman's musical treatment of the popular play *Auntie Mame*. Lansbury won a Tony for her spirited performance. Beatrice Arthur and Jane Connell were her hilarious sidekicks. The hit show ran for 1,508 performances, a new house record.

Hal Prince brought a most original musical to the Winter Garden in 1971: *Follies*. The title was meant to suggest both the glittering revues of the 1910s and 1920s, and the mistakes the main characters have made in their love lives. The musical focused on a reunion of a group of for-

Top left: Barbra Streisand triumphs as Fanny Brice in *Funny Girl* (1964).

Top right: The real Fanny Brice, as Baby Snooks, pesters Bob Hope in the 1936 edition of the *Ziegfeld Follies*.

mer *Follies* girls and their husbands on the stage of the theatre where they once performed. With an exciting score by Stephen Sondheim and a book by James Goldman, the surrealistic musical starred Alexis Smith, John McMartin, Dorothy Collins, Gene Nelson, and Yvonne De Carlo and featured old-timers Ethel Shutta and Fifi D'Orsay. *Follies* won seven Tony Awards.

In 1972 and 1973 Neil Diamond and Liza Minnelli made highly successful personal appearances at the Winter Garden. Also praised was the New York Shakespeare Festival's revival of Shakespeare's *Much Ado about Nothing*, imaginatively set in the early 1900s in the United States by director A. J. Antoon. Sam Waterston played Benedick, and Kathleen Widdoes was a radiant Beatrice.

Angela Lansbury returned to the Winter Garden in 1974 in a dynamic revival of *Gypsy*. Hal Prince and Stephen Sondheim came back in 1976 with the original musical *Pacific Overtures*, about the opening of Japan by Commodore Perry. Boris Aronson won a Tony for his splendid settings, and Florence Klotz won another Tony Award for her colorful costumes. Prince's Tony-

Above: PLAYBILL for the musical *Follies* (1971).

Above: PLAYBILL for the 1974 revival of *Gypsy*, starring Angela Lansbury.

Top: left to right, Karen Mason, Louise Pitre, and Judy Kaye in the original Broadway cast of *Mamma Mia!* (2001) (Photo by Joan Marcus)

Above: Opening night PLAYBILL for *Mamma Mia!* (2001)

Above: The *Cats* PLAYBILL, (1982).

nominated staging incorporated many conventions of Japanese Kabuki theatre.

Zero Mostel, who won a Tony in 1965 for his portrayal of Tevye in the award-winning musical *Fiddler on the Roof*, recreated his performance in a 1976 revival of the famous musical. It played for 167 performances. In 1977 a multimedia show called *Beatlemania* vividly recreated the career of the Beatles in remarkable fashion. It stayed at the Winter Garden until 1979.

A series of shows and personal appearances filled the theatre during 1979 and 1980, including *Zoot Suit*, *Gilda Radner—Live from New York*, and *Twyla Tharp and Dancers*. In August of 1980 David Merrick returned from producing films in Hollywood to bring glamour and excitement to the Winter Garden with an opulent tap-dancing musical based on the famous 1933 movie *42nd Street*. The brilliant opening night, Broadway's most exciting in years, was darkened by Merrick's announcement, at the show's curtain calls, without prior knowledge of the cast, that the musical's choreographer and director, Gower Champion, had died that afternoon.

In 1981 Richard Harris starred in a revival of *Camelot*, and in 1982 Christopher Plummer played a memorable Iago to James Earl Jones's powerful Othello.

In the summer of 1982 the Shuberts renovated the Winter Garden extensively, indoors and out. One feature that was retained was the blocklong billboard over the marquee, which has carried enormous advertisements for each show playing the theatre.

In preparation for the arrival of Andrew Lloyd Webber's British hit *Cats*, set designer John Napier and a battery of workmen transformed the theatre into a "cosmic garbage dump." The effort paid off. Not only did the unique *Cats* win seven Tony Awards, but by the time it closed on September 10, 2000, it had run for 7,485 performances, making it the longest-running show in Broadway history, a title it held for six years until eclipsed by another Andrew Lloyd Webber musical, *The Phantom of the Opera*, at the Majestic Theatre. For eighteen years the yellow eyes of the *Cats* logo (with tiny dancers as pupils) kept watch over Broadway from that huge billboard.

Based on T. S. Eliot's book *Old Possum's Book of Practical Cats*, about a tribe of anthropomorphized felines calling themselves "Jellicle Cats," the musical used spectacular choreography by Gillian Lynne to tell the stories of Rum Tum Tugger, Skimbleshanks, Mungojerrie, Rumpleteazer, Bustopher Jones, Mister Mistoffolees, Grizabella, and the rest of the nimble band. The song "Memory" became one of the few show tunes to achieve pop-standard status in the rock age. The show proved to be such a durable favorite with children and grownups alike that it advertised for more than a decade with the slogan "Now and Forever." For a generation of youngsters, *Cats*—and the Winter Garden—formed their introduction to Broadway.

In constant use for nearly two decades, the Winter Garden closed following Cats for another yearlong refurbishment. It reopened in fall 2001 with *Mamma Mia!*, a musical built around the 1970s-era hits of the Swedish rock group ABBA. Opening October 18, 2001, *Mamma Mia!* was one of the first new musicals to bow on Broadway following the terrorist attacks of September 11 of that year, and it provided audiences with a welcome burst of comedy and dance, telling the story of a young woman on a romantic Greek island who uses the occasion of her wedding to discover which of her disco-singer mother's three ex-boyfriends is her true father. At the time of this printing, *Mamma Mia!* was still near sellout in the ninth year of its run, well fulfilling the Winter Garden builders' original promise of "novel, international, spectacular and musical entertainments."

In 2002 the Shubert Organization signed a contract granting naming rights to Cadillac, a division of the Ford Motor Company, which had lent its name to Broadway's Ford Center (now the Hilton Theatre). The Winter Garden was rechristened the Cadillac Winter Garden from May 5, 2002, to January 1, 2007, when it reverted to simply the Winter Garden.

INDEX